FUNDAMENTALS OF SIGNALS AND SYSTEMS

Fundamentals of Signals and Systems

Benoit Boulet

DA VINCI ENGINEERING PRESS
Hingham, Massachusetts

Editor: David Pallai
Cover Design: Tyler Creative

DA VINCI ENGINEERING PRESS
CHARLES RIVER MEDIA, INC.
10 Downer Avenue
Hingham, Massachusetts 02043
781-740-0400
781-740-8816 (FAX)
info@charlesriver.com
www.charlesriver.com

This book is printed on acid-free paper.

Benoit Boulet. *Fundamentals of Signals and Systems.*
ISBN: 1-58450-381-5

Library of Congress Cataloging-in-Publication Data
Boulet, Benoit, 1967-
Fundamentals of signals and systems / Benoit Boulet.— 1st ed.
p. cm.
Includes index.
ISBN 1-58450-381-5 (hardcover with cd-rom : alk. paper)
1. Signal processing. 2. Signal generators. 3. Electric filters. 4. Signal detection. 5. System analysis.
I. Title.
TK5102.9.B68 2005
621.382'2—dc22
2005010054

05 7 6 5 4 3 2 First Edition

CHARLES RIVER MEDIA titles are available for site license or bulk purchase by institutions, user groups, corporations, etc. For additional information, please contact the Special Sales Department at 781-740-0400.

Contents

List of Lectures

Acknowledgments

I wish to acknowledge the contribution of Dr. Maier L. Blostein, emeritus professor in the Department of Electrical and Computer Engineering at McGill University. Our discussions over the past few years have led us to the current course syllabi for Signals & Systems I and II, essentially forming the table of contents of this textbook.

I would like to thank the many students whom, over the years, have reported mistakes and suggested useful revisions to my Signals & Systems I and II course notes.

The interesting and useful applets on the companion CD-ROM were programmed by the following students: Rafic El-Fakir (Bode plot applet) and Gul Pil Joo (Fourier series and convolution applets). I thank them for their excellent work and for letting me use their programs.

Acknowledgments

Preface

The study of signals and systems is considered to be a classic subject in the curriculum of most engineering schools throughout the world. The theory of signals and systems is a coherent and elegant collection of mathematical results that date back to the work of Fourier and Laplace and many other famous mathematicians and engineers. Signals and systems theory has proven to be an extremely valuable tool for the past 70 years in many fields of science and engineering, including power systems, automatic control, communications, circuit design, filtering, and signal processing. Fantastic advances in these fields have brought revolutionary changes into our lives.

At the heart of signals and systems theory is mankind's historical curiosity and need to analyze the behavior of physical systems with simple mathematical models describing the cause-and-effect relationship between quantities. For example, Isaac Newton discovered the second law of rigid-body dynamics over 300 years ago and described it mathematically as a relationship between the resulting force applied on a body (the input) and its acceleration (the output), from which one can also obtain the body's velocity and position with respect to time. The development of differential calculus by Leibniz and Newton provided a powerful tool for modeling physical systems in the form of differential equations implicitly relating the input variable to the output variable.

A fundamental issue in science and engineering is to predict what the behavior, or output response, of a system will be for a given input signal. Whereas science may seek to describe natural phenomena modeled as input-output systems, engineering seeks to design systems by modifying and analyzing such models. This issue is recurrent in the design of electrical or mechanical systems, where a system's output signal must typically respond in an appropriate way to selected input signals. In this case, a mathematical input-output model of the system would be analyzed to predict the behavior of the output of the system. For example, in the design of a simple resistor-capacitor electrical circuit to be used as a filter, the engineer would first specify the desired attenuation of a sinusoidal input voltage of a given frequency at the output of the filter. Then, the design would proceed by selecting the appropriate resistance R and capacitance C in the differential equation model of the filter in order to achieve the attenuation specification. The filter can then be built using actual electrical components.

A signal is defined as a function of time representing the evolution of a variable. Certain types of input and output signals have special properties with respect to linear time-invariant systems. Such signals include sinusoidal and exponential functions of time. These signals can be linearly combined to form virtually any other signal, which is the basis of the Fourier series representation of periodic signals and the Fourier transform representation of aperiodic signals.

The Fourier representation opens up a whole new interpretation of signals in terms of their frequency contents called the frequency spectrum. Furthermore, in the frequency domain, a linear time-invariant system acts as a filter on the frequency spectrum of the input signal, attenuating it at some frequencies while amplifying it at other frequencies. This effect is called the frequency response of the system. These frequency domain concepts are fundamental in electrical engineering, as they underpin the fields of communication systems, analog and digital filter design, feedback control, power engineering, etc. Well-trained electrical and computer engineers think of signals as being in the frequency domain probably just as much as they think of them as functions of time.

The Fourier transform can be further generalized to the Laplace transform in continuous-time and the z-transform in discrete-time. The idea here is to define such transforms even for signals that tend to infinity with time. We chose to adopt the notation $X(j\omega)$, instead of $X(\omega)$ or $X(f)$, for the Fourier transform of a continuous-time signal $x(t)$. This is consistent with the Laplace transform of the signal denoted as $X(s)$, since then $X(j\omega) = X(s)|_{s=j\omega}$. The same remark goes for the discrete-time Fourier transform: $X(e^{j\omega}) = X(z)|_{z=e^{j\omega}}$.

Nowadays, predicting a system's behavior is usually done through computer simulation. A simulation typically involves the recursive computation of the output signal of a discretized version of a continuous-time system model. A large part of this book is devoted to the issue of system discretization and discrete-time signals and systems. The MATLAB software package is used to compute and display the results of some of the examples. The companion CD-ROM contains the MATLAB script files, problem solutions, and interactive graphical applets that can help the student visualize difficult concepts such as the convolution and Fourier series.

Undergraduate students see the theory of signals and systems as a difficult subject. The reason may be that signals and systems is typically one of the first courses an engineering student encounters that has substantial mathematical content. So what is the required mathematical background that a student should have in order to learn from this book? Well, a good background in calculus and trigonometry definitely helps. Also, the student should know about complex numbers and complex functions. Finally, some linear algebra is used in the development of state-space representations of systems. The student is encouraged to review these topics carefully before reading this book.

My wish is that the reader will enjoy learning the theory of signals and systems by using this book. One of my goals is to present the theory in a direct and straightforward manner. Another goal is to instill interest in different areas of specialization of electrical and computer engineering. Learning about signals and systems and its applications is often the point at which an electrical or computer engineering student decides what she or he will specialize in.

Benoit Boulet
March 2005
Montréal, Canada

1 Elementary Continuous-Time and Discrete-Time Signals and Systems

In This Chapter

- Systems in Engineering
- Functions of Time as Signals
- Transformations of the Time Variable
- Periodic Signals
- Exponential Signals
- Periodic Complex Exponential and Sinusoidal Signals
- Finite-Energy and Finite-Power Signals
- Even and Odd Signals
- Discrete-Time Impulse and Step Signals
- Generalized Functions
- System Models and Basic Properties
- Summary
- To Probe Further
- Exercises

((Lecture 1: Signal Models))

In this first chapter, we introduce the concept of a signal as a real or complex function of time. We pay special attention to sinusoidal signals and to real and complex exponential signals, as they have the fundamental property of keeping their "identity" under the action of a linear time-invariant (LTI) system. We also introduce the concept of a system as a relationship between an input signal and an output signal.

SYSTEMS IN ENGINEERING

The word *system* refers to many different things in engineering. It can be used to designate such tangible objects as software systems, electronic systems, computer systems, or mechanical systems. It can also mean, in a more abstract way, theoretical objects such as a system of linear equations or a mathematical input-output model. In this book, we greatly reduce the scope of the definition of the word system to the latter; that is, a system is defined here as a mathematical relationship between an input signal and an output signal. Note that this definition of system is different from what we are used to. Namely, the system is usually understood to be the engineering device in the field, and a mathematical representation of this system is usually called a system model.

FUNCTIONS OF TIME AS SIGNALS

Signals are functions of time that represent the evolution of variables such as a furnace temperature, the speed of a car, a motor shaft position, or a voltage. There are two types of signals: *continuous-time* signals and *discrete-time* signals.

Continuous-time signals are functions of a continuous variable (time).

Example 1.1: The speed of a car $v(t)$ as shown in Figure 1.1.

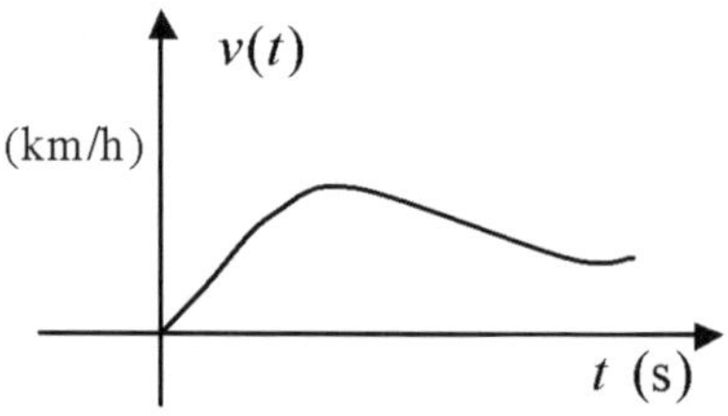

FIGURE 1.1 Continuous-time signal representing the speed of a car.

Discrete-time signals are functions of a discrete variable; that is, they are defined only for integer values of the independent variable (time steps).

Example 1.2: The value of a stock $x[n]$ at the end of month n, as shown in Figure 1.2.

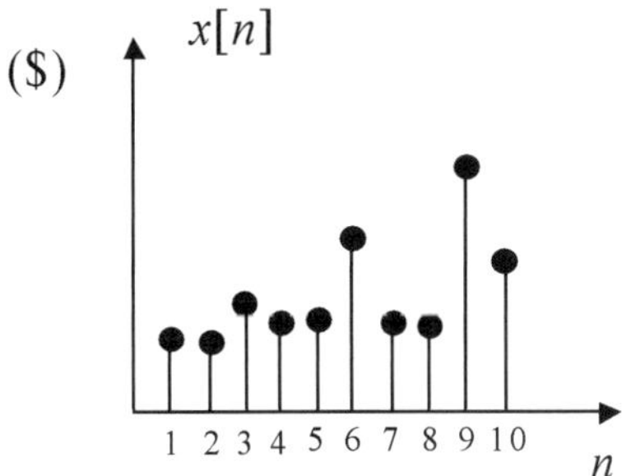

FIGURE 1.2 Discrete-time signal representing the value of a stock.

Note how the discrete values of the signal are represented by points linked to the time axis by vertical lines. This is done for the sake of clarity, as just showing a set of discrete points "floating" on the graph can be confusing to interpret.

Continuous-time and discrete-time functions map their *domain* $\mathcal{T}$ (time interval) into their *co-domain* $\mathcal{V}$ (set of values). This is expressed in mathematical notation as $f:\mathcal{T}\rightarrow\mathcal{V}$. The *range* of the function is the subset $\mathcal{R}\{f\}\subseteq\mathcal{V}$ of the co-domain, in which each element $v\in\mathcal{R}\{f\}$ has a corresponding time t in the domain $\mathcal{T}$ such that $v=f(t)$. This is illustrated in Figure 1.3.

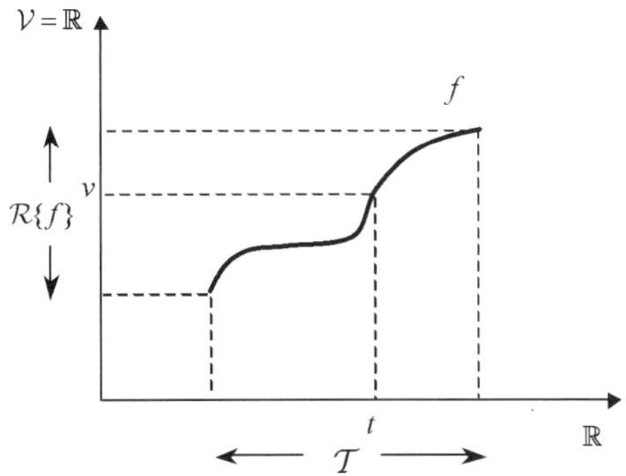

FIGURE 1.3 Domain, co-domain, and range of a real function of continuous time.

If the range $\mathcal{R}\{f\}$ is a subset of the real numbers $\mathbb{R}$, then f is said to be a real signal. If $\mathcal{R}\{f\}$ is a subset of the complex numbers $\mathbb{C}$, then f is said to be a complex signal. We will study both real and complex signals in this book. Note that we often use the notation $x(t)$ to designate a continuous-time signal (not just the value of x at time t) and $x[n]$ to designate a discrete-time signal (again for the whole signal, not just the value of x at time n).

For the car speed example above, the domain of $v(t)$ could be $\mathcal{T}=[0,+\infty)$ with units of seconds, assuming the car keeps on running forever, and the range is $\mathcal{V}=[0,+\infty)\subset\mathbb{R}$, the set of all non-negative speeds in units of kilometers per hour.

For the stock trend example, the domain of $x[n]$ is the set of positive natural numbers $\mathcal{T}=\{1,2,3,\ldots\}$, the co-domain is the non-negative reals $\mathcal{V}=[0,+\infty)\subset\mathbb{R}$, and the range could be $\mathcal{R}\{x\}=[0,100]$ in dollar unit.

An example of a complex signal is the complex exponential $x(t)=e^{j10t}$, for which $\mathcal{T}=\mathbb{R}$, $\mathcal{V}=\mathbb{C}$, and $\mathcal{R}\{x\}=\{z\in\mathbb{C}:|z|=1\}$; that is, the set of all complex numbers of magnitude equal to one.

TRANSFORMATIONS OF THE TIME VARIABLE

Consider the continuous-time signal $x(t)$ defined by its graph shown in Figure 1.4 and the discrete-time signal $x[n]$ defined by its graph in Figure 1.5. As an aside, these two signals are said to be of *finite support,* as they are nonzero only over a finite time interval, namely on $t\in[-2,2]$ for $x(t)$ and when $n\in\{-3,\ldots,3\}$ for $x[n]$. We will use these two signals to illustrate some useful transformations of the time variable, such as time scaling and time reversal.

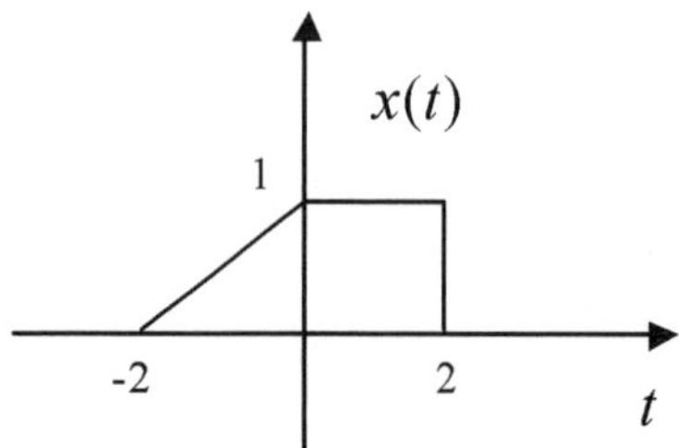

FIGURE 1.4 Graph of continuous time signal $x(t)$.

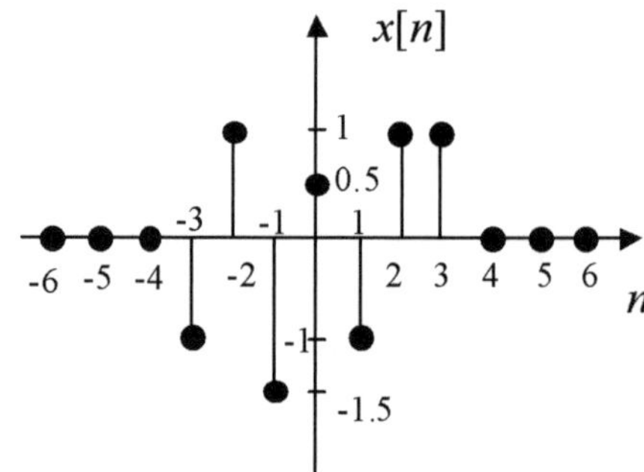

FIGURE 1.5 Graph of discrete-time signal $x[n]$.

Time Scaling

Time scaling refers to the multiplication of the time variable by a real positive constant α. In the continuous-time case, we can write

$$y(t)=x(\alpha t). \tag{1.1}$$

Case $0 < \alpha < 1$: The signal $x(t)$ is *slowed down* or *expanded* in time. Think of a tape recording played back at a slower speed than the nominal speed.

Example 1.3: Case $\alpha = \frac{1}{2}$ shown in Figure 1.6.

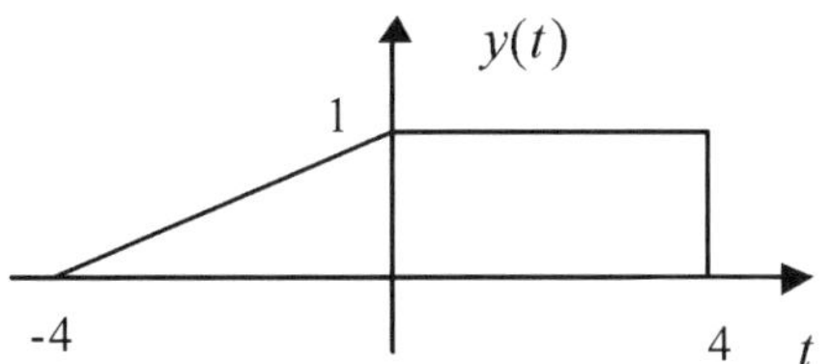

FIGURE 1.6 Graph of expanded signal $y(t) = x(0.5t)$.

Case $\alpha > 1$: The signal $x(t)$ is *sped up* or *compressed* in time. Think of a tape recording played back at twice the nominal speed.

Example 1.4: Case $\alpha = 2$ shown in Figure 1.7.

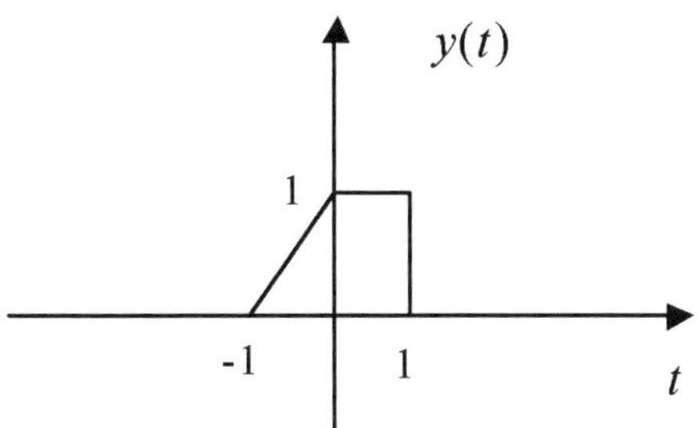

FIGURE 1.7 Graph of compressed signal $y(t) = x(2t)$.

For a discrete-time signal $x[n]$, we also have the time scaling

$$y[n] = x[\alpha n], \tag{1.2}$$

but only the case $\alpha > 1$, where α is an integer, makes sense, as $x[n]$ is undefined for fractional values of n. In this case, called *decimation* or *downsampling*, we not only get a time compression of the signal, but the signal can also lose part of its information; that is, some of its values may disappear in the resulting signal $y[n]$.

Example 1.5: Case $\alpha = 2$ shown in Figure 1.8.

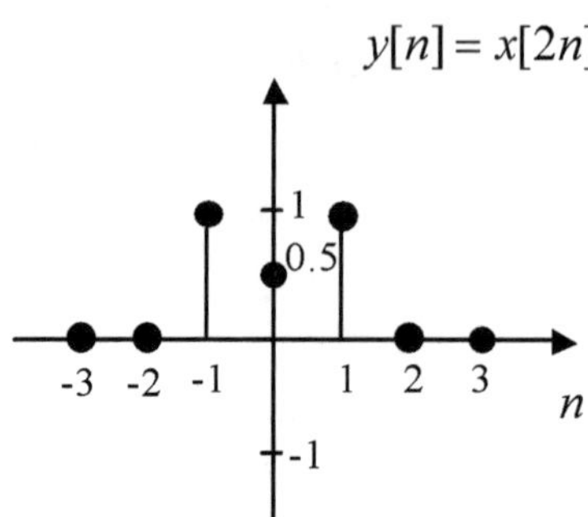

FIGURE 1.8 Graph of compressed signal $y[n] = x[2n]$.

In Chapter 12, *upsampling*, which involves inserting $m - 1$ zeros between consecutive samples, will be introduced as a form of time expansion of a discrete-time signal.

Time Reversal

A time reversal is achieved by multiplying the time variable by -1. The resulting continuous-time and discrete-time signals are shown in Figure 1.9 and Figure 1.10, respectively.

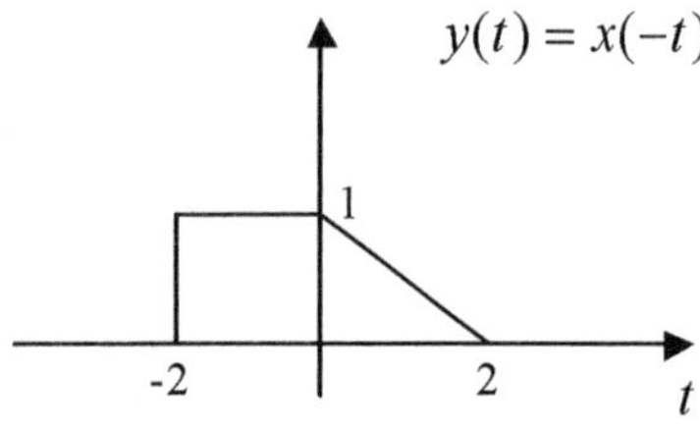

FIGURE 1.9 Graph of time-reversed signal $y(t) = x(-t)$.

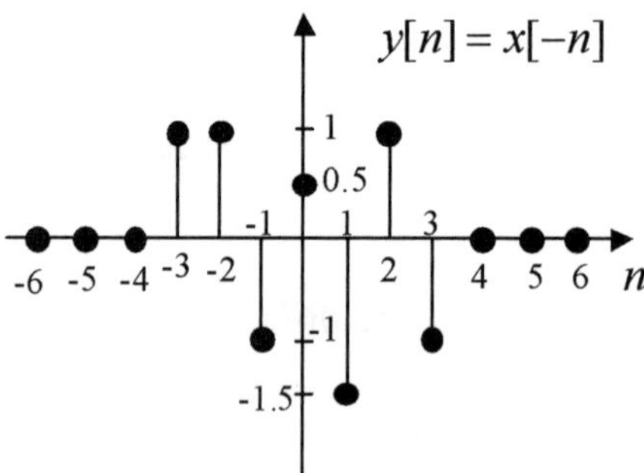

FIGURE 1.10 Graph of time-reversed signal $y[n] = x[-n]$.

Time Shift

A time shift delays or advances the signal in time by a continuous-time interval $T \in \mathbb{R}$:

$$y(t) = x(t+T). \tag{1.3}$$

For T positive, the signal is advanced; that is, it starts at time $t = -4$, which is before the time it originally started at, $t = -2$, as shown in Figure 1.11. For T negative, the signal is delayed, as shown in Figure 1.12.

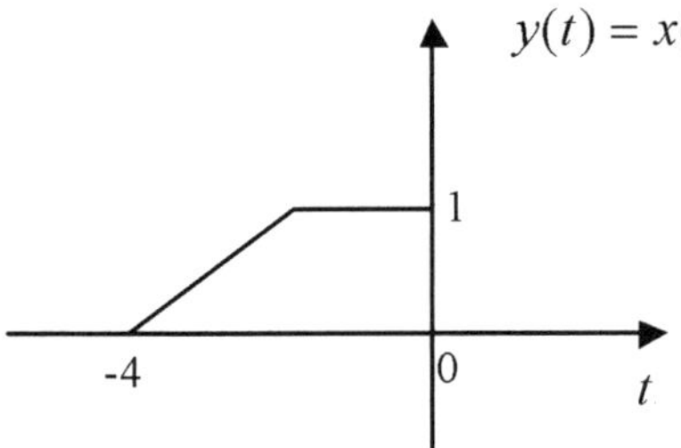

FIGURE 1.11 Graph of time-advanced signal $y(t) = x(t + 2)$.

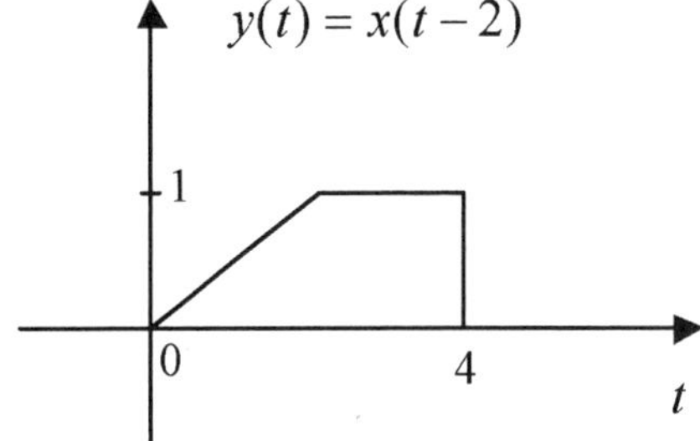

FIGURE 1.12 Graph of time-delayed signal $y(t) = x(t - 2)$.

Similarly, a time shift delays or advances a discrete-time signal by an integer discrete-time interval N:

$$y[n] = x[n+N]. \tag{1.4}$$

For N positive, the signal is advanced by N time steps, as shown in Figure 1.13. For N negative, the signal is delayed by $|N|$ time steps.

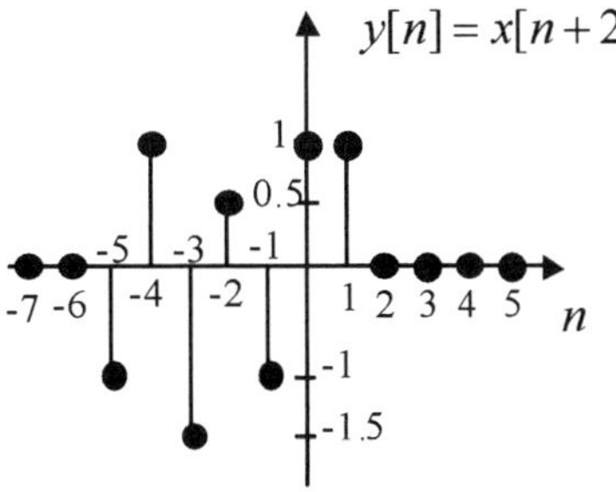

FIGURE 1.13 Graph of time-advanced signal $y[n] = x[n + 2]$.

PERIODIC SIGNALS

Intuitively, a signal is periodic when it repeats itself. This intuition is captured in the following definition: a continuous-time signal $x(t)$ is periodic if there exists a positive real T for which

$$x(t) = x(t+T), \quad \forall t \in \mathbb{R}. \tag{1.5}$$

A discrete-time signal $x[n]$ is periodic if there exists a positive integer N for which

$$x[n] = x[n+N], \quad \forall n \in \mathbb{Z}. \tag{1.6}$$

The smallest such T or N is called the *fundamental period* of the signal.

Example 1.6: The square wave signal in Figure 1.14 is periodic. The fundamental period of this square wave is $T = 4$, but 8, 12, and 16 are also periods of the signal.

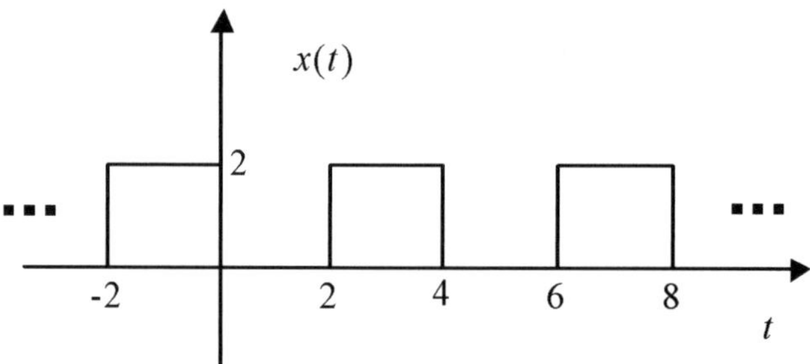

FIGURE 1.14 A continuous-time periodic square wave signal.

Example 1.7: The complex exponential signal $x(t) = e^{j\omega_0 t}$:

$$x(t+T) = e^{j\omega_0 (t+T)} = e^{j\omega_0 t} e^{j\omega_0 T}. \tag{1.7}$$

The right-hand side of Equation 1.7 is equal to $x(t) = e^{j\omega_0 t}$ for $T = \frac{2\pi k}{\omega_0}$, $k = \pm 1, \pm 2, \ldots$, so these are all periods of the complex exponential. The fundamental period is $T = \frac{2\pi}{\omega_0}$.

It may become more apparent that the complex exponential signal is periodic when it is expressed in its real/imaginary form:

$$x(t) = e^{j\omega_0 t} = \cos(\omega_0 t) + j\sin(\omega_0 t). \tag{1.8}$$

where it is clear that the real part, $\cos(\omega_0 t)$, and the imaginary part, $\sin(\omega_0 t)$, are periodic with fundamental period $T = \frac{2\pi}{\omega_0}$.

Example 1.8: The discrete-time signal $x[n] = (-1)^n$ in Figure 1.15 is periodic with fundamental period $N = 2$.

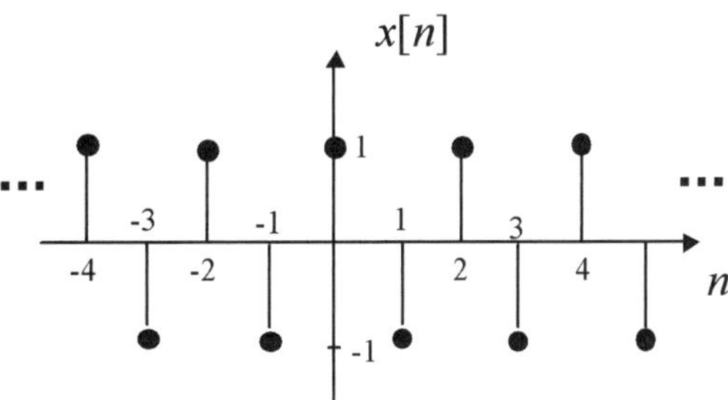

FIGURE 1.15 A discrete-time periodic signal.

EXPONENTIAL SIGNALS

Exponential signals are extremely important in signals and systems analysis because they are invariant under the action of linear time-invariant systems, which will be discussed in Chapter 2. This means that the output of an LTI system subjected to an exponential input signal will also be an exponential with the same exponent, but in general with a different real or complex amplitude.

Example 1.9: Consider the LTI system represented by a first-order differential equation initially at rest, with input $x(t) = e^{-2t}$:

$$\frac{dy(t)}{dt} + y(t) = x(t). \tag{1.9}$$

Its output signal is given by $y(t) = -e^{-2t}$. (Check it!)

Real Exponential Signals

Real exponential signals can be defined both in continuous time and in discrete time.

Continuous Time

We can define a general real exponential signal as follows:

$$x(t) = Ce^{\alpha t}, \quad 0 \neq C, \alpha \in \mathbb{R}. \tag{1.10}$$

We now look at different cases depending on the value of parameter α.

Case $\alpha = 0$: We simply get the constant signal $x(t) = C$.

Case $\alpha > 0$: The exponential tends to infinity as $t \to +\infty$, as shown in Figure 1.16, where $C > 0$. Notice that $x(0) = C$.

Case $\alpha < 0$: The exponential tends to zero as $t \to +\infty$; see Figure 1.17, where $C < 0$.

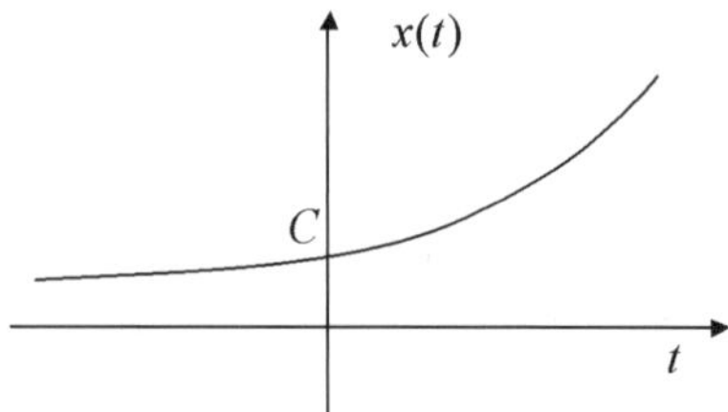

FIGURE 1.16 Continuous-time exponential signal growing unbounded with time.

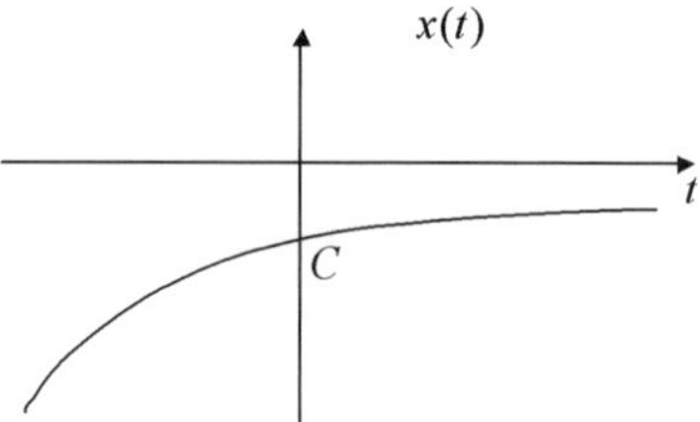

FIGURE 1.17 Continuous-time exponential signal tapering off to zero with time.

Discrete Time

We define a general real discrete-time exponential signal as follows:

$$x[n] = C\alpha^n, \quad C, \alpha \in \mathbb{R}. \tag{1.11}$$

There are six cases to consider, apart from the trivial cases $\alpha = 0$ or $C = 0$: $\alpha = 1$, $\alpha > 1$, $0 < \alpha < 1$, $\alpha < -1$, $\alpha = -1$, and $-1 < \alpha < 0$. Here we assume that $C > 0$, but for C negative, the graphs would simply be flipped images of the ones given around the time axis.

Case $\alpha = 1$: We get a constant signal $x[n] = C$.

Case $\alpha > 1$: We get a positive signal that grows exponentially, as shown in Figure 1.18.

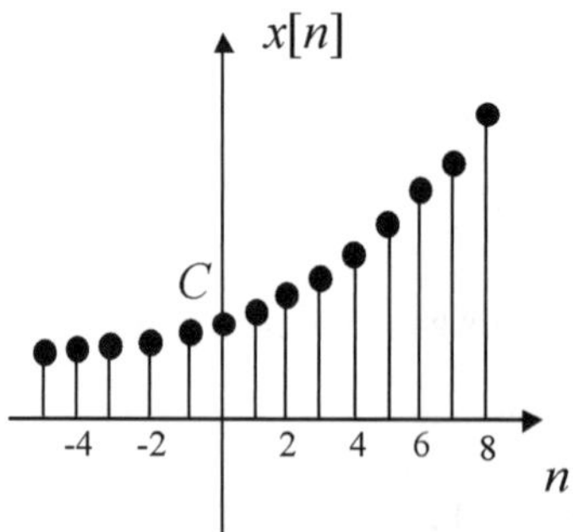

FIGURE 1.18 Discrete-time exponential signal growing unbounded with time.

Case $0<\alpha<1$: The signal $x[n]=C\alpha^n$ is positive and decays exponentially, as shown in Figure 1.19.

Case $\alpha<-1$: The signal $x[n]=C\alpha^n$ alternates between positive and negative values and grows exponentially in magnitude with time. This is shown in Figure 1.20.

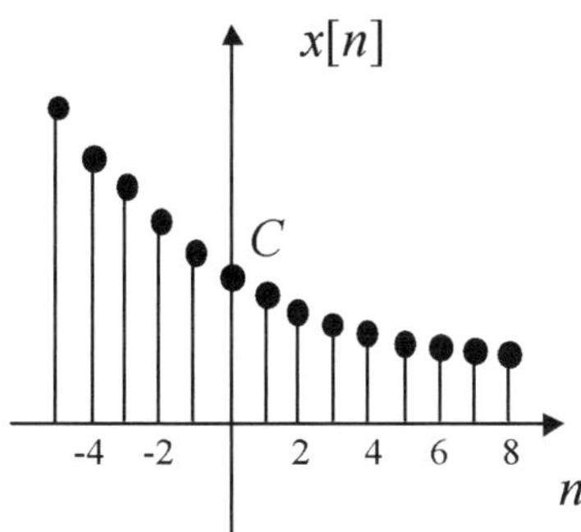

FIGURE 1.19 Discrete-time exponential signal tapering off to zero with time.

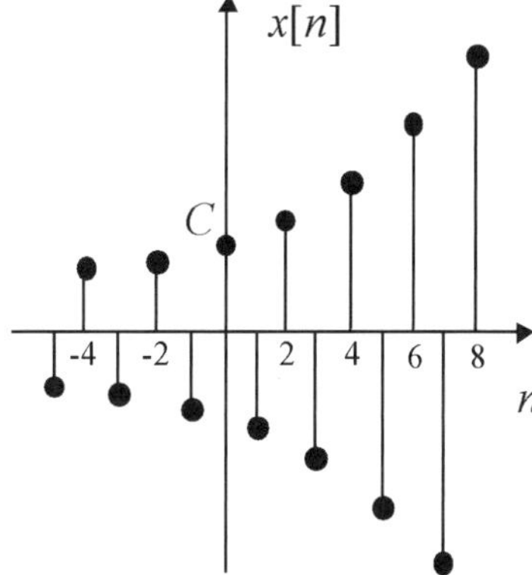

FIGURE 1.20 Discrete-time exponential signal alternating and growing unbounded with time.

Case $\alpha = -1$: The signal alternates between C and $-C$, as seen in Figure 1.21.

Case $-1<\alpha<0$: The signal alternates between positive and negative values and decays exponentially in magnitude with time, as shown in Figure 1.22.

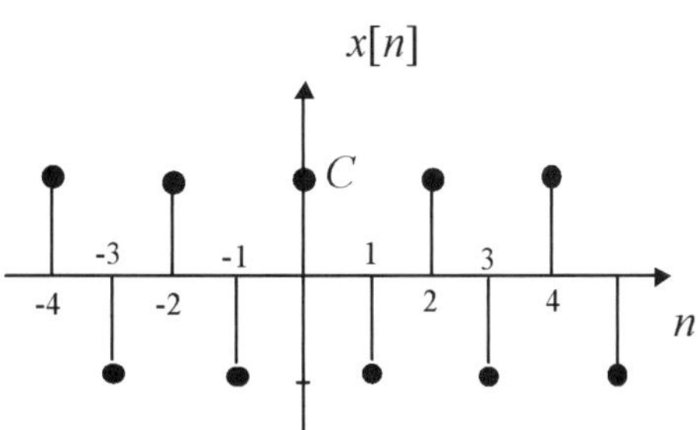

FIGURE 1.21 Discrete-time exponential signal reduced to an alternating periodic signal.

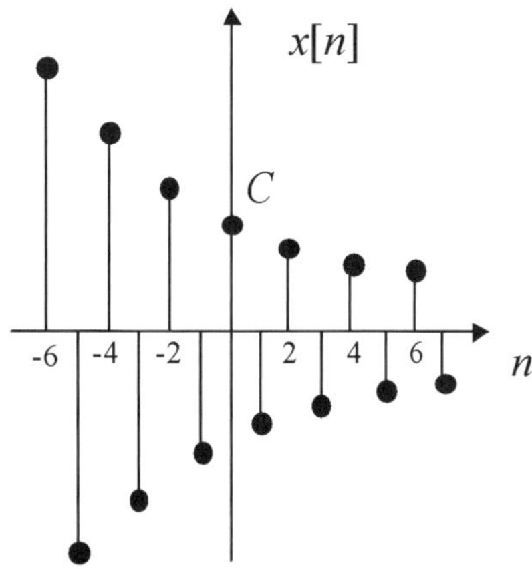

FIGURE 1.22 Discrete-time exponential signal alternating and tapering off to zero with time.

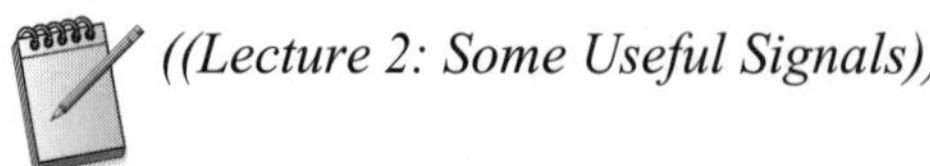

((Lecture 2: Some Useful Signals))

Complex Exponential Signals

Complex exponential signals can also be defined both in continuous time and in discrete time. They have real and imaginary parts with sinusoidal behavior.

Continuous Time

The continuous-time complex exponential signal can be defined as follows:

$$x(t) := Ce^{at}, \quad C, a \in \mathbb{C}, \tag{1.12}$$

where $C = Ae^{j\theta}$, $A, \theta \in \mathbb{R}, A > 0$ is expressed in polar form, and $a = \alpha + j\omega_0$, $\alpha, \omega_0 \in \mathbb{R}$ is expressed in rectangular form. Thus, we can write

$$\begin{aligned} x(t) &= Ae^{j\theta}e^{(\alpha + j\omega_0)t} \\ &= Ae^{\alpha t}e^{j(\omega_0 t + \theta)} \end{aligned} \tag{1.13}$$

If we look at the second part of Equation 1.13, we can see that $x(t)$ represents either a circular or a spiral trajectory in the complex plane, depending whether α is zero, negative, or positive. The term $e^{j(\omega_0 t + \theta)}$ describes a unit circle centered at the origin counterclockwise in the complex plane as time varies from $t = -\infty$ to $t = +\infty$, as shown in Figure 1.23 for the case $\theta = 0$. The times t_k indicated in the figure are the times when the complex point $e^{j\omega_0 t_k}$ has a phase of $\pi/4$.

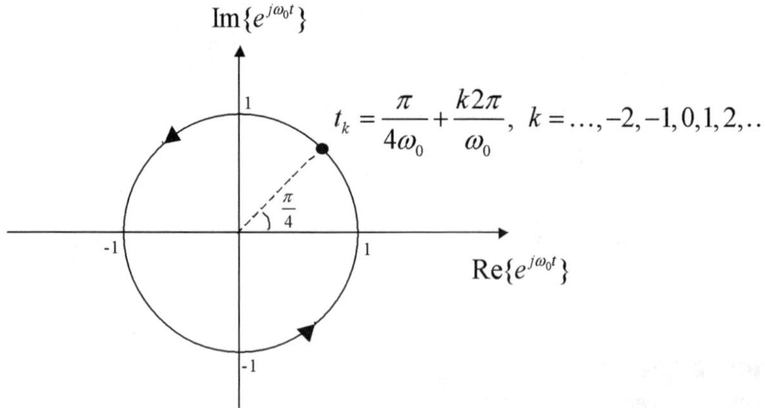

FIGURE 1.23 Trajectory described by the complex exponential.

Using Euler's relation, we obtain the signal in rectangular form:

$$x(t) = Ae^{\alpha t}\cos(\omega_0 t + \theta) + jAe^{\alpha t}\sin(\omega_0 t + \theta), \tag{1.14}$$

where $\mathrm{Re}\{x(t)\} = Ae^{\alpha t}\cos(\omega_0 t + \theta)$ and $\mathrm{Im}\{x(t)\} = Ae^{\alpha t}\sin(\omega_0 t + \theta)$ are the real part and imaginary part of the signal, respectively. Both are sinusoidal, with time-varying amplitude (or envelope) $Ae^{\alpha t}$. We can see that the exponent $\alpha = \mathrm{Re}\{a\}$ defines the type of real and imaginary parts we get for the signal.

For the case $\alpha = 0$, we obtain a complex periodic signal of period $T = \frac{2\pi}{\omega_0}$ (as shown in Figure 1.23 but with radius A) whose real and imaginary parts are sinusoidal:

$$x(t) = A\cos(\omega_0 t + \theta) + jA\sin(\omega_0 t + \theta). \tag{1.15}$$

The real part of this signal is shown in Figure 1.24.

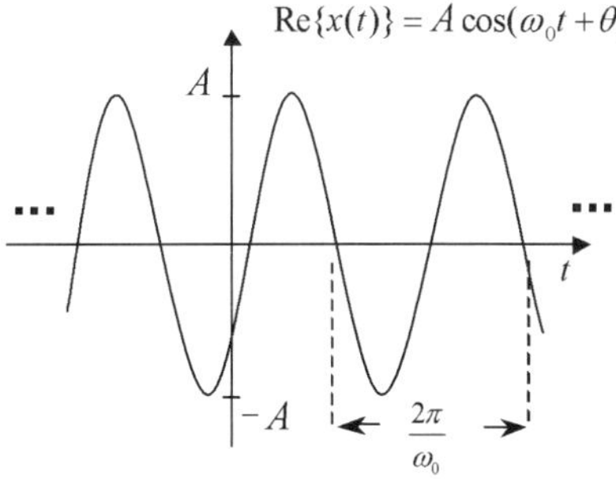

FIGURE 1.24 Real part of periodic complex exponential for $\alpha = 0$.

For the case $\alpha < 0$, we get a complex periodic signal multiplied by a decaying exponential. The real and imaginary parts are *damped sinusoids* that are signals that can describe, for example, the response of an *RLC* (resistance-inductance-capacitance) circuit or the response of a mass-spring-damper system such as a car suspension. The real part of $x(t)$ is shown in Figure 1.25.

For the case $\alpha > 0$, we get a complex periodic signal multiplied by a growing exponential. The real and imaginary parts are *growing sinusoids* that are signals that can describe the response of an unstable feedback control system. The real part of $x(t)$ is shown in Figure 1.26.

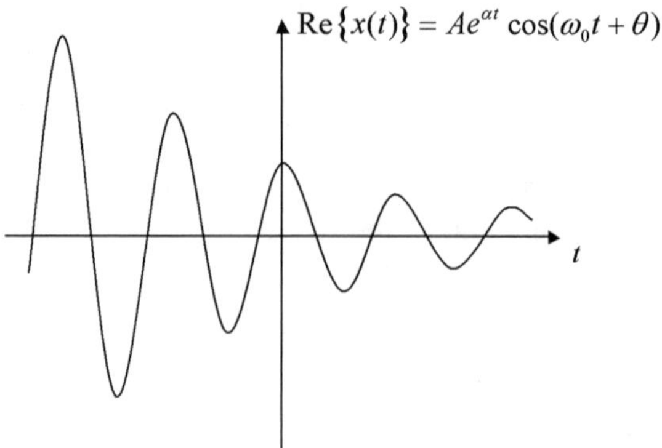

FIGURE 1.25 Real part of damped complex exponential for $\alpha < 0$.

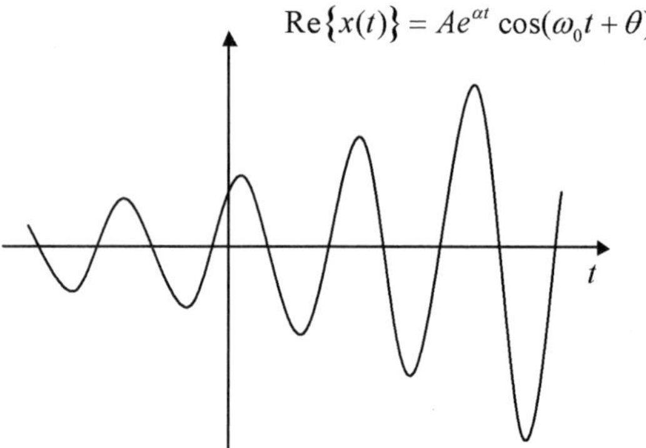

FIGURE 1.26 Real part of growing complex exponential for $\alpha > 0$.

The MATLAB script given below and located on the CD-ROM in D:\Chapter1\complexexp.m, where D: is assumed to be the CD-ROM drive, generates and plots the real and imaginary parts of a decaying complex exponential signal.

```
%% complexexp.m generates a complex exponential signal and plots
%% its real and imaginary parts.
% time vector
t=0:.005:1;
% signal parameters
A=1;
```

```
theta=pi/4;
C=A*exp(j*theta);
alpha=-3;
w0=20;
a=alpha+j*w0;
% Generate signal
x=C*exp(a*t);
%plot real and imaginary parts
figure(1)
plot(t,real(x))
figure(2)
plot(t,imag(x))
```

Discrete Time

The discrete-time complex exponential signal can be defined as follows:

$$x[n] = Ca^n, \tag{1.16}$$

where $C, a \in \mathbb{C}, \quad C = Ae^{j\theta}, A, \theta \in \mathbb{R}, A > 0 \quad a = re^{j\omega_0}, r, \omega_0 \in \mathbb{R}, r > 0$.

Substituting the polar forms of C and a in Equation 1.16, we obtain a useful expression for $x[n]$ with time-varying amplitude:

$$\begin{aligned} x[n] &= Ae^{j\theta} r^n e^{j\omega_0 n} \\ &= Ar^n e^{j(\omega_0 n + \theta)}, \end{aligned} \tag{1.17}$$

and using Euler's relation, we get the rectangular form of the discrete-time complex exponential:

$$x[n] = Ar^n \cos(\omega_0 n + \theta) + jAr^n \sin(\omega_0 n + \theta). \tag{1.18}$$

Clearly, the magnitude r of a determines whether the envelope of $x[n]$ grows, decreases, or remains constant with time.

For the case $r = 1$, we obtain a complex signal whose real and imaginary parts have a sinusoidal envelope (they are sampled cosine and sine waves), *but the signal is not necessarily periodic*! We will discuss this issue in the next section.

$$x[n] = A\cos(\omega_0 n + \theta) + jA\sin(\omega_0 n + \theta) \tag{1.19}$$

Figure 1.27 shows the real part of a complex exponential signal with $r = 1$.

For the case $r < 1$, we get a complex signal whose real and imaginary parts are damped sinusoidal signals (see Figure 1.28).

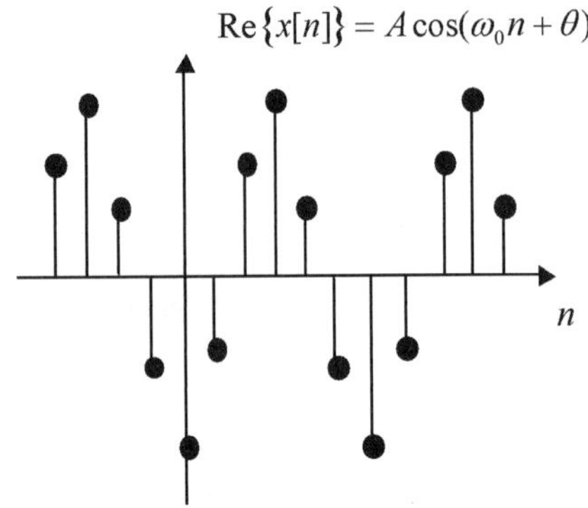

FIGURE 1.27 Real part of discrete-time complex exponential for $r = 1$.

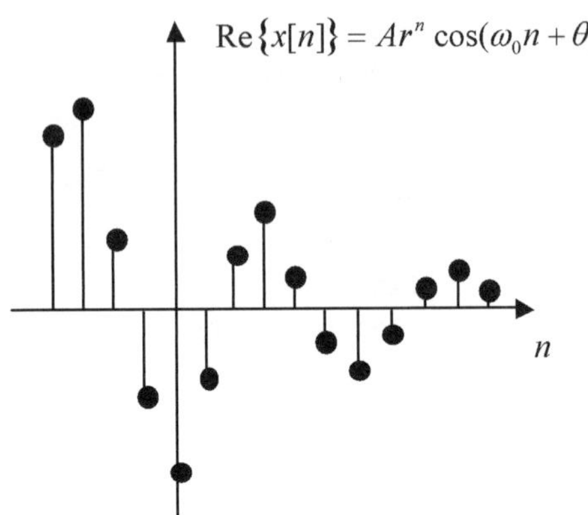

FIGURE 1.28 Real part of discrete-time damped complex exponential for $r < 1$.

For the case $r > 1$, we obtain a complex signal whose real and imaginary parts are growing sinusoidal sequences, as shown in Figure 1.29.

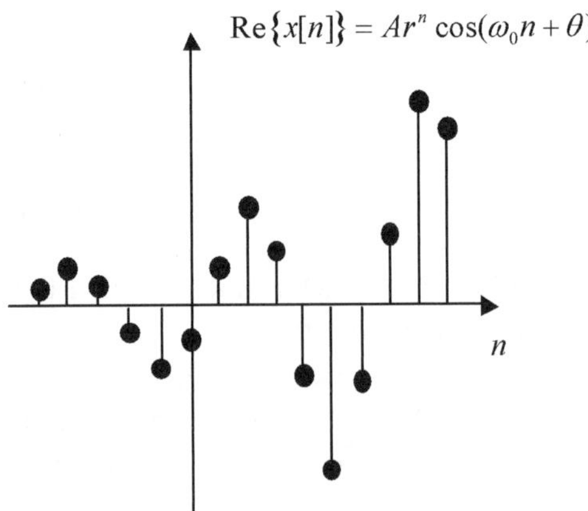

FIGURE 1.29 Real part of growing complex exponential for $r > 1$.

ON THE CD

The MATLAB script given below and located on the CD-ROM in D:\Chapter1\complexDTexp.m generates and plots the real and imaginary parts of a decaying discrete-time complex exponential signal.

```
%% complexDTexp.m generates a discrete-time
%% complex exponential signal and plots
%% its real and imaginary parts.
% time vector
n=0:1:20;
% signal parameters
A=1;
theta=pi/4;
C=A*exp(j*theta);
r=0.8;
w0=0.2*pi;
a=r*exp(j*w0);
% Generate signal
x=C*(a.^n);
%plot real and imaginary parts
figure(1)
stem(n,real(x))
figure(2)
stem(n,imag(x))
```

PERIODIC COMPLEX EXPONENTIAL AND SINUSOIDAL SIGNALS

In our study of complex exponential signals so far, we have found that in the cases $\alpha = \mathrm{Re}\{a\} = 0$ in continuous time and $r = |a| = 1$ in discrete time, we obtain signals whose trajectories lie on the unit circle in the complex plane. In particular, their real and imaginary parts are sinusoidal signals. We will see that in the continuous-time case, these signals are always periodic, but that is not necessarily the case in discrete time. Periodic complex exponentials can be used to define sets of harmonically related exponentials that have special properties that will be used later on to define the Fourier series.

Continuous Time

In continuous time, complex exponential and sinusoidal signals of constant amplitude are all periodic.

Periodic Complex Exponentials

Consider the complex exponential signal $e^{j\omega_0 t}$. We have already shown that this signal is periodic with fundamental period $T = \frac{2\pi}{\omega_0}$. Now let us consider *harmonically related complex exponential signals*:

$$\phi_k(t) := e^{jk\omega_0 t}, \quad k = \ldots,-2,-1,0,1,2,\ldots, \tag{1.20}$$

that is, complex exponentials with fundamental frequencies that are integer multiples of ω_0. These harmonically related signals have a very important property: they form an *orthogonal set*. Two signals $x(t)$, $y(t)$ are said to be orthogonal over an interval $[t_1,t_2]$ if their inner product, as defined in Equation 1.21, is equal to zero:

$$\int_{t_1}^{t_2} x(t)^* y(t)dt = 0, \tag{1.21}$$

where $x^*(t)$ is the complex conjugate of $x(t)$. This notion of orthogonality is a generalization of the concept of perpendicular vectors in three-dimensional Euclidean space $\mathbb{R}^3$. Two such perpendicular (or orthogonal) vectors $u=\begin{bmatrix} u_1 \\ u_2 \\ u_3 \end{bmatrix}, v=\begin{bmatrix} v_1 \\ v_2 \\ v_3 \end{bmatrix}$ have an inner product equal to zero:

$$u^T v = \begin{bmatrix} u_1 & u_2 & u_3 \end{bmatrix} \begin{bmatrix} v_1 \\ v_2 \\ v_3 \end{bmatrix} = u_1 v_1 + u_2 v_2 + u_3 v_3 = \sum_{i=1}^{3} u_i^T v_i = 0. \tag{1.22}$$

We know that a set of three orthogonal vectors can span the whole space $\mathbb{R}^3$ by forming linear combinations and therefore would constitute a basis for this space. It turns out that harmonically related complex exponentials (or *complex harmonics*) can also be seen as orthogonal vectors forming a basis for a space of vectors that are actually signals over the interval $[t_1,t_2]$. This space is infinite-dimensional, as there are infinitely many complex harmonics of increasing frequencies. It means that infinite linear combinations of the type $\sum_{k=-\infty}^{\infty} \alpha_k \phi_k(t)$ can basically represent any function of time in the signal space, which is the basis for the Fourier series representation of signals.

We now show that any two distinct complex harmonics $\phi_k(t) = e^{jk\omega_0 t}$ and $\phi_m(t) = e^{jm\omega_0 t}$, where $m \neq k$ are indeed orthogonal over their common period $T = \frac{2\pi}{\omega_0}$:

$$\begin{aligned} \int_0^{\frac{2\pi}{\omega_0}} \phi_k(t)^* \phi_m(t)dt &= \int_0^{\frac{2\pi}{\omega_0}} e^{-jk\omega_0 t} e^{jm\omega_0 t} dt = \int_0^{\frac{2\pi}{\omega_0}} e^{j(m-k)\omega_0 t} dt \\ &= \frac{1}{j(m-k)\omega_0} \Big[\underbrace{e^{j(m-k)2\pi}}_{=1} - 1 \Big] = 0. \end{aligned} \tag{1.23}$$

However, the inner product of a complex harmonic with itself evaluates to $T = \frac{2\pi}{\omega_0}$:

$$\int_0^{\frac{2\pi}{\omega_0}} \phi_k(t)^* \phi_k(t)dt = \int_0^{\frac{2\pi}{\omega_0}} e^{-jk\omega_0 t} e^{jk\omega_0 t} dt = \int_0^{\frac{2\pi}{\omega_0}} dt = \frac{2\pi}{\omega_0}. \tag{1.24}$$

Sinusoidal Signals

Continuous-time sinusoidal signals of the type $x(t) = A\cos(\omega_0 t + \theta)$ or $x(t) = A\sin(\omega_0 t + \theta)$ such as the one shown in Figure 1.30 are periodic with (fundamental) period $T = \frac{2\pi}{\omega_0}$, frequency $f_0 = \frac{\omega_0}{2\pi}$ in Hertz, angular frequency ω_0 in radians per second, and amplitude $|A|$. It is important to remember that in sinusoidal signals, or any other periodic signal, the shorter the period, the higher the frequency. For instance, in communication systems, a 1-MHz sine wave carrier has a period of 1 microsecond (10^{-6}s), while a 1-GHz sine wave carrier has a period of 1 nanosecond (10^{-9}s).

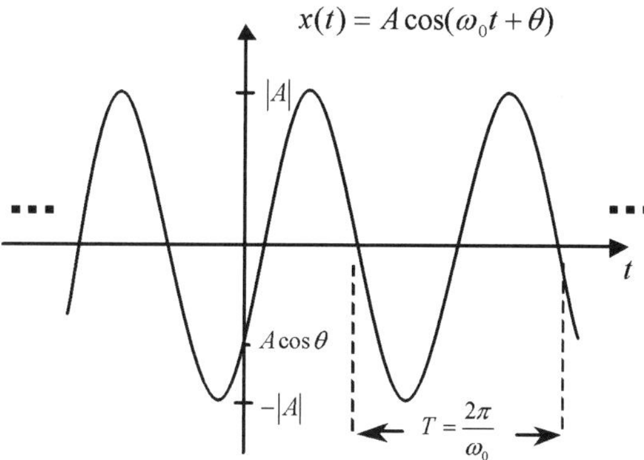

FIGURE 1.30 Continuous-time sinusoidal signal.

The following useful identities allow us to see the link between a periodic complex exponential and the sine and cosine waves of the same frequency and amplitude.

$$A\cos(\omega_0 t + \theta) = \frac{A}{2} e^{j\theta} e^{j\omega_0 t} + \frac{A}{2} e^{-j\theta} e^{-j\omega_0 t} = \mathrm{Re}\{Ae^{j(\omega_0 t + \theta)}\}, \tag{1.25}$$

$$A\sin(\omega_0 t + \theta) = \frac{A}{2j} e^{j\theta} e^{j\omega_0 t} - \frac{A}{2j} e^{-j\theta} e^{-j\omega_0 t} = \mathrm{Im}\{Ae^{j(\omega_0 t + \theta)}\}. \tag{1.26}$$

Discrete Time

In discrete time, complex exponential and sinusoidal signals of constant amplitude are not necessarily periodic.

Complex Exponential Signals

The complex exponential signal $Ae^{j\omega_0 n}$ is not periodic in general, although it seems like it is for any ω_0. The intuitive explanation is that the signal values, which are points on the unit circle in the complex plane, do not necessarily fall at the same locations as time evolves and the circle is described counterclockwise. When the signal values do always fall on the same points, then the discrete-time complex exponential is periodic. A more detailed analysis of periodicity is left for the next subsection on discrete-time sinusoidal signals, but it also applies to complex exponential signals.

The discrete-time complex harmonic signals defined by

$$\phi_k[n] := e^{jk\frac{2\pi}{N}n}, \quad k = 0,\ldots,N-1 \tag{1.27}$$

are periodic of (not necessarily fundamental) period N. They are also orthogonal, with the integral replaced by a sum in the inner product:

$$\begin{aligned}\sum_{n=0}^{N-1}\phi_k[n]^*\phi_m[n] &= \sum_{n=0}^{N-1}e^{-jk\frac{2\pi}{N}n}e^{jm\frac{2\pi}{N}n} = \sum_{n=0}^{N-1}e^{j(m-k)\frac{2\pi}{N}n} \\ &= \frac{1-e^{j(m-k)\frac{2\pi}{N}N}}{1-e^{j(m-k)\frac{2\pi}{N}}} = \frac{1-\overbrace{e^{j(m-k)2\pi}}^{=1}}{1-e^{j(m-k)\frac{2\pi}{N}}} = 0, \quad m \neq k.\end{aligned} \tag{1.28}$$

Here there are only N such distinct complex harmonics. For example, for $N =$ 8, we could easily check that $\phi_0[n] = \phi_8[n] = 1$. These signals will be used in Chapter 12 to define the discrete-time Fourier series.

Sinusoidal Signals

Discrete-time sinusoidal signals of the type $x[n] = A\cos(\omega_0 n + \theta)$ are *not always periodic*, although the *continuous envelope* of the signal $A\cos(\omega_0 t + \theta)$ *is* periodic of period $T = \frac{2\pi}{\omega_0}$. A periodic discrete-time sinusoid such as the one in Figure 1.31 is such that the signal values, which are samples of the continuous envelope, always repeat the same pattern over any period of the envelope.

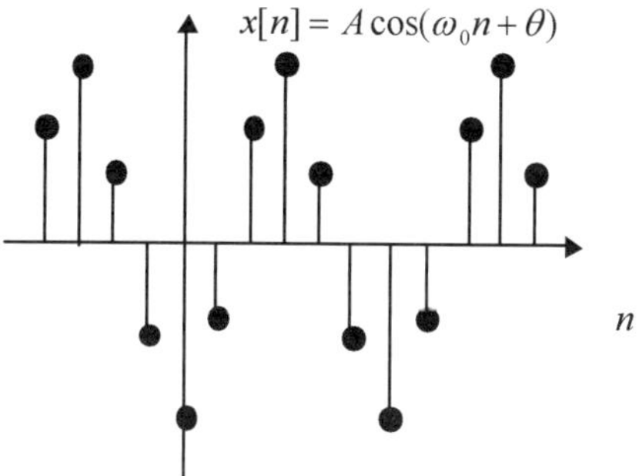

FIGURE 1.31 A periodic discrete-time sinusoidal signal.

Mathematically, we saw that $x[n]$ is periodic if there exists an integer $N > 0$ such that

$$x[n] = x[n+N] = A\cos(\omega_0 n + \omega_0 N + \theta). \quad (1.29)$$

That is, we must have $\omega_0 N = 2\pi m$ for some integer m, or equivalently:

$$\frac{\omega_0}{2\pi} = \frac{m}{N}; \quad (1.30)$$

that is, $\frac{\omega_0}{2\pi}$ must be a rational number (the ratio of two integers.) Then, the fundamental period $N > 0$ can also be expressed as $m\frac{2\pi}{\omega_0}$, assuming m and N have no common factor. The fundamental frequency defined by

$$\Omega_0 := \frac{2\pi}{N} = \frac{\omega_0}{m} \quad (1.31)$$

is expressed in radians. When the integers m and N have a common integer factor, that is, $m = m_0 q$ and $N = N_0 q$, then N_0 is the fundamental period of the sinusoid. These results hold for the complex exponential signal $e^{j(\omega_0 n + \theta)}$ as well.

FINITE-ENERGY AND FINITE-POWER SIGNALS

We defined signals as very general functions of time, although it is of interest to define classes of signals with special properties that make them significant in engineering. Such classes include signals with finite energy and signals of finite power.

The instantaneous power dissipated in a resistor of resistance R is simply the product of the voltage across and the current through the resistor:

$$p(t) = v(t)i(t) = \frac{v^2(t)}{R}, \tag{1.32}$$

and the *total energy* dissipated during a time interval $[t_1,t_2]$ is obtained by integrating the power

$$E_{[t_1,t_2]} = \int_{t_1}^{t_2} p(t)dt = \int_{t_1}^{t_2} \frac{v^2(t)}{R} dt. \tag{1.33}$$

The *average power* dissipated over that interval is the total energy divided by the time interval:

$$P_{[t_1,t_2]} = \frac{1}{t_2 - t_1} \int_{t_1}^{t_2} \frac{v^2(t)}{R} dt. \tag{1.34}$$

Analogously, the total energy and average power over $[t_1,t_2]$ of an arbitrary integrable continuous-time signal $x(t)$ are defined as though the signal were a voltage across a one-ohm resistor:

$$E_{[t_1,t_2]} := \int_{t_1}^{t_2} |x(t)|^2 \, dt, \tag{1.35}$$

$$P_{[t_1,t_2]} := \frac{1}{t_2 - t_1} \int_{t_1}^{t_2} |x(t)|^2 \, dt. \tag{1.36}$$

The total energy and total average power of a signal defined over $t \in \mathbb{R}$ are defined as

$$E_\infty := \lim_{T\to\infty} \int_{-T}^{T} |x(t)|^2 \, dt = \int_{-\infty}^{\infty} |x(t)|^2 \, dt, \tag{1.37}$$

$$P_\infty := \lim_{T\to\infty} \frac{1}{2T} \int_{-T}^{T} |x(t)|^2 \, dt. \tag{1.38}$$

The total energy and average power over $[n_1,n_2]$ of an arbitrary discrete-time signal $x[n]$ are defined as

$$E_{[n_1,n_2]} := \sum_{n=n_1}^{n_2} |x[n]|^2, \tag{1.39}$$

$$P_{[n_1,n_2]} := \frac{1}{n_2 - n_1 + 1}\sum_{n=n_1}^{n_2} |x[n]|^2. \tag{1.40}$$

Notice that $n_2 - n_1 + 1$ is the number of points in the signal over the interval $[n_1, n_2]$. The total energy and total average power of signal $x[n]$ defined over $n \in \mathbb{Z}$ are defined as

$$E_\infty := \lim_{N\to\infty}\sum_{n=-N}^{N} |x[n]|^2 = \sum_{n=-\infty}^{\infty} |x[n]|^2, \tag{1.41}$$

$$P_\infty := \lim_{N\to\infty}\frac{1}{2N+1}\sum_{n=-N}^{N} |x[n]|^2. \tag{1.42}$$

The class of continuous-time or discrete-time *finite-energy signals* is defined as the set of all signals for which $E_\infty < +\infty$.

Example 1.10: The discrete-time signal $x[n] := \begin{cases} 1, 0 \le n \le 10 \\ 0, \text{otherwise} \end{cases}$, for which $E_\infty = 11$ is a finite-energy signal.

The class of continuous-time or discrete-time *finite-power signals* is defined as the set of all signals for which $P_\infty < +\infty$.

Example 1.11: The constant signal $x(t) = 4$ has infinite energy, but a total average power of 16:

$$P_\infty := \lim_{T\to\infty}\frac{1}{2T}\int_{-T}^{T} 4^2\,dt = \lim_{T\to\infty}\frac{4^2}{2T}2T = 16. \tag{1.43}$$

The total average power of a periodic signal can be calculated over one period only as $P_\infty = \frac{1}{T}\int_0^T |x(t)|^2\,dt$.

Example 1.12: For $x(t) = Ce^{j\omega_0 t}$, the total average power is computed as

$$P_\infty = \frac{1}{T}\int_0^T |Ce^{j\omega_0 t}|^2\,dt = \frac{|C|^2}{T}\int_0^T dt = \frac{|C|^2}{T}\left[T - 0\right] = |C|^2. \tag{1.44}$$

Note that $e^{j\omega_0 t}$ has unit power.

EVEN AND ODD SIGNALS

A continuous-time signal is said to be *even* if $x(t) = x(-t)$, and a discrete-time signal is even if $x[n] = x[-n]$. An even signal is therefore symmetric with respect to the vertical axis.

A signal is said to be *odd* if $x(t) = -x(-t)$ or $x[n] = -x[-n]$. Odd signals are symmetric with respect to the origin. Another way to view odd signals is that their portion at positive times can be flipped with respect to the vertical axis, then with respect to the horizontal axis, and the result corresponds exactly to the portion of the signal at negative times. It implies that $x(0) = 0$ or $x[0] = 0$.

Figure 1.32 shows a continuous-time even signal, whereas Figure 1.33 shows a discrete-time odd signal.

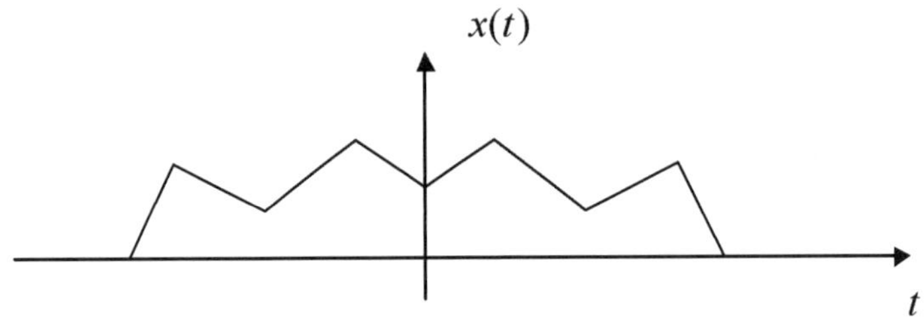

FIGURE 1.32 Even continuous-time signal.

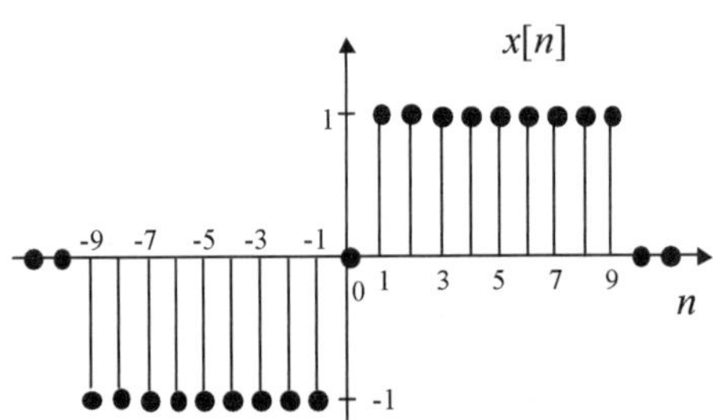

FIGURE 1.33 Odd discrete-time signal.

Any signal can be decomposed into its *even part* and its *odd part* as follows:

$$x(t) = x_e(t) + x_o(t) \tag{1.45}$$

Even part: $$x_e(t) := \frac{1}{2}[x(t) + x(-t)] \tag{1.46}$$

Odd part: $$x_o(t) := \frac{1}{2}[x(t) - x(-t)] \tag{1.47}$$

The even part and odd parts of a discrete-time signal are defined in the exact same way.

DISCRETE-TIME IMPULSE AND STEP SIGNALS

One of the simplest discrete-time signals is the *unit impulse* $\delta[n]$, also called the Dirac delta function, defined by

$$\delta[n] := \begin{cases} 1, & n = 0 \\ 0, & n \neq 0 \end{cases} \tag{1.48}$$

Its graph is shown in Figure 1.34.

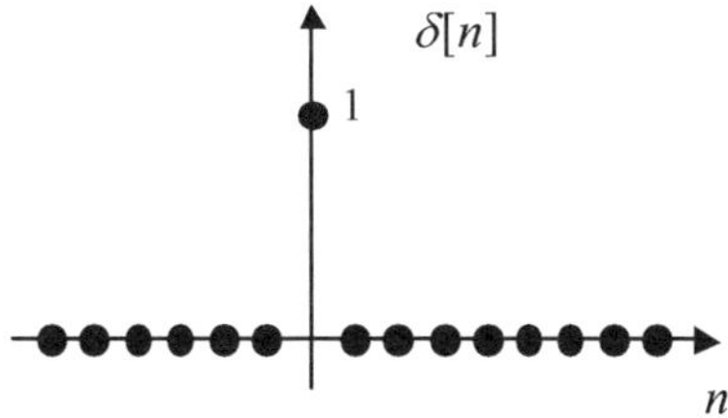

FIGURE 1.34 Discrete-time unit impulse.

The discrete-time *unit step* signal $u[n]$ is defined as follows:

$$u[n] := \begin{cases} 1, & n \geq 0 \\ 0, & n < 0 \end{cases} \tag{1.49}$$

The unit step is plotted in Figure 1.35.

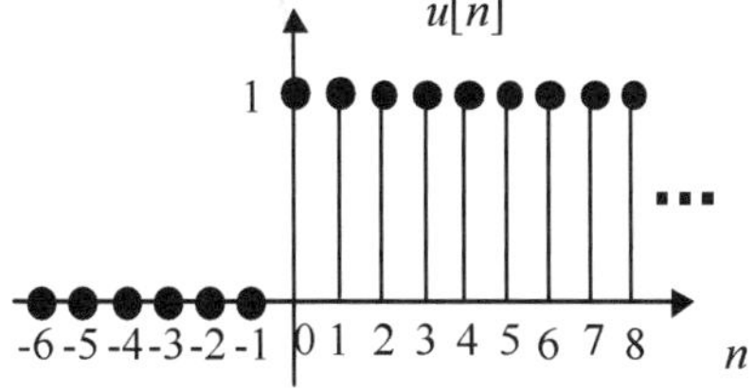

FIGURE 1.35 Discrete-time unit step signal.

The unit step is the running sum of the unit impulse:

$$u[n] = \sum_{k=-\infty}^{n} \delta[k], \tag{1.50}$$

and conversely, the unit impulse is the *first-difference* of a unit step:

$$\delta[n] = u[n] - u[n-1]. \tag{1.51}$$

Also, the unit step can be written as an infinite sum of time-delayed unit impulses:

$$u[n] = \sum_{k=0}^{\infty} \delta[n-k]. \tag{1.52}$$

The *sampling property* of the unit impulse is an important property in the theory of sampling and in the calculation of convolutions, both of which are discussed in later chapters. The sampling property basically says that when a signal $x[n]$ is multiplied by a unit impulse occurring at time n_0, then the resulting signal is an impulse at that same time, but with an amplitude equal to the signal value at time n_0:

$$x[n]\delta[n-n_0] = x[n_0]\delta[n-n_0]. \tag{1.53}$$

Another way to look at the sampling property is to take the sum of Equation 1.53 to obtain the signal sample at time n_0:

$$\sum_{k=-\infty}^{+\infty} x[k]\delta[k-n_0] = x[n_0]. \tag{1.54}$$

((Lecture 3: Generalized Functions and Input-Output System Models))

GENERALIZED FUNCTIONS

Continuous-Time Impulse and Step Signals

The continuous-time *unit step* function $u(t)$, plotted in Figure 1.36, is defined as follows:

$$u(t) := \begin{cases} 1, t > 0 \\ 0, t \leq 0 \end{cases} \tag{1.55}$$

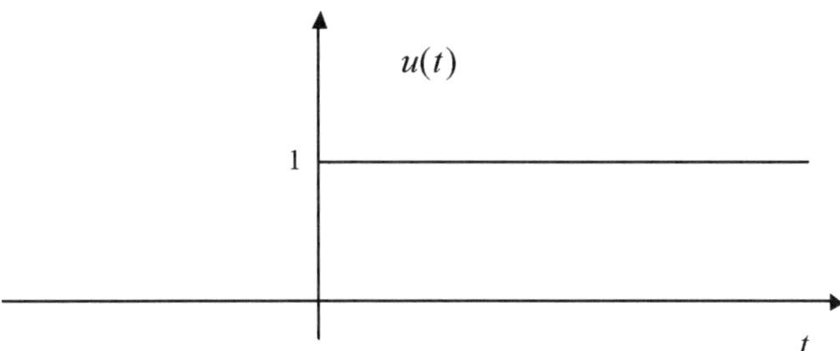

FIGURE 1.36 Continuous-time unit step signal.

Note that since $u(t)$ is discontinuous at the origin, it cannot be formally differentiated. We will nonetheless define the derivative of the step signal later and give its interpretation.

One of the uses of the step signal is to apply it at the input of a system in order to characterize its behavior. The resulting output signal is called the *step response* of the system. Another use is to truncate some parts of a signal by multiplication with time-shifted unit step signals.

Example 1.13: The finite-support signal $x(t)$ shown in Figure 1.37 can be written as $x(t) = e^t[u(t) - u(t-1)]$ or as $x(t) = e^t u(t)u(-t+1)$.

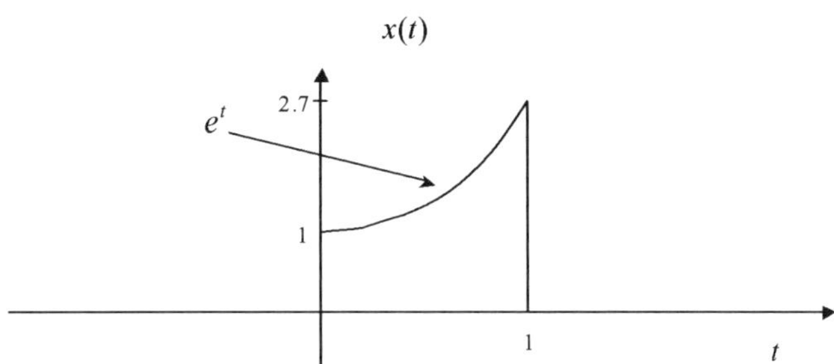

FIGURE 1.37 Truncated exponential signal.

The running integral of $u(t)$ is the *unit ramp* signal $tu(t)$ starting at $t = 0$, as shown in Figure 1.38:

$$\int_{-\infty}^{t} u(\tau)d\tau = tu(t) \qquad (1.56)$$

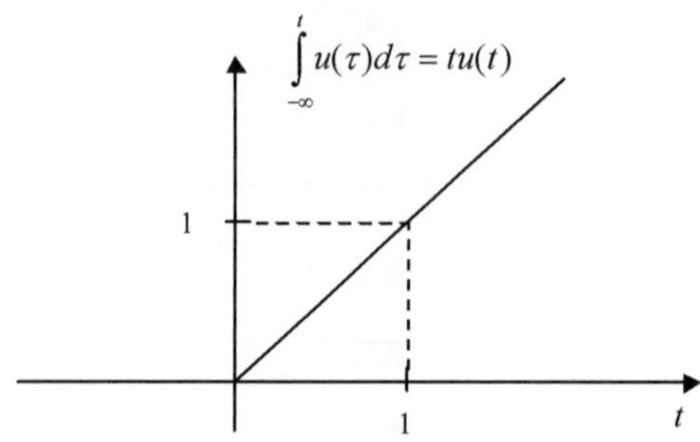

FIGURE 1.38 Continuous-time unit ramp signal.

Successive integrals of $u(t)$ yield signals with increasing powers of t:

$$\int_{-\infty}^{t}\int_{-\infty}^{\tau_{k-1}}\cdots\int_{-\infty}^{\tau_1} u(\tau)d\tau d\tau_1\cdots d\tau_{k-1} = \frac{1}{k!}t^k u(t) \tag{1.57}$$

The *unit impulse* $\delta(t)$, a generalized function that has infinite amplitude over an infinitesimal support at $t=0$, can be defined as follows. Consider a rectangular pulse function of unit area shown in Figure 1.39, defined as:

$$\delta_\Delta(t) := \begin{cases} \frac{1}{\Delta}, & 0 < t < \Delta \\ 0, & \text{otherwise} \end{cases} \tag{1.58}$$

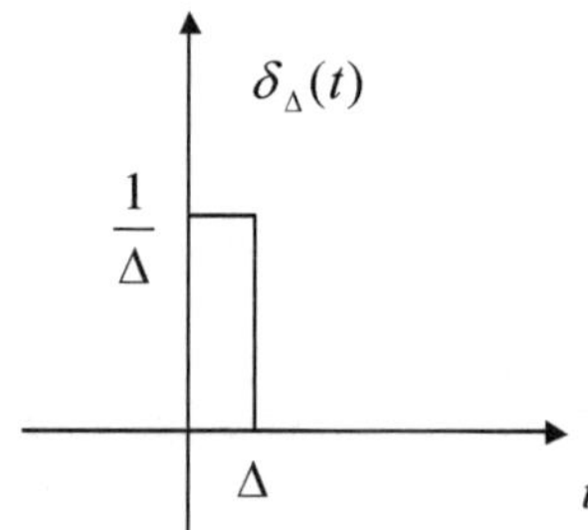

FIGURE 1.39 Continuous-time rectangular pulse signal.

The running integral of this pulse is an approximation to the unit step, as shown in Figure 1.40.

$$u_\Delta(t) := \int_{-\infty}^{t} \delta_\Delta(\tau)d\tau = \frac{1}{\Delta}tu(t) - \frac{1}{\Delta}(t-\Delta)u(t-\Delta) \tag{1.59}$$

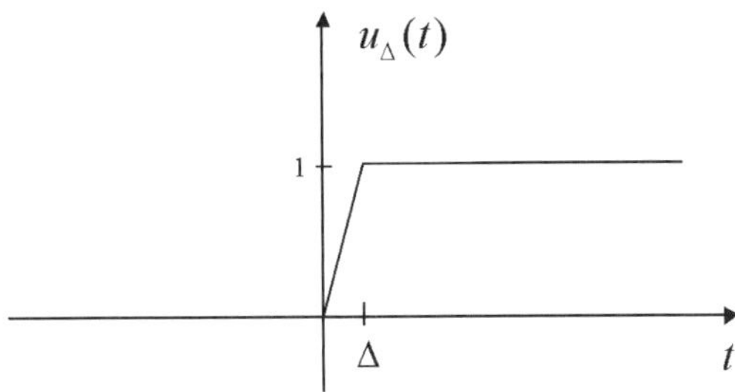

FIGURE 1.40 Integral of rectangular pulse signal approximating the unit step.

As Δ tends to 0, the pulse $\delta_\Delta(t)$ gets taller and thinner but keeps its unit area, which is the key property here, while $u_\Delta(t)$ approaches a unit step function. At the limit,

$$\delta(t) := \lim_{\Delta \to 0} \delta_\Delta(t) \tag{1.60}$$

$$u(t) = \lim_{\Delta \to 0} u_\Delta(t) \tag{1.61}$$

Note that $\delta_\Delta(t) = \frac{d}{dt}u_\Delta(t)$, and in this sense we can write $\delta(t) = \frac{d}{dt}u(t)$ at the limit, so that the impulse is the derivative of the step. Conversely, we have the important relationship stating that the unit step is the running integral of the unit impulse:

$$u(t) = \int_{-\infty}^{t} \delta(\tau)d\tau \tag{1.62}$$

Graphically, $\delta(t)$ is represented by an arrow "pointing to infinity" at $t = 0$ with *its length equal to the area of the impulse*, as shown in Figure 1.41.

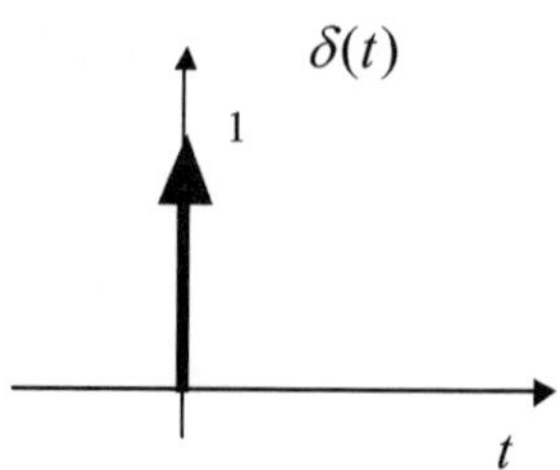

FIGURE 1.41 Unit impulse signal.

We mentioned earlier that the key property of the pulse $\delta_{\Delta}(t)$ is that its area is invariant as $\Delta \to 0$. This means that the impulse $\delta(t)$ packs significant "punch," enough to make a system react to it, even though it is zero at all times except at $t = 0$. The output of a system subjected to the unit impulse is called the *impulse response*.

Note that with the definition in Equation 1.60, the area of the impulse lies to the right of t = 0, so that integrating $A\delta(t)$ from t = 0 yields $\int_0^{\infty} A\delta(t)dt = A$. Had we defined the impulse as the limit of the pulse $\tilde{\delta}_{\Delta}(t) := \frac{1}{\Delta}[u(t+\Delta) - u(t)]$ whose area lies to the left of t = 0, we would have obtained $\int_0^{\infty} A\delta(t)dt = 0$. In order to "catch the impulse" in the integral, the trick is then to integrate from the left of the y-axis, but infinitesimally close to it. This time is denoted as $t = 0^-$. Similarly, the time $t = 0^+$ is to the right of t = 0 but infinitesimally close to it, so that for our definition of $\delta(t)$ in Equation 1.60, the above integral would have evaluated to zero: $\int_{0^+}^{\infty} A\delta(t)dt = 0$.

The following example provides motivation for the use of the impulse signal.

Example 1.14: Instantaneous discharge of a capacitor.

Consider the simple *RC* circuit depicted in Figure 1.42, with a constant voltage source V having fully charged a capacitor C through a resistor R_1. At time t = 0, the switch is thrown from position S_2 to position S_1 so that the capacitor starts discharging through resistor R. What happens to the current $i(t)$ as R tends to zero?

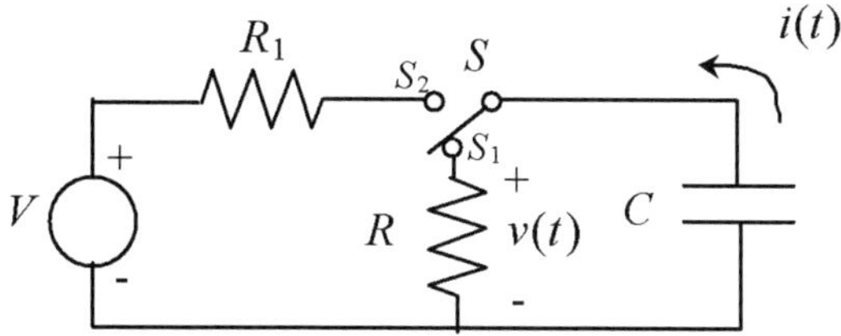

FIGURE 1.42 Simple *RC* circuit for analysis of capacitor discharge.

The capacitor is charged to a voltage V and a charge $Q = CV$ at $t = 0^-$. When the switch is thrown from S_2 to S_1 at $t = 0$, we have:

$$i(t) = \frac{v(t)}{R}, \tag{1.63}$$

$$i(t) = -C\frac{dv(t)}{dt}. \tag{1.64}$$

Combining Equation 1.63 and Equation 1.64, we get

$$RC\frac{dv(t)}{dt} + v(t) = 0. \tag{1.65}$$

The solution to this differential equation is

$$v(t) = Ve^{-t/RC}u(t), \tag{1.66}$$

and the current is simply

$$i(t) = \frac{V}{R}e^{-t/RC}u(t), \tag{1.67}$$

If we let R tend to 0, $i(t)$ tends to a tall, sharp pulse whose area remains constant at $Q = CV$, the initial charge in the capacitor (as $Q = \int_0^\infty i(t)dt$). We get an impulse. Of course if you tried this in reality, that is, shorting a charged capacitor, it would probably blow up, thereby demonstrating that the current flowing through the capacitor went "really high" in a very short time, burning the device.

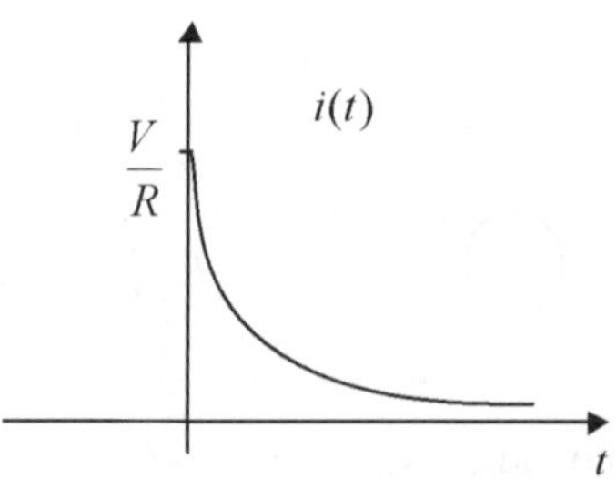

FIGURE 1.43 Capacitor discharge current in *RC* circuit.

Some Properties of the Impulse Signal

Sampling Property

The pulse function $\delta_\Delta(t)$ can be made narrow enough so that $x(t)\delta_\Delta(t) \approx x(0)\delta_\Delta(t)$, and at the limit, for an impulse at time t_0,

$$x(t)\delta(t-t_0) = x(t_0)\delta(t-t_0) \tag{1.68}$$

so that

$$\int_{-\infty}^{\infty} x(t)\delta(t-t_0)dt = x(t_0) \tag{1.69}$$

This last equation is often cited as the correct definition of an impulse, since it implicitly defines the impulse through what it does to any continuous function under the integral sign, rather than using a limiting argument pointwise, as we did in Equation 1.60.

Time Scaling

Time scaling of an impulse produces a change in its area. This is shown by calculating the integral in the sampling property with the time-scaled impulse. For $\alpha \in \mathbb{R}, \alpha \neq 0$:

$$\begin{aligned}\int_{-\infty}^{+\infty} x(t)\,\delta(\alpha t)dt &= \frac{1}{\alpha}\int_{-\infty}^{+\infty} x(\frac{\tau}{\alpha})\,\delta(\tau)d\tau \\ &= \begin{cases} \frac{1}{\alpha}\int_{-\infty}^{+\infty} x(\frac{\tau}{\alpha})\,\delta(\tau)d\tau, & \alpha>0 \\ \frac{1}{\alpha}\int_{+\infty}^{-\infty} x(\frac{\tau}{\alpha})\,\delta(\tau)d\tau, & \alpha<0 \end{cases} \\ &= \frac{1}{|\alpha|}\int_{-\infty}^{+\infty} x(\frac{\tau}{\alpha})\,\delta(\tau)d\tau \\ &= \frac{1}{|\alpha|}x(0) \end{aligned} \tag{1.70}$$

Hence,

$$\delta(\alpha t) = \frac{1}{|\alpha|}\delta(t). \tag{1.71}$$

Note that the equality sign in Equation 1.71 means that both of these impulses have the same effect under the integral in the sampling property.

Time Shift

The *convolution* of signals $x(t)$ and $y(t)$ is defined as

$$x(t) * y(t) := \int_{-\infty}^{\infty} x(\tau)y(t-\tau)d\tau = \int_{-\infty}^{\infty} y(\tau)x(t-\tau)d\tau \tag{1.72}$$

The convolution of signal $x(t)$ with the time-delayed impulse $\delta(t-T)$ delays the signal by T:

$$\delta(t-T) * x(t) = \int_{-\infty}^{\infty} \delta(\tau-T)x(t-\tau)d\tau = x(t-T) \tag{1.73}$$

Unit Doublet and Higher Order "Derivatives" of the Unit Impulse

What is $\delta'(t) := \frac{d\delta(t)}{dt}$, the *unit doublet*? That is, what does it do for a living? To answer this question, we look at the following integral, integrated by parts:

$$\int_{-\infty}^{\infty} \delta'(t)x(t)dt = \left[x(0)\delta(t)\right]_{-\infty}^{\infty} - \int_{-\infty}^{\infty} \delta(t)\frac{d}{dt}x(t)dt$$

$$= 0 - \frac{dx(0)}{dt} = -\frac{dx(0)}{dt}. \tag{1.74}$$

Thus, the unit doublet samples the *derivative of the signal* at time $t = 0$ (modulo the minus sign.) For higher order derivatives of $\delta(t)$, we have

$$\int_{-\infty}^{\infty} \delta^{(k)}(t)x(t)dt = (-1)^k \frac{d^k x(0)}{dt^k}. \tag{1.75}$$

Why is $\delta'(t)$ called a "doublet?" A possible representation of this generalized function comes from differentiating the pulse $\delta_\Delta(t)$, which produces two impulses, one negative and one positive. Then by letting $\Delta \to 0$, we get a "double impulse" at $t = 0$, as shown in Figure 1.44. Note that the resulting "impulses" are not regular impulses since their area is infinite.

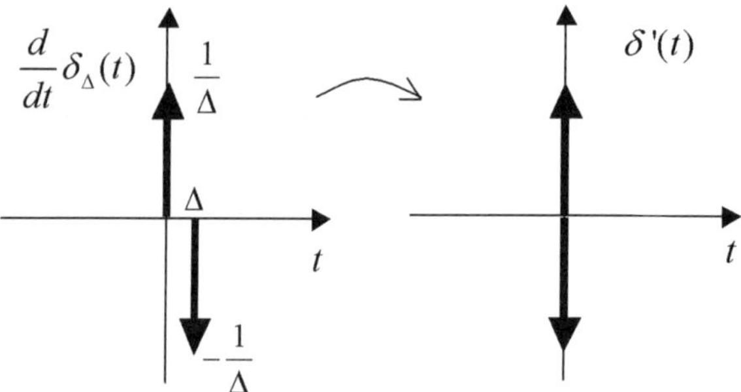

FIGURE 1.44 Representation of the unit doublet.

SYSTEM MODELS AND BASIC PROPERTIES

Recall that we defined signals as functions of time. In this book, a *system* is also simply defined as a mathematical relationship, that is, a function, between an input signal $x(t)$ or $x[n]$ and an output signal $y(t)$ or $y[n]$. Without going into too much d etail, recall that functions map their domain (set of input signals) into their co-domain (set of output signals, of which the range is a subset) and have the special property that any input signal in the domain of the system has a single associated output signal in the range of the system.

Input-Output System Models

The mathematical relationship of a system H between its input signal and its output signal can be formally written as $y = Hx$ (the time argument is dropped here, as this representation is used both for continuous-time and discrete-time systems). Note that this is not a multiplication by H—rather, it means that system (or function) H is applied to the input signal. For example, system H could represent a very complicated nonlinear differential equation linking $y(t)$ to $x(t)$.

A system is often conveniently represented by a block diagram, as shown in Figure 1.45 and Figure 1.46.

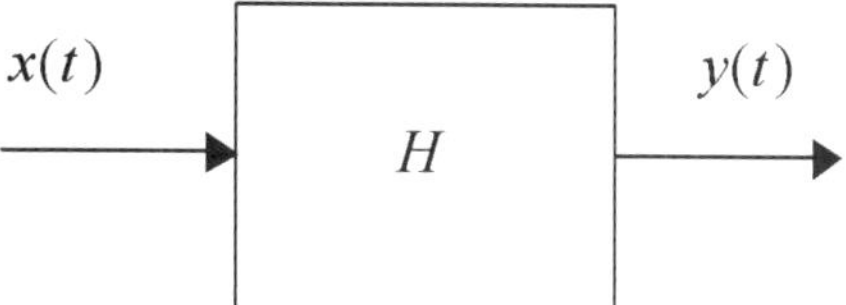

FIGURE 1.45 Block diagram representation of a continuous-time system *H*.

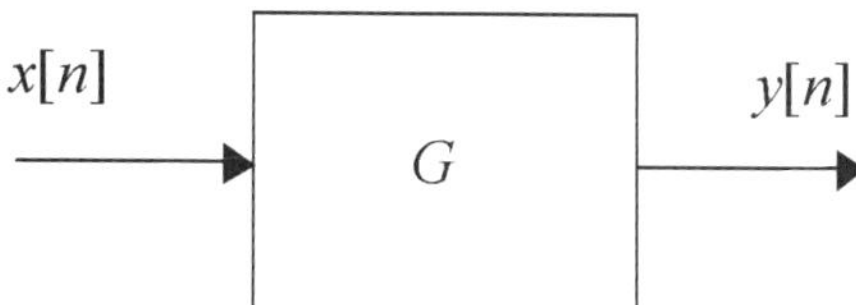

FIGURE 1.46 Block diagram representation of a discrete-time system *G*.

System Block Diagrams

Systems may be interconnections of other systems. For example, the discrete-time system $y[n] = Gx[n]$ shown as a block diagram in Figure 1.47 can be described by the following system equations:

$$\begin{aligned}
v[n] &= G_1x[n] \\
w[n] &= G_2v[n] \\
z[n] &= G_3x[n] \\
s[n] &= w[n] - z[n] \\
y[n] &= G_4s[n]
\end{aligned} \tag{1.76}$$

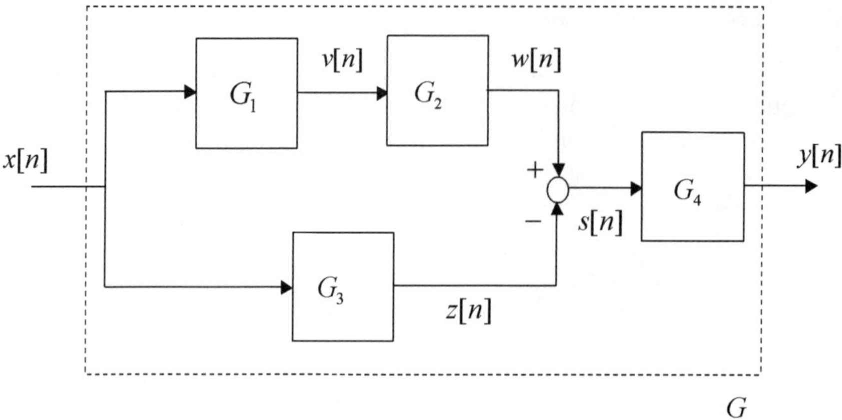

FIGURE 1.47 A discrete-time system composed of an interconnection of other systems.

We now look at some basic system interconnections, of which more complex systems are composed.

Cascade Interconnection

The cascade interconnection shown in Figure 1.48 is a successive application of two (or more) systems on an input signal:

$$y = G_2 \underbrace{(G_1 x)}_{y_1} \tag{1.77}$$

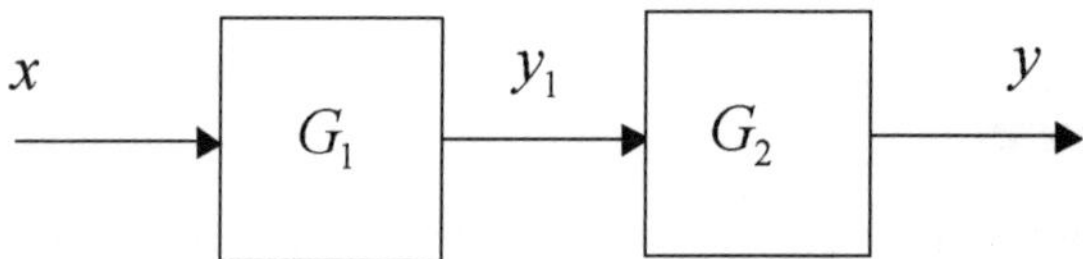

FIGURE 1.48 Cascade interconnection of systems.

Parallel Interconnection

The parallel interconnection shown in Figure 1.49 is an application of two (or more) systems to the same input signal, and the output is taken as the sum of the outputs of the individual systems.

$$y = G_1 x + G_2 x \tag{1.78}$$

Note that because there is no assumption of linearity or any other property for systems G_1, G_2, we are not allowed to write, for example, $y = (G_1 + G_2)x$. System properties will be defined later.

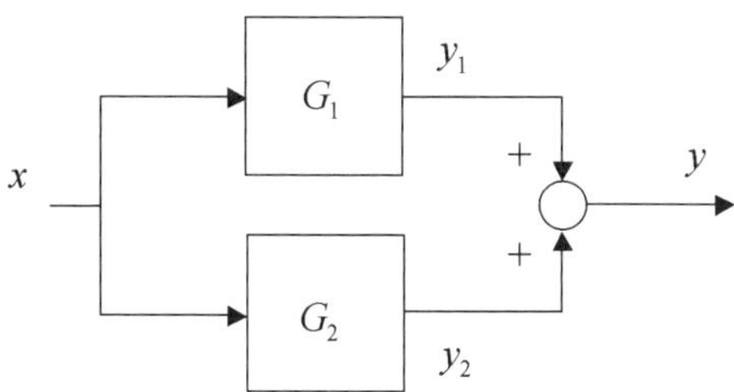

FIGURE 1.49 Parallel interconnection of systems.

Feedback Interconnection

The feedback interconnection of two systems as shown in Figure 1.50 is a feedback of the output of system G_1 to its input, through system G_2. This interconnection is quite useful in feedback control system analysis and design. In this context, signal e is the error between a desired output signal and a direct measurement of the output. The equations are

$$\begin{aligned} e &= x - G_2 y \\ y &= G_1 e \end{aligned} \tag{1.79}$$

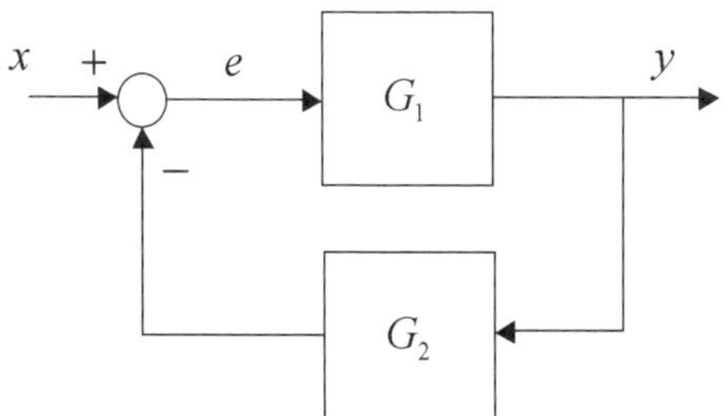

FIGURE 1.50 Feedback interconnection of systems.

Example 1.15: Consider the car cruise control system in Figure 1.51, whose task is to keep the car's velocity close to its setpoint. The system G is a model of the car's dynamics from the throttle input to the speed output, whereas system C is the controller, whose input is the velocity error e and whose output is the engine throttle.

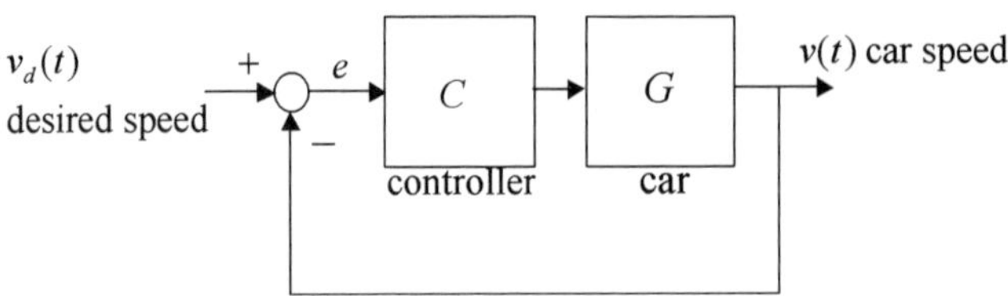

FIGURE 1.51 Feedback interconnection of a car cruise control system.

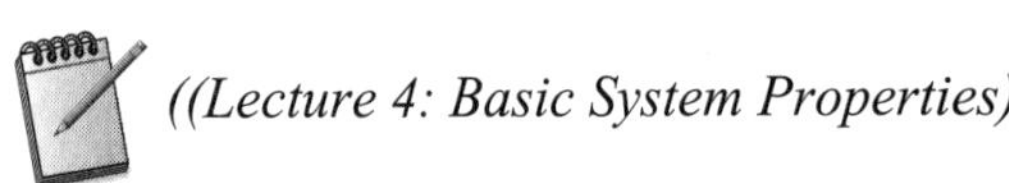
((Lecture 4: Basic System Properties))

Basic System Properties

All of the following system properties apply equally to continuous-time and discrete-time systems.

Linearity

A system S is *linear* if it has the *additivity* property *and* the *homogeneity* property. Let $y_1 := Sx_1$ and $y_2 := Sx_2$.

$$\text{Additivity: } y_1 + y_2 = S(x_1 + x_2) \tag{1.80}$$

That is, the response of S to the combined signal $x_1 + x_2$ is the sum of the individual responses y_1 and y_2.

$$\text{Homogeneity: } ay_1 = S(ax_1), \quad \forall a \in \mathbb{C} \tag{1.81}$$

Homogeneity means that the response of S to the scaled signal ax_1 is a times the response $y_1 = Sx_1$. An important consequence is that the response of a linear system to the 0 signal is the 0 signal. Thus, the system $y(t) = 2x(t) + 3$ is nonlinear because for $x(t) = 0$, we obtain $y(t) = 3$.

The linearity property (additivity and homogeneity combined) is summarized in the important *Principle of Superposition*: *the response to a linear combination of input signals is the same linear combination of the corresponding output signals.*

Example 1.16: Consider the ideal operational-amplifier (op-amp) integrator circuit shown in Figure 1.52.

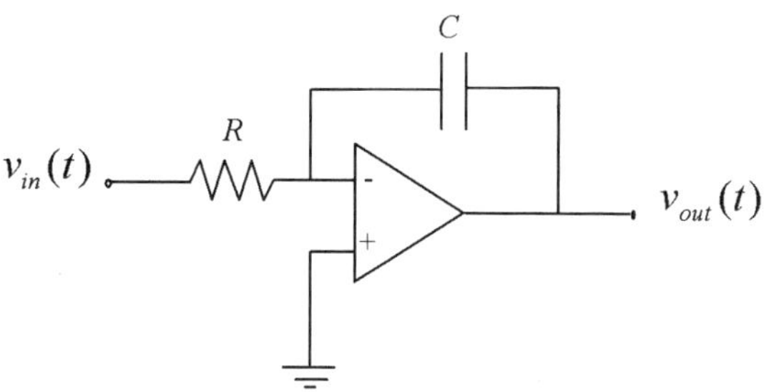

FIGURE 1.52 Ideal op-amp integrator circuit.

The output voltage of this circuit is given by a running integral of the input voltage:

$$v_{out}(t) = \frac{1}{RC}\int_{-\infty}^{t} v_{in}(\tau)d\tau \tag{1.82}$$

If $v_{in}(t) = av_1(t) + bv_2(t)$, then

$$v_{out}(t) = \frac{1}{RC}\int_{-\infty}^{t} v_{in}(\tau)d\tau = \frac{a}{RC}\int_{-\infty}^{t} v_1(\tau)d\tau + \frac{b}{RC}\int_{-\infty}^{t} v_2(\tau)d\tau \tag{1.83}$$

and hence this circuit is linear.

Time Invariance

A system S is *time-invariant* if its response to a time-shifted input signal $x[n-N]$ is equal to its original response $y[n]$ to $x[n]$, but also time shifted by N: $y[n-N]$. That is, if for $y[n] := Sx[n]$, $y_1[n] := Sx[n-N]$, the equality $y_1[n] = y[n-N]$ holds for any integer N, then the system is time-invariant.

Example 1.17: $y(t) = \sin(x(t))$ is time-invariant since $y_1(t) = \sin(x(t-T)) = y(t-T)$.

On the other hand, the system $y[n]=nx[n]$ is not time-invariant (it is *time-varying*) since $y_1[n]=nx[n-N]\neq(n-N)x[n-N]=y[n-N]$.

The time-invariance property of a system makes its analysis easier, as it is sufficient to study, for example, the impulse response or the step response starting at time $t = 0$. Then, we know that the response to a time-shifted impulse would have the exact same shape, except it would be shifted by the same interval of time as the impulse.

Memory

A system is *memoryless* if its output y at time t or n depends only on the input at that same time.

Examples of memoryless systems:

$$y[n]=x[n]^2$$

$$y(t)=\frac{x(t)}{1+x(t)}$$

Resistor: $v(t)=Ri(t)$.

Conversely, a system has *memory* if its output at time t or n depends on input values at some other times.

Examples of systems with memory:

$$y[n]=x[n+1]+x[n]+x[n-1]$$

$$y(t)=\int_{-\infty}^{t}x(\tau)d\tau$$

Causality

A system is *causal* if its output at time t or n depends only on past or current values of the input.

An important consequence is that if $y_1:=Sx_1$, $y_2:=Sx_2$ and $x_1(\tau)=x_2(\tau)$, $\forall\tau\in(-\infty,t]$, then $y_1(\tau)=y_2(\tau)$, $\forall\tau\in(-\infty,t]$. This means that a causal system subjected to two input signals that coincide up to the current time t produces outputs that also coincide up to time t. This is not the case for noncausal systems because their output up to time t depends on future values of the input signals, which may differ by assumption.

Examples of causal systems:
A car does not anticipate its driver's actions, or the road condition ahead.

$$y[n] = \sum_{k=-\infty}^{n} x[k-N], \quad N \geq 1$$

$$\frac{dy(t)}{dt} + ay(t) = bx(t) + cx(t-T) \quad T > 0$$

Example of a *noncausal* system:

$$y[n] = \sum_{k=-\infty}^{n} x[n-k]$$

Bounded-Input Bounded-Output Stability

A system S is *bounded-input bounded-output (BIBO) stable* if for any bounded input x, the corresponding output y is also bounded. Mathematically, the continuous-time system $y(t) = Sx(t)$ is BIBO stable if

$$\begin{aligned} &\forall K_1 > 0, \exists K_2 > 0 \text{ such that} \\ &|x(t)| < K_1, -\infty < t < \infty \quad \Rightarrow \quad |y(t)| < K_2, -\infty < t < \infty \end{aligned} \tag{1.84}$$

In this statement, $\Rightarrow$ means *implies*, $\forall$ means *for every*, and $\exists$ means *there exists*.

In other words, if we had a system S that we claimed was BIBO stable, then for any positive real number K_1 that someone challenges us with, we would have to find another positive real number K_2 such that, for *any input signal* $x(t)$ bounded in magnitude by K_1 at all times, the corresponding output signal $y(t)$ of S would also be bounded in magnitude by K_2 at all times. This is illustrated in Figure 1.53.

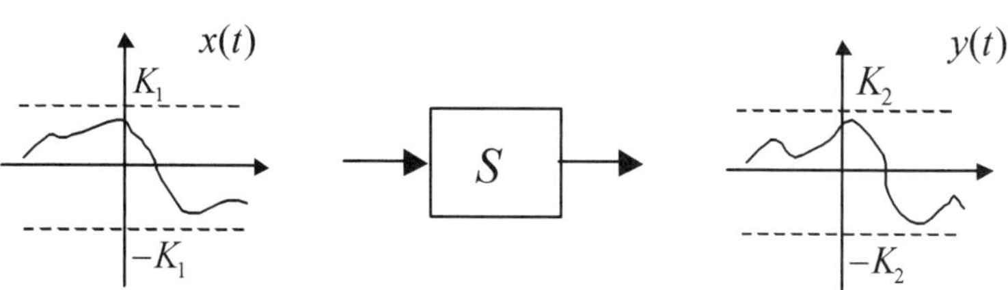

FIGURE 1.53 BIBO stability of a system.

Example 1.18: A resistor with characteristics $v(t) = Ri(t)$ is BIBO stable. For all currents $i(t)$ bounded by K_1 amperes in magnitude, the voltage is bounded by $K_2 = RK_1$ volts. However, the integrator op-amp circuit previously discussed is not BIBO stable, as a constant input would result in an output that tends to infinity as $t \to \infty$.

BIBO stability is very important to establish for feedback control systems and for analog and digital filters.

Invertibility

Recall that a system was defined as a function mapping a set of input signals (domain) into a set of output signals (co-domain). The range of the system is the subset of output signals in the co-domain that are actually possible to get.

It turns out that one can always restrict the co-domain of the system to be equal to its range, thereby making the system *onto* (surjective). Assuming this is the case, a system S is *invertible* if the input signal can always be uniquely recovered from the output signal. Mathematically, for $x_1 \neq x_2$, $y_1 = Sx_1$, $y_2 = Sx_2$, we have $y_1 \neq y_2$, which restricts the system to be *one-to-one* (injective). This means that two distinct input signals cannot lead to the same output signal. More generally, functions are invertible if and only if they are both one-to-one and onto.

The *inverse system*, formally written as S^{-1} (this is not the arithmetic inverse), is such that the cascade interconnection in Figure 1.54 is equivalent to the identity system, which leaves the input unchanged.

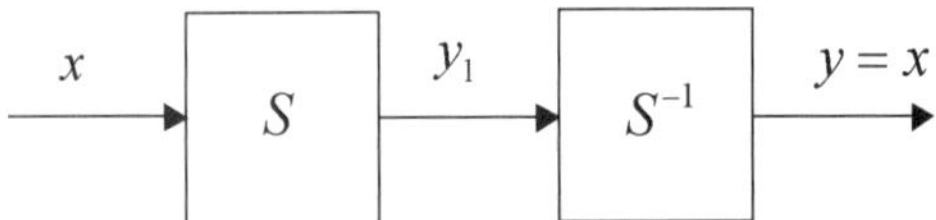

FIGURE 1.54 Cascade interconnection of a system and its inverse.

Example 1.19: The inverse system for $y = 2x$ is just $y = \frac{1}{2}x$.

Exercise: Check that the inverse system of the discrete-time running sum $y[n] = \sum_{k=-\infty}^{n} x[k]$ is the first-difference system $y[n] = x[n] - x[n-1]$.

SUMMARY

In this chapter, we introduced the following concepts.

- A signal was defined as a function of time, either continuous or discrete.
- A system was defined as a mathematical relationship between an input signal and an output signal.

- Special types of signals were studied: real and complex exponential signals, sinusoidal signals, impulse and step signals.
- The main properties of a system were introduced: linearity, memory, causality, time invariance, stability, and invertibility.

TO PROBE FURTHER

There are many introductory textbooks on signals and systems, each organizing and presenting the material in a particular way. See, for example, Oppenheim, Willsky, and Nawab 1997; Haykin & Van Veen, 2002; and Kamen & Heck, 1999. For applications of signal models to specific engineering fields, see, for example, Gold & Morgan, 1999 for speech and signal processing; Haykin, 2000 for modulated signals in telecommunications; and Bruce, 2000 for biomedical signals. For further details on system properties, see Chen, 1999.

EXERCISES

Exercises with Solutions

Exercise 1.1

Write the following complex signals in polar form, that is, in the form $x(t) = r(t)e^{j\theta(t)}$, $r(t), \theta(t) \in \mathbb{R}, r(t) > 0$ for continuous-time signals and $x[n] = r[n]e^{j\theta[n]}, r[n], \theta[n] \in \mathbb{R}, r[n] > 0$ for discrete-time signals.

(a) $x(t) = \dfrac{t}{1 + jt}$

Answer:

$$x(t) = \frac{t}{1 + jt} = \frac{|t|}{\sqrt{t^2 + 1}} e^{j\theta(t)}$$

$$\Rightarrow \quad r(t) = \frac{|t|}{\sqrt{t^2 + 1}}, \quad \theta(t) = \begin{cases} \arctan\left(\dfrac{-t}{1}\right), & t \geq 0 \\ \arctan\left(\dfrac{-t}{1}\right) + \pi, & t < 0 \end{cases}$$

(b) $x[n] = nje^{n+j},\ n > 0$

Answer:

$$x[n] = nje^{n+j} = ne^n e^{j(1+\pi/2)}, n > 0$$
$$\Rightarrow\ r[n] = ne^n,\ \theta[n] = 1 + \pi/2$$

Exercise 1.2

Determine whether the following systems are: (1) memoryless, (2) time-invariant, (3) linear, (4) causal, or (5) BIBO stable. Justify your answers.

(a) $y[n] = x[1-n]$

Answer:

1. Memoryless? No. For example, the output $y[0] = x[1]$ depends on a future value of the input.
2. Time-invariant? No.

$$\begin{aligned} y_1[n] &= Sx[n-N] = x[1-n-N] \\ &\neq x[1-(n-N)] = x[1-n+N)] = y[n-N] \end{aligned}$$

3. Linear? Yes. Let $y_1[n] := Sx_1[n] = x_1[1-n],\ y_2[n] := Sx_2[n] = x_2[1-n]$. Then, the output of the system with $x[n] := \alpha x_1[n] + \beta x_2[n]$ is given by:

$$\begin{aligned} y &= Sx: \\ y[n] &= x[1-n] = \alpha x_1[1-n] + \beta x_2[1-n] \\ &= \alpha y_1[n] + \beta y_2[n] \end{aligned}$$

4. Causal? No. For example, the output $y[0] = x[1]$ depends on a future value of the input.
5. Stable? Yes. $|x[n]| < B, \forall n \Rightarrow |y[n]| = |x[1-n]| < B, \forall n$.

(b) $y(t) = \dfrac{x(t)}{1 + x(t-1)}$

Answer:

1. Memoryless? No. The system has memory since at time t, it uses the past value of the input $x(t-1)$.
2. Time-invariant? Yes. $y_1(t) = Sx(t-T) = \dfrac{x(t-T)}{1 + x(t-1-T)} = y(t-T)$.

3. Linear? No. The system S is nonlinear since it does not have the superposition property:

For $x_1(t), x_2(t)$, let $y_1(t) = \dfrac{x_1(t)}{1 + x_1(t-1)}$, $y_2(t) = \dfrac{x_2(t)}{1 + x_2(t-1)}$

Define $x(t) = ax_1(t) + bx_2(t)$.

Then $y(t) = \dfrac{ax_1(t) + bx_2(t)}{1 + ax_1(t-1) + bx_2(t-1)} \neq \dfrac{ax_1(t)}{1 + x_1(t-1)} + \dfrac{bx_2(t)}{1 + x_2(t-1)} = ay_1(t) + by_2(t)$

4. Causal? Yes. The system is causal, as the output is a function of the past and current values of the input $x(t-1)$ and $x(t)$ only.
5. Stable? No. For the bounded input $x(t) = -1, \forall t \Rightarrow |y(t)| = \infty$, that is, the output is unbounded.

(c) $y(t) = tx(t)$

Answer:

1. Memoryless? Yes. The output at time t depends only on the current value of the input $x(t)$.
2. Time-invariant? No. $y_1(t) = Sx(t-T) = tx(t-T) \neq (t-T)x(t-T) = y(t-T)$.
3. Linear? Yes. Let $y_1(t) := Sx_1(t) = tx_1(t)$, $y_2(t) := Sx_2(t) = tx_2(t)$. Then,

$$\begin{aligned} y(t) &= S[ax_1(t) + bx_2(t)] = t[ax_1(t) + bx_2(t)] \\ &= atx_1(t) + btx_2(t) = ay_1(t) + by_2(t) \end{aligned}$$

4. Causal? Yes. The output at time t depends on the present value of the input only.
5. Stable? No. Consider the constant input $x(t) = B \Rightarrow$ for any K, $\exists T$ such that $|y(T)| = |TB| > K$, namely, $T > \frac{K}{|B|}$; that is, the output is unbounded.

(d) $y[n] = \sum_{k=-\infty}^{0} x[n-k]$

Answer:

1. Memoryless? No. The output $y[n]$ is computed using all future values of the input.
2. Time-invariant? Yes. $y_1[n] = Sx[n-N] = \sum_{k=-\infty}^{0} x[n-N-k] = y[n-N]$.

3. Linear? Yes. Let $y_1[n] := Sx_1[n] = \sum_{k=-\infty}^{0} x_1[n-k]$,

$y_2[n] := Sx_2[n] = \sum_{k=-\infty}^{0} x_2[n-k]$. Then, the output of the system with $x[n] := \alpha x_1[n] + \beta x_2[n]$ is given by

$$y[n] = \sum_{k=-\infty}^{0} x[n-k] = \sum_{k=-\infty}^{0} \alpha x_1[n-k] + \beta x_2[n-k] = \alpha \sum_{k=-\infty}^{0} x_1[n-k] + \beta \sum_{k=-\infty}^{0} x_2[n-k]$$
$$= \alpha y_1[n] + \beta y_2[n]$$

4. Causal? No. The output $y[n]$ depends on future values of the input $x[n+|k|]$.
5. Stable? No. For the input signal $x[n] = B, \forall n \Rightarrow |y[n]| = \left|\sum_{k=-\infty}^{0} x[n-k]\right| = \left|\sum_{k=-\infty}^{0} B\right| = +\infty$; that is, the output is unbounded.

Exercise 1.3

Find the fundamental periods (T for continuous-time signals, N for discrete-time signals) of the following periodic signals.

(a) $x(t) = \cos(13\pi t) + 2\sin(4\pi t)$

Answer:

$$x(t+T) = \cos(13\pi t + 13\pi T) + 2\sin(4\pi t + 4\pi T)$$

will equal $x(t)$ if $\exists k, p \in \mathbb{Z}$ such that $13\pi T = 2\pi k, 4\pi T = 2\pi p$, which yields $T = \frac{2k}{13} = \frac{p}{2} \Rightarrow \frac{p}{k} = \frac{4}{13}$. The numerator and denominator are coprime (no common divisor except 1); thus we take $p = 4, k = 13$, and the fundamental period is $T = \frac{p}{2} = 2$.

(b) $x[n] = e^{j7.351\pi n}$

Answer:

$x[n] = e^{j7.351\pi n} = e^{j\frac{7351}{1000}\pi n}$; thus the frequency is $\omega_0 = \frac{7351}{1000}\pi = \frac{7351}{2000}2\pi$ and the number 7351 is prime, so the fundamental period is $N = 20001$.

Exercise 1.4

Sketch the signals $x[n]=u[n+3]-u[n]+0.5^n u[n]-0.5^{n-4}u[n-4]$ and $y[n]=nu[-n]-\delta[n-1]-nu[n-3]+(n-4)u[n-6]$.

Answer: Signals $x[n]$ and $y[n]$ are sketched in Figure 1.55 and Figure 1.56.

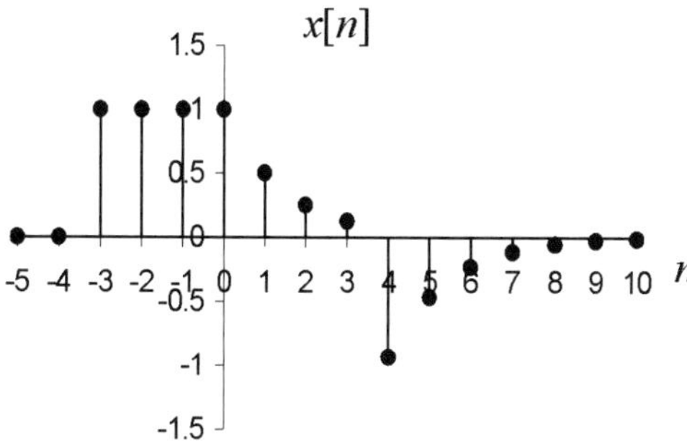

FIGURE 1.55 Signal $x[n]$.

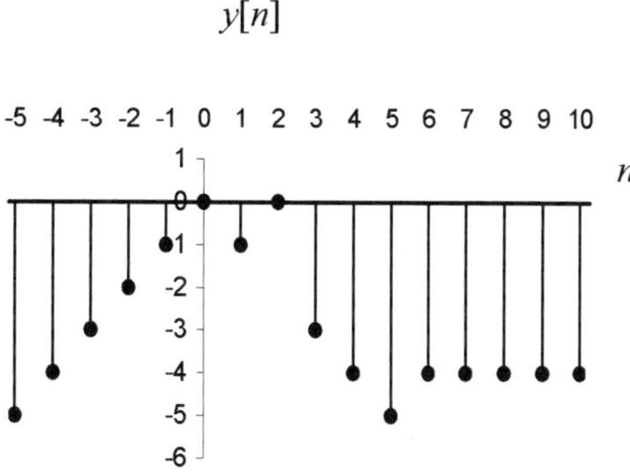

FIGURE 1.56 Signal $y[n]$.

(b) Find expressions for the signals shown in Figure 1.57.

Answer:

$$x(t)=\frac{2}{3}(t+3)u(t+3)-\frac{2}{3}(t+3)u(t)-u(t)+u(t-2)+2\delta(t+1)-\delta(t-3)$$

$$y(t)=\sum_{k=-\infty}^{\infty}2(t-3k)u(t-3k)-2(t-3k-1)u(t-3k-1)-2u(t-2-3k)$$

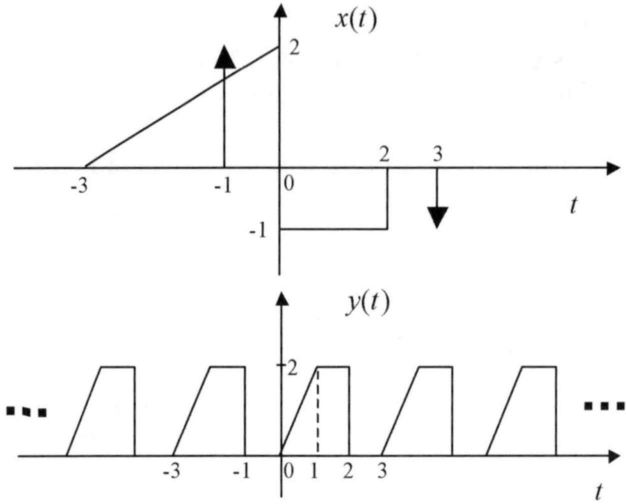

FIGURE 1.57 Plots of continuous-time signals $x(t)$ and $y(t)$.

Exercise 1.5

Properties of even and odd signals.

(a) Show that if $x[n]$ is an odd signal, then $\sum_{n=-\infty}^{+\infty} x[n] = 0$.

Answer:

For an odd signal,

$$x[n] = -x[-n] \Rightarrow x[0] = 0 \text{ and } \sum_{n=-\infty}^{+\infty} x[n] = x[0] + \sum_{n=1}^{+\infty}(x[n] + x[-n]) = \sum_{n=1}^{+\infty}(x[n] - x[n]) = 0$$

(b) Show that if $x_1[n]$ is odd and $x_2[n]$ is even, then their product is odd.

Answer:

$$x_1[n] = -x_1[-n], \quad x_2[n] = x_2[-n]$$
$$\Rightarrow \quad x_1[-n]x_2[-n] = -x_1[n]x_2[n]$$

(c) Let $x[n]$ be an arbitrary signal with even and odd parts $x_e[n], x_o[n]$. Show that $\sum_{n=-\infty}^{+\infty} x^2[n] = \sum_{n=-\infty}^{+\infty} x_e^2[n] + \sum_{n=-\infty}^{+\infty} x_o^2[n]$.

Answer:

$$\sum_{n=-\infty}^{+\infty} x^2[n] = \sum_{n=-\infty}^{+\infty} (x_e[n]+x_o[n])^2 = \sum_{n=-\infty}^{+\infty} x_e^{\,2}[n] + 2\underbrace{\sum_{n=-\infty}^{+\infty} x_e[n]x_o[n]}_{=0} + \sum_{n=-\infty}^{+\infty} x_o^{\,2}[n]$$

$$= \sum_{n=-\infty}^{+\infty} x_e^{\,2}[n] + \sum_{n=-\infty}^{+\infty} x_o^{\,2}[n]$$

(d) Similarly, show that $\int_{-\infty}^{+\infty} x^2(t)dt = \int_{-\infty}^{+\infty} x_e^{\,2}(t)dt + \int_{-\infty}^{+\infty} x_o^{\,2}(t)dt$.

Answer:

$$\int_{-\infty}^{+\infty} x^2(t)dt = \int_{-\infty}^{+\infty} (x_e(t)+x_o(t))^2\,dt = \int_{-\infty}^{+\infty} x_e^{\,2}(t)dt + 2\underbrace{\int_{-\infty}^{+\infty} x_e(t)x_o(t)dt}_{0} + \int_{-\infty}^{+\infty} x_o^{\,2}(t)dt$$

$$= \int_{-\infty}^{+\infty} x_e^{\,2}(t)dt + \int_{-\infty}^{+\infty} x_o^{\,2}(t)dt$$

Exercises

Exercise 1.6

Write the following complex signals in rectangular form: $x(t) = a(t) + jb(t),\ a(t),\ b(t) \in \mathbb{R}$ for continuous-time signals and $x[n] = a[n] + jb[n],\ a[n], b[n] \in \mathbb{R}$ for discrete-time signals.

(a) $x(t) = e^{(-2+j3)t}$

(b) $x(t) = e^{-j\pi t}u(t) + e^{(2+j\pi)t}u(-t)$

Exercise 1.7

Use the sampling property of the impulse to simplify the following expressions.

(a) $x(t) = e^{-t}\cos(10t)\delta(t)$

(b) $x(t) = \sin(2\pi t)\sum_{k=0}^{\infty}\delta(t-k)$

(c) $x[n] = \cos(0.2\pi n)\sum_{k=-\infty}^{0}\delta[n-10k]$

Answer:

ON THE CD

Exercise 1.8

Compute the convolution $\delta(t-T)*e^{-2t}u(t)=\int_{-\infty}^{\infty}\delta(\tau-T)e^{-2(t-\tau)}u(t-\tau)d\tau$.

Exercise 1.9

Write the following complex signals in (i) polar form and (ii) rectangular form.

Polar form: $x(t)=r(t)e^{j\theta(t)}, r(t),\theta(t)\in\mathbb{R}$ for continuous-time signals and $x[n]=r[n]e^{j\theta[n]}, r[n],\theta[n]\in\mathbb{R}$ for discrete-time signals.

Rectangular form: $x(t)=a(t)+jb(t), a(t),b(t)\in\mathbb{R}$ for continuous-time signals and $x[n]=a[n]+jb[n], a[n],b[n]\in\mathbb{R}$ for discrete-time signals.

(a) $x_1(t)=j+\dfrac{t}{1-j}$

(b) $x_2[n]=jn+e^{j2n}$

Answer:

ON THE CD

Exercise 1.10

Determine whether the following systems are (i) memoryless, (ii) time-invariant, (iii) linear, (iv) causal, or (v) BIBO stable. Justify your answers.

(a) $y(t)=\dfrac{d}{dt}x(t)$, where the time derivative of $x(t)$ is defined as

$$\frac{d}{dt}x(t):=\lim_{\Delta t\to 0}\frac{x(t)-x(t-\Delta t)}{\Delta t}.$$

(b) $y(t)=\dfrac{t}{1+x(t-1)}$

(c) $y(t)=2tx(2t)$

(d) $y[n]=\sum_{k=-\infty}^{n}x[k-n]$

(e) $y[n]=x[n]+nx[n+1]$

(f) $y[n]=x[n]+x[n-2]$

Exercise 1.11

Find the fundamental periods and fundamental frequencies of the following periodic signal.

(a) $x[n] = \cos(0.01\pi n)e^{j0.13\pi n}$

(b) $x(t) = \sum_{k=-\infty}^{\infty} e^{-(t-2k)} \cos\left(4\pi(t-2k)\right)\left[u(t-2k) - u(t-2k-1)\right]$. Sketch this signal.

Answer:

ON THE CD

2 Linear Time-Invariant Systems

In This Chapter

- Discrete-Time LTI Systems: The Convolution Sum
- Continuous-Time LTI Systems: The Convolution Integral
- Properties of Linear Time-Invariant Systems
- Summary
- To Probe Further
- Exercises

((Lecture 5: LTI Systems; Convolution Sum))

Many physical processes can be represented by, and successfully analyzed with, linear time-invariant (LTI) systems as models. For example, both a DC motor or a liquid mixing tank have constant dynamical behavior (time-invariant) and can be modeled by linear differential equations. Filter circuits designed with operational amplifiers are usually modeled as LTI systems for analysis. LTI models are also extremely useful for design. A process control engineer would typically design a level controller for the mixing tank based on a set of linearized, time-invariant differential equations. DC motors are often used in industrial robots and may be controlled using simple LTI controllers designed using LTI models of the motors and the robot.

DISCRETE-TIME LTI SYSTEMS: THE CONVOLUTION SUM

It is arguably easier to introduce the concept of convolution in discrete time, which amounts to a sum, rather than in continuous time, where the convolution is an integral. This is why we are starting the discussion of LTI systems in discrete time. We will see that the convolution sum is the mathematical relationship that links the input and output signals in any linear time-invariant discrete-time system. Given an LTI system and an input signal $x[n]$, the convolution sum will allow us to compute the corresponding output signal $y[n]$ of the system.

Representation of Discrete-Time Signals in Terms of Impulses

A discrete-time signal $x[n]$ can be viewed as a linear combination of time-shifted impulses:

$$x[n] = \sum_{k=-\infty}^{\infty} x[k]\delta[n-k]. \tag{2.1}$$

Example 2.1: The finite-support signal $x[n]$ shown in Figure 2.1 is the sum of four impulses.

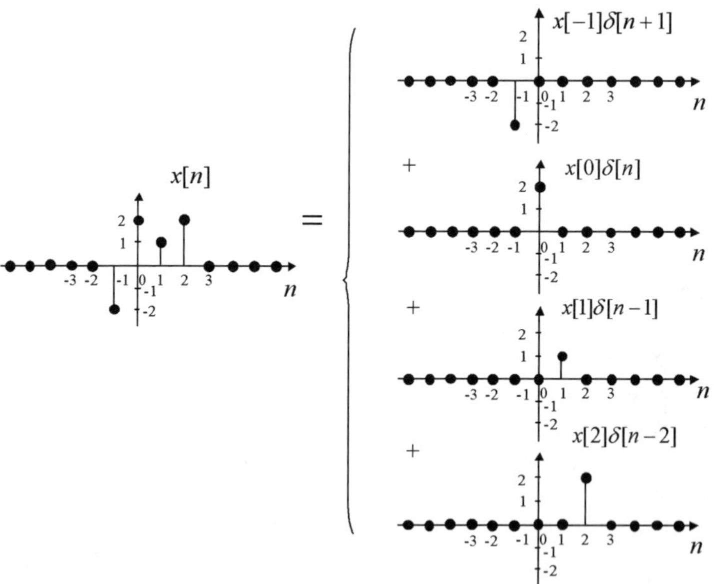

FIGURE 2.1 Decomposition of a discrete-time signal as a sum of shifted impulses.

Thus the signal can be written as $x[n] = -2\delta[n+1] + 2\delta[n] + \delta[n-1] + 2\delta[n-2]$.

Response of an LTI System as a Linear Combination of Impulse Responses

We now turn our attention to the class of linear discrete-time systems to which the Principle of Superposition applies.

By the Principle of Superposition, the response $y[n]$ of a discrete-time linear system is the sum of the responses to the individual shifted impulses making up the input signal $x[n]$.

Let $h_k[n]$ be the response of the LTI system to the shifted impulse $\delta[n-k]$.

Example 2.2: For $k = -4$, the response $h_{-4}[n]$ to $\delta[n+4]$ might look like the one in Figure 2.2.

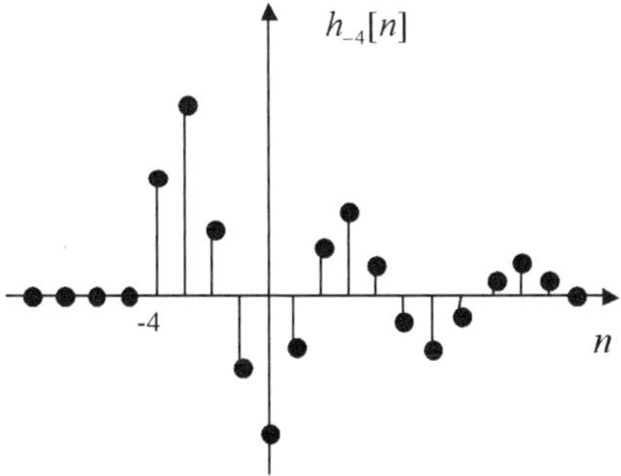

FIGURE 2.2 Impulse response for an impulse occurring at time −4.

Example 2.3: For the input signal $x[n] = -2\delta[n+1] + 2\delta[n] + \delta[n-1] + 2\delta[n-2]$ in Example 2.1, the response of a linear system would be $y[n] = -2h_{-1}[n] + 2h_0[n] + h_1[n] + 2h_2[n]$.

Thus, the response to the input $x[n]$ can be written as an infinite sum of all the impulse responses:

$$y[n] = \sum_{k=-\infty}^{\infty} x[k]h_k[n]. \tag{2.2}$$

If we knew the response of the system to each shifted impulse $\delta[n-k]$, we would be able to calculate the response to *any* input signal $x[n]$ using Equation 2.2. It gets better than this: for a linear *time-invariant* system (the time-invariance property is important here), the impulse responses $h_k[n]$ are just shifted versions of the same impulse response for $k = 0$:

$$h_k[n] = h_0[n-k] \tag{2.3}$$

Therefore, the impulse response $h[n] := h_0[n]$ *of an LTI system characterizes it completely*. This is not the case for a linear *time-varying* system: one has to specify all the impulse responses $h_k[n]$ (an infinite number) to characterize the system.

Example 2.4: Consider the first-order constant-coefficient causal differential equation

$$\frac{dy(t)}{dt} + 3y(t) = x(t) \tag{2.4}$$

and assume the input signal $x(t)$ is given. It is desired to compute the output signal $y(t)$. Suppose that this differential equation is discretized in time in the following manner for simulation purposes: the derivative $\frac{dy(t)}{dt}$ is approximated by $\frac{y(nT_s) - y((n-1)T_s)}{T_s}$, where T_s is the time step (or the sampling period) and nT_s, $n \in \mathbb{Z}$ is the discrete time at the sampling instant. Let $y[n] := y(nT_s)$, $x[n] := x(nT_s)$. Equation 2.4 then becomes the discrete-time LTI system described by the following causal constant-coefficient difference equation:

$$(1+3T_s)y[n] - y[n-1] = T_s x[n] \tag{2.5}$$

Its impulse response can be computed recursively with $x[n] = \delta[n]$ and the initial condition $y[-1] = 0$:

$$\begin{aligned}
h[n] &= y[n] = \frac{1}{1+3T_s} y[n-1] + \frac{T_s}{1+3T_s}\delta[n] \\
h[0] &= \frac{1}{1+3T_s} h[-1] + \frac{T_s}{1+3T_s} = \frac{T_s}{1+3T_s} \\
h[1] &= \frac{1}{1+3T_s} h[0] = \frac{T_s}{(1+3T_s)^2} \\
h[2] &= \frac{1}{1+3T_s} h[1] = \frac{T_s}{(1+3T_s)^3} \\
&\vdots \\
h[k] &= \frac{T_s}{(1+3T_s)^{k+1}} \\
&\vdots
\end{aligned} \tag{2.6}$$

Hence, the impulse response of the discretized version of the differential equation is $h[n]=\frac{T_s}{(1+3T_s)^{n+1}}u[n]$. It should become clear that this discrete-time system is indeed time-invariant by computing by recursion its response to the impulse $\delta[n-N]$ occurring at time N, with the initial condition $y[N-1]=0$, which yields

$$h_N[n]=h[n-N]=\frac{T_s}{(1+3T_s)^{n-N+1}}u[n-N]. \tag{2.7}$$

The Convolution Sum

If we substitute $h[n-k]$ for $h_k[n]$ in Equation 2.2, we obtain the *convolution sum* that gives the response of a discrete-time LTI system to an arbitrary input.

$$y[n]=\sum_{k=-\infty}^{\infty}x[k]h[n-k] \tag{2.8}$$

Remark: In general, for each time n, the summation for the single value $y[n]$ runs over all values (an infinite number) of the input signal $x[n]$ and of the impulse response $h[n]$.

The Convolution Operation

More generally, the *convolution* of two discrete-time signals $v[n]$ and $w[n]$, denoted as $v[n]*w[n]$ (or sometimes $(v*w)[n]$), is defined as follows:

$$v[n]*w[n]=\sum_{k=-\infty}^{\infty}v[k]w[n-k]. \tag{2.9}$$

The convolution operation has the following properties. It is

- Commutative:

$$v[n]*w[n]=\sum_{k=-\infty}^{\infty}v[k]w[n-k]=\sum_{m=\infty}^{-\infty}v[n-m]w[m]=\sum_{m=-\infty}^{+\infty}w[m]v[n-m]=w[n]*v[n] \tag{2.10}$$

(after the change of variables $m=n-k$)

- Associative:

$$\begin{aligned} v[n]*(w[n]*y[n]) &= v[n]*(y[n]*w[n]) \\ &= v[n]*\sum_{k=-\infty}^{+\infty} y[k]w[n-k] \\ &= \sum_{m=-\infty}^{+\infty} v[m]\left(\sum_{k=-\infty}^{+\infty} y[k]w[n-m-k]\right) \\ &= \sum_{m=-\infty}^{+\infty}\sum_{k=-\infty}^{+\infty} y[k]v[m]w[n-m-k] \\ &= \sum_{k=-\infty}^{+\infty}\sum_{m=-\infty}^{+\infty} y[k]v[m]w[n-m-k] \\ &= \sum_{k=-\infty}^{+\infty} y[k]\sum_{m=-\infty}^{+\infty} v[m]w[n-k-m] \\ &= y[n]*\left(\sum_{m=-\infty}^{+\infty} v[m]w[n-m]\right) \\ &= y[n]*(v[n]*w[n]) = (v[n]*w[n])*y[n] \end{aligned} \tag{2.11}$$

- Distributive:

$$\begin{aligned} x[n]*(v[n]+w[n]) &= \sum_{k=-\infty}^{+\infty} x[k](v[n-k]+w[n-k]) \\ &= \sum_{k=-\infty}^{+\infty} x[k]v[n-k] + \sum_{k=-\infty}^{+\infty} x[k]w[n-k] = x[n]*v[n]+x[n]*w[n] \end{aligned} \tag{2.12}$$

- Commutative with respect to multiplication by a scalar:

$$a(v[n]*w[n]) = (av[n])*w[n] = v[n]*(aw[n]) \tag{2.13}$$

- Time-shifted when one of the two signals is time-shifted:

$$v[n]*w[n-N] = \sum_{k=-\infty}^{\infty} v[k]w[n-N-k] = (v*w)[n-N] \tag{2.14}$$

- Finally, the convolution of a signal with a unit impulse $\delta[n]$ leaves the signal unchanged (this is just Equation 2.1), and therefore the LTI system defined by the impulse response $h[n]=\delta[n]$ is the identity system.

Graphical Computation of a Convolution

One way to visualize the convolution sum of Equation 2.8 for simple examples is to draw the weighted and shifted impulse responses one above the other and to add them up.

Example 2.5: Let us compute $y[n] = \sum_{k=-\infty}^{\infty} x[k]h[n-k] = \sum_{k=0}^{2} x[k]h[n-k]$ for the impulse response and input signal shown in Figure 2.3.

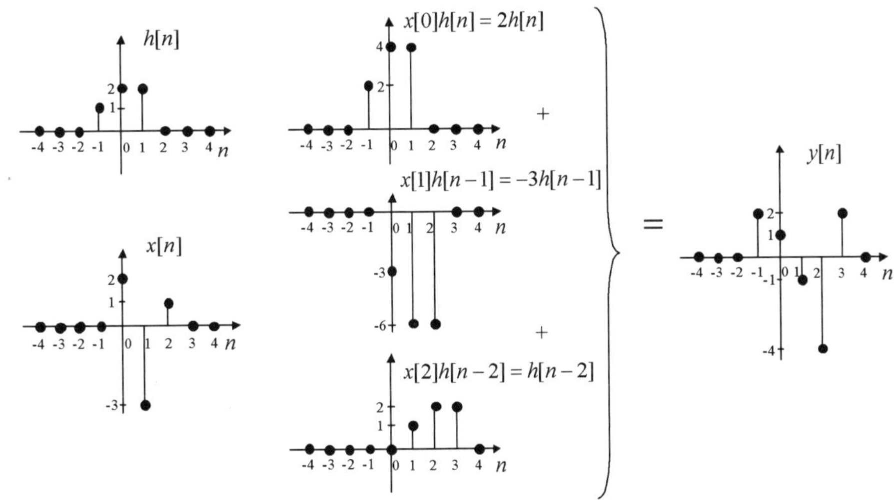

FIGURE 2.3 Graphical computation of a convolution.

Another way to visualize the convolution sum is to draw the signals $x[k]$ and $h[n-k]$ as functions of k (for a fixed n), multiply them to form the signal $g[k]$, and then sum all values of $g[k]$. Both of these approaches to computing a convolution are included in the interactive Java Convolution applet on the companion CD-ROM (in D:\Applets\Convolution\SignalGraph\Convolution.html).

Example 2.6: Let us compute $y[0]$ and $y[1]$ for the input signal and impulse response of an LTI system shown in Figure 2.4.

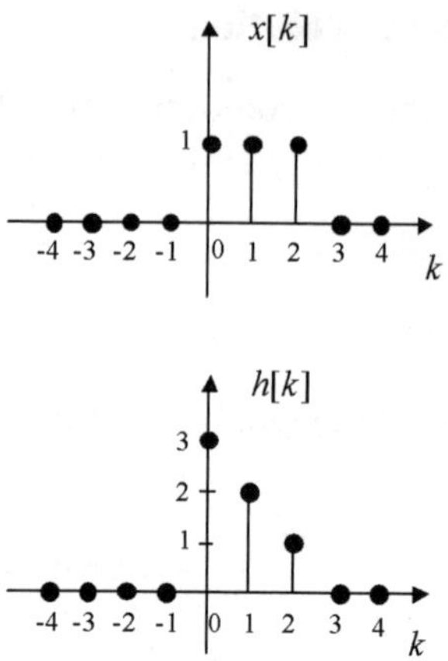

FIGURE 2.4 Convolution of an input signal with an impulse response.

Case $n = 0$:

Step 1: Sketch $x[k]$ and $h[0-k]=h[-k]$ as in Figure 2.5.

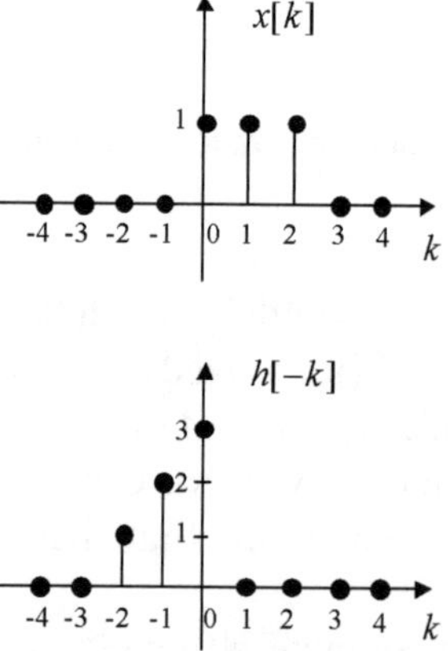

FIGURE 2.5 Impulse response flipped around the vertical axis.

Step 2: Multiply $x[k]$ and $h[-k]$ to get $g[k]$ shown in Figure 2.6.

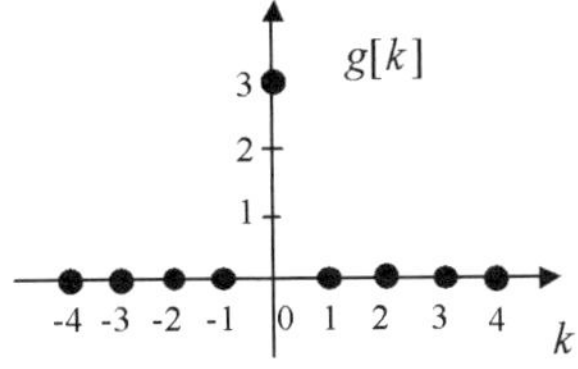

FIGURE 2.6 Product of flipped impulse response with input signal for $n = 0$.

Step 3: Sum all values of $g[k]$ from $k = -\infty$ to $+\infty$ to get $y[0]$:

$$y[0] = 3$$

Case $n = 1$:

Step 1: Sketch $x[k]$ and $h[1-k] = h[-(k-1)]$ (i.e., the signal $h[-k]$ delayed by 1) as in Figure 2.7.

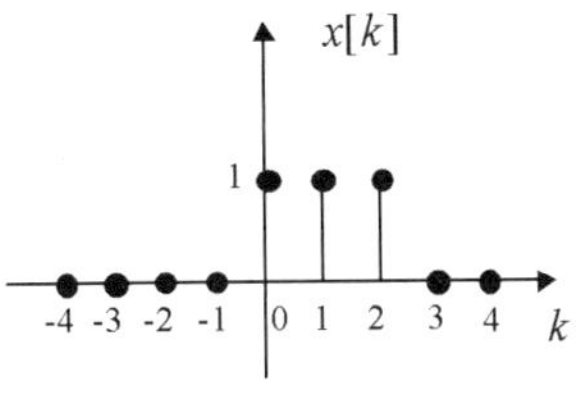

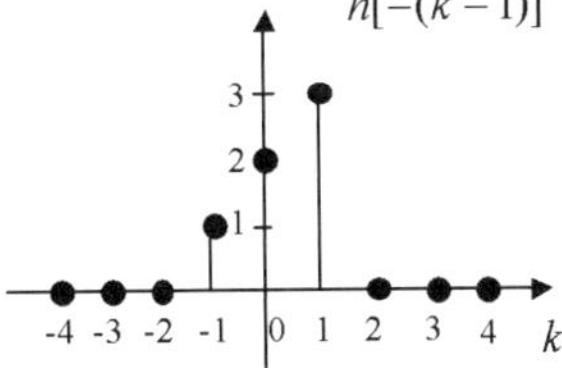

FIGURE 2.7 Time-reversed and shifted impulse response for $n = 1$.

Step 2: Multiply $x[k]$ and $h[1-k]$ to get $g[k]$ shown in Figure 2.8.

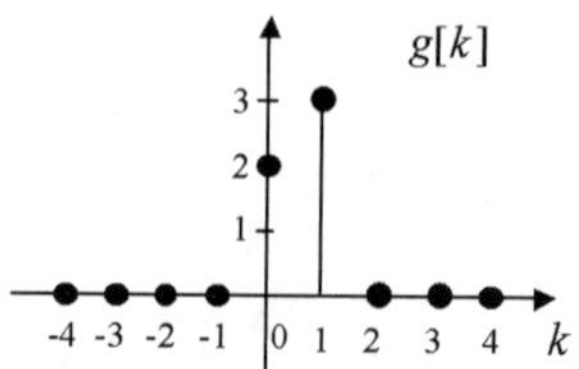

FIGURE 2.8 Product of flipped and shifted impulse response with input signal for $n = 1$.

Step 3: Sum all values of $g[k]$ from $k = -\infty$ to $+\infty$ to get $y[1]$:

$$y[1] = 2 + 3 = 5$$

((Lecture 6: Convolution Sum and Convolution Integral))

Numerical Computation of a Convolution

The numerical computation of a convolution sum $y[n] = \sum_{k=-\infty}^{\infty} x[k]h[n-k]$, is illustrated by means of an example. Let us compute the response of an LTI system described by its impulse response: $h[n] = \begin{cases} (0.8)^n, & 0 \le n \le 5 \\ 0, & \text{otherwise} \end{cases}$ to the input pulse signal $x[n]$ shown in Figure 2.9.

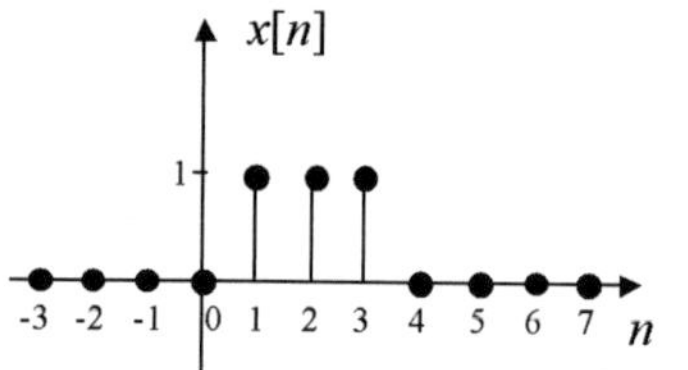

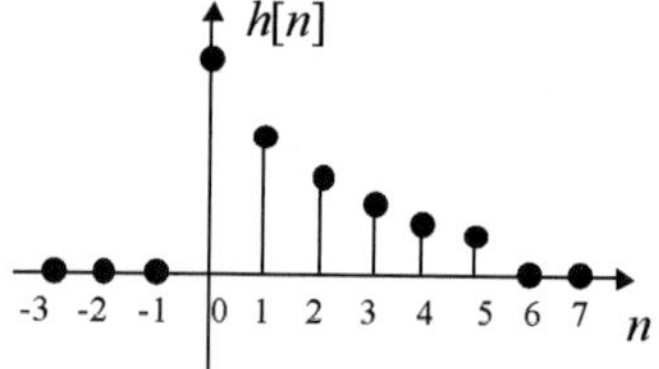

FIGURE 2.9 Impulse response and input signal for numerical computation of a convolution.

First, we sketch $h[-k]$ and $x[k]$, one above the other as shown in Figure 2.10, taking care to indicate where time n is (here $n = 0$) as a label attached to the time-reversed impulse response. The label will move with the impulse response as $h[-(k-n)] = h[n-k]$ is shifted left or right as n changes.

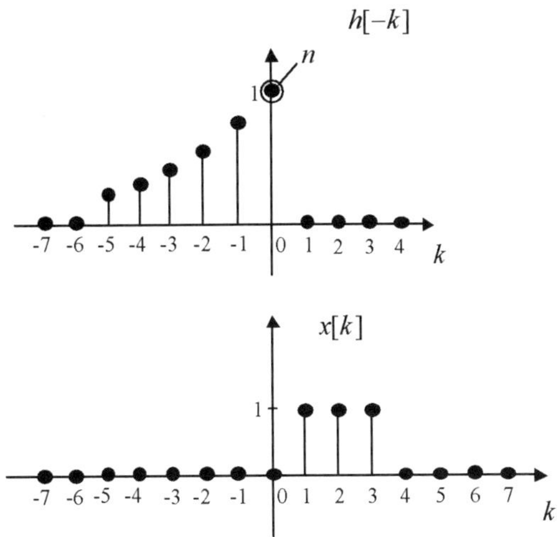

FIGURE 2.10 Time-reversed impulse response and input signal for numerical computation of a convolution.

Now, imagine grabbing the whole signal $h[-k]$ in your hands and bringing it to $k=-\infty$ by making $n\rightarrow-\infty$. Then, you gradually slide the signal back to the right by increasing n (as $h[-(k-n)]$ is a time delay by n of $h[-k]$), and you figure out for what values of n the signals $h[-(k-n)]$ and $x[k]$ start to overlap. The overlapping intervals in time k are used as limits in the convolution sum. What is important to determine is for what values of n these limits change so that the calculation of the convolution effectively changes.

In doing this for the above example, we find that the problem can be broken down into five intervals for n.

For $n < 0$: There is no overlap, so $x[k]h[n-k]$ is zero for all k, and hence $y[n]=0$. This is the situation in Figure 2.10.

For $1\leq n\leq 3$: There is some overlap as $g[k]=x[k]h[n-k]\neq 0$ for $k=1,\ldots,n$. The case $n=2$ is shown in Figure 2.11.

We get

$$\begin{aligned} y[n]&=\sum_{k=1}^{n}g[k]=\sum_{k=1}^{n}(0.8)^{n-k}=(0.8)^{n}\sum_{m=0}^{n-1}(0.8)^{-(m+1)}=(0.8)^{n-1}\sum_{m=0}^{n-1}(0.8)^{-m}\\ &=(0.8)^{n-1}\left(\frac{1-(0.8^{-1})^{n}}{1-(0.8)^{-1}}\right)=\frac{(0.8)^{n}-1}{-0.2}=5-5(0.8)^{n}, \end{aligned} \tag{2.15}$$

where we used the change of variable $m=k-1$.

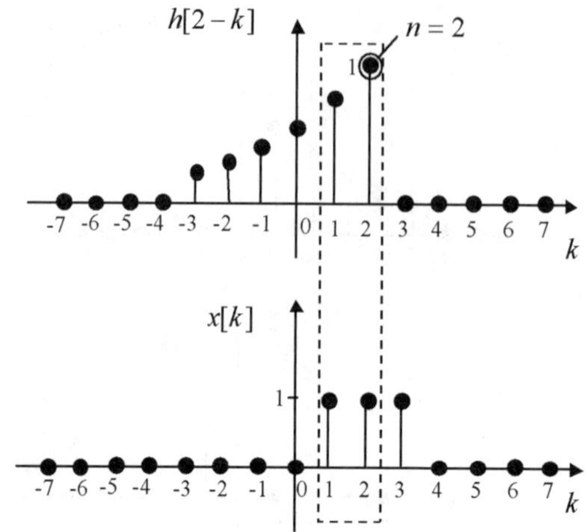

FIGURE 2.11 Time-reversed and shifted impulse response for $n = 2$ with interval of overlap.

For $4 \le n \le 6$: $g[k] = x[k]h[n-k] \neq 0$ for $k = 1,\ldots,3$. The case $n = 5$ is shown in Figure 2.12.

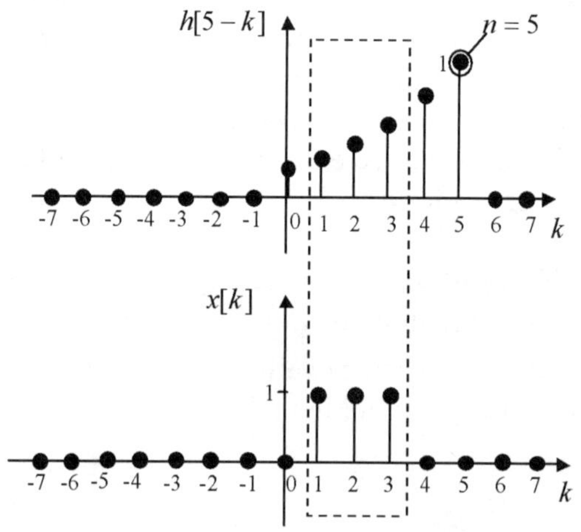

FIGURE 2.12 Time-reversed and shifted impulse response for $n = 5$ with interval of overlap.

We get

$$y[n]=\sum_{k=1}^{3}g[k]=\sum_{k=1}^{3}(0.8)^{n-k}=(0.8)^{n}\sum_{m=0}^{2}(0.8)^{-(m+1)}=(0.8)^{n-1}\sum_{m=0}^{2}(0.8)^{-m}$$
$$=(0.8)^{n-1}\left(\frac{1-(0.8^{-1})^{3}}{1-(0.8)^{-1}}\right)=\frac{(0.8)^{n}-(0.8)^{n-3}}{-0.2}=5(0.8)^{n-3}-5(0.8)^{n}=4.7656(0.8)^{n}, \quad (2.16)$$

where we used the change of variables $m=k-1$.

For $7\le n\le 8$: $g[k]=x[k]h[n-k]\neq 0$ for $n-5\le k\le 3$ (see Figure 2.13).

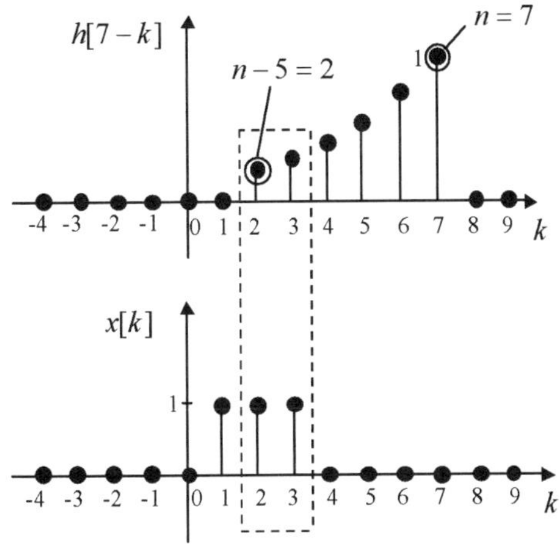

FIGURE 2.13 Time-reversed and shifted impulse response for $n=7$ with interval of overlap.

We have

$$y[n]=\sum_{k=n-5}^{3}g[k]=\sum_{k=n-5}^{3}(0.8)^{n-k}=\sum_{m=0}^{8-n}(0.8)^{n-(m+n-5)}=(0.8)^{5}\sum_{m=0}^{8-n}(0.8)^{-m}$$
$$=(0.8)^{5}\left(\frac{1-(0.8^{-1})^{9-n}}{1-(0.8)^{-1}}\right)=\frac{(0.8)^{6}-(0.8)^{n-3}}{-0.2}=5(0.8)^{n-3}-5(0.8)^{6}, \quad (2.17)$$

where we used the change of variables $m=k-(n-5)$.

For $n\ge 9$: the two signals $x[k], h[n-k]$ do not overlap, so $y[n]=0$.

In summary, the output signal $y[n]$ of the LTI system as given by $x[n]*h[n]$ is

$$y[n]=\begin{cases}0, & n\leq 0\\ 5-5(0.8)^{n}, & 1\leq n\leq 3\\ \left[5(0.8)^{-3}-5\right](0.8)^{n}, & 4\leq n\leq 6\\ 5(0.8)^{n-3}-5(0.8)^{6}, & 7\leq n\leq 8\\ 0, & n\geq 9\end{cases}\tag{2.18}$$

which is sketched in Figure 2.14.

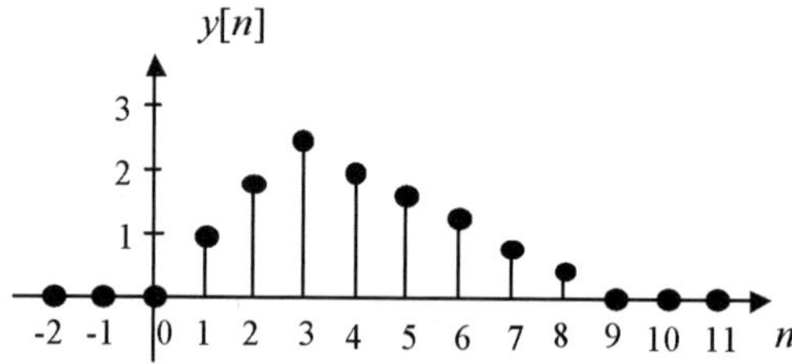

FIGURE 2.14 Output signal obtained by numerical computation of a convolution.

ON THE CD

The following MATLAB M-file located on the CD-ROM in D:\Chapter2\DTconv.m computes the convolution between two discrete-time signals.

```
%% DTconv.m computes the convolution of two discrete-time
%% signals and plots the resulting signal
% define the signals
% first value is for time n=0
x=[1 4 -3 -2 -1];
h=[2 2 2 2 -3 -3 -3 -3 -3];
% compute the convolution
y=conv(x,h);
% time vector
n=0:1:length(y)-1;
%plot real and imaginary parts
stem(n,y)
```

CONTINUOUS-TIME LTI SYSTEMS: THE CONVOLUTION INTEGRAL

In much the same way as for discrete-time systems, the response of a continuous-time LTI system can be computed by a convolution of the system's impulse response with the input signal, using a convolution *integral* rather than a sum.

Representation of Continuous-Time Signals in Terms of Impulses

A continuous-time signal $x(t)$ can be viewed as a linear combination of a continuum of impulses (an uncountable set of impulses infinitely close to one another):

$$x(t) = \int_{-\infty}^{+\infty} x(\tau)\delta(t-\tau)d\tau \tag{2.19}$$

We arrive at this result by "chopping up" the signal $x(t)$ in sections of width Δ as shown in Figure 2.15 and taking the sum in Equation 2.20 to an integral as $\Delta \to 0$.

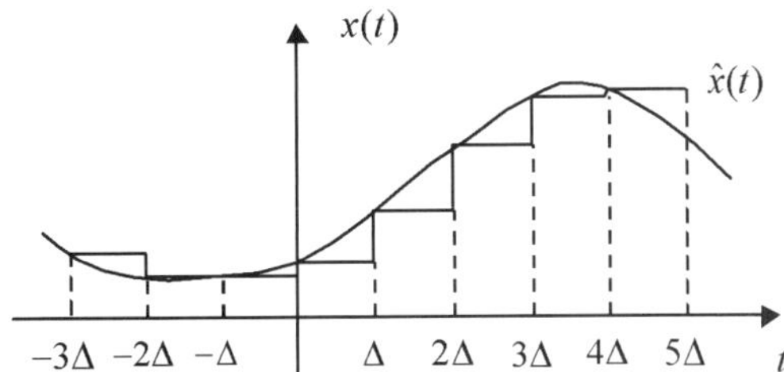

FIGURE 2.15 Staircase approximation to a continuous-time signal.

Recalling our definition of the unit pulse $\delta_\Delta(t)$ (width Δ and height Δ^{-1}), we can define a signal $\hat{x}(t)$ as a linear combination of delayed pulses of height $x(k\Delta)$ (each rectangular section in the above plot.)

$$\hat{x}(t) := \sum_{k=-\infty}^{\infty} x(k\Delta)\,\delta_\Delta(t-k\Delta)\Delta \tag{2.20}$$

Taking the limit as $\Delta \to 0$, we obtain the integral of Equation 2.19 above.

Remarks: As $\Delta \to 0$,

- The summation approaches an integral.
- $k\Delta \to \tau$, so $x(k\Delta) \to x(\tau)$.

- $\Delta \to d\tau$.
- $\delta_\Delta(t-k\Delta) \to \delta(t-\tau)$.

Equation 2.19 can also be arrived at by using the sampling property of the impulse function. If we consider t to be fixed and τ to be the time variable, then we have

$$x(\tau)\delta(t-\tau) = \underbrace{x(\tau)\delta(-(\tau-t)) = x(\tau)\delta(\tau-t)}_{\text{as } \delta(t)=\delta(-t)} \overbrace{= x(t)\delta(\tau-t)}^{\text{sampling property}} \tag{2.21}$$

Hence,

$$\int_{-\infty}^{+\infty} x(\tau)\delta(t-\tau)d\tau = \int_{-\infty}^{+\infty} x(t)\delta(\tau-t)d\tau = x(t)\int_{-\infty}^{+\infty} \delta(\tau-t)d\tau = x(t) \tag{2.22}$$

Impulse Response and the Convolution Integral Representation of a Continuous-Time LTI System

The linearity property of an LTI system allows us to apply the Principle of Superposition to calculate the system's response to the piecewise-constant input signal $\hat{x}(t)$ defined previously. Let $\hat{h}_{k\Delta}(t)$ be the "pulse responses" of the linear *time-varying* system S to the unit area pulses $\delta_\Delta(t-k\Delta)$ for $-\infty < k < +\infty$. Then, by linearity, the response of S to $\hat{x}(t)$ is simply given by

$$\hat{y}(t) := \sum_{k=-\infty}^{\infty} x(k\Delta)\hat{h}_{k\Delta}(t)\Delta \tag{2.23}$$

Note that the response $\hat{h}_{k\Delta}(t)$ tends to the impulse response $h_\tau(t)$ (corresponding to an impulse at time τ) as $\Delta \to 0$. Then, at the limit, we get the response of system S to the input signal $x(t) = \lim_{\Delta \to 0} \hat{x}(t)$:

$$y(t) = \lim_{\Delta \to 0} \hat{y}(t) = \int_{-\infty}^{+\infty} x(\tau)h_\tau(t)d\tau \tag{2.24}$$

For an LTI (not time-varying) system S, the impulse responses $h_\tau(t)$ are all the same as $h_0(t)$, except that they are shifted by τ, just like the discrete-time case. We define the *unit impulse response* (or *impulse response* for short) of the LTI system S as follows:

$$h(t) := h_0(t) \tag{2.25}$$

Then, the response of the LTI system S is given by the *convolution integral*

$$y(t) = \int_{-\infty}^{+\infty} x(\tau)h(t-\tau)d\tau \tag{2.26}$$

Note that an LTI system is completely determined by its impulse response.

The Convolution Operation

Recall that we defined the convolution operation for discrete-time signals in the previous section. The convolution operation for continuous-time signals is defined in an analogous manner. The convolution of $v(t)$ and $w(t)$, denoted as $v(t) * w(t)$, or sometimes $(v * w)(t)$, is defined as follows:

$$v(t) * w(t) = \int_{-\infty}^{+\infty} v(\tau)w(t-\tau)d\tau \tag{2.27}$$

Just like the discrete-time case, the convolution operation is (check as an exercise):

- Commutative: $v(t) * w(t) = w(t) * v(t)$
- Associative: $\left[r(t) * v(t)\right] * w(t) = r(t) * \left[v(t) * w(t)\right]$
- Distributive: $r(t) * \left[v(t) + w(t)\right] = r(t) * v(t) + r(t) * w(t)$
- Commutative with respect to multiplication by a scalar: $\left[\alpha v(t)\right] * w(t) = v(t) * \left[\alpha w(t)\right] = \alpha\left[v(t) * w(t)\right]$
- Finally, the convolution of any signal with a unit impulse leaves the signal unchanged: $v(t) * \delta(t) = v(t)$. Hence, if the impulse response of an LTI system is the unit impulse, then this system is the identity system. This is expressed in Equation 2.19.

((Lecture 7: Convolution Integral))

Calculation of the Convolution Integral

The calculation of a convolution integral is very similar to the calculation of a convolution sum. To evaluate the integral in Equation 2.26 for a specific value of t, we first obtain the signal $h(t-\tau)$ viewed as a function of τ, then we multiply it by $x(\tau)$ to obtain the function $g(\tau)$, and finally we integrate $g(\tau)$ to get $y(t)$.

We now introduce a method to obtain the graph of $h(t-\tau)$ from the graph of $h(\tau)$:

Step 1: Sketch the time-reversed impulse response $h(-\tau)$. This involves flipping the graph of $h(\tau)$ around the vertical axis.

Step 2: Then, shift this new function to the right by t (time delay) for $t > 0$ to obtain $h(-(\tau - t)) = h(t-\tau)$, or to the left by $|t|$ (time advance) for $t < 0$ to obtain $h(-(\tau + |t|)) = h(t-\tau)$.

This method has the advantage of always starting from a single sketch of $h(-\tau)$.

Example 2.7: Given $h(\tau)$ in Figure 2.16, sketch $h(t-\tau)$ for $t=-2$ and $t=2$.

Time reversal is shown in Figure 2.17, and the shifts to the left for $t=-2$ and to the right for $t=2$ are shown in Figure 2.18 and Figure 2.19, respectively.

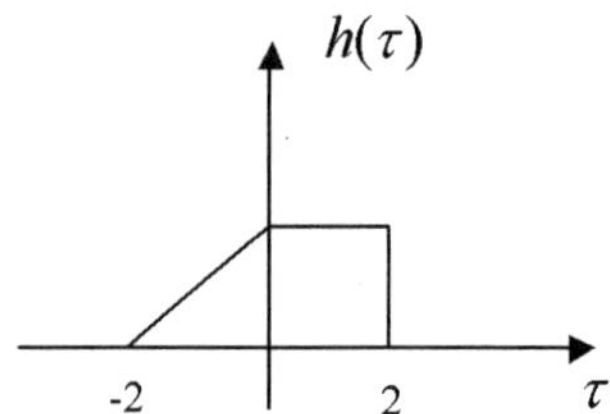

FIGURE 2.16 Impulse response of a continuous-time system.

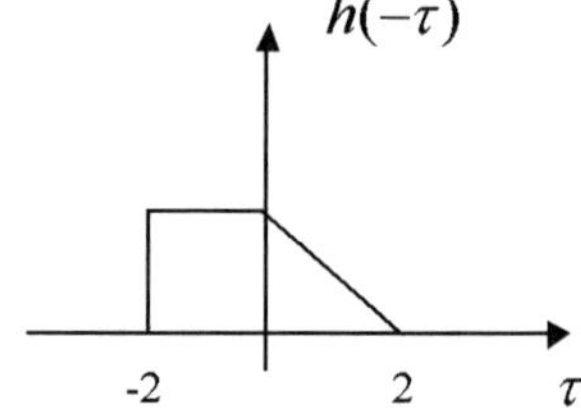

FIGURE 2.17 Time-reversed impulse response.

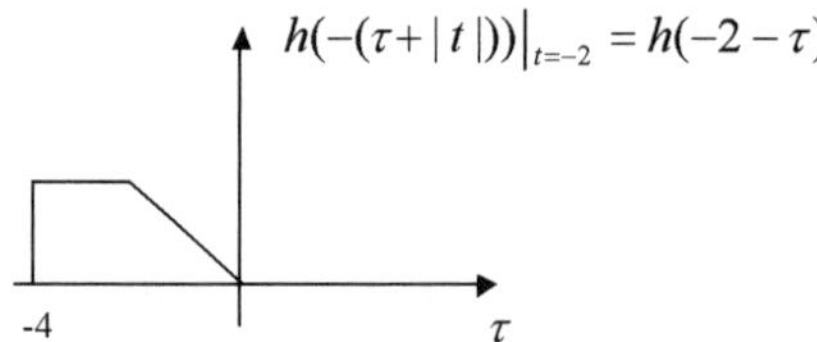

FIGURE 2.18 Time-reversed impulse response shifted to the left.

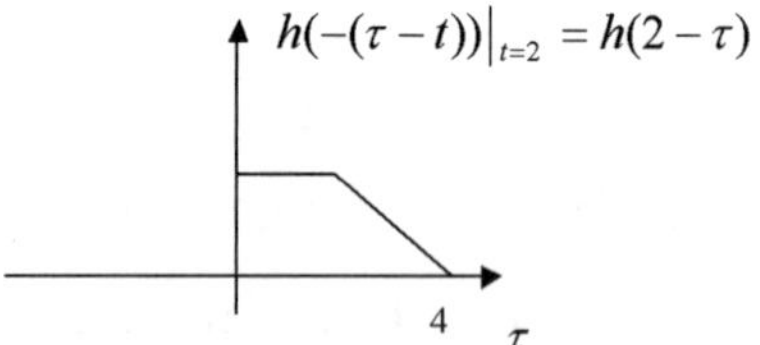

FIGURE 2.19 Time-reversed impulse response shifted to the right.

Remark: A convolution being commutative, sometimes it proves easier to work with $h(\tau)$ and $x(t-\tau)$, instead of $x(\tau)$ and $h(t-\tau)$.

Now, we look at a convolution example. We will compute the response of a continuous-time LTI system described by its impulse response $h(t)=e^{-at}u(t), a>0$ to the step input signal $x(t)=u(t)$, as shown in Figure 2.20.

Sketch $h(-\tau)$ as in Figure 2.21.

Immediately, we see that for $t\leq 0$ in Figure 2.22, the two signals $x(\tau)$ and $h(t-\tau)$ do not overlap, so $g(\tau)=x(\tau)h(t-\tau)=0$ and hence, $y(t)=0$ for $t\leq 0$.

However, for $t>0$, the two functions overlap, as can be seen in Figure 2.23, and $g(\tau)=x(\tau)h(t-\tau)\neq 0$ for $0<\tau<t$.

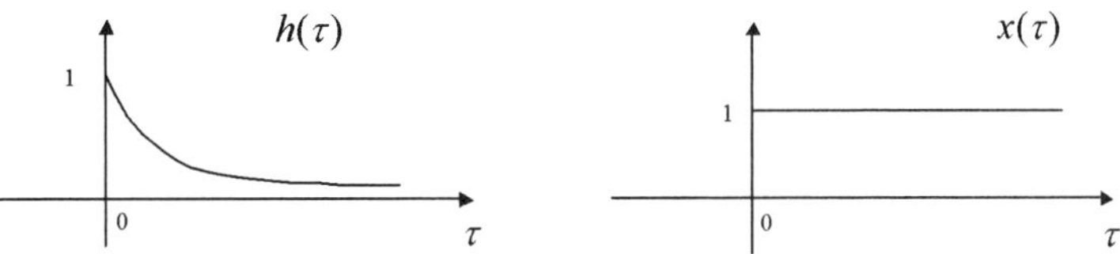

FIGURE 2.20 Exponential impulse response and unit step input to be convolved.

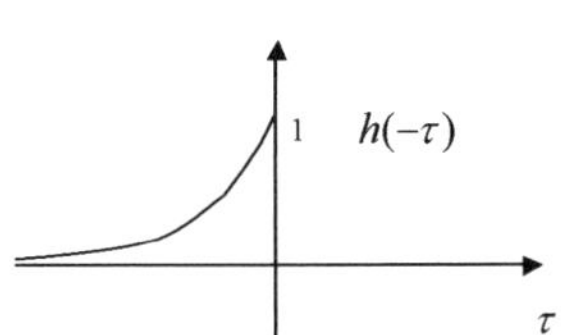

FIGURE 2.21 Time-reversed impulse response.

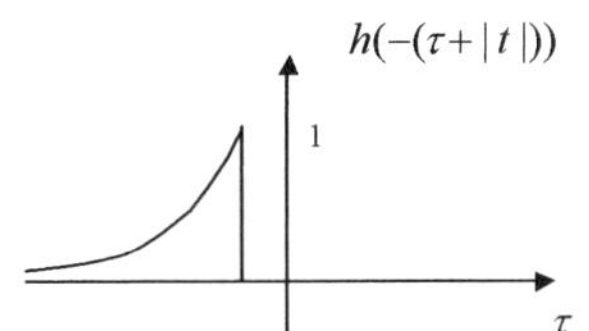

FIGURE 2.22 Time-reversed impulse response shifted to the left for negative times.

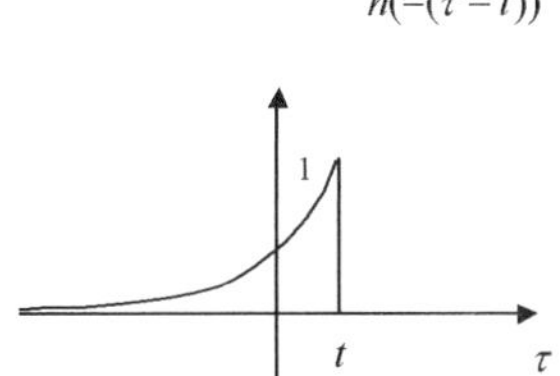

FIGURE 2.23 Time-reversed impulse response shifted to the right for positive times.

Thus, for $t>0$, we have

$$
\begin{aligned}
y(t) &= \int_{-\infty}^{+\infty} g(\tau)d\tau = \int_0^t g(\tau)d\tau \\
&= \int_0^t x(\tau)h(t-\tau)d\tau \\
&= \int_0^t e^{-a(t-\tau)}d\tau = e^{-at}\int_0^t e^{a\tau}d\tau = \frac{1}{a}\left[1-e^{-at}\right]
\end{aligned}
\tag{2.28}
$$

Finally, combining the results for $t \le 0$ and $t > 0$, we get the response

$$y(t) = \frac{1}{a}(1 - e^{-at})u(t), \quad -\infty < t < \infty. \tag{2.29}$$

Since "practice makes perfect," let us look at a second example.

Example 2.8: We want to calculate the response of the continuous-time LTI system described by its impulse response $h(t) = u(t+1)$ to the input signal $x(t) = -e^{2(t-1)}u(-(t-1))$ (see Figure 2.24).

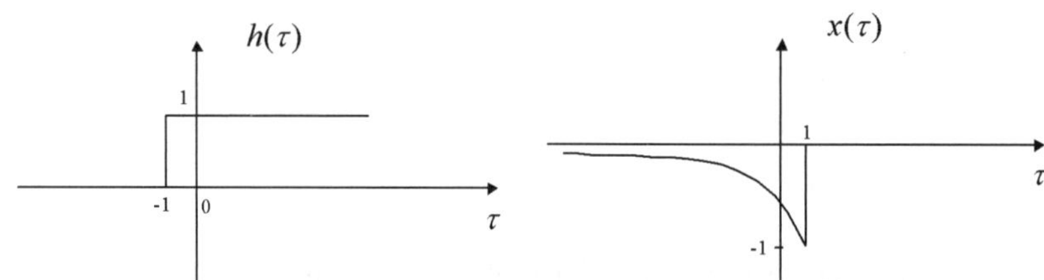

FIGURE 2.24 Impulse response and input signal to be convolved.

The time-reversed impulse response $h(-\tau)$ is plotted in Figure 2.25.

We can see from Figure 2.26 and Figure 2.24 that there are two distinct cases: for $t \le 0$, the two functions overlap over the interval $-\infty < \tau < t+1$.

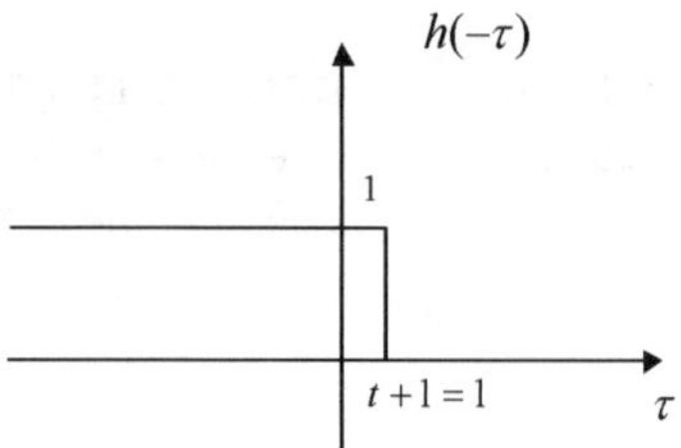

FIGURE 2.25 Time-reversed impulse response.

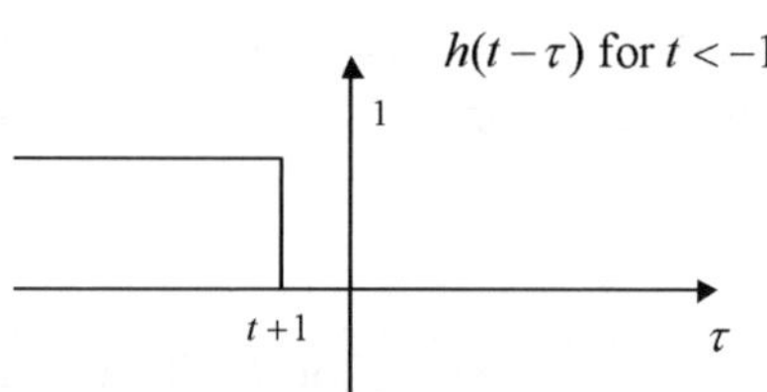

FIGURE 2.26 Time-reversed impulse response shifted to the left.

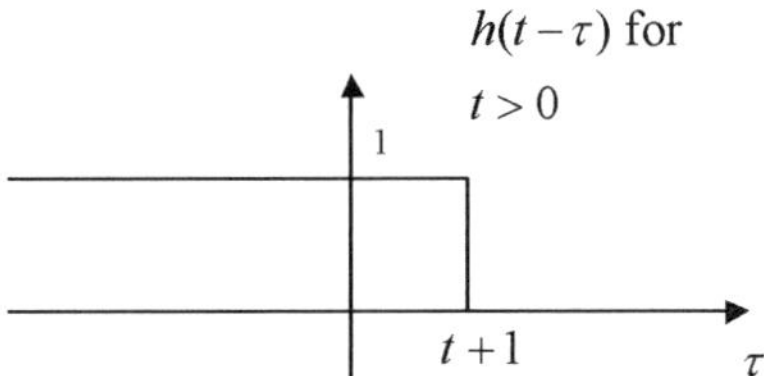

FIGURE 2.27 Time-reversed impulse response shifted to the right.

For $t>0$ the two functions overlap over the fixed interval $-\infty<\tau<1$ (see Figure 2.27). Thus, for $t\leq 0$, we get

$$y(t)=\int_{-\infty}^{+\infty} g(\tau)d\tau=\int_{-\infty}^{t+1} g(\tau)d\tau$$

$$=\int_{-\infty}^{t+1} x(\tau)h(t-\tau)d\tau$$

$$=\int_{-\infty}^{t+1} -e^{2(\tau-1)}d\tau=-\frac{1}{2}\left[e^{2t}-0\right]=-\frac{1}{2}e^{2t} \tag{2.30}$$

and for $t>0$ we get

$$y(t)=\int_{-\infty}^{+\infty} g(\tau)d\tau=\int_{-\infty}^{1} g(\tau)d\tau$$

$$=\int_{-\infty}^{1} x(\tau)h(t-\tau)d\tau$$

$$=\int_{-\infty}^{1} -e^{2(\tau-1)}d\tau=-\frac{1}{2}\left[e^{0}-0\right]=-\frac{1}{2}. \tag{2.31}$$

Piecing the two intervals together we obtain the response

$$y(t)=-\frac{1}{2}e^{2t}u(-t)-\frac{1}{2}u(t) \tag{2.32}$$

This sum of two signals forming the output is illustrated in Figure 2.28.

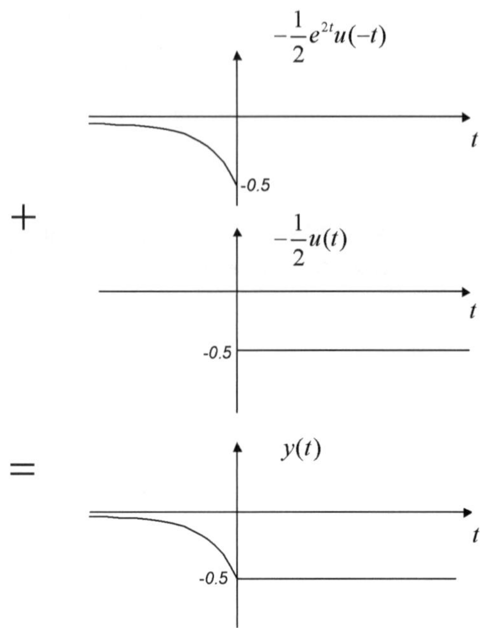

FIGURE 2.28 Overall response of the LTI system as a sum of two signals.

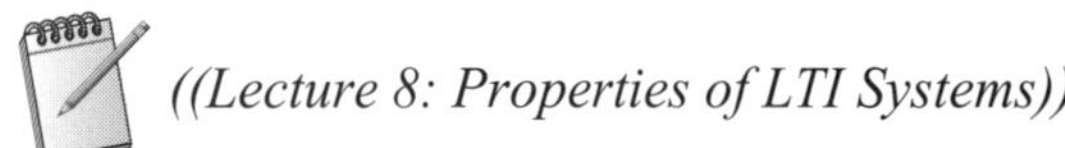

PROPERTIES OF LINEAR TIME-INVARIANT SYSTEMS

LTI systems are completely characterized by their impulse response (a *nonlinear* system is not). It should be no surprise that their properties are also characterized by their impulse response.

The Commutative Property of LTI Systems

The output of an LTI system with input x and impulse response h is identical to the output of an LTI system with input h and impulse response x, as suggested by the block diagrams in Figure 2.29. This results from the fact that a convolution is commutative, as we have already seen.

$$y[n] = \sum_{k=-\infty}^{\infty} x[k]h[n-k] = \sum_{k=-\infty}^{\infty} h[k]x[n-k] \tag{2.33}$$

$$y(t) = \int_{-\infty}^{+\infty} x(\tau)h(t-\tau)d\tau = \int_{-\infty}^{+\infty} h(\tau)x(t-\tau)d\tau \tag{2.34}$$

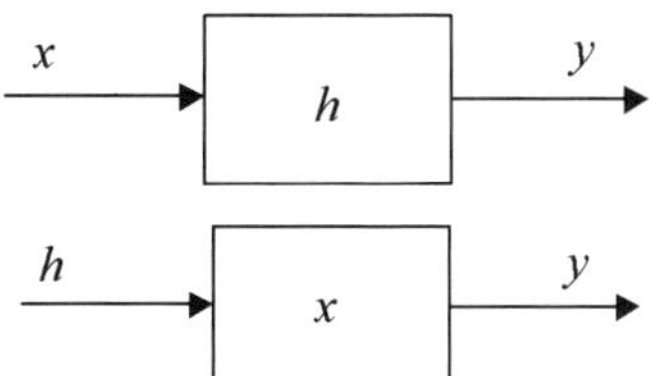

FIGURE 2.29 Equivalent block diagrams of LTI systems with respect to the output.

The Distributive Property of LTI Systems

The distributive property of LTI systems comes from the fact that a convolution is distributive:

$$x*(h_1+h_2) = x*h_1 + x*h_2 \tag{2.35}$$

which means that summing the outputs of two systems subjected to the same input is equivalent to a system with an impulse response equal to the sum of the impulse responses of the two individual systems, as shown in Figure 2.30.

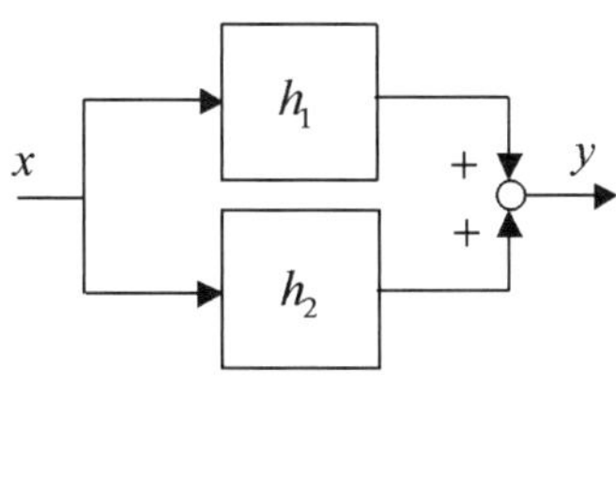

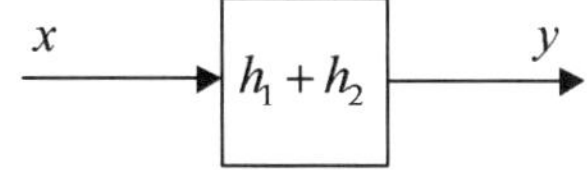

FIGURE 2.30 System equivalent to a parallel interconnection of LTI systems.

Application: The distributive property sometimes facilitates the evaluation of a convolution integral.

Example 2.9: Suppose we want to calculate the output of an LTI system with impulse response $h[n]=\left(\frac{1}{4}\right)^n u[n]+4^n u[-n]$ to the input signal $x[n]=u[n]$; it is easier to break down $h[n]$ as a sum of its two components, $h_1[n]=\left(\frac{1}{4}\right)^n u[n]$ and $h_2[n]=4^n u[-n]$, then calculate the two convolutions $y_1[n]=x[n]*h_1[n]$, $y_2[n]=x[n]*h_2[n]$ and sum them to obtain $y[n]$.

The Associative Property of LTI Systems

The associative property of LTI systems comes from the convolution operation being associative.

$$y=(x*h_1)*h_2=x*(h_1*h_2) \tag{2.36}$$

This implies that a cascade of two (or more) LTI systems can be reduced to a single system with impulse response equal to the convolution of the impulse responses of the cascaded systems. Furthermore, from the commutative property, the order of the systems in the cascade can be modified without changing the impulse response of the overall system.

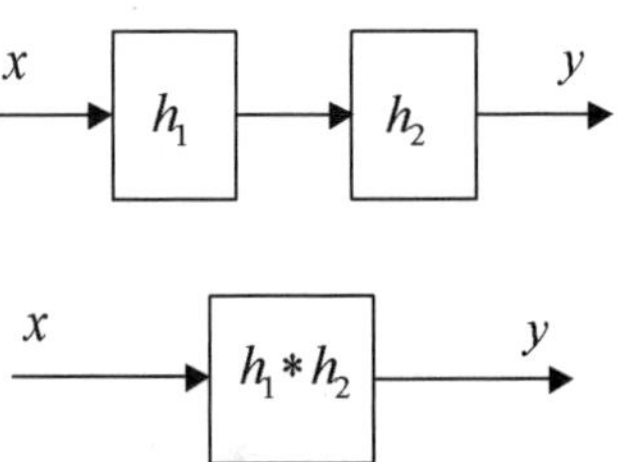

FIGURE 2.31 System equivalent to a cascade interconnection of LTI systems.

Application: A bandpass filter design problem is sometimes approached in two stages, where a first filter stage with impulse response $h_{lowpass}(t)$ would filter out the high frequencies in the input signal, while a high-pass stage with impulse response $h_{hipass}(t)$ would filter out the low frequencies and DC component of the input signal. Once the two stages are designed (i.e., their impulse responses have been determined), they are combined together as $h_{filter}(t) := h_{hipass}(t) * h_{lowpass}(t)$ for a more efficient implementation as an op-amp circuit (one may be able to save a few op-amps while reducing the potential sources of noise).

LTI Systems Without Memory

Recall that a system S is memoryless if its output at any time depends only on the value of its input at that same time.

For an LTI system, this property can only hold if its impulse response is itself an impulse, as is easily seen from the convolution Equations 2.8 and 2.26. When $h[n]$ and $h(t)$ are impulses, $h[n-k]$ and $h(t-\tau)$ are nonzero only for $k=n$ and $\tau = t$, and then $y[n] = x[n]h[0]$ and

$$y(t) = \int_{t^-}^{t^+} x(\tau)h(t-\tau)d\tau = \int_{t^-}^{t^+} x(\tau)A\delta(-(\tau-t))d\tau = Ax(t)\int_{t^-}^{t^+} \delta(\tau-t)d\tau = Ax(t) \quad (2.37)$$

Thus, to be memoryless, a continuous-time LTI system must have an impulse response of the form $h(t) = A\delta(t)$, and a discrete-time LTI system must have an impulse response of the form $h[n] = A\delta[n]$. The LTI system has memory otherwise.

Invertibility of LTI Systems

We have already seen that a system S is invertible if and only if there exists an inverse system S^{-1} for it such that $S^{-1}S$ is the identity system.

For an LTI system with impulse response h, this is equivalent to the existence of another system with impulse response h_1 such that $h * h_1 = \delta$, as shown in Figure 2.32.

FIGURE 2.32 Cascade of an LTI system and its inverse.

Application: For low-distortion transmission of a signal over a communication channel (telephone line, TV cable, radio link), the signal at the receiving end is often processed through a filter whose impulse response is designed to be the inverse of the impulse response of the communication channel.

Example 2.10: A system with impulse response $h(t)=\delta(t-T)$ delays its input signal by time T. Its inverse system is a time advance of T with impulse response $h_1(t)=\delta(t+T)$, as we now show. (Here we make use of the sampling property of the impulse function and we use the fact that $\delta(t)=\delta(-t)$.)

$$\begin{aligned}
h(t)*h_1(t) &= \int_{-\infty}^{+\infty} h(\tau)h_1(t-\tau)d\tau = \int_{-\infty}^{+\infty} \delta(\tau-T)\delta(t-\tau+T)d\tau \\
&= \int_{-\infty}^{+\infty} \delta(\tau-T)\delta(-(\tau-t-T))d\tau = \int_{-\infty}^{+\infty} \delta(\tau-T)\delta(\tau-t-T)d\tau \\
&= \int_{-\infty}^{+\infty} \delta(\tau-T)\delta(\tau-(t+T))d\tau = \delta(t+T-T)\int_{-\infty}^{+\infty} \delta(\tau-(t+T))d\tau \\
&= \delta(t)
\end{aligned} \tag{2.38}$$

Causality of an LTI System

Recall that a system is causal if its output depends only on past and/or present values of the input signal. Specifically, for a discrete-time LTI system, this requirement is that $y[n]$ should not depend on $x[k]$ for $k > n$. Thus, looking back at the convolution sum in Equation 2.8, the impulse response should satisfy $h[n-k]=0$ for $k > n$, which is equivalent to $h[k]=0$ for $k < 0$. Therefore, a discrete-time LTI system is causal if and only if its impulse response is zero for negative times. This makes sense, as a causal system should not exhibit a response before the impulse is applied at time $n = 0$.

A similar analysis for a continuous-time LTI system leads us to the same conclusion. Namely, a continuous-time LTI system is causal if and only if $h(t)=0, t<0$.

Example 2.11: A linear time-invariant circuit is causal. In fact, virtually all physical systems are causal since it is impossible for them to predict the future.

BIBO Stability of LTI Systems

Recall that a system is BIBO stable if for every bounded input, the output is also bounded. Let us consider a discrete-time system with impulse response $h[n]$. Assume that the discrete-time signal $x[n]$ is bounded by B for all n. Then, the magnitude of the system's output can be bounded using the triangle inequality as follows:

$$\begin{aligned}|y[n]| &= \left|\sum_{k=-\infty}^{\infty} x[k]h[n-k]\right| \le \sum_{k=-\infty}^{\infty} |h[k]||x[n-k]| \\ &< \sum_{k=-\infty}^{\infty} B|h[k]| = B\sum_{k=-\infty}^{\infty} |h[k]| \end{aligned} \tag{2.39}$$

and we conclude that if $\sum_{k=-\infty}^{+\infty} |h[k]| < +\infty$, then $|y[n]|$ is bounded and the LTI system is stable. It turns out that this condition on the impulse response is also necessary for BIBO stability, as we now show. Suppose that $\sum_{k=-\infty}^{+\infty} |h[k]| = +\infty$. Then we can construct an input signal using the so-called *signum* function $x[k] = \text{sgn}(h[-k]) = \begin{cases} 1, & h[-k] \ge 0 \\ -1, & h[-k] < 0 \end{cases}$, which is bounded by 1 and leads to an output that is unbounded at $n = 0$:

$$|y[0]| = \left|\sum_{k=-\infty}^{\infty} x[k]h[-k]\right| = \left|\sum_{k=-\infty}^{\infty} \text{sgn}(h[-k])h[-k]\right| = \sum_{k=-\infty}^{\infty} |h[k]| = +\infty \tag{2.40}$$

Therefore, a discrete-time LTI system is BIBO stable if and only if $\sum_{k=-\infty}^{+\infty} |h[k]| < +\infty$, that is, the impulse response must be *absolutely summable.*

The same analysis applies to continuous-time LTI systems for which BIBO stability is equivalent to $\int_{-\infty}^{+\infty} |h(\tau)| d\tau < +\infty$, that is, for which the impulse response is *absolutely integrable.*

Example 2.12: The discrete-time system with impulse response $h[n] = \frac{1}{n}u[n-1]$ is unstable because $\sum_{n=1}^{N} \frac{1}{n}$ does not converge as $N \to +\infty$.

Example 2.13: Is the continuous-time integrator system $y(t) = \int_{-\infty}^{t} x(\tau)d\tau$ stable?

Let us calculate its impulse response first: $h(t) = \int_{-\infty}^{t} \delta(\tau)d\tau = u(t)$, the unit step. A unit step is not absolutely integrable, so the system is unstable.

The Unit Step Response of an LTI System

The *step response* of an LTI system is simply the response of the system to a unit step. It conveys a lot of information about the system. For a discrete-time system with impulse response $h[n]$, the step response is $s[n] = u[n] * h[n] = h[n] * u[n]$. This convolution can be interpreted as the response of the accumulator system with impulse response $u[n]$ to the signal $h[n]$. Hence, the step response of a discrete-time LTI system is just the running sum of its impulse response:

$$s[n] = \sum_{-\infty}^{n} h[k]. \tag{2.41}$$

Conversely, the impulse response of the system is the output of the first-difference system with the step response as the input:

$$h[n] = s[n] - s[n-1]. \tag{2.42}$$

For a continuous-time system with impulse response $h(t)$, the step response is $s(t) = u(t) * h(t) = h(t) * u(t)$. This convolution can also be interpreted as the response of the integrator system with impulse response $u(t)$ to the signal $h(t)$. Again, the step response of a continuous-time LTI system is just the running integral of its impulse response:

$$s(t) = \int_{-\infty}^{t} h(\tau)d\tau. \tag{2.43}$$

Conversely, the first-order differentation system (the inverse system of the integrator), applied to the step response, yields the impulse response of the system:

$$h(t) = \frac{d}{dt}s(t). \tag{2.44}$$

Example 2.14: The impulse response and the step response of the *RC* circuit of Figure 2.33 are shown in Figure 2.34.

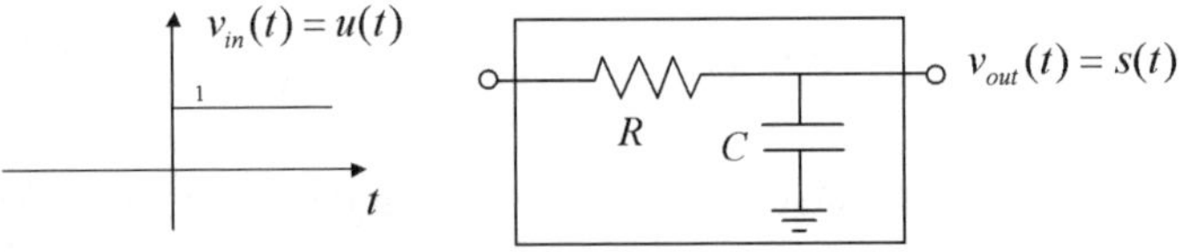

FIGURE 2.33 Setup for step response of an *RC* circuit.

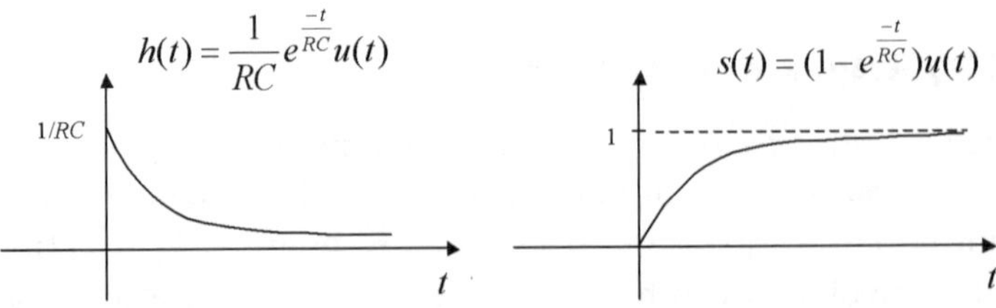

FIGURE 2.34 Impulse response and step response of the *RC* circuit.

SUMMARY

In this chapter, we have studied linear time-invariant systems.

- An LTI system is completely characterized by its impulse response.
- The input-output relationship of an LTI discrete-time system is given by the convolution sum of the system's impulse response with the input signal.
- The input-output relationship of an LTI continuous-time system is given by the convolution integral of the system's impulse response with the input signal.
- Given the impulse response of an LTI system and a specific input signal, the convolution giving the output signal can be computed using a graphical approach or a numerical approach.
- The main properties of an LTI system were derived in terms of its impulse response.

TO PROBE FURTHER

For a more detailed presentation of linear time-invariant and time-varying systems, including multi-input multi-output systems, see Chen, 1999.

EXERCISES

Exercises with Solutions

Exercise 2.1

Compute the convolutions $y[n]=x[n]*h[n]$:

(a) $x[n]=\alpha^n u[n],\ h[n]=\beta^n u[n],\quad \alpha\neq\beta$. Sketch the output signal $y[n]$ for the case $\alpha=0.8$, $\beta=0.9$.

Answer:

$$\begin{aligned} y[n] &= \sum_{k=-\infty}^{+\infty} x[k]h[n-k] \\ &= \sum_{k=-\infty}^{+\infty} \alpha^k u[k]\beta^{n-k}u[n-k] \\ &= \beta^n \sum_{k=0}^{n}\left(\frac{\alpha}{\beta}\right)^k, \quad n\geq 0 \end{aligned}$$

$$= \beta^n \left(\frac{1-\left(\frac{\alpha}{\beta}\right)^{n+1}}{1-\left(\frac{\alpha}{\beta}\right)} \right) u[n]$$

$$= \left(\frac{\beta^{n+1}-\alpha^{n+1}}{\beta-\alpha} \right) u[n], \quad \alpha \neq \beta$$

For $\alpha = 0.8,\ \beta = 0.9$, we obtain

$$y[n] = \left(\frac{(0.9)^{n+1}-(0.8)^{n+1}}{0.1} \right) u[n] = \left[9(0.9)^n - 8(0.8)^n \right] u[n]$$

which is plotted in Figure 2.35.

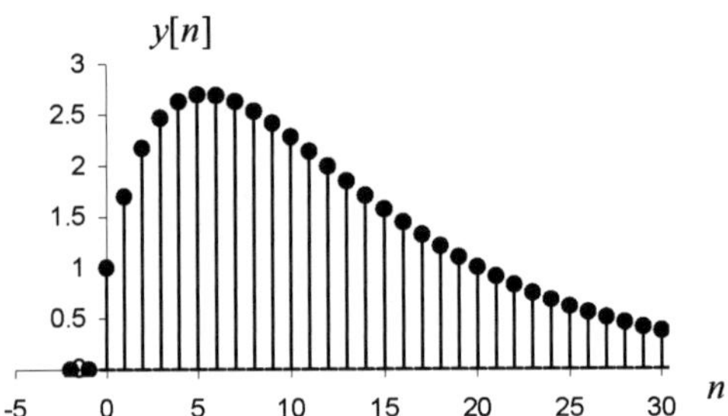

FIGURE 2.35 Output of discrete-time LTI system obtained by convolution in Exercise 2.1(a).

(b) $x[n] = \delta[n] - \delta[n-2],\ h[n] = u[n]$

Answer:

$$y[n] = \sum_{k=-\infty}^{+\infty} x[k]h[n-k] = \sum_{k=-\infty}^{+\infty} \left(\delta[k] - \delta[k-2]\right) u[n-k] = u[n] - u[n-2].$$

(c) The input signal and impulse response depicted in Figure 2.36. Sketch the output signal $y[n]$.

Answer:

Let us compute this one by time-reversing and shifting $x[k]$ (note that time-reversing and shifting $h[k]$ would lead to the same answer) as shown in Figure 2.37.

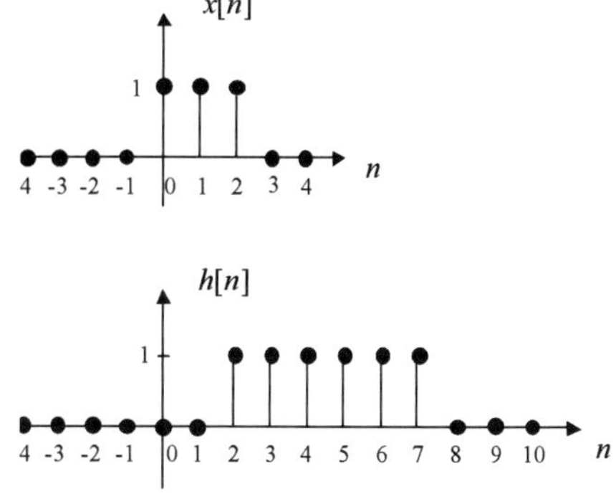

FIGURE 2.36 Input signal and impulse response in Problem 2.1(c).

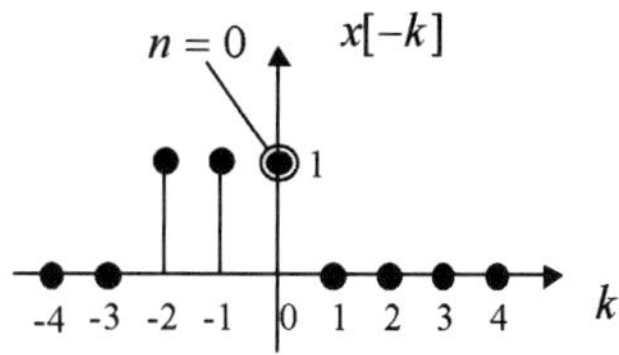

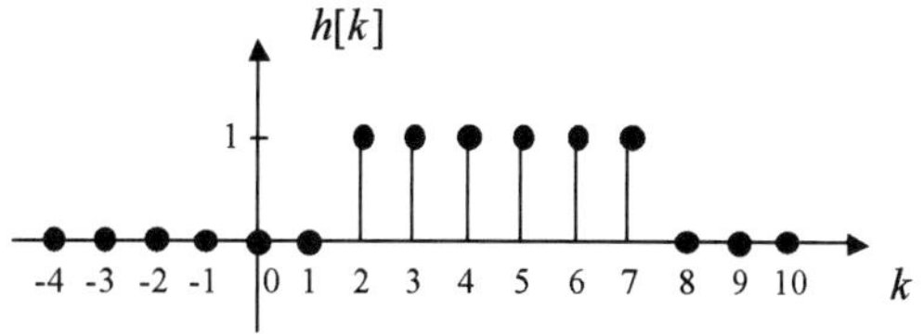

FIGURE 2.37 Time-reversing and shifting the input signal to compute the convolution in Exercise 2.1(c).

Intervals:

$n<2 \qquad h[k]x[k-n]=0, \forall k \qquad y[n]=0$

$2\le n\le 4: \quad h[k]x[k-n]=1, 2\le k\le n \qquad y[n]=\sum_{k=2}^{n} 1 = n-(2)+1 = n-1$

$5\le n\le 7: \quad h[k]x[k-n]=1, n-2\le k\le n \qquad y[n]=\sum_{k=n-2}^{n} 1 = 3$

$8\le n\le 9: \quad h[k]x[k-n]=1, n-2\le k\le 7 \qquad y[n]=\sum_{k=n-2}^{7} 1 = 7-(n-2)+1 = 10-n$

$n\ge 10 \qquad h[k]x[k-n]=0, \forall k \qquad y[n]=0$

Figure 2.38 shows a plot of the output signal:

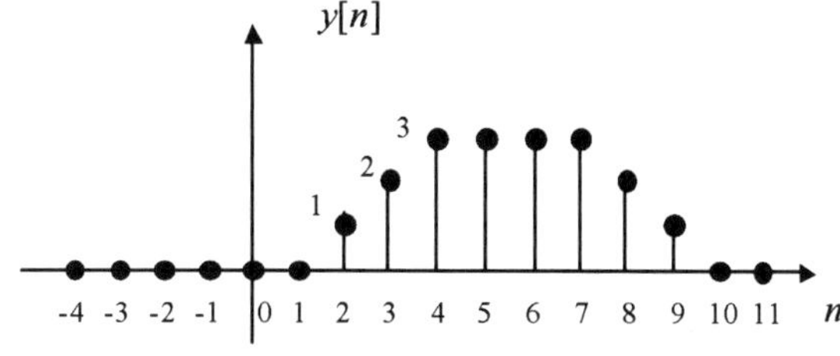

FIGURE 2.38 Output of discrete-time LTI system obtained by convolution in Exercise 2.1(c).

(d) $x[n]=u[n],\ h[n]=u[n]$

Answer:

$$\begin{aligned}
y[n] &= \sum_{k=-\infty}^{+\infty} x[k]h[n-k] \\
&= \sum_{k=-\infty}^{+\infty} u[k]u[n-k] \\
&= \sum_{k=-\infty}^{+\infty} u[k]u[-(k-n)] \\
&= \begin{cases} \sum_{k=0}^{n} 1 = n+1, & n \geq 0 \\ 0, & n<0 \end{cases} \\
&= (n+1)u[n]
\end{aligned}$$

Exercise 2.2

Compute and sketch the output $y(t)$ of the continuous-time LTI system with impulse response $h(t)$ for an input signal $x(t)$ as depicted in Figure 2.39.

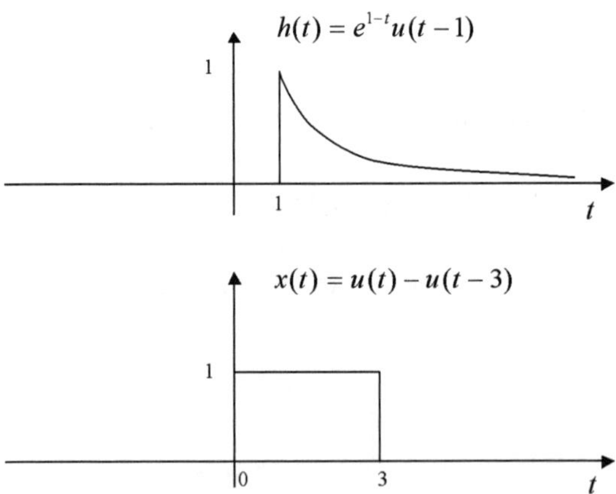

FIGURE 2.39 Input signal and impulse response in Exercise 2.2.

Answer: Let us time-reverse and shift the impulse response. The intervals of interest are

$t < 1$: no overlap as seen in Figure 2.40, so $y(t) = 0$.

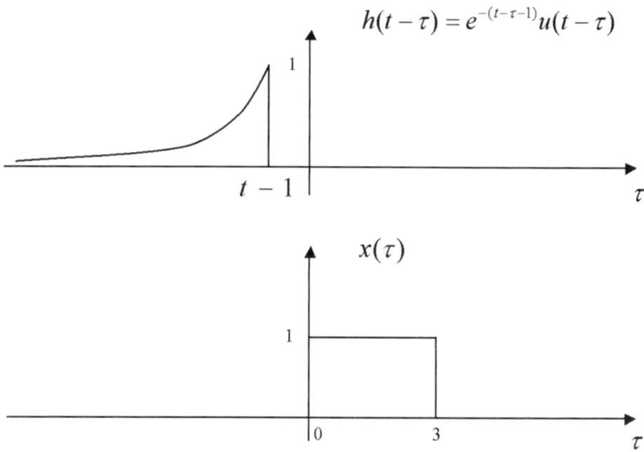

FIGURE 2.40 Time-reversed and shifted impulse response and input signal do not overlap for $t < 1$, Exercise 2.2.

$1 \le t < 4$: overlap for $0 < \tau < t-1$ as shown in Figure 2.41. Then,

$$y(t) = \int_0^{t-1} h(t-\tau)x(\tau)d\tau = \int_0^{t-1} e^{-(t-\tau-1)}d\tau = e^{-(t-\tau-1)}\Big|_0^{t-1} = (1-e^{-(t-1)}), \quad 1 \le t < 4$$

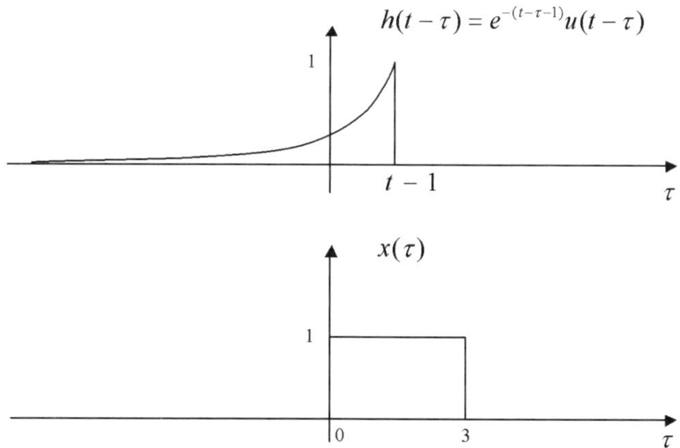

FIGURE 2.41 Overlap between the impulse response and the input for $1 \le t < 4$ in Exercise 2.2.

$t \geq 4$: overlap for $0 < \tau < 3$ as shown in Figure 2.42. Then,

$$y(t) = \int_0^3 h(t-\tau)x(\tau)d\tau = \int_0^3 e^{-(t-\tau-1)}d\tau = e^{-(t-\tau-1)}\Big|_0^3 = (e^{4-t} - e^{1-t}) = (e^4 - e^1)e^{-t}, \quad t \geq 4$$

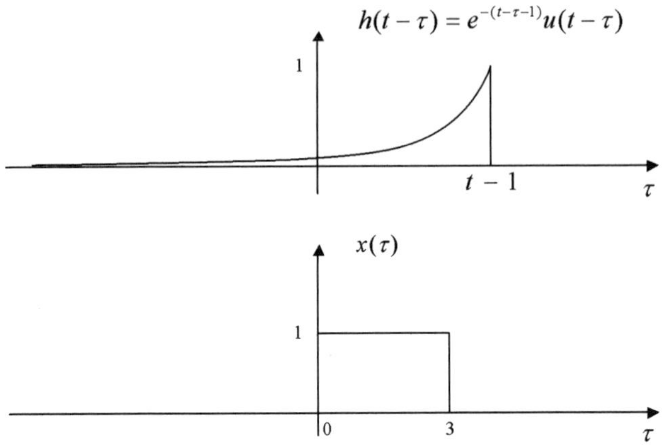

FIGURE 2.42 Overlap between the impulse response and the input for $t \geq 4$ in Exercise 2.2.

Finally, the output signal shown in Figure 2.43 can be written as follows:

$$y(t) = \begin{cases} 0 & t < 1 \\ 1 - e^{-(t-1)} & 1 \leq t < 4 \\ (e^4 - e^1)e^{-t}, & t \geq 4 \end{cases}$$

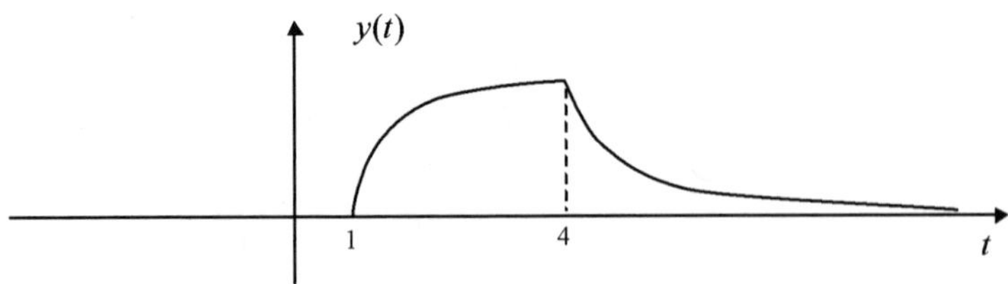

FIGURE 2.43 Output signal in Exercise 2.2.

Exercises

Exercise 2.3

Compute the output $y(t)$ of the continuous-time LTI system with impulse response $h(t) = u(t+1) - u(t-1)$ subjected to the input signal $x(t) = u(t+1) - u(t-1)$.

Answer:

ON THE CD

Exercise 2.4

Determine whether the discrete-time LTI system with impulse response $h[n] = (-0.9)^n u[n-4]$ is BIBO stable. Is it causal?

Exercise 2.5

Compute the step response of the LTI system with impulse response $h(t) = e^{-t}\cos(2t)u(t)$.

Answer:

ON THE CD

Exercise 2.6

Compute the output $y(t)$ of the continuous-time LTI system with impulse response $h(t)$ for an input signal $x(t)$ as depicted in Figure 2.44.

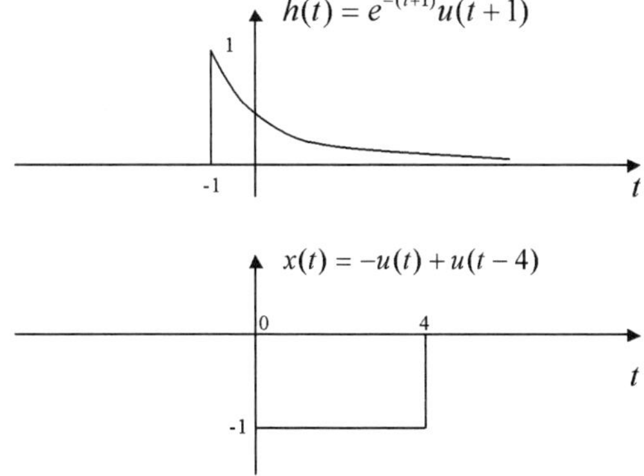

FIGURE 2.44 Impulse response and input signal in Exercise 2.6.

Exercise 2.7

Compute the convolutions $y[n] = x[n] * h[n]$.

(a) The input signal $x[n]$ and impulse response $h[n]$ are depicted in Figure 2.45. Sketch the output signal $y[n]$.

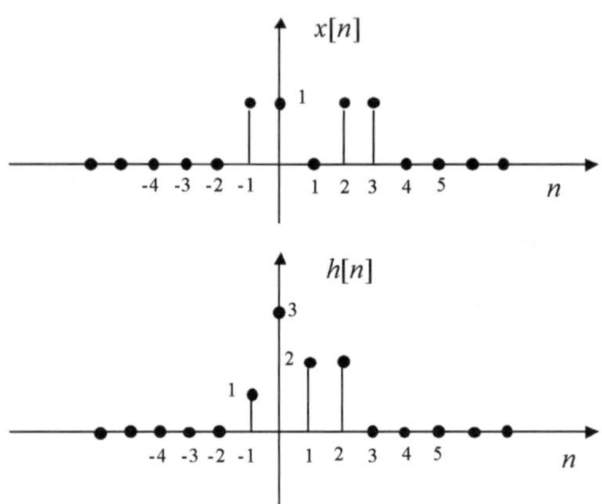

FIGURE 2.45 Input signal and impulse response in Exercise 2.7.

(b) $x[n] = u[n] - u[n-4]$, $h[n] = u[n+4] - u[n]$. Sketch the input signal $x[n]$, the impulse response $h[n]$, and the output signal $y[n]$.

Answer:

Exercise 2.8

Compute and sketch the output $y(t)$ of the continuous-time LTI system with impulse response $h(t)$ for an input signal $x(t)$ as depicted in Figure 2.46.

Exercise 2.9

Compute the response of an LTI system described by its impulse response $h[n] = \begin{cases} (0.8)^n, & 0 \leq n \leq 5 \\ 0, & \text{otherwise} \end{cases}$ to the input signal shown in Figure 2.47.

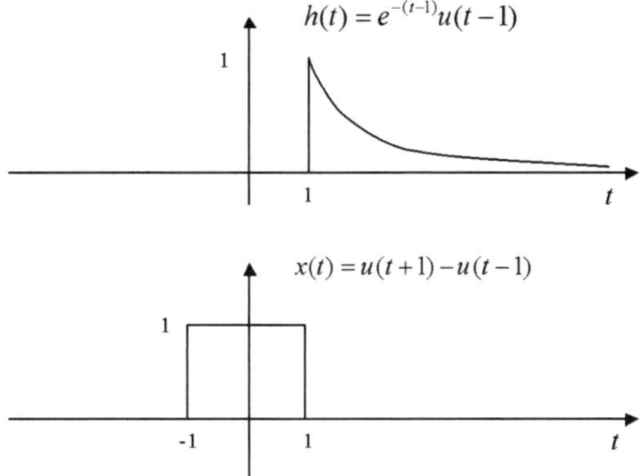

FIGURE 2.46 Impulse response and input signal in Exercise 2.8.

FIGURE 2.47 Input signal and impulse response in Exercise 2.9.

Answer:

Problem 2.10

The input signal of the LTI system shown in Figure 2.48 is the following:

$$x(t) = u(t) - u(t-2) + \delta(t+1)$$

The impulse responses of the subsystems are $h_1(t) = e^{-t}u(t), \quad h_2(t) = e^{-2t}u(t)$.

(a) Compute the impulse response $h(t)$ of the overall system.

(b) Find an equivalent system (same impulse response) configured as a parallel interconnection of two LTI subsystems.

(c) Sketch the input signal $x(t)$. Compute the output signal $y(t)$.

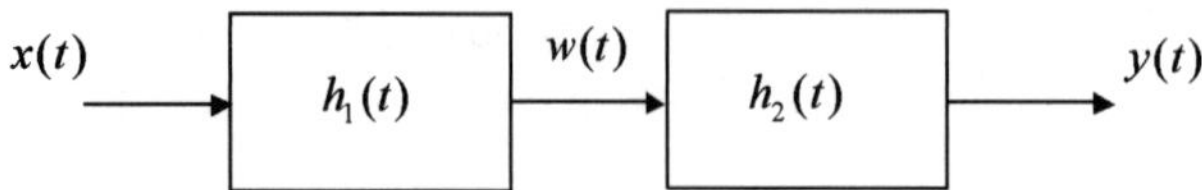

FIGURE 2.48 Cascaded LTI systems in Exercise 2.10.

3 Differential and Difference LTI Systems

In This Chapter

- Causal LTI Systems Described by Differential Equations
- Causal LTI Systems Described by Difference Equations
- Impulse Response of a Differential LTI System
- Impulse Response of a Difference LTI System
- Characteristic Polynomials and Stability of Differential and Difference Systems
- Time Constant and Natural Frequency of a First-Order LTI Differential System
- Eigenfunctions of LTI Difference and Differential Systems
- Summary
- To Probe Further
- Exercises

((Lecture 9: Definition of Differential and Difference Systems))

Differential and difference linear time-invariant (LTI) systems constitute an extremely important class of systems in engineering. They are used in circuit analysis, filter design, controller design, process modeling, and in many other applications. We will review the classical solution approach for such systems. Figure 3.1 shows that differential systems form a subset of the set of continuous-time LTI systems. A consequence of this set diagram is that any differential system has an impulse response. The same is true for difference systems. We will show techniques to compute their impulse response.

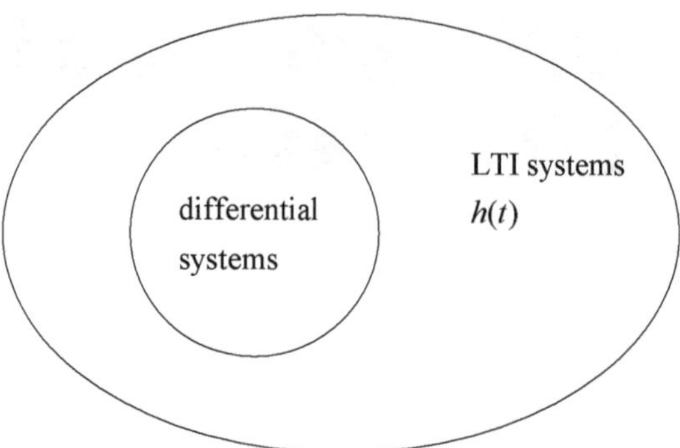

FIGURE 3.1 Differential systems form a subset of continuous-time LTI systems.

CAUSAL LTI SYSTEMS DESCRIBED BY DIFFERENTIAL EQUATIONS

Differential systems form the class of systems for which the input and output signals are related *implicitly* through a *linear, constant coefficient ordinary differential equation.* Note that partial differential equations, such as the heat equation, are excluded here, as they represent distributed-parameter or infinite-dimensional systems, which are out of the scope of this book.

Example 3.1: Consider a first-order differential equation relating the input $x(t)$ to the output $y(t)$:

$$1000\frac{dy(t)}{dt}+300y(t)=x(t) \tag{3.1}$$

This equation could represent the evolution of the velocity $y(t)$ in meters per second of a car of mass $m = 1000$ kg, subjected to an aerodynamic drag force proportional to its speed $Dy(t)$, where $D=300\,\frac{\mathrm{N}}{\mathrm{m/s}}$ and in which $x(t)$ is the tractive force in newtons applied on the car (Figure 3.2). According to Newton's law, the sum of forces accelerates the car so that we can write $m\,\frac{dy(t)}{dt}=-Dy(t)+x(t)$, where the derivative of the velocity $\frac{dy(t)}{dt}$ is the car's acceleration. Rearranging this equation, we obtain Equation 3.1. Note that the aerodynamic drag force is more typically modeled as being proportional to the square of the velocity of the vehicle, but this leads to a nonlinear differential equation, which is beyond the scope of this book. A version of the car's dynamics linearized around an operating velocity, such as given in Equation 3.1, would often be used in a preliminary analysis. Given the input signal $x(t)$, that is, the tractive force, we would normally have to solve the differential equation to obtain the output signal (the response) of the system, that is, the speed of the car.

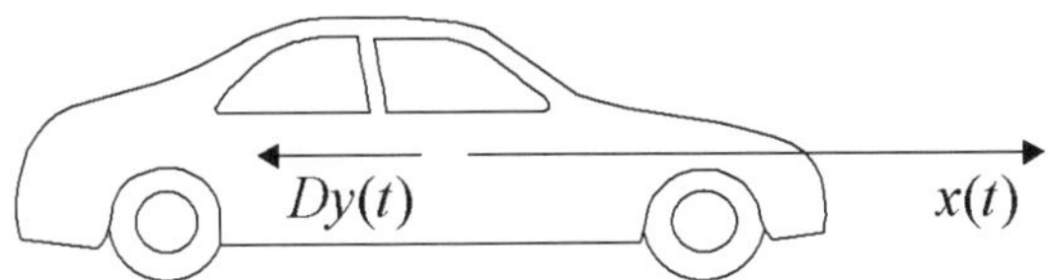

FIGURE 3.2 Forces acting on a car.

In general, an Nth-order linear constant coefficient differential equation has the form

$$\sum_{k=0}^{N} a_k \frac{d^k y(t)}{dt^k} = \sum_{k=0}^{M} b_k \frac{d^k x(t)}{dt^k} \tag{3.2}$$

which can be expanded to

$$a_N \frac{d^N y(t)}{dt^N} + \cdots + a_1 \frac{dy(t)}{dt} + a_0 y(t) = b_M \frac{d^M x(t)}{dt^M} + \cdots + b_1 \frac{dx(t)}{dt} + b_0 x(t). \tag{3.3}$$

The constant coefficients $\{a_i\}_{i=1}^{N}$ and $\{b_i\}_{i=1}^{M}$ are assumed to be real, and some of them may be equal to zero, although it is assumed that $a_N \neq 0$ without loss of generality. The order of the differential equation is defined as the order of the highest derivative of the output present in the equation. To find a solution to a differential equation of this form, we need more information than the equation provides. We need N initial conditions (or auxiliary conditions) on the output variable $y(t)$ and its derivatives to be able to calculate a solution.

Recall from previous math courses that the complete solution to Equation 3.2 is given by the sum of the *homogeneous solution* of the differential equation (a solution with the input signal set to zero) and of a *particular solution* (an output signal that satisfies the differential equation), also called the *forced response* of the system.

The usual terminology is as follows:

- Forced response of the system = particular solution (usually has the same form as the input signal)

- Natural response of the system = homogeneous solution (depends on initial conditions and forced response)

A few authors use the term *forced response* as meaning the system's response to the input with zero initial conditions. However, in this book, and in most of the relevant literature, such a response is called a zero-state response (more on this later.)

Example 3.2: Consider the LTI system described by the causal linear constant coefficient differential Equation 3.1. We will calculate the output of this system, that is, the car velocity, from a standstill, to the input tractive force signal $x(t) = 5000e^{-2t}u(t)\,\mathrm{N}$. This input signal could correspond to the driver stepping on the gas pedal from a standstill and then rapidly easing the throttle. As stated above, the solution is composed of a homogeneous response (natural response) and a particular solution (forced response) of the system:

$$y(t) = y_h(t) + y_p(t), \tag{3.4}$$

where the particular solution satisfies Equation 3.1, and the homogeneous solution $y_h(t)$ satisfies

$$1000\frac{dy_h(t)}{dt} + 300y_h(t) = 0. \tag{3.5}$$

Step 1: For the particular solution for $t > 0$, we consider a signal $y_p(t)$ of the same form as $x(t)$ for $t > 0$: $y_p(t) = Ce^{-2t}$, where coefficient $C \in \mathbb{R}$ is to be determined. Substituting the exponentials for $x(t)$ and $y_p(t)$ in Equation 3.1, we get

$$-2000Ce^{-2t} + 300Ce^{-2t} = 5000e^{-2t}, \tag{3.6}$$

which simplifies to $-2000C + 300C = 5000$ and yields $C = -{}^{5000}\!/\!_{1700} = -2.941$. Thus, we have

$$y_p(t) = -2.941e^{-2t},\ t > 0. \tag{3.7}$$

Remark: The particular solution seems to indicate a negative velocity, that is, the car moving backward, which would not make sense, but the full solution needs to be considered, not just the particular solution.

Step 2: Now we want to determine $y_h(t)$, the natural response of the system. We assume a solution of the form of an exponential: $y_h(t) = Ae^{st}$, where $A \neq 0$. Substituting this exponential into Equation 3.5, we get

$$0 = 1000Ase^{st} + 300Ae^{st} = A(1000s + 300)e^{st}, \tag{3.8}$$

which simplifies to $s + 0.3 = 0$. This equation holds for $s = -0.3$. Also, with this value for s, $Ae^{-0.3t}$ is a solution to the homogeneous Equation 3.5 for any choice of A.

Combining the natural response and the forced response, we find the solution to the differential Equation 3.1:

$$y(t) = y_h(t) + y_p(t) = Ae^{-0.3t} - 2.941e^{-2t}, \quad t > 0. \tag{3.9}$$

Now, because we have not yet specified an initial condition on $y(t)$, this response is not completely determined, as the value of A is still unknown.

Strictly speaking, for causal LTI systems defined by linear constant-coefficient differential equations, the initial conditions must be $y(0) = \frac{dy(0)}{dt} = \cdots = \frac{d^{N-1}y(0)}{dt^{N-1}} = 0$, what is called *initial rest*. That is, if at least one initial condition is nonzero, then strictly speaking, the system is nonlinear. In practice, we often encounter nonzero initial conditions and still refer to the system as being linear.

In Example 3.2, initial rest implies that $y(0) = 0$, so that

$$y(0) = A - 2.941 = 0, \tag{3.10}$$

and we get $A = 2.941$. Thus, for $t > 0$, the car velocity is given by

$$y(t) = 2.941(e^{-0.3t} - e^{-2t}), \quad t > 0. \tag{3.11}$$

What about the negative times $t < 0$? The condition of initial rest and the causality of the system imply that $y(t) = 0,\ t < 0$ since $x(t) = 0,\ t < 0$. Therefore, we can write the speed of the car $\forall t \in \mathbb{R}$ as follows:

$$y(t) = 2.941(e^{-0.3t} - e^{-2t})u(t). \tag{3.12}$$

This speed signal is plotted in Figure 3.3, and we can see that the car is moving forward, as expected.

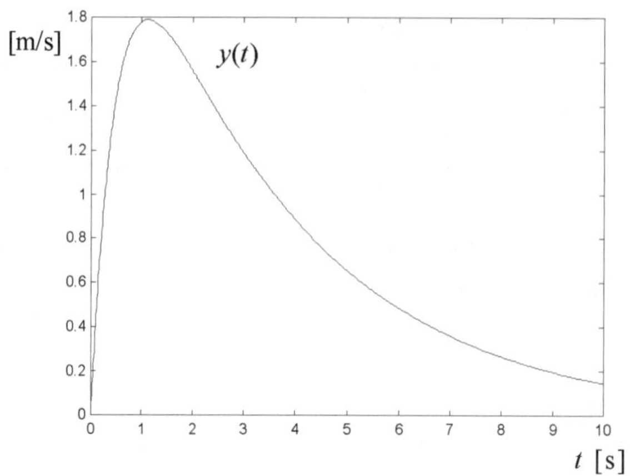

FIGURE 3.3 Car speed signal as the solution of a differential equation.

The above remark on initial rest is true in general for causal LTI systems, as we now show. A linear system is causal if its output depends only on past and present values of $x(t)$, but for a linear system $y = Sx$, the output to the zero input is zero, as $S(0x) = 0Sx = 0y = 0$. Since we assumed that $x(t) = 0,\ t < 0$ and that $y(t)$ only depends on past or current values of the input, then we have $y(t) = 0,\ t < 0$.

The condition of initial rest means that the output of the causal system is zero until the time when the input becomes nonzero.

CAUSAL LTI SYSTEMS DESCRIBED BY DIFFERENCE EQUATIONS

In a causal LTI difference system, the discrete-time input and output signals are related *implicitly* through a *linear constant-coefficient difference equation.*

In general, an Nth-order linear constant coefficient difference equation has the form:

$$\sum_{k=0}^{N} a_k y[n-k] = \sum_{k=0}^{M} b_k x[n-k], \tag{3.13}$$

which can be expanded to

$$a_N y[n-N] + \cdots + a_1 y[n-1] + a_0 y[n] = b_M x[n-M] + \cdots + b_1 x[n-1] + b_0 x[n]. \tag{3.14}$$

The constant coefficients $\{a_i\}_{i=1}^{N}$ and $\{b_i\}_{i=1}^{M}$ are assumed to be real, and although some of them may be equal to zero, it is assumed that $a_N \neq 0$ without loss of generality. The order of the difference equation is defined as the longest time delay of the output present in the equation. To find a solution to the difference equation, we need more information than what the equation provides. We need N initial conditions (or auxiliary conditions) on the output variable (its N past values) to be able to compute a specific solution.

General Solution

A general solution to Equation 3.13 can be expressed as the sum of a homogeneous solution (natural response) to $\sum_{k=0}^{N} a_k y[n-k]=0$ and a particular solution (forced response), in a manner analogous to the continuous-time case.

$$y[n]=y_h[n]+y_p[n]. \tag{3.15}$$

The concept of *initial rest* of the LTI causal system described by the difference equation here means that $x[n]=0,\ \forall n<n_0$ implies $y[n]=0,\ \forall n<n_0$.

Example 3.3: Consider the first-order difference equation initially at rest:

$$y[n]+0.5y[n-1]=(-0.8)^n u[n]. \tag{3.16}$$

The solution is composed of a homogeneous response (natural response), and a particular solution (forced response) of the system:

$$y[n]=y_h[n]+y_p[n], \tag{3.17}$$

where the particular solution satisfies Equation 3.16 for $n \geq 0$, and the homogeneous solution satisfies

$$y_h[n]+0.5y_h[n-1]=0. \tag{3.18}$$

For the particular solution for $n \geq 0$, we look for a signal $y_p[n]$ of the same form as $x[n]$: $y_p[n]=Y(-0.8)^n$. Then, we get

$$\begin{aligned}
&Y(-0.8)^n+0.5Y(-0.8)^{n-1}=(-0.8)^n \\
&\Leftrightarrow \\
&Y\left[1+0.5(-0.8)^{-1}\right]=1 \\
&Y=\frac{8}{3},
\end{aligned} \tag{3.19}$$

which yields

$$y_p[n] = \frac{8}{3}(-0.8)^n. \tag{3.20}$$

Now let us determine $y_h[n]$, the natural response of the system. We hypothesize a solution of the form of an exponential signal: $y_h[n] = Az^n$. Substituting this exponential in Equation 3.18, we get

$$\begin{aligned} &Az^n + 0.5Az^{n-1} = 0 \\ &\Leftrightarrow \\ &1 + 0.5z^{-1} = 0 \\ &z = -0.5. \end{aligned} \tag{3.21}$$

With this value for z, $y_h[n] = A(-0.5)^n$ is a solution to the homogeneous equation for any choice of A. Combining the natural response and the forced response, we find the solution to the difference Equation 3.16 for $n \geq 0$:

$$y[n] = y_h[n] + y_p[n] = A(-0.5)^n + \frac{8}{3}(-0.8)^n. \tag{3.22}$$

The assumption of initial rest implies $y[-1] = 0$, *but we need to use an initial condition at a time where the forced response exists* (*for* $n \geq 0$), that is, $y[0]$, which can be obtained by a simple recursion.

$$\begin{aligned} &y[n] = -0.5y[n-1] + (-0.8)^n u[n] \\ &n = 0: \quad y[0] = -0.5y[-1] + (-0.8)^0 = 0 + 1 = 1 \end{aligned} \tag{3.23}$$

Note that this remark also holds for higher-order systems. For instance, the response of a second-order system initially at rest satisfies the conditions $y[-2] = y[-1] = 0$, but $y[0], y[1]$ must be computed recursively and used as new initial conditions in order to obtain the correct coefficients in the homogeneous response. In our example, the coefficient is computed as follows:

$$\begin{aligned} &y[0] = 1 = A(-0.5)^0 + \frac{8}{3}(-0.8)^0 = A + \frac{8}{3} \\ &\Rightarrow A = -\frac{5}{3} \end{aligned} \tag{3.24}$$

Therefore, the complete solution is (check that it satisfies Equation 3.16 as an exercise)

$$y[n] = -\frac{5}{3}(-0.5)^n u[n] + \frac{8}{3}(-0.8)^n u[n]. \tag{3.25}$$

Recursive Solution

In the discrete-time case, we have an alternative to compute $y[n]$: we can compute it recursively using Equation 3.13 rearranged so that all the terms are brought to the right-hand side, except $y[n]$:

$$y[n] = \frac{1}{a_0}\left(\sum_{k=0}^{M} b_k x[n-k] - \sum_{k=1}^{N} a_k y[n-k]\right). \tag{3.26}$$

Suppose that the system is initially at rest and that $x[n]$ has nonzero values starting at $n = 0$. Then, the condition of initial rest means that $y[-1] = y[-2] = \cdots = y[-N] = 0$, and one can start computing $y[n]$ recursively. This is often how digital filters are implemented on a computer or a digital signal processor board. This is also how a simulation of the response of a differential equation is typically computed: first, the differential equation is discretized at a given sampling rate to obtain a difference equation, and then the response of the difference equation is computed recursively. We will talk about sampling and system discretization in some detail in subsequent chapters.

Example 3.4: Consider the difference equation:

$$y[n] - \frac{5}{6}y[n-1] + \frac{1}{6}y[n-2] = 3x[n] - 2x[n-1]. \tag{3.27}$$

Taking the second and third terms on the left-hand side of Equation 3.27 to the right-hand side, we obtain the recursive form of the difference equation:

$$y[n] = \frac{5}{6}y[n-1] - \frac{1}{6}y[n-2] + 3x[n] - 2x[n-1]. \tag{3.28}$$

Assuming initial rest and that the input is an impulse $x[n] = \delta[n]$, we have $y[-2] = y[-1] = 0$, and the recursion can be started:

$$
\begin{aligned}
y[0] &= \frac{5}{6}y[-1] - \frac{1}{6}y[-2] + 3x[0] - 2x[-1] \\
&= \frac{5}{6}(0) - \frac{1}{6}(0) + 3(1) - 2(0) = 3 \\
y[1] &= \frac{5}{6}y[0] - \frac{1}{6}y[-1] + 3x[1] - 2x[0] \\
&= \frac{5}{6}(3) - \frac{1}{6}(0) + 3(0) - 2(1) = \frac{1}{2} \\
y[2] &= \frac{5}{6}y[1] - \frac{1}{6}y[0] + 3x[2] - 2x[1] \\
&= \frac{5}{6}(\frac{1}{2}) - \frac{1}{6}(3) + 3(0) - 2(0) = -\frac{1}{12} \\
&\vdots
\end{aligned} \tag{3.29}
$$

ON THE CD

The following MATLAB program, which can be found on the CD-ROM in D:\Chapter3\recursion.m, computes and plots the response of the difference system in Example 3.4 by recursion.

```
%% recursion.m computes the response of a difference system recursively
% time vector
n=0:1:15;
% define the input signal
x=[1 zeros(1,length(n)-1)];
y=zeros(1,length(n));
% initial conditions
yn_1=0;
yn_2=0;
xn_1=0;
xn=0;
% recursion
for k=1:length(n)
xn=x(k);
yn=(5/6)*yn_1-(1/6)*yn_2+3*xn-2*xn_1;
y(k)=yn;
yn_2=yn_1;
yn_1=yn;
xn_1=xn;
end
% plot output
stem(n,y)
```

Note that because this system is LTI, it is completely determined by its impulse response. Thus, the response to the unit impulse that we obtain here numerically by recursion is actually the impulse response of the system. For a simpler first-order system, it is often easy to find the "general term" describing the impulse response $h[n]$ for any time step n. For example, you can check that the causal LTI system described by the difference equation,

$$y[n]+2y[n-1]=x[n], \tag{3.30}$$

has an impulse response given by $h[n]=(-2)^n u[n]$.

((Lecture 10: Impulse Response of a Differential System))

IMPULSE RESPONSE OF A DIFFERENTIAL LTI SYSTEM

Consider again the general form of a causal LTI differential system of order N:

$$\sum_{k=0}^{N} a_k \frac{d^k y(t)}{dt^k} = \sum_{k=0}^{M} b_k \frac{d^k x(t)}{dt^k}. \tag{3.31}$$

In this section, we give two methods to compute the impulse response of such a system.

Method 1: Impulse Response Obtained by Linear Combination of Impulse Responses of the Left-Hand Side of the Differential Equation

The step-by-step procedure to find the impulse response of a differential LTI system is as follows:

1. Replace the whole right-hand side of the differential Equation 3.31 by $\delta(t)$.
2. Integrate this new equation from $t = 0^-$ to $t = 0^+$ to find a set of initial conditions at $t = 0$.
3. Calculate the homogeneous response $h_a(t)$ to the homogeneous equation with these initial conditions.
4. Finally, differentiate the homogeneous response $h_a(t)$ and use linear superposition according to the right-hand side of the differential equation to form the overall response of the system.

The procedure is based on the properties of linearity and commutativity of LTI systems. Differential systems can be seen as the combination of two subsystems, each one defined by a side of the differential equation, as illustrated in Figure 3.4. The first subsystem processes the input signal by implementing the right-hand side of the equation, that is, by forming a linear combination of the input and its derivatives. The second subsystem implements the left-hand side of the differential equation, with its input being the output of the first subsystem. Both of these subsystems are LTI, and therefore each one has an impulse response. Let the impulse response of the second one be denoted as $h_a(t)$. Another consequence of the LTI properties is that, by commutativity, the order of the subsystems can be interchanged, as shown in Figure 3.5.

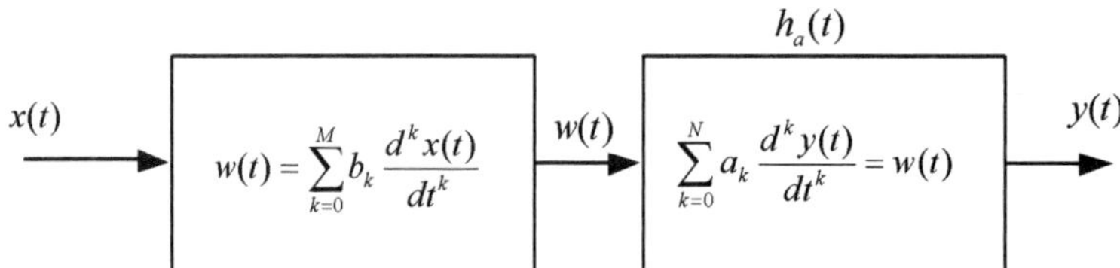

FIGURE 3.4 Differential system as the cascade of two LTI subsystems.

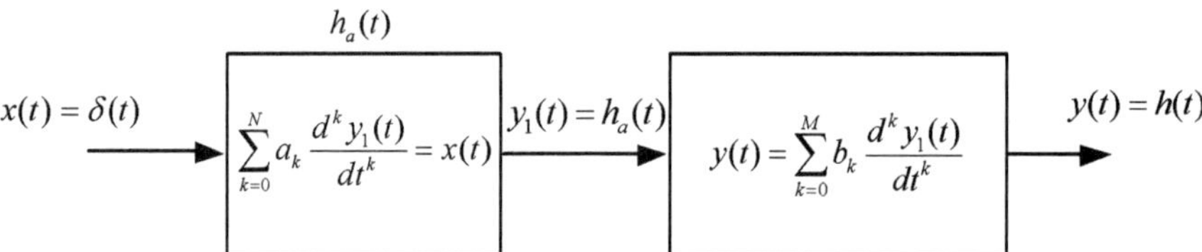

FIGURE 3.5 Cascade of two LTI subsystems equivalent to the differential system.

The block diagram in Figure 3.5 suggests how the procedure works. Steps 1–3 compute the impulse response $h_a(t)$ of the first block, and Step 4 computes the impulse response of the overall differential system by applying the second block (the right-hand side of the differential equation) to $h_a(t)$ in order to get $h(t)$.

Step 1: Under the assumption that $N \geq M$ and the system is initially at rest, that is,

$$y(0^-) = \frac{dy(0^-)}{dt} = \cdots = \frac{d^{N-1}y(0^-)}{dt^{N-1}} = 0,$$

we first replace the right-hand side of Equation 3.31 with a single unit impulse:

$$\sum_{k=0}^{N} a_k \frac{d^k h_a(t)}{dt^k} = \delta(t). \tag{3.32}$$

Step 2: To solve this equation for $h_a(t)$, we first observe that the impulse can only be generated by the highest-order derivative (i.e., $k = N$) of $h_a(t)$. Otherwise, we would have *derivatives* of the impulse function in the right-hand side of Equation 3.5. This means that the functions $h_a(t), \frac{dh_a(t)}{dt}, \ldots, \frac{d^{N-1}h_a(t)}{dt^{N-1}}$ are smooth or have finite discontinuities at worst. Such functions integrated over an infinitesimally small interval simply vanish. This important observation (make sure you understand it!) gives us the first $N-1$ initial conditions for $h_a(t)$ when we integrate those functions from $t = 0^-$ to $t = 0^+$:

$$\int_{0^-}^{0^+} \frac{d^k h_a(\tau)}{dt^k} d\tau = \frac{d^{k-1} h_a(0^+)}{dt^{k-1}} = 0, \quad k = 1, \ldots, N-1. \tag{3.33}$$

Then, integrating both sides of Equation 3.32 from $t = 0^-$ to $t = 0^+$, we obtain

$$\sum_{k=0}^{N} a_k \int_{0^-}^{0^+} \frac{d^k h_a(\tau)}{dt^k} d\tau = a_N \int_{0^-}^{0^+} \frac{d^N h_a(\tau)}{dt^N} d\tau = a_N \frac{d^{N-1} h_a(0^+)}{dt^{N-1}} = 1, \tag{3.34}$$

which gives us our N^{th} initial condition at $t = 0^+$:

$$\frac{d^{N-1} h_a(0^+)}{dt^{N-1}} = \frac{1}{a_N}. \tag{3.35}$$

Step 3: Thus, starting at time $t = 0^+$, we need to solve the homogeneous equation,

$$\sum_{k=0}^{N} a_k \frac{d^k h_a(t)}{dt^k} = 0, \tag{3.36}$$

subject to the above initial conditions. Assume that the solution has the form of a complex exponential Ae^{st} for $t > 0$, where $A, s \in \mathbb{C}$. Substituting this exponential into Equation 3.36, we get a polynomial in s multiplying an exponential on the left-hand side:

$$Ae^{st} \sum_{k=0}^{N} a_k s^k = 0. \tag{3.37}$$

With the assumption that $A \neq 0$, this equation holds if and only if the *characteristic polynomial* $p(s) := \sum_{k=0}^{N} a_k s^k$ vanishes at the complex number s:

$$p(s) = \sum_{k=0}^{N} a_k s^k = a_N s^N + a_{N-1} s^{N-1} + \cdots + a_0 = 0. \quad (3.38)$$

By the fundamental theorem of algebra, Equation 3.38 has at most N distinct complex roots. Assume for simplicity that the N roots are distinct, and let them be denoted as $\{s_k\}_{k=1}^{N}$. This means that there are N distinct functions $A_k e^{s_k t}$ that satisfy the homogeneous Equation 3.36. Then, the solution to Equation 3.36 can be written as a linear combination of these complex exponentials:

$$h_a(t) = \sum_{k=1}^{N} A_k e^{s_k t}. \quad (3.39)$$

The N complex coefficients $\{A_k\}_{k=1}^{N}$ can be computed using the initial conditions:

$$\begin{aligned} 0 &= h_a(0^+) = \sum_{k=1}^{N} A_k e^{s_k 0^+} = \sum_{k=1}^{N} A_k \\ 0 &= \frac{dh_a(0^+)}{dt} = \sum_{k=1}^{N} A_k s_k \\ &\vdots \\ \frac{1}{a_N} &= \frac{d^{N-1} h_a(0^+)}{dt^{N-1}} = \sum_{k=1}^{N} A_k s_k^{N-1}. \end{aligned} \quad (3.40)$$

This set of linear equations can be written as follows:

$$\begin{bmatrix} 0 \\ 0 \\ 0 \\ \vdots \\ 1/a_N \end{bmatrix} = \begin{bmatrix} 1 & 1 & \cdots & 1 \\ s_1 & s_2 & \cdots & s_N \\ s_1^2 & s_2^2 & \cdots & s_N^2 \\ \vdots & \vdots & \vdots & \vdots \\ s_1^N & s_2^N & \cdots & s_N^N \end{bmatrix} \begin{bmatrix} A_1 \\ A_2 \\ A_3 \\ \vdots \\ A_N \end{bmatrix}. \quad (3.41)$$

The $N \times N$ matrix with complex entries in this equation is called a *Vandermonde matrix* and it can be shown to be nonsingular (invertible). Thus, a unique solution always exists for the A_k's, which gives us the unique solution $h_a(t)$ through Equation 3.39.

Step 4: Finally, the impulse response of the general causal LTI system described by Equation 3.31 is a linear combination of $h_a(t)$ and its derivatives as shown in the second block of Figure 3.4. Hence, the impulse response is given by

$$h(t)=\sum_{k=0}^{M} b_k \frac{d^k h_a(t)}{dt^k}. \tag{3.42}$$

Example 3.5: Consider the first-order system initially at rest with time constant $\tau_0 > 0$:

$$\tau_0 \frac{dy(t)}{dt}+y(t)=\frac{d}{dt}x(t)+x(t). \tag{3.43}$$

Step 1: Set up the first problem of calculating the impulse response of the left-hand side of the differential equation.

$$\tau_0 \frac{dh_a(t)}{dt}+h_a(t)=\delta(t) \tag{3.44}$$

Step 2: Find the initial condition of the homogeneous equation at $t = 0^+$ by integrating on both sides of Equation 3.2 from $t = 0^-$ to $t = 0^+$. Note that the impulse is produced by the term $\tau_0 \frac{dh_a(t)}{dt}$, so $h_a(t)$ will have a finite jump at most. Thus we have

$$\int_{0^-}^{0^+} \tau_0 \frac{dh_a(\tau)}{dt} d\tau + \underbrace{\int_{0^-}^{0^+} h_a(\tau) d\tau}_{=0} = \tau_0 h_a(0^+) = 1, \tag{3.45}$$

and hence $h_a(0^+)=\frac{1}{\tau_0}$ is our initial condition for the homogeneous equation:

$$\tau_0 \frac{dh_a(t)}{dt}+h_a(t)=0. \tag{3.46}$$

Step 3: The characteristic polynomial is $p(s)=\tau_0 s+1$ and it has one zero at $s = -\tau_0^{-1}$ which means that the homogeneous response has the form $h_a(t)=Ae^{-\frac{t}{\tau_0}}$ for $t > 0$. The initial condition allows us to determine the constant A:

$$h_a(0^+)=A=\frac{1}{\tau_0}, \tag{3.47}$$

so that

$$h_a(t) = \frac{1}{\tau_0} e^{-\frac{t}{\tau_0}} u(t). \tag{3.48}$$

Step 4: Finally, the impulse response of the differential system of Equation 3.43 is computed by applying the right-hand side of Equation 3.43 to $h_a(t)$ as follows:

$$\begin{aligned} h(t) &= \frac{dh_a(t)}{dt} + h_a(t) \\ &= \frac{d}{dt}\left(\frac{1}{\tau_0} e^{-\frac{t}{\tau_0}} u(t)\right) + \frac{1}{\tau_0} e^{-\frac{t}{\tau_0}} u(t) \\ &= -\frac{1}{\tau_0^2} e^{-\frac{t}{\tau_0}} u(t) + \frac{1}{\tau_0} e^{-\frac{t}{\tau_0}} \delta(t) + \frac{1}{\tau_0} e^{-\frac{t}{\tau_0}} u(t) \\ &= \left(\frac{1}{\tau_0} - \frac{1}{\tau_0^2}\right) e^{-\frac{t}{\tau_0}} u(t) + \frac{1}{\tau_0} \delta(t). \end{aligned} \tag{3.49}$$

Notice how the chain rule and the sampling property of the impulse are applied in differentiating $h_a(t) = \frac{1}{\tau_0} e^{-\frac{t}{\tau_0}} u(t)$, which gives rise to the impulse in the bottom equality of Equation 3.49. The impulse response is shown in Figure 3.6.

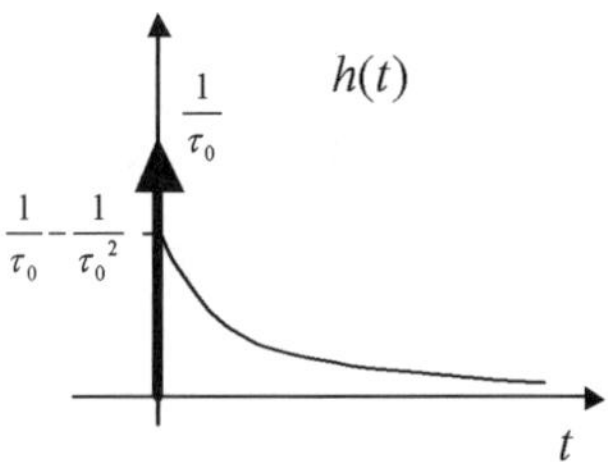

FIGURE 3.6 Impulse response of a first-order system.

Method 2: Impulse Response Obtained by Differentiation of the Step Response

We have seen that the impulse response of an LTI system is the derivative of its step response, that is, $h(t) = \frac{ds(t)}{dt}$. Thus, we can obtain the impulse response of an LTI differential system by first calculating its step response and then differentiating it. This method is useful when the right-hand side of the differential equation does not have derivatives of the input signal.

Example 3.6: We will illustrate this technique with an example of a second-order system. Consider the following causal LTI differential system initially at rest:

$$\frac{d^2y(t)}{dt^2} + 3\frac{dy(t)}{dt} + 2y(t) = x(t). \tag{3.50}$$

Let $x(t) = u(t)$. The characteristic polynomial of this system is

$$p(s) = s^2 + 3s + 2 = (s+2)(s+1), \tag{3.51}$$

and its *zeros* (values of s for which $p(s) = 0$) are $s = -2$ and $s = -1$. Hence, the homogeneous solution has the form

$$y_h(t) = A_1e^{-2t} + A_2e^{-t}. \tag{3.52}$$

We look for a particular solution of the form $y_p(t) = K$ for $t > 0$ when $x(t) = 1$. Substituting in Equation 3.50, we find

$$y_p(t) = \frac{1}{2}. \tag{3.53}$$

By adding the homogeneous and particular solutions, we obtain the overall step response for $t > 0$:

$$s(t) = A_1e^{-2t} + A_2e^{-t} + \frac{1}{2}. \tag{3.54}$$

The initial conditions at $t = 0^-$ are $\frac{dy(0^-)}{dt} = 0,\ y(0^-) = 0$. Because the input signal has a finite jump at $t = 0^+$, it will be included in $\frac{d^2y(t)}{dt^2}$ only, and $\frac{dy(t)}{dt}$, $y(t)$ will be continuous. Hence, $\frac{dy(0^-)}{dt} = \frac{dy(0^+)}{dt} = 0$, and we have

$$\begin{aligned} y(0^+) &= A_1 + A_2 + \frac{1}{2} = 0 \\ \frac{dy(0^+)}{dt} &= -2A_1 - A_2 = 0. \end{aligned} \tag{3.55}$$

The solution to these two linear algebraic equations is $A_1 = \frac{1}{2}, A_2 = -1$, which means that the step response of the system is

$$s(t) = \left(\frac{1}{2}e^{-2t} - e^{-t} + \frac{1}{2}\right)u(t). \tag{3.56}$$

This step response is shown in Figure 3.7.

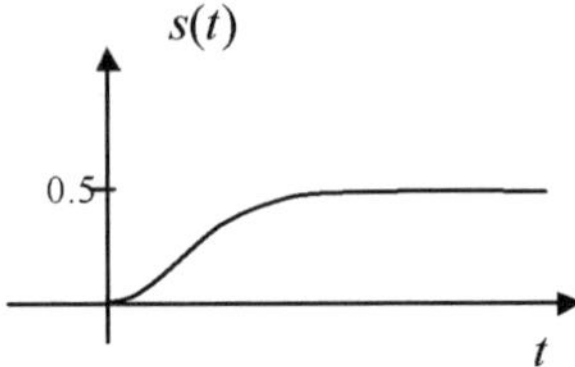

FIGURE 3.7 Step response of the second-order system.

Finally, the impulse response of the second-order system is obtained by differentiating its step response. It is interesting to look around the origin to see whether or not there is a jump in the derivative of the step response. The derivative is obviously 0 for $t < 0$. For $t > 0$,

$$h(t) = \frac{d}{dt}s(t) = \left(e^{-t} - e^{-2t}\right),\ t > 0, \tag{3.57}$$

which evaluates to 0 at time $t = 0^+$. Hence there is no jump, and the impulse response, shown in Figure 3.8 is given by (check that it solves Equation 3.50)

$$h(t) = \left(e^{-t} - e^{-2t}\right)u(t). \tag{3.58}$$

Of course, we can directly differentiate the step response as given in Equation 3.56 using the chain rule and the sampling property of the impulse, which yields the same impulse response shown in Figure 3.8:

$$\begin{aligned} h(t) &= \frac{d}{dt}s(t) = \left(e^{-t} - e^{-2t}\right)u(t) + \underbrace{\left(\frac{1}{2}e^{-2t} - e^{-t} + \frac{1}{2}\right)_{t=0}}_{=0}\delta(t) \\ &= \left(e^{-t} - e^{-2t}\right)u(t). \end{aligned} \tag{3.59}$$

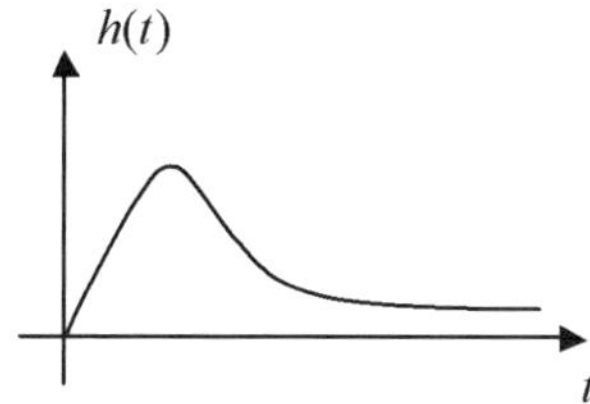

FIGURE 3.8 Impulse response obtained by differentiating the step response.

((Lecture 11: Impulse Response of a Difference System; Characteristic Polynomial and Stability))

IMPULSE RESPONSE OF A DIFFERENCE LTI SYSTEM

Consider the general form of a causal LTI difference system:

$$\sum_{k=0}^{N} a_k y[n-k] = \sum_{k=0}^{M} b_k x[n-k]. \tag{3.60}$$

We briefly discuss one method to obtain the impulse response of this general causal LTI difference system initially at rest. It is similar to Method 1 for a continuous-time differential system, but it is simpler, as there is no integration involved.

Impulse Response Obtained by Linear Combination of Shifted Impulse Responses of the Left-Hand Side of the Difference Equation

The step-by-step procedure to find the impulse response of a difference LTI system is as follows.

1. Replace the whole right-hand side of the difference Equation 3.60 by $\delta[n]$.
2. Find initial conditions on $y[n]$ at times $n = 0, -1, \ldots, -N+1$ for a homogeneous response starting at time $n = 1$.
3. Calculate the homogeneous response $h_a[n]$ to the homogeneous equation with these initial conditions.
4. Finally, calculate $h[n]$ as a linear combination of the current and delayed versions of $h_a[n]$ according to the right-hand side of the difference Equation 3.60.

Step 1: Under the assumption that the system is initially at rest, that is, $y[-1]=y[-2]=\cdots=y[-N]=0$, let $h_a[n]=y[n]$ and replace the right-hand side of Equation 3.60 with a single unit impulse:

$$\sum_{k=0}^{N} a_k h_a[n-k]=\delta[n]. \tag{3.61}$$

Step 2: To solve this equation for $h_a[n]$, we first observe that, by causality, the impulse can only be part of $h_a[n]$, not its delayed versions $h_a[n-k]$, $k \neq 0$. This immediately gives us $h_a[0]=\frac{1}{a_0}$. Causality and the initial rest condition yield the remaining initial conditions $h_a[-1]=h_a[-2]=\cdots=h_a[-N+1]=0$.

Step 3: Thus, starting at time $n = 1$, we need to solve the homogeneous equation for $n > 0$:

$$\sum_{k=0}^{N} a_k h_a[n-k]=0, \tag{3.62}$$

subject to the N initial conditions obtained in Step 2. Assume that the solution has the form of a complex exponential Cz^n for $n > 0$. Substituting this exponential into Equation 3.62, we get a polynomial in z^{-1}, multiplying an exponential on the left-hand side. Dividing both sides by Cz^n and multiplying both sides by z^N, we get an equivalent equation:

$$Cz^n \sum_{k=0}^{N} a_k z^{-k}=0 \Leftrightarrow \sum_{k=0}^{N} a_k z^{N-k}=0, \tag{3.63}$$

and this equation holds if and only if the *characteristic polynomial* $p(z):=\sum_{k=0}^{N} a_k z^{N-k}$ vanishes at the complex number z; that is,

$$p(z)=\sum_{k=0}^{N} a_k z^{N-k}=a_0 z^N + a_1 z^{N-1} + \cdots + a_N = 0. \tag{3.64}$$

By the fundamental theorem of algebra, this equation has at most N distinct roots. Assume that the N roots are distinct for simplicity and let them be denoted as $\{z_k\}_{k=1}^{N}$. This means that there are N distinct exponential signals $C_k z_k^{\,n}$ that satisfy the homogeneous Equation 3.62. Then the solution to Equation 3.62 can be written as a linear combination of these complex exponentials:

$$h_a[n]=\sum_{k=1}^{N} C_k z_k^{\,n}. \tag{3.65}$$

The complex coefficients $\{C_k\}_{k=1}^{N}$ can be computed using the initial conditions:

$$\frac{1}{a_0} = h_a[0] = \sum_{k=1}^{N} C_k$$

$$0 = h_a[-1] = \sum_{k=1}^{N} C_k z_k^{-1}$$

$$\vdots$$

$$0 = h_a[-N+1] = \sum_{k=1}^{N} C_k z_k^{-N+1} \tag{3.66}$$

This set of linear equations can be written as

$$\begin{bmatrix} \frac{1}{a_0} \\ 0 \\ 0 \\ \vdots \\ 0 \end{bmatrix} = \begin{bmatrix} 1 & 1 & \cdots & 1 \\ z_1^{-1} & z_2^{-1} & \cdots & z_N^{-1} \\ z_1^{-2} & z_2^{-2} & \cdots & z_N^{-2} \\ \vdots & \vdots & \vdots & \vdots \\ z_1^{1-N} & z_2^{1-N} & \cdots & z_N^{1-N} \end{bmatrix} \begin{bmatrix} C_1 \\ C_2 \\ C_3 \\ \vdots \\ C_N \end{bmatrix}. \tag{3.67}$$

The Vandermonde matrix on the right-hand side of Equation 3.67 can be shown to be nonsingular. Hence, a unique solution always exists for the C_ks, which gives us the unique solution $h_a[n]$ through Equation 3.65.

Step 4: Finally, by the LTI properties of the difference system, the response of the left-hand side of Equation 3.60 to its right-hand side is a linear combination of $h_a[n]$ and delayed versions of it. Therefore, the impulse response of the general causal LTI system described by the difference Equation 3.60 is given by

$$h[n] = \sum_{k=0}^{M} b_k h_a[n-k]. \tag{3.68}$$

Example 3.7: Consider the following second-order, causal LTI difference system initially at rest:

$$y[n] - 0.5y[n-1] + 0.06y[n-2] = x[n-1]. \tag{3.69}$$

The characteristic polynomial is given by

$$p(z) = z^2 - 0.5z + 0.06 = (z - 0.2)(z - 0.3), \tag{3.70}$$

and its zeros are $z_1 = 0.2,\ z_2 = 0.3$. The homogeneous response is given by

$$h_a[n] = A(0.2)^n + B(0.3)^n,\ n > 0. \tag{3.71}$$

The initial conditions for the homogeneous equation for $n > 0$ are $h_a[-1] = 0$ and $h_a[0] = \delta[0] = 1$. Now, we can compute the coefficients A and B:

$$h_a[-1] = A(0.2)^{-1} + B(0.3)^{-1} = 5A + \frac{10}{3}B = 0, \tag{3.72}$$

$$h_a[0] = A + B = 1. \tag{3.73}$$

Hence, $A = -2,\ B = 3$, and the impulse response is obtained by performing Step 4:

$$h[n] = h_a[n-1] = \left[-2(0.2)^{n-1} + 3(0.3)^{n-1}\right]u[n-1]. \tag{3.74}$$

CHARACTERISTIC POLYNOMIALS AND STABILITY OF DIFFERENTIAL AND DIFFERENCE SYSTEMS

The BIBO stability of differential and difference systems can be determined by analyzing their characteristic polynomials.

The Characteristic Polynomial of an LTI Differential System

Recall that the characteristic polynomial of a causal differential LTI system of the type

$$\sum_{k=0}^{N} a_k \frac{d^k y(t)}{dt^k} = \sum_{k=0}^{M} b_k \frac{d^k x(t)}{dt^k} \tag{3.75}$$

is given by

$$p(s) := a_N s^N + a_{N-1} s^{N-1} + \cdots + a_0. \tag{3.76}$$

This polynomial depends only on the coefficients on the left-hand side of the differential equation. It characterizes the intrinsic properties of the differential system, as it does not depend on the input. The zeros of the characteristic polynomial $\{s_k\}_{k=1}^{N}$ are the exponents of the exponentials forming the homogeneous response, so they give us an indication of the system properties, such as stability.

Stability of an LTI Differential System

We have seen that an LTI system is BIBO stable if and only if its impulse response is absolutely integrable, that is, $\int_{-\infty}^{+\infty} |h(t)|\,dt < +\infty$. We have also figured out that a general formula for the impulse response of the system described by Equation 3.31 is given by

$$h(t) = \sum_{k=0}^{M} b_k \frac{d^k}{dt^k} \underbrace{\left(\sum_{m=1}^{N} A_m e^{s_m t} u(t) \right)}_{h_a(t)}, \tag{3.77}$$

where the zeros $\{s_m\}_{m=1}^{N}$ of the characteristic polynomial are assumed to be distinct. Now we have to be concerned with the possibility of derivatives of impulses at time $t = 0$ in $h(t)$. Recall that the first $N - 1$ derivatives of $h_a(t)$ are either smooth functions or may have a finite jump (for $k = N - 1$), while the impulse appears in $\frac{d^N h_a(t)}{dt^N}$. Thus, under the assumption that $N \geq M$, the impulse response $h(t)$ will have at worst a single impulse at $t = 0$, which integrates to a finite value when integrated from $t = -\infty$ to $t = 0^+$. Under these conditions, the stability of the system is entirely determined by the exponentials in Equation 3.77. To show this, let us find an upper bound on $\int_{0^+}^{+\infty} |h(t)|\,dt$:

$$\begin{aligned}
\int_{0^+}^{\infty} |h(t)|\,dt &= \int_{0^+}^{\infty} \left| \sum_{k=0}^{M} b_k \frac{d^k}{dt^k} \left(\sum_{m=1}^{N} A_m e^{s_m t} \right) \right| dt \\
&\leq \int_{0^+}^{\infty} \sum_{k=0}^{M} |b_k| \left| \frac{d^k}{dt^k} \left(\sum_{m=1}^{N} A_m e^{s_m t} \right) \right| dt \\
&= \sum_{k=0}^{M} |b_k| \int_{0^+}^{\infty} \left| \frac{d^k}{dt^k} \left(\sum_{m=1}^{N} A_m e^{s_m t} \right) \right| dt \\
&= \sum_{k=0}^{M} |b_k| \int_{0^+}^{\infty} \left| \sum_{m=1}^{N} A_m s_m{}^k e^{s_m t} \right| dt \\
&\leq \sum_{k=0}^{M} |b_k| \int_{0^+}^{\infty} \sum_{m=1}^{N} \left| A_m s_m{}^k e^{s_m t} \right| dt \\
&\leq \sum_{k=0}^{M} |b_k| \sum_{m=1}^{N} \left| A_m s_m{}^k \right| \int_{0^+}^{\infty} e^{\mathrm{Re}\{s_m\} t}\,dt.
\end{aligned} \tag{3.78}$$

We can see from the last upper bound in Equation 3.78 that the integral of the magnitude of the impulse response is infinite only if $\int_{0^+}^{\infty} e^{\mathrm{Re}\{s_m\} t}\,dt$ is infinite for some $m \in \{1,\ldots,M\}$. This occurs only if $\mathrm{Re}\{s_m\} \geq 0$. It can be shown that this necessary condition of stability is also sufficient modulo the next remark. That is, if at least one of the zeros of the characteristic polynomial has a nonnegative real part, then the system is unstable.

With the earlier assumptions that the zeros of the characteristic polynomial are distinct and that $N \geq M$, a causal LTI differential system is BIBO stable if and only if the real part of all of the zeros of its characteristic polynomial are negative (we say that they lie in the left half of the complex plane).

Remark: The purist might say that the causal differential system described by

$$\frac{dy(t)}{dt} - y(t) = \frac{d}{dt}x(t) - x(t) \tag{3.79}$$

is BIBO stable, even though the zero $s_1 = 1$ of its characteristic polynomial lies in the right half of the complex plane. Indeed, if one computed the impulse response of this system by using the procedure outlined above, one would get the identity system $h(t) = \delta(t)$, whose impulse response is absolutely integrable. Thus, strictly speaking, the system of Equation 3.79 is BIBO stable, but as engineers, we must be aware that even if the input signal is identically zero for all times, any nonzero initial condition on the output signal, even infinitesimal, or any perturbation of the coefficients will excite the unstable exponential e^t in the homogeneous response and will drive the output to infinity. Therefore, this type of system must be considered unstable. We will describe such systems in subsequent chapters as having a pole canceling a zero in the closed right half of the complex plane. A physical system described by such a differential equation will surely be unstable in practice.

Example 3.8: Let us assess the stability of the causal LTI differential system defined as

$$\frac{dy(t)}{dt} - 2y(t) = x(t). \tag{3.80}$$

The characteristic polynomial is $p(s) = s - 2$, which has its zero at $s = 2$. This system is therefore BIBO unstable, which is easy to see with an impulse response of the form $Ae^{2t}u(t)$, a growing exponential.

The Characteristic Polynomial of an LTI Difference System

Recall that the characteristic polynomial of a causal difference LTI system of the type

$$\sum_{k=0}^{N} a_k y[n-k] = \sum_{k=0}^{M} b_k x[n-k] \tag{3.81}$$

is given by

$$p(z) = \sum_{k=0}^{N} a_k z^{N-k} = a_0 z^N + a_1 z^{N-1} + \cdots + a_N = 0. \tag{3.82}$$

This polynomial depends only on the coefficients on the left-hand side of the difference equation. The zeros $\{z_k\}_{k=1}^{N}$ (assumed to be distinct) of the characteristic polynomial are the arguments of the exponentials forming the homogeneous response, so they also give us an indication of system properties, such as stability.

Stability of an LTI Difference System

Recall that a discrete-time LTI system is stable if and only if its impulse response is absolutely summable, that is, $\sum_{n=-\infty}^{+\infty} |h[n]| < +\infty$. For the causal difference system above, this leads to the following upper bound:

$$\begin{aligned}
\sum_{n=0}^{+\infty} |h[n]| &= \sum_{n=0}^{+\infty} \left| \sum_{k=0}^{M} b_k h_a[n-k] \right| \\
&\le \sum_{n=0}^{+\infty} \sum_{k=0}^{M} |b_k| |h_a[n-k]| \\
&= \sum_{k=0}^{M} \sum_{n=k}^{+\infty} |b_k| |h_a[n-k]| \\
&= \sum_{k=0}^{M} \sum_{n=k}^{+\infty} |b_k| \left| \sum_{m=1}^{N} C_m z_m^{\,n-k} \right| \\
&\le \sum_{k=0}^{M} \sum_{n=k}^{+\infty} |b_k| \sum_{m=1}^{N} |C_m| \left| z_m^{\,n-k} \right| \\
&= \sum_{k=0}^{M} |b_k| \sum_{m=1}^{N} |C_m| \sum_{n=k}^{+\infty} |z_m|^{n-k} \\
&= \sum_{k=0}^{M} |b_k| \sum_{m=1}^{N} |C_m| \sum_{r=0}^{+\infty} |z_m|^{r},
\end{aligned} \tag{3.83}$$

and this last upper bound is finite if and only if $|z_m| < 1$, for all $m = 1, \ldots, N$. Hence, the causal LTI difference system is BIBO stable only if all the zeros of its characteristic polynomial have a magnitude less than 1. This necessary condition for stability turns out to be sufficient as well, and hence BIBO stability is equivalent to having all the zeros have a magnitude less than 1. Note that the previous remark also applies to discrete-time difference systems: a system of the type $y[n]+2y[n-1]=x[n]+2x[n-1]$ must be considered unstable even though its impulse response $h[n]=\delta[n]$ is absolutely summable. Round-off errors in a digital implementation of such a difference system would destabilize it.

Example 3.9: Consider the causal first-order LTI difference system:

$$y[n]-0.9y[n-1]=x[n]. \tag{3.84}$$

Its characteristic polynomial is $p(z)=z-0.9$, which has a single zero at $z_1=0.9$. Hence, this system is stable, as $|z_1|=0.9<1$. Its impulse response is shown in Figure 3.9.

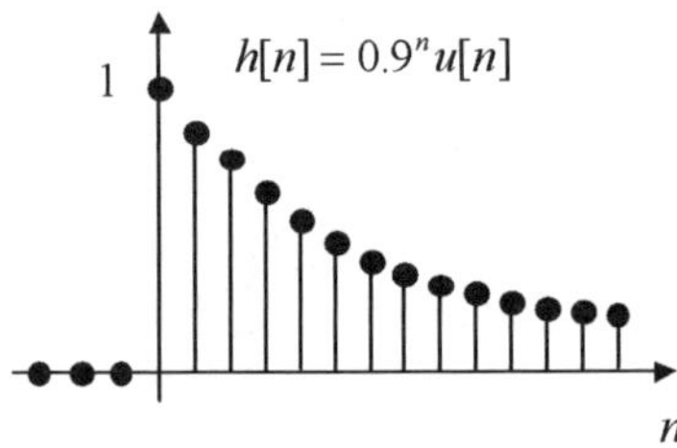

FIGURE 3.9 Impulse response of the first-order system.

TIME CONSTANT AND NATURAL FREQUENCY OF A FIRST-ORDER LTI DIFFERENTIAL SYSTEM

In general, the impulse response of an LTI differential system is a linear combination of complex exponentials of the type $Ae^{st}u(t)$ and their derivatives. Consider the stable, causal first-order LTI differential system:

$$a_1\frac{dy(t)}{dt}+a_0y(t)=Kx(t). \tag{3.85}$$

Its impulse response is a single exponential, $h(t)=Ae^{s_1t}u(t)$, where $s_1=-\frac{a_0}{a_1}$ and $A=\frac{K}{a_1}$. The real number $\omega_n:=|s_1|$ is called the *natural frequency* of the first-order system, and its inverse $\tau_0:=\frac{1}{\omega_n}=\frac{a_1}{a_0}$ is called the *time constant* of the first-order system. The time constant indicates the decay rate of the impulse response and the rise time of the step response. At time $t = \tau_0$, the impulse response is $h(\tau_0) = Ae^{-\frac{\tau_0}{\tau_0}} = Ae^{-1} = 0.37A$, so the impulse response has decayed to 37% of its initial value, as shown in Figure 3.10. The step response is also shown in this figure, and it can be seen that it has risen to 63% of its settling value after one time constant.

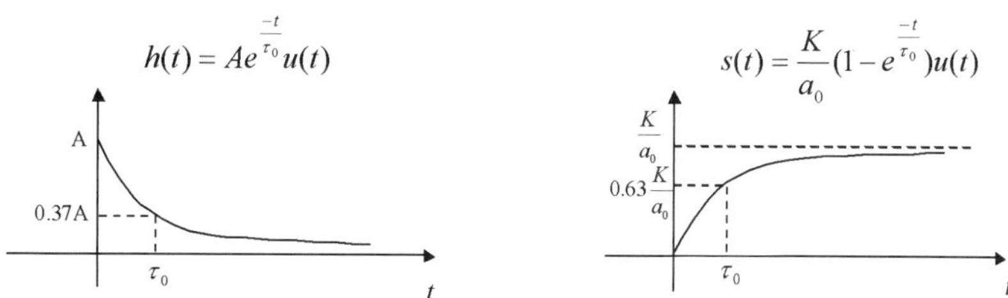

FIGURE 3.10 Impulse response and step response of the first-order system.

EIGENFUNCTIONS OF LTI DIFFERENCE AND DIFFERENTIAL SYSTEMS

We have used the fact that complex exponential signals of the type Cz^n and Ae^{st} remain basically invariant under the action of time shifts and derivatives, respectively, to find the homogeneous responses of LTI difference and differential systems.

The response of an LTI system to a complex exponential input is the same complex exponential, with only a change in (complex) amplitude.

$$\text{Continuous-time LTI system: } e^{st} * h(t) = H(s)e^{st} \tag{3.86}$$

$$\text{Discrete-time LTI system: } z^n * h[n] = H(z)z^n \tag{3.87}$$

The complex amplitude factors $H(s)$ and $H(z)$ are in general functions of the complex variables s and z.

Input signals like $x[n] = z^n$ and $x(t) = e^{st}$ for which the system output is a complex constant times the input signal are called *eigenfunctions* of the LTI system, and the complex gains are the system's *eigenvalues* corresponding to the eigenfunctions. To show that e^{st} is indeed an eigenfunction of any LTI system of impulse response $h(t)$, we look at the following convolution integral:

$$y(t) = \int_{-\infty}^{+\infty} h(\tau)x(t-\tau)d\tau = \int_{-\infty}^{+\infty} h(\tau)e^{s(t-\tau)}d\tau$$
$$= e^{st} \int_{-\infty}^{+\infty} h(\tau)e^{-s\tau}d\tau \qquad (3.88)$$

The system's response has the form $y(t) = H(s)e^{st}$, where $H(s) := \int_{-\infty}^{+\infty} h(\tau)e^{-s\tau}d\tau$, assuming the integral converges. For LTI discrete-time systems, the complex exponential z^n is an eigenfunction:

$$y[n] = \sum_{k=-\infty}^{+\infty} h[k]x[n-k] = \sum_{k=-\infty}^{+\infty} h[k]z^{n-k}$$
$$= z^n \sum_{k=-\infty}^{+\infty} h[k]z^{-k} \qquad (3.89)$$

The system's response has the form $y[n] = H(z)z^n$, where $H(z) = \sum_{k=-\infty}^{+\infty} h[k]z^{-k}$, assuming that the sum converges. The functions $H(s)$ and $H(z)$ are, respectively, the Laplace transform and the z-transform of the system's impulse response. Each is called the *transfer function* of the system; more on this in Chapter 6 and Chapter 13.

SUMMARY

In this chapter, we introduced special classes of LTI systems: differential and difference systems.

- The classical solution composed of the sum of the forced response and the natural response was reviewed for both differential and difference systems.
- Since an LTI system is completely characterized by its impulse response, we gave step-by-step techniques to compute the impulse responses of differential and difference systems.
- The BIBO stability of differential and difference systems was analyzed with respect to the characteristic polynomial.
- The time constant of a first-order differential system and its corresponding natural frequency were introduced.
- Finally, it was pointed out that exponential signals are basically invariant (only their complex amplitude varies) when processed by a differential or difference system.

TO PROBE FURTHER

The classical subject of linear constant-coefficient ordinary differential equations can be found in many basic mathematics textbooks, for example, Boyce and Diprima, 2004. An advanced treatment of difference equations can be found in Kelley and Peterson, 2001.

EXERCISES

Exercises with Solutions

Exercise 3.1

Consider the following first-order, causal LTI differential system S_1 initially at rest:

$$S_1: \quad \frac{dy(t)}{dt} + ay(t) = \frac{dx(t)}{dt} - 2x(t), \quad a > 0 \text{ is real.}$$

(a) Calculate the impulse response $h_1(t)$ of the system S_1. Sketch it for $a = 2$.

Answer:

Step 1: Set up the problem to calculate the impulse response of the left-hand side of the equation:

$$\frac{dh_a(t)}{dt} + ah_a(t) = \delta(t). \tag{3.59}$$

Step 2: Find the initial condition of the corresponding homogeneous equation at $t = 0^+$ by integrating the above differential equation from $t = 0^-$ to $t = 0^+$. Note that the impulse will be in the term $\frac{dh_a(t)}{dt}$, so $h_a(t)$ will have a finite jump at most. Thus, we have $\int_{0^-}^{0^+} \frac{dh_a(\tau)}{d\tau} d\tau = h_1(0^+) = 1$, and hence $h_1(0^+) = 1$ is our initial condition for the homogeneous equation for $t > 0$:

$$\frac{dh_a(t)}{dt} + ah_a(t) = 0.$$

Step 3: The characteristic polynomial is $p(s) = s + a$, and it has one zero at $s = -a$, which means that the homogeneous response has the form $h_a(t) = Ae^{-at}$ for $t > 0$. The initial condition allows us to determine the constant A: $h_a(0^+) = A = 1$, so that

$$h_a(t) = e^{-at}u(t).$$

Step 4: LTI systems are commutative, so we can apply the right-hand side of the differential equation to $h_a(t)$ in order to obtain $h_1(t)$:

$$\begin{aligned} h_1(t) &= \frac{dh_a(t)}{dt} - 2h_a(t) \\ &= \frac{d}{dt}\left(e^{-at}u(t)\right) - 2e^{-at}u(t) \\ &= -(2 + a)e^{-at}u(t) + \delta(t) \end{aligned}$$

This impulse response is plotted in Figure 3.11 for $a = 2$.
(b) Is the system S_1 BIBO stable? Justify your answer.

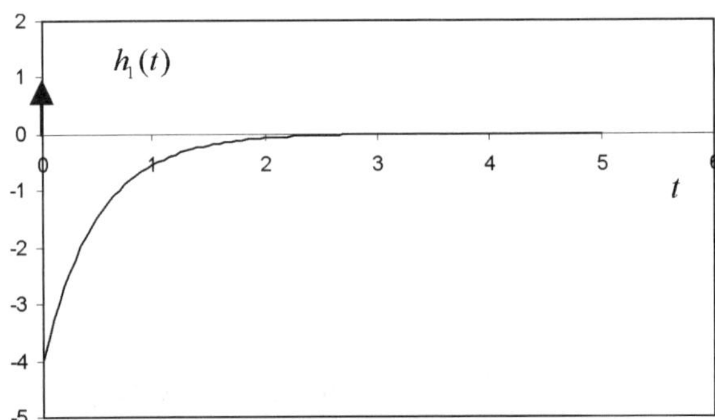

FIGURE 3.11 Impulse response of the first-order differential system.

Answer:
Yes, it is stable. The single real zero of its characteristic polynomial is negative: $s = -a < 0$.

Exercise 3.2

Consider the following second-order, causal LTI differential system S_2 initially at rest:

$$S_2: \quad \frac{d^2y(t)}{dt^2} + 5\frac{dy(t)}{dt} + 6y(t) = x(t).$$

Calculate the impulse response of the system S_2.

Answer:

Solution 1:

Step 1: Set up the problem to calculate the impulse response of the system:

$$\frac{d^2h_2(t)}{dt^2} + 5\frac{dh_2(t)}{dt} + 6h_2(t) = \delta(t)$$

Step 2: Find the initial conditions of the corresponding homogeneous equation at $t = 0^+$ by integrating the above differential equation from $t = 0^-$ to $t = 0^+$. Note that the impulse will be in the term $\frac{d^2h_2(t)}{dt^2}$, so $dh_2(t)$ will have a finite jump at most. Thus we have

$$\int_{0^-}^{0^+} \frac{d^2h_2(\tau)}{d\tau^2} d\tau = \frac{dh_2(0^+)}{dt} = 1.$$

Hence, $\frac{dh_2(0^+)}{dt} = 1$ is one of our two initial conditions for the homogeneous equation for $t > 0$:

$$\frac{d^2h_2(t)}{dt^2} + 5\frac{dh_2(t)}{dt} + 6h_2(t) = 0.$$

Since $\frac{dh_2(t)}{dt}$ has a finite jump from $t = 0^-$ to $t = 0^+$, the other initial condition is $h_2(0^+) = 0$.

Step 3: The characteristic polynomial is $p(s) = s^2 + 5s + 6$ and it has zeros at $s_1 = -2, s_2 = -3$, which means that the homogeneous response has the form $h_2(t) = Ae^{-2t} + Be^{-3t}$ for $t > 0$. The initial conditions allow us to determine constants A and B:

$$h_2(0^+) = 0 = A + B,$$

$$\frac{dh_2(0^+)}{dt} = 1 = -2A - 3B,$$

so that $A = 1, B = -1$, and finally,

$$h_2(t) = \left(e^{-2t} - e^{-3t}\right)u(t).$$

Solution 2 (step response approach):

Step 1: Set up the problem to calculate the step response of the system:

$$\frac{d^2 h_2(t)}{dt^2} + 5\frac{dh_2(t)}{dt} + 6h_2(t) = u(t).$$

Step 2: Compute the step response as the sum of a forced response and a homogeneous response.
The characteristic polynomial of this system is

$$p(s) = s^2 + 5s + 6 = (s+2)(s+3).$$

Hence, the homogeneous solution has the form

$$y_h(t) = Ae^{-2t} + Be^{-3t}.$$

We look for a particular solution of the form $y_p(t) = K$ for $t > 0$ when $x(t) = 1$. We find

$$y_p(t) = \frac{1}{6}.$$

Adding the homogeneous and particular solutions, we obtain the overall step response for $t > 0$:

$$s(t) = Ae^{-2t} + Be^{-3t} + \frac{1}{6}.$$

The initial conditions at $t = 0^-$ are $s(0^-) = 0, \frac{ds}{dt}(0^-) = 0$. Thus,

$$s(0^-) = 0 = A + B + \frac{1}{6},$$

which means that the step response of the system is

$$s(t)=\left(-\frac{1}{2}e^{-2t}+\frac{1}{3}e^{-3t}+\frac{1}{6}\right)u(t).$$

Step 3: Differentiating, we obtain the impulse response,

$$h(t)=\frac{d}{dt}s(t)=\left(e^{-2t}-e^{-3t}\right)u(t).$$

Exercise 3.3

Consider the following second-order, causal LTI differential system S initially at rest:

$$\frac{d^2y(t)}{dt^2}+\frac{dy(t)}{dt}+y(t)=x(t).$$

(a) Compute the response $y(t)$ of the system to the input $x(t)=2u(t)$ using the basic approach of the sum of the forced response and the natural response.

Answer:

First we seek to find a forced response of the same form as the input: $y_p(t)=A$. This yields $A=2$. Then, the natural response of the homogeneous equation

$$\frac{d^2y_h(t)}{dt^2}+\frac{dy_h(t)}{dt}+y_h(t)=0$$

will be a linear combination of terms of the form e^{st}. Substituting, we get the characteristic equation with complex roots:

$$s^2+s+1=(s+\frac{1}{2}-j\frac{\sqrt{3}}{2})(s+\frac{1}{2}+j\frac{\sqrt{3}}{2})=0.$$

Thus, the natural response is given by

$$y_h(t)=A_1e^{(-\frac{1}{2}-j\frac{\sqrt{3}}{2})t}+A_2e^{(-\frac{1}{2}+j\frac{\sqrt{3}}{2})t}.$$

The response of the system is the sum of the forced response and the natural response:

$$y(t)=y_h(t)+y_p(t)=A_1e^{(-\frac{1}{2}-j\frac{\sqrt{3}}{2})t}+A_2e^{(-\frac{1}{2}+j\frac{\sqrt{3}}{2})t}+2.$$

The initial conditions (zero) allow us to compute the remaining two unknown coefficients:

$$y(0^+)=A_1+A_2+2=0$$
$$\frac{dy}{dt}(0^+)=(-\frac{1}{2}-j\frac{\sqrt{3}}{2})A_1+(-\frac{1}{2}+j\frac{\sqrt{3}}{2})A_2=0.$$

We find $A_1=-1-j\frac{1}{\sqrt{3}}$, $A_2=-1+j\frac{1}{\sqrt{3}}$, which are complex conjugates of each other, as expected. Finally the response of the system is the signal

$$y(t)=y_h(t)+y_p(t)=\left((-1-j\frac{1}{\sqrt{3}})e^{(-\frac{1}{2}-j\frac{\sqrt{3}}{2})t}+(-1+j\frac{1}{\sqrt{3}})e^{(-\frac{1}{2}+j\frac{\sqrt{3}}{2})t}+2\right)u(t)$$
$$=\left(2\,\mathrm{Re}\left\{(-1+j\frac{1}{\sqrt{3}})e^{j\frac{\sqrt{3}}{2}t}\right\}e^{-\frac{1}{2}t}+2\right)u(t)$$
$$=2e^{-\frac{1}{2}t}\left(-\cos\frac{\sqrt{3}}{2}t-\frac{1}{\sqrt{3}}\sin\frac{\sqrt{3}}{2}t\right)u(t)+2u(t).$$

(b) Calculate the impulse response $h(t)$ of the system.

Answer:

Step 1: Set up the problem to calculate the impulse response of the left-hand side of the equation. Note that this will directly give us the impulse response of the system:

$$\frac{d^2h(t)}{dt^2}+\frac{dh(t)}{dt}+h(t)=\delta(t).$$

Step 2: Find the initial conditions of the corresponding homogeneous equation at $t=0^+$ by integrating the above differential equation from $t=0^-$ to $t=0^+$. Note that the impulse will be in the term $\frac{d^2h(t)}{dt^2}$, so $\frac{dh(t)}{dt}$ will have a finite jump at most. Thus we have

$$\int_{0^-}^{0^+}\frac{d^2h(\tau)}{d\tau^2}d\tau=\frac{dh(0^+)}{dt}=1.$$

Hence, $\frac{dh(0^+)}{dt} = 1$ is one of the two initial conditions for the homogeneous equation for $t > 0$:

$$\frac{d^2h(t)}{dt^2} + \frac{dh(t)}{dt} + h(t) = 0.$$

Since $\frac{dh(t)}{dt}$ has a finite jump from $t = 0^-$ to $t = 0^+$, the other initial condition is $h(0^+) = 0$.

Step 3: From (a), the natural response is given by

$$h(t) = A_1 e^{(-\frac{1}{2} - j\frac{\sqrt{3}}{2})t} + A_2 e^{(-\frac{1}{2} + j\frac{\sqrt{3}}{2})t}, \qquad t > 0.$$

The initial conditions allow us to determine the constants:

$$h(0^+) = 0 = A_1 + A_2,$$

$$\frac{dh(0^+)}{dt} = 1 = A_1(-\frac{1}{2} - j\frac{\sqrt{3}}{2}) + A_2(-\frac{1}{2} + j\frac{\sqrt{3}}{2}),$$

so that $A_1 = \frac{j}{\sqrt{3}}$, $A_2 = -\frac{j}{\sqrt{3}}$, and finally,

$$\begin{aligned} h(t) &= \left(\frac{j}{\sqrt{3}} e^{(-\frac{1}{2} - j\frac{\sqrt{3}}{2})t} - \frac{j}{\sqrt{3}} e^{(-\frac{1}{2} + j\frac{\sqrt{3}}{2})t} \right) u(t) \\ &= 2\,\mathrm{Re}\left(\frac{j}{\sqrt{3}} e^{-j\frac{\sqrt{3}}{2}t} \right) e^{-\frac{1}{2}t} u(t) \\ &= \frac{2}{\sqrt{3}} \sin\left(\frac{\sqrt{3}}{2} t \right) e^{-\frac{1}{2}t} u(t) \end{aligned}$$

Exercise 3.4

Consider the following second-order, causal difference LTI system S initially at rest:

$$S: \qquad y[n] - 0.64y[n-2] = x[n] + x[n-1].$$

Compute the response of the system to the input $x[n] = (0.2)^n u[n]$.

Answer:
The characteristic polynomial is $z^2 - 0.64 = (z - 0.8)(z + 0.8)$, with zeros $z_1 = -0.8, z_2 = 0.8$. The homogeneous response is given by

$$h_a[n] = A(-0.8)^n + B(0.8)^n,\ n \geq 0.$$

The forced response for $n \geq 1$ has the form $y_p[n] = C(0.2)^n$:

$$\begin{aligned} C(0.2)^n - 0.64C(0.2)^{n-2} &= (0.2)^n + (0.2)^{n-1} \\ C(1 - 0.64(0.2)^{-2}) &= 1 + (0.2)^{-1} \\ C &= \frac{6}{-15} = -0.4. \end{aligned}$$

Notice here that we assume that $n \geq 1$ so that all the terms on the right-hand side of the difference equation are present in the computation of the coefficient C. The assumption of initial rest implies $y[-2] = y[-1] = 0$, but we need to use initial conditions at times when the forced response exists (for $n \geq 1$), that is, $y[1]$, $y[2]$, which can be obtained by a simple recursion:

$$\begin{aligned} &y[n] = 0.64y[n-2] + (0.2)^n u[n] + (0.2)^{n-1} u[n-1] \\ &n = 0:\quad y[0] = 0.64(0) + (0.2)^0 + 0 = 1 \\ &n = 1:\quad y[1] = 0.64(0) + (0.2)^1 + (0.2)^0 = 1.2 \\ &n = 2:\quad y[2] = 0.64(1) + (0.2)^2 + (0.2)^1 = 0.88. \end{aligned}$$

Now, we can compute the coefficients A and B:

$$\begin{aligned} &y[1] = A(-0.8)^1 + B(0.8)^1 - 0.4(0.2)^1 = 1.2 \\ &\Rightarrow -0.8A + 0.8B = 1.28 \\ &y[2] = A(-0.8)^2 + B(0.8)^2 - 0.4(0.2)^2 = 0.88 \\ &\Rightarrow 0.64A + 0.64B = 0.896 \end{aligned}$$

This yields $A = -0.1,\quad B = 1.5$. Finally, the overall response is

$$y[n] = \left[-0.1(-0.8)^n + 1.5(0.8)^n - 0.4(0.2)^n\right]u[n].$$

Exercise 3.5

Consider the causal LTI system initially at rest and described by the difference equation

$$y[n]+0.4y[n-1]=x[n]+x[n-1].$$

Find the response of this system to the input depicted in Figure 3.12 by convolution.

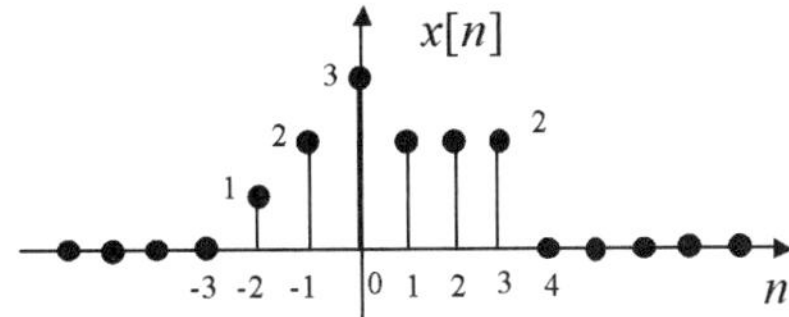

FIGURE 3.12 Input signal of the difference system.

Answer:
First we need to find the impulse response of the difference system. The characteristic polynomial is given by

$$p(z)=z+0.4,$$

and its zero is $z_1=-0.4$. The homogeneous response is given by

$$h_a[n]=A(-0.4)^n,\ \ n>0.$$

The initial condition for the homogeneous equation for $n>0$ is $h_a[0]=\delta[0]=1$. Now, we can compute the coefficient A:

$$h_a[0]=A=1.$$

Hence, $h_a[n]=(-0.4)^n u[n]$, and the impulse response is obtained as follows:

$$h[n]=h_a[n]+h_a[n-1]=(-0.4)^n u[n]+(-0.4)^{n-1}u[n-1].$$

Secondly, we compute the convolution $y[n]=h[n]*x[n]$. Perhaps the easiest way to compute it is to write

$$
\begin{aligned}
y[n] &= \sum_{k=-\infty}^{\infty} x[k]h[n-k] \\
&= x[-2]h[n+2]+x[-1]h[n+1]+x[0]h[n]+x[1]h[n-1]+x[2]h[n-2]+x[3]h[n-3] \\
&= h[n+2]+2h[n+1]+3h[n]+2h[n-1]+2h[n-2]+2h[n-3] \\
&= (-0.4)^{n+2}u[n+2]+(-0.4)^{n+1}u[n+1]+2(-0.4)^{n+1}u[n+1]+2(-0.4)^{n}u[n]+3(-0.4)^{n}u[n] \\
&\quad +3(-0.4)^{n-1}u[n-1]+2(-0.4)^{n-1}u[n-1]+2(-0.4)^{n-2}u[n-2]+2(-0.4)^{n-2}u[n-2] \\
&\quad +2(-0.4)^{n-3}u[n-3]+2(-0.4)^{n-3}u[n-3]+2(-0.4)^{n-4}u[n-4] \\
&= (-0.4)^{n+2}u[n+2]+3(-0.4)^{n+1}u[n+1]+5(-0.4)^{n}u[n]+5(-0.4)^{n-1}u[n-1] \\
&\quad +4(-0.4)^{n-2}u[n-2]+4(-0.4)^{n-3}u[n-3]+2(-0.4)^{n-4}u[n-4].
\end{aligned}
$$

Exercises

Exercise 3.6

Determine whether the following causal LTI second-order differential system is stable:

$$2\frac{d^2y(t)}{dt^2}-2\frac{dy(t)}{dt}-24y(t)=\frac{d}{dt}x(t)-4x(t).$$

Exercise 3.7

Consider the following first-order, causal LTI difference system:

$$2y[n]+1.2y[n-1]=x[n-1].$$

Compute the impulse response $h[n]$ of the system by using recursion.

Answer:

ON THE CD

Exercise 3.8

Suppose that a \$1000 deposit is made at the beginning of each year in a bank account carrying an annual interest rate of $r = 6\%$. The interest is vested in the account at the end of each year. Write the difference equation describing the evolution of the account and find the amount accrued at the end of the 50th year.

Exercise 3.9

Find the impulse response $h(t)$ of the following second-order, causal LTI differential system:

$$\frac{d^2y(t)}{dt^2}+\sqrt{2}\frac{dy(t)}{dt}+y(t)=\frac{dx(t)}{dt}+x(t).$$

Answer:

ON THE CD

Exercise 3.10

Compute and sketch the impulse response $h(t)$ of the following causal LTI, first-order differential system initially at rest:

$$2\frac{dy(t)}{dt}+4y(t)=3\frac{d}{dt}x(t)+2x(t).$$

Exercise 3.11

Compute the impulse response $h[n]$ of the following causal LTI, second-order difference system initially at rest:

$$y[n]+\sqrt{3}y[n-1]+y[n-2]=x[n-1]+x[n-2].$$

Simplify your expression of $h[n]$ to obtain a real function of time.

Answer:

ON THE CD

Exercise 3.12

Calculate the impulse response $h(t)$ of the following second-order, causal LTI differential system initially at rest:

$$\frac{d^2y(t)}{dt^2}+2\frac{dy(t)}{dt}+2y(t)=-3\frac{dx(t)}{dt}+x(t).$$

Exercise 3.13

Consider the following second-order, causal difference LTI system S initially at rest:

$$S: \quad y[n]-0.9y[n-1]+0.2y[n-2]=x[n-1].$$

(a) What is the characteristic polynomial of S? What are its zeros? Is the system stable?

(b) Compute the impulse response of S for all n.

(c) Compute the response of S for all n for the input signal $x[n]=2u[n]$ using the conventional solution (sum of particular solution and homogeneous solution).

Answer:

ON THE CD

4 Fourier Series Representation of Periodic Continuous-Time Signals

In This Chapter

- Linear Combinations of Harmonically Related Complex Exponentials
- Determination of the Fourier Series Representation of a Continuous-Time Periodic Signal
- Graph of the Fourier Series Coefficients: The Line Spectrum
- Properties of Continuous-Time Fourier Series
- Fourier Series of a Periodic Rectangular Wave
- Optimality and Convergence of the Fourier Series
- Existence of a Fourier Series Representation
- Gibbs Phenomenon
- Fourier Series of a Periodic Train of Impulses
- Parseval Theorem
- Power Spectrum
- Total Harmonic Distortion
- Steady-State Response of an LTI System to a Periodic Signal
- Summary
- To Probe Further
- Exercises

((Lecture 12: Definition and Properties of the Fourier Series))

A signal is defined as a function of time representing the evolution of a variable. Certain types of signals have the special property of remaining basically invariant under the action of linear time-invariant systems. Such signals include sinusoids and exponential functions of time. These signals can be linearly combined to form virtually any other signal, which is the basis of the Fourier series representation of periodic signals and the Fourier transform representation of aperiodic signals.

The Fourier representation opens up a whole new interpretation of signals in terms of their frequency contents, called their frequency spectrum. Furthermore, in the frequency domain, a linear time-invariant system acts as a filter on the frequency spectrum of the input signal, attenuating it at some frequencies while amplifying it at other frequencies. This property is called the frequency response of the system. These frequency domain concepts are fundamental in electrical engineering, as they underpin the fields of communication systems, analog and digital filter design, feedback control, power engineering, etc.

Well-trained electrical and computer engineers think of signals in terms of their frequency spectrum probably just as much as they think of them as functions of time.

LINEAR COMBINATIONS OF HARMONICALLY RELATED COMPLEX EXPONENTIALS

Recall that periodic signals satisfy $x(t) = x(t+T), -\infty < t < +\infty$ for some positive value of T. The smallest such T is called the fundamental period of the signal, and its fundamental frequency is defined as $\omega_0 = \frac{2\pi}{T}$ rad/s. One thing to remember is that the periodic signal $x(t)$ is entirely determined by its values over one period T. Also recall that we looked at harmonically related complex exponentials with frequencies that are integer multiples of ω_0:

$$\phi_k(t) := e^{jk\omega_0 t}, \quad k = 0, \pm 1, \pm 2, \ldots \tag{4.1}$$

We saw that these harmonically related signals have a very important property: they form an *orthogonal set*. That is,

$$\int_0^{\frac{2\pi}{\omega_0}} \phi_k(t)\phi_{-m}(t)dt = \int_0^{\frac{2\pi}{\omega_0}} e^{jk\omega_0 t}e^{-jm\omega_0 t}dt = \int_0^{\frac{2\pi}{\omega_0}} e^{j(m-k)\omega_0 t}dt$$

$$= \frac{1}{j(m-k)\omega_0}\left[e^{j(m-k)2\pi} - 1\right] = \begin{cases} \frac{2\pi}{\omega_0}, & m = k \\ 0, & m \neq k \end{cases}. \tag{4.2}$$

Each of these signals has a fundamental frequency that is a multiple of ω_0, and therefore each is periodic with period T (although for $|k| > 1$, the fundamental period of $\phi_k(t)$ is T). Let us look at the imaginary part of $\phi_k(t)$ for $k = 0,1,2$ and $T = 1\text{s}$ shown in Figure 4.1.

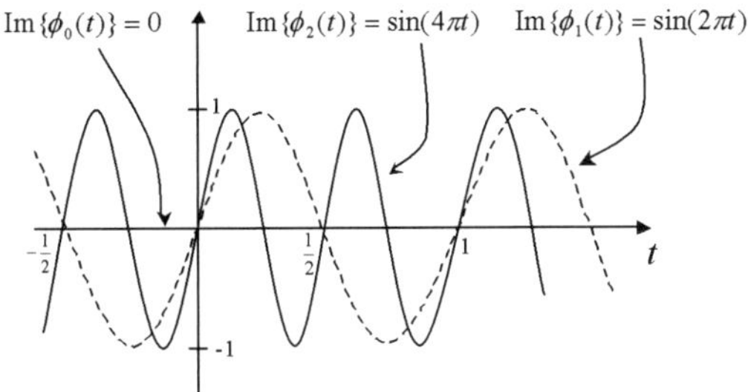

FIGURE 4.1 Imaginary parts of complex harmonics.

A linear combination of the complex exponentials $\phi_k(t)$ is also periodic with fundamental period T:

$$x(t)=\sum_{k=-\infty}^{+\infty} a_k e^{jk\omega_0 t}=\sum_{k=-\infty}^{+\infty} a_k e^{jk(\frac{2\pi}{T})t}. \tag{4.3}$$

The two terms with $k=\pm 1$ in this series are collectively called the *fundamental components,* or the *first harmonic components,* of the signal. The two terms with $k=\pm 2$ are referred to as the *second harmonic components* (with fundamental frequency $2\omega_0$), and more generally the components for $k=\pm N$ are called the *N^{th} harmonic components*.

Example 4.1: Consider the periodic signal with fundamental frequency $\omega_0=\pi/2$ rad/s made up of the sum of five harmonic components:

$$\begin{aligned}
&x(t)=\sum_{k=-5}^{5} a_k e^{jk\frac{\pi}{2}t},\\
&a_0=0,\ a_{\pm 1}=-0.2026,\ a_{\pm 2}=0,\\
&a_{\pm 3}=-0.0225,\ a_{\pm 4}=0,\ a_{\pm 5}=-0.0081.
\end{aligned} \tag{4.4}$$

Collecting the harmonic components together, we obtain

$$\begin{aligned}
x(t)&=-0.2026(e^{j\frac{\pi}{2}t}+e^{-j\frac{\pi}{2}t})-0.0225(e^{j\frac{3\pi}{2}t}+e^{-j\frac{3\pi}{2}t})-0.0081(e^{j\frac{5\pi}{2}t}+e^{-j\frac{5\pi}{2}t})\\
&=-0.4052\cos(\frac{\pi}{2}t)-0.0450\cos(\frac{3\pi}{2}t)-0.0162\cos(\frac{5\pi}{2}t)
\end{aligned} \tag{4.5}$$

The resulting signal represents an approximation to a triangular wave, as seen in Figure 4.2.

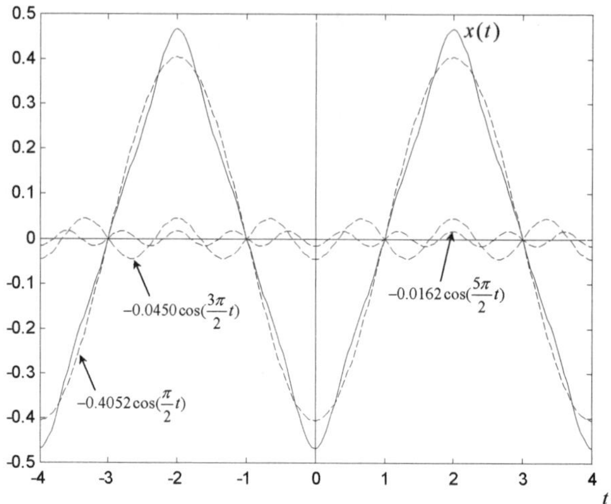

FIGURE 4.2 Signal as a sum of five harmonic components.

DETERMINATION OF THE FOURIER SERIES REPRESENTATION OF A CONTINUOUS-TIME PERIODIC SIGNAL

Assume that a periodic signal can be expressed as a linear combination of harmonically related signals as in Equation 4.3. Then, by the orthogonality property of the harmonically related complex exponentials, we can easily compute the a_k coefficients. To obtain a_n, we just have to multiply both sides of Equation 4.3 by $e^{-jn\omega_0 t}$ and integrate over one fundamental period of the signal (here from 0 to T, but it could be from any time t_0 to time $t_0 + T$, which is denoted as $\int_T (\cdot)dt$):

$$\begin{aligned} \int_0^T x(t)e^{-jn\omega_0 t}dt &= \int_0^T \sum_{k=-\infty}^{+\infty} a_k e^{jk\omega_0 t} e^{-jn\omega_0 t} dt \\ &= \sum_{k=-\infty}^{+\infty} a_k \int_0^T e^{jk\omega_0 t} e^{-jn\omega_0 t} dt \\ &= Ta_n. \end{aligned} \tag{4.6}$$

Thus, $a_n = \frac{1}{T}\int_0^T x(t)e^{-jn\omega_0 t}dt.$

To recap, if a periodic signal $x(t)$ has a Fourier series representation, then we have the equation pair

$$x(t) = \sum_{k=-\infty}^{+\infty} a_k e^{jk\omega_0 t} = \sum_{k=-\infty}^{+\infty} a_k e^{jk(\frac{2\pi}{T})t}, \tag{4.7}$$

$$a_k = \frac{1}{T}\int_T x(t)e^{-jk\omega_0 t}dt = \frac{1}{T}\int_T x(t)e^{-jk(\frac{2\pi}{T})t}dt, \tag{4.8}$$

which gives us two representations of the signal. Equation 4.7 is a time-domain representation of the signal as a sum of periodic complex exponential signals. This is the *synthesis equation*. Equation 4.8, called the *analysis equation*, gives us a frequency-domain representation of the signal as the *Fourier series coefficients*, also referred to as the *spectral coefficients* of $x(t)$. That is, each one of these complex coefficients tells us how much the corresponding harmonic component of a given frequency contributes to the signal.

Remarks:

- The coefficient $a_0 = \frac{1}{T}\int_T x(t)dt$ is the DC component of the signal (average value of the signal over one period). It should always be computed separately from a_k to avoid indeterminacies of the type 0/0 in the expression for a_k evaluated at $k = 0$.
- For a *real* signal $x(t)$, we have $a_{-k} = a_k^*$. Let $a_k = A_k e^{j\theta_k}$, $A_k, \theta_k \in \mathbb{R}$. Then we have a real form of the Fourier series:

$$\begin{aligned} x(t) &= \sum_{k=-\infty}^{+\infty} a_k e^{jk\omega_0 t} = a_0 + \sum_{k=1}^{+\infty} a_k e^{jk\omega_0 t} + a_k^* e^{-jk\omega_0 t} \\ &= a_0 + \sum_{k=1}^{+\infty} 2\,\mathrm{Re}\{a_k e^{jk\omega_0 t}\} \\ &= a_0 + 2\sum_{k=1}^{+\infty} A_k \cos(k\omega_0 t + \theta_k). \end{aligned} \tag{4.9}$$

- For a real signal $x(t)$, if we represent the Fourier series coefficients as $a_k = B_k + jC_k$, $B_k, C_k \in \mathbb{R}$, we obtain another real form of the Fourier series:

$$
\begin{aligned}
x(t) &= \sum_{k=-\infty}^{+\infty} a_k e^{jk\omega_0 t} = a_0 + \sum_{k=1}^{+\infty} a_k e^{jk\omega_0 t} + a_k^* e^{-jk\omega_0 t} \\
&= a_0 + \sum_{k=1}^{+\infty} 2\,\mathrm{Re}\{a_k e^{jk\omega_0 t}\} \\
&= a_0 + \sum_{k=1}^{+\infty} 2\,\mathrm{Re}\{(B_k + jC_k)[\cos(k\omega_0 t) + j\sin(k\omega_0 t)]\} \\
&= a_0 + 2\sum_{k=1}^{+\infty} [B_k \cos(k\omega_0 t) - C_k \sin(k\omega_0 t)] \qquad (4.10)
\end{aligned}
$$

Example 4.2: Let us find the fundamental period T, the fundamental frequency ω_0, and the Fourier series coefficients a_k of the periodic "sawtooth" signal $x(t)$ shown in Figure 4.3. Then, we will express $x(t)$ as a Fourier series.

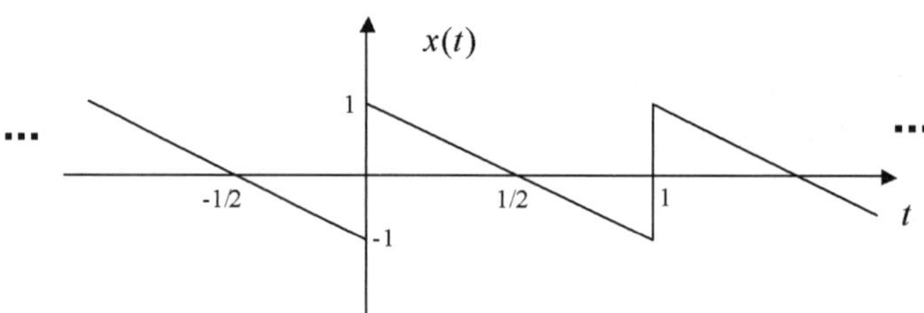

FIGURE 4.3 Periodic "sawtooth" signal.

The fundamental period is $T = 1\text{s}$; hence $\omega_0 = 2\pi$ rad/s. First, the average over one period (the DC value of the signal) is 0, so $a_0 = 0$. For $k \neq 0$,

$$
\begin{aligned}
a_k &= \frac{1}{T}\int_0^1 x(t)e^{-jk2\pi t}\,dt \\
&= \int_0^1 (1-2t)e^{-jk2\pi t}\,dt \\
&= \frac{-1}{jk2\pi}\Big[(1-2t)e^{-jk2\pi t}\Big]_0^1 - \frac{1}{jk\pi}\underbrace{\int_0^1 e^{-jk2\pi t}\,dt}_{=0} \text{ (integration by parts)}
\end{aligned}
$$

$$= \frac{1}{jk2\pi} + \frac{1}{jk2\pi}$$
$$= \frac{1}{jk\pi}$$
$$= \frac{-j}{k\pi}. \qquad (4.11)$$

Note that the coefficients $a_k = \frac{-j}{k\pi}$ are purely imaginary and form an odd sequence, which is consistent with our real, odd signal. The Fourier series representation of $x(t)$ is

$$x(t) = \sum_{k=-\infty}^{+\infty} a_k e^{jk2\pi t} = \sum_{\substack{k=-\infty \\ k\neq 0}}^{+\infty} \frac{-j}{k\pi} e^{jk2\pi t}. \qquad (4.12)$$

GRAPH OF THE FOURIER SERIES COEFFICIENTS: THE LINE SPECTRUM

The set of complex Fourier series coefficients $\{a_k\}_{k=-\infty}^{+\infty}$ of a signal can be plotted with separate graphs for their magnitude and phase. The combination of both plots is called the *line spectrum* of the signal.

Example 4.3: Consider the Fourier series coefficients of the sawtooth signal obtained in the previous example. Their magnitudes are given by $|a_k| = \frac{1}{|k|\pi}$, $k \neq 0$, and $|a_0| = 0$, and their phases are given by $\angle a_k = \begin{cases} -\frac{\pi}{2}, & k > 0 \\ \frac{\pi}{2}, & k < 0 \end{cases}$ and $\angle a_0 = 0$. The corresponding line spectrum is shown in Figure 4.4.

The following MATLAB M-file located in D:\Chapter4\linespectrum.m displays the line spectrum of the sawtooth signal.

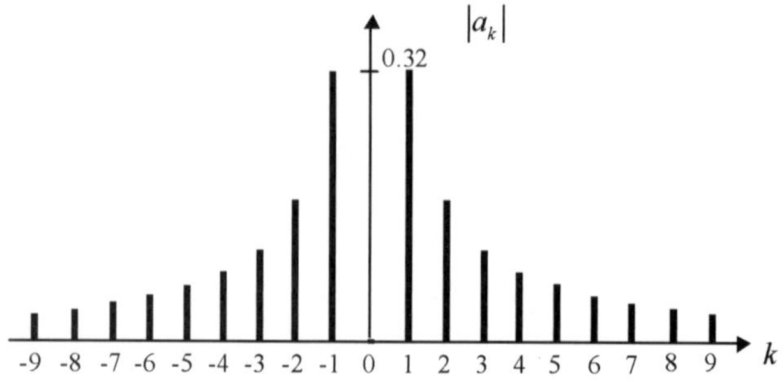

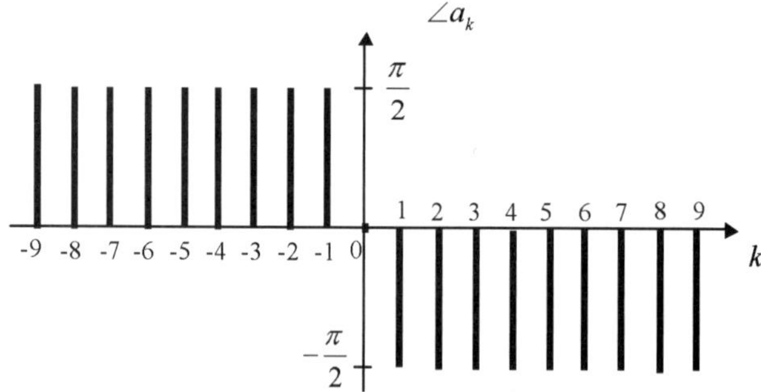

FIGURE 4.4 Line spectrum of the sawtooth signal.

```
%% Line spectrum of Fourier series coefficients
% signal amplitude and period
A=1;
T=1;
% number of harmonics
N=10;
% first compute the ak's
a0=0;
spectrum=zeros(1,2*N+1);
for k=-N:N
% spectral coefficients of sawtooth signal
if k>0
eval(['a' num2str(k) '=-j*A/(k*pi)'])
eval(['spectrum(k+N+1)=a' num2str(k)]);
elseif k<0
eval(['a_' num2str(abs(k)) '=-j*A/(k*pi)'])
eval(['spectrum(k+N+1)=a_' num2str(abs(k))]);
end
```

```
eval(['spectrum(N+1)=a0']);
end
% line spectrum
K=[-N:N];
subplot(211)
stem(K,abs(spectrum),'.-')
subplot(212)
stem(K,phase(spectrum),'.-')
```

Remark: A common mistake is to forget that the magnitude line spectrum must always be nonnegative. This mistake might arise, for example, when one writes $|a_k| = \frac{1}{k\pi}$, which is obviously wrong since k can be negative.

PROPERTIES OF CONTINUOUS-TIME FOURIER SERIES

Note that if the periodic signal $x(t)$ admits a Fourier series representation, then its set of spectral coefficients $\{a_k\}_{k=-\infty}^{+\infty}$ determines $x(t)$ completely. The duality between the signal and its spectral representation is denoted as $x(t) \overset{FS}{\leftrightarrow} a_k$. The following properties of the Fourier series are easy to show using Equations 4.7 and 4.8. (Do it as an exercise.) Note that these properties are also listed in Table D.3 of Appendix D.

Linearity

The operation of calculating the Fourier series coefficients of a periodic signal is linear. For $x(t) \overset{FS}{\leftrightarrow} a_k$, $y(t) \overset{FS}{\leftrightarrow} b_k$, if we form the linear combination $z(t) = \alpha x(t) + \beta y(t)$, $\alpha, \beta \in \mathbb{C}$, then

$$z(t) \overset{FS}{\leftrightarrow} \alpha a_k + \beta b_k. \tag{4.13}$$

Time Shifting

Time shifting leads to a multiplication by a complex exponential. For $x(t) \overset{FS}{\leftrightarrow} a_k$,

$$x(t - t_0) \overset{FS}{\leftrightarrow} e^{-jk\omega_0 t_0} a_k. \tag{4.14}$$

Remark: The magnitudes of the Fourier series coefficients are not changed, only their phases.

Time Reversal

Time reversal leads to a "sequence reversal" of the corresponding sequence of Fourier series coefficients:

$$x(-t) \overset{FS}{\leftrightarrow} a_{-k}. \tag{4.15}$$

Interesting consequences are that

- For $x(t)$ even, the sequence of coefficients is also even ($a_{-k} = a_k$).
- For $x(t)$ odd, the sequence of coefficients is also odd ($a_{-k} = -a_k$).

Time Scaling

Time scaling applied on a periodic signal changes the fundamental frequency of the signal (but it remains periodic "with the same shape"). For example, $x(\alpha t)$ has fundamental frequency $\alpha\omega_0$ and fundamental period $\alpha^{-1}T$. The Fourier series coefficients do not change:

$$x(\alpha t) \overset{FS}{\leftrightarrow} a_k, \tag{4.16}$$

but the Fourier series itself *has changed,* as the harmonic components are now at the frequencies $\pm\alpha\omega_0, \pm 2\alpha\omega_0, \pm 3\alpha\omega_0, \ldots$.

Application: For a given periodic signal (a specific waveform) such as a square wave, one can compute the Fourier series coefficients for a single normalized fundamental frequency. Then, the Fourier series of a square wave of any frequency has the same coefficients.

Multiplication of Two Signals

Suppose that $x(t)$ and $y(t)$ are both periodic with period T. For $x(t) \overset{FS}{\leftrightarrow} a_k$, $y(t) \overset{FS}{\leftrightarrow} b_k$, we have

$$x(t)y(t) \overset{FS}{\leftrightarrow} \sum_{l=-\infty}^{+\infty} a_l b_{k-l}, \tag{4.17}$$

that is, a convolution of the two sequences of spectral coefficients.

Conjugation and Conjugate Symmetry

Taking the conjugate of a periodic signal has the effect of conjugation and index reversal on the spectral coefficients:

$$x^*(t) \overset{FS}{\leftrightarrow} a^*_{-k}. \tag{4.18}$$

Interesting consequences are that

- For $x(t)$ real, $x(t) = x^*(t)$ and the sequence of coefficients is *conjugate symmetric*; that is, $a_{-k} = a^*_k$. This implies $|a_{-k}| = |a_k|$ (magnitude is even), $\angle a_{-k} = -\angle a_k$ (phase is odd), $a_0 \in \mathbb{R}$, $\mathrm{Re}\{a_{-k}\} = \mathrm{Re}\{a_k\}$, $\mathrm{Im}\{a_{-k}\} = -\mathrm{Im}\{a_k\}$.
- For $x(t)$ real and even, the sequence of coefficients is also real and even ($a_{-k} = a_k \in \mathbb{R}$).
- For $x(t)$ real and odd, the sequence of coefficients is imaginary and odd ($a_{-k} = -a^*_k$ purely imaginary).
- For an even-odd decomposition of the signal $x(t) = x_e(t) + x_o(t)$, we have $x_e(t) \overset{FS}{\leftrightarrow} \mathrm{Re}\{a_k\}$, $x_o(t) \overset{FS}{\leftrightarrow} j\,\mathrm{Im}\{a_k\}$.

((Lecture 13: Convergence of the Fourier Series))

FOURIER SERIES OF A PERIODIC RECTANGULAR WAVE

Consider the following periodic rectangular wave (or square wave) of fundamental period T and fundamental frequency $\omega_0 = \frac{2\pi}{T}$ (see Figure 4.5).

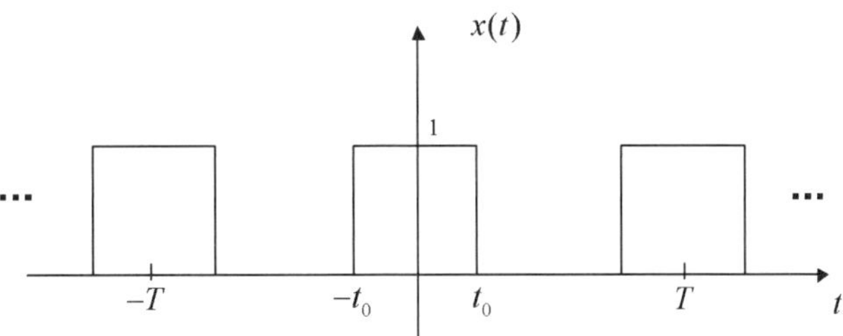

FIGURE 4.5 Periodic rectangular wave.

This signal is even and real and hence its Fourier series coefficients are also real and form an even sequence. Its DC value is equal to the area of one rectangle divided by the period: $a_0 = \frac{2t_0}{T}$. The other spectral coefficients are obtained as follows:

$$
\begin{aligned}
a_k &= \frac{1}{T}\int_{-T/2}^{T/2} x(t)e^{-jk\omega_0 t}\,dt = \frac{1}{T}\int_{-t_0}^{t_0} e^{-jk\omega_0 t}\,dt \\
&= -\frac{1}{jk\omega_0 T}\left[e^{-jk\omega_0 t}\right]_{-t_0}^{t_0} = -\frac{1}{jk\omega_0 T}\left(e^{-jk\omega_0 t_0} - e^{jk\omega_0 t_0}\right) \\
&= \frac{2}{k\omega_0 T}\left(\frac{e^{jk\omega_0 t_0} - e^{-jk\omega_0 t_0}}{2j}\right) = \frac{2\sin(k\omega_0 t_0)}{k\omega_0 T} \\
&= \frac{\sin\left(\pi k \frac{2t_0}{T}\right)}{\pi k}, \quad k \neq 0.
\end{aligned}
\tag{4.19}
$$

As previously mentioned, the coefficient a_0 is the signal average over one period. The other coefficients are scaled *samples* of the real continuous *sinc* function defined as follows:

$$
\operatorname{sinc}(u) := \frac{\sin \pi u}{\pi u}, \quad u \in \mathbb{R}. \tag{4.20}
$$

This function is equal to one at $u = 0$ and has zero crossings at $u = \pm n$, $n = 1,2,3,\ldots$, as shown in Figure 4.6.

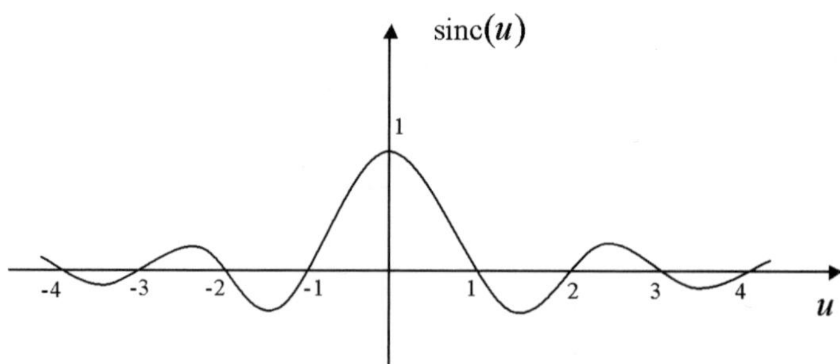

FIGURE 4.6 Graph of the sinc function.

Now, define the duty cycle $\eta := \frac{2t_0}{T}$ of the rectangular wave as the fraction of time the signal is "on" (equal to one) over one period. The duty cycle is often given as a percentage. The spectral coefficients expressed using the sinc function and the duty cycle can be written as

$$\begin{aligned} a_k &= \frac{2t_0}{T}\frac{\sin\left(\frac{\pi k 2t_0}{T}\right)}{\frac{\pi k 2t_0}{T}} = \frac{2t_0}{T}\operatorname{sinc}\left(\frac{k2t_0}{T}\right) \\ &= \eta \operatorname{sinc}(k\eta). \end{aligned} \tag{4.21}$$

For a 50% duty cycle, that is, $\eta = \frac{1}{2}$, we get the Fourier series coefficients given in Equation 4.22 and whose line spectrum is shown in Figure 4.7. Note that the coefficients are real, so a single plot suffices. However, one could also choose to sketch the magnitude (absolute value of a_k) and the phase (0 for a_k nonnegative, $-\pi/2$ for a_k negative) on two separate graphs.

$$a_k = \frac{1}{2}\operatorname{sinc}\left(\frac{k}{2}\right). \tag{4.22}$$

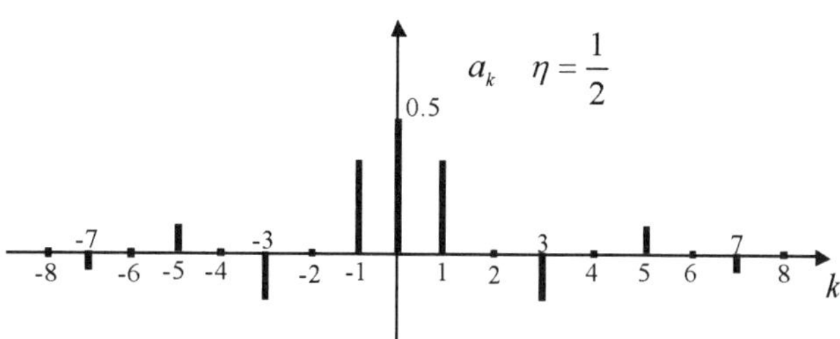

FIGURE 4.7 Spectral coefficients of the rectangular wave for a 50% duty cycle.

Remember that k is a multiple of the fundamental frequency. So for a 60 Hz (120π rad/s) square wave, the coefficients $a_{\pm 1}$ are the fundamental components at 60 Hz, $a_{\pm 2}$ are the second harmonic components at 120 Hz, etc.

For shorter duty cycles (shorter pulses with respect to the fundamental period), the "sinc envelope" of the spectral coefficients expands, and we get more coefficients in each lobe. For example, the real line spectrum of a rectangular wave with $\eta = \frac{1}{8}$ is shown in Figure 4.8.

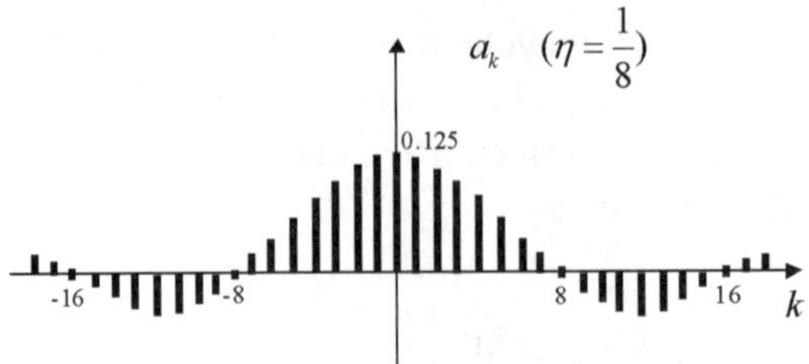

FIGURE 4.8 Spectral coefficients of the rectangular wave for a duty cycle $\eta = \frac{1}{8}$.

Remarks:

- In general, the coefficients are complex, and one would have to sketch two graphs to represent them (magnitude and phase).
- For a long duty cycle tending to 1, the waveform approaches a constant signal, and at the limit all the spectral coefficients vanish except the DC value: $a_0 = 1$.
- For a short duty cycle tending to 0, there are more and more lines in the main lobe of the sinc envelope. In fact, the first zero crossings bounding the main lobe are at $k = \pm\frac{1}{\eta}$ when these numbers turn out to be integers. This means that a periodic signal with short pulses has several significant harmonic components at high frequencies. This observation holds true in general for other signals in that signals with fast variations display significant high-frequency harmonics.

- The interactive Fourier Series Applet on the companion CD-ROM located in D:\Applets\FourierSeries\FourierApplet.html can help visualize the decomposition of a signal as a sum of harmonic components.

OPTIMALITY AND CONVERGENCE OF THE FOURIER SERIES

To study the convergence of the Fourier series, let us first look at the problem of approximating a periodic signal with a *finite* sum of harmonics (a truncated version of the infinite sum). The question here is as follows: What coefficients will give us the "best" approximation to the signal? Let the truncated Fourier sum be defined as

$$x_N(t) := \sum_{k=-N}^{+N} a_k e^{jk\omega_0 t}, \tag{4.23}$$

and define the approximation error as

$$e_N(t) := x(t) - x_N(t) = x(t) - \sum_{k=-N}^{+N} a_k e^{jk\omega_0 t}. \tag{4.24}$$

Now, consider the energy in one period of the error signal as the quantity to minimize to get the best approximation.

$$E_N = \int_T \left| e_N(t) \right|^2 dt. \tag{4.25}$$

We proceed by first expanding this equation:

$$\begin{aligned}
E_N &= \int_0^T \left(x(t) - \sum_{k=-N}^{+N} a_k e^{jk\omega_0 t} \right)\left(x^*(t) - \sum_{k=-N}^{+N} a_k^* e^{-jk\omega_0 t} \right) dt \\
&= \int_0^T x(t)x^*(t)dt + \int_0^T \left(\sum_{k=-N}^{+N} a_k e^{jk\omega_0 t} \right)\left(\sum_{n=-N}^{+N} a_n^* e^{-jn\omega_0 t} \right) dt - \int_0^T x(t) \sum_{k=-N}^{+N} a_k^* e^{-jk\omega_0 t} dt - \int_0^T x^*(t) \sum_{k=-N}^{+N} a_k e^{jk\omega_0 t} dt \\
&= \int_0^T \left| x(t) \right|^2 dt + \sum_{k=-N}^{+N} \sum_{n=-N}^{N} a_k a_n^* \int_0^T e^{j(k-n)\omega_0 t} dt - \sum_{k=-N}^{+N} a_k^* \int_0^T x(t) e^{-jk\omega_0 t} dt - \sum_{k=-N}^{+N} a_k \int_0^T x^*(t) e^{jk\omega_0 t} dt \\
&= \int_0^T \left| x(t) \right|^2 dt + T \sum_{k=-N}^{+N} a_k a_k^* - \sum_{k=-N}^{+N} a_k^* \int_0^T x(t) e^{-jk\omega_0 t} dt - \sum_{k=-N}^{+N} a_k \int_0^T x^*(t) e^{jk\omega_0 t} dt.
\end{aligned} \tag{4.26}$$

Then, we write the coefficients in rectangular coordinates $a_k = \alpha_k + j\beta_k$ and seek to minimize the energy $E_N(\alpha_k, \beta_k)$ by taking its partial derivatives with respect to α_k and β_k and setting them equal to zero. Let us do it for the real part α_k:

$$\begin{aligned}
E_N &= \int_0^T \left| x(t) \right|^2 dt + T \sum_{k=-N}^{+N} (\alpha_k^2 + \beta_k^2) - \sum_{k=-N}^{+N} (\alpha_k - j\beta_k) \int_0^T x(t) e^{-jk\omega_0 t} dt - \sum_{k=-N}^{+N} (\alpha_k + j\beta_k) \int_0^T x^*(t) e^{jk\omega_0 t} dt \\
&= \int_0^T \left| x(t) \right|^2 dt + T \sum_{k=-N}^{+N} (\alpha_k^2 + \beta_k^2) - 2\sum_{k=-N}^{+N} \alpha_k \operatorname{Re}\left\{ \int_0^T x(t) e^{-jk\omega_0 t} dt \right\} - 2\sum_{k=-N}^{+N} \beta_k \operatorname{Im}\left\{ \int_0^T x(t) e^{-jk\omega_0 t} dt \right\}.
\end{aligned} \tag{4.27}$$

Differentiating with respect to α_k, we obtain

$$\frac{\partial E_N}{\partial \alpha_k} = 2T \sum_{k=-N}^{+N} \alpha_k - 2\sum_{k=-N}^{+N} \operatorname{Re}\left\{ \int_0^T x(t) e^{-jk\omega_0 t} dt \right\} = 0. \tag{4.28}$$

This equation is satisfied with $\alpha_k = \operatorname{Re}\left\{ \frac{1}{T} \int_0^T x(t) e^{-jk\omega_0 t} dt \right\}$. Similarly, minimizing the energy of the approximation error with respect to β_k yields $\beta_k = \operatorname{Im}\left\{ \frac{1}{T} \int_0^T x(t) e^{-jk\omega_0 t} dt \right\}$. Therefore, the complex coefficients $a_k = \frac{1}{T} \int_0^T x(t) e^{-jk\omega_0 t} dt$ minimize the approximation error.

If the signal $x(t)$ has a Fourier series representation, then the limit of the energy in the approximation error $E_N = \int_T \left|e_N(t)\right|^2 dt$ as N tends to infinity is zero. In this sense, the Fourier series converges to the signal $x(t)$.

EXISTENCE OF A FOURIER SERIES REPRESENTATION

What classes of periodic signals have Fourier series representation? One that does is the class of periodic signals with finite energy over one period (finite total average power), that is, signals for which

$$\int_T \left|x(t)\right|^2 dt < \infty. \tag{4.29}$$

These signals have Fourier series that converge in the sense that the power in the difference between the signal and its Fourier series representation is zero. Note that this *does not* imply that the signal $x(t)$ and its corresponding Fourier series are equal at every value of time t. The class of periodic signals with finite energy over one period is broad and quite useful for us.

Another broad class of signals that have Fourier series representation are signals that satisfy the three *Dirichlet conditions.* These signals *equal* their Fourier series representation, except at isolated values of t where $x(t)$ has finite discontinuities. At these times, the Fourier series converges to the average of the signal values on either side of the discontinuity.

Dirichlet Conditions

Condition 1: Over any period, $x(t)$ must be absolutely integrable; that is, $\int_T \left|x(t)\right| dt < \infty$.

Condition 2: In any finite interval of time, $x(t)$ must be of bounded variations. This means that $x(t)$ must have a finite number of maxima and minima during any single period.

Example 4.4: The signal $x(t) = \sin\left(\frac{2\pi}{t}\right),\ 0 < t \le 1$ does not meet this requirement, as it has an infinite number of oscillations as time approaches zero.

Condition 3: In any finite interval of time, $x(t)$ has a finite number of discontinuities. Furthermore, each of these discontinuities is finite.

GIBBS PHENOMENON

An interesting observation can be made when one looks at the graph of a truncated Fourier series of a square wave. This is easy to do using, for example, MATLAB: compute the spectral coefficients as given in Equation 4.21 and up to $k = \pm 7$ ($N = 7$) and plot the real approximation to the square wave signal. The MATLAB M-file Fourierseries.m located in D:\Chapter4 on the companion CD-ROM can be used.

ON THE CD

$$x_N(t) := \sum_{k=-N}^{+N} a_k e^{jk\omega_0 t} = a_0 + 2\sum_{k=1}^{7} a_k \cos(k\omega_0 t). \tag{4.30}$$

The graph over one period looks like the one in Figure 4.9.

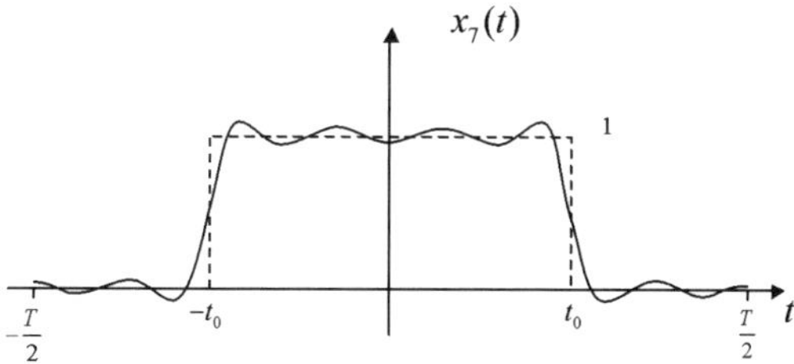

FIGURE 4.9 Gibbs phenomenon for truncated Fourier series of a square wave with seven harmonic components.

We can see that there are ripples of a certain amplitude in the approximation, especially close to the discontinuities in the signal. The surprising thing is that the peak amplitude of these ripples does not diminish when we add more terms in the truncated Fourier series. For example, for $N = 19$ in Figure 4.10; the approximation gets closer to a square wave, but we can still see rather large, but narrow, ripples around the discontinuities.

This is called the *Gibbs phenomenon* after the mathematical physicist who first provided an explanation of this phenomenon at the turn of the twentieth century. Indeed, the peak amplitude does not diminish as N grows larger, and the first overshoot on both sides of the discontinuity remains at 9% of the height of the discontinuity. However, the energy in these ripples vanishes as $N \to +\infty$. Also, for any fixed time t_1 (not at the discontinuity), the approximation tends to the signal value $x_N(t_1) \underset{N\to+\infty}{\to} x(t_1)$ (this is called *pointwise convergence*). At the discontinuity for time t_0, the approximation converges to a value corresponding to half of the jump.

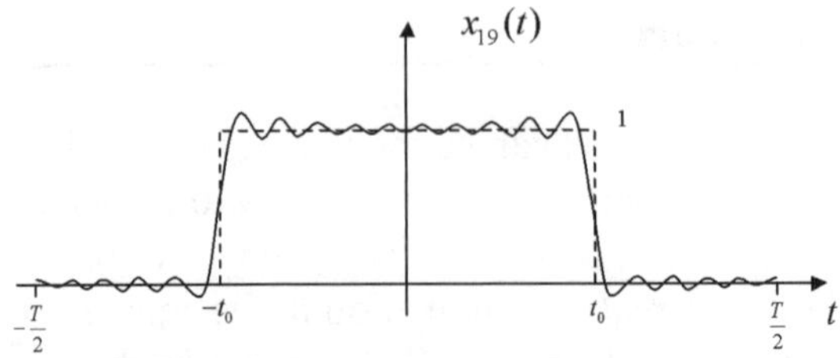

FIGURE 4.10 Gibbs phenomenon for a truncated Fourier series of a square wave with 19 harmonic components.

((Lecture 14: Parseval Theorem, Power Spectrum, Response of LTI System to Periodic Input))

FOURIER SERIES OF A PERIODIC TRAIN OF IMPULSES

It would be useful to have a Fourier series representation of a periodic train of impulses, called an *impulse train* as shown in Figure 4.11.

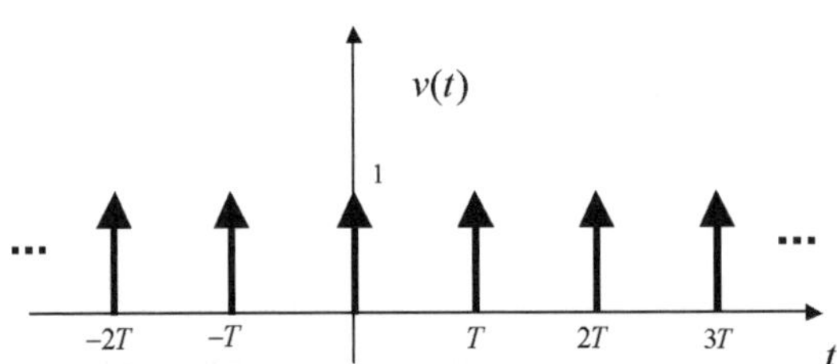

FIGURE 4.11 Impulse train.

A train of singularity functions such as impulses does not meet the Dirichlet conditions, nor is it of finite energy over one period. We can nevertheless calculate the Fourier series coefficients of the impulse train $v(t) = \sum_{n=-\infty}^{+\infty} \delta(t - nT)$ by using the formula

$$a_k = \frac{1}{T} \int_{-T/2}^{T/2} \delta(t) e^{-jk\omega_0 t} dt = \frac{1}{T}. \tag{4.31}$$

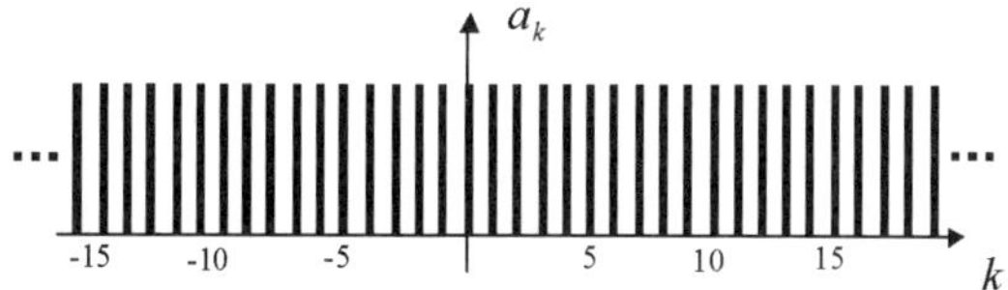

FIGURE 4.12 Spectral coefficients of the impulse train.

We can see in Figure 4.12 that the spectrum of an impulse train is a real, constant sequence. This means that the impulse train contains harmonics of equal strength at all frequencies, up to infinity.

Example 4.5: A periodic signal $x(t)$ can be described as a convolution of a single period of the signal with a train of impulses as shown in Figure 4.13. Let $x_T(t) := \begin{cases} x(t), & 0 \le t < T \\ 0, & \text{otherwise} \end{cases}$. Then,

$$\begin{aligned} x(t) &= \sum_{n=-\infty}^{+\infty} \delta(t-nT) * x_T(t) \\ &= \int_{-\infty}^{+\infty} \sum_{n=-\infty}^{+\infty} \delta(\tau - nT) x_T(t-\tau) d\tau \\ &= \sum_{n=-\infty}^{+\infty} \int_{-\infty}^{+\infty} \delta(\tau - nT) x_T(t-\tau) d\tau \\ &= \sum_{n=-\infty}^{+\infty} x_T(t-nT). \end{aligned} \tag{4.32}$$

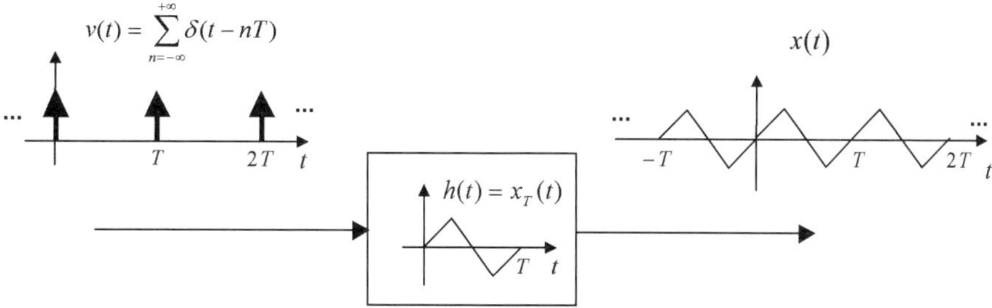

FIGURE 4.13 Conceptual setup for generating a periodic signal.

The Fourier series coefficients of the periodic signal $x(t)$ are obtained by multiplying the spectrum (Fourier transform) of $x_T(t)$ by the spectrum of the impulse train (more on this later when we study the Fourier transform).

The operation of periodically sampling a continuous-time signal can also be conveniently represented by a multiplication of an impulse train with the signal, as depicted in Figure 4.14. Sampling will be studied in detail in Chapter 15.

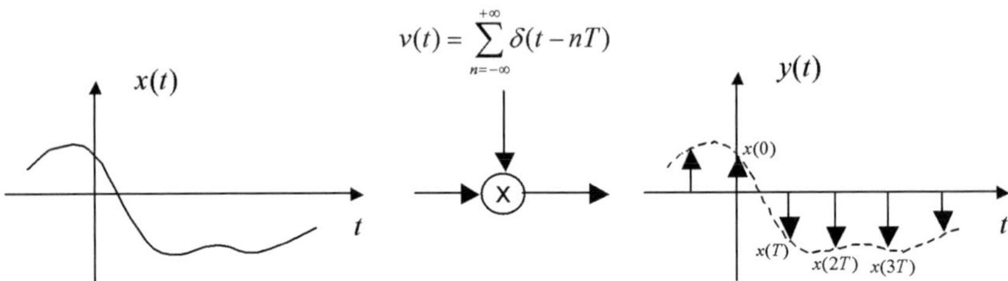

FIGURE 4.14 Conceptual setup for signal sampling.

PARSEVAL THEOREM

The Parseval theorem or Parseval equality simply says that the total average power of a periodic signal $x(t)$ is equal to the sum of the average powers in all of its harmonic components.

The power in the kth complex harmonic $a_k e^{jk\omega_0 t}$ of a periodic signal is given by

$$P_k = \frac{1}{T}\int_0^T \left|a_k e^{jk\omega_0 t}\right|^2 dt = \frac{1}{T}\int_0^T \left|a_k\right|^2 dt = \left|a_k\right|^2. \tag{4.33}$$

Note that $P_k = P_{-k}$, so the total power of the kth harmonic components of the signal (i.e., the total power at frequency $k\omega_0$) is $2P_k$.

The total average signal power is given in the frequency domain by the Parseval theorem, which can be derived using the orthogonality property of the complex harmonics:

$$P = \frac{1}{T}\int_T \left|x(t)\right|^2 dt = \sum_{k=-\infty}^{\infty}\left|a_k\right|^2. \tag{4.34}$$

This elegant result basically states that the total average power of a signal can be computed using its frequency domain representation. We will see in the next section that we can compute the average power of a signal in different frequency bands. It makes the Parseval theorem very useful to, for example, electrical engineers trying to figure out the power losses of a signal transmitted over a communication channel at various frequencies.

Example 4.6: Let us compute the total average power in the unit-amplitude square wave of period T and 50% duty cycle. We have already computed its spectral coefficients: $a_k = \frac{1}{2}\operatorname{sinc}\left(\frac{k}{2}\right)$. First, using Parseval's relation in the frequency domain, we obtain

$$\begin{aligned} P &= \sum_{k=-\infty}^{\infty}|a_k|^2 = \sum_{k=-\infty}^{\infty}\left|\frac{1}{2}\operatorname{sinc}\frac{k}{2}\right|^2 = \frac{1}{4}+2\sum_{k=1}^{\infty}\frac{1}{4}\left|\operatorname{sinc}\frac{k}{2}\right|^2 \\ &= \frac{1}{4}+\frac{1}{2}\sum_{k=1,3,5,\ldots}\left|\operatorname{sinc}\frac{k}{2}\right|^2 = \frac{1}{4}+\frac{1}{2}\sum_{k=1,3,5,\ldots}\left|\frac{\sin\frac{k\pi}{2}}{\frac{k\pi}{2}}\right|^2 \\ &= \frac{1}{4}+2\sum_{k=1,3,5,\ldots}\frac{1}{k^2\pi^2} = \frac{1}{4}+\frac{2}{\pi^2}\left[1+\frac{1}{9}+\frac{1}{25}+\cdots\right] = \frac{1}{4}+\frac{2}{\pi^2}\left[\frac{\pi^2}{8}\right] \\ &= \frac{1}{2}. \end{aligned} \tag{4.35}$$

Now we check this result against the time-domain formula to compute the power:

$$P = \frac{1}{T}\int_T |x(t)|^2\,dt = \frac{1}{T}\int_{-T/4}^{T/4} 1^2\,dt = \frac{1}{T}\left(\frac{T}{4}+\frac{T}{4}\right) = \frac{1}{2}. \tag{4.36}$$

POWER SPECTRUM

The power spectrum of a signal is the sequence of average powers in each complex harmonic: $|a_k|^2$. For real periodic signals, the power spectrum is a real even sequence, as $|a_{-k}|^2 = |a_k^*|^2 = |a_k|^2$.

Example 4.7: The power spectrum of the unit-amplitude rectangular wave with duty cycle $\eta = \frac{1}{8}$ is given by $|a_k|^2 = \eta^2\operatorname{sinc}^2(k\eta) = \frac{1}{64}\operatorname{sinc}^2(\frac{k}{8})$. This power spectrum is shown in Figure 4.15. We can see that most of the power is concentrated at DC and in the first seven harmonic components, that is, in the frequency range $[-\frac{14\pi}{T},\frac{14\pi}{T}]$ rad/s.

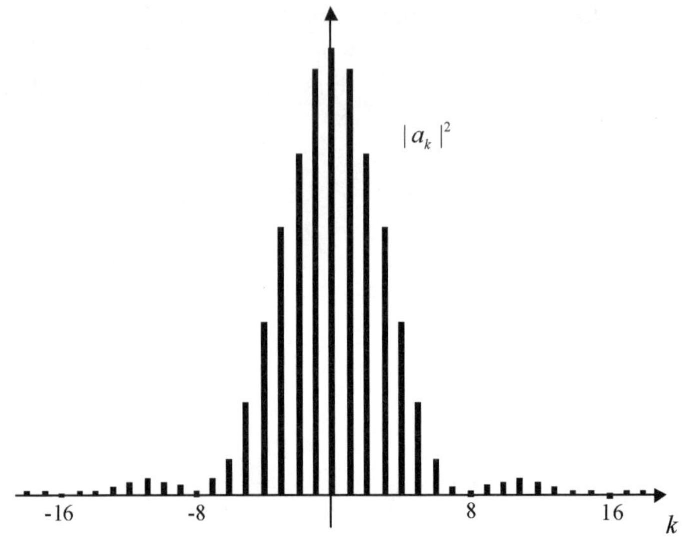

FIGURE 4.15 Power spectrum of the rectangular wave of duty cycle $\eta=\frac{1}{8}$.

Example 4.8: The Fourier series coefficients and the power spectrum of the sine wave $x(t)=A\sin(\omega_0 t)$ can be easily computed using Euler's formula: $x(t)=A\sin(\omega_0 t)=\frac{A}{2j}(e^{j\omega_0 t}-e^{-j\omega_0 t})$, so that $a_1=-j\frac{A}{2}$, $a_{-1}=j\frac{A}{2}$, $a_k=0$, $k\neq\pm 1$. The power spectrum shown in Figure 4.16 is given by $|a_1|^2=|a_{-1}|^2=\frac{A^2}{4}$ and $|a_k|^2=0$, $k\neq\pm 1$, and the total average power is $P=\frac{A^2}{2}$.

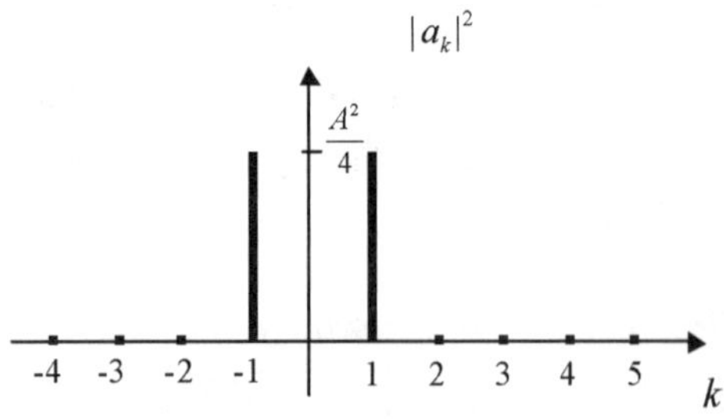

FIGURE 4.16 Power spectrum of a sine wave.

TOTAL HARMONIC DISTORTION

Suppose that a signal that was supposed to be a pure sine wave of amplitude A is distorted, as shown in Figure 4.17. This can occur in the line voltages of an industrial plant making heavy use of nonlinear loads such as electric arc furnaces, solid state relays, motor drives, etc.

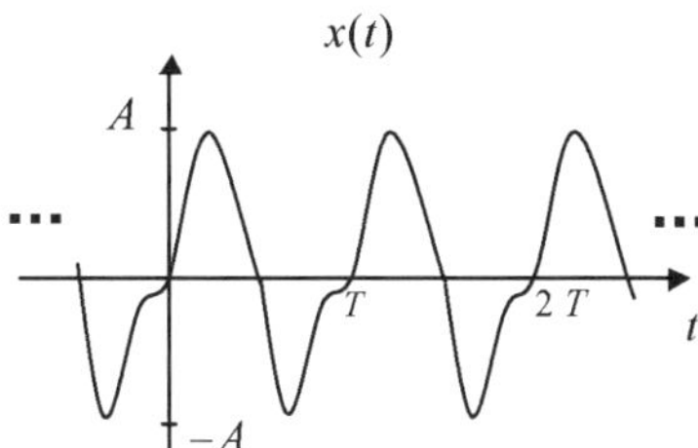

FIGURE 4.17 Distorted sine wave.

Clearly, some of the harmonics for $k \neq \pm 1$ are nonzero in the signal $x(t)$ shown in Figure 4.17. One way to characterize the distortion in the signal is to compute the ratio of average power in all the harmonics that "should not be there," that is, for $|k| > 1$, to the total average power of the sine wave, that is, the power in its fundamental components. The square root of this ratio is called the *total harmonic distortion* (THD) in the signal.

Let us first define a classical quantity in electrical engineering called the *RMS value* of a periodic signal (RMS stands for root mean square):

$$X_{RMS} := \sqrt{\frac{1}{T}\int_0^T |x(t)|^2 \, dt}. \tag{4.37}$$

The RMS value is a measure of the power in a signal, but the square root is taken to get back to the units of volt or ampere when one works with voltage or current signals.

Notice that the quantity inside the square root is nothing but the total average power P_∞. From the Parseval theorem, we have

$$X_{RMS} = \sqrt{\sum_{k=-\infty}^{+\infty} |a_k|^2}. \tag{4.38}$$

Thus, assuming that the signal is real and $a_0 = 0$, we have $X_{RMS} = \sqrt{\sum_{k=1}^{+\infty} 2|a_k|^2}$ and we can define the total harmonic distortion in this periodic signal as the ratio of the RMS value of all the higher harmonics for $k > 1$ (the distortion) to the RMS value of the fundamental (the pure sine wave) which is $\sqrt{2|a_1|^2}$:

$$THD := 100\sqrt{\frac{\sum_{k=2}^{+\infty}|a_k|^2}{|a_1|^2}}\ \%. \tag{4.39}$$

This definition of THD is the one generally adopted in power engineering, and other areas of engineering, although audio engineers often use a different definition, which compares the RMS value of the distortion to the RMS value of the *distorted* sine wave:

$$THD_a := 100\sqrt{\frac{\sum_{k=2}^{+\infty}|a_k|^2}{\sum_{k=1}^{+\infty}|a_k|^2}}\ \%. \tag{4.40}$$

Example 4.9: For the distorted sine wave of Figure 4.17, suppose the power spectrum is as given in Figure 4.18, where $|a_k|^2 = 0, |k| \geq 5$. Figure 4.18 illustrates how the THD is computed.

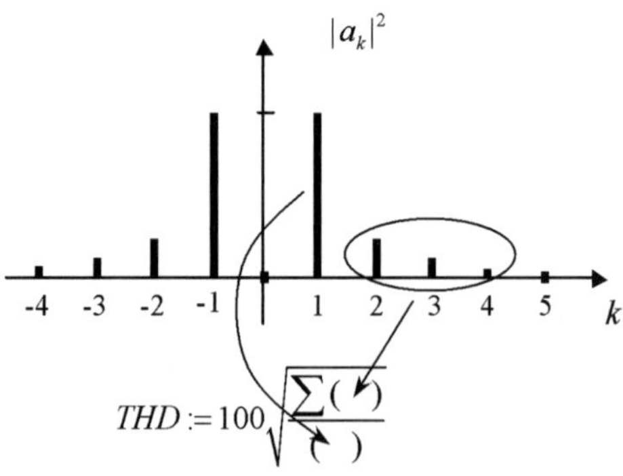

FIGURE 4.18 Computation of THD for a distorted sine wave.

STEADY-STATE RESPONSE OF AN LTI SYSTEM TO A PERIODIC SIGNAL

We have seen that the response of an LTI system with impulse response $h(t)$ to a complex exponential signal e^{st} is the same complex exponential multiplied by a complex gain: $y(t) = H(s)e^{st}$, where

$$H(s) = \int_{-\infty}^{+\infty} h(\tau)e^{-s\tau}\,d\tau. \tag{4.41}$$

In particular, for $s = j\omega$, the output is simply $y(t) = H(j\omega)e^{j\omega t}$. The complex functions $H(s)$ and $H(j\omega)$ are called the system's *transfer function* and *frequency response*, respectively.

By superposition, the output of an LTI system to a periodic input signal represented by a Fourier series $x(t) = \sum_{k=-\infty}^{+\infty} a_k e^{jk\omega_0 t}$ is given by

$$y(t) = \sum_{k=-\infty}^{+\infty} a_k H(jk\omega_0)e^{jk\omega_0 t}, \tag{4.42}$$

which is itself a Fourier series. That is, the Fourier series coefficients b_k of the periodic output $y(t)$ are given by:

$$b_k = a_k H(jk\omega_0). \tag{4.43}$$

This is an important fact: The effect of an LTI system on a periodic input signal is to modify its Fourier series coefficients through a multiplication by its frequency response evaluated at the harmonic frequencies.

Example 4.10: Consider a periodic square wave as the input to an LTI system of impulse response $h(t)$ and frequency response $H(j\omega)$. The spectrum of the output signal of the system is shown in Figure 4.19.

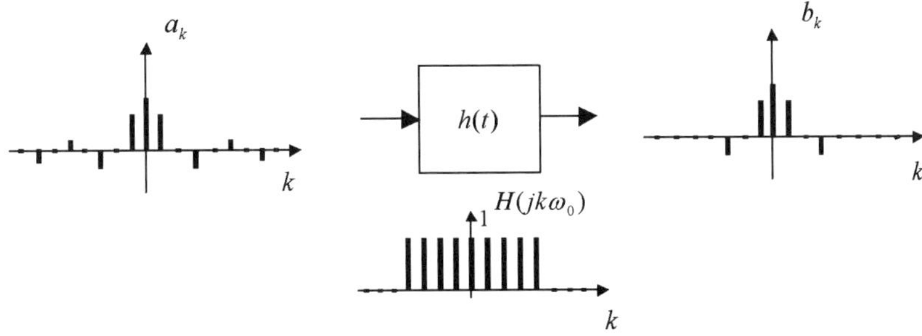

FIGURE 4.19 Effect of an LTI system on a periodic input in the frequency domain.

Remarks:

- It is assumed that the system is in steady-state; that is, it has been submitted to the same input from time $t=-\infty$. Thus, there is no transient response from initial conditions in the output signal.
- If the system is unstable, then the output would tend to infinity, so we assume that the system is stable.

Filtering

Filtering is based on the concepts described earlier. Filtering a periodic signal with an LTI system involves the design of a filter with a desirable frequency spectrum $H(jk\omega_0)$ that retains certain frequencies and cuts off others.

Example 4.11: A first-order lowpass filter with impulse response $h(t)=e^{-t}u(t)$ (a simple RC circuit with $RC=1$) cuts off the high-frequency harmonics in a periodic input signal, while low-frequency harmonics are mostly left intact. The frequency response of this filter is computed as follows:

$$H(j\omega)=\int_0^{+\infty} e^{-\tau}e^{-j\omega\tau}\,d\tau=\frac{1}{1+j\omega} \tag{4.44}$$

We can see that as the frequency ω increases, the magnitude of the frequency response of the filter $\left|H(j\omega)\right|=\frac{1}{\sqrt{1+\omega^2}}$ decreases. If the periodic input signal is a unit-amplitude rectangular wave of duty cycle η, then the output signal will have its Fourier series coefficients b_k given by:

$$b_k=a_kH(jk\omega_0)=\frac{\eta\,\mathrm{sinc}(\eta k)}{(1+jk\omega_0)},\quad k\neq 0, \tag{4.45}$$

$$b_0=a_0H(0)=a_0=\eta. \tag{4.46}$$

The reduced power at high frequencies produces an output signal that is "smoother" than the input signal. Remember that discontinuities can only result from a significant contribution of high-frequency harmonic components in the Fourier series, so when these harmonics are filtered out, the result is a smoother signal, as shown in Figure 4.20.

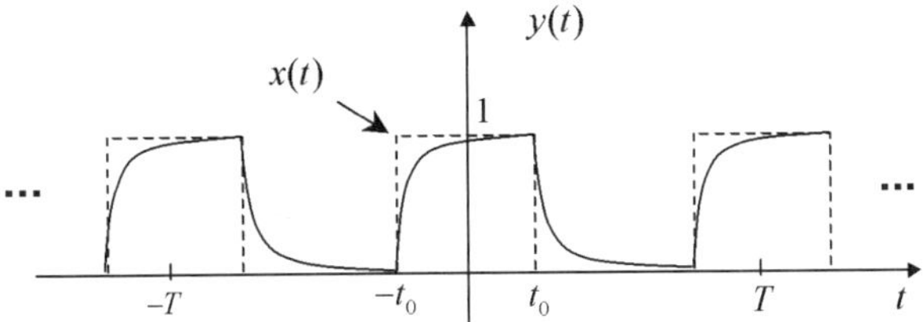

FIGURE 4.20 Effect of a first-order, low-pass filter on a rectangular wave.

SUMMARY

This chapter introduced the frequency-domain interpretation of periodic continuous-time signals.

- We have shown that most periodic continuous-time signals can be decomposed as an infinite sum of complex harmonics using the Fourier series. These include finite-power signals and signals satisfying the Dirichlet conditions.
- Complex harmonics are periodic complex exponential signals of fundamental frequency equal to an integer times the fundamental frequency of the signal. These harmonics were shown to be orthogonal.
- The line spectrum and power spectrum plots of a periodic signal are based on its Fourier series coefficients and indicate the relative importance of the different harmonic components making up the signal. The total harmonic distortion in a signal approximating a pure sine wave can be computed from the power spectrum of the signal.
- The Gibbs phenomenon was shown to produce oscillations in the truncated Fourier series approximation of a signal around first-order discontinuities.
- Finally, filtering was introduced as the action of an LTI system on the Fourier series coefficients of the input signal to either amplify or attenuate the harmonic components at different frequencies.

TO PROBE FURTHER

Further information on Fourier series can be found in Brown and Churchill, 2001.

EXERCISES

Exercises with Solutions

Exercise 4.1: Fourier Series of the Output Voltage of an Ideal Full-Wave Diode Bridge Rectifier

The nonlinear circuit in Figure 4.21 is a full-wave rectifier. It is often used as a first stage of a power supply to generate a constant voltage from the 60 Hz sinusoidal line voltage for all kinds of electronic devices. Here the input voltage is not sinusoidal.

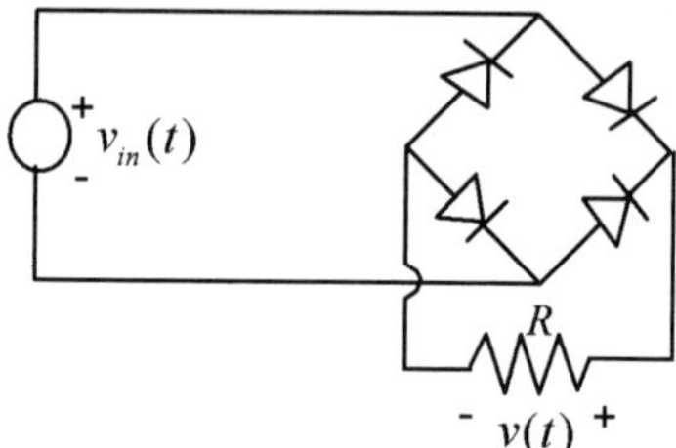

FIGURE 4.21 Full-wave rectifier circuit.

The voltages are $v_{in}(t)=\sum_{k=-\infty}^{+\infty}\delta(t-kT)*\left(A\frac{2}{T}t\right)\left(u(t+\frac{T}{2})-u(t-\frac{T}{2})\right)$, and $v(t)=\left|v_{in}(t)\right|$.

(a) Let T_1 be the fundamental period of the rectified voltage signal $v(t)$ and let $\omega_1=2\pi/T_1$ be its fundamental frequency. Find the fundamental period T_1. Sketch the input and output voltages $v_{in}(t), v(t)$.

Answer:

Let us first sketch the input voltage, which is the periodic sawtooth signal shown in Figure 4.22. Then the output voltage is simply the absolute value of the input signal that results in a triangular wave as shown in Figure 4.23.

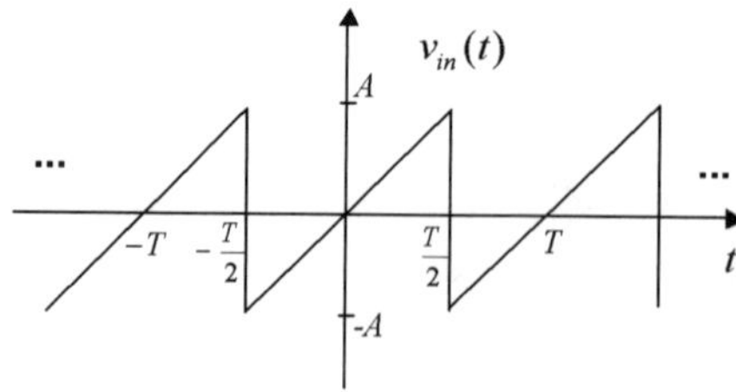

FIGURE 4.22 Input voltage of the full-wave rectifier.

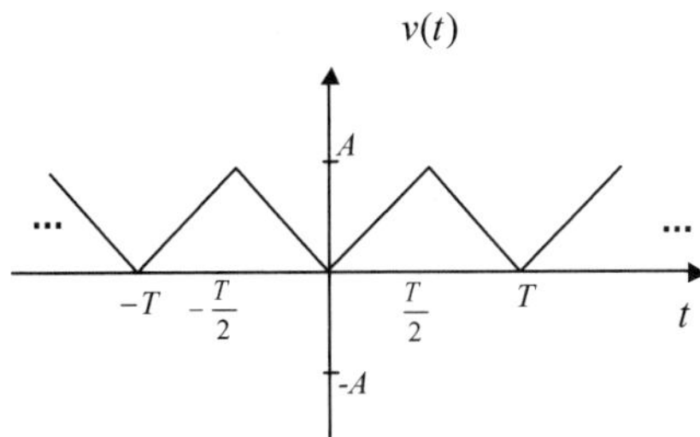

FIGURE 4.23 Output voltage of the full-wave rectifier.

We can see that the fundamental period of the output signal is the same as that of the input: $T_1 = T$.

(b) Compute the Fourier series coefficients of $v_{in}(t)$. Sketch the spectrum for $A = 1$.

Answer:

The DC component of the input is obviously 0:

$$a_0 = \frac{A}{T_1}\int_{-T_1/2}^{T_1/2} \frac{2}{T_1} t dt = \frac{A}{T_1^2}\left[t^2\right]_{-T_1/2}^{T_1/2} = \frac{A}{T_1^2}\left[\frac{T_1^2}{4} - \frac{T_1^2}{4}\right] = 0$$

for $k \neq 0$:

$$\begin{aligned} a_k &= \frac{A}{T_1}\int_{-T_1/2}^{T_1/2} \frac{2}{T_1} t e^{-jk\omega_1 t} dt \\ &= \frac{jA}{k\pi T_1}\left[\left(te^{-jk\omega_1 t}\right)_{-T_1/2}^{T_1/2} - \int_{-T_1/2}^{T_1/2} e^{-jk\omega_1 t} dt\right] \\ &= \frac{jA}{k\pi T_1}\left[\left(\frac{T_1}{2}e^{-jk\pi} + \frac{T_1}{2}e^{jk\pi}\right) - 0\right] \\ &= \frac{jA}{k\pi}\cos k\pi \\ &= \frac{jA(-1)^k}{k\pi}. \end{aligned}$$

The spectrum is imaginary, so we can use a single plot to represent it as in Figure 4.24.

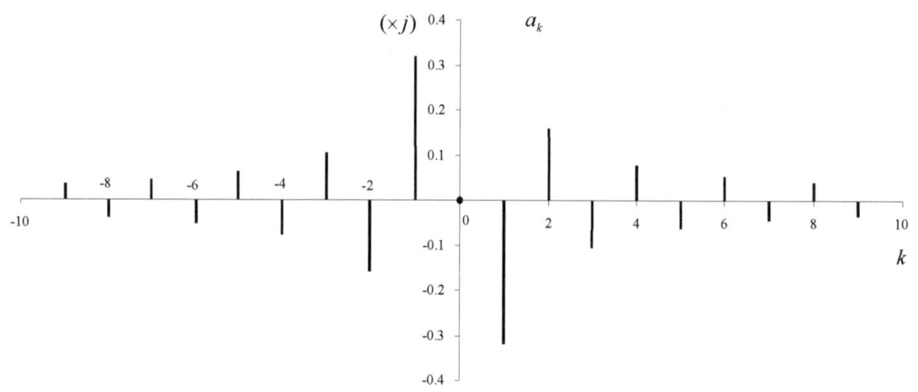

FIGURE 4.24 Line spectrum of input voltage, case A = 1.

(c) Compute the Fourier series coefficients of $v(t)$. Write $v(t)$ as a Fourier series. Sketch the spectrum for $A = 1$.

Answer:
Let us first compute the DC component of the output signal:

$$a_0 = \frac{A}{T_1}\int_{-T_1/2}^{T_1/2}\frac{2}{T_1}|t|\,dt = \frac{4A}{T_1^2}\int_{0}^{T_1/2} t\,dt = \frac{4A}{T_1^2}\frac{T_1^2}{8} = \frac{1}{2}A.$$

For $k \neq 0$, the spectral coefficients are computed as follows:

$$\begin{aligned} a_k &= \frac{A}{T_1}\int_{-T_1/2}^{T_1/2}\frac{2}{T_1}|t|e^{-jk\omega_1 t}\,dt \\ &= \frac{A}{T_1}\left[\int_{0}^{T_1/2}\frac{2}{T_1}te^{-jk\omega_1 t}\,dt - \int_{-T_1/2}^{0}\frac{2}{T_1}te^{-jk\omega_1 t}\,dt\right] \\ &= \frac{A}{T_1}\int_{0}^{T_1/2}\frac{2}{T_1}t(e^{-jk\omega_1 t} + e^{jk\omega_1 t})\,dt \end{aligned}$$

$$
\begin{aligned}
&= \frac{2A}{T_1}\int_0^{T_1/2} \frac{2}{T_1} t\cos(k\omega_1 t)dt \\
&= \frac{2A}{k\pi T_1}\int_0^{T_1/2} (k\omega_1)t\cos(k\omega_1 t)dt \\
&= \frac{2A}{k\pi T_1}\left[\left(t\sin(k\omega_1 t)\right)_0^{T_1/2} - \int_0^{T_1/2}\sin(k\omega_1 t)dt\right] \\
&= \frac{2A}{k\pi T_1}\left[\underbrace{\left(\frac{T_1}{2}\sin k\pi - 0\right)}_{0} + \frac{1}{k\omega_1}\cos(k\omega_1 t)_0^{T_1/2}\right] \\
&= \frac{A}{(k\pi)^2}\left(\cos k\pi - 1\right) \\
&= \frac{A}{(k\pi)^2}\left((-1)^k - 1\right).
\end{aligned}
$$

The spectrum of the triangular wave is real and even (because the signal is real and even), so we can use a single plot to represent it as in Figure 4.25.

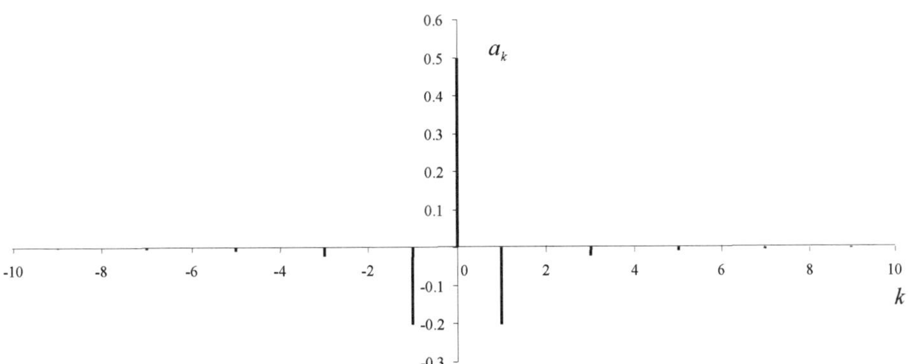

FIGURE 4.25 Line spectrum of output voltage, case $A = 1$.

Thus,

$$
v(t) = \sum_{k=-\infty}^{+\infty} \frac{A}{(k\pi)^2}\left((-1)^k - 1\right)e^{jk\omega_1 t}
$$

is the Fourier series expansion of the full-wave rectified voltage.

(d) What is the average power of the input voltage $v_{in}(t)$ at frequencies higher than or equal to its fundamental frequency? Answer the same question for the output voltage $v(t)$. Discuss the difference in power.

Answer:

Since $a_0 = 0$, and given the Parseval theorem, the average power of the input voltage $v_{in}(t)$ at frequencies higher than or equal to its fundamental frequency is equal to its total average power computed in the time domain:

$$\begin{aligned} P_{in} &= \sum_{k=-\infty}^{+\infty} |a_k|^2 = \frac{1}{T}\int_{-T/2}^{T/2} \frac{4A^2}{T^2} t^2 \, dt \\ &= \frac{4A^2}{3T^3}\left[t^3\right]_{-T/2}^{T/2} \\ &= \frac{4A^2}{24T^3}\left[T^3 + T^3\right] \\ &= \frac{A^2}{3}. \end{aligned}$$

The average power in all harmonic components of $v(t)$ excluding the DC component (call it P_{out}) is computed as follows:

$$\begin{aligned} P_{out} &= \sum_{k=-\infty}^{+\infty} |a_k|^2 - |a_0|^2 = \frac{1}{T}\int_{-T/2}^{T/2} \frac{4A^2}{T^2} t^2 \, dt - |a_0|^2 \\ &= \frac{A^2}{3} - \frac{A^2}{4} = \frac{A^2}{12}. \end{aligned}$$

Note that the input and output signals have the same total average power, but some of the power in the input voltage (namely $A^2/4$) was transferred over to DC by the nonlinear circuit.

Exercise 4.2

Given periodic signals with spectra $x(t) \overset{FS}{\leftrightarrow} a_k$ and $y(t) \overset{FS}{\leftrightarrow} b_k$, show the following properties:

(a) Multiplication: $x(t)y(t) \overset{FS}{\leftrightarrow} \sum_{l=-\infty}^{+\infty} a_l b_{k-l}$

Answer:

$$\begin{aligned} x(t)y(t) &= \sum_{k=-\infty}^{+\infty} a_k e^{-jk\omega_0 t} \sum_{n=-\infty}^{+\infty} b_n e^{-jn\omega_0 t} \\ &= \sum_{k=-\infty}^{+\infty} \sum_{n=-\infty}^{+\infty} a_k b_n e^{-j(k+n)\omega_0 t} \\ &= \sum_{k=-\infty}^{+\infty} \sum_{p=-\infty}^{+\infty} a_k b_{p-k} e^{-jp\omega_0 t} \\ &= \sum_{p=-\infty}^{+\infty} \underbrace{\left(\sum_{k=-\infty}^{+\infty} a_k b_{p-k} \right)}_{\text{FS coeff. } c_p} e^{-jp\omega_0 t} \end{aligned}$$

Therefore, $x(t)y(t) \overset{FS}{\leftrightarrow} \sum_{l=-\infty}^{+\infty} a_l b_{k-l}$.

(b) Periodic convolution: $\int_T x(\tau)y(t-\tau)d\tau \overset{FS}{\leftrightarrow} Ta_k b_k$

Answer:

$$\begin{aligned} \int_T x(\tau)y(t-\tau)d\tau &= \int_T \sum_{k=-\infty}^{+\infty} a_k e^{jk\omega_0 \tau} \sum_{p=-\infty}^{+\infty} b_p e^{jp\omega_0 (t-\tau)} d\tau \\ &= \int_T \sum_{k=-\infty}^{+\infty} a_k e^{jk\omega_0 \tau} \sum_{p=-\infty}^{+\infty} b_p e^{-jp\omega_0 \tau} e^{jp\omega_0 t} d\tau \\ &= \int_T \sum_{k=-\infty}^{+\infty} \sum_{p=-\infty}^{+\infty} a_k b_p e^{j(k-p)\omega_0 \tau} d\tau e^{jp\omega_0 t} \\ &= \sum_{k=-\infty}^{+\infty} \sum_{p=-\infty}^{+\infty} a_k b_p \int_T e^{j(k-p)\omega_0 \tau} d\tau \, e^{jp\omega_0 t} \\ &= \sum_{k=-\infty}^{+\infty} a_k b_k T e^{jk\omega_0 t} \end{aligned}$$

Therefore, $\int_T x(\tau)y(t-\tau)d\tau \overset{FS}{\leftrightarrow} Ta_k b_k$.

Exercise 4.3: Fourier Series of the Output of an LTI System

Consider the familiar rectangular waveform $x(t)$ in Figure 4.26 of period T and duty cycle $\eta = \frac{2t_0}{T}$. This signal is the input to an LTI system with impulse response $h(t) = e^{-5t}\sin(10\pi t)u(t)$.

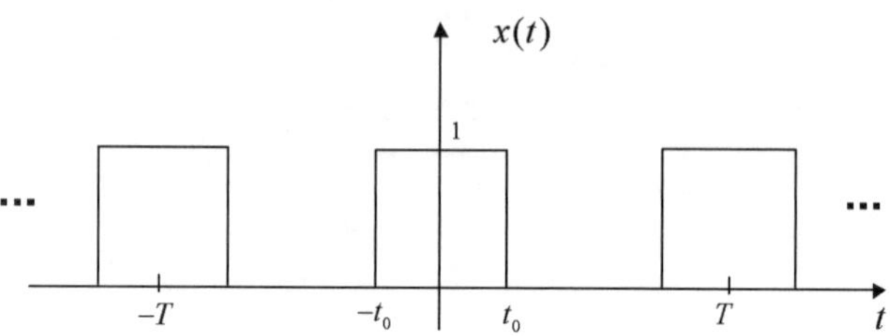

FIGURE 4.26 Rectangular wave input to an LTI system.

(a) Find the frequency response $H(j\omega)$ of the LTI system. Give expressions for its magnitude $|H(j\omega)|$ and phase $\angle H(j\omega)$ as functions of ω.

Answer:

The frequency response of the system is given by

$$
\begin{aligned}
H(j\omega) &= \int_0^{+\infty} e^{-5t}\sin(10\pi t)e^{-j\omega t}\,dt \\
&= \frac{1}{2j}\int_0^{+\infty} (e^{j10\pi t} - e^{-j10\pi t})e^{-(5+j\omega)t}\,dt \\
&= \frac{1}{2j}\int_0^{+\infty} (e^{-(5+j(\omega-10\pi))t} - e^{-(5+j(\omega+10\pi))t})\,dt \\
&= \frac{1}{2j(5+j(\omega-10\pi))} - \frac{1}{2j(5+j(\omega+10\pi))} \\
&= \frac{(5+j(\omega+10\pi))-(5+j(\omega-10\pi))}{2j(5+j(\omega-10\pi))(5+j(\omega+10\pi))} \\
&= \frac{10\pi}{25-\omega^2+100\pi^2+j10\omega}.
\end{aligned}
$$

Magnitude: $|H(j\omega)| = \dfrac{10\pi}{\left[(25-\omega^2+100\pi^2)^2+100\omega^2\right]^{\frac{1}{2}}}$

Phase: $\angle H(j\omega) = \arctan\left(\dfrac{-10\omega}{25-\omega^2+100\pi^2}\right)$

(b) Find the Fourier series coefficients a_k of the input voltage $x(t)$ for $T = 1\text{s}$ and a 60% duty cycle.

Answer:

The period given corresponds to a signal frequency of 1 Hz, and the 60% duty cycle means that $\eta = \frac{3}{5}$, so that the spectral coefficients of the rectangular wave are given by $a_k = \frac{3}{5}\,\mathrm{sinc}(\frac{3k}{5})$.

(c) Compute the Fourier series coefficients b_k of the output signal $y(t)$ (for the input described in (b) above) and sketch its power spectrum.

Answer:

$$
\begin{aligned}
b_k = H(jk\omega_0)a_k &= \tfrac{3}{5}\mathrm{sinc}(\tfrac{3k}{5})\frac{10\pi}{25-(k\omega_0)^2+100\pi^2+j10k\omega_0} \\
&= \frac{6\pi\mathrm{sinc}(\tfrac{3k}{5})}{25-(k2\pi)^2+100\pi^2+j20\pi k}
\end{aligned}
$$

The power spectrum of the output signal is given by the expression below and shown in Figure 4.27.

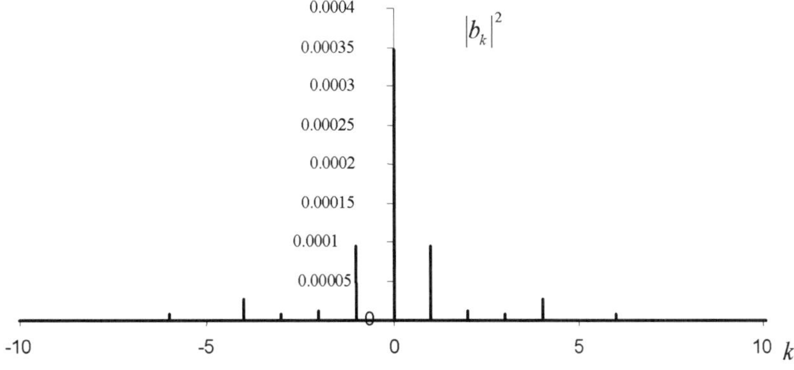

FIGURE 4.27 Power spectrum of the output signal.

$$\left|b_k\right|^2 = \frac{36\pi^2 \text{sinc}^2(\frac{3k}{5})}{\left[25-(k2\pi)^2+100\pi^2\right]^2+400\pi^2k^2}$$

(d) Using MATLAB, plot an approximation to the output signal over three periods by summing the first 100 harmonics of $y(t)$, that is, by plotting

$$\tilde{y}(t) = \sum_{-100}^{+100} b_k e^{jk\frac{2\pi}{T}t}.$$

Answer:

$$\begin{aligned}
\tilde{y}(t) &= \sum_{k=-100}^{+100} b_k e^{jk2\pi t} \\
&= \sum_{k=-100}^{+100} \tfrac{3}{5}\text{sinc}(\tfrac{3k}{5}) \frac{10\pi}{25-(k2\pi)^2+100\pi^2+j20k\pi} e^{jk2\pi t} \\
&= b_0 + \sum_{k=1}^{100} \tfrac{6}{5}\text{sinc}(\tfrac{3k}{5}) \frac{10\pi}{\sqrt{\left[25-(k2\pi)^2+100\pi^2\right]^2+400\pi^2k^2}} \cos\left[k2\pi t + \arctan\left(\frac{-20k\pi}{25-(k2\pi)^2+100\pi^2}\right)\right] \\
&= \frac{6\pi}{25+100\pi^2} + \sum_{k=1}^{100} \tfrac{6}{5}\text{sinc}(\tfrac{3k}{5}) \frac{10\pi}{\sqrt{\left[25-(k2\pi)^2+100\pi^2\right]^2+400\pi^2k^2}} \cos\left[k2\pi t + \arctan\left(\frac{-20k\pi}{25-(k2\pi)^2+100\pi^2}\right)\right]
\end{aligned}$$

ON THE CD

Figure 4.28 shows a plot of $\tilde{y}(t)$ from 0 s to 3 s that was made using the MATLAB M-file Fourierseries.m located in D:\Chapter4 on the companion CD-ROM.

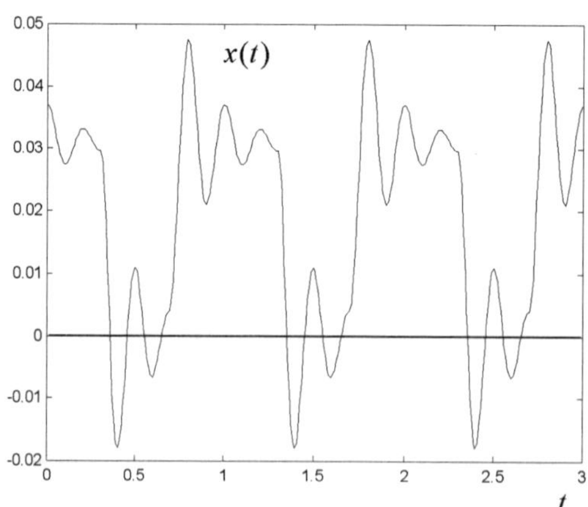

FIGURE 4.28 Approximation of the output signal using a truncated 100-harmonic Fourier series.

Exercise 4.4: Digital Sine Wave Generator

A programmable digital signal generator generates a sinusoidal waveform by filtering the staircase approximation to a sine wave shown in Figure 4.29.

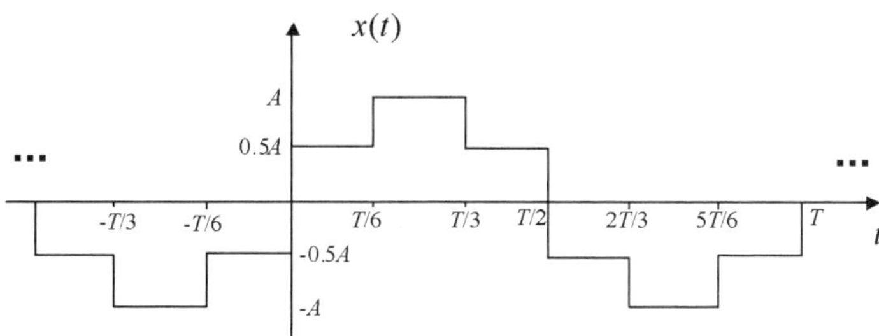

FIGURE 4.29 Staircase approximation to a sinusoidal wave in Exercise 4.4.

(a) Find the Fourier series coefficients a_k of the periodic signal $x(t)$. Show that the even harmonics vanish. Express $x(t)$ as a Fourier series.

Answer:

First, the average over one period is 0, so $a_0 = 0$. For $k \neq 0$,

$$a_k = \frac{1}{T}\int_{-\frac{T}{2}}^{\frac{T}{2}} x(t)e^{-jk\frac{2\pi}{T}t}\,dt$$

$$= -\frac{A}{2T}\int_{-\frac{T}{2}}^{-\frac{T}{3}} e^{-jk\frac{2\pi}{T}t}\,dt - \frac{A}{T}\int_{-\frac{T}{3}}^{-\frac{T}{6}} e^{-jk\frac{2\pi}{T}t}\,dt - \frac{A}{2T}\int_{-\frac{T}{6}}^{0} e^{-jk\frac{2\pi}{T}t}\,dt$$

$$+\frac{A}{2T}\int_{\frac{T}{3}}^{\frac{T}{2}} e^{-jk\frac{2\pi}{T}t}\,dt + \frac{A}{T}\int_{\frac{T}{6}}^{\frac{T}{3}} e^{-jk\frac{2\pi}{T}t}\,dt + \frac{A}{2T}\int_{0}^{\frac{T}{6}} e^{-jk\frac{2\pi}{T}t}\,dt$$

$$= \frac{A}{2T}\int_{0}^{\frac{T}{6}}\left(e^{-jk\frac{2\pi}{T}t} - e^{jk\frac{2\pi}{T}t}\right)dt + \frac{A}{2T}\int_{\frac{T}{3}}^{\frac{T}{2}}\left(e^{-jk\frac{2\pi}{T}t} - e^{jk\frac{2\pi}{T}t}\right)dt + \frac{A}{T}\int_{\frac{T}{6}}^{\frac{T}{3}}\left(e^{-jk\frac{2\pi}{T}t} - e^{jk\frac{2\pi}{T}t}\right)dt$$

$$= \frac{-jA}{T}\int_0^{\frac{T}{6}} \sin\left(k\frac{2\pi}{T}t\right)dt - \frac{j2A}{T}\int_{\frac{T}{6}}^{\frac{T}{3}} \sin\left(k\frac{2\pi}{T}t\right)dt - \frac{jA}{T}\int_{\frac{T}{3}}^{\frac{T}{2}} \sin\left(k\frac{2\pi}{T}t\right)dt$$

$$= \frac{jA}{T}\left(\frac{T}{2\pi k}\right)\cos\left(k\frac{2\pi}{T}t\right)\Bigg|_0^{\frac{T}{6}} + \frac{j2A}{T}\left(\frac{T}{2\pi k}\right)\cos\left(k\frac{2\pi}{T}t\right)\Bigg|_{\frac{T}{6}}^{\frac{T}{3}} + \frac{jA}{T}\left(\frac{T}{2\pi k}\right)\cos\left(k\frac{2\pi}{T}t\right)\Bigg|_{\frac{T}{3}}^{\frac{T}{2}}$$

$$= \frac{jA}{2\pi k}\left[\cos\left(k\frac{\pi}{3}\right) - 1 + 2\cos\left(k\frac{2\pi}{3}\right) - 2\cos\left(k\frac{\pi}{3}\right) + \cos(k\pi) - \cos\left(k\frac{2\pi}{3}\right)\right]$$

$$= \frac{jA}{2\pi k}\left[-\cos\left(k\frac{\pi}{3}\right) + \cos\left(k\frac{2\pi}{3}\right) - 1 + \cos(k\pi)\right].$$

Note that the coefficients are purely imaginary, which is consistent with our real, odd signal. The even spectral coefficients are for:

$$a_k = a_{2m} = \frac{jA}{2\pi 2m}\left[-\cos\left(m\frac{2\pi}{3}\right) + \cos\left(m\frac{4\pi}{3}\right) - 1 + \cos(m2\pi)\right]$$

$$= \frac{jA}{2\pi 2m}\left[-\cos\left(-m\frac{\pi}{3} + m\pi\right) + \cos\left(m\frac{\pi}{3} + m\pi\right)\right]$$

$$= \frac{jA}{2\pi 2m}\left[\cos\left(m\frac{\pi}{3}\right) - \cos\left(m\frac{\pi}{3}\right)\right]\cos(m\pi) = 0$$

Figure 4.30 shows a plot of $x(t)$ computed using 250 harmonics in the MATLAB program Fourierseries.m, which can be found in the Chapter 4 folder on the companion CD-ROM.

ON THE CD

The Fourier series representation of $x(t)$ is

$$x(t) = \sum_{k=-\infty}^{+\infty} a_k e^{jk\frac{2\pi}{T}t} = \sum_{\substack{k=-\infty \\ k\neq 0}}^{+\infty} \frac{jA}{2\pi k}\left[-\cos\left(k\frac{\pi}{3}\right) + \cos\left(k\frac{2\pi}{3}\right) - 1 + \cos(k\pi)\right]e^{jk\frac{2\pi}{T}t}.$$

(b) Write $x(t)$ using the real form of the Fourier series.

$$x(t) = a_0 + 2\sum_{k=1}^{+\infty}[B_k \cos(k\omega_0 t) - C_k \sin(k\omega_0 t)]$$

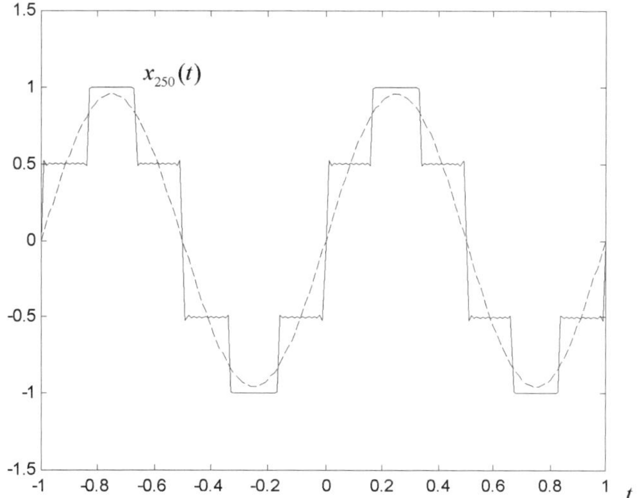

FIGURE 4.30 Truncated Fourier series approximation to the staircase signal and first harmonic in Exercise 4.4(a).

Recall that the C_k coefficients are the imaginary parts of the a_ks. Hence

$$x(t) = \sum_{k=1}^{+\infty} \frac{-A}{\pi k}\left[-\cos\left(k\frac{\pi}{3}\right) + \cos\left(k\frac{2\pi}{3}\right) - 1 + \cos\left(k\pi\right)\right]\sin(k\omega_0 t).$$

(c) Design an ideal lowpass filter that will produce the perfect sinusoidal waveform $y(t) = \sin\frac{2\pi}{T}t$ at its output, with $x(t)$ as its input. Sketch its frequency response and specify its gain K and cutoff frequency ω_c.

Answer:
The frequency response of the lowpass filter is shown in Figure 4.31.

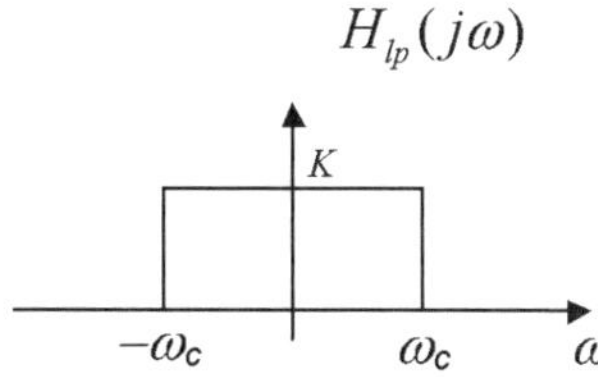

FIGURE 4.31 Frequency response of the lowpass filter.

The cutoff should be between the fundamental and the second harmonic, for example, $\omega_c = \frac{3\pi}{T}$. The gain should be

$$K = \frac{-\pi}{A}\left[-\cos\left(\frac{\pi}{3}\right)+\cos\left(\frac{2\pi}{3}\right)-2\right]^{-1}$$

$$= \frac{-\pi}{A}\left[-\frac{1}{2}-\frac{1}{2}-2\right]^{-1} = \frac{\pi}{3A}.$$

(d) Now suppose that the first-order lowpass filter whose differential equation follows is used to filter $x(t)$:

$$\tau\frac{dy(t)}{dt} + y(t) = Bx(t),$$

where the time constant is chosen to be $\tau = \frac{T}{2\pi}$. Give the Fourier series representation of the output $y(t)$. Compute the total average power in the fundamental components P_{1tot} and in the third harmonic components P_{3tot}. Find the value of the DC gain B such that the output $w(t)$ produced by the fundamental harmonic of the real Fourier series of $x(t)$ has unit amplitude.

Answer:

$$H(s) = \frac{B}{\tau s+1}$$

$$H(j\omega) = \frac{B}{\tau j\omega+1}$$

$$y(t) = \sum_{k=-\infty}^{+\infty} a_k H(jk\frac{2\pi}{T})e^{jk2\pi t} = \sum_{\substack{k=-\infty \\ k\neq 0}}^{+\infty} \frac{B}{jk+1}\frac{jA}{2\pi k}\left[-\cos\left(k\frac{\pi}{3}\right)+\cos\left(k\frac{2\pi}{3}\right)-1+\cos(k\pi)\right]e^{jk\frac{2\pi}{T}t}$$

Power:

$$P_{1tot} = 2\left|\frac{B}{j+1}\frac{jA}{2\pi}\left[-\cos\left(\frac{\pi}{3}\right)+\cos\left(\frac{2\pi}{3}\right)-1+\cos(\pi)\right]\right|^2$$

$$= 2\left|\frac{B}{j+1}\frac{j3A}{2\pi}\right|^2 = A^2B^2\frac{9}{4\pi^2}$$

$$P_{3tot} = 2\left|\frac{B}{j3+1}\frac{jA}{2\pi}\left[-\cos(\pi)+\cos(2\pi)-1+\cos(3\pi)\right]\right|^2$$

$$= 2\left|\frac{B}{j3+1}\frac{jA}{2\pi}\left[-2\right]\right|^2 = 2\frac{4A^2B^2}{40\pi^2} = \frac{A^2B^2}{5\pi^2}$$

For the filter's DC gain B, we found that the gain at ω_0 should be

$$\frac{\pi}{3A} = \left|H(j\omega_0)\right| = \frac{B}{\left|\tau j\omega_0 + 1\right|} = \frac{B}{\sqrt{(\tau\omega_0)^2+1}}$$

$$\Leftrightarrow B = \frac{\pi\sqrt{(\tau\omega_0)^2+1}}{3A}.$$

Exercises

Exercise 4.5

The output voltage of a half-wave rectifier is given by $v(t) = \begin{cases} v_{in}(t), & v_{in}(t) > 0 \\ 0, & v_{in}(t) \le 0 \end{cases}$.

Suppose that the periodic input voltage signal is $v_{in}(t) = A\sin(\omega_1 t)$, $\omega_1 = 2\pi/T_1$. Find the fundamental period T and the fundamental frequency ω_0 of the half-wave rectified voltage signal $v(t)$. Compute the Fourier series coefficients of $v(t)$ and write the voltage as a Fourier series.

Answer:

Exercise 4.6

Suppose that the voltages in the full-wave bridge rectifier circuit of Figure 4.21 are $v_{in}(t) = A\sin(\omega_0 t)$, $\omega_0 = 2\pi/T$, and $v(t) = \left|v_{in}(t)\right|$. Let $T_1 = T/2$ be the fundamental period of the rectified voltage signal $v(t)$ and let $\omega_1 = 2\pi/T_1$ be its fundamental frequency.

(a) Compute the Fourier series coefficients of $v(t)$ and write $v(t)$ as a Fourier series.

(b) Express $v(t)$ as a real Fourier series of the form $v(t) = a_0 + 2\sum_{k=1}^{+\infty}[B_k\cos(k\omega_1 t) - C_k\sin(k\omega_1 t)]$.

Exercise 4.7: Fourier Series of a Train of RF Pulses

Consider the following signal $x(t)$ of fundamental frequency $\omega_0 = \frac{2\pi}{T}$, a periodic train of radio frequency (RF) pulses. Over one period from $-T/2$ to $T/2$, the signal is given by

$$x(t) = \begin{cases} A\cos(\omega_c t), & -T_1 < t < T_1 \\ 0, & -T/2 < t < -T_1 \\ 0, & T_1 < t < T/2 \end{cases}.$$

This signal could be used to test a transmitter-receiver radio communication system. Assume that the pulse frequency is an integer multiple of the signal frequency; that is, $\omega_c = N\omega_0$. Compute the Fourier series coefficients of $x(t)$.

Answer:

Exercise 4.8

(a) Compute and sketch (magnitude and phase) the Fourier series coefficients of the sawtooth signal of Figure 4.32.

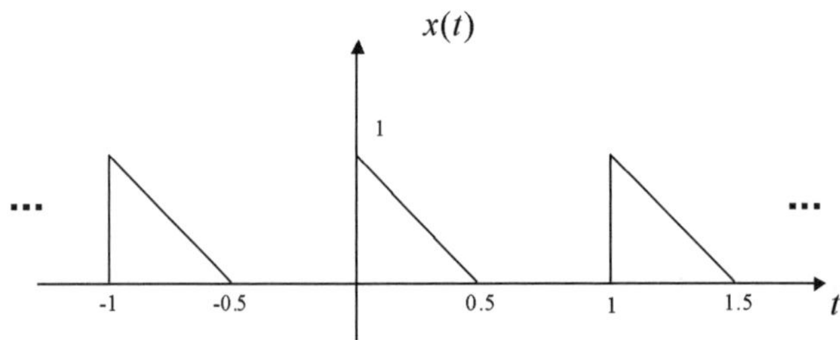

FIGURE 4.32 Periodic sawtooth signal in Exercise 4.8(a).

(b) Express $x(t)$ as its real Fourier series of the form

$$x(t) = a_0 + 2\sum_{k=1}^{+\infty}[B_k \cos(k\omega_0 t) - C_k \sin(k\omega_0 t)].$$

(c) Use MATLAB to plot, superimposed on the same figure, approximations to the signal over two periods by summing the first 5 and the first 50 harmonic components of $x(t)$, that is, by plotting $\tilde{x}(t)=\sum_{-N}^{N}a_k e^{jk\frac{2\pi}{T}t}$. Discuss your results.

(d) The sawtooth signal $x(t)$ is the input to an LTI system with impulse response $h(t)=e^{-t}\sin(2\pi t)u(t)$. Let $y(t)$ denote the resulting periodic output. Find the frequency response $H(j\omega)$ of the LTI system. Give expressions for its magnitude $|H(j\omega)|$ and phase $\angle H(j\omega)$ as functions of ω. Find the Fourier series coefficients b_k of the output $y(t)$. Use your computer program of (c) to plot an approximation to the output signal over two periods by summing the first 50 harmonic components of $y(t)$. Discuss your results.

Exercise 4.9

Consider the sawtooth signal $y(t)$ in Figure 4.33.

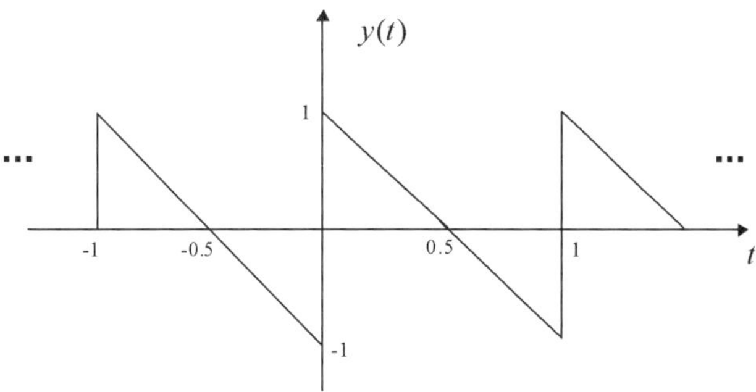

FIGURE 4.33 Periodic sawtooth signal in Exercise 4.9.

(a) Compute the Fourier series coefficients of $y(t)$ using a direct computation.

(b) Compute the Fourier series coefficients of $y(t)$ using properties of Fourier series, your result of Exercise 4.8(a) for $x(t)$, and the fact that $y(t) = x(t)-x(-t)$.

Answer:

Exercise 4.10

Compute and sketch (magnitude and phase) the Fourier series coefficients of the following signals:

(a) Signal $x(t)$ shown in Figure 4.34.

(b) $x(t) = \sin(10\pi t) + \cos(20\pi t)$

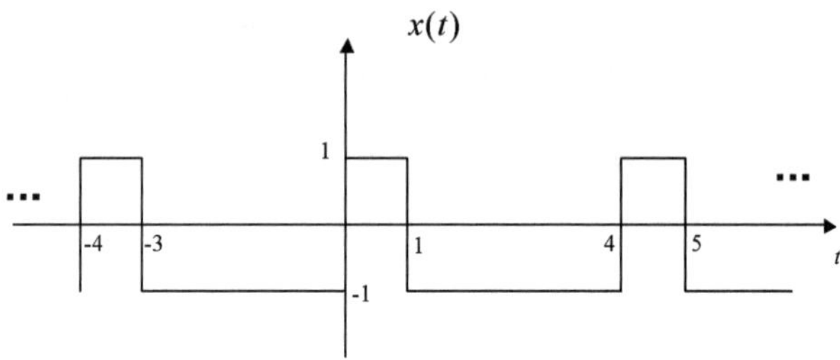

FIGURE 4.34 Periodic rectangular signal in Exercise 4.10(a).

5 The Continuous-Time Fourier Transform

In This Chapter

((Lecture 15: Definition and Properties of the Continuous-Time Fourier Transform))

The Fourier series is a frequency-domain representation of a continuous-time periodic signal. What about aperiodic signals? The concept of Fourier series can be extended to the Fourier transform, which applies to many aperiodic signals. For instance, all signals of finite energy have a Fourier transform, also called a *spectrum*.

As mentioned earlier, engineers often like to think of a signal as a spectrum whose energy is mostly contained in certain frequency bands. For instance, the

Fourier transform of a human voice signal would show that most of the spectral contents of the signal are contained between 300 Hz and 3400 Hz. This is why the old telephone lines, seen here as linear time-invariant (LTI) systems that transmit continuous-time voice signals as voltage signals, were designed to have a flat frequency response over that band so as to maintain signal integrity.

FOURIER TRANSFORM AS THE LIMIT OF A FOURIER SERIES

In order to introduce the Fourier transform, we will use the specific example of a periodic rectangular signal, and we will let the period tend to infinity so as to have only the base period effectively remaining, that is, the part of the waveform around time $t = 0$. We will see that the Fourier transform in this particular case is nothing but the sinc envelope of the Fourier series coefficients.

Consider the Fourier series representation of the rectangular wave $\tilde{x}(t)$ shown in Figure 5.1.

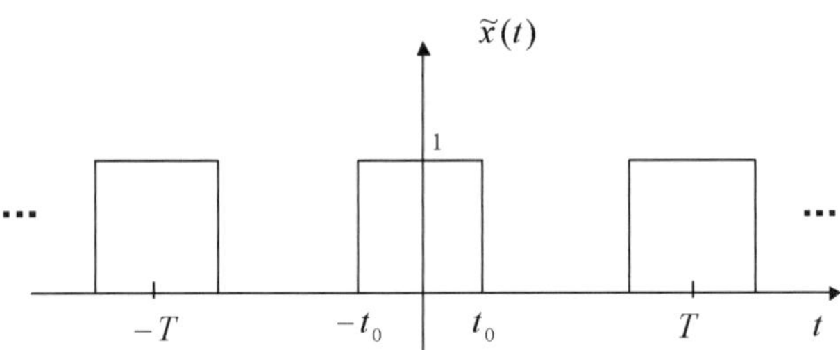

FIGURE 5.1 Periodic rectangular waveform.

Suppose we normalize the spectral coefficients of $\tilde{x}(t)$ by multiplying them by T, and we assume that t_0 is fixed, so that the duty cycle $\eta = \frac{2t_0}{T}$ will decrease with an increase in T:

$$Ta_k = T\eta \operatorname{sinc}(k\eta) = 2t_0 \operatorname{sinc}\left(k\frac{2t_0}{T}\right). \tag{5.1}$$

Then, the normalized coefficients Ta_k of the rectangular wave have a sinc envelope with a constant amplitude at the origin equal to $2t_0$ and a zero crossing at the fixed frequency $\frac{\pi}{t_0}$ rad/s, both independent of the value of T. This is illustrated in Figure 5.2 with a 50% duty cycle and in Figure 5.3 for a 12.5% duty cycle; that is, the fundamental period T in Figure 5.3 is four times as long as T in Figure 5.2.

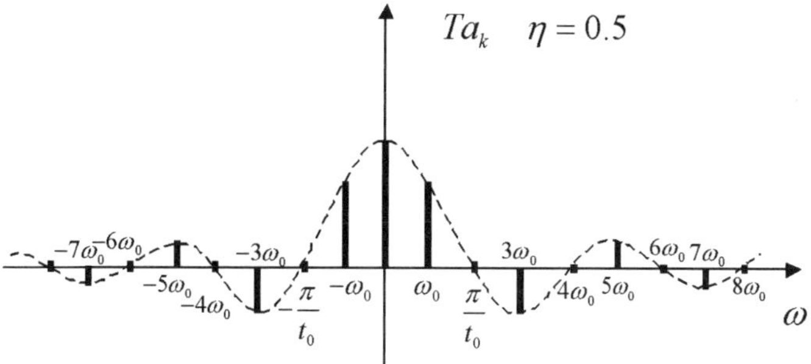

FIGURE 5.2 Sinc envelope of the spectral coefficients of a rectangular wave with a 50% duty cycle.

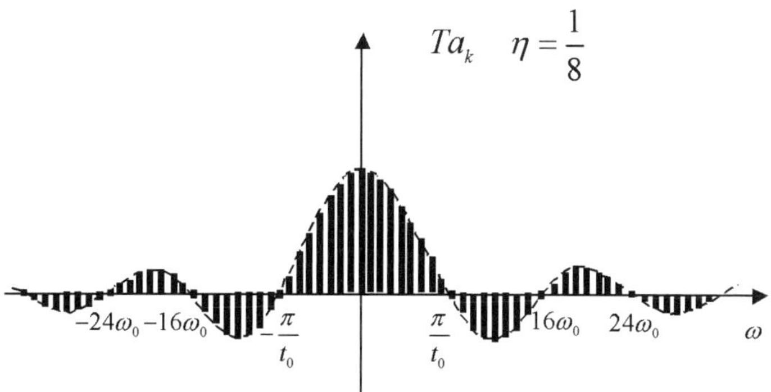

FIGURE 5.3 Sinc envelope of the spectral coefficients of a rectangular wave with a 12.5% duty cycle.

We see that as the fundamental period increases, we get more and more lines packed in the lobes of the sinc envelope. These normalized spectral coefficients turn out to be samples of the continuous sinc function in the line spectrum of $\tilde{x}(t)$. Also, note that the two above spectra are plotted against the frequency variable $k\omega_0$ with units of rad/s, rather than the index of each harmonic component. We can see that the first zeros on each side of the main lobe are at frequencies $\omega = \pm\frac{\pi}{t_0}$ rad/s and these frequencies are invariant with respect to the period T. They only depend on the width of the pulse.

Thus, our intuition tells us the following:

- An aperiodic signal of finite support that has been made periodic by "repeating its graph" every T seconds will have a line spectrum that becomes more and more dense as the fundamental period T is made longer and longer, but the line spectrum has the same continuous envelope.
- As T goes to infinity, the line spectrum will become a continuous function of frequency ω: the envelope.

It turns out that this intuition is right, and the resulting continuous function of frequency is the Fourier transform. Recall that the Fourier series coefficients for the rectangular wave were computed using the formula

$$a_k = \frac{1}{T}\int_{-t_0/2}^{t_0/2} \tilde{x}(t)e^{-jk\omega_0 t}\,dt, \tag{5.2}$$

where $\omega_0 = \frac{2\pi}{T}$ as usual. Now define a signal $x(t)$ equal to $\tilde{x}(t)$ over one period and zero elsewhere, as shown in Figure 5.4.

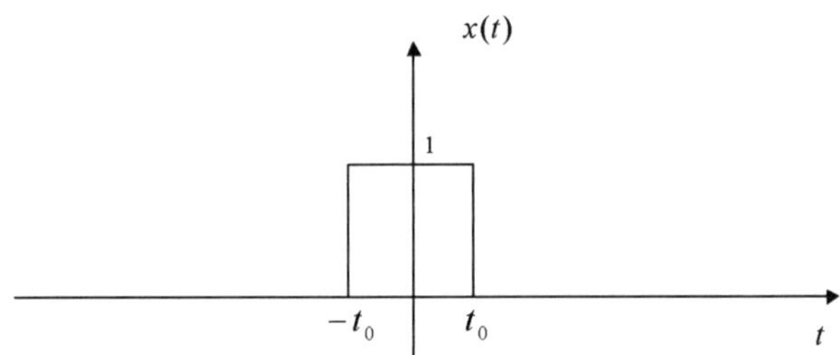

FIGURE 5.4 An aperiodic rectangular pulse signal corresponding to one period of $\tilde{x}(t)$.

This aperiodic signal, a single rectangular pulse, can be thought of as being periodic with an infinite fundamental period (we will let $T \to +\infty$ later). Since $\tilde{x}(t) = x(t)$ over $t \in [-T/2, T/2]$, the spectral coefficients a_k of the periodic signal $\tilde{x}(t)$ can be written in terms of the aperiodic signal $x(t)$ as follows:

$$a_k = \frac{1}{T}\int_{-\infty}^{+\infty} x(t)e^{-jk\omega_0 t}\,dt. \tag{5.3}$$

Let us define the envelope $X(j\omega)$ of Ta_k (we already know that it is the sinc function):

$$X(j\omega) := \int_{-\infty}^{+\infty} x(t)e^{-j\omega t}dt = \int_{-t_0}^{+t_0} e^{-j\omega t}dt = 2t_0\text{sinc}(\frac{t_0}{\pi}\omega). \tag{5.4}$$

The coefficients a_k are therefore samples of the continuous envelope $X(j\omega)$:

$$a_k = \frac{1}{T}X(jk\omega_0). \tag{5.5}$$

Now, the periodic signal $\tilde{x}(t)$ has the Fourier series representation

$$\tilde{x}(t) = \sum_{k=-\infty}^{+\infty} \frac{1}{T}X(jk\omega_0)e^{jk\omega_0 t}. \tag{5.6}$$

Or, equivalently, since $\omega_0 = \frac{2\pi}{T}$,

$$\tilde{x}(t) = \frac{1}{2\pi}\sum_{k=-\infty}^{+\infty} X(jk\omega_0)e^{jk\omega_0 t}\omega_0. \tag{5.7}$$

At the limit, as $T \to +\infty$ in Equation 5.7, we get

- $\omega_0 \to d\omega$ (The fundamental frequency becomes infinitesimally small.)
- $k\omega_0 \to \omega$ (Harmonic frequencies get so close together that they become a continuum.)
- The summation tends to an integral.
- $\tilde{x}(t) \to x(t)$ (The periodic signal tends to the aperiodic signal.)

All of these elements put together give us an expression for the aperiodic signal in terms of its Fourier transform:

$$\text{Inverse Fourier Transform: } x(t) = \frac{1}{2\pi}\int_{-\infty}^{+\infty} X(j\omega)e^{j\omega t}d\omega. \tag{5.8}$$

Let us rewrite Equation 5.4 for an arbitrary $x(t)$ here for convenience:

$$\text{Fourier Transform: } X(j\omega) = \int_{-\infty}^{+\infty} x(t)e^{-j\omega t}dt \tag{5.9}$$

These two equations are called the *Fourier transform pair*. Equation 5.9 gives the *Fourier transform* or the *spectrum* of signal $x(t)$, while Equation 5.8 is the *inverse Fourier transform* equation. Thus, the Fourier transform of the rectangular pulse signal of Figure 5.4 is $X(j\omega) = 2t_0\text{sinc}(\frac{t_0}{\pi}\omega)$, as obtained in Equation 5.4.

PROPERTIES OF THE FOURIER TRANSFORM

We denote the relationship between a signal and its Fourier transform as $x(t)\overset{FT}{\leftrightarrow}X(j\omega)$. Try to derive the following properties of the Fourier transform by using Equation 5.8 and Equation 5.9 as an exercise. Note that these properties are summarized in Table D.2 of Appendix D.

Linearity

The Fourier transform is a linear operation:

$$ax(t)+by(t)\overset{FT}{\leftrightarrow}aX(j\omega)+bY(j\omega),\ \ a,b\in\mathbb{C}. \tag{5.10}$$

Time Shifting

A time shift results in a phase shift in the Fourier transform:

$$x(t-t_0)\overset{FT}{\leftrightarrow}e^{-j\omega t_0}X(j\omega). \tag{5.11}$$

Time/Frequency Scaling

Scaling the time variable with $\alpha\in\mathbb{R}$ either expands or contracts the Fourier transform:

$$x(\alpha t)\overset{FT}{\leftrightarrow}\frac{1}{|\alpha|}X(j\omega/\alpha). \tag{5.12}$$

For $\alpha > 1$, the signal $x(\alpha t)$ is sped up (or compressed in time), so intuitively its frequency contents should extend to higher frequencies. This is exactly what happens: the spectrum (Fourier transform) of the signal expands to higher frequencies. On the other hand, when the signal is slowed down ($\alpha < 1$), the Fourier transform gets compressed to lower frequencies.

Conjugation and Conjugate Symmetry

In general, the signal is complex, so we can take its conjugate and we obtain

$$x^*(t)\overset{FT}{\leftrightarrow}X^*(-j\omega). \tag{5.13}$$

In particular, if the signal is real, that is, $x^*(t)=x(t)$, then the Fourier transform has conjugate symmetry $X^*(j\omega)=X(-j\omega)$. Other interesting consequences include

- $\mathrm{Re}\{X(j\omega)\} = \mathrm{Re}\{X(-j\omega)\}$, an even function of ω
- $\mathrm{Im}\{X(j\omega)\} = -\mathrm{Im}\{X(-j\omega)\}$, an odd function of ω
- $|X(j\omega)| = |X(-j\omega)|$, an even function of ω
- $\angle X(j\omega) = -\angle X(-j\omega)$, an odd function of ω

Furthermore, if $x(t)$ is real and even, then we can show that

- $X(j\omega) = X(-j\omega) = X^*(j\omega)$, that is, the spectrum is even and real.

Similarly, if $x(t)$ is real and odd, we have

- $X(j\omega) = -X(-j\omega) = -X^*(j\omega)$, that is, the spectrum is odd and purely imaginary.

Differentiation

Differentiating a signal results in a multiplication of the Fourier transform by $j\omega$:

$$\frac{d}{dt}x(t) \overset{FT}{\leftrightarrow} j\omega X(j\omega). \tag{5.14}$$

Integration

Integration of a signal results in a division of the Fourier transform by $j\omega$. However, to account for the possibility that $x(t)$ has a nonzero, but finite, average value, that is, $X(j0) = X(0) = \int_{-\infty}^{+\infty} x(t)dt \neq 0$, we must add the term $\pi X(0)\delta(\omega)$ to the Fourier transform. That is, upon integrating $x(t)$, the nonzero average value of $x(t)$ produces a constant part with finite power concentrated at DC ($\omega = 0$), and this is represented as an impulse at that frequency.

$$\int_{-\infty}^{t} x(\tau)d\tau \overset{FT}{\leftrightarrow} \frac{1}{j\omega}X(j\omega) + \pi X(0)\delta(\omega). \tag{5.15}$$

Convolution

The convolution of two signals results in the multiplication of their Fourier transforms in the frequency domain:

$$x(t) * y(t) \overset{FT}{\leftrightarrow} X(j\omega)Y(j\omega). \tag{5.16}$$

A direct application of this property is the calculation of the response of an LTI system with impulse response $h(t)$ to an arbitrary input signal $x(t)$, which is given by the convolution $y(t) = x(t) * h(t)$. The Fourier transform of the output $Y(j\omega)$ is obtained by multiplying the Fourier transform of the input signal $X(j\omega)$ with the frequency response of the system $H(j\omega)$ (the Fourier transform of its impulse response). The output signal in the time domain is obtained by taking the inverse Fourier transform of its spectrum.

Multiplication

The multiplication property is the dual of the convolution property. The multiplication of two signals results in the convolution of their spectra:

$$x(t)y(t)\overset{FT}{\leftrightarrow}\frac{1}{2\pi}X(j\omega)*Y(j\omega). \tag{5.17}$$

Amplitude modulation is based on this property. For example, consider the modulation system described by

$$y(t)=\cos(\omega_0 t)x(t), \tag{5.18}$$

where the signal $x(t)$ is modulated by multiplying it with a sinusoidal wave of frequency ω_0. We will see later that the Fourier transform of the *carrier* $c(t):=\cos(\omega_0 t)$ is composed of two impulses of area π, one at $-\omega_0$ and the other at ω_0, as shown on the right in Figure 5.5. Suppose that the spectrum of $x(t)$ has a triangular shape as shown on the left in Figure 5.5.

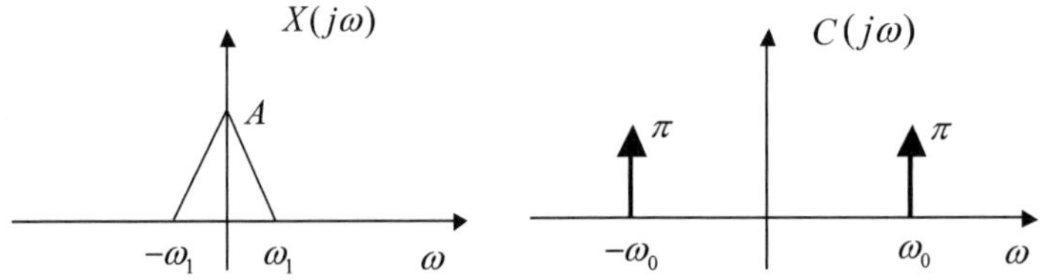

FIGURE 5.5 Spectra of the signal and the carrier.

Recall that the convolution of a function with an impulse simply shifts the function to the location of the impulse. For a time-domain signal, this amounts to a time shift, and for a Fourier transform, it amounts to a frequency shift. Thus, the Fourier transform of the resulting amplitude modulated signal $y(t)$ is as shown in Figure 5.6.

Multiplication of a signal by a sinusoid shifts its spectrum to another frequency band (it also creates a mirror image at the negative frequencies) for easier transmission over a communication channel. For example, music (bandwidth less than

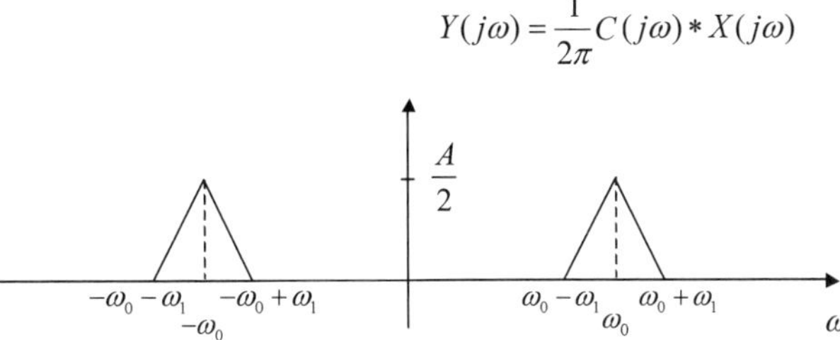

FIGURE 5.6 Spectrum of an amplitude modulated signal.

20 kHz) transmitted over typical AM radio has modulation frequencies in the range of 500 kHz to 1500 kHz. Modulated signals in this range can be conveniently transmitted at reasonable power by using "reasonable size" antennas (actually they seem large by today's standards!). The basic theory of modulation is presented in Chapter 16.

Energy-Density Spectrum

Recall that the power spectrum of a periodic signal is defined as the squared magnitudes of its Fourier series coefficients. A plot of the power spectrum of a signal gives us an idea of the density of power at different frequencies (harmonics).

Similarly, the *energy-density spectrum* of an aperiodic signal is defined as the magnitude squared of its spectrum; that is, $\left|X(j\omega)\right|^2$ is the energy-density spectrum of $x(t)$. We can find the energy of a signal in a given frequency band by integrating its energy-density spectrum over the interval of frequencies.

For example,

$$E_{[\omega_a,\omega_b]} := \frac{1}{2\pi}\int_{\omega_a}^{\omega_b}\left|X(j\omega)\right|^2 d\omega. \tag{5.19}$$

Note that for real signals, it is customary to include the negative frequency band as well. For example, if we wanted to compute the energy contained in a real signal between, for example, 5 kHz and 10 kHz, we would compute

$$E^r_{[10000\pi,20000\pi]} = \frac{1}{2\pi}\left[\int_{10000\pi}^{20000\pi}\left|X(j\omega)\right|^2 d\omega + \int_{-20000\pi}^{-10000\pi}\left|X(j\omega)\right|^2 d\omega\right] = \frac{1}{\pi}\int_{10000\pi}^{20000\pi}\left|X(j\omega)\right|^2 d\omega \tag{5.20}$$

Parseval Equality

Just like the total average power of a periodic signal is equal to the sum of the powers of all its harmonics, the total energy in an aperiodic signal is equal to the total energy in its spectrum. This is the Parseval equality for Fourier transforms:

$$\int_{-\infty}^{+\infty} |x(t)|^2 \, dt = \frac{1}{2\pi} \int_{-\infty}^{+\infty} |X(j\omega)|^2 \, d\omega. \tag{5.21}$$

((Lecture 16: Examples of Fourier Transforms, Inverse Fourier Transform))

EXAMPLES OF FOURIER TRANSFORMS

Let us compute the Fourier transforms of a few signals.

Fourier Transform of the Complex Exponential Signal

The Fourier transform of $e^{-at}u(t),\ a = \alpha + j\beta \in \mathbb{C}, \alpha > 0$ is computed as follows:

$$\begin{aligned}
X(j\omega) &= \int_{-\infty}^{+\infty} e^{-at} u(t) e^{-j\omega t} dt \\
&= \int_{0}^{+\infty} e^{-(a+j\omega)t} dt = \int_{0}^{+\infty} e^{-(\alpha + j\beta + j\omega)t} dt = \overbrace{\int_{0}^{+\infty} e^{-\alpha t} e^{-j(\beta+\omega)t} dt}^{\text{converges for } \alpha>0} \\
&= \frac{1}{j\omega + a}, \quad \mathrm{Re}\{a\} > 0 \\
&= \frac{1}{j(\omega + \beta) + \alpha}, \quad \alpha > 0
\end{aligned} \tag{5.22}$$

Figure 5.7 shows a plot of the magnitude and phase of $X(j\omega)$ for the important case $a > 0$ real ($a = \alpha$). Call it $X_1(j\omega)$.

Remarks:

- For the case where $x(t)$ is the impulse response $h(t)$ of a first-order differential LTI system:
  - The system is a lowpass filter with DC gain of $1/\alpha$.
  - High frequencies in the input signal are attenuated.

- The *cutoff frequency* of the filter is $\omega_c = \alpha$, where frequency components of the input signal are attenuated by a factor $1/\sqrt{2}$.
- The maximum phase added to the input signal is $-\pi/2$ for $\omega \to +\infty$.

■ In the case of $a = \alpha + j\beta,\ \alpha > 0, \beta \neq 0$, the Fourier transform of the complex exponential $X_2(j\omega)$ can be obtained by shifting the magnitude and phase of $X_1(j\omega)$:

$$X_2(j\omega) = X_1(j(\omega+\beta)) = \frac{1}{j(\omega+\beta)+\alpha}. \tag{5.23}$$

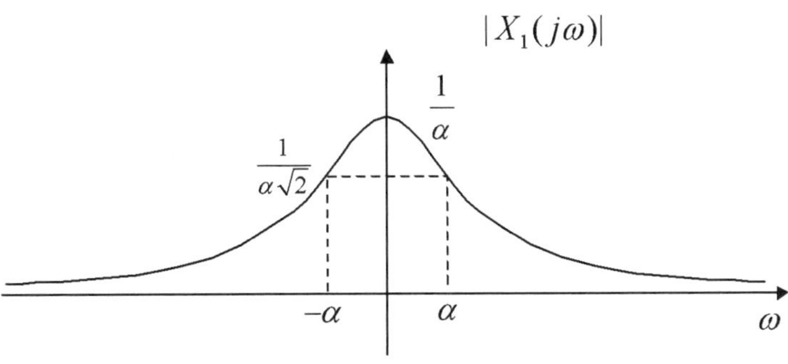

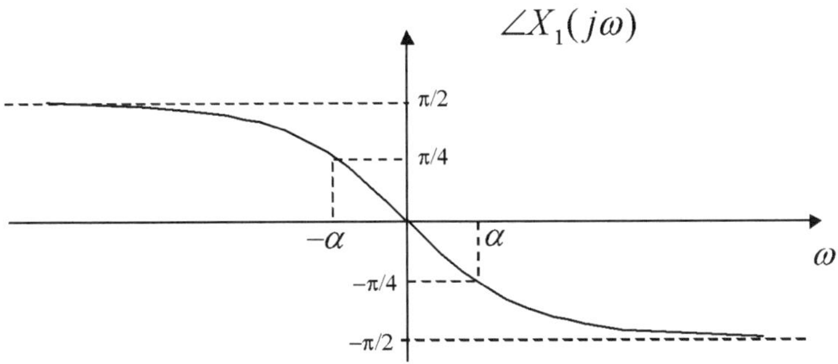

FIGURE 5.7 Fourier transform of a real exponential signal.

Note that this is a shift to the left in the frequency domain when $\beta > 0$, so in this case the magnitude and phase of $X_2(j\omega)$ would look like the ones plotted in Figure 5.8.

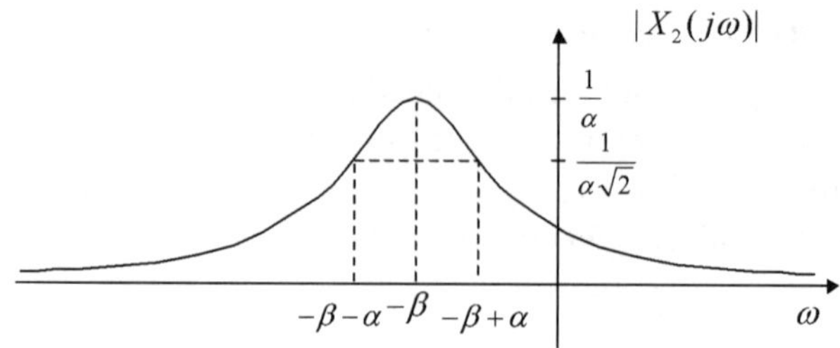

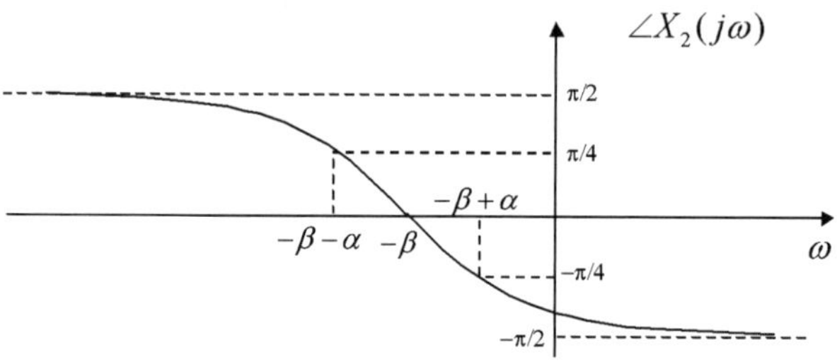

FIGURE 5.8 Fourier transform of a complex exponential signal.

Suppose we want to calculate the Fourier transform of the damped sinusoid $x_3(t) = \mathrm{Im}\{e^{(-\alpha+j\omega_0)t}\} = e^{-\alpha t}\sin(\omega_0 t)$. By the linearity and conjugation properties and by using our result for a complex exponential signal, we can write

$$x_3(t) = e^{-\alpha t}\sin(\omega_0 t)u(t) = \frac{1}{2j}\left[e^{-(\alpha-j\omega_0)t}u(t) - e^{-(\alpha+j\omega_0)t}u(t)\right]$$

$$\overset{FT}{\leftrightarrow}$$

$$\begin{aligned} X_3(j\omega) &= \frac{1}{2j}\left(\frac{1}{j(\omega-\omega_0)+\alpha} - \frac{1}{j(\omega+\omega_0)+\alpha}\right) \\ &= \frac{1}{2j}\left(\frac{j(\omega+\omega_0)+\alpha-[j(\omega-\omega_0)+\alpha]}{[j(\omega-\omega_0)+\alpha][j(\omega+\omega_0)+\alpha]}\right) \\ &= \frac{\omega_0}{(j\omega+\alpha)^2+\omega_0^2} \end{aligned} \tag{5.24}$$

Here, the damped sinusoid signal is real, so we should get an even $|X_3(j\omega)|$ and an odd $\angle X_3(j\omega)$. This turns out to be the case as shown in Figure 5.9. If we assume that $\omega_0 > \alpha$, it can be shown that the magnitude peaks to $\frac{1}{2\alpha}$ at the frequencies $\omega = \pm\sqrt{\omega_0^2-\alpha^2}$. The phase tends to $-\pi$ as $\omega \to +\infty$, and it is equal to $-\pi/2$ and $\pi/2$ at the frequencies $\omega = \sqrt{\omega_0^2+\alpha^2}$ and $\omega = -\sqrt{\omega_0^2+\alpha^2}$, respectively.

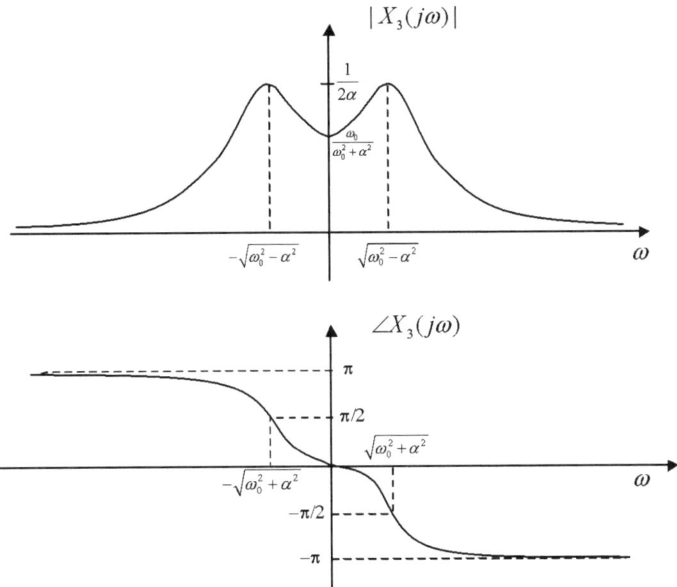

FIGURE 5.9 Fourier transform of a damped sinusoid.

Fourier Transform of an Aperiodic Sawtooth Signal

Let us calculate the Fourier transform of the aperiodic sawtooth signal $x(t)$ shown in Figure 5.10.

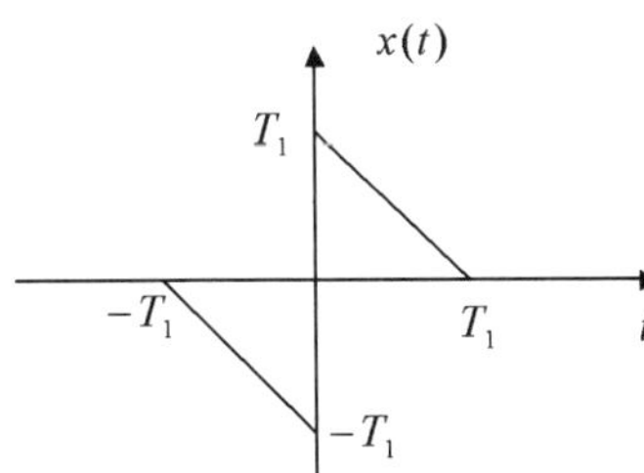

FIGURE 5.10 Aperiodic sawtooth signal.

$$
\begin{aligned}
X(j\omega) &= \int_{-\infty}^{+\infty} x(t)e^{-j\omega t}\,dt \\
&= \int_{-T_1}^{0} (-T_1 - t)e^{-j\omega t}\,dt + \int_{0}^{T_1} (T_1 - t)e^{-j\omega t}\,dt \\
&= \int_{0}^{T_1} -\tau e^{-j\omega(\tau - T_1)}\,d\tau + \int_{0}^{T_1} (T_1 - \tau)e^{-j\omega\tau}\,d\tau \quad (\tau = t + T_1 \text{ in first integral, } \tau = t \text{ in second integral}) \\
&= T_1\int_{0}^{T_1} e^{-j\omega\tau}\,d\tau - (e^{j\omega T_1} + 1)\int_{0}^{T_1} \tau e^{-j\omega\tau}\,d\tau \\
&= \frac{T_1}{-j\omega}(e^{-j\omega T_1} - 1) - \frac{(e^{j\omega T_1} + 1)}{-j\omega}\left[\left[te^{-j\omega t}\right]_0^{T_1} - \int_0^{T_1} e^{-j\omega\tau}\,d\tau\right] \\
&= \frac{T_1}{-j\omega}(e^{-j\omega T_1} - 1) - \frac{(e^{j\omega T_1} + 1)}{-j\omega}\left[T_1 e^{-j\omega T_1} + \frac{(e^{-j\omega T_1} - 1)}{j\omega}\right] \\
&= \frac{T_1}{-j\omega}(e^{-j\omega T_1} - 1) - \frac{T_1(e^{-j\omega T_1} + 1)}{-j\omega} - \frac{(e^{-j\omega T_1} - e^{j\omega T_1})}{-(j\omega)^2} \\
&= \frac{2T_1}{j\omega} + \frac{(e^{-j\omega T_1} - e^{j\omega T_1})}{(j\omega)^2} \\
&= \frac{2T_1}{j\omega} - \frac{2j\sin(\omega T_1)}{(j\omega)^2} \\
&= j\left(\frac{2\sin(\omega T_1)}{\omega^2} - \frac{2T_1}{\omega}\right) \qquad (5.25)
\end{aligned}
$$

This Fourier transform is purely imaginary and odd, as we would expect since the signal is real and odd. Hence, this Fourier transform is equal to zero at $\omega = 0$; that is, the signal's average value is zero (apply L'Hopital's rule twice).

THE INVERSE FOURIER TRANSFORM

In general, one would have to use the integral of Equation 5.8 to obtain the time-domain representation of a signal from its Fourier transform.

Example 5.1: Consider the ideal lowpass filter with cutoff frequency ω_c and given by its spectrum $H(j\omega) = \begin{cases} 1, & |\omega| < \omega_c \\ 0, & |\omega| \geq \omega_c \end{cases}$. The corresponding impulse response is calculated as follows.

$$h(t)=\frac{1}{2\pi}\int_{-\infty}^{+\infty}H(j\omega)e^{j\omega t}d\omega=\frac{1}{2\pi}\int_{-\omega_c}^{+\omega_c}e^{j\omega t}d\omega$$

$$=\frac{1}{2\pi(jt)}\left[e^{j\omega t}\right]_{-\omega_c}^{\omega_c}=\frac{\sin(\omega_c t)}{\pi t}=\frac{\omega_c}{\pi}\frac{\sin(\frac{\omega_c}{\pi}t\pi)}{\frac{\omega_c\pi t}{\pi}}$$

$$=\frac{\omega_c}{\pi}\text{sinc}\left(\frac{\omega_c}{\pi}t\right) \tag{5.26}$$

Thus, the impulse response of an ideal lowpass filter is a real-valued sinc function extending from $t=-\infty$ to $t=+\infty$, as shown in Figure 5.11.

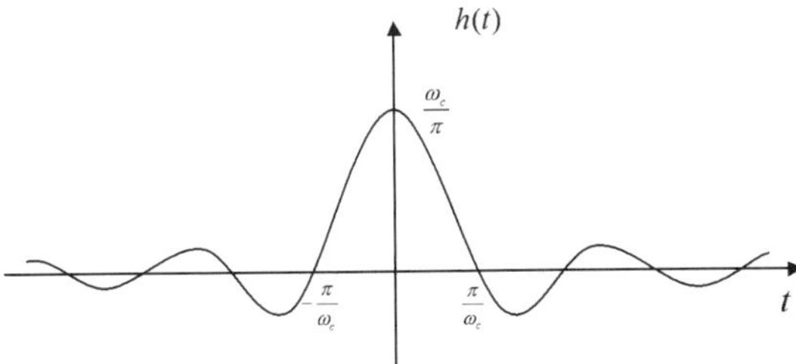

FIGURE 5.11 Impulse response of a perfect lowpass filter.

Very often, the Fourier transform will be in the form of a rational function of $j\omega$ (a ratio of two polynomials in $j\omega$). In this case, it is much easier to perform a *partial fraction expansion* of the Fourier transform and then to identify each term in this expansion using a table of Fourier transforms and their corresponding time-domain signals. This method is usually preferred to obtain the output response of a stable differential LTI system using the convolution property.

Example 5.2: Consider the response of an LTI system with impulse response $h(t)=e^{-2t}u(t)$, (which meets the Dirichlet conditions) to the input $x(t)=e^{-3t}u(t)$. Rather than computing their convolution, we will find the response by multiplying the Fourier transforms of the input and the impulse response. From Equation 5.22, we have

$$X(j\omega)=\frac{1}{j\omega+3},\qquad H(j\omega)=\frac{1}{j\omega+2}. \tag{5.27}$$

Then,

$$Y(j\omega) = X(j\omega)H(j\omega) = \frac{1}{(j\omega+3)(j\omega+2)}. \tag{5.28}$$

The partial fraction expansion consists of expressing this transform as a sum of simple first-order terms.

$$Y(j\omega) = \frac{A}{j\omega+2} + \frac{B}{j\omega+3} \tag{5.29}$$

The constants *A, B* can be determined by substituting values for the frequency ω (e.g., 0) and solving the resulting system of linear equations. An easier technique consists of applying the following procedure.

1. Equate the right-hand sides of Equations 5.28 and 5.29 and let $s := j\omega$.

$$\frac{1}{(s+2)(s+3)} = \frac{A}{s+2} + \frac{B}{s+3} \tag{5.30}$$

2. To obtain *A*, multiply both sides of the equation by $(s+2)$ and evaluate for $s = -2$.

$$\left.\frac{1}{s+3}\right|_{s=-2} = A + \left.\frac{(s+2)B}{(s+3)}\right|_{s=-2}$$

$$\Rightarrow \quad A = \frac{1}{-2+3} = 1 \tag{5.31}$$

Applying Step 2 for the constant *B*, we obtain

$$\left.\frac{1}{s+2}\right|_{s=-3} = \left.\frac{(s+3)A}{s+2}\right|_{s=-3} + B$$

$$\Rightarrow \quad B = \frac{1}{-3+2} = -1 \tag{5.32}$$

3. Finally, the partial fraction expansion of the Fourier transform of the output is given by

$$Y(j\omega) = \frac{1}{j\omega+2} - \frac{1}{j\omega+3}. \tag{5.33}$$

Using Table D.1 of basic Fourier transform pairs in Appendix D, we find that

$$y(t) = e^{-2t}u(t) - e^{-3t}u(t). \tag{5.34}$$

For the case where the two exponents are equal, for example, $h(t) = e^{-2t}u(t)$ and $x(t) = e^{-2t}u(t)$, the partial fraction expansion of Equation 5.33 is not valid. On the other hand, in this case the spectrum of $y(t)$ is given by $Y(j\omega) = \frac{1}{(j\omega+2)^2}$, which in the table corresponds to the signal $y(t) = te^{-2t}u(t)$. The partial fraction expansion technique will be reviewed in more detail in Chapter 6.

DUALITY

The Fourier transform pair is quite symmetric. This results in a duality between the time domain and the frequency domain. For example, Figure 5.12 shows that a rectangular pulse signal in the time domain has a Fourier transform that takes the form of a sinc function of frequency. The dual of this situation is a rectangular spectrum that turns out to be the Fourier transform of a signal that is a sinc function of time.

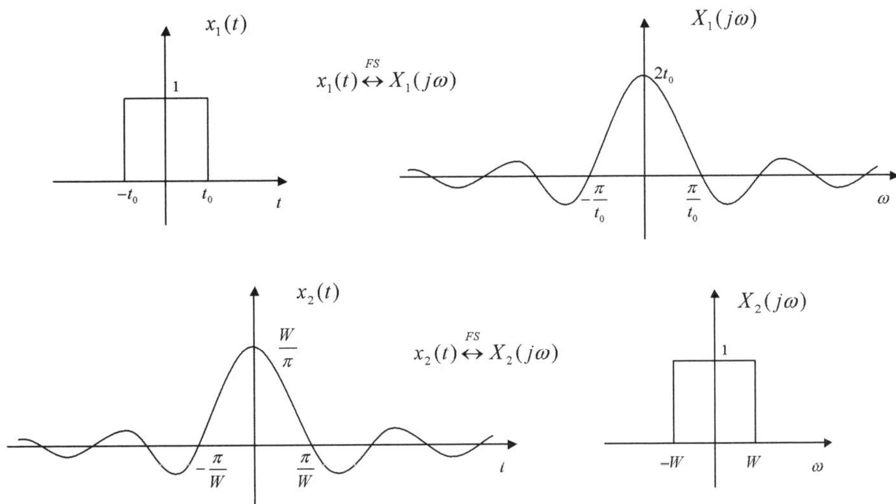

FIGURE 5.12 Duality between time-domain and frequency-domain functions.

When such a rectangular spectrum centered at $\omega = 0$ is the frequency response of an LTI system, it is often referred to as an *ideal lowpass filter* because it lets the low frequency components pass undistorted while the high frequencies are completely cut off. The problem is that the impulse response of this LTI system, the time-domain sinc function, is noncausal. Filter design will be discussed in more detail later on.

((Lecture 17: Convergence of the Fourier Transform, Convolution Property and LTI Systems))

CONVERGENCE OF THE FOURIER TRANSFORM

There are two important classes of signals for which the Fourier transform converges:

1. Signals of finite total energy, that is, signals for which $\int_{-\infty}^{+\infty} |x(t)|^2 \, dt < +\infty$
2. Signals that satisfy the Dirichlet conditions:
   a. $x(t)$ is absolutely integrable, that is, $\int_{-\infty}^{+\infty} |x(t)| \, dt < +\infty$.
   b. $x(t)$ has a finite number of maxima and minima over any finite interval of time.
   c. $x(t)$ has a finite number of discontinuities over any finite interval of time. Furthermore, each one of these discontinuities must be finite.

The type of convergence that we get for signals of finite energy is similar to the convergence of Fourier series for signals of finite power. That is, there is no energy in the error between a signal $x(t)$ and its inverse Fourier transform $\tilde{x}(t) = \frac{1}{2\pi}\int_{-\infty}^{+\infty} X(j\omega)e^{j\omega t} d\omega$. For signals $x(t)$ satisfying the Dirichlet conditions, it is guaranteed that $\tilde{x}(t)$ is equal to $x(t)$ at every time t, except at discontinuities where $\tilde{x}(t)$ will take on the average of the values on either side of the discontinuity.

Later, we will extend the Fourier transform to include periodic signals (infinite energy, finite power) by allowing the use of impulse functions in the frequency domain.

THE CONVOLUTION PROPERTY IN THE ANALYSIS OF LTI SYSTEMS

General LTI Systems

We have seen that the response of a stable LTI system to a complex exponential of the type $e^{j\omega t}$ is simply the same exponential multiplied by the frequency response of the system $H(j\omega)e^{j\omega t}$. We used this fact to find the Fourier series coefficients of the output of an LTI system as the product $b_k = H(jk\omega_0)a_k$ for a periodic input of frequency ω_0 with spectral coefficients a_k.

In Example 5.2, we computed the output signal of an LTI system by using the convolution property of the Fourier transform. That is, even though the output $y(t)$ of a stable LTI system with impulse response $h(t)$ and subjected to an input $x(t)$ is given by the convolution $y(t)=\int_{-\infty}^{+\infty} x(\tau)h(t-\tau)d\tau$, we can also compute it by taking the inverse Fourier transform of $Y(j\omega)=H(j\omega)X(j\omega)$. This is represented in the block diagram of Figure 5.13.

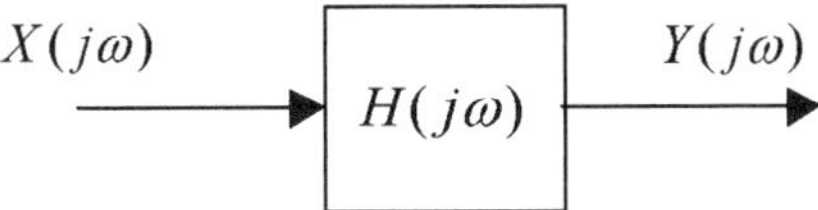

FIGURE 5.13 Block diagram of an LTI system in the frequency domain.

For a cascade of two stable LTI systems with impulse responses $h_1(t)$, $h_2(t)$, we have

$$Y(j\omega)=H_2(j\omega)H_1(j\omega)X(j\omega). \tag{5.35}$$

This is illustrated in Figure 5.14.

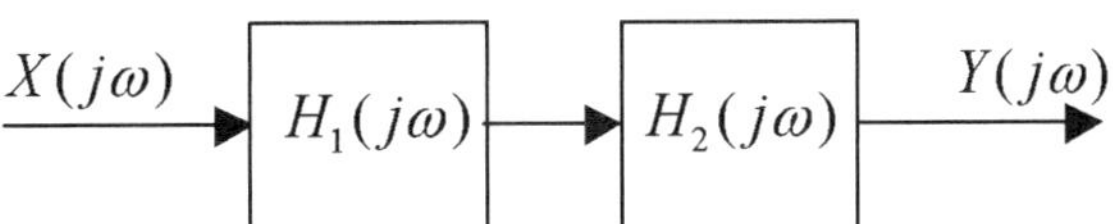

FIGURE 5.14 Cascade interconnection of two LTI systems in the frequency domain.

For a parallel interconnection of two stable LTI systems with impulse responses $h_1(t)$, $h_2(t)$, we have

$$Y(j\omega)=[H_1(j\omega)+H_2(j\omega)]X(j\omega). \tag{5.36}$$

This parallel interconnection is shown in Figure 5.15.

For a feedback interconnection of two stable LTI systems with impulse responses $h_1(t)$, $h_2(t)$, we have

$$Y(j\omega)=\frac{H_1(j\omega)}{1+H_1(j\omega)H_2(j\omega)}X(j\omega). \tag{5.37}$$

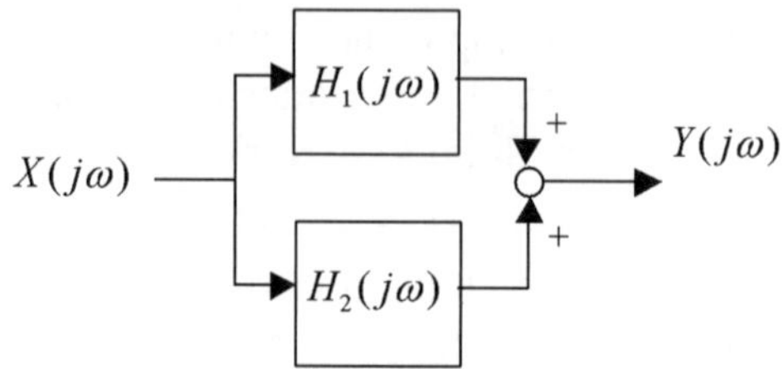

FIGURE 5.15 Parallel interconnection of two LTI systems in the frequency domain.

This feedback interconnection is shown in Figure 5.16.

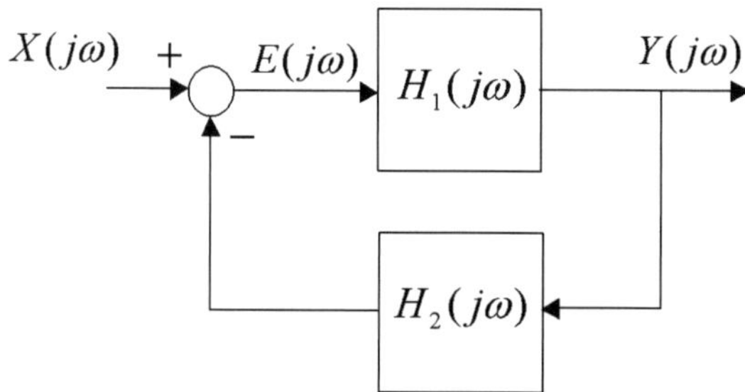

FIGURE 5.16 Feedback interconnection of two LTI systems in the frequency domain.

LTI Differential Systems

We already know how to solve for the response of an LTI differential system, which, in general, is given by the sum of a forced response and a natural response. However, it is often easier to use a Fourier transform approach, provided the system is known to be *stable*.

Consider the stable LTI system defined by an Nth-order linear constant-coefficient causal differential equation initially at rest:

$$\sum_{k=0}^{N} a_k \frac{d^k y(t)}{dt^k} = \sum_{k=0}^{M} b_k \frac{d^k x(t)}{dt^k}. \tag{5.38}$$

Assume that $X(j\omega)$, $Y(j\omega)$ denote the Fourier transforms of the input $x(t)$ and the output $y(t)$, respectively. Recall that differentiation in the time domain is equivalent to a multiplication of the Fourier transform by $j\omega$. Thus, if we take the Fourier transform of both sides of Equation 5.38, we get

$$\sum_{k=0}^{N} a_k (j\omega)^k Y(j\omega) = \sum_{k=0}^{M} b_k (j\omega)^k X(j\omega). \tag{5.39}$$

Since $H(j\omega) = \frac{Y(j\omega)}{X(j\omega)}$, the frequency response of the system is given by

$$H(j\omega) = \frac{Y(j\omega)}{X(j\omega)} = \frac{\sum_{k=0}^{M} b_k (j\omega)^k}{\sum_{k=0}^{N} a_k (j\omega)^k}. \tag{5.40}$$

Example 5.3 The frequency response of the causal second-order LTI differential system,

$$\frac{d^2 y(t)}{dt^2} + 3\frac{dy(t)}{dt} + 2y(t) = \frac{dx(t)}{dt} - x(t), \tag{5.41}$$

is calculated as follows:

$$[(j\omega)^2 + 3j\omega + 2]Y(j\omega) = (j\omega - 1)X(j\omega) \tag{5.42}$$

$$H(j\omega) = \frac{Y(j\omega)}{X(j\omega)} = \frac{j\omega - 1}{(j\omega)^2 + 3j\omega + 2}. \tag{5.43}$$

Note that the order of the system is the highest power of $j\omega$ in the denominator of the frequency response. Now, suppose we want to obtain the system's response when the input signal is a unit step function. From Table D.1, The Fourier transform of the step function has the form

$$X(j\omega) = \frac{1}{j\omega} + \pi\delta(\omega), \tag{5.44}$$

so that

$$\begin{aligned} Y(j\omega) &= \frac{j\omega - 1}{(j\omega)^2 + 3j\omega + 2} X(j\omega) \\ &= \frac{j\omega - 1}{(j\omega)^2 + 3j\omega + 2}\left[\frac{1}{j\omega} + \pi\delta(\omega)\right] \\ &= \frac{j\omega - 1}{\left[(j\omega)^2 + 3j\omega + 2\right] j\omega} \underbrace{- \frac{1}{2}\pi\delta(\omega)}_{\text{sampling property}} \end{aligned} \tag{5.45}$$

Letting $s = j\omega$ and expanding the rational function on the right-hand side into partial fractions, we get

$$\frac{s-1}{\left[s^2 + 3s + 2\right]s} = \frac{s-1}{(s+1)(s+2)s} = \frac{A}{s} + \frac{B}{s+1} + \frac{C}{s+2}, \tag{5.46}$$

and the coefficients are computed as follows:

$$A = \left.\frac{s-1}{(s+1)(s+2)}\right|_{s=0} = -\frac{1}{2} \tag{5.47}$$

$$B = \left.\frac{s-1}{s(s+2)}\right|_{s=-1} = \frac{-2}{-1} = 2 \tag{5.48}$$

$$C = \left.\frac{s-1}{s(s+1)}\right|_{s=-2} = -\frac{3}{2} \tag{5.49}$$

Hence,

$$\begin{aligned} Y(j\omega) &= \frac{j\omega - 1}{\left[(j\omega)^2 + 3j\omega + 2\right] j\omega} - \frac{1}{2}\pi\delta(\omega) \\ &= -\frac{1}{2}\left(\frac{1}{j\omega} + \pi\delta(\omega)\right) + 2\left(\frac{1}{j\omega + 1}\right) - \frac{3}{2}\left(\frac{1}{j\omega + 2}\right) \end{aligned} \tag{5.50}$$

and using Table D.1 of Fourier transform pairs, we find the output by inspection:

$$y(t) = \left[-\frac{1}{2} + 2e^{-t} - \frac{3}{2}e^{-2t}\right]u(t). \tag{5.51}$$

Remark: When $M \geq N$ in differential Equation 5.38, the frequency response has a numerator of equal or higher order than the denominator polynomial. It is then necessary to express the frequency response as a sum of a *strictly proper* rational function (it means that the numerator polynomial is of lower order than the denominator) and a polynomial in $j\omega$ of order $M-N$. Each term of this polynomial is associated either with an impulse (constant term), a doublet (term in $j\omega$), or a kth-order derivative of the impulse (term in $(j\omega)^k$). Then, one only needs to perform a partial fraction expansion of the resulting strictly proper rational function to find the other time-domain components of the response.

((Lecture 18: LTI Systems, Fourier Transform of Periodic Signals))

Example 5.4: Consider the causal LTI differential system initially at rest described by

$$2\frac{dy(t)}{dt} + y(t) = \frac{d^2x(t)}{dt^2} - \frac{dx(t)}{dt} - 2x(t). \tag{5.52}$$

The frequency response of this system is

$$H(j\omega) = \frac{(j\omega)^2 - j\omega - 2}{2(j\omega + 0.5)} = \frac{(j\omega - 2)(j\omega + 1)}{2(j\omega + 0.5)}. \tag{5.53}$$

Let $s = j\omega$ and write $H(s)$ as

$$H(s) = \frac{s^2 - s - 2}{2(s + 0.5)} = As + B + \frac{C}{(s + 0.5)} \tag{5.54}$$

Multiplying both sides by $2(s + 0.5)$, we can identify each coefficient:

$$s^2 - s - 2 = 2(s + 0.5)(As + B) + 2C = 2As^2 + (A + 2B)s + 2C + B \tag{5.55}$$

$$A = \frac{1}{2}, \quad B = -\frac{3}{4}, \quad C = -\frac{5}{8}. \tag{5.56}$$

Thus,

$$H(s) = \frac{s^2 - s - 2}{2(s + 0.5)} = \frac{1}{2}s - \frac{3}{4} - \frac{5}{8}\frac{1}{(s + 0.5)} \tag{5.57}$$

and

$$H(j\omega) = \frac{1}{2} j\omega - \frac{3}{4} - \frac{5}{8} \frac{1}{(j\omega + 0.5)}. \tag{5.58}$$

Finally, the inverse Fourier transform of Equation 5.58 gives us the impulse response

$$h(t) = \frac{1}{2} \frac{d}{dt} \delta(t) - \frac{3}{4} \delta(t) - \frac{5}{8} e^{-0.5t} u(t). \tag{5.59}$$

Example 5.5: Consider a stable causal second-order LTI differential system whose characteristic polynomial has complex zeros:

$$\frac{d^2 y(t)}{dt^2} + \frac{dy(t)}{dt} + y(t) = x(t) \tag{5.60}$$

The frequency response of this system is given by

$$H(j\omega) = \frac{Y(j\omega)}{X(j\omega)} = \frac{1}{(j\omega)^2 + j\omega + 1} = \frac{1}{(j\omega + \frac{1}{2} - j\frac{\sqrt{3}}{2})(j\omega + \frac{1}{2} + j\frac{\sqrt{3}}{2})} \tag{5.61}$$

Letting $s = j\omega$ and expanding the right-hand side into partial fractions, we get

$$\frac{1}{s^2 + 1s + 1} = \frac{1}{(s + \frac{1}{2} + j\frac{\sqrt{3}}{2})(s + \frac{1}{2} - j\frac{\sqrt{3}}{2})} = \frac{A}{s + \frac{1}{2} + j\frac{\sqrt{3}}{2}} + \frac{B}{s + \frac{1}{2} - j\frac{\sqrt{3}}{2}}. \tag{5.62}$$

The coefficients are computed as follows:

$$A = \left. \frac{1}{s + \frac{1}{2} - j\frac{\sqrt{3}}{2}} \right|_{s = -\frac{1}{2} - j\frac{\sqrt{3}}{2}} = j\frac{1}{\sqrt{3}}, \tag{5.63}$$

$$B = \left. \frac{1}{s + \frac{1}{2} + j\frac{\sqrt{3}}{2}} \right|_{s = -\frac{1}{2} + j\frac{\sqrt{3}}{2}} = -j\frac{1}{\sqrt{3}}. \tag{5.64}$$

Hence,

$$H(j\omega)=\frac{1}{(j\omega+\frac{1}{2}+j\frac{\sqrt{3}}{2})(j\omega+\frac{1}{2}-j\frac{\sqrt{3}}{2})}=j\frac{1}{\sqrt{3}}\frac{1}{j\omega+\frac{1}{2}+j\frac{\sqrt{3}}{2}}-j\frac{1}{\sqrt{3}}\frac{1}{j\omega+\frac{1}{2}-j\frac{\sqrt{3}}{2}} \quad (5.65)$$

and using Table D.1 of Fourier transform pairs, we find the output by inspection:

$$\begin{aligned}h(t)&=\left[\frac{j}{\sqrt{3}}e^{-\frac{1}{2}t-j\frac{\sqrt{3}}{2}t}-\frac{j}{\sqrt{3}}e^{-\frac{1}{2}t+j\frac{\sqrt{3}}{2}t}\right]u(t)\\&=\frac{2}{\sqrt{3}}e^{-\frac{1}{2}t}\operatorname{Re}\left\{e^{-j(\frac{\sqrt{3}}{2}t-\frac{\pi}{2})}\right\}u(t)\\&=\frac{2}{\sqrt{3}}e^{-\frac{1}{2}t}\cos(\frac{\sqrt{3}}{2}t-\frac{\pi}{2})u(t)\\&=\frac{2}{\sqrt{3}}e^{-\frac{1}{2}t}\sin(\frac{\sqrt{3}}{2}t)u(t)\end{aligned} \quad (5.66)$$

Remarks:

- For complex conjugate zeros of the characteristic polynomial, the two coefficients of the first-order terms in the partial fraction expansion are also complex conjugates of each other. Therefore it is sufficient to compute only one, that is, $A=j\frac{1}{\sqrt{3}}$ in the above example, and then one can write directly $B=A^*=-j\frac{1}{\sqrt{3}}$. However, it is good practice to compute the second coefficient just to double-check that the calculation is correct.
- It is usually not sufficient to write the impulse response as a sum of two complex signals as in the first line of Equation 5.66. These signals are complex conjugates of each other, so that their sum can be simplified to get a real signal at the end. More generally, if the differential system has real coefficients, the impulse response can always be expressed as a sum of real signals.

FOURIER TRANSFORMS OF PERIODIC SIGNALS

Periodic signals are neither finite-energy, nor do they meet the Dirichlet conditions. We will nonetheless use the Fourier transform to represent them by using singularity functions such as impulses in the frequency domain. We have already studied the Fourier series representation of periodic signals with their spectra. We will see that the Fourier transforms of these signals are the same spectra, but the coefficients (times 2π) now represent the impulse areas at the harmonic frequencies $k\omega_0$.

Let us consider a signal $x(t)$ with Fourier transform that is a single impulse of area 2π at frequency $k\omega_0$:

$$X(j\omega) = 2\pi\delta(\omega - k\omega_0). \tag{5.67}$$

Taking the inverse Fourier transform of this impulse, we obtain by using the sampling property:

$$\begin{aligned} x(t) &= \frac{1}{2\pi}\int_{-\infty}^{+\infty} 2\pi\delta(\omega - k\omega_0)e^{j\omega t}\,d\omega \\ &= e^{jk\omega_0 t}. \end{aligned} \tag{5.68}$$

Thus, the frequency-domain impulse corresponds to a single complex harmonic component whose amplitude is one. Therefore, by linearity, a more general signal with Fourier transform,

$$X(j\omega) = \sum_{k=-\infty}^{+\infty} 2\pi a_k \delta(\omega - k\omega_0), \tag{5.69}$$

has the time-domain form

$$x(t) = \sum_{k=-\infty}^{+\infty} a_k e^{jk\omega_0 t}, \tag{5.70}$$

which is the Fourier series representation of $x(t)$. Therefore the Fourier transform of a periodic signal with Fourier series coefficients a_k is a train of impulses of areas $2\pi a_k$ occurring at the frequencies $k\omega_0$.

Example 5.6: The Fourier transform of a sinusoidal signal of the form $x(t) = A\sin(\omega_0 t)$ is $X(j\omega) = jA\pi\delta(\omega + \omega_0) - jA\pi\delta(\omega - \omega_0)$.

Fourier Transform of a Periodic Impulse Train

Consider the impulse train signal shown in Figure 5.17, which can be written as

$$x(t) = \sum_{k=-\infty}^{+\infty} \delta(t - kT). \tag{5.71}$$

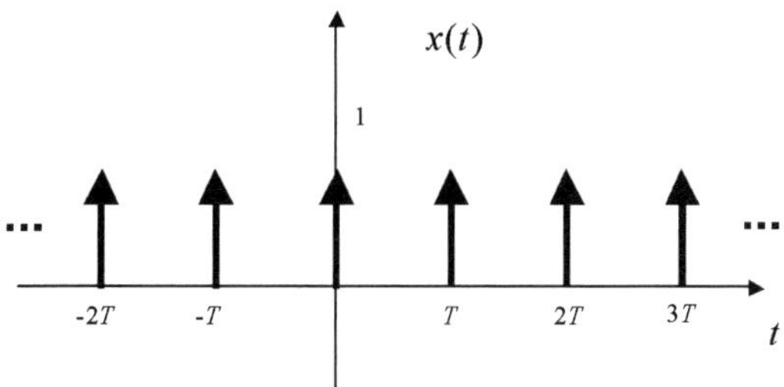

FIGURE 5.17 Impulse train signal.

There are two ways to derive the Fourier transform of an impulse train. The first method is the one introduced above: use the Fourier series coefficients times 2π as the areas of a periodic train of impulses in the frequency domain of frequency $\omega_0 = 2\pi/T$. We know that the spectral coefficients of the impulse train are $a_k = 1/T$; hence,

$$X(j\omega) = \frac{2\pi}{T} \sum_{k=-\infty}^{+\infty} \delta(\omega - k\omega_0). \tag{5.72}$$

The second method consists of calculating the Fourier transform of the impulse train using the integral formula. This yields

$$\begin{aligned} X(j\omega) &= \int_{-\infty}^{+\infty} \sum_{k=-\infty}^{+\infty} \delta(t - kT) e^{-j\omega t}\, dt \\ &= \sum_{k=-\infty}^{+\infty} \int_{-\infty}^{+\infty} \delta(t - kT) e^{-j\omega t}\, dt \\ &= \sum_{k=-\infty}^{+\infty} e^{-j\omega kT}. \end{aligned} \tag{5.73}$$

This Fourier transform, shown in Figure 5.18, is actually a periodic train of impulses of period $\omega_0 = 2\pi/T$ (note that the period is a frequency) in the frequency domain. That is, the series in Equation 5.73 converges to the impulse train of Equation 5.72.

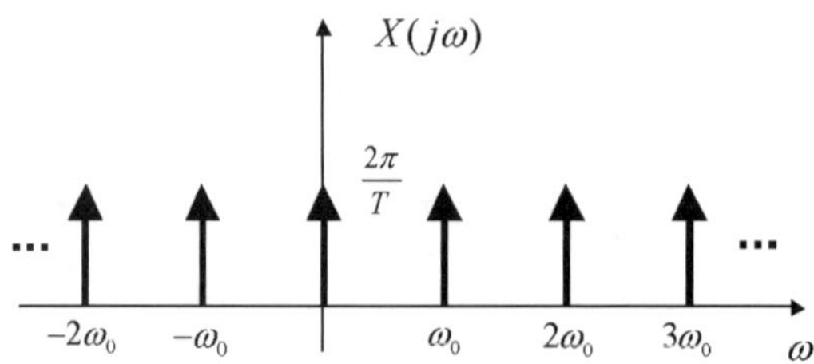

FIGURE 5.18 Fourier transform of an impulse train signal.

FILTERING

In this section, we discuss an important application of the Fourier transform: filtering. Filtering is a rich topic often taught in graduate courses in electrical and computer engineering. We only give a rudimentary introduction to filtering to show how the frequency-domain viewpoint can help us understand the concept of shaping the spectrum of a signal by using filters. Sampling and modulation are also important applications of the Fourier transform. They will be studied in Chapters 15 and 16, respectively.

Frequency-Selective Filters

Ideal frequency-selective filters are filters that let frequency components over a given frequency band (the *passband*) pass through undistorted, while components at other frequencies (the *stopband*) are completely cut off. A typical scenario shown in Figure 5.19, where filtering is needed, is when a noise $n(t)$ is added to a signal $x(t)$, but the noise has most, or all, of its energy at frequencies outside of the bandwidth of the signal. By linearity of the Fourier transform, the spectra of the signal and the noise are also summed together. We want to recover the original signal from its noisy measurement $x_1(t)$.

Here the noise spectrum is assumed to have all of its energy at higher frequencies than the bandwidth W of the signal. Thus, an ideal lowpass filter would perfectly recover the signal, that is, $\tilde{x}(t) = x(t)$, as seen in Figure 5.20.

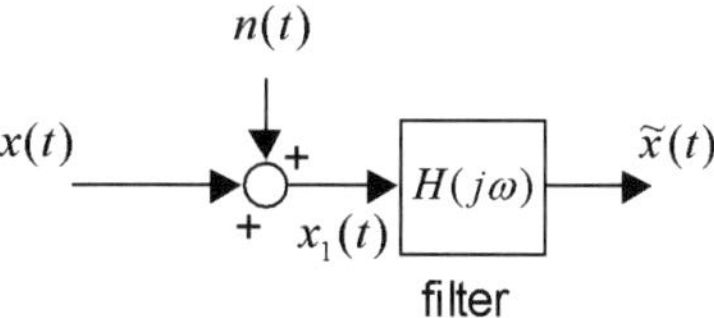

FIGURE 5.19 Typical filtering problem.

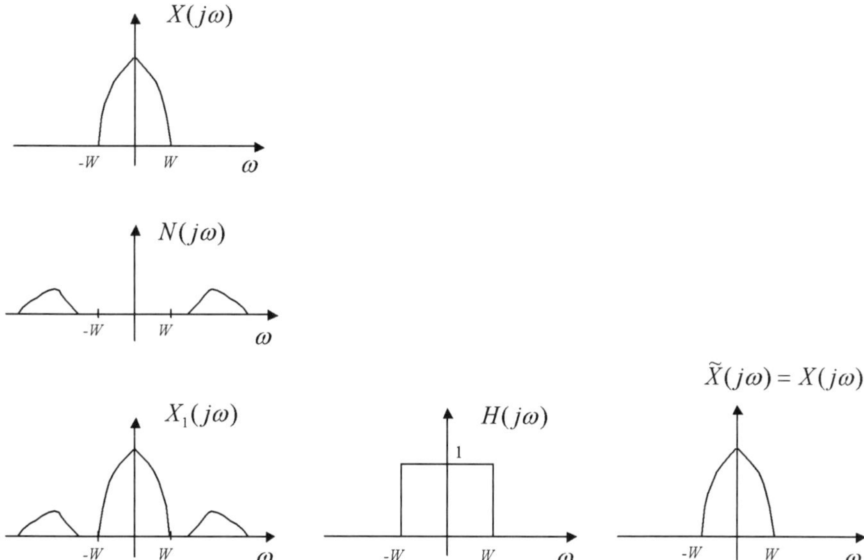

FIGURE 5.20 Effect of filtering in the frequency domain.

Lowpass Filters

An ideal lowpass filter cuts off frequencies higher than its *cutoff frequency,* ω_c. The frequency response of this filter, shown in Figure 5.21, is given by

$$H_{lp}(j\omega) := \begin{cases} 1, & |\omega| < \omega_c \\ 0, & |\omega| \geq \omega_c \end{cases}. \tag{5.74}$$

The impulse response $h_{lp}(t)$ of the ideal lowpass filter shown in Figure 5.22 was found to be a sinc function of time (it is even and real, as expected):

$$h_{lp}(t) = \frac{\omega_c}{\pi}\operatorname{sinc}\left(\frac{\omega_c}{\pi}t\right). \tag{5.75}$$

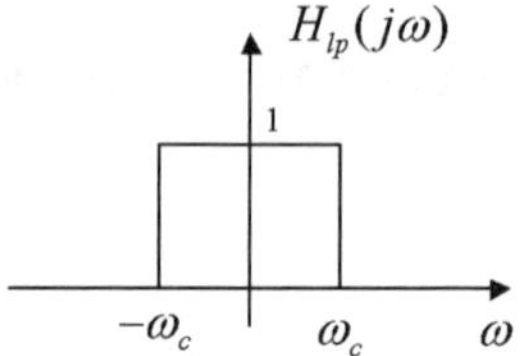

FIGURE 5.21 Frequency response of an ideal lowpass filter.

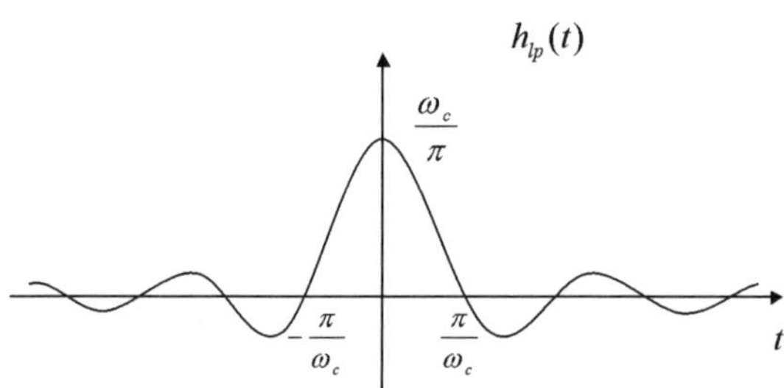

FIGURE 5.22 Impulse response of an ideal lowpass filter.

Recall that the convolution property of the Fourier transform is the basis for filtering: the output of an LTI system with impulse response $h(t) \overset{FT}{\leftrightarrow} H(j\omega)$ subjected to an input signal $x(t) \overset{FT}{\leftrightarrow} X(j\omega)$ is given by $y(t) = x(t) * h(t) \overset{FT}{\leftrightarrow} Y(j\omega) = H(j\omega)X(j\omega)$.

Even though the above filter is termed "ideal" in reference to its frequency response, it may not be so desirable in the time domain for some applications because of the ripples in its impulse response. For example, the step response of the ideal lowpass filter is the running integral of the sinc function shown in Figure 5.22. Its plot in Figure 5.23 indicates that there are potentially undesirable oscillations before (because the impulse response is noncausal) and after the discontinuity. Such a signal in an electronic circuit might cause improper switching of a binary latch.

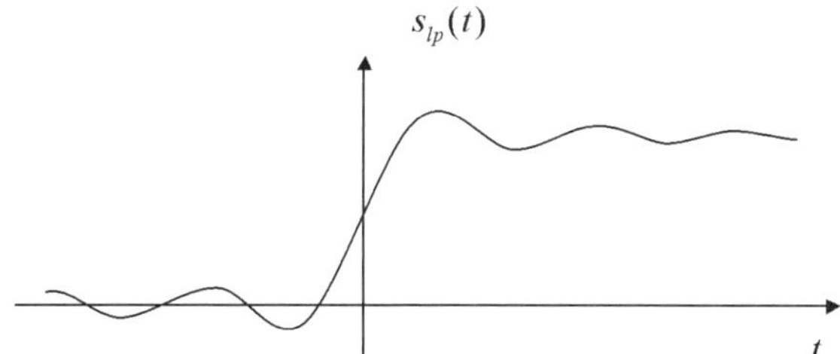

FIGURE 5.23 Step response of an ideal lowpass filter.

As mentioned before, the impulse response of the ideal lowpass filter is not realizable, as it is noncausal. Approximations to the ideal lowpass filter that can be realized by stable causal LTI differential equations have been proposed in the past, and some of them have found widespread use. One of these filters is the *Butterworth filter*. The magnitude of the frequency response of an Nth-order Butterworth filter with cutoff frequency ω_c is given by

$$|H_B(j\omega)| = \frac{1}{\left(1+\left(\frac{\omega}{\omega_c}\right)^{2N}\right)^{\frac{1}{2}}}. \tag{5.76}$$

Remarks:

- The DC gain is $|H_B(j0)| = 1$.
- The attenuation at the cutoff frequency is $|H_B(j\omega_c)| = \frac{1}{\sqrt{2}}$ for any order N.

Figure 5.24 shows a plot of the filter's magnitude for $N = 2$ (second-order) compared to the ideal "brick wall" magnitude. The *transition band* is the frequency band around ω_c, where the magnitude rolls off. The higher the order of the Butterworth filter, the narrower the transition band gets.

The second-order Butterworth filter is defined by its characteristic polynomial:

$$\begin{aligned} p(s) &= (s-\omega_c e^{j3\pi/4})(s-\omega_c e^{-j3\pi/4}) \\ &= \left[s-\omega_c\left(-\frac{1}{\sqrt{2}}+j\frac{1}{\sqrt{2}}\right)\right]\left[s-\omega_c\left(-\frac{1}{\sqrt{2}}-j\frac{1}{\sqrt{2}}\right)\right] \\ &= s^2+\omega_c\sqrt{2}s+\omega_c^2. \end{aligned} \tag{5.77}$$

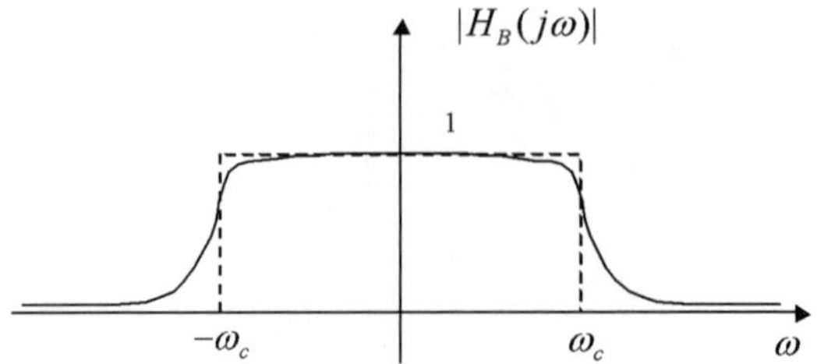

FIGURE 5.24 Magnitude of frequency response of a second-order Butterworth filter.

Therefore the differential equation relating the input and output signals of this filter must have the form

$$\frac{d^2y(t)}{dt^2}+\omega_c\sqrt{2}\frac{dy(t)}{dt}+\omega_c^2 y(t)=\omega_c^2 x(t). \tag{5.78}$$

Note that it is necessary to add a gain of ω_c^2, multiplying the input signal to obtain a DC gain of 1 for the filter. Recall that the DC gain is the gain of the filter when the input and output signals are constant, which means that the derivatives of $y(t)$ are zero in Equation 5.78.

Let us check that the frequency response of this differential equation has the magnitude of Equation 5.76. The frequency response of the second-order Butterworth filter is obtained from Equation 5.78:

$$\begin{aligned} H_B(j\omega) &= \frac{Y(j\omega)}{X(j\omega)} \\ &= \frac{\omega_c^2}{(j\omega)^2+\omega_c\sqrt{2}j\omega+\omega_c^2} \\ &= \frac{1}{1+(\frac{j\omega}{\omega_c})^2+\frac{\sqrt{2}j\omega}{\omega_c}} \\ &= \frac{1}{1-(\frac{\omega}{\omega_c})^2+\frac{\sqrt{2}j\omega}{\omega_c}} \end{aligned} \tag{5.79}$$

and the magnitude is

$$\left|H_B(j\omega)\right| = \frac{1}{\sqrt{\left[1-(\frac{\omega}{\omega_c})^2\right]^2 + \frac{2\omega^2}{\omega_c^2}}}$$
$$= \frac{1}{\sqrt{1+(\frac{\omega}{\omega_c})^4}} \tag{5.80}$$

The impulse response of a Butterworth filter is given by (following a partial fraction expansion of the frequency response):

$$h_B(t) = \sqrt{2}\omega_c e^{-\frac{\omega_c}{\sqrt{2}}t} \sin(\frac{\omega_c}{\sqrt{2}}t)u(t). \tag{5.81}$$

This impulse response does not oscillate much even though it is a damped sinusoid. The decay rate is fast enough to damp out the oscillations. For example, if we plot the step response of this second-order Butterworth filter, we obtain the graph of Figure 5.25 with a single overshoot.

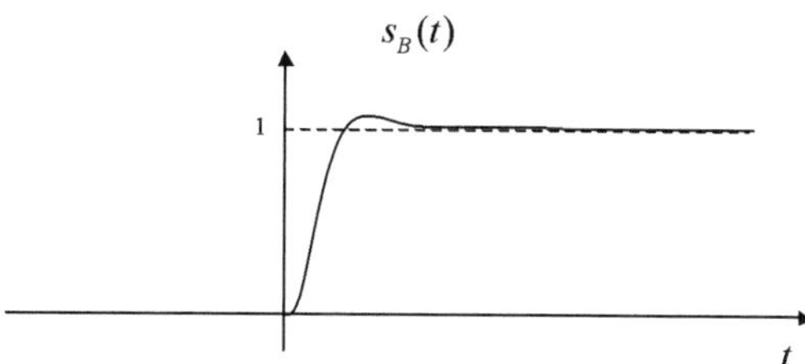

FIGURE 5.25 Step response of a second-order Butterworth filter.

Highpass Filters

An ideal highpass filter cuts off the part of the input signal's spectrum that is at lower frequencies than the filter's cutoff frequency, ω_c. The frequency response of this filter, shown in Figure 5.26, is given by

$$H_{hp}(j\omega) := \begin{cases} 0, & \left|\omega\right| \le \omega_c \\ 1, & \left|\omega\right| > \omega_c \end{cases}. \tag{5.82}$$

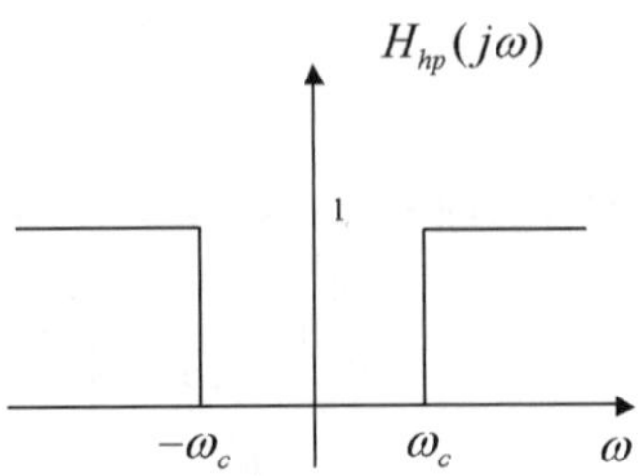

FIGURE 5.26 Frequency response of an ideal highpass filter.

Notice that the frequency response of an ideal highpass filter can be written as the difference between 1 and the frequency response of an ideal lowpass filter:

$$H_{hp}(j\omega) = 1 - H_{lp}(j\omega). \tag{5.83}$$

The resulting impulse response is simply

$$h_{hp}(t) = \delta(t) - h_{lp}(t). \tag{5.84}$$

This suggests one possible, but naïve, approach to obtaining a realizable highpass filter. First, design a lowpass filter with cutoff frequency ω_c and desirable characteristics in the transition band and the stopband. Second, form the frequency response of the highpass filter using Equation 5.83.

Example 5.7: We can design a highpass filter using the second-order lowpass Butterworth filter of the above example. The resulting highpass magnitude of the frequency response of the filter is shown in Figure 5.27.

$$\begin{aligned} H_{Bhp}(j\omega) &= 1 - H_B(j\omega) \\ &= 1 - \frac{\omega_c^2}{(j\omega)^2 + \omega_c\sqrt{2}j\omega + \omega_c^2} \\ &= \frac{(j\omega)^2 + \omega_c\sqrt{2}j\omega + \omega_c^2 - \omega_c^2}{(j\omega)^2 + \omega_c\sqrt{2}j\omega + \omega_c^2} \\ &= \frac{(j\omega)^2 + \omega_c\sqrt{2}j\omega}{(j\omega)^2 + \omega_c\sqrt{2}j\omega + \omega_c^2} \end{aligned} \tag{5.85}$$

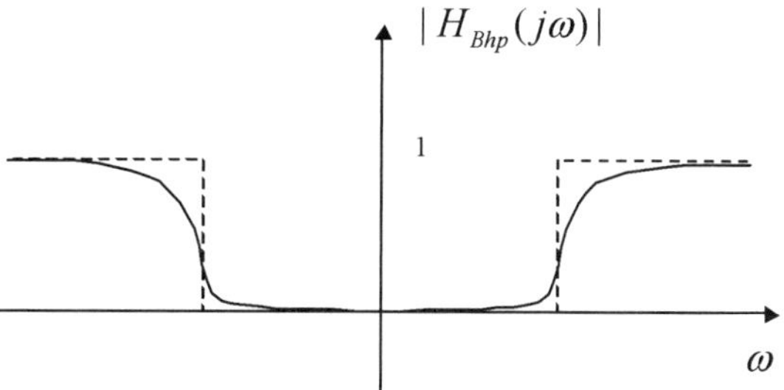

FIGURE 5.27 Magnitude of frequency response of a second-order highpass filter.

The causal LTI differential system corresponding to this highpass filter is the following:

$$\frac{d^2y(t)}{dt^2}+\omega_c\sqrt{2}\frac{dy(t)}{dt}+\omega_c^2y(t)=\frac{d^2x(t)}{dt^2}+\omega_c\sqrt{2}\frac{dx(t)}{dt}, \tag{5.86}$$

and the impulse response is as given by Equation 5.87:

$$h_{Bhp}(t)=\delta(t)-\sqrt{2}\omega_c e^{-\frac{\omega_c}{\sqrt{2}}t}\sin(\frac{\omega_c}{\sqrt{2}}t)u(t). \tag{5.87}$$

Bandpass Filters

An ideal bandpass filter cuts off frequencies lower than its first cutoff frequency ω_{c1} and higher than its second cutoff frequency ω_{c2}, as shown in Figure 5.28. The frequency response of such a filter is given by

$$H_{bp}(j\omega):=\begin{cases}1, & \omega_{c1}<|\omega|<\omega_{c2}\\ 0, & \text{otherwise}\end{cases}. \tag{5.88}$$

The frequency response of an ideal bandpass filter can be written as the product of the frequency responses of overlapping ideal lowpass and highpass filters. The highpass filter should have a cutoff frequency of ω_{c1} and the lowpass filter ω_{c2}.

$$H_{bp}(j\omega)=H_{hp}(j\omega)H_{lp}(j\omega). \tag{5.89}$$

This is one approach to designing bandpass filters.

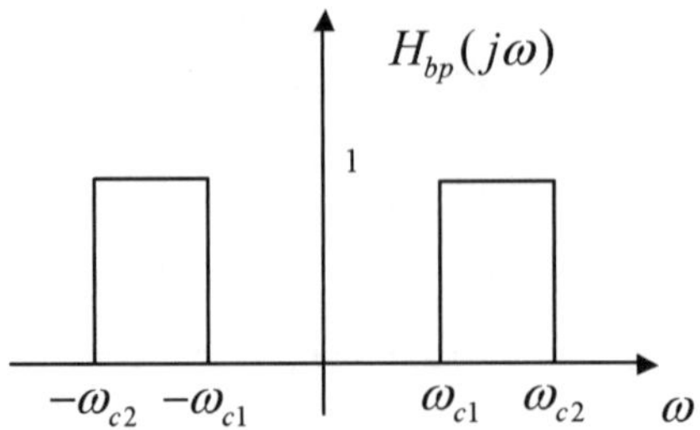

FIGURE 5.28 Frequency response of an ideal bandpass filter.

SUMMARY

In this chapter, we have extended the concept of Fourier series to aperiodic continuous-time signals, which resulted in the Fourier transform.

- The Fourier transform was derived as the limit of the Fourier series of a periodic signal whose period tends to infinity. Classes of signals that have a Fourier transform include finite-energy signals and signals satisfying the Dirichlet conditions.
- The Fourier transform of a signal, also called a spectrum, is in most cases a complex-valued continuous function of frequency. Its magnitude and phase are usually plotted separately. The energy-density spectrum plot of a signal is the squared magnitude of its spectrum.
- The inverse Fourier transform is given by an integral formula. However, a partial fraction expansion of a Fourier transform can often be performed, and the time-domain signal is then obtained from a table of Fourier transform pairs.
- The Fourier transform of a periodic signal can be defined with frequency-domain impulses located at the harmonic frequencies, whose areas are a constant times the Fourier series coefficients of the signal.
- In the frequency domain, signal filtering using an LTI system is simply the multiplication of the frequency response of the system with the spectrum of the input signal to either amplify or attenuate different frequencies. We briefly discussed lowpass, bandpass, and highpass filters.

TO PROBE FURTHER

For a more detailed treatment of the Fourier transform and its applications, see Bracewell, 2000. For a specialized treatment of filtering and filter design, see Schaumann and Van Valkenburg, 2001 and Winder, 2002.

EXERCISES

Exercises with Solutions

Exercise 5.1

Sketch the following signals and find their Fourier transforms.

(a) $x(t)=\left(1-e^{-|t|}\right)\left[u(t+1)-u(t-1)\right]$. Show that $X(j\omega)$ is real and even.

Answer:

The signal is sketched in Figure 5.29.

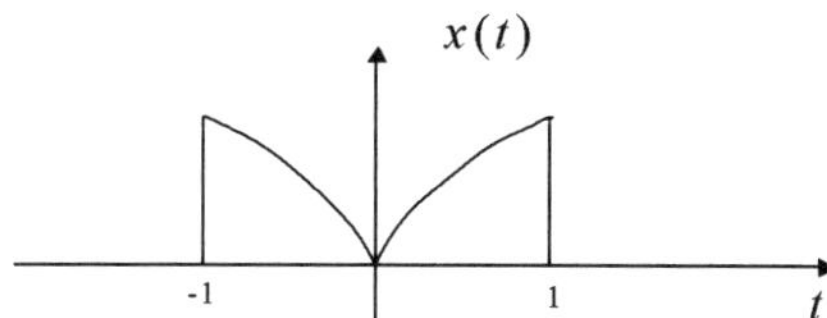

FIGURE 5.29 Signal of Exercise 5.1(a).

Its Fourier transform is computed as follows:

$$
\begin{aligned}
X(j\omega) &= \int_{-1}^{1} x(t)e^{-j\omega t}\,dt \\
&= \int_{-1}^{1} \left(1-e^{-|t|}\right)e^{-j\omega t}\,dt \\
&= \int_{-1}^{1} e^{-j\omega t}\,dt - \int_{-1}^{0} e^{(1-j\omega)t}\,dt - \int_{0}^{1} e^{-(1+j\omega)t}\,dt \\
&= -\frac{1}{j\omega}\left[e^{-j\omega t}\right]_{-1}^{1} - \frac{1}{1-j\omega}\left[e^{(1-j\omega)t}\right]_{-1}^{0} + \frac{1}{1+j\omega}\left[e^{-(1+j\omega)t}\right]_{0}^{1}
\end{aligned}
$$

$$
\begin{aligned}
&= \frac{e^{j\omega} - e^{-j\omega}}{j\omega} - \frac{1 - e^{-1}e^{j\omega}}{1 - j\omega} + \frac{e^{-1}e^{-j\omega} - 1}{1 + j\omega} \\
&= \frac{2\sin\omega}{\omega} + \frac{(1 + j\omega)(-1 + e^{-1}e^{j\omega}) + (1 - j\omega)(-1 + e^{-1}e^{-j\omega})}{1 + \omega^2} \\
&= \frac{2\sin\omega}{\omega} + \frac{(-1 - j\omega + e^{-1}e^{j\omega} + j\omega e^{-1}e^{j\omega}) + (-1 + j\omega + e^{-1}e^{-j\omega} - j\omega e^{-1}e^{-j\omega})}{1 + \omega^2} \\
&= \frac{2\sin\omega}{\omega} + \frac{-2 + e^{-1}(e^{j\omega} + e^{-j\omega}) + j\omega e^{-1}(e^{j\omega} - e^{-j\omega})}{1 + \omega^2} \\
&= \frac{2\sin\omega}{\omega} + \frac{-2 + 2e^{-1}(\cos\omega - \omega\sin\omega)}{1 + \omega^2}.
\end{aligned}
$$

This Fourier transform is obviously real. To show that it is even, we consider $X(-j\omega)$:

$$
\begin{aligned}
X(-j\omega) &= \frac{2\sin(-\omega)}{-\omega} + \frac{-2 + 2e^{-1}(\cos(-\omega) + \omega\sin(-\omega))}{1 + (-\omega)^2} \\
&= \frac{-2\sin(\omega)}{-\omega} + \frac{-2 + 2e^{-1}(\cos(\omega) - \omega\sin(\omega))}{1 + \omega^2} = X(j\omega).
\end{aligned}
$$

(b) Periodic signal $x(t)$ in Figure 5.30.

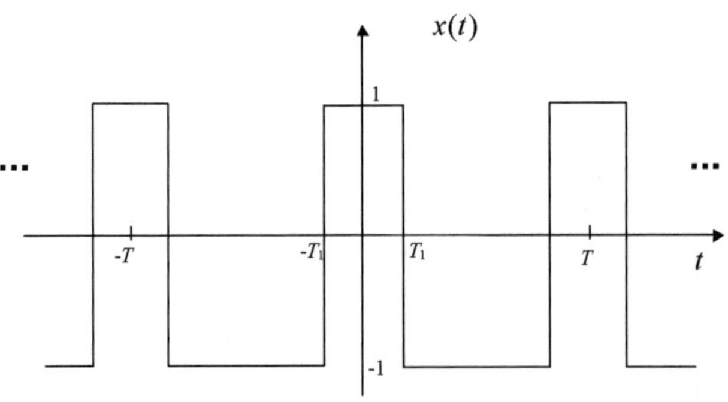

FIGURE 5.30 Signal of Exercise 5.1(b).

Answer:

This signal is the sum of the constant signal –1 with our familiar rectangular wave of amplitude 2 and duty cycle $\eta = \frac{2T_1}{T}$. Therefore, its Fourier series coefficients are

$$a_k = 2\frac{2T_1}{T}\operatorname{sinc}\left(\frac{k2T_1}{T}\right), \quad k \neq 0$$

$$a_0 = \frac{4T_1}{T} - 1.$$

Note that since $0 < T_1 < \frac{T}{2}$, then $-1 < a_0 < 1$ depending on the duty cycle. The Fourier transform of the signal is given by

$$X(j\omega) = 2\pi \sum_{\substack{k=-\infty \\ k\neq 0}}^{+\infty} \frac{4T_1}{T}\operatorname{sinc}(\frac{k2T_1}{T})\delta(\omega - k\frac{2\pi}{T}) + 2\pi(\frac{4T_1}{T} - 1)\delta(\omega).$$

Exercise 5.2

Sketch the following signals and compute their Fourier transforms using the integral formula.

(a) $x_1(t) = \begin{cases} \sin\omega_0 t, & -\frac{2\pi}{\omega_0} \leq t \leq \frac{2\pi}{\omega_0} \\ 0, & \text{otherwise} \end{cases}$

Answer:

This real, odd signal is composed of two periods of a sine wave. Its sketch is in Figure 5.31.

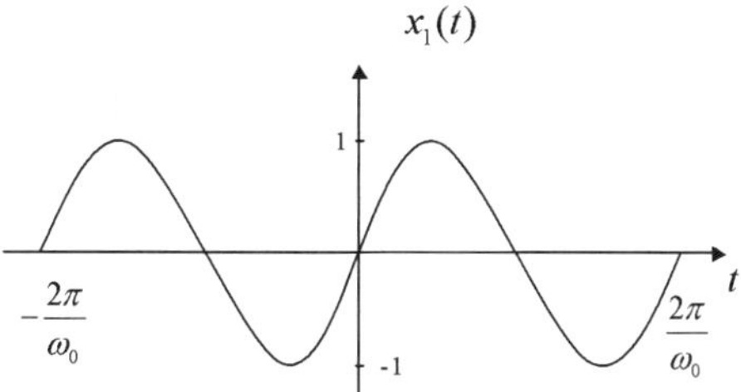

FIGURE 5.31 Signal composed of two periods of a sine wave in Exercise 5.2(a).

Let us compute its Fourier transform:

$$X_1(j\omega) = \int_{-\frac{2\pi}{\omega_0}}^{\frac{2\pi}{\omega_0}} x(t)e^{-j\omega t}dt = \int_{-\frac{2\pi}{\omega_0}}^{\frac{2\pi}{\omega_0}} \sin(\omega_0 t)e^{-j\omega t}dt$$

$$= \frac{1}{2j}\int_{-\frac{2\pi}{\omega_0}}^{\frac{2\pi}{\omega_0}} \left(e^{j(\omega_0-\omega)t} - e^{j(-\omega_0-\omega)t}\right)dt$$

$$= -\frac{j}{2j(\omega_0-\omega)}\left[e^{j(\omega_0-\omega)t}\right]_{-\frac{2\pi}{\omega_0}}^{\frac{2\pi}{\omega_0}} + \frac{j}{2j(-\omega_0-\omega)}\left[e^{j(-\omega_0-\omega)t}\right]_{-\frac{2\pi}{\omega_0}}^{\frac{2\pi}{\omega_0}}$$

$$= \frac{1}{2(\omega-\omega_0)}\left[e^{j(\omega_0-\omega)\frac{2\pi}{\omega_0}} - e^{-j(\omega_0-\omega)\frac{2\pi}{\omega_0}}\right] - \frac{1}{2(\omega_0+\omega)}\left[e^{-j(\omega_0+\omega)\frac{2\pi}{\omega_0}} - e^{j(\omega_0+\omega)\frac{2\pi}{\omega_0}}\right]$$

$$= \frac{1}{2(\omega-\omega_0)}\left[e^{-j\omega\frac{2\pi}{\omega_0}} - e^{j\omega\frac{2\pi}{\omega_0}}\right] - \frac{1}{2(\omega_0+\omega)}\left[e^{-j\omega\frac{2\pi}{\omega_0}} - e^{j\omega\frac{2\pi}{\omega_0}}\right]$$

$$= \frac{1}{2(\omega-\omega_0)(\omega_0+\omega)}\left[2\omega_0 e^{-j\omega\frac{2\pi}{\omega_0}} - 2\omega_0 e^{j\omega\frac{2\pi}{\omega_0}}\right]$$

$$= \frac{2j\omega_0\sin(\frac{2\pi}{\omega_0}\omega)}{\omega_0^2-\omega^2}$$

This Fourier transform is imaginary and odd, as expected.

(b) $x_2(t) = x_1(t) * p(t)$, where $x_1(t)$ is as defined in (a) and

$p(t) = \sum_{k=-\infty}^{+\infty}\delta(t-k\frac{4\pi}{\omega_0})$ is an impulse train.

Answer:

Note that $x_2(t) = x_1(t) * p(t)$ is just the regular sine wave of frequency ω_0 since $x_2(t) = x_1(t) * p(t) = x_1(t) * \sum_{k=-\infty}^{+\infty}\delta(t-k\frac{4\pi}{\omega_0}) = \sum_{k=-\infty}^{+\infty}x_1(t-k\frac{4\pi}{\omega_0}) = \sin\left(\omega_0 t\right)$. Thus,

$$X_2(j\omega) = \int_{-\infty}^{\infty}\sin(\omega_0 t)e^{-j\omega t}dt$$

$$= \frac{1}{2j}\int_{-\infty}^{\infty}e^{j\omega_0 t}e^{-j\omega t}dt - \frac{1}{2j}\int_{-\infty}^{\infty}e^{-j\omega_0 t}e^{-j\omega t}dt$$

We know that the Fourier transform of $e^{j\omega_0 t}$ is given by $2\pi\delta(\omega-\omega_0)$, so

$$\begin{aligned} X_2(j\omega) &= -\frac{1}{2j}2\pi\delta(\omega+\omega_0)+\frac{1}{2j}2\pi\delta(\omega-\omega_0) \\ &= j\pi\delta(\omega+\omega_0)-j\pi\delta(\omega-\omega_0) \end{aligned}$$

We can obtain the same result by applying the convolution property:

$$x_2(t)=x_1(t)*p(t)\overset{FT}{\leftrightarrow}X_1(j\omega)P(j\omega)=X_2(j\omega).$$

Thus,

$$\begin{aligned} X_2(j\omega) &= X_1(j\omega)P(j\omega)=X_1(j\omega)\frac{\omega_0}{2}\sum_{k=-\infty}^{+\infty}\delta(\omega-k\frac{\omega_0}{2}) \\ &= \frac{\omega_0}{2}\sum_{k=-\infty}^{+\infty}X_1(jk\frac{\omega_0}{2})\delta(\omega-k\frac{\omega_0}{2}) \\ &= \frac{\omega_0}{2}\sum_{k=-\infty}^{+\infty}\frac{2j\omega_0\sin(k\frac{2\pi}{\omega_0}\frac{\omega_0}{2})}{\omega_0^2-\frac{1}{4}k^2\omega_0^2}\delta(\omega-k\frac{\omega_0}{2}) \\ &= \frac{\omega_0}{2}\sum_{k=-\infty}^{+\infty}\underbrace{\frac{2j\omega_0\sin(k\pi)}{\omega_0^2-\frac{1}{4}k^2\omega_0^2}}_{=0\text{ for }k\neq\pm 2}\delta(\omega-k\frac{\omega_0}{2}) \end{aligned}$$

The term in the above summation for $X_2(j\omega)$ is equal to zero for all integers $k\neq\pm2$. In the case of $k=2$, we have a $0/0$ indeterminacy, and using l'Hopital's rule we find that

$$\left.\frac{2j\omega_0\sin(k\pi)}{\omega_0^2-\frac{1}{4}k^2\omega_0^2}\right|_{k=2}=\left.\frac{2j\omega_0\pi\cos(k\pi)}{-\frac{1}{2}k\omega_0^2}\right|_{k=2}=\frac{2j\omega_0\pi}{-\omega_0^2}=-j\frac{2\pi}{\omega_0}$$

Similarly, for $k=-2$, we get $\left.\frac{2j\omega_0\sin(k\pi)}{\omega_0^2-\frac{1}{4}k^2\omega_0^2}\right|_{k=-2}=j\frac{2\pi}{\omega_0}$, and therefore,

$$X_2(j\omega)=\frac{\omega_0}{2}\sum_{k=-\infty}^{+\infty}\frac{2j\omega_0\sin(k\pi)}{\omega_0^{\,2}-\frac{1}{4}k^2\omega_0^{\,2}}\delta(\omega-k\frac{\omega_0}{2})$$
$$=\frac{\omega_0}{2}\left(j\frac{2\pi}{\omega_0}\right)\delta(\omega+\omega_0)+\frac{\omega_0}{2}\left(-j\frac{2\pi}{\omega_0}\right)\delta(\omega-\omega_0)$$
$$=j\pi\delta(\omega+\omega_0)-j\pi\delta(\omega-\omega_0)$$

Exercise 5.3

Find the time-domain signals corresponding to the following Fourier transforms.

(a) $X(j\omega)=\dfrac{j\sqrt{2}\omega+1-\omega^2}{(j\omega)(j2\sqrt{2}\omega+4-\omega^2)}+\dfrac{\pi}{4}\delta(\omega)$

Answer:

$$X(j\omega)=\frac{j\sqrt{2}\omega+1-\omega^2}{(j\omega)(j2\sqrt{2}\omega+4-\omega^2)}+\frac{\pi}{4}\delta(\omega)$$
$$=\frac{(j\omega)^2+\sqrt{2}j\omega+1}{(j\omega)\left[(j\omega)^2+2\sqrt{2}j\omega+4\right]}+\frac{\pi}{4}\delta(\omega)$$
$$=\frac{\frac{3}{8}+j\frac{1}{8}}{(j\omega+\sqrt{2}-j\sqrt{2})}+\frac{\frac{3}{8}-j\frac{1}{8}}{(j\omega+\sqrt{2}+j\sqrt{2})}+\frac{1}{4j\omega}+\frac{\pi}{4}\delta(\omega)$$

From Table D.1 (Appendix D) of Fourier transform pairs,

$$X(j\omega)\overset{FT}{\leftrightarrow}$$
$$x(t)=\left(\frac{3}{8}+j\frac{1}{8}\right)e^{(-\sqrt{2}+j\sqrt{2})t}u(t)+\left(\frac{3}{8}-j\frac{1}{8}\right)e^{(-\sqrt{2}-j\sqrt{2})t}u(t)+\frac{1}{4}u(t)$$
$$x(t)=2\,\mathrm{Re}\left\{\left(\frac{3}{8}+j\frac{1}{8}\right)e^{(-\sqrt{2}+j\sqrt{2})t}\right\}u(t)+\frac{1}{4}u(t)$$
$$x(t)=e^{-\sqrt{2}t}\left(\frac{3}{4}\cos(\sqrt{2}t)-\frac{1}{4}\sin(\sqrt{2}t)\right)u(t)+\frac{1}{4}u(t)$$

(b) $X(j\omega) = \dfrac{(j\omega+2)^2(j\omega)}{(j\omega+3)(j\omega+1)}$

Answer:
Let $s = j\omega$. Partial fraction expansion:

$$
\begin{aligned}
X(s) &= \frac{(s+2)^2 s}{(s+3)(s+1)} \\
&= As + B + \frac{C}{s+1} + \frac{D}{s+3} \\
&= s + \frac{-0.5}{s+1} + \frac{1.5}{s+3} \\
X(j\omega) &= j\omega + \frac{-0.5}{j\omega+1} + \frac{1.5}{j\omega+3}
\end{aligned}
$$

Thus, $X(j\omega) \overset{FT}{\leftrightarrow} x(t) = \delta'(t) + \left(-\frac{1}{2}e^{-t} + \frac{3}{2}e^{-3t}\right)u(t).$

Exercise 5.4

Consider the feedback interconnection in Figure 5.32 of two causal LTI differential systems defined by $S_1: \frac{dy(t)}{dt} + y(t) = x(t)$, $S_2: \frac{dy(t)}{dt} + 2y(t) = \frac{dx(t)}{dt} + x(t)$.

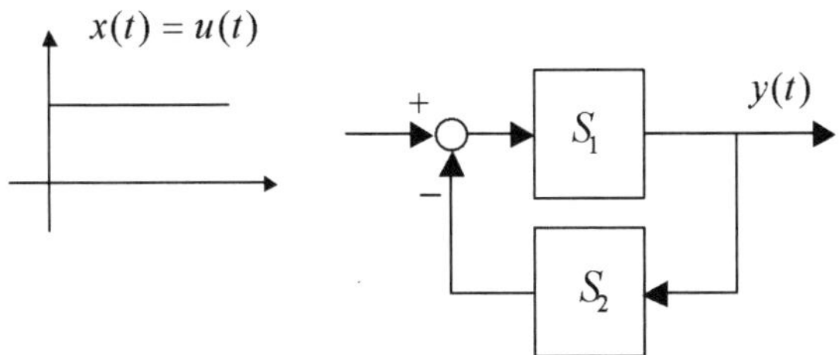

FIGURE 5.32 Feedback interconnection of two LTI systems in Exercise 5.4.

(a) Find the frequency response of the overall system $H(j\omega)$ and plot its magnitude and phase using MATLAB.

Answer:

$$S_1: \ (j\omega)Y(j\omega)+Y(j\omega)=X(j\omega)$$
$$\Rightarrow H_1(j\omega)=\frac{Y(j\omega)}{X(j\omega)}=\frac{1}{j\omega+1}$$
$$S_2: \ (j\omega)Y(j\omega)+2Y(j\omega)=(j\omega)X(j\omega)+X(j\omega)$$
$$\Rightarrow H_2(j\omega)=\frac{Y(j\omega)}{X(j\omega)}=\frac{j\omega+1}{j\omega+2}$$

The overall closed-loop frequency response is obtained by first writing the loop equations for the error signal $e(t)$ (output of the summing junction) and the output.

$$E(j\omega)=X(j\omega)+H_2(j\omega)H_1(j\omega)E(j\omega)$$
$$Y(j\omega)=H_1(j\omega)E(j\omega)$$

Solving the first equation for $E(j\omega)$, we obtain

$$E(j\omega)=\frac{1}{1+H_2(j\omega)H_1(j\omega)}X(j\omega)$$
$$Y(j\omega)=\underbrace{\frac{H_1(j\omega)}{1+H_2(j\omega)H_1(j\omega)}}_{H(j\omega)}X(j\omega).$$

Thus,

$$H(j\omega)=\frac{H_1(j\omega)}{1+H_2(j\omega)H_1(j\omega)}=\frac{\frac{1}{j\omega+1}}{1+\frac{1}{j\omega+1}\frac{j\omega+1}{j\omega+2}}$$
$$=\frac{\frac{1}{j\omega+1}}{1+\frac{1}{j\omega+2}}=\frac{j\omega+2}{(j\omega+3)(j\omega+1)}.$$

Magnitude and phase:

$$|H(j\omega)| = \frac{\sqrt{\omega^2+4}}{\sqrt{\omega^2+9}\sqrt{\omega^2+1}}$$

$$\angle H(j\omega) = \arctan\left(\frac{\omega}{2}\right) + \arctan\left(\frac{-\omega}{3}\right) + \arctan\left(\frac{-\omega}{1}\right)$$

Using MATLAB, we obtain the frequency response plots of Figure 5.33. These so-called Bode plots have a logarithmic frequency axis and a logarithmic scale for the magnitude as well (more on Bode plots in Chapter 8.)

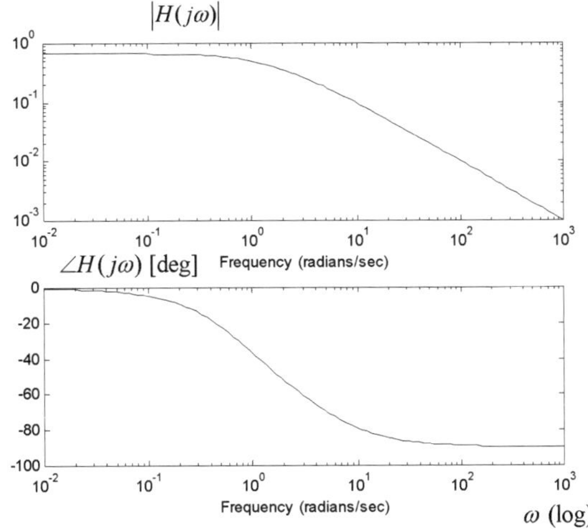

FIGURE 5.33 Frequency response of feedback system in Exercise 5.4(a).

(b) Find the output signal $y(t)$ (the step response) using the Fourier transform technique and sketch it.

Answer:

$$Y(j\omega) = H(j\omega)X(j\omega) = \frac{j\omega+2}{(j\omega+3)(j\omega+1)}\left(\frac{1}{j\omega} + \pi\delta(\omega)\right)$$

$$= \frac{j\omega+2}{(j\omega)(j\omega+3)(j\omega+1)} + \frac{2}{3}\pi\delta(\omega)$$

$$= \frac{-\frac{1}{6}}{j\omega+3} + \frac{-\frac{1}{2}}{j\omega+1} + \frac{\frac{2}{3}}{j\omega} + \frac{2}{3}\pi\delta(\omega)$$

Taking the inverse transform, we obtain the step response shown in Figure 5.34.

$$y(t)=\frac{2}{3}u(t)+\left[-\frac{1}{6}e^{-3t}-\frac{1}{2}e^{-t}\right]u(t)$$

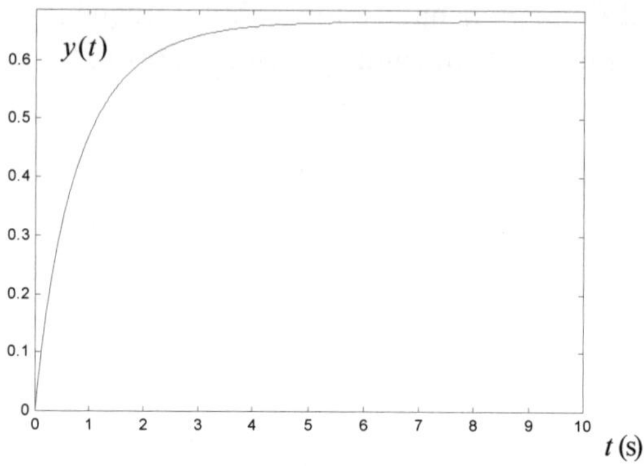

FIGURE 5.34 Step response of feedback system in Exercise 5.4(b).

Exercises

Exercise 5.5

Compute the energy-density spectrum of the signal $x(t)=e^{-5(t-2)}u(t-2)$. Now, suppose that this signal is filtered by a unit-gain ideal bandpass filter with cutoff frequencies $\omega_{c1}=2\,\text{rad/s}$, $\omega_{c2}=4\,\text{rad/s}$. Compute the total energy contained in the output signal of the filter.

Answer:

ON THE CD

Exercise 5.6

Compute the Fourier transform of the signal $x(t)$ shown in Figure 5.35.

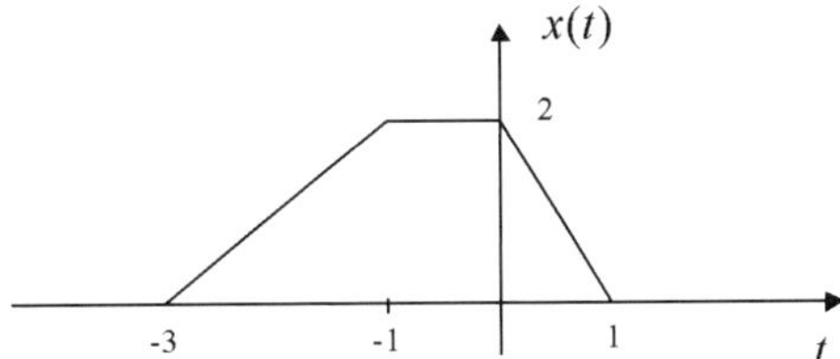

FIGURE 5.35 Signal in Exercise 5.6.

Exercise 5.7

Find the time-domain signal corresponding to the Fourier transform:

$$X(j\omega) = \frac{j\omega + 1}{j4\omega + 4 - \omega^2}.$$

Answer:

Exercise 5.8

Sketch the signal $x(t) = e^{(t-1)}\left[u(t) - u(t-1)\right] + e^{-(t-1)}\left[u(t-1) - u(t-3)\right]$ and compute its Fourier transform.

Exercise 5.9

Find the time-domain signals corresponding to the following Fourier transforms. You can use Table D.1 of Fourier transform pairs.

(a) $X(j\omega) = \dfrac{j\omega + 2}{j\omega(j\omega + 5)} + \dfrac{2\pi}{5}\delta(\omega)$

(b) $X(j\omega) = \dfrac{j\omega + 1}{-\omega^2 + j2\sqrt{2}\omega + 4}$

(c) $X(j\omega) = \dfrac{\sin(\omega)}{\omega}$

(d) $H(j\omega) = \begin{cases} 1, & \omega_{c1} < |\omega| < \omega_{c2} \\ 0, & \text{otherwise} \end{cases}$, where $\omega_{c1} < \omega_{c2}$

Answer:

Exercise 5.10

Compute the Fourier transform of the periodic signal $x(t)$ shown in Figure 5.36.

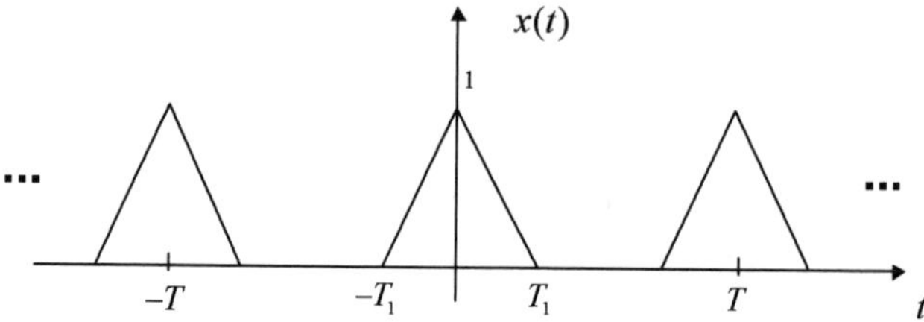

FIGURE 5.36 Periodic triangular waveform of Exercise 5.10.

Exercise 5.11

Find the inverse Fourier transform $x(t)$ of $X(j\omega)$, whose magnitude and phase are shown in Figure 5.37.

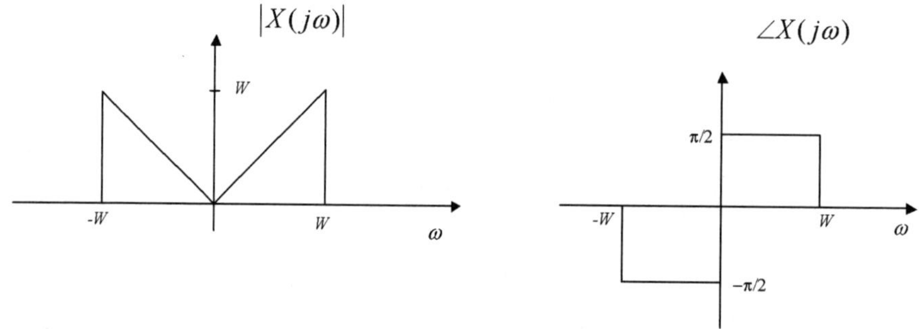

FIGURE 5.37 Magnitude and phase of Fourier transform in Exercise 5.11.

Answer:

6 The Laplace Transform

In This Chapter

((Lecture 20: Definition of the Laplace Transform))

So far, we have studied the Fourier series and the Fourier transform for the analysis of periodic and aperiodic signals, and linear time-invariant (LTI) systems. These tools are useful because they allow us to analyze continuous-time signals and systems in the frequency domain. In particular, signals can be represented as linear combinations of periodic complex exponentials, which are eigenfunctions of LTI systems, but if we replace $j\omega$ with the more general complex variable s in the Fourier transform equations, we obtain the Laplace transform, a generalization of the Fourier transform.

The Fourier transform was defined only for signals that taper off at infinity, that is, signals of finite energy or signals that are absolutely integrable. On the other hand, the Laplace transform of an unbounded signal or of an unstable impulse response can be defined. The Laplace transform can also be used to analyze differential LTI systems with nonzero initial conditions.

DEFINITION OF THE TWO-SIDED LAPLACE TRANSFORM

The two-sided Laplace transform of $x(t)$ is defined as follows:

$$X(s) := \int_{-\infty}^{+\infty} x(t)e^{-st}\,dt, \tag{6.1}$$

where s is a complex variable. Notice that the Fourier transform is given by the same equation, but with $s = j\omega$.

Let the complex variable be written as $s = \sigma + j\omega$. Then the Laplace transform can be interpreted as the Fourier transform of the signal $x(t)e^{-\sigma t}$:

$$X(\sigma + j\omega) = \int_{-\infty}^{+\infty} \left[x(t)e^{-\sigma t} \right] e^{-j\omega t}\,dt. \tag{6.2}$$

Given $x(t)$, this integral may or may not converge, depending on the value of σ (the real part of s).

Example 6.1: Let us find the Laplace transform of the signal $x(t) = e^{-at}u(t),\ a \in \mathbb{R}$ shown in Figure 6.1.

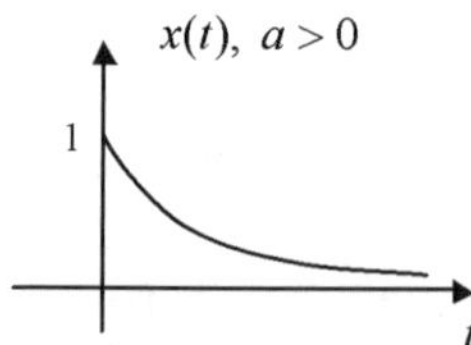

FIGURE 6.1 Real decaying exponential signal.

$$
\begin{aligned}
X(s) &= \int_{-\infty}^{+\infty} e^{-at}u(t)e^{-st}\,dt \\
&= \int_{0}^{+\infty} e^{-(s+a)t}\,dt \\
&= \frac{1}{s+a}, \quad \operatorname{Re}\{s\} > -a
\end{aligned}
\tag{6.3}
$$

This Laplace transform converges only for values of s in the open half-plane to the right of $s=-a$. This half-plane is the region of convergence (ROC) of the Laplace transform. It is depicted in Figure 6.2.

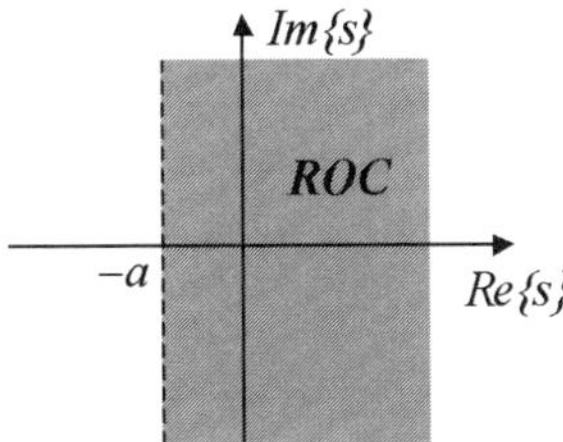

FIGURE 6.2 Region of convergence of Laplace transform of $x(t) = e^{-at}u(t)$, $a \in \mathbb{R}$.

Recall that the Fourier transform of $x(t)=e^{-at}u(t)$, $a \in \mathbb{R}$ converges only for $a>0$ (decaying exponential), whereas its Laplace transform converges for any a (even for growing exponentials), as long as $\operatorname{Re}\{s\}>-a$. In other words, the Fourier transform of $x(t)e^{-\sigma t} = e^{-(a+\sigma)t}u(t)$ converges for $\sigma > -a$.

Example 6.2: Find the Laplace transform of the signal $x(t)=e^{-at}u(-t)$, $a \in \mathbb{R}$ shown in Figure 6.3.

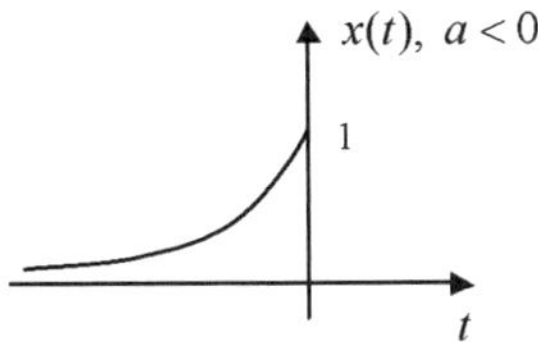

FIGURE 6.3 Real growing exponential signal identically zero at positive times.

$$
\begin{aligned}
X(s) &= \int_{-\infty}^{+\infty} e^{-at}u(-t)e^{-st}\,dt \\
&= \int_{-\infty}^{0} e^{-(s+a)t}\,dt \\
&= -\frac{1}{s+a}, \quad \operatorname{Re}\{s\} < -a
\end{aligned} \tag{6.4}
$$

This Laplace transform converges only in the ROC that is the open half-plane to the left of $s=-a$ (see Figure 6.4).

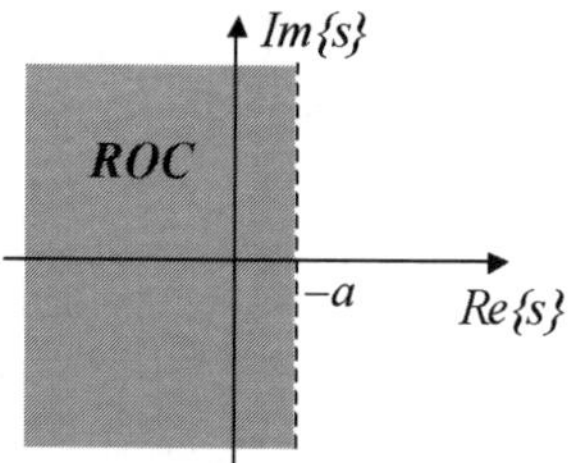

FIGURE 6.4 Region of convergence of Laplace transform of $x(t) = e^{-at}u(-t)$, $a \in \mathbb{R}$.

Important note: *The ROC is an integral part of a Laplace transform. It must be specified. Without it, we cannot tell what the corresponding time-domain signal is.*

INVERSE LAPLACE TRANSFORM

The inverse Laplace transform is in general given by the following integral:

$$
x(t) := \frac{1}{2\pi j}\int_{\sigma-j\infty}^{\sigma+j\infty} X(s)e^{st}\,ds. \tag{6.5}
$$

This contour integral, where the contour in the ROC is parallel to the imaginary axis and wraps around at infinity on the side that includes all the poles of $X(s)$ within the contour, is rarely used because we are mostly dealing with linear systems and standard signals whose Laplace transforms are found in tables of Laplace transform pairs such as Table D.4 in Appendix D. Thus, in this book we will mainly use the partial fraction expansion technique to find the continuous-time signal corresponding to a Laplace transform.

Before turning our attention to partial fraction expansion, let us look at one example of how the contour integral and the residue theorem are used to compute the inverse Laplace transform of a simple rational function $X(s), s \in \text{ROC}$. Assume for simplicity that all the poles of $X(s)$ are distinct. Recall that in the theory of complex functions, the residue at the simple pole s_0 of a given analytic function $X(s)$ is given by $\text{Res}_{s=s_0}\{X(s)\} = \left[(s-s_0)X(s)\right]_{s=s_0}$. For instance, if $X(s) = \frac{1}{(s+1)(s+2)}$, then the residue at the pole –2 is given by $\text{Res}_{s=-2}\{X(s)\} = \left[(s+2)X(s)\right]_{s=-2} = -1$.

The well-known residue theorem in the context of the Laplace transform basically states that, given an analytic function $F(s)$ with N poles $\{p_k\}_{k=1}^{N}$, and given a simple closed contour C lying in the region of analyticity of $F(s)$ (here the ROC) but encircling all of its poles, the following contour integral evaluates to

$$\oint_C F(s)ds = 2\pi j \sum_{k=1}^{N} \text{Res}_{s=p_k}\{F(s)\}. \tag{6.6}$$

The residue theorem can be directly applied to the contour integral of Equation 6.5 with $F(s) = X(s)e^{st}$ and the contour C defined as a vertical line in the ROC, wrapping around at infinity in the complex plane so as to encircle all the poles of $X(s)e^{st}$, which turn out to be the same as the poles of $X(s)$.

Example 6.3: Let us compute the inverse Laplace transform of $X(s) = \frac{1}{s-a}$, $a \in \mathbb{C}, \quad \text{Re}\{s\} > \text{Re}\{a\}$. We will see later that the first piece of information that we can use is that the ROC is specified to be a right half-plane, which tells us that $x(t)$ will be right-sided. In addition, this Laplace transform is rational, so $x(t)$ will be zero at negative times.

Using Equation 6.5, we get

$$\begin{aligned} x(t) &= u(t)\frac{1}{2\pi j}\int_{\sigma-j\infty}^{\sigma+j\infty} \frac{1}{s-a}e^{st}ds, \quad \sigma > \text{Re}\{a\} \\ &= u(t)\frac{1}{2\pi j}\underbrace{(2\pi j)\text{Res}_{s=a}\left\{\frac{1}{s-a}e^{st}\right\}}_{\text{residue theorem}} \\ &= e^{at}u(t). \end{aligned} \tag{6.7}$$

Similarly, for $X(s) = \frac{1}{s-a}$, $a \in \mathbb{C}, \quad \text{Re}\{s\} < \text{Re}\{a\}$, that is, the ROC is specified to be a left half-plane to the left of the pole a, we would use a contour C consisting of a vertical line in the ROC wrapping around at infinity in the right half-plane to encircle the pole, in the clockwise direction, and we would finally compute the signal to be $x(t) = -e^{at}u(-t)$, where the negative sign in front comes from the fact that the contour must be traversed clockwise instead of counterclockwise.

Partial Fraction Expansion

In the previous example, we were able to find the inverse Laplace transforms of two first-order Laplace transforms, one leading to a right-sided complex exponential signal, and the other leading to a left-sided complex exponential signal. These two inverse transforms are the foundation for a technique known as *partial fraction expansion*. Assuming there is no multiple-order pole in the set of poles $\{p_k\}_{k=1}^{N}$ of the rational transform $X(s)$, and assuming that the order of the denominator polynomial is greater than the order of the numerator polynomial, we can always expand $X(s)$ as a sum of partial fractions:

$$X(s) = \sum_{k=1}^{N} \frac{A_k}{s - p_k}. \tag{6.8}$$

From the ROC of $X(s)$, the ROC of each of the individual terms in Equation 6.8 can be found, and then the inverse transform of each one of these terms can be determined. If the ROC of the term $\frac{A_i}{s-p_i}$ is to the right of the pole at $s = p_i$, then the inverse transform of this term is $A_i e^{p_i t}u(t)$, a right-sided signal. If, on the other hand, the ROC is to the left of the pole at $s = p_i$ for the term $\frac{A_i}{s-p_i}$, then its inverse transform is $-A_i e^{p_i t}u(-t)$, a left-sided signal. Note that the poles and their associated coefficients can be real or complex. Adding the inverse transforms of the individual terms in Equation 6.8 yields the inverse transform of $X(s)$.

The technique of partial fraction expansion of a rational Laplace transform is introduced here and will be illustrated by means of a few examples. As discussed above, the idea behind the partial fraction expansion is to expand a Laplace transform $X(s)$ as a sum of first-order rational functions. Assuming for the moment that $X(s)$ has distinct poles $\{p_k\}_{k=1}^{N}$, each one of the first-order fractions contains one of the poles:

$$X(s) = \underbrace{\sum_{k=1}^{N} \frac{A_k}{s - p_k}}_{s \in ROC} = \underbrace{\frac{A_1}{s - p_1}}_{s \in ROC_1} + \underbrace{\frac{A_2}{s - p_2}}_{s \in ROC_2} + \cdots + \underbrace{\frac{A_N}{s - p_N}}_{s \in ROC_N}. \tag{6.9}$$

Then, using Table D.4 of Laplace transform pairs, one can easily obtain the time-domain signal $x(t)$. Assuming that the ROC of $X(s)$ is an open right half-plane, then all the ROCs of the partial fractions must also be open right half-planes for consistency. In fact, ROC of $X(s)$ must at least contain the intersection of all the ROCs of the fractions $\text{ROC} \supseteq \bigcap_{i=1,\ldots,N} \text{ROC}_i$. Then we have

$$x(t) = A_1 e^{p_1 t} u(t) + A_2 e^{p_2 t} u(t) + \cdots + A_N e^{p_N t} u(t). \tag{6.10}$$

If the ROC of $X(s)$ is an open left half-plane, then all the ROCs of the partial fractions must also be open left half-planes, and we get

$$x(t) = -A_1 e^{p_1 t} u(-t) - A_2 e^{p_2 t} u(-t) - \cdots - A_N e^{p_N t} u(-t). \tag{6.11}$$

The last case to consider for $X(s)$ with distinct poles is when the ROC of $X(s)$ is an open vertical strip between two adjacent poles, for example, p_m to the left and p_{m+1} to the right, without loss of generality. In this case, all the poles to the left of, and including, p_m must have their ROCs as open right half-planes, and all the poles to the right of, and including, p_{m+1} must have their ROCs as open left half-planes. Then, $\text{ROC} \supseteq \bigcap_{i=1,\ldots,N} \text{ROC}_i$ holds and we have

$$\underbrace{X(s)}_{\text{Re}\{p_m\}<\text{Re}\{s\}<\text{Re}\{p_{m+1}\}} = \underbrace{\frac{A_1}{s-p_1}}_{\text{Re}\{s\}>\text{Re}\{p_1\}} + \underbrace{\frac{A_2}{s-p_2}}_{\text{Re}\{s\}>\text{Re}\{p_2\}} + \cdots + \underbrace{\frac{A_m}{s-p_m}}_{\text{Re}\{s\}>\text{Re}\{p_m\}} + \underbrace{\frac{A_{m+1}}{s-p_{m+1}}}_{\text{Re}\{s\}<\text{Re}\{p_{m+1}\}} + \cdots + \underbrace{\frac{A_N}{s-p_N}}_{\text{Re}\{s\}<\text{Re}\{p_N\}}. \tag{6.12}$$

For multiple poles in $X(s)$, the partial fraction expansion must contain fractions with all the powers of the multiple poles up to their multiplicity. To illustrate this, consider $X(s)$ with ROC $\text{Re}\{s\} > \text{Re}\{p_N\}$ and with one multiple pole p_m of multiplicity r, that is,

$$X(s) = \frac{n(s)}{(s-p_1)\cdots(s-p_{m-1})(s-p_m)^r(s-p_{m+1})\cdots(s-p_N)}, \tag{6.13}$$

where $n(s)$ is the numerator polynomial. Its partial fraction expansion is

$$\begin{aligned} \underbrace{X(s)}_{\text{Re}\{s\}>\text{Re}\{p_N\}} = {} & \underbrace{\frac{A_1}{s-p_1}}_{\text{Re}\{s\}>\text{Re}\{p_1\}} + \cdots + \underbrace{\frac{A_m}{s-p_m}}_{\text{Re}\{s\}>\text{Re}\{p_m\}} + \underbrace{\frac{A_{m+1}}{(s-p_m)^2}}_{\text{Re}\{s\}>\text{Re}\{p_m\}} + \cdots + \underbrace{\frac{A_{m+r-1}}{(s-p_m)^r}}_{\text{Re}\{s\}>\text{Re}\{p_m\}} \\ & + \underbrace{\frac{A_{m+r}}{s-p_{m+1}}}_{\text{Re}\{s\}>\text{Re}\{p_{m+1}\}} + \cdots + \underbrace{\frac{A_{N+r-1}}{s-p_N}}_{\text{Re}\{s\}>\text{Re}\{p_N\}}. \end{aligned} \tag{6.14}$$

The question now is, How do we compute the coefficients A_i for a given Laplace transform? For a single pole p_k, coefficient A_k is simply the residue at the pole, that is,

$$A_k = \operatorname{Res}_{s=p_k}\{X(s)\} = \left[(s-p_k)X(s)\right]_{s=p_k}.$$

Example 6.4: Let us compute the inverse of the following Laplace transform:

$$X(s) = \frac{s+3}{s(s+1)(s-2)}, \quad 0 < \operatorname{Re}\{s\} < 2. \tag{6.15}$$

$$\begin{aligned} X(s) &= \frac{s+3}{s(s+1)(s-2)}, \quad 0 < \operatorname{Re}\{s\} < 2 \\ &= \underbrace{\frac{A_1}{s+1}}_{s\in ROC_1} + \underbrace{\frac{A_2}{s}}_{s\in ROC_2} + \underbrace{\frac{A_3}{s-2}}_{s\in ROC_3} \end{aligned} \tag{6.16}$$

In order to have $\mathrm{ROC} \supseteq \mathrm{ROC}_1 \cap \mathrm{ROC}_2 \cap \mathrm{ROC}_3$, the only possibility for the individual fractions' ROCs is the following:

$$\mathrm{ROC}_1 = \{s \in \mathbb{C} : \operatorname{Re}\{s\} > -1\},\ \mathrm{ROC}_2 = \{s \in \mathbb{C} : \operatorname{Re}\{s\} > 0\},\ \mathrm{ROC}_3 = \{s \in \mathbb{C} : \operatorname{Re}\{s\} < 2\}.$$

Thus,

$$X(s) = \underbrace{\frac{A_1}{s+1}}_{\operatorname{Re}\{s\}>-1} + \underbrace{\frac{A_2}{s}}_{\operatorname{Re}\{s\}>0} + \underbrace{\frac{A_3}{s-2}}_{\operatorname{Re}\{s\}<2}. \tag{6.17}$$

We compute coefficient A_1:

$$A_1 = (s+1)\left(\frac{(s+3)}{s(s+1)(s-2)}\right)_{s=-1} = \frac{2}{(-1)(-3)} = \frac{2}{3}, \tag{6.18}$$

Then, we obtain coefficient A_2:

$$A_2 = s\left(\frac{(s+3)}{s(s+1)(s-2)}\right)_{s=0} = \frac{3}{(1)(-2)} = -\frac{3}{2}. \tag{6.19}$$

Finally, coefficient A_3 is computed:

$$A_3 = (s-2)\left(\frac{(s+3)}{s(s+1)(s-2)}\right)_{s=2} = \frac{5}{(2)(3)} = \frac{5}{6}. \tag{6.20}$$

Hence, the transfer function can be expanded as

$$X(s) = \frac{2}{3}\underbrace{\frac{1}{s+1}}_{\text{Re}\{s\}>-1} - \frac{3}{2}\underbrace{\frac{1}{s}}_{\text{Re}\{s\}>0} + \frac{5}{6}\underbrace{\frac{1}{s-2}}_{\text{Re}\{s\}<2}, \tag{6.21}$$

and from Table D.4 of Laplace transform pairs, we obtain the signal

$$x(t) = \frac{2}{3}e^{-t}u(t) - \frac{3}{2}u(t) - \frac{5}{6}e^{2t}u(-t). \tag{6.22}$$

For a multiple pole p_m of multiplicity r, the coefficients $A_m, \ldots, A_{m+r-1}$ are computed as follows:

$$A_{m+r-i} = \frac{1}{(i-1)!}\frac{d^{i-1}}{ds^{i-1}}\left[(s-p_m)^r X(s)\right]_{s=p_m}, i = 1, \ldots, r, \tag{6.23}$$

where $0! = 1$ by convention. To compute the coefficient of the term with the highest power of the repeated pole, we simply have to compute

$$A_{m+r-1} = \left[(s-p_m)^r X(s)\right]_{s=p_m}. \tag{6.24}$$

It should be clear that after multiplication by $(s-p_m)^r$ on both sides of Equation 6.14, all the terms on the right-hand side will vanish upon letting $s = p_m$, except the term $\frac{A_{m+r-1}}{(s-p_m)^r}$, which yields A_{m+r-1}. Now, consider the computation of A_{m+r-2} using the formula $A_{m+r-2} = \frac{d}{ds}\left[(s-p_m)^r X(s)\right]_{s=p_m}$. After multiplication by $(s-p_m)^r$, the terms on the right-hand side corresponding to the multiple pole become

$$(s-p_m)^{r-1} A_m + (s-p_m)^{r-2} A_{m+1} + \cdots + (s-p_m)A_{m+r-2} + A_{m+r-1}. \tag{6.25}$$

After differentiating with respect to s and letting $s = p_m$, we obtain

$$\left[(r-1)(s-p_m)^{r-2} A_m + (r-2)(s-p_m)^{r-3} A_{m+1} + \cdots + 2(s-p_m)A_{m+r-3} + A_{m+r-2}\right]_{s=p_m} = A_{m+r-2} \tag{6.26}$$

All the other terms of the partial fraction expansion disappear.

In practice, differentiating $X(s)$ can be tedious. Thus, at least for a pen and paper solution of a simple problem with only one double pole, one can compute coefficient A_{m+1} as in Equation 6.24, and the other coefficient A_m can be computed by multiplying both sides of the partial fraction equation by $(s-p_m)$ and by letting $s\to\infty$, which yields

$$A_m=\left[(s-p_m)X(s)\right]_{s\to\infty}-\left(A_1+A_2+\cdots+A_{m-1}+A_{m+2}+\cdots+A_N\right). \qquad (6.27)$$

Example 6.5:

$$X(s)=\frac{s-2}{(s+1)(s+3)^2}=\frac{A_1}{s+3}+\frac{A_2}{(s+3)^2}+\frac{A_3}{s+1},\ \mathrm{Re}\{s\}>-1 \qquad (6.28)$$

Let us compute coefficient A_3 first:

$$A_3=\left.\frac{s-2}{(s+3)^2}\right|_{s=-1}=-\frac{3}{4}. \qquad (6.29)$$

We then compute coefficient A_2:

$$A_2=\left.\frac{s-2}{s+1}\right|_{s=-3}=\frac{5}{2}. \qquad (6.30)$$

Finally, coefficient A_1 is found:

$$A_1=\left.\frac{s-2}{(s+1)(s+3)}\right|_{s\to\infty}-\left(-\frac{3}{4}\right)=\frac{3}{4}. \qquad (6.31)$$

Hence, we have

$$X(s)=\frac{3}{4}\underbrace{\frac{1}{s+3}}_{\mathrm{Re}\{s\}>-3}+\frac{5}{2}\underbrace{\frac{1}{(s+3)^2}}_{\mathrm{Re}\{s\}>-3}-\frac{3}{4}\underbrace{\frac{1}{s+1}}_{\mathrm{Re}\{s\}>-1}. \qquad (6.32)$$

We can check that this partial fraction expansion is correct by bringing all the terms together with a common denominator:

$$\begin{aligned}
X(s) &= \frac{3}{4}\frac{1}{s+3} + \frac{5}{2}\frac{1}{(s+3)^2} - \frac{3}{4}\frac{1}{s+1} \\
&= \frac{3(s+1)(s+3)+10(s+1)-3(s+3)^2}{4(s+1)(s+3)^2} \\
&= \frac{3s^2+12s+9+10s+10-3s^2-18s-27}{4(s+1)(s+3)^2} \\
&= \frac{4s-8}{4(s+1)(s+3)^2} = \frac{s-2}{(s+1)(s+3)^2}.
\end{aligned} \tag{6.33}$$

Finally, using Table D.4 of Laplace transform pairs, we obtain

$$x(t) = \left[\frac{3}{4}e^{-3t} + \frac{5}{2}te^{-3t} - \frac{3}{4}e^{-t}\right]u(t) \tag{6.34}$$

A pair of complex conjugate poles in a Laplace transform can be dealt with individually using the residue technique outlined above. The two complex coefficients obtained are complex conjugates of each other. A pair of complex conjugate poles can also be treated by including a second-order term in the partial fraction expansion. The idea is to make use of the damped or growing sinusoids in the table of Laplace transforms, such as

$$e^{-\alpha t}\sin(\omega_0 t) \overset{L}{\leftrightarrow} \frac{\omega_0}{(s+\alpha)^2+\omega_0{}^2}, \quad \mathrm{Re}\{s\} > -\alpha, \tag{6.35}$$

$$e^{-\alpha t}\cos(\omega_0 t) \overset{L}{\leftrightarrow} \frac{s+\alpha}{(s+\alpha)^2+\omega_0{}^2}, \quad \mathrm{Re}\{s\} > -\alpha \tag{6.36}$$

by creating a term $\frac{A\omega_0 + B(s+\alpha)}{(s+\alpha)^2+\omega_0{}^2}$ in the partial fraction expansion. It is perhaps best to explain this technique by means of an example.

Example 6.6: Let us compute the inverse of the following Laplace transform:

$$X(s) = \frac{2s^2+3s-2}{\left(s^2+2s+4\right)s}, \quad \mathrm{Re}\{s\} > 0. \tag{6.37}$$

Note that $s^2+2s+4 = (s+1)^2 + (\sqrt{3})^2$, so that the complex poles are $p_1 = -1 + j\sqrt{3}$ and $p_1 = -1 - j\sqrt{3}$. The transform $X(s)$ can be expanded as follows:

$$X(s)=\frac{2s^2+3s-2}{\left(s^2+2s+4\right)s}=\underbrace{\frac{A\sqrt{3}+B(s+1)}{(s+1)^2+3}}_{\mathrm{Re}\{s\}>-1}+\underbrace{\frac{C}{s}}_{\mathrm{Re}\{s\}>0}. \tag{6.38}$$

Coefficient C is easily obtained with the residue technique: $C=\frac{1}{2}$. Now, let $s=-1$ to compute $\frac{-3}{-3}=\frac{1}{\sqrt{3}}A+\frac{1}{2}\Rightarrow A=\frac{\sqrt{3}}{2}$, and then multiply both sides by s and let $s\to\infty$ to get $B=5/2$. Then we have the following expansion:

$$\begin{aligned}X(s)&=\underbrace{\frac{\frac{\sqrt{3}}{2}(\sqrt{3})+\frac{5}{2}(s+1)}{(s+1)^2+3}}_{\mathrm{Re}\{s\}>-1}-\underbrace{\frac{1/2}{s}}_{\mathrm{Re}\{s\}>0}\\&=\underbrace{\frac{\frac{\sqrt{3}}{2}(\sqrt{3})}{(s+1)^2+3}}_{\mathrm{Re}\{s\}>-1}+\underbrace{\frac{\frac{5}{2}(s+1)}{(s+1)^2+3}}_{\mathrm{Re}\{s\}>-1}-\underbrace{\frac{1/2}{s}}_{\mathrm{Re}\{s\}>0}.\end{aligned} \tag{6.39}$$

Taking the inverse Laplace transform using Table D.4, we obtain

$$x(t)=\left[\frac{\sqrt{3}}{2}e^{-t}\sin(\sqrt{3}t)+\frac{5}{2}e^{-t}\cos(\sqrt{3}t)\right]u(t)-\frac{1}{2}u(t). \tag{6.40}$$

CONVERGENCE OF THE TWO-SIDED LAPLACE TRANSFORM

As mentioned above, the convergence of the integral in Equation 6.1 depends on the value of the real part of the complex Laplace variable. Thus, the ROC in the complex plane or s-plane is either a vertical half-plane, a vertical strip, or nothing. We have seen two examples above that led to open half-plane ROCs. Here is a signal for which the Laplace transform only converges in an open vertical strip.

Example 6.7: Consider the double-sided signal $x(t)=e^{-2t}u(t)+e^{t}u(-t)$ shown in Figure 6.5.

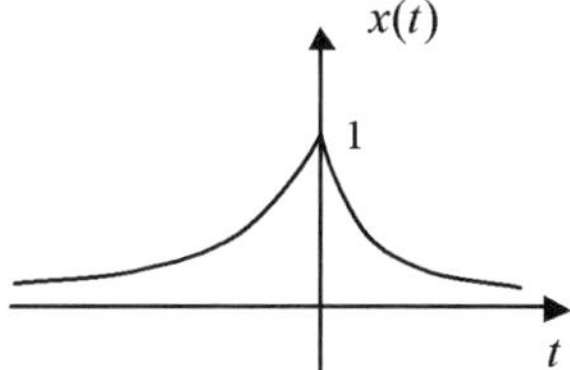

FIGURE 6.5 Double-sided signal.

Its Laplace transform is given by

$$X(s) = \int_{-\infty}^{+\infty} e^{-2t}u(t)e^{-st}dt + \int_{-\infty}^{+\infty} e^{t}u(-t)e^{-st}dt$$

$$= \int_{0}^{+\infty} e^{-(s+2)t}dt + \int_{-\infty}^{0} e^{-(s-1)t}dt$$

$$= \frac{1}{s+2} - \frac{1}{s-1}, \quad \text{Re}\{s\} > -2 \text{ and } \text{Re}\{s\} < 1$$

$$= \frac{-3}{s^2+s-2}, \quad -2 < \text{Re}\{s\} < 1 \qquad (6.41)$$

The ROC is a vertical strip between the real parts –2 and 1, as shown in Figure 6.6.

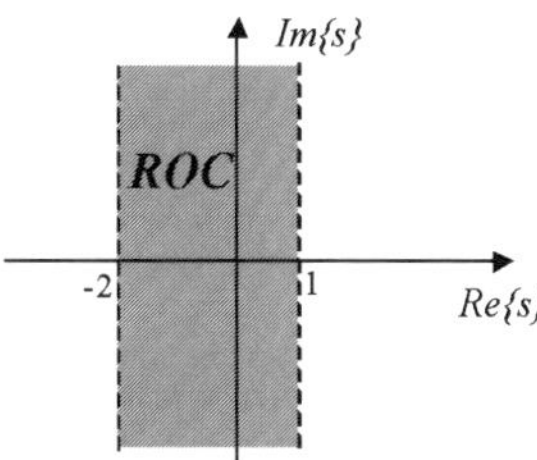

FIGURE 6.6 Region of convergence of Laplace transform of the double-sided signal.

POLES AND ZEROS OF RATIONAL LAPLACE TRANSFORMS

Complex or real exponential signals have rational Laplace transforms. That is, they are ratios of a numerator polynomial and a denominator polynomial.

$$X(s) = \frac{n(s)}{d(s)} \tag{6.42}$$

The zeros of the numerator $n(s)$ are called the *zeros* of the Laplace transform. If z_1 is a zero, then $X(z_1) = 0$. The zeros of the denominator $d(s)$ are called the *poles* of the Laplace transform. If p_1 is a pole, then $X(p_1) = \infty$.

Example 6.8: $X(s) = \frac{2s+1}{s^2+s-2}$, $-2 < \mathrm{Re}\{s\} < 1$ has poles at $p_1 = 1,\ p_2 = -2$.

For differential LTI systems, the zeros of the characteristic polynomial are equal to the poles of the Laplace transform of the impulse response.

((Lecture 21: Properties of the Laplace Transform, Transfer Function of an LTI System))

PROPERTIES OF THE TWO-SIDED LAPLACE TRANSFORM

The properties of the two-sided Laplace transform are similar to those of the Fourier transform, but one must pay attention to the ROCs. Take for example the sum of two Laplace transforms: the resulting Laplace transform exists if and only if the two original ROCs have a nonempty intersection in the complex plane. Note that the properties of the Laplace transform described in this section are summarized in Table D.5 of Appendix D.

Linearity

The Laplace transform is linear. If $x_1(t) \overset{L}{\leftrightarrow} X_1(s),\ s \in \mathrm{ROC}_1$ and $x_2(t) \overset{L}{\leftrightarrow} X_2(s)$, $s \in \mathrm{ROC}_2$, then

$$ax_1(t) + bx_2(t) \overset{L}{\leftrightarrow} aX_1(s) + bX_2(s),\ s \in \mathrm{ROC} \supseteq \mathrm{ROC}_1 \cap \mathrm{ROC}_2. \tag{6.43}$$

Time Shifting

If $x(t) \overset{L}{\leftrightarrow} X(s),\ s \in \mathrm{ROC}$, then

$$x(t - t_0) \overset{L}{\leftrightarrow} e^{-st_0} X(s),\ s \in \mathrm{ROC}. \tag{6.44}$$

Example 6.9: Consider an LTI system with an impulse response that is a unit rectangular pulse of duration T: $h(t) = u(t) - u(t - T)$. Then

$$H(s) = \frac{1}{s} - e^{-sT}\frac{1}{s} = \frac{1-e^{-sT}}{s}, \quad \forall s. \tag{6.45}$$

Note that the ROC is the whole complex plane because the impulse response is of finite support. There is no pole at $s = 0$.

Shifting in the s-Domain

If $x(t) \overset{L}{\leftrightarrow} X(s),\ s \in \text{ROC}$, then

$$e^{s_0 t}x(t) \overset{L}{\leftrightarrow} X(s - s_0),\ s \in \text{ROC+Re}\{s_0\}, \tag{6.46}$$

where the new ROC is the original one shifted by $\text{Re}\{s_0\}$, to the right if this number is positive, to the left otherwise.

Time Scaling

If $x(t) \overset{L}{\leftrightarrow} X(s),\ s \in \text{ROC}$, then

$$x(\alpha t) \overset{L}{\leftrightarrow} \frac{1}{|\alpha|} X\left(\frac{s}{\alpha}\right),\ s \in \frac{1}{\alpha}\text{ROC}, \tag{6.47}$$

where the new ROC is the original one, expanded or contracted by $1/|\alpha|$ and flipped around the imaginary axis if $\alpha < 0$.

Example 6.10: Consider a signal $x(t)$ whose Laplace transform has the ROC shown on the left in Figure 6.7. After the time expansion and reversal $x(-0.5t)$, the resulting Laplace transform has the ROC shown on the right in Figure 6.7.

$$x(-0.5t) \overset{L}{\leftrightarrow} 2X(-2s),\ s \in -2\text{ROC} \tag{6.48}$$

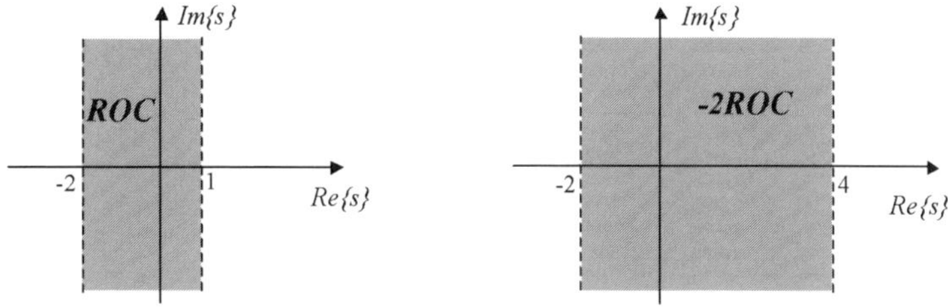

FIGURE 6.7 Expansion of region of convergence after time scaling.

Conjugation

If $x(t) \overset{L}{\leftrightarrow} X(s),\ s \in \text{ROC}$, then

$$x^*(t) \overset{L}{\leftrightarrow} X^*(s^*),\ s \in \text{ROC}. \tag{6.49}$$

Therefore, for $x(t)$ real, $X(s) = X^*(s^*)$.

An important consequence is that if $x(t)$ is real and $X(s)$ has a pole (or zero) at $s = s_0$, then $X(s)$ has also a pole (or zero) at the complex conjugate point $s = s_0^*$. Thus, *the complex poles and zeros of the Laplace transform of a real signal always come in conjugate pairs.*

Convolution Property

If $x_1(t) \overset{L}{\leftrightarrow} X_1(s),\ s \in \text{ROC}_1$ and $x_2(t) \overset{L}{\leftrightarrow} X_2(s),\ s \in \text{ROC}_2$, then

$$x_1(t) * x_2(t) \overset{L}{\leftrightarrow} X_1(s)X_2(s),\ s \in \text{ROC} \supseteq \text{ROC}_1 \cap \text{ROC}_2. \tag{6.50}$$

This is of course an extremely useful property for LTI system analysis. Note that the resulting ROC includes the intersection of the two original ROCs, but it may be larger, for example, when a pole-zero cancellation occurs.

Example 6.11: The response of the LTI system with $h(t) = \left[e^{-2t} + e^{-t}\right]u(t)$ to the input $x(t) = -e^{-2t}u(t) + \delta(t)$ is given by the inverse Laplace transform of $Y(s)$:

$$\begin{aligned} h(t) &\overset{L}{\leftrightarrow} H(s) = \frac{2s+3}{(s+2)(s+1)},\ \text{Re}\{s\} > -1 \\ x(t) &\overset{L}{\leftrightarrow} X(s) = \frac{-1}{s+2} + 1 = \frac{s+1}{s+2},\ \text{Re}\{s\} > -2 \end{aligned} \tag{6.51}$$

and

$$\begin{aligned} Y(s) = H(s)X(s) &= \frac{(2s+3)}{(s+2)(s+1)}\frac{(s+1)}{(s+2)},\ \{s : \text{Re}\{s\} > -2\} \cap \{s : \text{Re}\{s\} > -1\} = \{s : \text{Re}\{s\} > -1\} \\ &= \frac{(2s+3)}{(s+2)^2},\ \text{Re}\{s\} > -2 \text{ (after the pole-zero cancellation).} \end{aligned} \tag{6.52}$$

Expanding this transform into partial fractions, we get

$$Y(s) = \frac{(2s+3)}{(s+2)^2} = \frac{A}{(s+2)} + \frac{B}{(s+2)^2},\ \text{Re}\{s\} > -2. \tag{6.53}$$

We find coefficient B first:

$$\left.\frac{(2s+3)}{1}\right|_{s=-2} = -1 = B, \tag{6.54}$$

and coefficient A is then obtained:

$$\left.\frac{2s+3}{s+2}\right|_{s=+\infty} = 2 = A. \tag{6.55}$$

Therefore, using Table D.4 of Laplace transform pairs, we obtain

$$y(t) = \left[2e^{-2t} - te^{-2t}\right]u(t). \tag{6.56}$$

Differentiation in the Time Domain

If $x(t) \overset{L}{\leftrightarrow} X(s),\ s \in \text{ROC}$, then

$$\frac{dx(t)}{dt} \overset{L}{\leftrightarrow} sX(s),\ s \in \text{ROC}_1 \supseteq \text{ROC}, \tag{6.57}$$

ROC_1 can be larger than ROC, namely when there is a pole-zero cancellation at $s = 0$.

Differentiation in the Frequency Domain

If $x(t) \overset{L}{\leftrightarrow} X(s),\ s \in \text{ROC}$, then

$$-tx(t) \overset{L}{\leftrightarrow} \frac{dX(s)}{ds},\ s \in \text{ROC}. \tag{6.58}$$

This property is useful to obtain the Laplace transform of signals of the form $x(t) = te^{-at}u(t)$.

Integration in the Time Domain

If $x(t) \overset{L}{\leftrightarrow} X(s),\ s \in \text{ROC}$, then:

$$\int_{-\infty}^{t} x(\tau)d\tau \overset{L}{\leftrightarrow} \frac{1}{s}X(s),\ s \in \text{ROC}_1 \supseteq \text{ROC} \cap \left\{s{:}\text{Re}\{s\}{>}0\right\}. \tag{6.59}$$

For example, since the unit step response of an LTI system is given by the running integral of its impulse response $s(t)=\int_{-\infty}^{t} h(\tau)d\tau$, we have $S(s)=\frac{1}{s}H(s)$ with the appropriate ROC. Note that ROC_1 can be bigger than the intersection, namely when there is a pole-zero cancellation at $s=0$.

The Initial and Final Value Theorems

Under the assumptions that $x(t)=0$ for $t<0$ and that it contains no impulse or higher order singularity, one can directly calculate the initial value $x(0^+)$ and the final value $x(+\infty)$ using the Laplace transform.

The *initial-value theorem* states that

$$x(0^+)=\lim_{s\to+\infty} sX(s), \tag{6.60}$$

and the *final-value theorem* states that

$$\lim_{t\to+\infty} x(t)=\lim_{s\to 0} sX(s). \tag{6.61}$$

A typical use of the final-value theorem is to find the settling value of the output of a system.

Example 6.12: Let us find the final value of the step response of the causal LTI system with $h(t)\overset{L}{\leftrightarrow}H(s)=\frac{s+1}{s+4}$, $\mathrm{Re}\{s\}>-4$, shown in Figure 6.8.

$$y(+\infty)=\lim_{s\to 0} sY(s)=\lim_{s\to 0} s\frac{1}{s}\frac{(s+1)}{(s+4)}=\frac{1}{4} \tag{6.62}$$

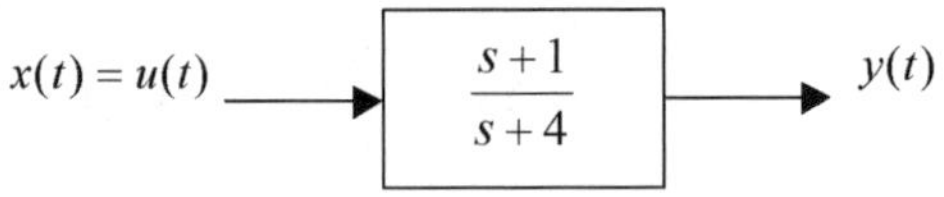

FIGURE 6.8 System subjected to a step input.

Note that in the above example, the multiplication by s cancels out the output's pole at the origin. Thus, it is sufficient to evaluate the system's Laplace transform at $s=0$ to obtain the final value. This is true for most problems of this type, that is, finding the final value of the step response of a system.

ANALYSIS AND CHARACTERIZATION OF LTI SYSTEMS USING THE LAPLACE TRANSFORM

We have seen that the convolution property makes the Laplace transform useful to obtain the response of an LTI system to an arbitrary input (with a Laplace transform). Specifically, the Laplace transform of the output of an LTI system with impulse response $h(t)$ is simply given by

$$Y(s) = H(s)X(s), \quad \mathrm{ROC}_Y \supseteq \mathrm{ROC}_H \cap \mathrm{ROC}_X. \tag{6.63}$$

Also recall that the frequency response of the system is $H(j\omega) = H(s)\big|_{s=j\omega}$.

The Laplace transform $H(s)$ of the impulse response is called the *transfer function*. Many properties of LTI systems are associated with the characteristics of their transfer functions.

Causality

Recall that $h(t) = 0$ for $t < 0$ for a causal system and thus is right-sided. Therefore, *the ROC associated with the transfer function of a causal system is a right half-plane.*

The converse is not true. For example, a right-sided signal starting at $t = -10$ also leads to an ROC that is a right half-plane. However, if we know that the transfer function is *rational*, then it suffices to check that the ROC is the right half-plane to the right of the rightmost pole in the s-plane to conclude that the system is causal.

Example 6.13: The transfer function $H(s) = \frac{1}{s+1}$, $\mathrm{Re}\{s\} > -1$ corresponds to a causal system. On the other hand, the transfer function $H_1(s) = \frac{e^s}{s+1}$, $\mathrm{Re}\{s\} > -1$ is noncausal (causal $h(t)$ time-advanced by 1), whereas $H_2(s) = \frac{e^{-s}}{s+1}$, $\mathrm{Re}\{s\} > -1$ is causal (causal $h(t)$ time-delayed by 1).

Stability

So far, we have seen that bounded-input bounded-output (BIBO) stability of a continuous-time LTI system is equivalent to its impulse response being absolutely integrable, in which case its Fourier transform converges. Also, the stability of an LTI *differential* system is equivalent to having all the zeros of its characteristic polynomial having a negative real part.

For the Laplace transform, the first stability condition translates into the following:

- An LTI system is stable if and only if the ROC of its transfer function contains the $j\omega$-axis.

Example 6.14: Consider an LTI system with proper transfer function:

$$H(s)=\frac{s(s+1)}{(s+2)(s-1)}. \tag{6.64}$$

Three possible ROCs could be associated with this transfer function. Table 6.1 gives the impulse response for each ROC. Only one ROC leads to a stable system. Note that the system poles are marked with an X and the system zeros are marked with an O in the *s*-plane.

First, let us compute the partial fraction expansion of *H*(*s*):

$$H(s)=\frac{s(s+1)}{(s+2)(s-1)}=A+\frac{B}{s-1}+\frac{C}{s+2}. \tag{6.65}$$

To obtain *A*, let $s\rightarrow\infty$: *A* = 1. Then, we find the coefficient *B*:

$$B=\left.\frac{s(s+1)}{(s+2)}\right|_{s=1}=\frac{2}{3}, \tag{6.66}$$

and finally we get coefficient *C*:

$$C=\left.\frac{s(s+1)}{(s-1)}\right|_{s=-2}=-\frac{2}{3}. \tag{6.67}$$

Hence, the transfer function can be expanded as

$$H(s)=\frac{s(s+1)}{(s+2)(s-1)}=1+\frac{2}{3}\frac{1}{s-1}-\frac{2}{3}\frac{1}{s+2}. \tag{6.68}$$

The first term is constant and corresponds to an impulse $\delta(t)$. The two other terms are partial fractions that can correspond to right-sided or left-sided signals, depending on the chosen ROCs, as presented in Table 6.1.

The stability condition for a *causal* LTI system with a *proper, rational* transfer function is stated as follows. Note that a large class of causal differential LTI systems have rational transfer functions.

- A causal system with a proper rational transfer function *H*(*s*) is stable if and only if all of its poles are in the left-half of the *s*-plane; that is, if all of the poles have negative real parts.

TABLE 6.1 Correspondence Between a Transfer Function and Its Impulse Response Depending on the ROC

ROC	h(t)	Causal	Stable
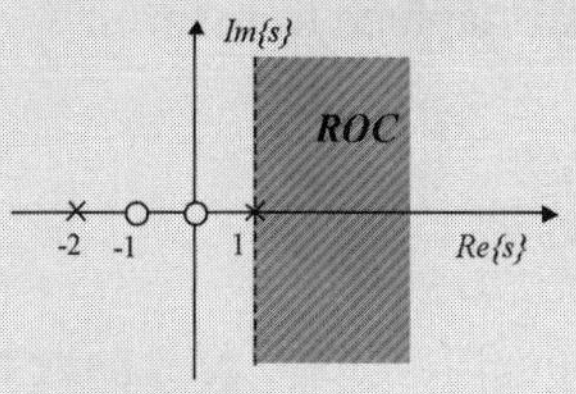	$h(t)=\left[\frac{2}{3}e^{t}-\frac{2}{3}e^{-2t}\right]u(t)+\delta(t)$	Yes ROC is a right half-plane	No
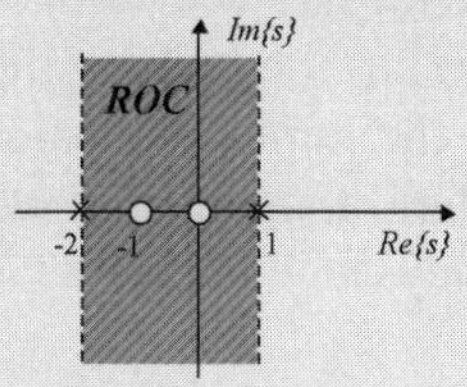	$h(t)=-\frac{2}{3}e^{t}u(-t)-\frac{2}{3}e^{-2t}u(t)$ $+\delta(t)$	No	Yes $j\omega$-axis lies in the ROC
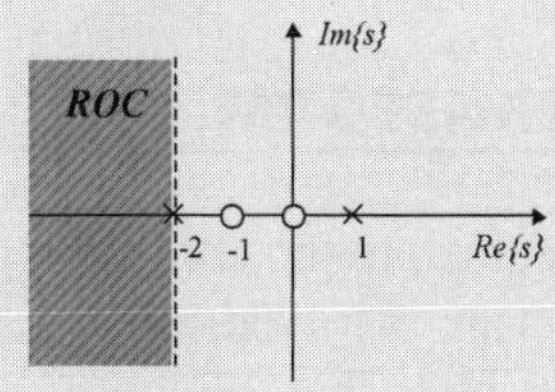	$h(t)=\left[-\frac{2}{3}e^{t}+\frac{2}{3}e^{-2t}\right]u(-t)$ $+\delta(t)$	No	No

Notice that the transfer function must be proper; otherwise when the degree of the numerator exceeds that of the denominator, the impulse response contains the derivative of an impulse that is not absolutely integrable.

((Lecture 22: Definition and Properties of the Unilateral Laplace Transform))

DEFINITION OF THE UNILATERAL LAPLACE TRANSFORM

The *one-sided,* or *unilateral,* Laplace transform of $x(t)$ is defined as follows:

$$\mathcal{X}(s) := \int_{0^-}^{+\infty} x(t)e^{-st}\,dt, \qquad (6.69)$$

where s is a complex variable. Notice that this transform considers only the signal for nonnegative times. The lower limit of integration is $t=0^-$, which means that singular functions such as impulses at $t = 0$ will be taken into account in the unilateral Laplace transform.

We will use the following notation for the unilateral Laplace transform:

$$x(t)\overset{UL}{\leftrightarrow}\mathcal{X}(s)=\mathcal{UL}\{x(t)\}. \tag{6.70}$$

Note that two signals that differ for $t < 0$ but are equal for $t\geq 0$ will have the same unilateral Laplace transform. Also note that the unilateral Laplace transform of $x(t)$ is identical to the two-sided Laplace transform of $x(t)u(t)$, assuming there is no impulse at $t = 0$. A direct consequence of this is that the Laplace transform properties for causal, right-sided signals apply to the unilateral transform as well. Moreover, the ROC of a unilateral Laplace transform is always an open right half-plane or the entire s-plane.

PROPERTIES OF THE UNILATERAL LAPLACE TRANSFORM

The properties of the unilateral Laplace transform are identical to those of the regular two-sided Laplace transform, except when time shifts are involved, which can make part of the signal "disappear" to the negative times. Note that the following properties are summarized in Table D.6 of Appendix D.

Linearity

The unilateral Laplace transform is linear. If $x_1(t)\overset{UL}{\leftrightarrow}\mathcal{X}_1(s),\ s\in \text{ROC}_1$ and $x_2(t)\overset{UL}{\leftrightarrow}\mathcal{X}_2(s),\ s\in \text{ROC}_2$, then

$$ax_1(t)+bx_2(t)\overset{UL}{\leftrightarrow}a\mathcal{X}_1(s)+b\mathcal{X}_2(s),\ s\in \text{ROC}\supseteq \text{ROC}_1\cap \text{ROC}_2. \tag{6.71}$$

Time Delay

For $x(t)=0, t<0$, if $x(t)\overset{UL}{\leftrightarrow}\mathcal{X}(s),\ s\in \text{ROC}$, then for a time delay of $t_0>0$,

$$x(t-t_0)\overset{UL}{\leftrightarrow}e^{-st_0}\mathcal{X}(s),\ s\in \text{ROC}, t_0>0. \tag{6.72}$$

Thus, for a time delay, this time-shifting property is exactly the same as that for the two-sided Laplace transform. In the case where $x(t)$ is nonzero at negative times, a time delay can make a part of the signal "appear" at positive times, which could change the unilateral Laplace transform. For a time advance, the part of the signal shifted to negative times is lost. In both of these cases there is no simple relationship between the resulting and the original unilateral transforms.

Shifting in the s-Domain

If $x(t) \overset{UL}{\leftrightarrow} \mathcal{X}(s),\ s \in \text{ROC}$, then

$$e^{s_0 t} x(t) \overset{UL}{\leftrightarrow} \mathcal{X}(s - s_0),\ s \in \text{ROC+Re}\{s_0\}, \tag{6.73}$$

where the new ROC is the original one shifted by $\text{Re}\{s_0\}$, to the right if this number is positive, to the left otherwise.

Time Scaling

If $x(t) \overset{UL}{\leftrightarrow} \mathcal{X}(s),\ s \in \text{ROC}$, then for $\alpha > 0$,

$$x(\alpha t) \overset{UL}{\leftrightarrow} \frac{1}{\alpha}\mathcal{X}\left(\frac{s}{\alpha}\right),\ s \in \frac{1}{\alpha}\text{ROC}, \tag{6.64}$$

where the new ROC is the original one, expanded or contracted by $1/\alpha$.

Conjugation

If $x(t) \overset{UL}{\leftrightarrow} \mathcal{X}(s),\ s \in \text{ROC}$, then

$$x^*(t) \overset{UL}{\leftrightarrow} \mathcal{X}^*(s^*),\ s \in \text{ROC}. \tag{6.75}$$

Therefore, for $x(t)$ real, $\mathcal{X}(s) = \mathcal{X}^*(s^*)$, and we have the important consequence that *the complex poles and zeros of the unilateral Laplace transform of a real signal always come in conjugate pairs.*

Convolution Property

Assume that $x_1(t) = x_2(t) = 0$ for $t < 0$. If $x_1(t) \overset{UL}{\leftrightarrow} \mathcal{X}_1(s),\ s \in \text{ROC}_1$ and $x_2(t) \overset{UL}{\leftrightarrow} \mathcal{X}_2(s),\ s \in \text{ROC}_2$, then

$$x_1(t) * x_2(t) \overset{UL}{\leftrightarrow} \mathcal{X}_1(s)\mathcal{X}_2(s),\ s \in \text{ROC} \supseteq \text{ROC}_1 \cap \text{ROC}_2. \tag{6.76}$$

This is a useful property for *causal* LTI system analysis with signals that are identically zero at negative times.

Differentiation in the Time Domain

The differentiation property of the unilateral Laplace transform is particularly useful for analyzing the response of causal differential systems to nonzero initial conditions.

If $x(t) \overset{UL}{\leftrightarrow} \mathcal{X}(s),\ s \in \text{ROC}$, then

$$\frac{dx(t)}{dt} \overset{UL}{\leftrightarrow} s\mathcal{X}(s) - x(0^-),\ s \in \text{ROC}_1 \supseteq \text{ROC}. \tag{6.77}$$

ROC_1 can be larger than ROC when there is a pole-zero cancellation at $s = 0$. Note that the value $x(0^-)$ is 0 for signals that are identically 0 for $t < 0$, but not for signals that extend to negative times. Furthermore, $x(0^-)$ can be used to set an initial condition on the output of a causal differential system as shown in Example 6.15.

Example 6.15: Let us calculate the output of the following homogeneous causal LTI differential system with initial condition $y(0^-)$:

$$\tau_0 \frac{dy(t)}{dt} + y(t) = 0. \tag{6.78}$$

We take the unilateral Laplace transform on both sides:

$$\tau_0 \left[s\mathcal{Y}(s) - y(0^-) \right] + \mathcal{Y}(s) = 0. \tag{6.79}$$

Solving for $\mathcal{Y}(s)$, we obtain

$$\mathcal{Y}(s) = \frac{y(0^-)}{s + \frac{1}{\tau_0}},\ \text{Re}\{s\} > -\frac{1}{\tau_0}, \tag{6.80}$$

which corresponds to the time-domain output signal:

$$y(t) = y(0^-) e^{-\frac{t}{\tau_0}} u(t). \tag{6.81}$$

Note that the unilateral Laplace transform of the nth-order derivative of $x(t)$ is given by the following formula, which is derived by successive applications of Equation 6.77.

$$\frac{d^n x(t)}{dt^n} \overset{UL}{\leftrightarrow} s^n \mathcal{X}(s) - s^{n-1} x(0^-) - \ldots - s \frac{d^{n-2} x(0^-)}{dt^{n-2}} - \frac{d^{n-1} x(0^-)}{dt^{n-1}},$$
$$s \in \text{ROC}_1 \supseteq \text{ROC} \tag{6.82}$$

Differentiation in the Frequency Domain

If $x(t)\overset{UL}{\leftrightarrow}\mathcal{X}(s),\ s\in \text{ROC}$, then

$$-tx(t)\overset{UL}{\leftrightarrow}\frac{d\mathcal{X}(s)}{ds},\quad s\in \text{ROC}. \tag{6.83}$$

Integration in the Time Domain

If $x(t)\overset{UL}{\leftrightarrow}\mathcal{X}(s),\ s\in \text{ROC}$, then

$$\int_0^t x(\tau)d\tau \overset{UL}{\leftrightarrow}\frac{1}{s}\mathcal{X}(s),\quad s\in \text{ROC}_1 \supseteq \text{ROC}\cap\{s:\text{Re}\{s\}>0\}. \tag{6.84}$$

The Initial and Final Value Theorems

Even though these theorems were introduced as two-sided Laplace transform properties, they are basically unilateral transform properties, as they apply only to signals that are identically 0 for $t<0$.

The *initial-value theorem* states that

$$x(0^+) = \lim_{s\to+\infty} s\mathcal{X}(s), \tag{6.85}$$

and the *final-value theorem* states that

$$\lim_{s\to+\infty} x(t) = \lim_{s\to 0} s\mathcal{X}(s). \tag{6.86}$$

Example 6.16: Let us find the initial value $x(0^+)$ of the signal whose unilateral Laplace transform is $\mathcal{X}(s)=\frac{10}{s-3},\ \text{Re}\{s\}>3$:

$$x(0^+) = \lim_{s\to+\infty} s\mathcal{X}(s) = \lim_{s\to+\infty} s\frac{10}{s-3} = 10. \tag{6.87}$$

SUMMARY

In this chapter, we introduced the Laplace transform of a continuous-time signal as a generalization of the Fourier transform.

- The Laplace transform can be defined for signals that tend to infinity, as long as the integral converges for some values of the complex variable s. The set of all such values in the complex plane is the region of convergence of the Laplace transform.
- The inverse Laplace transform is given by a contour integral in the complex plane, and the residue theorem can be used to solve it. However, the Laplace transforms that we have to deal with in engineering are often rational functions, and these can be inverted by first expanding the transform into a sum of partial fractions, and then by using a table of basic Laplace transform pairs. The region of convergence of each individual fraction must be found to select the correct time-domain signal in the table.
- We discussed many of the properties of Laplace transforms, but one is particularly useful in engineering: the convolution property, which states that the Laplace transform of the convolution of two signals is equal to the product of their Laplace transforms. This allows us to compute a convolution, for example, to obtain the output signal of an LTI system, simply by forming and inverting the product of two Laplace transforms.
- The Fourier transform of a signal is simply equal to its Laplace transform evaluated on the $j\omega$-axis, provided that it is included in the region of convergence.
- The unilateral Laplace transform was introduced mostly for its differentiation property, which proves particularly useful in solving for the response of differential systems with initial conditions.

TO PROBE FURTHER

References on the Laplace transform include Oppenheim, Willsky, and Nawab, 1997; Kamen and Heck, 1999; and Haykin and Van Veen, 2002. The theory of complex variables and complex functions is covered in Brown and Churchill, 2004.

EXERCISES

Exercises with Solutions

Exercise 6.1

Compute the Laplace transforms of the following three signals (find the numerical values of ω_0 and θ in (c) first). Specify their ROC. Find their Fourier transforms if they exist.

(a) $x_1(t) = 10e^{-(t-2)}u(t-2) + 10e^{0.5(t-2)}u(-t+2)$ as shown in Figure 6.9.

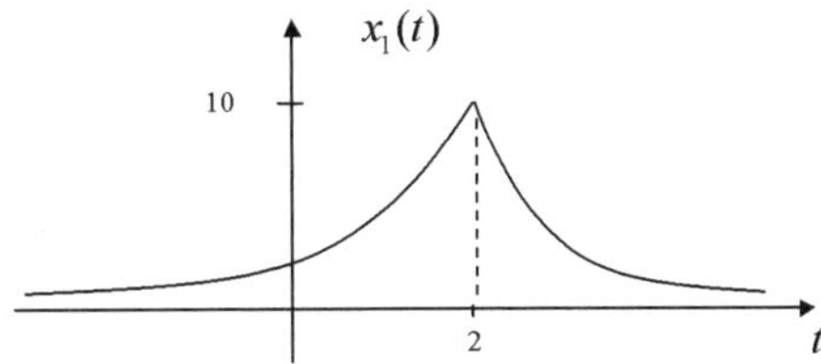

FIGURE 6.9 Double-sided signal of Exercise 6.1(a).

Answer:
Using Table D.4 and the time-shifting property, we get

$$\begin{aligned} x_1(t) &= 10e^{-(t-2)}u(t-2) + 10e^{0.5(t-2)}u(-t+2) \\ &= 10e^{-(t-2)}u(t-2) + 10e^{0.5(t-2)}u(-(t-2)) \end{aligned}$$

$$\begin{aligned} X_1(s) &= 10\underbrace{\frac{e^{-2s}}{s+1}}_{\mathrm{Re}\{s\}>-1} - 10\underbrace{\frac{e^{-2s}}{s-0.5}}_{\mathrm{Re}\{s\}<0.5} \\ &= 10e^{-2s}\frac{s-0.5-s-1}{(s+1)(s-0.5)}, \quad -1<\mathrm{Re}\{s\}<0.5 \\ &= \frac{-15e^{-2s}}{(s+1)(s-0.5)}, \quad -1<\mathrm{Re}\{s\}<0.5. \end{aligned}$$

The Fourier transform exists since the ROC contains the imaginary axis, that is, $s = j\omega$. It is given by

$$\begin{aligned} X_1(j\omega) &= \frac{-15e^{-2j\omega}}{(j\omega+1)(j\omega-0.5)} \\ &= \frac{15e^{-2j\omega}}{(0.5+\omega^2)-0.5j\omega}. \end{aligned}$$

(b) Signal $x_2(t)$ shown in Figure 6.10.

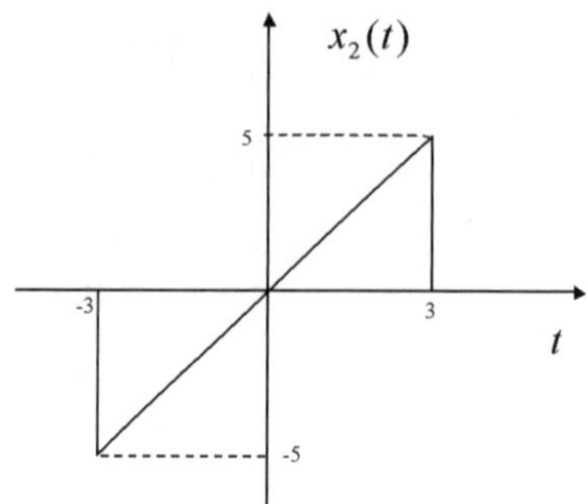

FIGURE 6.10 Sawtooth signal of Exercise 6.1(b).

Answer:

We can compute this one by using the integral defining the Laplace transform. Here $x_2(t)$ has finite support; hence the Laplace transform integral converges for all s.

$$
\begin{aligned}
X_2(s) &= \frac{5}{3}\int_{-3}^{3} te^{-st}\,dt \\
&= -\frac{5}{3}\frac{te^{-st}}{s}\bigg|_{-3}^{3} + \frac{5}{3s}\int_{-3}^{3} e^{-st}\,dt \\
&= -\frac{5}{3}\frac{3e^{-3s}+3e^{3s}}{s} - \frac{5}{3}\frac{(e^{-3s}-e^{3s})}{s^2}, \quad \forall s \\
&= -\frac{5e^{-3s}+5e^{3s}}{s} - \frac{5}{3}\frac{(e^{-3s}-e^{3s})}{s^2}, \quad \forall s \\
&= \frac{(-15s-5)e^{-3s}-(15s-5)e^{3s}}{3s^2}, \quad \forall s \\
&= \frac{(-5s-5/3)e^{-3s}-(5s-5/3)e^{3s}}{s^2}, \quad \forall s
\end{aligned}
$$

The Fourier transform of this signal is given by

$$\begin{aligned}
X_2(j\omega) &= \frac{(-5j\omega - 5/3)e^{-3j\omega} - (5j\omega - 5/3)e^{3j\omega}}{-\omega^2} \\
&= \frac{-5j\omega(e^{3j\omega} + e^{-3j\omega}) + 5/3(e^{3j\omega} - e^{-3j\omega})}{-\omega^2} \\
&= \frac{5j(e^{3j\omega} + e^{-3j\omega})}{\omega} - \frac{5/3(e^{3j\omega} - e^{-3j\omega})}{\omega^2} \\
&= \frac{10j\cos(3\omega)}{\omega} - \frac{10j\sin(3\omega)}{3\omega^2} \\
&= 10j\frac{3\omega\cos(3\omega) - \sin(3\omega)}{3\omega^2}
\end{aligned}$$

It is odd and purely imaginary, as expected. Applying L'Hopital's rule twice, we can also check that $X_2(j0)$ is finite, as it should be.

(c) Damped sinusoid signal $x_3(t) = e^{-10t}\sin(\omega_0 t + \theta)u(t)$ of Figure 6.11.

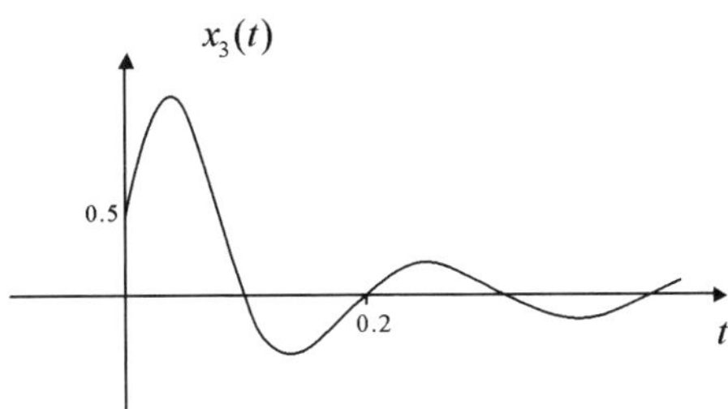

FIGURE 6.11 Damped sinusoid signal of Exercise 6.1(c).

Answer:
Let us first find the values of the parameters θ and ω_0. We have

$$\begin{aligned}
x_3(0) &= 0.5 = \sin(\theta) \\
\theta &= \arcsin(0.5) \\
\theta &= \frac{\pi}{6}
\end{aligned}$$

and

$$x_3(0.2) = 0 = e^{-2}\sin(0.2\omega_0 + \frac{\pi}{6})$$

$$\Leftrightarrow 0.2\omega_0 + \frac{\pi}{6} = k\pi,\ k \in \mathbb{Z}$$

here $k = 2$

$$\omega_0 = 5\left(2\pi - \frac{\pi}{6}\right) = \frac{55\pi}{6}\text{ rad/s}$$

The signal's Laplace transform can be obtained as follows:

$$\begin{aligned}
x_3(t) &= e^{-10t}\sin(\frac{55\pi}{6}t + \frac{\pi}{6})u(t) \\
&= e^{-10t}\left(\frac{e^{j\frac{55\pi}{6}t + j\frac{\pi}{6}} - e^{-j\frac{55\pi}{6}t - j\frac{\pi}{6}}}{2j}\right)u(t) \\
&= e^{-10t}\left(\frac{e^{j\frac{\pi}{6}}e^{j\frac{55\pi}{6}t} - e^{-j\frac{\pi}{6}}e^{-j\frac{55\pi}{6}t}}{2j}\right)u(t) \\
&= e^{-10t}\left(\frac{2j\,\mathrm{Im}\left\{e^{j\frac{\pi}{6}}e^{j\frac{55\pi}{6}t}\right\}}{2j}\right)u(t) \\
&= e^{-10t}\left(\cos\frac{\pi}{6}\sin\frac{55\pi}{6}t + \sin\frac{\pi}{6}\cos\frac{55\pi}{6}t\right)u(t) \\
&= e^{-10t}\left(\frac{\sqrt{3}}{2}\sin\frac{55\pi}{6}t + \frac{1}{2}\cos\frac{55\pi}{6}t\right)u(t) \\
&= \left(\frac{\sqrt{3}}{2}e^{-10t}\sin\frac{55\pi}{6}t + \frac{1}{2}e^{-10t}\cos\frac{55\pi}{6}t\right)u(t)
\end{aligned}$$

Using Table D.4, we get

$$X_3(s) = \frac{\sqrt{3}}{2}\underbrace{\frac{\frac{55\pi}{6}}{(s+10)^2 + \left(\frac{55\pi}{6}\right)^2}}_{\mathrm{Re}\{s\}>-10} + \frac{1}{2}\underbrace{\frac{s+10}{(s+10)^2 + \left(\frac{55\pi}{6}\right)^2}}_{\mathrm{Re}\{s\}>-10}$$

$$= \frac{1}{2}\frac{s + \frac{55\pi\sqrt{3}}{6} + 10}{(s+10)^2 + \left(\frac{55\pi}{6}\right)^2}, \quad \mathrm{Re}\{s\} > -10$$

$$= \frac{1}{2}\frac{s + 59.88}{s^2 + 20s + 929.3}, \quad \mathrm{Re}\{s\} > -10$$

The Fourier transform of $x_3(t)$ exists since the imaginary axis lies in the ROC.

$$X_3(j\omega) = \frac{1}{2}\frac{j\omega + 59.88}{929.3 - \omega^2 + 20\,j\omega}$$

Exercise 6.2

For the causal LTI system $H(s) = \frac{1}{s+1}$, $\mathrm{Re}\{s\} > -1$ shown in Figure 6.12, find the output responses $y_1(t)$ and $y_3(t)$ to the input signals $x_1(t)$ and $x_3(t)$ of Exercise 6.1.

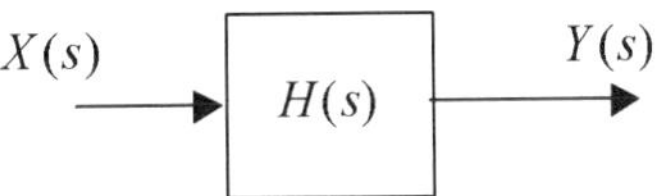

FIGURE 6.12 Causal LTI system of Exercise 6.2.

The Laplace transform of the output response $y_1(t)$ is given by

$$Y_1(s) = H(s)X_1(s)$$

$$= \frac{-15e^{-2s}}{(s+1)^2(s-0.5)}, \quad -1 < \mathrm{Re}\{s\} < 0.5$$

$$= e^{-2s}\left[\underbrace{\frac{A}{(s+1)^2}}_{\mathrm{Re}\{s\}>-1} + \underbrace{\frac{B}{s+1}}_{\mathrm{Re}\{s\}>-1} + \underbrace{\frac{C}{s-0.5}}_{\mathrm{Re}\{s\}<0.5}\right]$$

The coefficients are computed:

$$Y_1(s) = e^{-2s}\left[\underbrace{\frac{10}{(s+1)^2}}_{\mathrm{Re}\{s\}>-1} + \underbrace{\frac{6.667}{s+1}}_{\mathrm{Re}\{s\}>-1} - \underbrace{\frac{6.667}{s-0.5}}_{\mathrm{Re}\{s\}<0.5}\right],$$

and taking the inverse Laplace transform, we get

$$y_1(t) = 10(t-2)e^{-(t-2)}u(t-2) + 6.667e^{-(t-2)}u(t-2) + 6.667e^{0.5(t-2)}u(-t+2).$$

The Laplace transform of the output response $y_3(t)$ is given by

$$\begin{aligned} Y_3(s) &= H(s)X_3(s) \\ &= \frac{1}{2}\frac{s+59.88}{(s+1)(s^2+20s+929.3)}, \quad \mathrm{Re}\{s\} > -1 \\ &= \underbrace{\frac{A}{s+1}}_{\mathrm{Re}\{s\}>-1} + \underbrace{\frac{B(s+10)+28.80C}{s^2+20s+929.3}}_{\mathrm{Re}\{s\}>-10} \end{aligned}$$

We find the coefficients by first multiplying on both sides by the common denominator and then by identifying the coefficients of the polynomials.

$$\begin{aligned} s+59.88 &= 2A\left(s^2+20s+929.3\right) + 2\left[B(s+10)+28.80C\right](s+1) \\ &= 2(A+B)s^2 + \left(40A+22B+57.6C\right)s + 1858.6A + 20B + 57.6C \end{aligned}$$

We obtain the linear vector equation:

$$\begin{bmatrix} 1 & 1 & 0 \\ 40 & 22 & 57.6 \\ 1858.6 & 20 & 57.6 \end{bmatrix}\begin{bmatrix} A \\ B \\ C \end{bmatrix} = \begin{bmatrix} 0 \\ 1 \\ 59.88 \end{bmatrix},$$

from which we compute

$$\begin{bmatrix} A \\ B \\ C \end{bmatrix} = \begin{bmatrix} 0.0323 \\ -0.0323 \\ 0.0073 \end{bmatrix}.$$

Thus,

$$Y_3(s) = \underbrace{\frac{0.0323}{s+1}}_{\mathrm{Re}\{s\}>-1} + \underbrace{\frac{-0.0323(s+10)+28.8(0.0073)}{s^2+20s+929.3}}_{\mathrm{Re}\{s\}>-10},$$

and taking the inverse Laplace transform, we get

$$y_3(t) = 0.0323e^{-t}u(t) - 0.0323e^{-10t}\cos(28.8t)u(t) + 0.0073e^{-10t}\sin(28.8t)u(t).$$

Exercise 6.3

Find all possible ROCs for the transfer function $H(s) = \frac{1}{(s^2+3s+3)(s-3)}$ and give the corresponding impulse responses. Specify for each ROC whether the corresponding system is causal and stable.

Answer:

The complex poles are found by identifying the damping ratio ζ and undamped natural frequency ω_n of the second-order denominator factor with the standard second-order polynomial $s^2 + 2\zeta\omega_n + \omega_n^2$. Here $\omega_n = \sqrt{3},\ \zeta = \frac{\sqrt{3}}{2}$. Thus, the poles are

$$p_1 = 3$$

$$p_2 = -\zeta\omega_n + j\omega_n\sqrt{1-\zeta^2} = -\frac{3}{2} + j\frac{\sqrt{3}}{2}$$

$$p_3 = p_2^* = -\frac{3}{2} - j\frac{\sqrt{3}}{2}$$

There are three possible ROCs: $\mathrm{Re}\{s\} < -1.5,\quad -1.5 < \mathrm{Re}\{s\} < 3,\quad \mathrm{Re}\{s\} > 3$. The partial fraction expansion of $H(s)$ yields

$$H(s) = \left(-\frac{1}{42} + j\frac{\sqrt{3}}{14}\right)\frac{1}{s+\frac{3}{2}-j\frac{\sqrt{3}}{2}} + \left(-\frac{1}{42} - j\frac{\sqrt{3}}{14}\right)\frac{1}{s+\frac{3}{2}+j\frac{\sqrt{3}}{2}} + \frac{1}{21}\frac{1}{s-3}.$$

Using Table D.4 and simplifying, we find the following impulse responses:

$$\mathrm{ROC}_1 = \{s \in \mathbb{C} : \mathrm{Re}\{s\} > 3\}$$

$$h(t) = \left(-\frac{1}{42} + j\frac{\sqrt{3}}{14}\right)e^{(-3/2+j\sqrt{3}/2)t}u(t) + \left(-\frac{1}{42} - j\frac{\sqrt{3}}{14}\right)e^{(-3/2-j\sqrt{3}/2)t}u(t) + \frac{1}{21}e^{3t}u(t)$$

$$\mathrm{ROC}_2 = \{s \in \mathbb{C} : -1.5 < \mathrm{Re}\{s\} < 3\}$$

$$h(t) = \left(-\frac{1}{42} + j\frac{\sqrt{3}}{14}\right)e^{(-3/2 + j\sqrt{3}/2)t}u(t) + \left(-\frac{1}{42} - j\frac{\sqrt{3}}{14}\right)e^{(-3/2 - j\sqrt{3}/2)t}u(t) - \frac{1}{21}e^{3t}u(-t)$$

$$\mathrm{ROC}_3 = \{s \in \mathbb{C} : \mathrm{Re}\{s\} < -1.5\}$$

$$h(t) = \left(\frac{1}{42} - j\frac{\sqrt{3}}{14}\right)e^{(-3/2 + j\sqrt{3}/2)t}u(-t) + \left(\frac{1}{42} + j\frac{\sqrt{3}}{14}\right)e^{(-3/2 - j\sqrt{3}/2)t}u(-t) - \frac{1}{21}e^{3t}u(-t).$$

These are further simplified to their real form in Table 6.2.

TABLE 6.2 Impulse Responses in Exercise 6.3 for the Three Possible ROCs

ROC	$h(t)$	Causal	Stable
Im{s} ROC -1.5 3 Re{s}	$h(t) = \frac{-1}{21}e^{-1.5t}\left[3\sqrt{3}\sin\frac{\sqrt{3}}{2}t + \cos\frac{\sqrt{3}}{2}t\right]u(t) + \frac{1}{21}e^{3t}u(t)$	Yes ROC is a right half-plane	No $j\omega$ -axis out of ROC
Im{s} ROC -1.5 3 Re{s}	$h(t) = \frac{-1}{21}e^{-1.5t}\left[3\sqrt{3}\sin\frac{\sqrt{3}}{2}t + \cos\frac{\sqrt{3}}{2}t\right]u(t) - \frac{1}{21}e^{3t}u(-t)$	No	Yes
Im{s} ROC -1.5 3 Re{s}	$h(t) = \frac{1}{21}e^{-1.5t}\left[3\sqrt{3}\sin\frac{\sqrt{3}}{2}t + \cos\frac{\sqrt{3}}{2}t\right]u(-t) - \frac{1}{21}e^{3t}u(-t)$	No	No

Exercises

Exercise 6.4

Compute the step response of the LTI system $H(s) = \frac{6(s+1)}{s(s+3)}$, $\mathrm{Re}\{s\} > 0$.

Exercise 6.5

Compute the output $y(t)$ of the LTI system $H(s)=\frac{100}{s^2+10s+100}$, $\mathrm{Re}\{s\}>-5$ for the input signal $x(t)=e^{4t}u(-t)$.

Answer:

ON THE CD

Exercise 6.6

Suppose that the LTI system described by $H(s)=\frac{2}{(s+3)(s-1)}$ is known to be stable. Is this system causal? Compute its impulse response $h(t)$.

Exercise 6.7

Consider an LTI system with transfer function $H(s)=\frac{s^2-s-2}{s^2+5s+6}$. Sketch all possible regions of convergence of $H(s)$ on pole-zero plots and compute the associated impulse responses $h(t)$. Indicate for each impulse response whether it corresponds to a system that is causal/stable.

Answer:

ON THE CD

Exercise 6.8

Consider an LTI system with transfer function $H(s)=\frac{s(s-1)}{s^2+\sqrt{2}s+1}$. Sketch all possible ROCs of $H(s)$ on a pole-zero plot and compute the associated impulse responses $h(t)$. Indicate for each impulse response whether it corresponds to a system that is causal/stable.

Exercise 6.9

Suppose we know that the input of an LTI system is $x(t)=e^{t}u(-t)$. The output was measured to be $y(t)=e^{-t}\sin(t)u(t)+e^{-t}u(t)+2e^{t}u(-t)$. Find the transfer function $H(s)$ of the system and its ROC and sketch its pole-zero plot. Is the system causal? Is it stable? Justify your answers.

Answer:

ON THE CD

Exercise 6.10

(a) Find the impulse response of the system $H(s)=\frac{3s^2-3s-6}{s^3+12s^2+120s+200}$, $\mathrm{Re}\{s\}>-2$. Hint: this system has a pole at –2.

(b) Find the settling value of the step response of *H*(*s*) given in (a).

7 Application of the Laplace Transform to LTI Differential Systems

In This Chapter

- The Transfer Function of an LTI Differential System
- Block Diagram Realizations of LTI Differential Systems
- Analysis of LTI Differential Systems With Initial Conditions Using the Unilateral Laplace Transform
- Transient and Steady-State Responses of LTI Differential Systems
- Summary
- To Probe Further
- Exercises

((Lecture 23: LTI Differential Systems and Rational Transfer Functions))

The Laplace transform is a powerful tool to solve linear time-invariant (LTI) differential equations. We have used the Fourier transform for the same purpose, but the Laplace transform, whether bilateral or unilateral, is applicable in more cases, for example, to unstable systems or unbounded signals.

THE TRANSFER FUNCTION OF AN LTI DIFFERENTIAL SYSTEM

We have seen that the transfer function of an LTI system is the Laplace transform of its impulse response. For a *differential* LTI system, the transfer function can be readily written by inspecting the differential equation, just like its frequency response can be obtained by inspection.

Consider the general form of an LTI differential system:

$$\sum_{k=0}^{N} a_k \frac{d^k y(t)}{dt^k} = \sum_{k=0}^{M} b_k \frac{d^k x(t)}{dt^k}. \tag{7.1}$$

We use the differentiation and linearity properties of the Laplace transform to obtain the transfer function $H(s) = Y(s)/X(s)$:

$$\sum_{k=0}^{N} a_k s^k Y(s) = \sum_{k=0}^{M} b_k s^k X(s), \tag{7.2}$$

$$H(s) = \frac{Y(s)}{X(s)} = \frac{\sum_{k=0}^{M} b_k s^k}{\sum_{k=0}^{N} a_k s^k}. \tag{7.3}$$

Note that we have not specified a region of convergence (ROC) yet. This means that differential Equation 7.1 can have many different impulse responses; that is, it is not a complete specification of the LTI system. If we know that the differential system is causal, then the ROC is the open right half-plane to the right of the rightmost pole in the *s*-plane. The impulse response is then uniquely defined.

Poles and Zeros of the Transfer Function

Let $n(s) := \sum_{k=0}^{M} b_k s^k$ be the numerator polynomial of the transfer function $H(s)$ in Equation 7.3 and let $d(s) := \sum_{k=0}^{N} a_k s^k$ be its denominator polynomial. Then,

- The *poles* of $H(s)$ are the N roots of the *characteristic equation* $d(s) = 0$, or, equivalently, the N zeros of the characteristic polynomial.
- The *zeros* of $H(s)$ are the M roots of equation $n(s) = 0$.
- If $M > N$, then $\lim_{s\to\infty} H(s) = \infty$, and the transfer function is sometimes said to have $M - N$ poles at ∞.
- If $M < N$, then $\lim_{s\to\infty} H(s) = 0$, and the transfer function is sometimes said to have $N - M$ zeros at ∞.

Example 7.1: Find the transfer function poles of the following causal differential LTI system.

$$\frac{d^2y(t)}{dt^2}+\omega_c\sqrt{2}\frac{dy(t)}{dt}+\omega_c^2y(t)=\frac{d^2x(t)}{dt^2}+\omega_c\sqrt{2}\frac{dx(t)}{dt} \tag{7.4}$$

Taking the Laplace transform on both sides, we get

$$s^2Y(s)+\omega_c\sqrt{2}sY(s)+\omega_c^2Y(s)=s^2X(s)+\omega_c\sqrt{2}sX(s), \tag{7.5}$$

which yields

$$H(s)=\frac{Y(s)}{X(s)}=\frac{s^2+\omega_c\sqrt{2}s}{s^2+\omega_c\sqrt{2}s+\omega_c^2}. \tag{7.6}$$

The poles are the roots of $s^2+\omega_c\sqrt{2}s+\omega_c^2=0$ (note that this is the second-order Butterworth characteristic polynomial). Identifying the coefficients with the standard second-order denominator $s^2+2\zeta\omega_n s+\omega_n^2$, one finds the *damping ratio* $\zeta=\sqrt{2}/2=0.707$ and the *undamped natural frequency* $\omega_n=\omega_c$. The poles of $H(s)$ are then given by the following formulas:

$$\begin{aligned} p_1&=-\zeta\omega_n+\omega_n\sqrt{\zeta^2-1}=-\frac{\sqrt{2}}{2}\omega_c+j\frac{\sqrt{2}}{2}\omega_c=\omega_c e^{j\frac{3\pi}{4}},\\ p_2&=-\zeta\omega_n-\omega_n\sqrt{\zeta^2-1}=-\frac{\sqrt{2}}{2}\omega_c-j\frac{\sqrt{2}}{2}\omega_c=\omega_c e^{-j\frac{3\pi}{4}} \end{aligned} \tag{7.7}$$

and its two zeros are

$$z_1=-\omega_c\sqrt{2}, \qquad z_2=0. \tag{7.8}$$

The poles and zeros of a transfer function are usually denoted with the symbols X and O, respectively, in the s-plane, as shown in Figure 7.1, which is the pole-zero plot of $H(s)$.

Causality

The transfer function of an LTI system by itself does not determine whether the system is causal or not. We have seen that for rational Laplace transforms, causality is equivalent to the ROC being an open right half-plane (open means that the half-plane's boundary is not included) to the right of the rightmost pole. Hence, since differential LTI systems considered in this section have rational transforms, *the LTI differential system of Equation 7.1 is causal if and only if the ROC of its transfer function is an open right half-plane located to the right of the rightmost pole.*

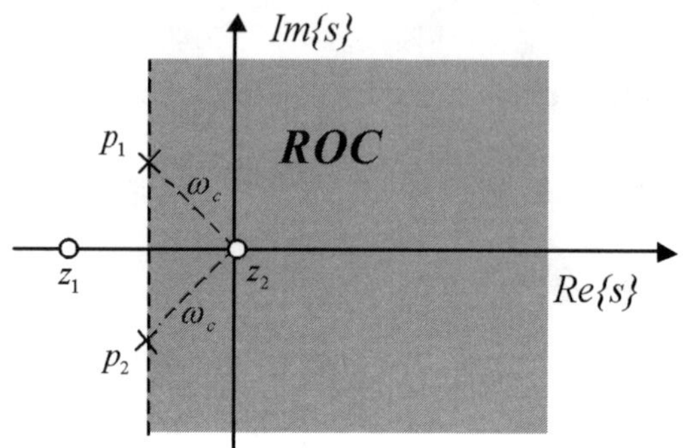

FIGURE 7.1 Pole-zero plot of transfer function in Example 7.1.

We normally deal with causal differential systems, as analog engineering systems are naturally causal.

BIBO Stability

The stability of an LTI differential system is directly related to the poles of the transfer function and its region of convergence. Recall that an LTI system (including a *differential* LTI system) is stable if and only if the ROC of its transfer function includes the $j\omega$-axis. Assume there is no pole-zero cancellation in the *closed right half-plane* when $H(s) = n(s)/d(s)$ is formed. Then, *a causal LTI differential system is stable if and only if the poles of its transfer function all lie in the open left half-plane.*

Remark: It is customary to refer to the set $\{s : \mathrm{Re}\{s\} \geq 0\}$ as *the right half-plane* (or to $\{s : \mathrm{Re}\{s\} > 0\}$ as *the open right half-plane*) and to $\{s : \mathrm{Re}\{s\} \leq 0\}$ as *the left half-plane* (or to $\{s : \mathrm{Re}\{s\} < 0\}$ as *the open left half-plane*).

Recall that for the case where a zero cancels out an unstable pole (call it p_0) in the transfer function, the corresponding differential LTI system is considered to be unstable. The reason is that any nonzero initial condition would cause the output to either grow unbounded (case $\mathrm{Re}\{p_0\} > 0$), oscillate forever (case p_0 imaginary), or settle down to a nonzero value (case $p_0 = 0$).

In Example 7.1, the two complex conjugate poles are in the open left half-plane, so the system is stable.

Example: System Identification

Suppose we know that the input of the differential LTI system depicted in Figure 7.2 is $x(t) = 2e^{-t}u(t)$.

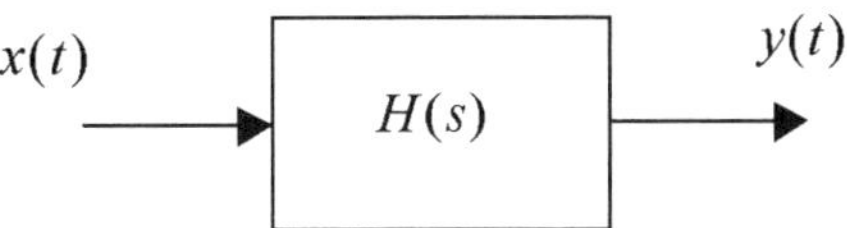

FIGURE 7.2 Finding the transfer function of an LTI system.

If the output was measured to be $y(t) = e^{-2t}\sin(2t)u(t) - te^{-t}u(t)$, let us find the transfer function *H*(*s*) of the system and its ROC and sketch its pole-zero plot. Let us also determine whether the system is causal and stable. This is known as *system identification*, studied here in its simplest, noise-free form.

First, let us take the Laplace transforms of the input and output signals using Table D.4 in Appendix D:

$$X(s) = \frac{2}{s+1}, \quad \mathrm{Re}\{s\} > -1 \tag{7.9}$$

$$\begin{aligned} Y(s) &= \underbrace{\frac{2}{(s+2)^2 + 2^2}}_{\mathrm{Re}\{s\}>-2} - \underbrace{\frac{1}{(s+1)^2}}_{\mathrm{Re}\{s\}>-1} \\ &= \frac{(2s^2+4s+2) - (s^2+4s+8)}{(s^2+4s+8)(s+1)^2}, \quad \mathrm{Re}\{s\} > -1 \\ &= \frac{s^2-6}{(s^2+4s+8)(s+1)^2}, \quad \mathrm{Re}\{s\} > -1. \end{aligned} \tag{7.10}$$

Then, the transfer function is simply

$$H(s) = \frac{Y(s)}{X(s)} = \frac{\dfrac{s^2-6}{(s^2+4s+8)(s+1)^2}}{\dfrac{2}{(s+1)}} = \frac{(s-\sqrt{6})(s+\sqrt{6})}{2(s^2+4s+8)(s+1)}. \tag{7.11}$$

To determine the ROC, first note that the ROC of $Y(s)$ should contain the intersection of the ROCs of $H(s)$ and $X(s)$. There are three possible ROCs for $H(s)$:

ROC_1: an open left half-plane to the left of $\mathrm{Re}\{s\}=-2$

ROC_2: an open right half-plane to the right of $\mathrm{Re}\{s\}=-1$

ROC_3: a vertical strip between $\mathrm{Re}\{s\}=-2$ and $\mathrm{Re}\{s\}=-1$

Since the ROC of $X(s)$ is an open right half-plane to the right of $\mathrm{Re}\{s\}=-1$, the only possible choice is ROC_2. Hence, the ROC of $H(s)$ is $\{s\in\mathbb{C}:\mathrm{Re}\{s\}>-1\}$.

The system is causal, as the transfer function is rational and the ROC is a right half-plane. It is also stable, as the transfer function is proper and all three poles $p_{1,2}=-2\pm j2,\ p_3=-1$ are in the open left half-plane, as shown in Figure 7.3.

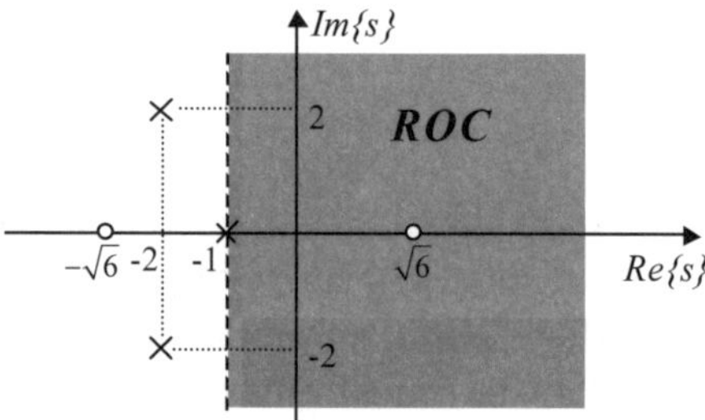

FIGURE 7.3 Pole-zero plot of identified transfer function.

A causal LTI differential equation representing the system is obtained by inspection of the transfer function:

$$2\frac{d^3y(t)}{dt^3}+10\frac{d^2y(t)}{dt^2}+24\frac{dy(t)}{dt}+16y(t)=\frac{d^2x(t)}{dt^2}-6x(t). \tag{7.12}$$

((Lecture 24: Analysis of LTI Differential Systems with Block Diagrams))

BLOCK DIAGRAM REALIZATIONS OF LTI DIFFERENTIAL SYSTEMS

Block diagrams are useful to analyze LTI differential systems composed of subsystems. They are also used to represent a *realization* of an LTI differential system as a combination of three basic elements: the integrator, the gain, and the summing junction.

System Interconnections

We have already studied system interconnections using block diagrams in the context of general systems (not necessarily linear) and also in the context of LTI systems with the convolution property and Fourier transforms. However, this approach to analyzing complex systems becomes quite powerful when one uses transfer functions to describe the interconnected LTI systems. The reason is that the space of all transfer functions forms an *algebra* with the usual arithmetic operations (+,-,×,/). That is, the sum, difference, multiplication, or division of two transfer functions yield another transfer function.

Example 7.2: Find the step response of the car cruise control system depicted in Figure 7.4 to a step in the desired velocity input v_{des} from 0 km/h to 100 km/h, where

$$\begin{aligned} P(s) &= \frac{1}{s+3}, \quad \mathrm{Re}\{s\} > -3 \\ K(s) &= \frac{10}{s}, \quad \mathrm{Re}\{s\} > 0 \\ F(s) &= 2, \quad \forall s \in \mathbb{C} \end{aligned} \tag{7.13}$$

and the time unit is the minute.

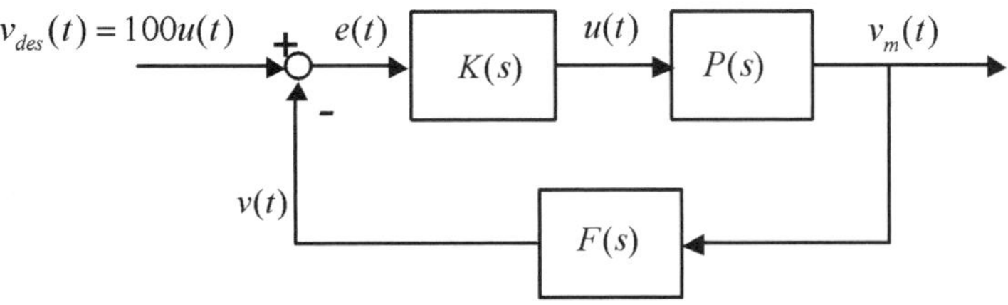

FIGURE 7.4 Block diagram of a car cruise control system.

This feedback system represents a car cruise control system where $P(s)$ is the car's dynamics from the engine throttle input to the speed output, $F(s)$ is a scaling factor on the tachometer speed measurement to get, for example, kilometer per hour units, and $K(s)$ is the controller, here a pure integrator that integrates the error between the desired speed and the actual car speed to obtain a throttle command $u(t)$ for the engine.

It is interesting to note that the theory of Laplace transforms and transfer functions allows us to analyze within a single framework a mechanical system (the car), an electromechanical sensor (the tachometer), and a control circuit or a control algorithm residing in a microcontroller chip.

The first task of a control engineer would be to check that this system is stable. We do not want the car to accelerate out of control when the driver switches the cruise control system on. Thus, we need to find the transfer function relating the input $v_{des}(t)$ to the scaled measured speed of the car $v(t)$ and compute its poles. Let us denote the Laplace transforms of the signals with "hats." We have

$$\begin{aligned}\hat{v}(s) &= F(s)P(s)K(s)\hat{e}(s)\\ \hat{e}(s) &= \hat{v}_{des}(s) - \hat{v}(s).\end{aligned} \tag{7.14}$$

Thus, the error can be expressed as

$$\begin{aligned}\hat{e}(s) &= \hat{v}_{des}(s) - F(s)P(s)K(s)\hat{e}(s)\\ &= \frac{1}{1+F(s)P(s)K(s)}\hat{v}_{des}(s).\end{aligned} \tag{7.15}$$

and substituting this expression back into the first equation of Equation 7.14, we obtain

$$\hat{v}(s) = \underbrace{\frac{F(s)P(s)K(s)}{1+F(s)P(s)K(s)}}_{H(s)}\hat{v}_{des}(s) = H(s)\hat{v}_{des}(s). \tag{7.16}$$

This is the transfer function relating the desired car velocity to its measurement. Using the actual transfer functions provided above, we get

$$H(s) = \frac{2\frac{1}{s+3}\frac{10}{s}}{1+2\frac{1}{s+3}\frac{10}{s}} = \frac{20}{s^2+3s+20}. \tag{7.17}$$

This is a second-order transfer function with undamped natural frequency $\omega_n = \sqrt{20}$ rad/min and damping ratio $\zeta = \frac{3}{2\sqrt{20}} = 0.34$. Hence, the poles are in the open left-half plane:

$$\begin{aligned}p_1 &= -\zeta\omega_n + \omega_n\sqrt{\zeta^2-1} = -1.5 + j4.2131\\ p_2 &= -\zeta\omega_n - \omega_n\sqrt{\zeta^2-1} = -1.5 - j4.2131,\end{aligned} \tag{7.18}$$

which means that the system is stable and the ROC of $H(s)$ is $\mathrm{Re}\{s\} > -1.5$. The Laplace transform of the car speed response to a step in the desired velocity input v_{des} from 0 km/h to 100 km/h is

$$\begin{aligned}\hat{v}(s) &= H(s)\hat{v}_{des}(s) \\ &= \frac{20}{s^2+3s+20}\frac{100}{s}, \quad \mathrm{Re}\{s\}>0 \\ &= \underbrace{\frac{A(s+1.5)+B4.2131}{(s+1.5)^2+(4.2131)^2}}_{\mathrm{Re}\{s\}>-1.5} + \underbrace{\frac{C}{s}}_{\mathrm{Re}\{s\}>0},\end{aligned} \tag{7.19}$$

where the second-order term of the partial fraction expansion was written to match the form of the Laplace transform of the sum of a damped sine and cosine (see Table D.4). We find

$$\hat{v}(s) = \frac{-100(s+1.5)-35.603(4.2131)}{(s+1.5)^2+(4.2131)^2} + \frac{100}{s}, \tag{7.20}$$

which, for the ROCs of Equation 7.19 and using the table, corresponds to

$$v(t) = \left[100 - 100e^{-1.5t}\cos 4.2131t - 35.603e^{-1.5t}\sin 4.2131t\right]u(t)\ \text{km/h} \tag{7.21}$$

This speed response is shown in Figure 7.5.

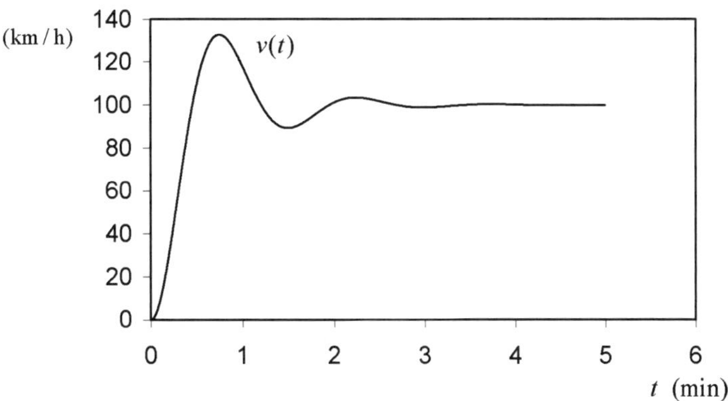

FIGURE 7.5 Step response of car cruise control system.

It can be seen on this plot that there is too much overshoot in the speed response. By choosing a smaller integrator gain in $K(s)$, we would obtain a smoother response with less overshoot. This is a problem typical to the area of control engineering introduced in Chapter 11.

Realization of a Transfer Function

It is possible to obtain a *realization* of the transfer function of an LTI differential system as a combination of three basic elements shown in Figure 7.6: the integrator, the gain, and the summing junction.

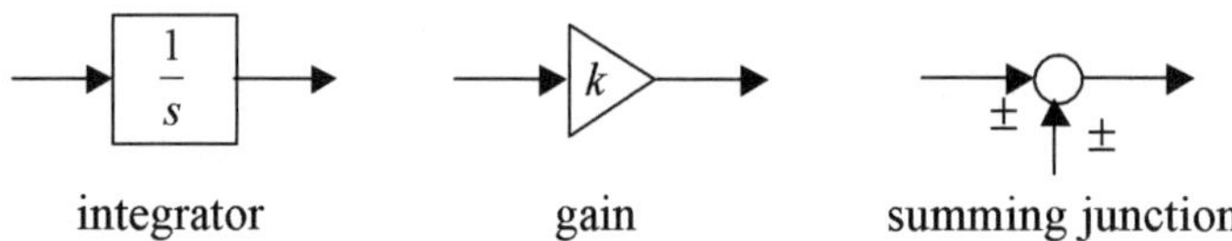

FIGURE 7.6 Basic elements to realize any transfer function.

Simple First-Order Transfer Function

Consider the transfer function $H(s)=\frac{1}{s+a}$. It can be realized with a feedback interconnection of the three basic elements, as shown in Figure 7.7.

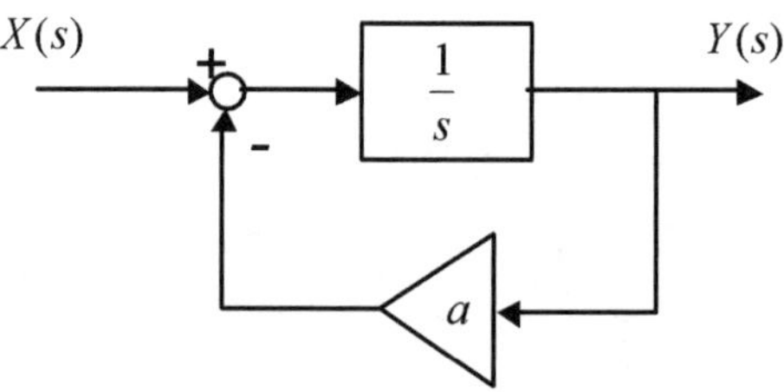

FIGURE 7.7 Realization of first-order transfer function.

The feedback equation associated with this block diagram is as follows:

$$\begin{aligned} Y(s) &= -a\frac{1}{s}Y(s)+\frac{1}{s}X(s) \\ &= \frac{\frac{1}{s}}{1+a\frac{1}{s}}X(s)=\frac{1}{s+a}X(s)=H(s)X(s). \end{aligned} \tag{7.22}$$

With this simple block diagram, we can realize any transfer function of any order after it is written as a partial fraction expansion. This leads to the parallel form introduced below.

Simple Second-Order Transfer Function

Consider the transfer function $H(s)=\frac{1}{s^2+a_1s+a_0}$. It can be realized with a feedback interconnection of the three basic elements in a number of ways. One way is to expand the transfer function as a sum of two first-order transfer functions (partial fraction expansion). The resulting form is called the *parallel form* and is discussed below. Another way is to break up the transfer function as a cascade (multiplication) of two first-order transfer functions. This cascade form is also discussed below. Yet another way to realize the second-order transfer function is the so-called *direct form* or *controllable canonical form*. To develop this form, consider the system equation

$$s^2Y(s)=-a_1sY(s)-a_0Y(s)+X(s). \tag{7.23}$$

This equation can be realized as in Figure 7.8. The idea is that the variable at the input of an integrator is thought of as the derivative of its output.

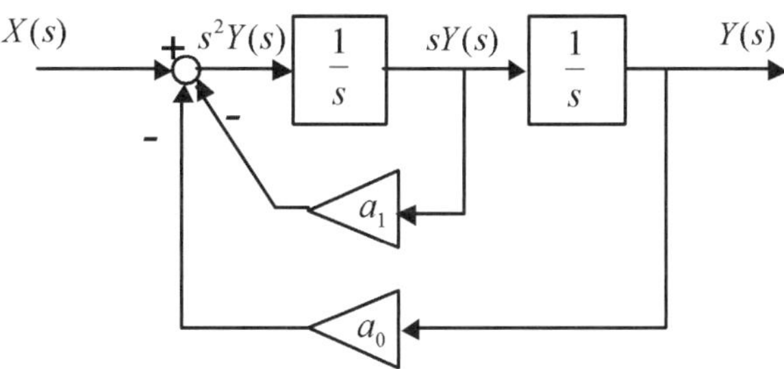

FIGURE 7.8 Direct form realization of a second-order transfer function.

Parallel Realization

A parallel realization can be obtained by expanding the transfer function into partial first-order fractions with real coefficients or complex coefficients for complex poles.

Example 7.3: Consider the system $H(s)=\frac{s-1}{(s+1)(s-2)}=\frac{2/3}{s+1}+\frac{1/3}{s-2}$. Its parallel realization is shown in Figure 7.9.

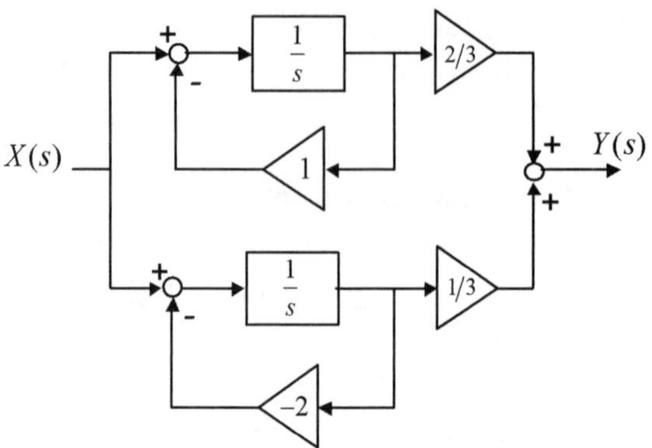

FIGURE 7.9 Parallel realization of a second-order transfer function.

Cascade Realization

A cascade realization can be obtained by expressing the numerator and denominator of the transfer function as a product of zeros of the form $(s - z_i)$ and of poles of the form $(s - p_i)$, respectively, and by arbitrarily grouping a pole with a zero until all zeros are matched to form first-order subsystems. The poles left at the end of this procedure are taken as first-order subsystems with constant numerators.

Example 7.4: Consider the system $H(s) = \frac{s-1}{(s+1)(s-2)}$. Its cascade form is shown in Figure 7.10 for the grouping $H(s) = \left(\frac{1}{s+1}\right)\left(\frac{s-1}{s-2}\right)$. The zero in the first first-order subsystem is implemented using a feedthrough term. This first subsystem is actually realized in a direct form, which is explained next.

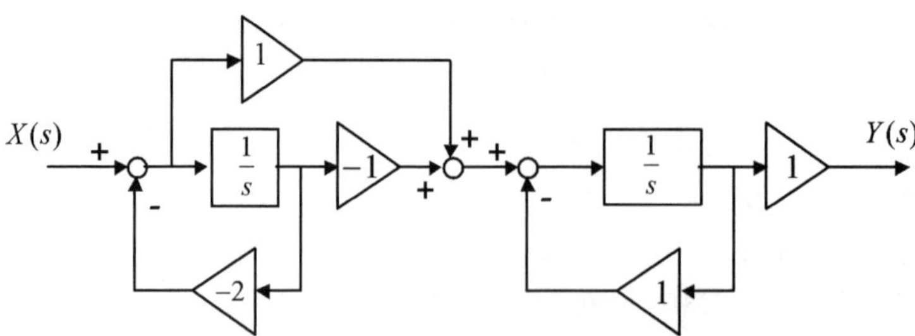

FIGURE 7.10 Cascade realization of a second-order transfer function.

Direct Form (Controllable Canonical Form)

The direct form, also called the controllable canonical form, can be obtained by breaking up a general transfer function into two subsystems as in Figure 7.11.

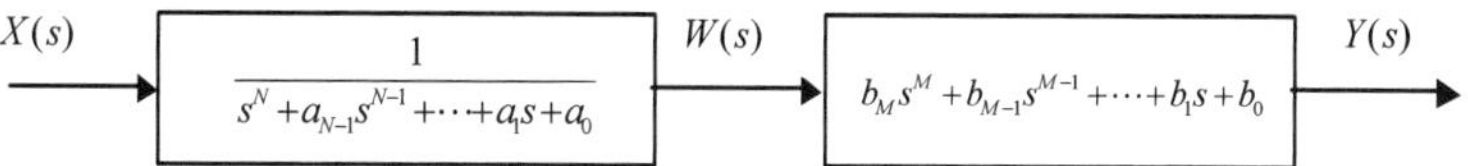

FIGURE 7.11 Transfer function as a cascade of two LTI subsystems.

The input-output system equation of the first subsystem is

$$s^N W(s) = -a_{N-1}s^{N-1}W(s) - \cdots - a_1 sW(s) - a_0 W(s) + X(s), \qquad (7.24)$$

and for the second subsystem, we have

$$Y(s) = b_M s^M W(s) + b_{M-1}s^{M-1}W(s) + \cdots + b_1 sW(s) + b_0 W(s). \qquad (7.25)$$

To get the direct form realization, a cascade of N integrators is first sketched, and the input to the first integrator is labeled $s^N W(s)$. The output of this first integrator is $\frac{1}{s}s^N W(s) = s^{N-1}W(s)$. The outputs of the remaining integrators are labeled successively from the left: $s^{N-2}W(s)$, etc. Then, the feedback paths with gains equal to the coefficients of the denominator as expressed in Equation 7.24 are added. Finally, Equation 7.25 is implemented by tapping the signals $s^k W(s)$, multiplying them with coefficients of the numerator of the transfer function, and summing them. Figure 7.12 shows a direct form realization of a second-order transfer function.

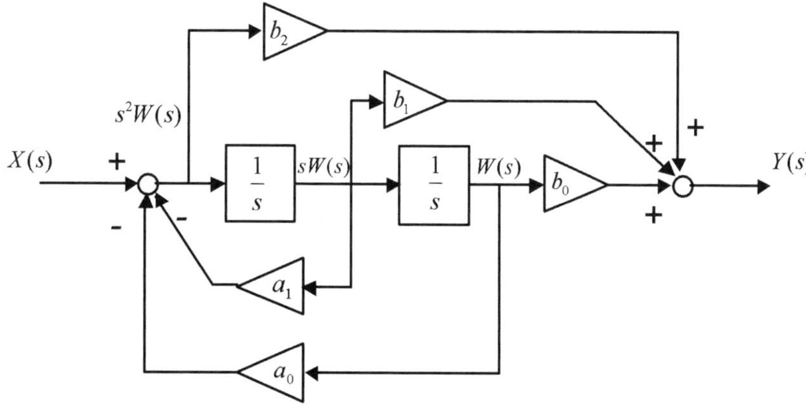

FIGURE 7.12 Direct form realization of a second-order transfer function

((Lecture 25: Response of LTI Differential Systems with Initial Conditions))

ANALYSIS OF LTI DIFFERENTIAL SYSTEMS WITH INITIAL CONDITIONS USING THE UNILATERAL LAPLACE TRANSFORM

Recall the differentiation property of the unilateral Laplace transform:

If $x(t) \overset{UL}{\leftrightarrow} \mathcal{X}(s),\ s \in \text{ROC}$, then

$$\frac{dx(t)}{dt} \overset{UL}{\leftrightarrow} s\mathcal{X}(s) - x(0^-),\ s \in \text{ROC}_1 \supseteq \text{ROC}. \tag{7.26}$$

We have already solved a first-order system with an initial condition. Let us now look at a second-order LTI differential system with initial conditions and a nonzero input.

Example 7.5: Consider the causal second-order system described by

$$\frac{d^2y(t)}{dt^2} + 3\frac{dy(t)}{dt} + 2y(t) = \frac{dx(t)}{dt} + 3x(t) \tag{7.27}$$

and with initial conditions $\frac{dy(0^-)}{dt} = 2,\quad y(0^-) = 1$. Suppose that this system is subjected to the input signal:

$$x(t) = e^{-5t}u(t). \tag{7.28}$$

What is the output of the system? Take the unilateral Laplace transform on both sides of Equation 7.27.

$$\left[s^2\mathcal{Y}(s) - sy(0^-) - \frac{dy(0^-)}{dt}\right] + 3\left[s\mathcal{Y}(s) - y(0^-)\right] + 2\mathcal{Y}(s) = s\mathcal{X}(s) - x(0^-) + 3\mathcal{X}(s) \tag{7.29}$$

Note that $x(0^-) = 0$. Collecting the terms containing $\mathcal{Y}(s)$ on the left-hand side and putting everything else on the right-hand side, we can solve for $\mathcal{Y}(s)$.

$$\left(s^2 + 3s + 2\right)\mathcal{Y}(s) = \left(s+3\right)\mathcal{X}(s) + sy(0^-) + 3y(0^-) + \frac{dy(0^-)}{dt}$$

$$\mathcal{Y}(s) = \frac{\left(s+3\right)\mathcal{X}(s)}{s^2 + 3s + 2} + \frac{sy(0^-) + 3y(0^-) + \frac{dy(0^-)}{dt}}{s^2 + 3s + 2} \tag{7.30}$$

We have,

$$\mathcal{X}(s)=\frac{1}{s+5},\quad \mathrm{Re}\{s\}>-5, \tag{7.31}$$

and thus,

$$\begin{aligned}\mathcal{Y}(s)&=\frac{s+3}{\left(s^2+3s+2\right)\left(s+5\right)}+\frac{s+5}{s^2+3s+2},\quad \mathrm{Re}\{s\}>-1\\&=\frac{s^2+11s+28}{\left(s^2+3s+2\right)\left(s+5\right)},\quad \mathrm{Re}\{s\}>-1\\&=\frac{\frac{9}{2}}{s+1}-\frac{\frac{10}{3}}{s+2}-\frac{\frac{1}{6}}{s+5}.\end{aligned} \tag{7.32}$$

Taking the inverse Laplace transform of each term, we obtain

$$y(t)=\left[\frac{9}{2}e^{-t}-\frac{10}{3}e^{-2t}-\frac{1}{6}e^{-5t}\right]u(t). \tag{7.33}$$

Zero-Input Response and Zero-State Response

The response of a causal LTI differential system with initial conditions and a nonzero input can be decomposed as the sum of a *zero-input response* and a *zero-state response.* As these names imply, the zero-input response is due to the initial conditions only, whereas the zero-state response is produced by the input only. Note that the term *state* refers to the initial state in a state-space description of a differential system. We will study state-space systems in Chapter 10.

In Example 7.5, the zero-input and zero-state responses in the Laplace domain are identified as follows.

$$\mathcal{Y}(s)=\underbrace{\frac{(s+3)\mathcal{X}(s)}{s^2+3s+2}}_{\text{zero-state resp.}}+\underbrace{\frac{sy(0^-)+3y(0^-)+\dfrac{dy(0^-)}{dt}}{s^2+3s+2}}_{\text{zero-input resp.}} \tag{7.34}$$

TRANSIENT AND STEADY-STATE RESPONSES OF LTI DIFFERENTIAL SYSTEMS

The *transient response* (also called natural response) of a causal, stable LTI differential system is the homogeneous response.

The *steady-state response* (or forced response) is the particular solution corresponding to a constant or periodic input. We say that a stable system is in steady-state when the transient component of the output has practically disappeared. For example, consider the step response

$$s(t) = u(t) - e^{-5t}u(t). \tag{7.35}$$

The transient part of this response is the term $e^{-5t}u(t)$, and the steady-state part is $u(t)$.

As another example, assume that a causal LTI differential system is subjected to the sinusoidal input signal $x(t) = \sin(\omega_0 t)u(t)$. Suppose that the resulting output is

$$y(t) = 2\sin(\omega_0 t - \phi)u(t) + e^{-2t}\cos(2t + \theta)u(t). \tag{7.36}$$

Then the transient response of the system to the input is $e^{-2t}\cos(2t + \theta)u(t)$, while $2\sin(\omega_0 t - \phi)u(t)$ is the steady-state response.

The steady-state response of a causal, stable LTI system to a sinusoidal input of frequency ω_0 is also a sinusoid of frequency ω_0, although in general with a different amplitude and phase.

Transient and Steady-State Analysis Using the Laplace Transform

For a causal, stable LTI system with a real-rational transfer function, a partial fraction expansion of the transfer function allows us to determine which terms correspond to transients (the terms with the system poles) and which correspond to the steady-state response (terms with the input poles).

Example 7.6: Consider the step response.

$$\begin{aligned} Y(s) &= \frac{s+3}{\left(s^2+3s+2\right)} X(s), \quad \mathrm{Re}\{s\} > -1 \\ &= \frac{s+3}{\left(s^2+3s+2\right)s}, \quad \mathrm{Re}\{s\} > 0 \\ &= \underbrace{\frac{A}{s+1}}_{\mathrm{Re}\{s\}>-1} + \underbrace{\frac{B}{s+2}}_{\mathrm{Re}\{s\}>-2} + \underbrace{\frac{C}{s}}_{\mathrm{Re}\{s\}>0} \end{aligned} \tag{7.37}$$

The steady-state response corresponds to the last term, C, which in the time-domain is $Cu(t)$. The other two terms correspond to the transient response $Ae^{-t}u(t)+Be^{-2t}u(t)$.

If we are only interested in the steady-state response of an LTI system, there is no need to do a partial fraction expansion. The transfer function and the frequency response of the system (which is the transfer function evaluated at $s=j\omega$) directly give us the answer.

Step Response

We can use the final value theorem to determine the steady-state component of a step response. In general, this component is a step function $Au(t)$. The "gain" A is given by

$$A=\lim_{s\to 0} sH(s)\frac{1}{s}=H(0) \tag{7.38}$$

Response to a Sinusoid or a Periodic Complex Exponential

The frequency response of the system directly gives us the steady-state response to a sinusoid or a periodic complex exponential signal. For the latter, $x(t)=Ae^{j\omega_0 t}$, the steady-state response is

$$\begin{aligned} y_{ss}(t) &= H(j\omega_0)Ae^{j\omega_0 t} \\ &= \left|H(j\omega_0)\right| Ae^{j(\omega_0 t+\angle H(j\omega_0))}. \end{aligned} \tag{7.39}$$

For a sinusoidal input, say $x(t)=A\sin(\omega_0 t)$, the steady-state response is as follows (the same for a cosine signal):

$$\begin{aligned} y_{ss}(t) &= \frac{A}{2j}(H(j\omega_0)e^{j\omega_0 t}-H(-j\omega_0)e^{-j\omega_0 t}) \\ &= \frac{A}{2j}(\left|H(j\omega_0)\right|e^{j(\omega_0 t+\angle H(j\omega_0))}-\left|H(-j\omega_0)\right|e^{-j(\omega_0 t-\angle H(-j\omega_0))}) \\ &= \frac{A}{2j}(\left|H(j\omega_0)\right|e^{j(\omega_0 t+\angle H(j\omega_0))}-\left|H(j\omega_0)\right|e^{-j(\omega_0 t+\angle H(j\omega_0))}) \\ &= \left|H(j\omega_0)\right|A\sin\left(\omega_0 t+\angle H(j\omega_0)\right), \end{aligned} \tag{7.40}$$

where we used the fact that the frequency response magnitude is even and the phase is odd for a real-rational transfer function. An important application is the steady-state analysis of circuits at a fixed frequency, for instance, 60 Hz. For example, if a circuit is described by its impedance, $Z(s)$, seen as a transfer function, then its steady-state response to a 60 Hz sinusoidal current is characterized by the complex number $Z(j2\pi 60)$.

Response to a Periodic Signal

Again, the frequency response of the system gives us the steady-state response to a periodic signal admitting a Fourier series representation. For $x(t)=\sum_{k=-\infty}^{+\infty} a_k e^{jk\omega_0 t}$, the steady-state response is the periodic signal:

$$y_{ss}(t)=\sum_{k=-\infty}^{+\infty} H(jk\omega_0)a_k e^{jk\omega_0 t}. \tag{7.41}$$

SUMMARY

In this chapter, we studied the application of the Laplace transform to differential systems.

- The transfer function of an LTI differential system can be obtained by inspection of the differential equation.
- The zeros and poles of a transfer function were defined as the zeros of its numerator and denominator, respectively.
- Transfer functions can be interconnected in block diagrams to form more complex systems whose transfer functions can be obtained using simple rules.
- Any proper real-rational transfer function can be realized using an interconnection of three basic elements: the gain, the summing junction, and the integrator. We discussed the parallel, cascade, and direct form realizations.
- The unilateral Laplace transform can be used to compute the response of a differential system with initial conditions. The overall response is composed of a zero-state response coming from the input only (assuming zero initial conditions) and of a zero-input response caused by the initial conditions only. Another way to decompose the overall response of the system is to identify the transient response and the steady-state response.

TO PROBE FURTHER

On the response of LTI differential systems, see, for example, Oppenheim, Willsky, and Nawab, 1997. We will revisit realization theory in the context of state-space systems in Chapter 10.

EXERCISES

Exercises with Solutions

Exercise 7.1

Consider the system described by

$$H(s)=\frac{3s^2-3s-6}{s^3+12s^2+120s+200},\quad \mathrm{Re}\{s\}>-2.$$

(a) Find the direct form realization of the transfer function $H(s)$. Is this system BIBO stable? Is it causal? Why?

Answer:
The direct form realization is obtained by splitting up the system into two systems as in Figure 7.13.

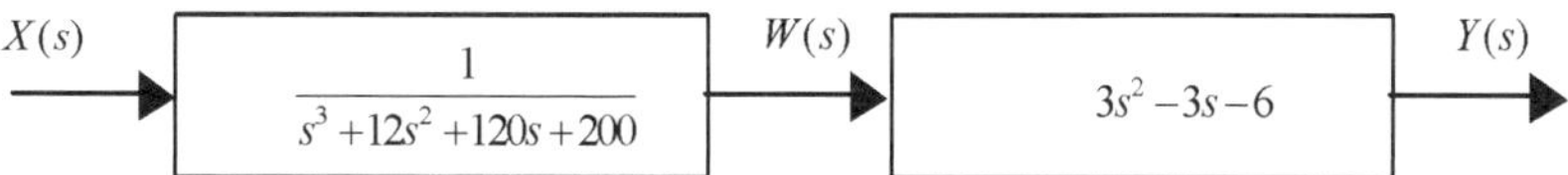

FIGURE 7.13 Transfer function split up as a cascade of two subsystems, Exercise 7.1(a).

The input-output system equation of the first subsystem is

$$s^3W(s)=-12s^2W(s)-120sW(s)-200W(s)+X(s),$$

and we begin the diagram by drawing a cascade of three integrators with their inputs labeled as $s^3W(s)$, $s^2W(s)$, $sW(s)$. Then, we can draw the feedbacks to a summing junction whose output is the input of the first integrator, labeled $s^3W(s)$. The input signal is also an input to that summing junction. For the second subsystem we have

$$Y(s)=3s^2W(s)-3sW(s)-6W(s),$$

which can be drawn as taps on the integrator inputs, summed up to form the output signal. The resulting direct form realization is shown in Figure 7.14.

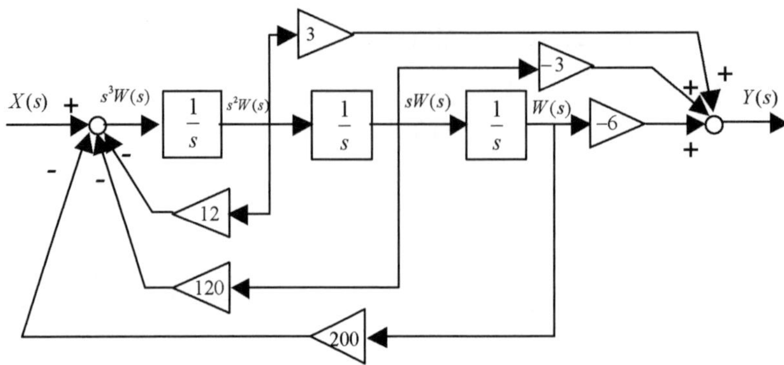

FIGURE 7.14 Direct form realization of transfer function, Exercise 7.1(a).

The system is BIBO stable, as its rational transfer function is proper and its ROC contains the $j\omega$-axis. It is also causal because its ROC is an open right-half plane *and* its transfer function is rational.

(b) Give a parallel form realization of $H(s)$ with (possibly complex-rational) first-order blocks.

Answer:

The partial fraction expansion for the parallel realization of the transfer function is as follows. Figure 7.15 shows the corresponding parallel realization.

$$\begin{aligned}H(s) &= \frac{3s^2-3s-6}{s^3+12s^2+120s+200},\ \text{Re}\{s\}>-2\\ &= \frac{3s^2-3s-6}{(s+2)(s^2+10s+100)},\ \text{Re}\{s\}>-2\\ &= \underbrace{\frac{0.14286}{s+2}}_{\text{Re}\{s\}>-2}+\underbrace{\frac{1.4286+j1.4104}{s+5-j5\sqrt{3}}}_{\text{Re}\{s\}>-5}+\underbrace{\frac{1.4286-j1.4104}{s+5+j5\sqrt{3}}}_{\text{Re}\{s\}>-5}.\end{aligned}$$

(c) Give a parallel form realization of $H(s)$ using a real-rational first-order block and a real-rational second-order block.

Answer:

The transfer function can be expanded as follows:

$$H(s)=\underbrace{\frac{0.14286}{s+2}}_{\text{Re}\{s\}>-2}+\underbrace{\frac{2.857s-10.14287}{s^2+10s+100}}_{\text{Re}\{s\}>-5},$$

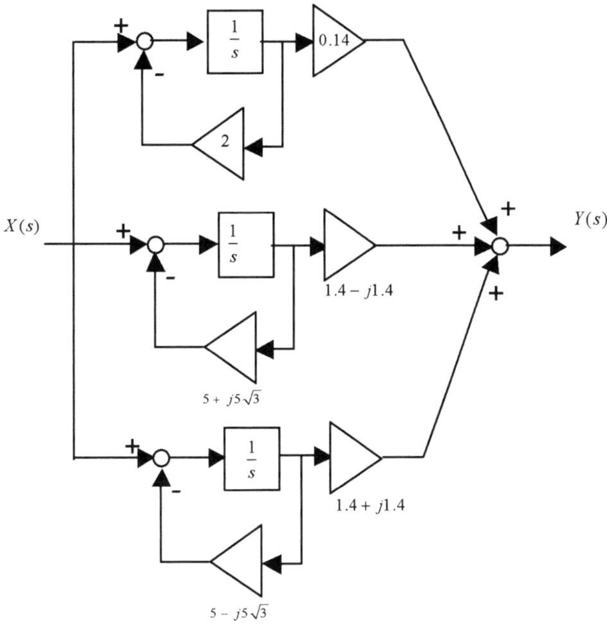

FIGURE 7.15 Parallel form realization of transfer function in Exercise 7.1(b).

which corresponds to the desired parallel realization in Figure 7.16.

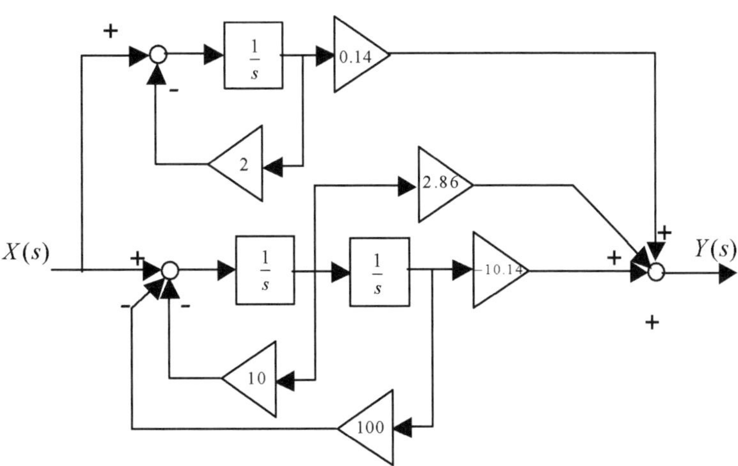

FIGURE 7.16 Real-rational parallel form realization of transfer function in Exercise 7.1(c).

Exercise 7.2

Consider the causal differential system described by

$$\frac{d^2y(t)}{dt^2}+3\frac{dy(t)}{dt}+25y(t)=\frac{d^2x(t)}{dt^2}-\frac{dx(t)}{dt}+x(t),$$

with initial conditions $\frac{dy(0^-)}{dt}=3,\quad y(0^-)=-1$. Suppose this system is subjected to a unit step input signal $x(t)=u(t)$.

Find the system's damping ratio ζ and undamped natural frequency ω_n. Give the transfer function of the system and specify its ROC. Compute the steady-state response $y_{ss}(t)$ and the transient response $y_{tr}(t)$ for $t\geq 0$. Compute the zero-input response $y_{zi}(t)$ and the zero-state response $y_{zs}(t)$.

Answer:

Let us take the unilateral Laplace transform on both sides of the differential equation.

$$\left[s^2\mathcal{Y}(s)-sy(0^-)-\frac{dy(0^-)}{dt}\right]+3\left[s\mathcal{Y}(s)-y(0^-)\right]+25\mathcal{Y}(s)=s^2\mathcal{X}(s)-s\mathcal{X}(s)+\mathcal{X}(s)$$

Collecting the terms containing $\mathcal{Y}(s)$ on the left-hand side and putting everything else on the right-hand side, we can solve for $\mathcal{Y}(s)$.

$$\left(s^2+3s+25\right)\mathcal{Y}(s)=s^2\mathcal{X}(s)-s\mathcal{X}(s)+\mathcal{X}(s)+sy(0^-)+3y(0^-)+\frac{dy(0^-)}{dt}$$

$$\mathcal{Y}(s)=\underbrace{\frac{(s^2-s+1)\mathcal{X}(s)}{s^2+3s+25}}_{\text{zero-state resp.}}+\underbrace{\frac{(s+3)y(0^-)+\frac{dy(0^-)}{dt}}{s^2+3s+25}}_{\text{zero-input resp.}}$$

The transfer function is $H(s)=\frac{s^2-s+1}{s^2+3s+25}$, and since the system is causal, the ROC is an open right half-plane to the right of the rightmost pole. The poles are $p_{1,2}=-1.5\pm j4.77$. Therefore, the ROC is $\mathrm{Re}\{s\}>-1.5$. The unilateral Laplace transform of the input is given by

$$\mathcal{X}(s)=\frac{1}{s},\quad \mathrm{Re}\{s\}>0,$$

and thus,

$$\mathcal{Y}(s) = \underbrace{\frac{s^2 - s + 1}{s(s^2 + 3s + 25)}}_{\text{zero-state resp.}} + \underbrace{\frac{-s}{s^2 + 3s + 25}}_{\text{zero-input resp.}}$$
$$= \frac{-s + 1}{s(s^2 + 3s + 25)}.$$

Let us compute the zero-state response first:

$$\mathcal{Y}_{zs}(s) = \frac{s^2 - s + 1}{s(s^2 + 3s + 25)}, \quad \mathrm{Re}\{s\} > 0$$
$$= \underbrace{\frac{A(4.77) + B(s + 1.5)}{(s + 1.5)^2 + 22.75}}_{\mathrm{Re}\{s\} > -1.5} + \underbrace{\frac{C}{s}}_{\mathrm{Re}\{s\} > 0}$$
$$= \underbrace{\frac{A(4.77) + B(s + 1.5)}{(s + 1.5)^2 + 22.75}}_{\mathrm{Re}\{s\} > -1.5} + \underbrace{\frac{0.04}{s}}_{\mathrm{Re}\{s\} > 0}.$$

Let $s = -1.5$ to compute $\frac{(-1.5)^2 + 1.5 + 1}{(-1.5)(22.75)} = \frac{4.77}{22.75} A - 0.0267 \Rightarrow A = -0.5365$, then multiply both sides by s and let $s \to \infty$ to get $1 = B + 0.04 \quad \Rightarrow B = 0.96$:

$$\mathcal{Y}_{zs} = \underbrace{\frac{-0.5365(4.77) + 0.96(s + 1.5)}{(s + 1.5)^2 + 22.75}}_{\mathrm{Re}\{s\} > -1.5} + \underbrace{\frac{0.04}{s}}_{\mathrm{Re}\{s\} > 0}.$$

Notice that the second term, $\frac{0.04}{s}$, is the steady-state response, and thus, $y_{ss}(t) = 0.04u(t)$.

Taking the inverse Laplace transform using Table D.4, we obtain

$$y_{zs}(t) = \left[-0.5365e^{-1.5t}\sin(4.77t) + 0.96e^{-1.5t}\cos(4.77t)\right]u(t) + 0.04u(t).$$

Let us compute the zero-input response:

$$\mathcal{Y}_{zi}(s) = \frac{-s}{s^2 + 3s + 25}, \quad \mathrm{Re}\{s\} > -1.5$$
$$= \frac{\frac{1.5}{4.77}(4.77) - (s + 1.5)}{(s + 1.5)^2 + 22.75}, \quad \mathrm{Re}\{s\} > -1.5$$

The inverse Laplace transform using the table yields

$$y_{zi}(t) = \left[0.3145e^{-1.5t}\sin(4.77t) - e^{-1.5t}\cos(4.77t)\right]u(t).$$

Finally, the transient response is the sum of the zero-input and zero-state responses minus the steady-state response.

$$\begin{aligned} y_{tr}(t) &= \left[(0.3145 - 0.5365)e^{-1.5t}\sin(4.77t) + (0.96 - 1)e^{-1.5t}\cos(4.77t)\right]u(t) \\ &= \left[-0.222e^{-1.5t}\sin(4.77t) - 0.04e^{-1.5t}\cos(4.77t)\right]u(t). \end{aligned}$$

Exercises

Exercise 7.3

Consider the causal differential system described by

$$\frac{1}{4}\frac{d^2y(t)}{dt^2} + \frac{1}{\sqrt{2}}\frac{dy(t)}{dt} + y(t) = \frac{dx(t)}{dt} + x(t),$$

with initial conditions $\frac{dy(0^-)}{dt} = 3,\quad y(0^-) = 0w$. Suppose that this system is subjected to the input signal, $x(t) = e^{-2t}u(t)$. Find the system's damping ratio ζ and undamped natural frequency ω_n. Compute the output of the system $y(t)$ for $t \geq 0$. Find the steady-state response $y_{ss}(t)$, the transient response $y_{tr}(t)$, the zero-input response $y_{zi}(t)$, and the zero-state response $y_{zs}(t)$ for $t \geq 0$.

Answer:

ON THE CD

Exercise 7.4

Use the unilateral Laplace transform to compute the output response $y(t)$ to the input $x(t) = \cos(10t)u(t)$ of the following causal LTI differential system with initial conditions $y(0^-) = 1,\ \frac{dy(0^-)}{dt} = 1$:

$$\frac{d^2y(t)}{dt^2} + 5\frac{dy(t)}{dt} + 6y(t) = x(t).$$

Exercise 7.5

Compute the steady-state response of the causal LTI differential system $5\frac{dy(t)}{dt} + y(t) = 10x(t)$ to the input $x(t) = \sin(20t)$.

Answer:

Exercise 7.6

(a) Find the direct form realization of the transfer function $H(s)=\frac{s^2-3s+12}{3s^2+9s+6}$, $\mathrm{Re}\{s\}>-1$. Is this system BIBO stable? Is it causal? Why? Let *y*(*t*) be the step response of the system. Compute $y(0^+)$ and $y(+\infty)$.

(b) Give a parallel form realization of *H*(*s*) given in (a) with first-order blocks.

Exercise 7.7

(a) Find the direct form realization of the following transfer function. Is this system BIBO stable? Is it causal? Why?

$$H(s)=\frac{s^2+4s-6}{s^3+2s^2-5s-6},\quad -1<\mathrm{Re}\{s\}<2$$

(b) Give a parallel form realization of *H*(*s*) with first-order blocks.

(c) Give a cascade form realization of *H*(*s*) with first-order blocks.

Answer:

Exercise 7.8

Consider the causal differential system described by

$$\frac{1}{2}\frac{d^2y(t)}{dt^2}+\frac{dy(t)}{dt}+2y(t)=-\frac{dx(t)}{dt}-x(t),$$

with initial conditions $\frac{dy(0^-)}{dt}=1,\quad y(0^-)=2$. Suppose this system is subjected to the input signal $x(t)=u(t)$. Give the transfer function of the system and specify its ROC. Compute the steady-state response $y_{ss}(t)$ and the transient response $y_{tr}(t)$ for $t\geq 0$.

8 Time and Frequency Analysis of BIBO Stable, Continuous-Time LTI Systems

In This Chapter

((Lecture 26: Qualitative Evaluation of the Frequency Response from the Pole-Zero Plot))

In this chapter, we will analyze the behavior of stable continuous-time linear time-invariant (LTI) systems by looking at both the time-domain and the frequency-domain points of view. We will see how to get a feel for the frequency response of a system by looking at its transfer function in pole-zero form. We will also introduce the Bode plot, which is a representation of the frequency response of a system that can be sketched by hand.

RELATION OF POLES AND ZEROS OF THE TRANSFER FUNCTION TO THE FREQUENCY RESPONSE

A standing assumption here is that the causal LTI system is *stable*. This means that all the poles of the transfer function lie in the open left half-plane. On the other hand, the zeros do not have this restriction.

We want to be able to characterize qualitatively the system's frequency response from the knowledge of the poles and zeros of the transfer function. Consider a transfer function written in its pole-zero form:

$$H(s)=\frac{K(s-z_1)\cdots(s-z_M)}{(s-p_1)\cdots(s-p_N)}. \tag{8.1}$$

When we let $s=j\omega$, each first-order pole and zero factor can be seen as a vector whose origin is at the pole (zero) and whose endpoint is at $j\omega$. For a fixed frequency ω, each of these vectors adds a phase contribution and a magnitude factor to the overall frequency response. Let us illustrate this by means of two examples.

Example 8.1: A stable first-order system with transfer function

$$H(s)=\frac{1}{s+2},\ \mathrm{Re}\{s\}>-2 \tag{8.2}$$

has the frequency response

$$H(j\omega)=\frac{1}{j\omega+2}. \tag{8.3}$$

In the s-plane, the complex denominator $2+j\omega$ can be seen as a vector-valued function of ω, with the vector's origin at the pole and its endpoint at $j\omega$ on the imaginary axis, as depicted in Figure 8.1 for $\omega=-1,0,1$ rad/s.

Thus, as ω goes from $-\infty$ to 0 rad/s, the magnitude of $2+j\omega$ (the vector's length) goes from ∞ to 2, while its phase goes from $-\pi/2$ to 0 rad. This in turn implies that the magnitude of $H(j\omega)=(2+j\omega)^{-1}$ varies from 0 to 0.5, while its phase goes from $\pi/2$ to 0 rad.

Then, as ω goes from 0 to ∞ rad/s, the magnitude of $2+j\omega$ (the vector's length) goes from 2 to ∞, while its phase goes from 0 to $\pi/2$ rad. This implies that the magnitude of $H(j\omega)=(2+j\omega)^{-1}$ varies from 0.5 to 0, while its phase goes from 0 to $-\pi/2$ rad. Using this information, we can roughly sketch the magnitude and phase of the frequency response as shown in Figure 8.2.

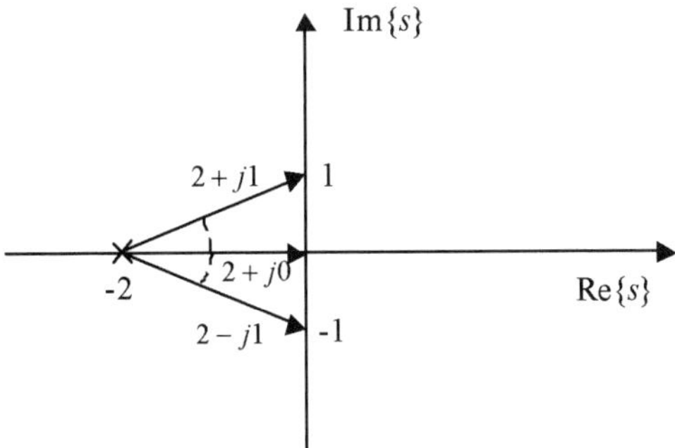

FIGURE 8.1 Denominator $j\omega + 2$ seen as a vector-valued function of frequency in the complex plane.

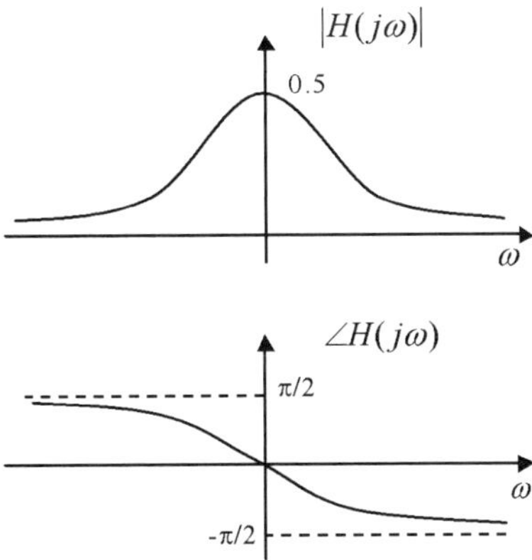

FIGURE 8.2 Sketch of the frequency response of $1/(s + 2)$.

Of course, for this simple example we know that

$$H(j\omega) = \frac{1}{j\omega + 2} = \frac{1}{\sqrt{\omega^2 + 4}} e^{j\arctan\left(\frac{-\omega}{2}\right)}. \tag{8.4}$$

For a higher-order system, the vector representation of each first-order pole and zero factor can help us visualize its contribution to the overall frequency response of the system.

Example 8.2: A stable third-order system with transfer function

$$H(s)=\frac{(s+1)(s-2)}{(s+3)(s+\sqrt{2}-j\sqrt{2})(s+\sqrt{2}+j\sqrt{2})},\ \mathrm{Re}\{s\}>-\sqrt{2} \tag{8.5}$$

has the frequency response

$$H(j\omega)=\frac{(j\omega+1)(j\omega-2)}{(j\omega+3)(j\omega+\sqrt{2}-j\sqrt{2})(j\omega+\sqrt{2}+j\sqrt{2})}. \tag{8.6}$$

In the s-plane, the vector-valued functions of ω originating at the poles and zeros are depicted in Figure 8.3.

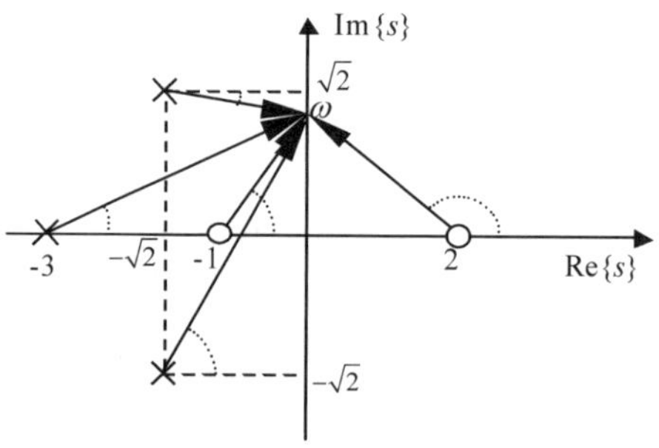

FIGURE 8.3 Vector representation of the first-order terms in the pole-zero form of the transfer function.

The phase at frequency ω is given by the sum of the angles of the vectors originating at the zeros minus the sum of the angles of the vectors originating at the poles.

The magnitude at frequency ω is given by the product of the lengths of the vectors originating at the zeros divided by the product of the lengths of the vectors originating at the poles.

For Example 8.2, we can make the following qualitative observations:

- At $\omega = 0$ rad/s, the lengths of the vectors originating from the two zeros are minimized, and hence we would expect that the DC gain would be somewhat lower than the gain at medium frequencies.
- At $\omega = \pm\sqrt{2}$ rad/s, the lengths of the vectors originating from the poles $p_{1,2} = -\sqrt{2} \pm j\sqrt{2}$ are minimized, and hence we could expect that the gain at those frequencies would be somewhat higher than the gain at low and high frequencies.

- The phase at $\omega = 0$ is $-\pi$ rad and has a net contribution of $-\pi$ rad only from the zero $z_1 = 2$. This is to be expected since the transfer function of Equation 8.5 at $s = 0$ is equal to $-1/6$. The angles of the two vectors originating from the complex conjugate poles cancel each other out.
- The phase around $\omega = \pm\sqrt{2}$ rad/s should be more sensitive to a small change in ω than elsewhere. This is even more noticeable when the complex poles are closer to the imaginary axis. For $\omega = \sqrt{2}$ rad/s, the angle of the vector originating from the pole $p_1 = -\sqrt{2} + j\sqrt{2}$ quickly goes from a significant negative angle to a significant positive angle as ω varies from $\sqrt{2} - \Delta$ to $\sqrt{2} + \Delta$ rad/s. This implies a relatively fast negative drop in the phase plot of the frequency response around $\omega = \sqrt{2}$ rad/s.
- At $\omega = +\infty$, the phase is $-\pi/2$ rad. This comes from a contribution of $-\pi/2$ from the three pole vectors, a contribution of $\pi/2$ from the right half-plane (RHP) zero vector, and a contribution of $\pi/2$ from the left half-plane (LHP) zero vector. The magnitude at $\omega = +\infty$ is 0 as the two zero vectors tending to infinity in length are not sufficient to counteract the three pole vectors also tending to infinity in length.
- At $\omega = -\infty$, the phase is $\pi/2$ rad. This comes from a contribution of $\pi/2$ from the three pole vectors, a contribution of $-\pi/2$ from the RHP zero vector, and a contribution of $-\pi/2$from the LHP zero vector. The magnitude at $\omega = -\infty$ is 0.

A portion of the magnitude of the transfer function $H(s)$ of Equation 8.5, which is represented as a surface over the complex plane, is shown in Figure 8.4. The edge of that surface along the imaginary axis is nothing but the magnitude of the frequency response of the system.

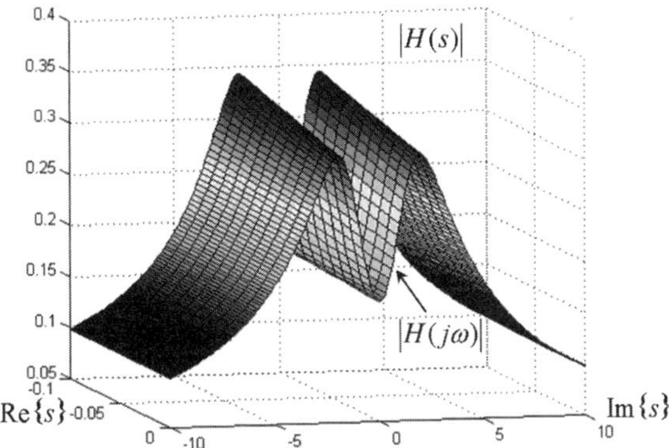

FIGURE 8.4 Magnitudes of the transfer function and its frequency response over a portion of the complex plane.

Remark: The definition of an angle is sometimes ambiguous. In Example 8.2, we have defined the angle of the right half-plane zero vector as being measured counterclockwise along positive angles for $\omega > 0$ and as being measured clockwise along negative angles for $\omega < 0$. This allowed us to obtain $\angle H(j\infty) = -\angle H(-j\infty) = -\pi/2$ rad, which is consistent with the fact that the frequency-response phase of an LTI differential system with real coefficients is an odd function of frequency. However, for most purposes, the angle $\pi/2$ rad can be considered the same as $-3\pi/2$ rad.

((Lecture 27: The Bode Plot))

BODE PLOTS

It is often convenient to use a logarithmic scale to plot the magnitude of a frequency response. One reason is that frequency responses can have a wide dynamic range covering many orders of magnitude. Some frequencies may be amplified by a factor of 1000, while others may be attenuated by a factor of 10^{-4}. Another reason is that using a log scale, we can *add* rather than multiply the magnitudes of cascaded Fourier transforms, which is easier to do graphically:

$$\log\left|Y(j\omega)\right| = \log\left|H(j\omega)\right| + \log\left|X(j\omega)\right|. \tag{8.7}$$

It is customary to use the decibel (dB) as the logarithmic unit. The bel (B) was defined (after Alexander Graham Bell) as a power amplification of $\left|H(j\omega)\right|^2 = 10$ for a system. The decibel is one tenth of a bel. Therefore, for a system with a power gain of 10 at frequency ω, its power gain in dB is

$$10\,\frac{\text{dB}}{\text{B}} \times \log_{10}\left|H(j\omega)\right|^2\ \text{B} = 10\log_{10}10\ \text{dB} = 10\ \text{dB}. \tag{8.8}$$

To measure the actual magnitude gain (not the power gain) of a system, we use the identity

$$10\log_{10}\left|H(j\omega)\right|^2\ \text{dB} = 20\log_{10}\left|H(j\omega)\right|\ \text{dB}. \tag{8.9}$$

Thus, a magnitude plot of $\left|H(j\omega)\right|$ is represented as $20\log_{10}\left|H(j\omega)\right|$ dB using a linear scale in dB. Table 8.1 shows the correspondence between some gains and their values expressed in dB.

TABLE 8.1 Gain Values Expressed in Decibels

Gain	Gain (dB)
0	–∞ dB
0.01	–40 dB
0.1	–20 dB
1	0 dB
10	20 dB
100	40 dB
1000	60 dB

It is also convenient to use a log scale for the frequency, as features of a frequency response can be spread over a wide frequency band.

A *Bode plot* is the combination of a magnitude plot and a phase plot using log scales for the magnitude and the frequency and using a linear scale (in radians or degrees) for the phase. Only positive frequencies are normally considered. As stated above, the Bode plot is quite useful since the overall frequency response of cascaded systems is simply the graphical summation of the Bode plots of the individual systems. In particular, this property is used to hand sketch a Bode plot of a rational transfer function in pole-zero form by considering each first-order factor corresponding to a pole or a zero to be an individual system with its own Bode plot.

Example 8.3: Consider again the first-order system with transfer function

$$H(s)=\frac{1}{s+2},\ \mathrm{Re}\{s\}>-2, \tag{8.10}$$

which has the frequency response

$$H(j\omega)=\frac{1}{j\omega+2}. \tag{8.11}$$

It is convenient to write this frequency response as the product of a gain and a first-order transfer function with unity gain (0 dB) at DC:

$$H(j\omega)=\frac{1}{2}\frac{1}{j\omega/2+1}. \tag{8.12}$$

The *break frequency* is 2 rad/s. The Bode magnitude plot is the graph of:

$$\begin{aligned}20\log_{10}|H(j\omega)| &= 20\log_{10}\left|\frac{1}{2}\right| + 20\log_{10}\left|\frac{1}{\frac{j\omega}{2}+1}\right| \text{ dB} \\ &= -20\log_{10}2 - 20\log_{10}\left|\tfrac{j\omega}{2}+1\right| \text{ dB} \\ &= -6 \text{ dB} - 20\log_{10}\left|\tfrac{j\omega}{2}+1\right| \text{ dB}. \end{aligned} \tag{8.13}$$

Note that for low frequencies, that is, $\omega << 2$,

$$20\log_{10}|H(j\omega)| \approx -6 \text{ dB} - 20\log_{10}|1| \text{ dB} = -6 \text{ dB}, \tag{8.14}$$

and for high frequencies, that is, $\omega >> 2$,

$$\begin{aligned}20\log_{10}|H(j\omega)| &\approx -6 \text{ dB} - 20\log_{10}\left|\frac{\omega}{2}\right| \text{ dB} \\ &= -6 \text{ dB} - 20\log_{10}|\omega| \text{ dB} + 20\log_{10}2 \text{ dB} \\ &= -20\log_{10}|\omega| \text{ dB}. \end{aligned} \tag{8.15}$$

For $\omega = 10$ rad/s in Equation 8.15, we get –20 dB, for $\omega = 100$ rad/s, we get –40 dB, etc. The slope of the asymptote $-20\log_{10}|\omega|$ dB is therefore –20 decibels per decade of frequency (a decade is an increase by a factor of 10.) With the asymptotes meeting at the break frequency 2 rad/s, we can sketch the magnitude Bode plot as shown in Figure 8.5 (dotted line: actual magnitude.)

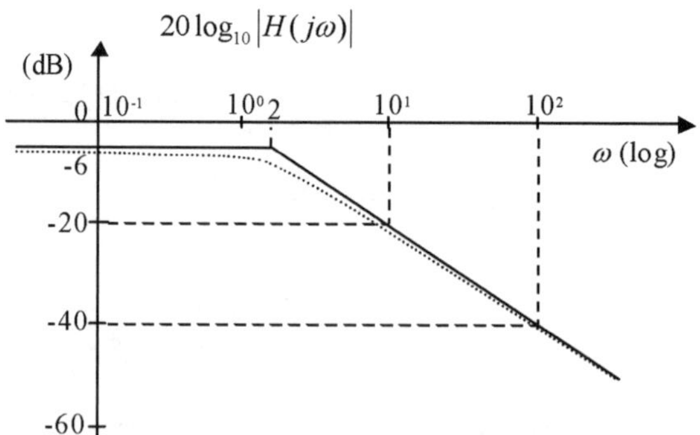

FIGURE 8.5 Bode magnitude plot of a first-order transfer function.

The Bode phase plot is the graph of

$$\angle H(j\omega) = \angle \frac{1}{2} \frac{1}{j\omega/2+1} = \angle \frac{1}{j\omega/2+1} = \arctan\left(\frac{-\frac{\omega}{2}}{1}\right). \tag{8.16}$$

We know that the phase is 0 at $\omega = 0$ and π at $\omega = \infty$. A piecewise linear approximation (with a log frequency scale) to the phase that helps us sketch it is given by

$$\angle H(j\omega) \cong \begin{cases} 0, & \omega \leq \frac{2}{10} \\ -\frac{\pi}{4}\left[\log_{10}\left(\frac{\omega}{2}\right)+1\right], & \frac{2}{10} < \omega < 20. \\ -\frac{\pi}{2}, & \omega \geq 20 \end{cases} \tag{8.17}$$

The approximation given by Equation 8.17 deserves some explanations. The phase approximation is constructed as follows:

- At frequencies lower than one decade below the break frequency, the phase is 0.
- At frequencies higher than one decade above the break frequency, the phase is –π/2.
- In the interval from one decade below to one decade above the break frequency, the phase is linear and goes from 0 to –π/2 with a slope –π/4 radian per decade.

The Bode phase plot is shown in Figure 8.6. The interactive Bode applet on the companion CD-ROM located in D:\Applets\BodePlot\Bode.exe lets the user enter poles and zeros of a transfer function on a pole-zero plot and it then produces a Bode plot of the transfer function. Both the actual frequency response plot and the broken line approximation obtained using the above rules are shown on the applet's Bode plot for comparison.

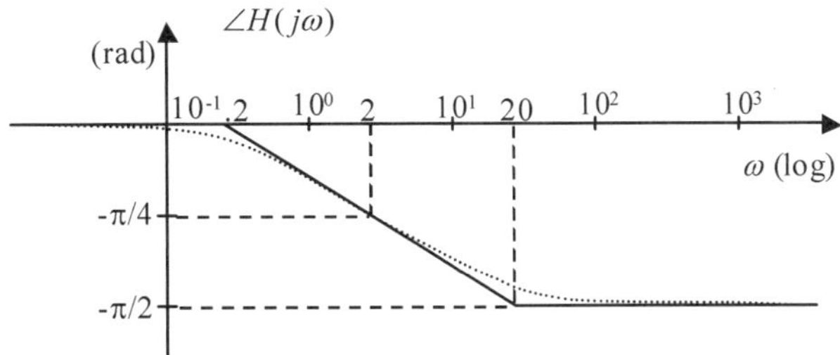

FIGURE 8.6 Bode phase plot of a first-order transfer function.

Note that the Bode magnitude plot of $s + 2$ (the inverse of $H(s)$) is simply the above magnitude plot flipped around the frequency axis (see Figure 8.7), and likewise for the phase plot in Figure 8.8.

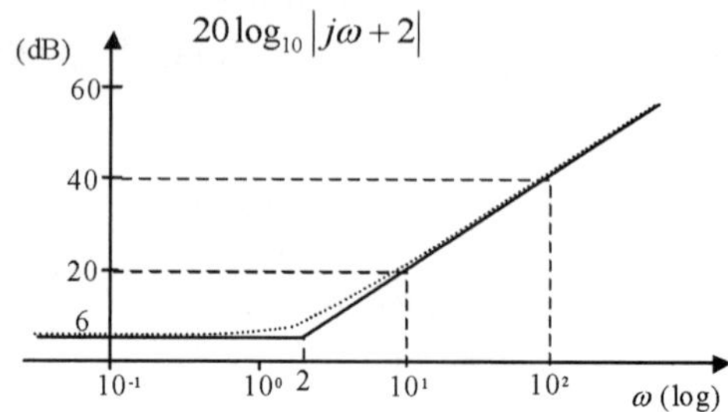

FIGURE 8.7 Bode magnitude plot of $s + 2$.

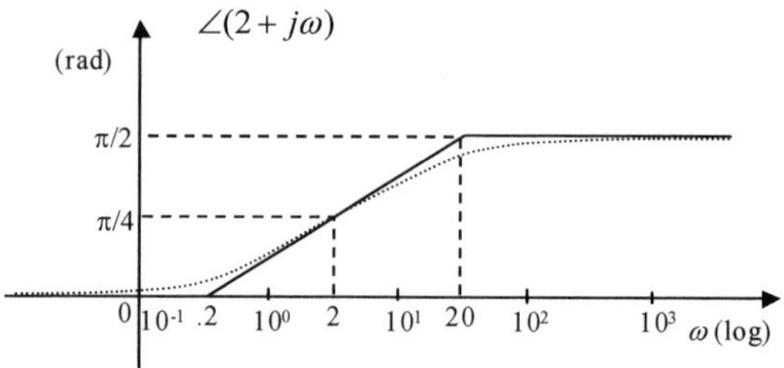

FIGURE 8.8 Bode phase plot of $s + 2$.

Example 8.4: Consider the second-order stable system with transfer function

$$H(s)=\frac{s+100}{\left(s^2+11s+10\right)}=10\frac{\frac{s}{100}+1}{(s+1)\left(\frac{s}{10}+1\right)},\ \mathrm{Re}\{s\}>-1, \tag{8.18}$$

which has the frequency response

$$H(j\omega)=10\frac{\frac{j\omega}{100}+1}{\left(j\omega+1\right)\left(\frac{j\omega}{10}+1\right)}. \tag{8.19}$$

The break frequencies are at 1, 10, and 100 rad/s. For the Bode magnitude plot, we can sketch the asymptotes of each first-order term in Equation 8.19 on the same magnitude graph (as dashed lines) and then add them together as shown in Figure 8.9.

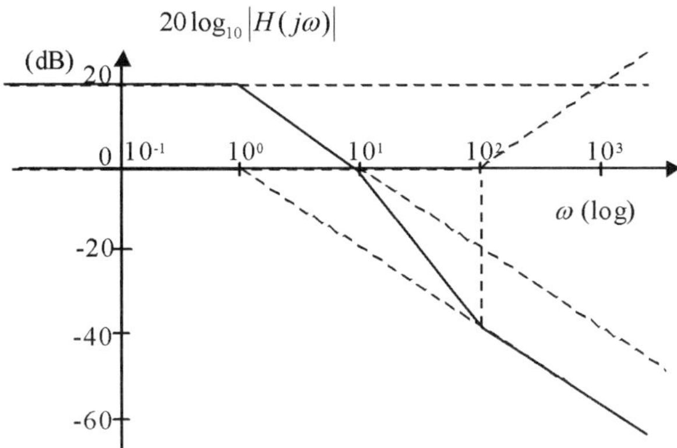

FIGURE 8.9 Bode magnitude plot of a second-order example.

We proceed in a similar fashion to obtain the Bode phase plot of Figure 8.10.

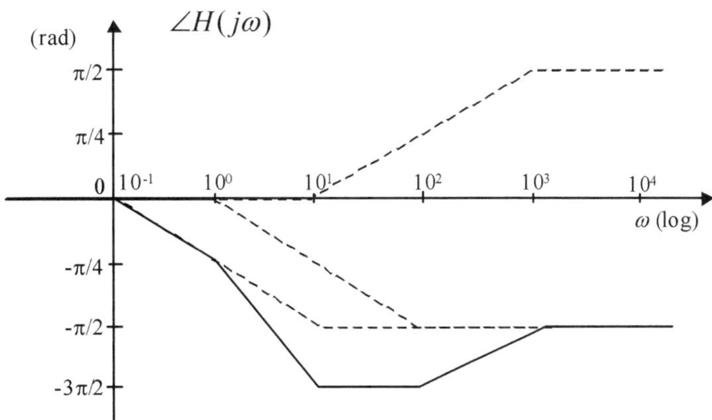

FIGURE 8.10 Bode phase plot of a second-order example.

A Bode plot can easily be obtained in MATLAB. The following MATLAB script bodeplot.m, which is located on the CD-ROM in D:\Chapter8, produces the Bode plot of Example 8.4.

```
%% bodeplot.m Bode plot of a transfer function
% transfer function numerator and denominator
num=[1 100];
den=[1 11 10];
sys=tf(num,den);
% frequency vector
w=logspace(-2,4,200);
% Bode plot
bode(sys,w)
```

((Lecture 28: Frequency Responses of Lead, Lag, and Lead-Lag Systems))

FREQUENCY RESPONSE OF FIRST-ORDER LAG, LEAD, AND SECOND-ORDER LEAD-LAG SYSTEMS

First-order lag systems and lead systems can be considered as building blocks in filter and controller design. They have simple transfer functions with lowpass and highpass frequency responses, respectively, which can be combined into a second-order lead-lag system that has applications in sound equalization and feedback control design.

First-Order Lag

A first-order lag has a transfer function of the form

$$H(s)=\frac{\alpha\tau s+1}{\tau s+1},\quad \mathrm{Re}\{s\}>-\frac{1}{\tau}, \tag{8.20}$$

where $0\le\alpha<1$, $\tau>0$ is the time constant and τ^{-1} (the absolute value of the pole) is called either the natural frequency, the cutoff frequency, or the break frequency, depending on the application. This system is called a *lag* because it has an effect similar to a pure delay of τ seconds $e^{-\tau s}$ at low frequencies, especially for $\alpha = 0$. To see this, expand $H(s)$ as a Taylor series around $s = 0$:

$$\frac{1}{\tau s+1}=1-\tau s+(\tau s)^2-(\tau s)^3+\ldots \tag{8.21}$$

$$e^{-\tau s}=1-\tau s+\frac{(\tau s)^2}{2}-\frac{(\tau s)^3}{3!}+\ldots. \tag{8.22}$$

To first order, these systems are identical. In the previous section, we studied the frequency response of a first-order lag as an example with $\tau = 1/2$ and $\alpha = 0$. In the case $\alpha \neq 0$, the Bode plot is as shown in Figure 8.11 and Figure 8.12.

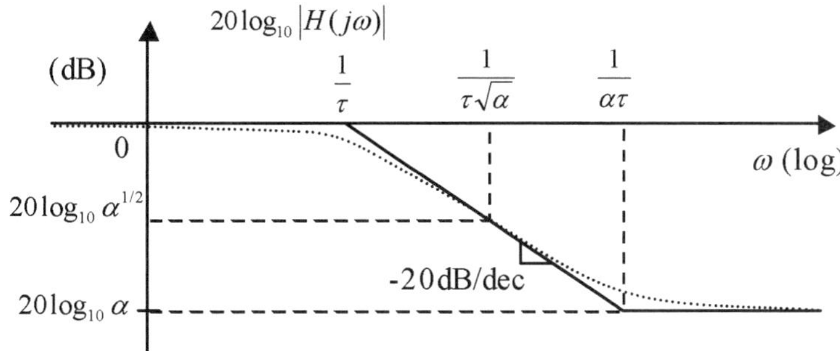

FIGURE 8.11 Bode magnitude plot of a first-order lag.

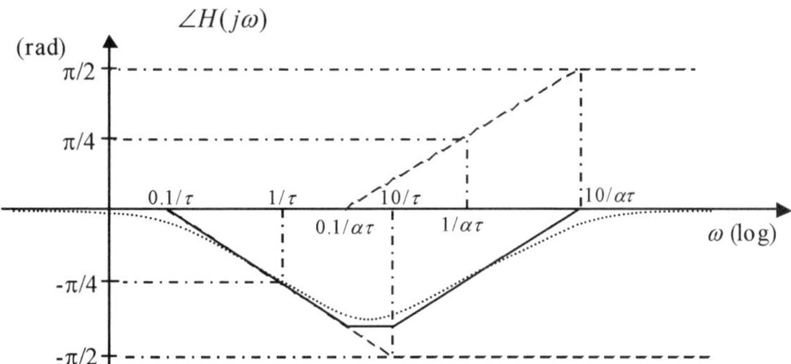

FIGURE 8.12 Bode phase plot of a first-order lag.

The general first-order lag can be thought of as a lowpass filter. Note that the high-frequency gain is α, and the phase tends to 0 at high frequencies, unless $\alpha = 0$, in which case it tends to $-\pi/2$. A first-order lag can be realized with the block diagram shown in Figure 8.13.

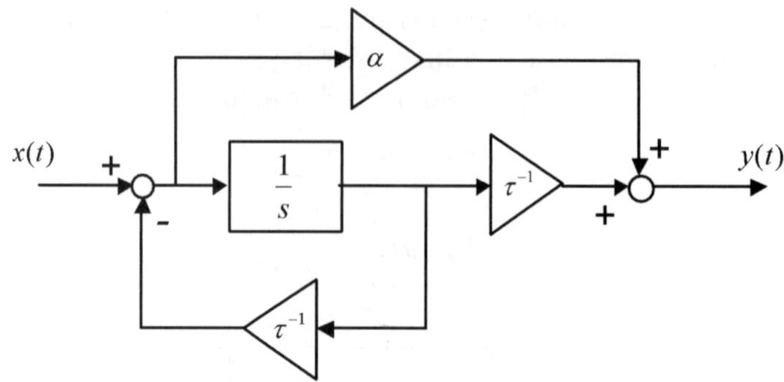

FIGURE 8.13 Realization of a first-order lag.

First-Order Lead

A first-order lead also has a transfer function of the form

$$H(s)=\frac{\alpha\tau s+1}{\tau s+1},\quad \mathrm{Re}\{s\}>-\frac{1}{\tau}, \tag{8.23}$$

where $\tau>0$ but $\alpha > 1$. The Bode plot for this system (assuming that $\alpha > 10$) is shown in Figure 8.14 and Figure 8.15.

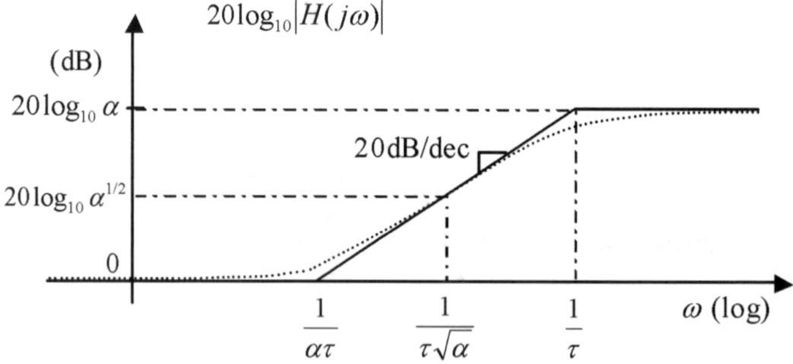

FIGURE 8.14 Bode magnitude plot of a first-order lead.

For the case where $\tau\to 0,\ \alpha\tau\to T$, the first-order lead is equivalent to a differentiator with gain T in parallel with the identity system:

$$H(s)=Ts+1, \tag{8.24}$$

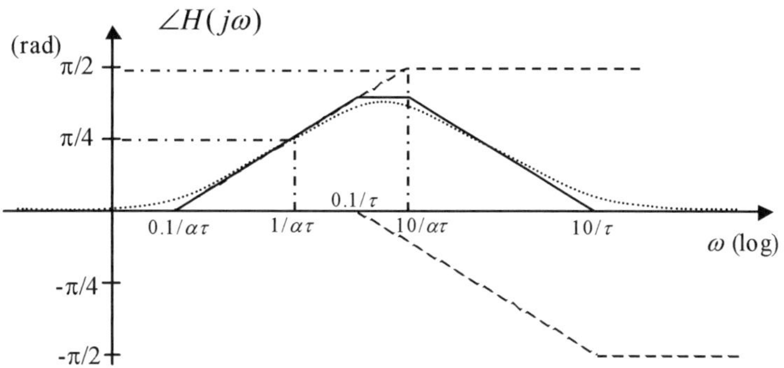

FIGURE 8.15 Bode phase plot of a first-order lead.

and its Bode plot is given in Figure 8.16. Note that the high frequencies are amplified: the higher the frequency, the higher the gain of the system is. This is a property of differentiators, and it explains why high-frequency noise is greatly amplified by such devices. The maximum positive phase is $\pi/2$ rad for $\omega = +\infty$.

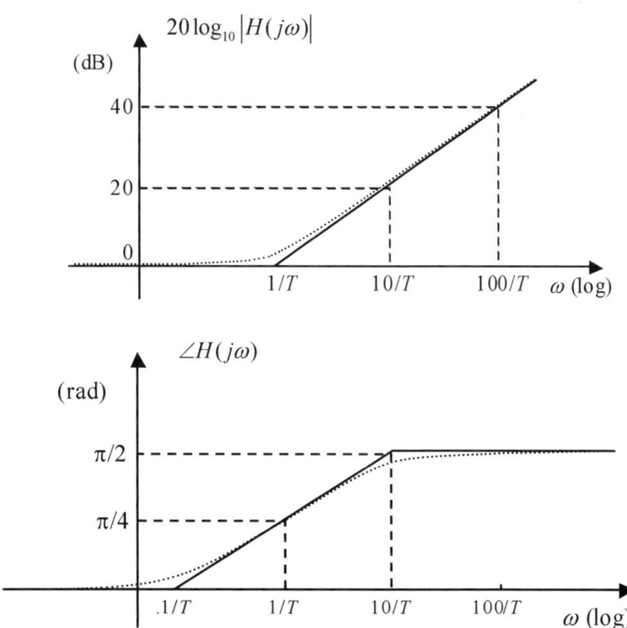

FIGURE 8.16 Bode plot of a limit case of first-order lead $H(s) = Ts + 1$.

Applications: The first-order lead may be used to "differentiate" signals at frequencies higher than $(\alpha\tau)^{-1}$ rad/s but lower than τ^{-1} rad/s. It can help "reshape" pulses that have been distorted by a communication channel with a lowpass frequency response. It is also often used as a controller because it adds positive phase to the overall loop transfer function (more on this in Chapter 11.) A first-order lead system can be realized with the same interconnection as that shown in Figure 8.13 for a first-order lag.

Second-Order Lead-Lag

A second-order lead-lag system has a transfer function of the form

$$H(s) = \frac{K(\alpha\tau_a s+1)(\beta\tau_b s+1)}{(\tau_a s+1)(\tau_b s+1)}, \quad \mathrm{Re}\{s\} > -\frac{1}{\tau_b}, \tag{8.25}$$

where $\tau_a^{-1} > \tau_b^{-1} > 0$ are the lead and lag frequencies, respectively, and $\alpha > 1,\ 0 \le \beta < 1$. This system amplifies the low frequencies and the high frequencies, like a rudimentary equalizer in a stereo system. It is often used as a feedback controller to get more gain at low frequencies and positive phase at the mid-frequencies. This should become clear in Chapter 11, where feedback control theory is introduced. The Bode magnitude plot for this lead-lag system, where $K = \beta^{-1}$, is shown in Figure 8.17.

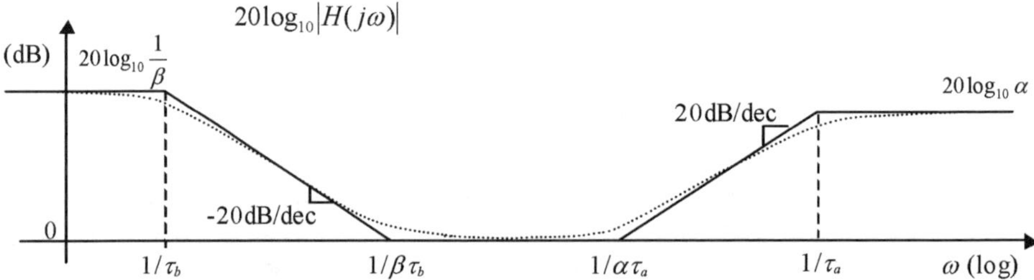

FIGURE 8.17 Bode magnitude plot of a second-order lead-lag.

((Lecture 29: Frequency Response of Second-Order Systems))

FREQUENCY RESPONSE OF SECOND-ORDER SYSTEMS

A general second-order system has a transfer function of the form

$$H(s) = \frac{b_2 s^2 + b_1 s + b_0}{a_2 s^2 + a_1 s + a_0}. \tag{8.26}$$

It can be stable, unstable, causal, or not causal, depending on the signs of the coefficients and the specified region of convergence (ROC). Let us restrict our attention to causal, stable LTI second-order systems of this type. A necessary and sufficient condition for stability is that the coefficients a_i be either all positive or all negative, which ensures that the poles are in the open left half-plane. This is also a necessary, but not sufficient, condition for stability of higher-order systems. Let us also assume that $b_2 = b_1 = 0$; that is, we basically have a lowpass system with two poles and no finite zero. Under these conditions, the transfer function can be expressed as

$$H(s) = \frac{A\omega_n^2}{s^2 + 2\zeta\omega_n s + \omega_n^2}, \tag{8.27}$$

where ζ is the damping ratio and ω_n is the undamped natural frequency of the second-order system. Systems that can be modeled by this transfer function include the mechanical mass-spring-damper system, and the lowpass second-order *RLC* filter, which is a circuit combining an inductance *L*, a capacitance *C*, and a resistance *R*.

Example 8.5: Consider the causal second-order transfer function

$$\begin{aligned} H(s) &= \frac{1}{-2s^2 - 6s - 9} \\ &= -\frac{1}{2}\frac{1}{s^2 + 3s + 9/2}. \end{aligned} \tag{8.28}$$

Its undamped natural frequency is $\omega_n = 3\sqrt{2}/2$, and its damping ratio is

$$\zeta = \frac{3}{2\omega_n} = \frac{3}{2\frac{3\sqrt{2}}{2}} = \frac{1}{\sqrt{2}} = \frac{\sqrt{2}}{2} = 0.707. \tag{8.29}$$

Since the damping ratio is less than one, the two poles are complex. The poles are given by

$$\begin{aligned} p_1 &= -\zeta\omega_n + j\omega_n\sqrt{1-\zeta^2} = -\frac{3\sqrt{2}}{2}\frac{\sqrt{2}}{2} + j\frac{3\sqrt{2}}{2}\sqrt{1-\frac{1}{2}} = -\frac{3}{2} + j\frac{3}{2} \\ p_2 &= -\zeta\omega_n - j\omega_n\sqrt{1-\zeta^2} = -\frac{3}{2} - j\frac{3}{2}. \end{aligned} \tag{8.30}$$

There are three cases of interest for the damping ratio that lead to different pole patterns and frequency response types.

Case $\zeta > 1$

In the case $\zeta > 1$, the system is said to be *overdamped*. The step response does not exhibit any oscillation. The two poles are real, negative, and distinct: $p_1 = -\zeta\omega_n + \omega_n\sqrt{\zeta^2 - 1}$ and $p_2 = -\zeta\omega_n - \omega_n\sqrt{\zeta^2 - 1}$. The second-order system can then be seen as a cascade of two standard first-order systems:

$$H(s) = \frac{A\omega_n^2}{s^2 + 2\zeta\omega_n s + \omega_n^2} = \frac{A\omega_n^2}{p_1 p_2}\left(\frac{1}{\frac{s}{-p_1}+1}\right)\left(\frac{1}{\frac{s}{-p_2}+1}\right) = A\left(\frac{1}{\frac{s}{-p_1}+1}\right)\left(\frac{1}{\frac{s}{-p_2}+1}\right). \quad (8.31)$$

The Bode plot of $H(j\omega) = A\cdot\frac{1}{\frac{j\omega}{-p_1}+1}\frac{1}{\frac{j\omega}{-p_2}+1}$ can be sketched using the technique presented in the previous section for systems with real poles and zeros.

Case $\zeta = 1$

In the case $\zeta = 1$, the system is said to be *critically damped*. The two poles are negative and real, but they are identical. We say that it is a repeated pole; $p_1 = -\zeta\omega_n + j\omega_n\sqrt{1-\zeta^2} = -\zeta\omega_n = p_2$. In this situation, the second-order system can also be seen as a cascade of two first-order transfer functions with the same pole:

$$H(s) = A\frac{1}{(\frac{s}{-p_1}+1)^2}. \quad (8.32)$$

Case $\zeta < 1$

In the case $\zeta < 1$, the system is said to be *underdamped*. The step response exhibits some oscillations, although they really become visible only for $\zeta < 1/\sqrt{2} = 0.707$. The two poles are complex and conjugates of each other: $p_1 = -\zeta\omega_n + j\omega_n\sqrt{1-\zeta^2}$, $p_2 = -\zeta\omega_n - j\omega_n\sqrt{1-\zeta^2}$.

The magnitude and phase of the frequency response

$$H(j\omega) = \frac{A\omega_n^2}{(j\omega)^2 + 2\zeta\omega_n(j\omega) + \omega_n^2} = \frac{A}{\frac{(j\omega)^2}{\omega_n^2} + \frac{2\zeta}{\omega_n}(j\omega) + 1} \quad (8.33)$$

are given by

$$20\log_{10}|H(j\omega)| = 20\log_{10} A - 10\log_{10}\left\{\left(1-\frac{\omega^2}{\omega_n^2}\right)^2 + 4\zeta^2\frac{\omega^2}{\omega_n^2}\right\} \tag{8.34}$$

$$\angle H(j\omega) = -\arctan\left\{\frac{2\zeta\frac{\omega}{\omega_n}}{\left(1-\frac{\omega^2}{\omega_n^2}\right)}\right\}. \tag{8.35}$$

Notice that the denominator in Equation 8.33 was written in such a way that its DC gain is 1. The break frequency is simply the undamped natural frequency. At this frequency, the magnitude is

$$20\log_{10}|H(j\omega_n)| = -20\log_{10}\{2\zeta\}. \tag{8.36}$$

For example, with $\zeta = 0.1$ and $A = 1$, the magnitude at ω_n is 13.98 dB. Note that this is not the maximum of the magnitude, as it occurs at the *resonant frequency,*

$$\omega_{\max} := \omega_n\sqrt{1-2\zeta^2}, \tag{8.37}$$

which is close to ω_n for low damping ratios. At the resonant frequency, the magnitude of the peak resonance is given by

$$\begin{aligned} 20\log_{10}|H(j\omega_{\max})| &= -10\log_{10}\left\{\left(1-\frac{\omega_n^2(1-2\zeta^2)}{\omega_n^2}\right)^2 + 4\zeta^2\frac{\omega_n^2(1-2\zeta^2)}{\omega_n^2}\right\} \\ &= -10\log_{10}\left\{4\zeta^4 + 4\zeta^2(1-2\zeta^2)\right\} \\ &= -10\log_{10}\left\{4\zeta^2(1-\zeta^2)\right\} \\ &= -20\log_{10}\left\{2\zeta\sqrt{1-\zeta^2}\right\} \end{aligned} \tag{8.38}$$

and thus for our example with $\zeta = 0.1$ and $A = 1$, $20\log_{10}|H(j\omega_{\max})| = 16.20$ dB.

The Bode plot for the case $\zeta < 1$ can be sketched using the asymptotes as in Figure 8.18, but at the cost of an approximation error around ω_n that increases as the damping ratio decreases. The roll-off rate past the break frequency is –40 dB/decade. The phase starts at 0 and tends to $-\pi$ at high frequencies.

The Bode plot approximation using the asymptotes does not convey the information about the resonance in the system caused by the complex poles. That is, the damping ratio was not used to draw the asymptotes for the magnitude and phase plots. The peak resonances in the magnitude produced by different values of $\zeta \le 1$ are shown in Figure 8.19. This figure also shows that the phase drop around the normalized undamped natural frequency $\omega_n = 1$ becomes steeper as the damping ratio is decreased.

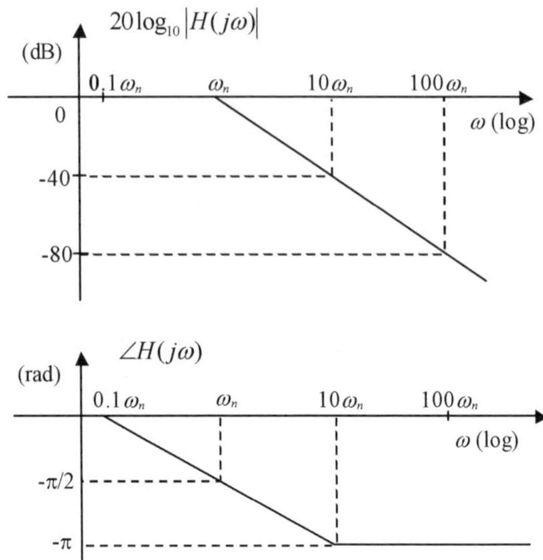

FIGURE 8.18 Bode plot of a second-order system: broken line approximation.

ON THE CD

The following MATLAB script, zetas.m, located on the CD-ROM in D:\Chapter8, was used to produce the Bode plots in Figure 8.19.

```
%% zetas.m Script used to produce the Bode plots of second-order
systems
%% with different damping ratios
zeta=[0.01 [.1:.2:0.9] 1]
num=1;
w=logspace(-1,1,1000);
for k=1:length(zeta)
den(k,:)=[1 2*zeta(k) 1];
[mag(:,k), ph(:,k)]=bode(num,den(k,:),w);
end
figure(1)
semilogx(w,20*log10(mag),'-k')
figure(2)
semilogx(w,pi*ph/180,'-k')
```

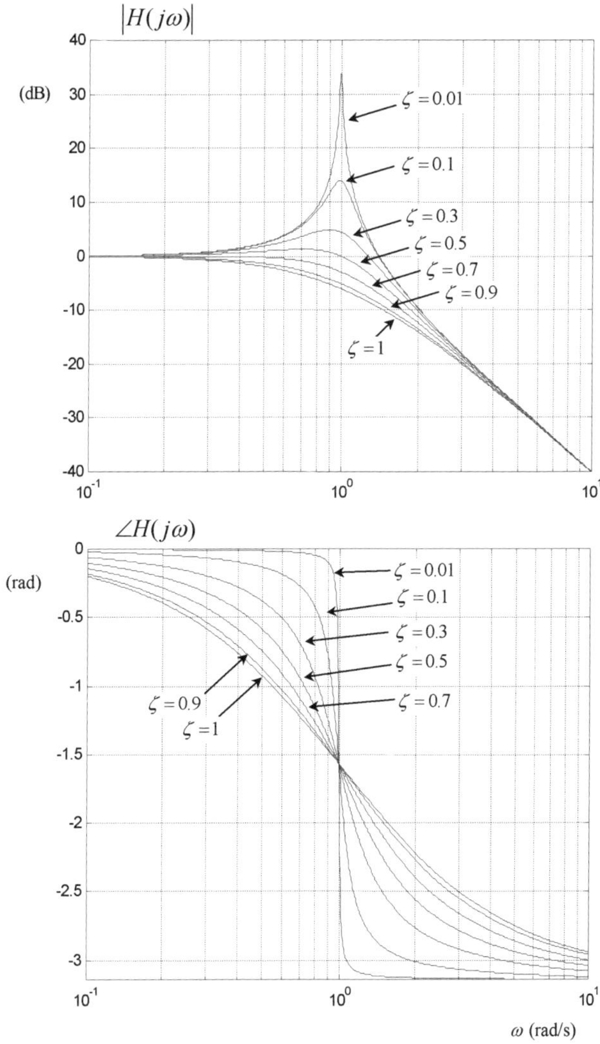

FIGURE 8.19 Bode plots of second-order system $H(s)=\frac{1}{s^2+2\zeta s+1}$ for various damping ratios.

Quality Q

In the field of communications engineering, the underdamped second-order filter has played an important role as a simple frequency-selective bandpass filter. When the damping ratio is very low, the filter becomes highly selective due to its high peak resonance at ω_{max}. The *quality* Q of the filter is defined as

$$Q := \frac{1}{2\zeta}. \tag{8.39}$$

The higher the quality, the more selective the bandpass filter is. To support this claim, the –3 dB bandwidth (frequency band between the two frequencies where the magnitude is 3 dB lower than $20\log_{10}\left|H(j\omega_{\max})\right|$) of the bandpass second-order filter shown in Figure 8.20 is given by

$$\Delta\omega \approx \frac{\omega_{\max}}{Q} = 2\zeta\omega_{\max}. \tag{8.40}$$

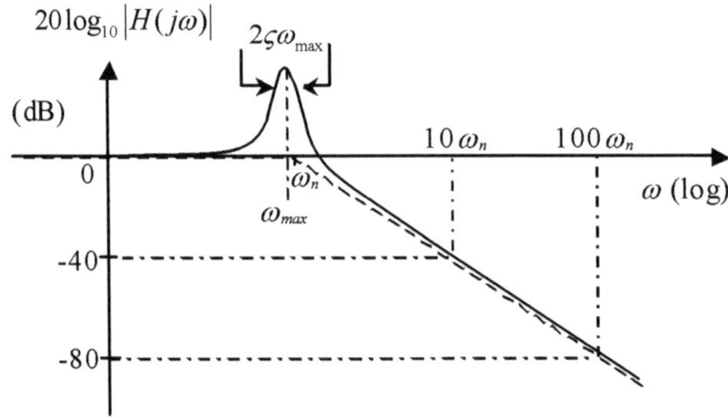

FIGURE 8.20 Bode magnitude plot of a second-order bandpass system.

Maximal Flatness and the Butterworth Filter

In the transition from a second-order system without resonance to one that starts to exhibit a peak, there must be an optimal damping ratio ζ for which the magnitude stays flat over the widest possible bandwidth before rolling off. It turns out that this occurs for $\zeta = 1/\sqrt{2} = 0.707$. For this damping ratio, the real part and imaginary part of the two poles have the same absolute value, and the poles can be expressed as

$$p_1 = \omega_n e^{j\frac{3\pi}{4}}, \quad p_2 = \omega_n e^{-j\frac{3\pi}{4}}. \tag{8.41}$$

We recognize the poles of a lowpass second-order Butterworth filter with cutoff at ω_n. Thus, a Butterworth filter is optimized for its magnitude to be *maximally flat*, as can be seen in Figure 8.19 for the case $\zeta = 0.7$.

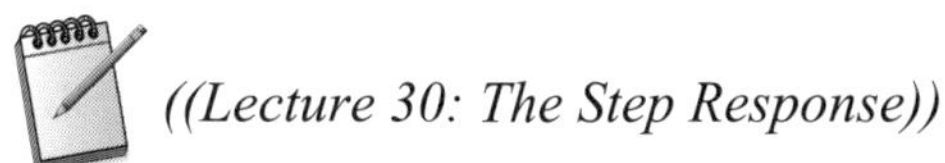

STEP RESPONSE OF STABLE LTI SYSTEMS

A step response experiment is a simple way to characterize a stable LTI system. It is often used in the process industry to help identify an LTI model for the process. Theoretically, the step response conveys all the dynamical information required to characterize the system uniquely, since it is the integral of the impulse response. Note that only step responses of lowpass systems with nonzero DC gains are of interest here. We are not really interested in step responses of highpass or bandpass systems, or more generally of systems with a DC gain of 0.

As engineers, we would like to be able to perform quick quantitative and qualitative analyses on the step response of a system without first having to transform it to the Laplace domain. Qualitative observations can be made about the rise time (fast, sluggish), the overshoot and ringing, etc. On the other hand, more quantitative observations can also be made once unequivocal definitions for quantities like the rise time and the settling time are given.

Rise Time

The rise time of a step response is often used as a qualitative measure of how fast or sluggish a system is, but we can define it unambiguously and use this definition to compare systems between them. One typical definition for the rise time t_r of a system initially at rest is the time taken by the output to rise from 5 to 95% of its final value, as illustrated in Figure 8.21.

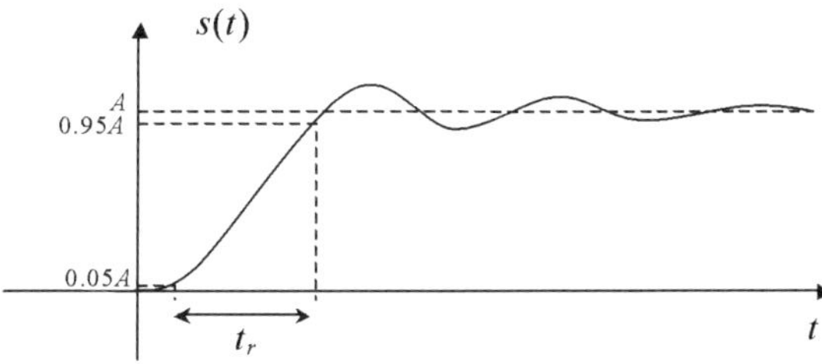

FIGURE 8.21 Definition of rise time.

Note that a step response could have a desirably fast rise time but so much overshoot and ringing that the corresponding system may be judged to have poor performance. A measure of overshoot is given in the next section.

One thing to remember is that the larger the frequency bandwidth of a system, the shorter the rise time. For instance, the step response of a lowpass filter with a cutoff frequency of 1 MHz will have a fast, sub-microsecond rise time.

First-Order Lag

For a first-order lag with $\alpha = 0$ and time constant τ, that is,

$$H(s) = \frac{1}{\tau s + 1}, \tag{8.42}$$

the step response is

$$s(t) = (1 - e^{-\frac{t}{\tau}})u(t). \tag{8.43}$$

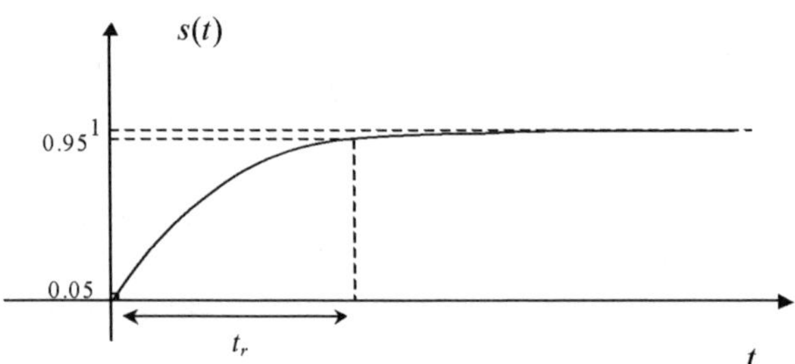

FIGURE 8.22 Rise time of a first-order lag with $\alpha = 0$.

The 95% rise time is given by the difference between the times when the response reaches the value 0.95 and the value 0.05, as shown in Figure 8.22:

$$0.95 = 1 - e^{-\frac{t_{95\%}}{\tau}} \quad \Rightarrow \quad t_{95\%} = -\tau \ln 0.05 = 2.9957\tau. \tag{8.44}$$

$$0.05 = 1 - e^{-\frac{t_{5\%}}{\tau}} \quad \Rightarrow \quad t_{5\%} = -\tau \ln 0.95 = 0.0513\tau. \tag{8.45}$$

$$t_r = 2.9957\tau - 0.0513\tau = 2.9444\tau. \tag{8.46}$$

For the case $0 < \alpha < 1$ and time constant τ, that is,

$$\begin{aligned} H(s) &= \frac{\alpha\tau s+1}{\tau s+1} \\ &= \alpha + \frac{1-\alpha}{\tau s+1} \end{aligned} \tag{8.47}$$

the step response is

$$s(t) = \alpha u(t) + (1-\alpha)(1-e^{-\frac{t}{\tau}})u(t). \tag{8.48}$$

The 95% rise time is given by the difference between the times when the response reaches the value 0.95 and the value 0.05. If $\alpha > 0.05$, then the output is already larger than 0.05 at $t = 0^+$ (see Figure 8.23).

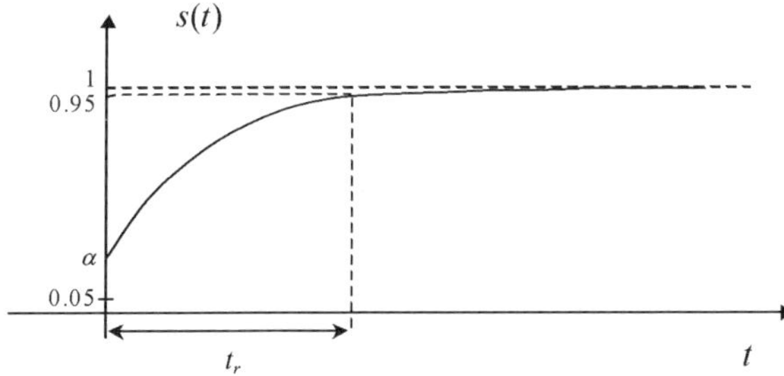

FIGURE 8.23 Rise time for a first-order lag.

On the other hand, if $\alpha > 0.95$, then the rise time is 0.

$$\begin{aligned} &0.95 = \alpha + (1-\alpha)(1-e^{-\frac{t_{95\%}}{\tau}}) \\ &\Rightarrow \quad t_{95\%} = -\tau(\ln 0.05 - \ln(1-\alpha)) = [2.9957 + \ln(1-\alpha)]\tau \end{aligned} \tag{8.49}$$

$$\begin{aligned} &0.05 = \alpha + (1-\alpha)(1-e^{-\frac{t_{5\%}}{\tau}}) \\ &\Rightarrow \quad t_{5\%} = -\tau(\ln 0.95 - \ln(1-\alpha)) = [0.0513 + \ln(1-\alpha)]\tau \end{aligned} \tag{8.50}$$

For the case $0 < \alpha < 0.05$, the rise time is

$$t_r = t_{95\%} - t_{5\%} = -\tau(\ln 0.05 - \ln 0.95) = 2.9957\tau - 0.0513\tau = 2.9444\tau \tag{8.51}$$

For the case $0.05 < \alpha < 0.95$, the rise time is

$$t_r = t_{95\%} = [2.9957 + \ln(1-\alpha)]\tau. \tag{8.52}$$

Notice that the rise time is 0 for $\alpha = 0.95$, as expected.

For the case $-1 < \alpha < 0$ and time constant τ, the system has an open right half-plane (RHP) zero,

$$\begin{aligned} H(s) &= \frac{\alpha\tau s + 1}{\tau s + 1} \\ &= \alpha + \frac{1-\alpha}{\tau s + 1} \end{aligned} \tag{8.53}$$

and the step response is (see Figure 8.24)

$$s(t) = \alpha u(t) + (1-\alpha)(1 - e^{-\frac{t}{\tau}})u(t). \tag{8.54}$$

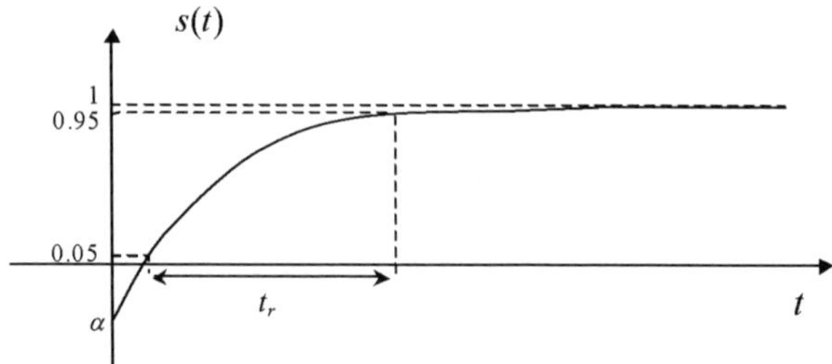

FIGURE 8.24 Rise time of a non-minimum phase system.

According to our definition, the 95% rise time is given by the difference between the times when the response reaches the value 0.95 and the value 0.05:

$$0.95 = 1 - (1-\alpha)e^{-\frac{t_{95\%}}{\tau}} \quad \Rightarrow \quad t_{95\%} = -\tau(\ln 0.05 - \ln(1-\alpha)). \tag{8.55}$$

$$0.05 = 1 - (1-\alpha)e^{-\frac{t_{5\%}}{\tau}} \quad \Rightarrow \quad t_{5\%} = -\tau(\ln 0.95 - \ln(1-\alpha)). \tag{8.56}$$

$$t_r = t_{95\%} - t_{5\%} = -\tau(\ln 0.05 - \ln 0.95) = 2.9957\tau - 0.0513\tau = 2.9444\tau. \tag{8.57}$$

An important thing to notice in Figure 8.24 is that the step response starts in the "wrong direction." That is, we want the output to go to 1, but it actually goes negative first before rising toward 1. This phenomenon, which causes problems for feedback control systems, is associated with systems with RHP zeros, which are also called *non-minimum phase systems.*

Second-Order Systems

We could do a similar analysis for the step response of second-order systems, although it is perhaps better to do it on a case-by-case basis. Suffice it to say that the rise time primarily depends on the undamped natural frequency, but also on the damping ratio. For a given ω_n, the rise time is fastest for $\zeta << 1$, at the expense of a large overshoot. A good tradeoff for a relatively fast rise time with low or no overshoot is obtained for $0.5 \le \zeta \le 1$.

Overshoot

A step response is said to overshoot if it goes past its settling value (see Figure 8.25). The amount of overshoot (we usually consider the first overshoot) can be measured as a percentage of the final value of the output signal.

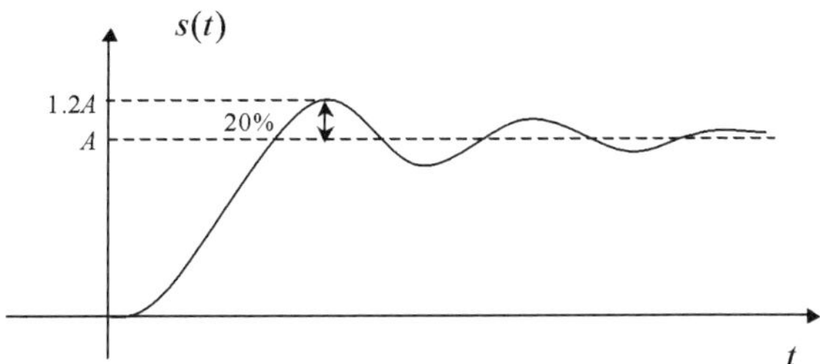

FIGURE 8.25 Definition of overshoot in the step response.

There is no overshoot to speak of for first-order systems, except for first-order leads. Step responses of lead systems have an initial value that is larger than the final value (use the initial value theorem to show this).

The step response of a second-order order system of the form

$$H(s) = \frac{A\omega_n^2}{s^2 + 2\zeta\omega_n s + \omega_n^2} \tag{8.58}$$

overshoots if $\zeta < 1$. The percentage overshoot OS can be computed by finding the maximum value of the step response of the system. The maximum occurs for

$$0 = \frac{ds(t)}{dt} = h(t), \tag{8.59}$$

and thus, we must solve Equation 8.59 for $t_{\max}$. The impulse response $h(t)$ of the second-order system of Equation 8.58 is given by

$$h(t) = A\frac{\omega_n e^{-\zeta\omega_n t}}{\sqrt{1-\zeta^2}}\sin(\omega_n\sqrt{1-\zeta^2}t). \tag{8.60}$$

Note that $\omega_n\sqrt{1-\zeta^2}$ is called the damped natural frequency. Solving Equation 8.59, we find

$$h(t_{\max}) = A\frac{\omega_n e^{-\zeta\omega_n t_{\max}}}{\sqrt{1-\zeta^2}}\sin(\omega_n\sqrt{1-\zeta^2}t_{\max}) \tag{8.61}$$

It can be shown that the step response of the system is given by the right-hand side of the first equality in Equation 8.62. We now have to evaluate $s(t_{\max})$:

$$\begin{aligned} s(t_{\max}) &= A\left\{u(t) - e^{-\zeta\omega_n t}\left[\cos(\omega_n\sqrt{1-\zeta^2}t) + \frac{\zeta}{\sqrt{1-\zeta^2}}\sin(\omega_n\sqrt{1-\zeta^2}t)\right]u(t)\right\}_{t=t_{\max}} \\ &= A\left\{1 - e^{-\frac{\zeta\pi}{\sqrt{1-\zeta^2}}}\left[\cos(\pi) + \frac{\zeta}{\sqrt{1-\zeta^2}}\sin(\pi)\right]u(t)\right\} \\ &= A(1 + e^{-\frac{\zeta\pi}{\sqrt{1-\zeta^2}}}). \end{aligned} \tag{8.62}$$

Finally, the percentage overshoot is given by

$$OS = 100\frac{s(t_{\max}) - A}{A} = 100e^{-\frac{\zeta\pi}{\sqrt{1-\zeta^2}}}\%. \tag{8.63}$$

The percentage overshoot is given for different values of the damping ratio in Table 8.2.

TABLE 8.2 Percentage Overshoot Versus Damping Ratio

ζ	OS (%)
0.1	72.9
0.2	52.7
0.3	37.2
0.4	25.4
0.5	16.3
0.6	9.5
0.707	4.3
0.8	1.5
0.9	0.2
1	0.0

Settling Time

The settling time measures how fast the response practically reaches steady-state. It is defined as the time when the response first reaches the final value to a certain percentage and stays within that percentage of the final value for all subsequent times. For example, the ±5% settling time t_s is the time when the response gets to within 5% of its final value for all subsequent times, as depicted in Figure 8.26.

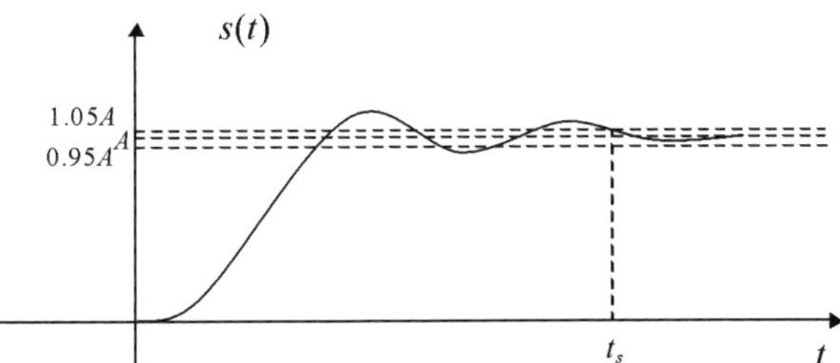

FIGURE 8.26 Definition of settling time.

First-Order Lag

For a first-order lag with $\alpha = 0$ and time constant τ, that is,

$$H(s) = \frac{1}{\tau s + 1}, \tag{8.64}$$

the step response is (see Figure 8.27)

$$s(t) = (1 - e^{-\frac{t}{\tau}})u(t). \tag{8.65}$$

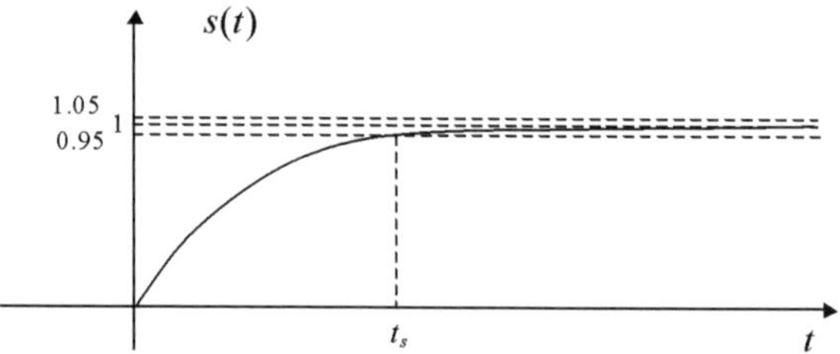

FIGURE 8.27 Settling time for a first-order lag with $\alpha = 0$.

We know that this step response increases monotonically toward 1. Hence the ±5% settling time is given by

$$0.95 = 1 - e^{-\frac{t_s}{\tau}} \quad \Rightarrow \quad t_s = -\tau \ln 0.05 = 2.9957\tau \cong 3\tau, \tag{8.66}$$

and we have the following rule of thumb:

- The ±5% settling time of a first-order lag of the form of Equation 8.64 is equal to three time constants.

Note that the settling time for first-order lags with different values of α considered above is equal to $t_{95\%}$.

Second-Order Systems

The settling time for a second-order system depends primarily on the undamped natural frequency, but also on the damping ratio. It should be determined on a case-by-case basis because for a given ω_n, the settling time is a nonlinear function of ζ.

We can see this from the step response plot in Figure 8.26. The response enters the ±5% band from the top, but if we gradually increased the damping ratio, then the response would eventually enter that band from below, causing a discontinuity in the settling time as a function of ζ.

Remark: The step response of a system is easy to plot in MATLAB. Consider, for example, the M-file D:\Chapter8\stepresp.m given below.

```
%% stepresp.m Plots the step response of a system
% numerator and denominator of transfer function
num=[1];
den=[1 3 9];
sys=tf(num,den);
% time vector
tfinal=10;
step(sys,tfinal);
```

IDEAL DELAY SYSTEMS

The transfer function of an ideal delay of T time units is

$$H(s) = e^{-sT}. \qquad (8.67)$$

The magnitude of its frequency response $H(j\omega) = e^{-j\omega T}$ is 1 for all frequencies, whereas its phase is linear and negative for positive frequencies. The Bode plot of a pure delay system is shown in Figure 8.28. Note that the phase appears to be nonlinear because of the logarithmic frequency scale.

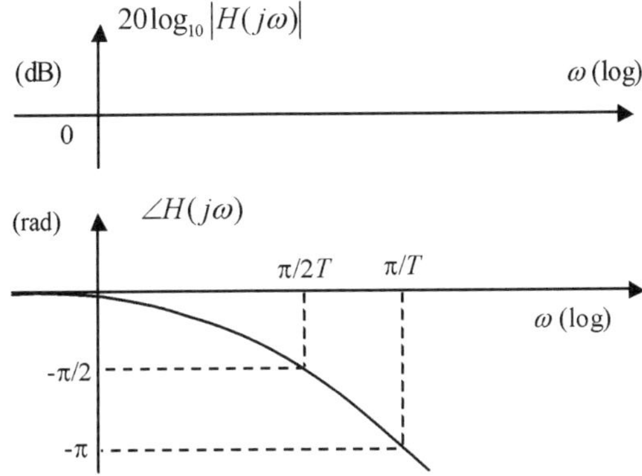

FIGURE 8.28 Bode plot of an ideal delay system.

GROUP DELAY

We have just seen that a pure delay corresponds to a linear negative phase shift. A lowpass system also has a negative phase, so it must have an effect similar to a time delay on the input signal. If we look at a narrow frequency band where the phase is almost linear, then an input signal with energy restricted to that band will be delayed by a value given by the slope of the phase function. This is called the *group delay,* and it is defined as follows:

$$\tau(\omega) := -\frac{d}{d\omega}\angle H(j\omega). \tag{8.68}$$

Suppose that the magnitude of a system is constant, but its phase is not. The output signal will be distorted if the group delay is not constant, that is, if the phase is nonlinear. In this case, the complex exponentials at different frequencies that compose the input signal get delayed by different amounts of time, thereby causing distortion in the output signal.

NON-MINIMUM PHASE AND ALL-PASS SYSTEMS

Systems whose transfer functions have RHP zeros are said to be *non-minimum phase*. This comes from the Bode phase plot of such systems. There always exists a minimum-phase system whose Bode magnitude plot is exactly the same as that of the non-minimum phase system but whose phase is "less negative."

Hendrik Bode showed that for a given magnitude plot, there exists only one minimum-phase system that has this magnitude. Moreover, the phase of this system can be uniquely determined from the magnitude plot. There also exists an infinite number of non-minimum phase systems that have the same magnitude plot, yet their phase plots are "more negative"; that is, they fall below the phase plot of the minimum-phase system.

Example 8.6: Consider the minimum-phase system $H(s) = 1$. The magnitude of its frequency response if 1, and its phase is zero for all frequencies. Now consider the system

$$H_1(s) = \frac{-s+1}{s+1}. \tag{8.69}$$

This is a non-minimum phase system whose magnitude of the frequency response is 1 for all frequencies. Its phase is given by

$$\angle H_1(j\omega) = \arctan\left(\frac{-\omega}{1}\right) + \arctan\left(\frac{-\omega}{1}\right) = -2\arctan(\omega), \tag{8.70}$$

which tends to $-\pi$ as $\omega \to \infty$. The Bode plot of this system is given in Figure 8.29.

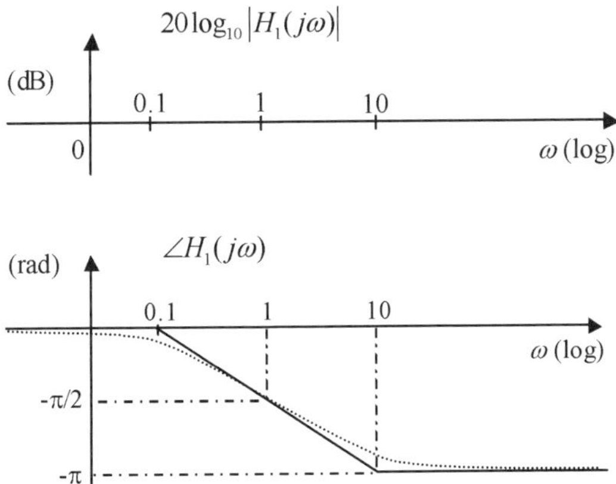

FIGURE 8.29 Bode plot of a first-order non-minimum phase system.

Such a system is called an *allpass system* because it passes all frequencies with unity gain. Thus an allpass system has unity magnitude for all frequencies but can have any phase function.

Example 8.7: The non-minimum phase system

$$H_1(s) = \frac{-s+100}{(s+1)(s+10)} \tag{8.71}$$

has the same magnitude as the minimum-phase system

$$H(s) = \frac{s+100}{(s+1)(s+10)} \tag{8.72}$$

given in Example 8.4, but its phase is more negative, as shown in the Bode phase plot of Figure 8.30. Note that any non-minimum phase transfer function can be expressed as the product of a minimum phase transfer function and an allpass transfer function. For the Example 8.7, we can write

$$H_1(s) = \underbrace{\frac{s+100}{(s+1)(s+10)}}_{\text{minimum-phase}} \underbrace{\frac{-s+100}{s+100}}_{\text{allpass}}. \tag{8.73}$$

The Bode phase plots of $H(s)$ and $H_1(s)$ are shown in Figure 8.30.

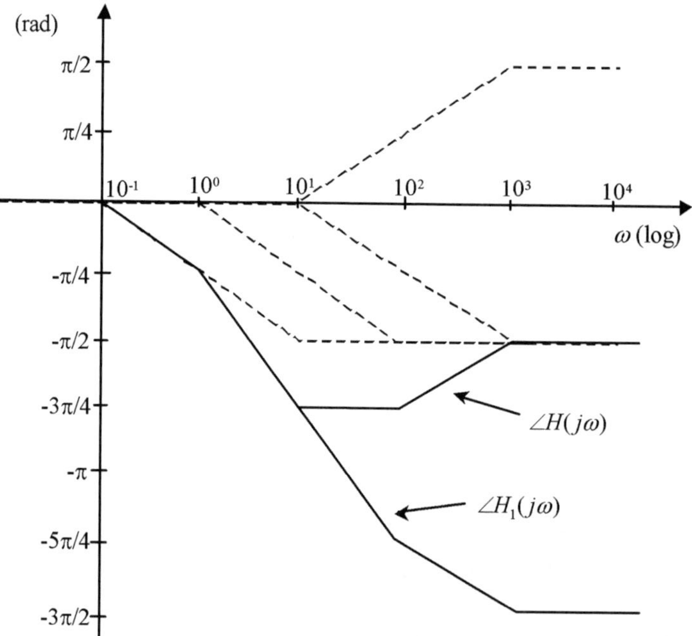

FIGURE 8.30 Bode phase plot of minimum phase and non-minimum phase systems.

Finally, as mentioned earlier, the step response of a non-minimum-phase system often starts off in the wrong direction, which makes these systems difficult to control.

SUMMARY

In this chapter, we analyzed stable continuous-time LTI systems in the frequency domain and in the time domain.

- A qualitative relationship between the pole-zero plot and the frequency response of a stable LTI system was established.
- The Bode plot was introduced as a convenient representation of the frequency response of a system that can be sketched by hand.
- We characterized the frequency responses of first-order lag and lead systems and of second-order systems.
- The time domain performance of first- and second-order systems was quantified using the step response. The classical performance criteria of rise time, settling time, and overshoot were discussed.
- We briefly discussed the issues of group delay, allpass systems, and non-minimum phase systems.

TO PROBE FURTHER

Bode plots can be used in the analysis of feedback control systems as we will find out in Chapter 11. See also Bélanger, 1995 and Kuo and Golnaraghi 2002. For further examples of step responses of LTI systems, see Kamen and Heck 1999.

EXERCISES

Exercises with Solutions

Exercise 8.1

Sketch the pole-zero plots in the s-plane and the Bode plots (magnitude and phase) for the following systems. Specify if the transfer functions have poles or zeros at infinity.

(a) $$H(s)=\frac{100(s-1)(s+10)}{(s+100)^2},\ \mathrm{Re}\{s\}>-100$$

Answer:

$$H(s)=\frac{100(s-1)(s+10)}{(s+100)^2}=\frac{-0.1(-s+1)(s/10+1)}{(0.01s+1)(0.01s+1)},\ \mathrm{Re}\{s\}>-100$$

The break frequencies are at $\omega_1 = 1, \omega_2 = 10$ (zeros); $\omega_3 = 100$ (double pole). The pole-zero plot is shown in Figure 8.31, and the Bode plot is shown in Figure 8.32.

(b) $H(s) = \dfrac{s+10}{s(0.001s+1)}$, $\mathrm{Re}\{s\} > 0$

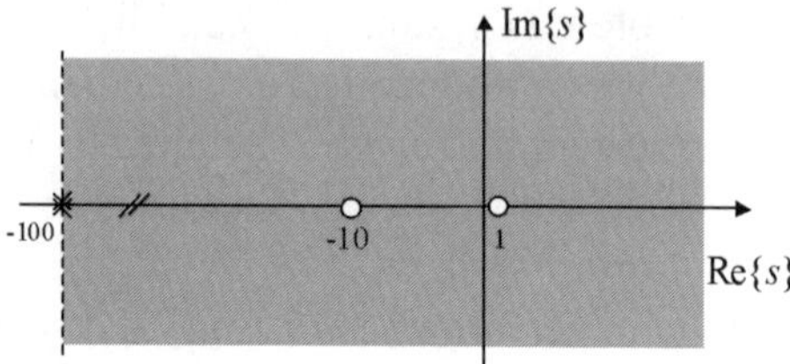

FIGURE 8.31 Pole-zero plot of the transfer function of Exercise 8.1(a).

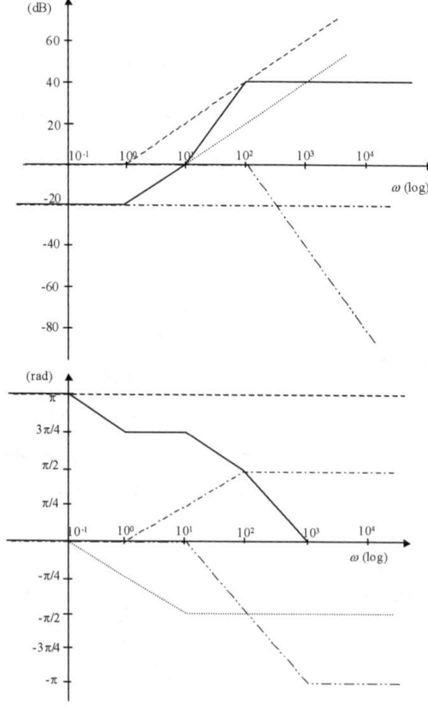

FIGURE 8.32 Bode plot of the transfer function of Exercise 8.1(a).

Answer:

$$H(s)=\frac{s+10}{s(0.001s+1)}=\frac{10(s/10+1)}{s(s/1000+1)},\ \mathrm{Re}\{s\}>0$$

The pole-zero plot is given in Figure 8.33.

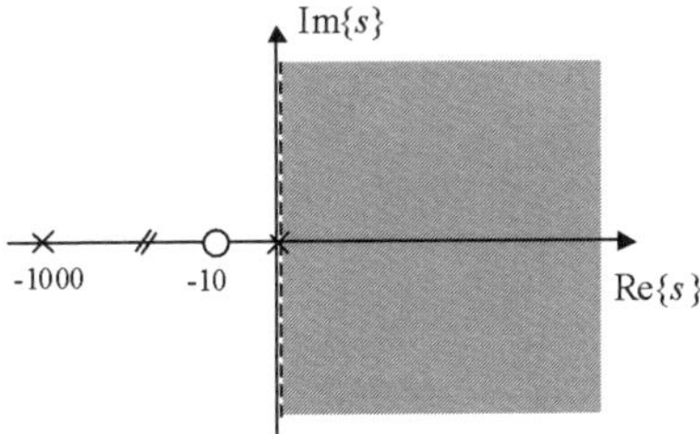

FIGURE 8.33 Pole-zero plot of the transfer function of Exercise 8.1(b).

The break frequencies are $\omega_1 = 10$ (zero); $\omega_2 = 0, \omega_3 = 1000$ (poles), and the transfer function has one zero at ∞. The Bode plot is shown in Figure 8.34.

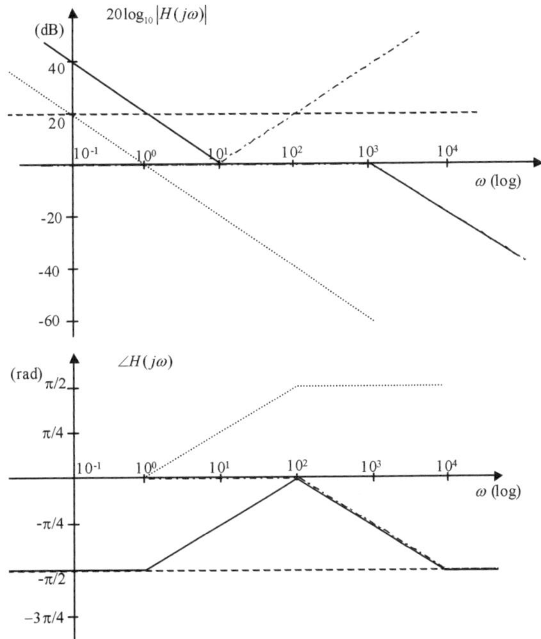

FIGURE 8.34 Bode plot of the transfer function of Exercise 8.1(b).

(c) $H(s)=\dfrac{s^2+2s+1}{(s+100)(s^2+10s+100)}, \ \text{Re}\{s\}>-5$

Answer:
We can write the transfer function as follows:

$$H(s)=\frac{0.0001(s+1)^2}{(0.01s+1)(0.01s^2+0.1s+1)}=\frac{0.01(s+1)^2}{(0.01s+1)(s+5-j5\sqrt{3})(s+5+j5\sqrt{3})}, \ \text{Re}\{s\}>-5$$

The pole zero plot is shown in Figure 8.35, and the Bode plot is shown in Figure 8.36.

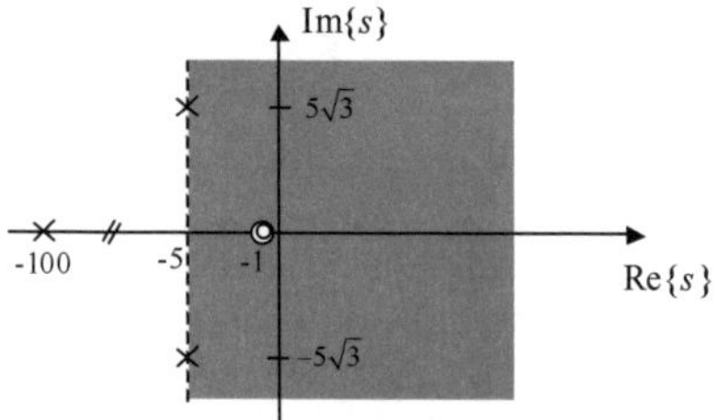

FIGURE 8.35 Pole-zero plot of the transfer function of Exercise 8.1(c).

Exercise 8.2

Consider the mechanical system in Figure 8.37 consisting of a mass m attached to a spring of stiffness k and a viscous damper (dashpot) of coefficient b, both rigidly connected to ground. This basic system model is quite useful for studying a number of systems, including a car's suspension or a flexible robot link.

Assume that the mass-spring-damper system is initially at rest, which means that the spring generates a force equal, but opposite to, the force of gravity to support the mass. The balance of forces on the mass causing motion is the following:

$$x(t)-F_k(t)-F_b(t)=m\frac{d^2y(t)}{dt^2}$$

(a) Write the differential equation governing the motion of the mass.

Answer:

$$m\frac{d^2y(t)}{dt^2}+b\frac{dy(t)}{dt}+ky(t)=x(t)$$

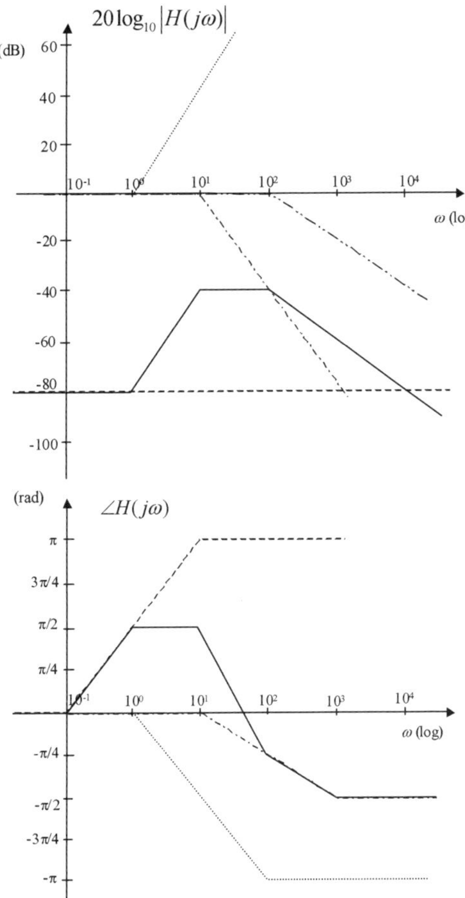

FIGURE 8.36 Bode plot of the transfer function of Exercise 8.1(c).

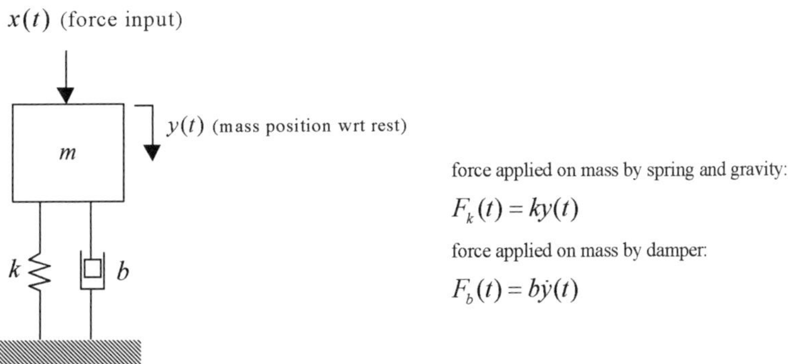

FIGURE 8.37 Mass-spring-damper system of Exercise 8.2.

(b) Find the transfer function of the system relating the applied force to the mass position. Express it in the form $H(s)=\frac{A\omega_n^2}{s^2+2\zeta\omega_n s+\omega_n^2}$. What is the damping ratio ζ for this mechanical system? What is its undamped natural frequency ω_n?

Answer:

$$H(s)=\frac{1}{ms^2+bs+k}$$
$$=\frac{(1/k)(k/m)}{s^2+\frac{b}{m}s+\frac{k}{m}}$$

The natural frequency is given by $\omega_n^2=\frac{k}{m}\Rightarrow\omega_n=\sqrt{\frac{k}{m}}$. Note that the larger the mass, the lower the undamped natural frequency; the stiffer the spring, the higher the undamped natural frequency. The damping ratio of the system is then

$$\zeta=\frac{\frac{b}{m}}{2\omega_n}=\frac{\frac{b}{m}}{2\sqrt{\frac{k}{m}}}=\frac{b}{2\sqrt{mk}}.$$

For a given dashpot, the larger the mass and/or spring constant, the less damped the system will be.

(c) Let the physical constants have numerical values $m=2\,\text{kg}$, $k=8\,\text{N/m}$, and $b=4\ \text{N}/{}^{\text{m}}\!/\!_{\text{s}}$. Suppose that the applied force is a step $x(t)=3u(t)\,\text{N}$. Compute and sketch the resulting mass position for all times. What is the mass position in steady-state? What is the percentage of the first overshoot in the step response? What is the $\pm5\%$ settling time of the mass? (a numerical answer will suffice.)

Answer:
With the numerical values given, the damping ratio and undamped natural frequencies are

$$\omega_n=\sqrt{\frac{k}{m}}=\sqrt{\frac{8\frac{\frac{\text{kgm}}{\text{s}^2}}{\text{m}}}{2\,\text{kg}}}=2\,\frac{\text{rad}}{\text{s}},$$

$$\zeta=\frac{b}{2\sqrt{mk}}=\frac{4\frac{\text{N}}{\text{m/s}}}{2\sqrt{16\,\text{kg}\frac{\text{N}}{\text{m}}}}=0.5.$$

The step input force is $x(t)=3u(t)\overset{L}{\leftrightarrow}\frac{3}{s}$, $\mathrm{Re}\{s\}>0$. The Laplace transform of the step response is given by

$$\begin{aligned}Y(s)&=\frac{1.5}{s(s^2+2s+4)}\\&=\frac{-0.18750\ +\ j0.10826}{s+1-j\sqrt{3}}+\frac{-0.18750\ \text{-}\ j0.10826}{s+1+j\sqrt{3}}+\frac{0.375}{s}.\end{aligned}$$

Taking the inverse Laplace transforms of the partial fractions and simplifying, we get

$$\begin{aligned}y(t)&=\Big[(-0.18750+j0.10826)e^{(-1+j\sqrt{3})t}+(-0.18750-j0.10826)e^{(-1-j\sqrt{3})t}\Big]u(t)+0.375u(t)\\&=2e^{-t}\,\mathrm{Re}\Big[(-0.18750+j0.10826)e^{j\sqrt{3}t}\Big]u(t)+0.375u(t)\\&=2e^{-t}\Big[-0.18750\cos\sqrt{3}t-0.10826\sin\sqrt{3}t\Big]u(t)+0.375u(t)\ \text{m}.\end{aligned}$$

This step response is plotted in Figure 8.38. The mass position in steady state is 0.375 m.

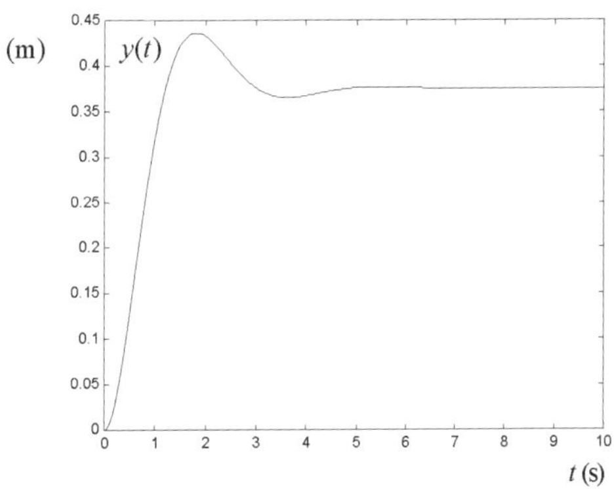

FIGURE 8.38 Step response of the mass-spring-damper system of Exercise 8.2.

The ±5% settling time of the mass is found to be $t_s=2.65$ s. The percentage of overshoot is

$$OS=100e^{-\frac{\zeta\pi}{\sqrt{1-\zeta^2}}}\%=100e^{-\frac{0.5\pi}{\sqrt{0.75}}}\%=16.3\%.$$

Exercises

Exercise 8.3

Compute the 95% rise time t_r and the ±5% settling time t_s of the step response of the system $H(s)=\frac{0.001s+1}{0.1s+1}$, $\mathrm{Re}\{s\}>-10$.

Answer:

Exercise 8.4

Compute the DC gain in decibels, the peak resonance in decibels, and the quality Q of the second-order causal filter with transfer function $H(s)=\frac{1000}{s^2+2s+100}$.

Exercise 8.5

Compute the actual value of the first overshoot in the step response of the causal LTI system

$$H(s)=\frac{5}{3s^2+3s+6}.$$

Answer:

Exercise 8.6

Compute the group delay of a communication channel represented by the causal first-order system $H(s)=\frac{1}{0.01s+1}$, $\mathrm{Re}\{s\}>-100$. Compute the approximate value of the channel's delay at very low frequencies.

Exercise 8.7

Sketch the pole-zero plots in the s-plane and the Bode plots (magnitude and phase) for the following systems. Specify whether the transfer functions have poles or zeros at infinity.

(a) $H(s)=\dfrac{100(s-20)}{(s+5)(s+100)^2}$, $\mathrm{Re}\{s\}>-5$

(b) $H(s)=\dfrac{-s+10}{s(0.005s+1)}$, $\mathrm{Re}\{s\}>0$

(c) $H(s)=\dfrac{s^2}{s^2+30s+900},\ \operatorname{Re}\{s\}>-15$

Answer:

Exercise 8.8

Sketch the pole-zero plots in the s-plane and the Bode plots (magnitude and phase) for the following systems. Specify if the transfer functions have poles or zeros at infinity.

(a) $H(s)=\dfrac{100(s-10)}{(s+1)(s+10)(s+100)},\ \operatorname{Re}\{s\}>-1$

(b) $H(s)=\dfrac{s+1}{s(0.01s+1)},\ \operatorname{Re}\{s\}>0$

(c) $H(s)=\dfrac{s(s^2-9)}{(s+100)(s^2+10s+100)},\ \operatorname{Re}\{s\}>-5$

Exercise 8.9

Consider the causal differential system described by

$$\frac{1}{4}\frac{d^2y(t)}{dt^2}+\frac{1}{\sqrt{2}}\frac{dy(t)}{dt}+y(t)=\frac{dx(t)}{dt}+x(t),$$

with initial conditions $\frac{dy(0^-)}{dt}=3,\quad y(0^-)=0$. Suppose that this system is subjected to the input signal $x(t)=e^{-2t}u(t)$.

(a) Find the system's damping ratio ζ and undamped natural frequency ω_n. Compute the output of the system $y(t)$ for $t\geq 0$. Find the steady-state response $y_{ss}(t)$, the transient response $y_{tr}(t)$, the zero-input response $y_{zi}(t)$, and the zero-state response $y_{zs}(t)$ for $t\geq 0$.

(b) Plot $y_{ss}(t)$, $y_{tr}(t)$, $y_{zi}(t)$, and $y_{zs}(t)$ for $t\geq 0$, all on the same figure using MATLAB or any other software of your choice.

(c) Find the frequency response of the system and sketch its Bode plot.

Answer:

Exercise 8.10

Consider the causal differential system described by its direct form realization shown in Figure 8.39.

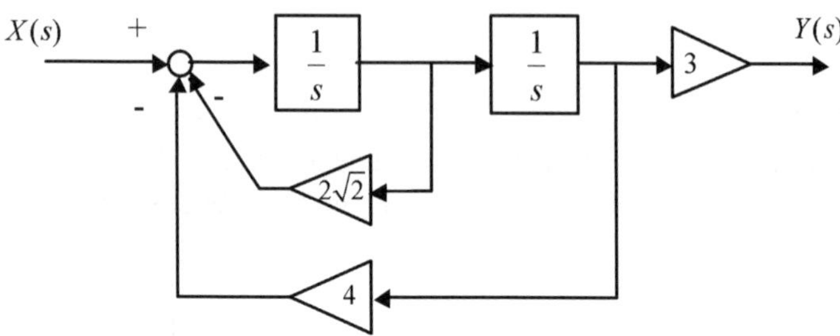

FIGURE 8.39 System of Exercise 8.10.

This system has initial conditions $\frac{dy(0^-)}{dt} = -1, \quad y(0^-) = 2$. Suppose that the system is subjected to the unit step input signal $x(t) = u(t)$.

(a) Write the differential equation of the system. Find the system's damping ratio ζ and undamped natural frequency ω_n. Give the transfer function of the system and specify its ROC. Sketch its pole-zero plot. Is the system stable? Justify.

(b) Compute the step response of the system (including the effect of initial conditions), its steady-state response $y_{ss}(t)$, and its transient response $y_{tr}(t)$ for $t \geq 0$. Identify the zero-state response and the zero-input response in the Laplace domain.

(c) Compute the percentage of first overshoot in the step response of the system assumed this time to be initially at rest.

9 Application of Laplace Transform Techniques to Electric Circuit Analysis

In This Chapter

- Review of Nodal Analysis and Mesh Analysis of Circuits
- Transform Circuit Diagrams: Transient and Steady-State Analysis
- Operational Amplifier Circuits
- Summary
- To Probe Further
- Exercises

((Lecture 31: Review of Nodal Analysis and Mesh Analysis of Circuits))

The Laplace transform is a very useful tool for analyzing linear time-invariant (LTI) electric circuits. It can be used to solve the differential equation relating an input voltage or current signal to another output signal in the circuit. It can also be used to analyze the circuit directly in the Laplace domain, where circuit components are replaced by their impedances seen as transfer functions.

REVIEW OF NODAL ANALYSIS AND MESH ANALYSIS OF CIRCUITS

Let us quickly review some of the fundamentals of circuit analysis, such as nodal and mesh analysis based on Kirchhoff's current and voltage laws.

Nodal Analysis

Kirchhoff's Current Law (KCL) states that the sum of all currents entering a node is equal to zero. This law can be used to analyze a circuit by writing the current equations at the nodes (nodal analysis) and solving for the node voltages. Nodal analysis is usually applied when the unknowns are voltages. For a circuit with N nodes and $N-1$ unknown node voltages, one needs to solve $N-1$ nodal equations.

Example 9.1: Suppose we have the resistor-inductor-capacitor (RLC) circuit of Figure 9.1 and we want to solve for the voltage across the resistor $v(t)$.

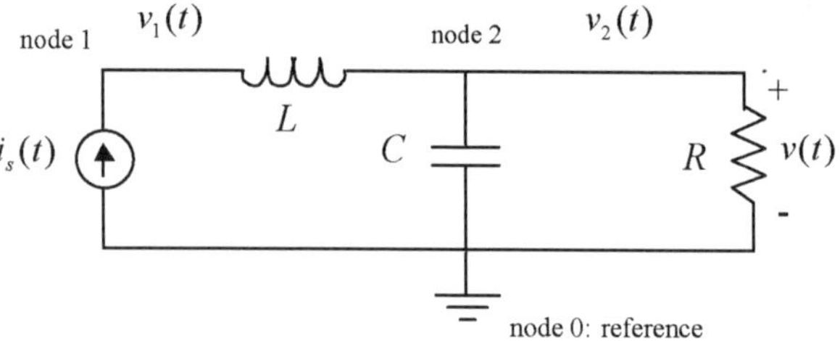

FIGURE 9.1 *RLC* circuit with a current source input.

There are three nodes. The bottom one is taken to be the reference node (voltage = 0). We can solve this circuit by writing the node equations at the other two nodes by applying KCL.

Node 1:

$$i_s(t)+\frac{1}{L}\int_{-\infty}^{t}[v_2(\tau)-v_1(\tau)]d\tau=0$$

$$\Rightarrow \quad L\frac{di_s(t)}{dt}=v_1(t)-v_2(t) \tag{9.1}$$

Node 2:

$$i_s(t)-C\frac{dv_2(t)}{dt}-\frac{1}{R}v_2(t)=0$$

$$\Rightarrow \quad i_s(t)=C\frac{dv_2(t)}{dt}+\frac{1}{R}v_2(t) \tag{9.2}$$

Given the source current $i_s(t)$, the voltage $v(t) = v_2(t)$ is obtained by solving the first-order differential Equation (9.2). Suppose there is an initial condition $v(0^-)$ on the capacitor voltage and the current is a unit step function. We use the unilateral Laplace transform to obtain

$$\begin{aligned}
&Cs\mathcal{V}(s) - Cv(0^-) + \frac{1}{R}\mathcal{V}(s) = \mathcal{V}_s(s) \\
\Rightarrow \quad &\mathcal{V}(s) = \frac{R}{RCs+1}\mathcal{V}_s(s) + \frac{RC}{RCs+1}v(0^-) \\
&= \frac{R}{s(RCs+1)} + \frac{RC}{RCs+1}v(0^-) \\
&= \frac{R}{s} + \frac{-R}{s+\frac{1}{RC}} + \frac{1}{s+\frac{1}{RC}}v(0^-).
\end{aligned} \tag{9.3}$$

Taking the inverse Laplace transform, we get

$$v(t) = R(1 - e^{-\frac{t}{RC}})u(t) + v(0^-)e^{-\frac{t}{RC}}u(t) \tag{9.4}$$

When voltage sources are present in the circuit, we can create "supernodes" around them. KCL applies to these supernodes. However, there are two node voltages associated with them, not just one.

Example 9.2: Consider the *RLC* circuit of Figure 9.2.

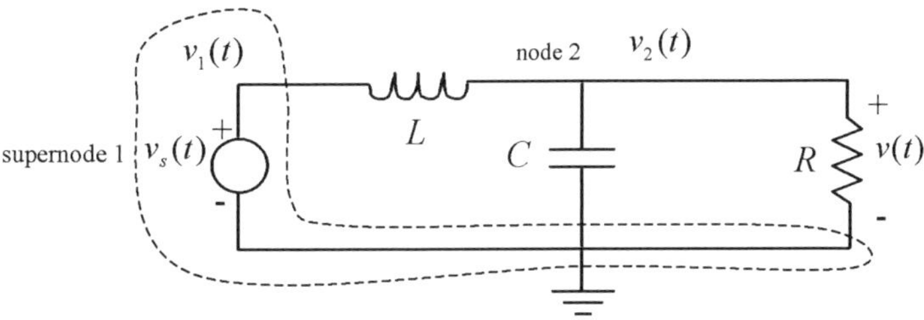

FIGURE 9.2 *RLC* circuit with voltage source input and supernode.

Since there is one supernode for which we know that $v_1(t) = v_s(t)$ and one ordinary node, we need only one node equation:

Node 1:

$$\frac{1}{L}\int_{-\infty}^{t}[v_s(\tau)-v_2(\tau)]d\tau - C\frac{dv_2(t)}{dt} - \frac{1}{R}v_2(t) = 0$$

$$\Rightarrow \frac{1}{L}[v_s(t)-v_2(t)] = C\frac{d^2v_2(t)}{dt^2} + \frac{1}{R}\frac{dv_2(t)}{dt}$$

$$v_s(t) = LC\frac{d^2v_2(t)}{dt^2} + \frac{L}{R}\frac{dv_2(t)}{dt} + v_2(t) \qquad (9.5)$$

Mesh Analysis

Kirchhoff's Voltage Law (KVL) states that the sum of all voltages around a mesh (a loop that has no element within it) is equal to zero. This law can be used to analyze a circuit by writing the voltage equation for each mesh (mesh analysis) and solving for the mesh currents. Mesh analysis is usually applied when the unknowns are currents.

Example 9.3: Suppose that we have the circuit in Figure 9.3 and we want to solve for the current $i(t) = i_1(t) - i_2(t)$ flowing in the capacitor.

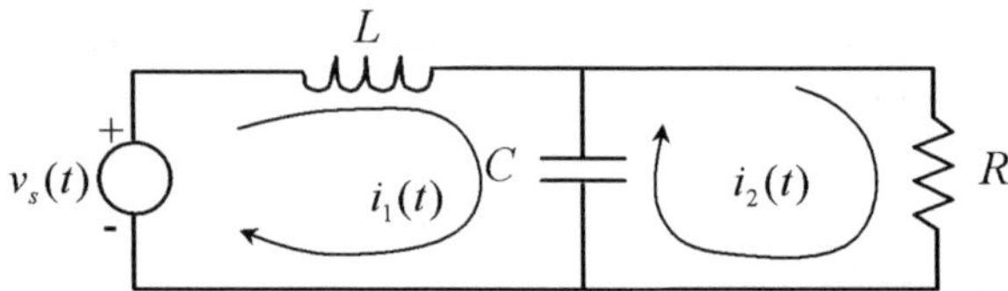

FIGURE 9.3 *RLC* circuit with voltage source input and mesh currents

Mesh 1:

$$v_s(t) - L\frac{di_1(t)}{dt} - \frac{1}{C}\int_{-\infty}^{t}[i_1(\tau)-i_2(\tau)]d\tau = 0$$

$$\Rightarrow \frac{1}{C}[i_1(t)-i_2(t)] + L\frac{d^2i_1(t)}{dt^2} = \frac{dv_s(t)}{dt} \qquad (9.6)$$

Mesh 2:

$$\frac{1}{C}\int_{-\infty}^{t}[i_1(\tau)-i_2(\tau)]d\tau - Ri_2(t) = 0$$

$$\Rightarrow \frac{1}{C}[i_1(t)-i_2(t)] = R\frac{di_2(t)}{dt} \qquad (9.7)$$

We can transform these two equations to the Laplace domain before solving them for the mesh currents. Equation 9.6 becomes

$$\begin{aligned} I_1(s) - I_2(s) + LCs^2 I_1(s) &= CsV_s(s) \\ (1 + LCs^2)I_1(s) - CsV_s(s) &= I_2(s) \end{aligned} \tag{9.8}$$

and Equation 9.7 becomes

$$\begin{aligned} I_1(s) - I_2(s) &= RCsI_2(s) \\ (1 + RCs)I_2(s) &= I_1(s) \end{aligned} \tag{9.9}$$

Substituting for $I_1(s)$ in Equation 9.8, we get

$$\begin{aligned} [(1 + LCs^2)(1 + RCs) - 1]I_2(s) &= CsV_s(s) \\ I_2(s) &= \frac{CV_s(s)}{RLC^2s^2 + LCs + RC} \end{aligned} \tag{9.10}$$

and

$$I_1(s) = \frac{(1 + RCs)CV_s(s)}{RLC^2s^2 + LCs + RC} \tag{9.11}$$

Now, we find the Laplace transform of the capacitor current to be

$$\begin{aligned} I(s) &= I_1(s) - I_2(s) \\ &= \frac{[(1 + RCs) - 1]CV_s(s)}{RLC^2s^2 + LCs + RC} \\ &= \frac{CsV_s(s)}{LCs^2 + \frac{L}{R}s + 1}. \end{aligned} \tag{9.12}$$

When current sources are present in the circuit, it actually simplifies the mesh analysis.

Example 9.4: Consider the circuit shown in Figure 9.4.
The current source specifies mesh current $i_1(t)$:

$$i_s(t) = i_1(t) \tag{9.13}$$

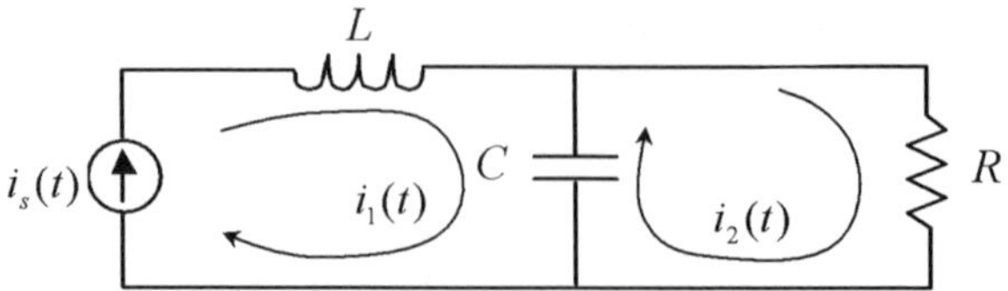

FIGURE 9.4 *RLC* circuit with current source input and mesh currents.

and we only need the other mesh equation:

Mesh 2:
$$\frac{1}{C}[i_s(t)-i_2(t)]=R\frac{di_2(t)}{dt} \tag{9.14}$$

which is a simple first-order equation expressed in the Laplace domain as

$$\begin{aligned}(1+RCs)I_2(s)&=I_s(s)\\ I_2(s)&=\frac{1}{1+RCs}I_s(s)\end{aligned} \tag{9.15}$$

((Lecture 32: Transform Circuit Diagrams, Op-Amp Circuits))

TRANSFORM CIRCUIT DIAGRAMS: TRANSIENT AND STEADY-STATE ANALYSIS

The nice thing about using the Laplace transform for circuit analysis is that we can replace each impedance in a circuit by its equivalent unilateral Laplace transform, and solve the circuit as if all the impedances were simple resistors. Initial conditions can also be treated easily as additional sources.

Transform Circuit for Nodal Analysis

As we have just seen in the previous section, nodal analysis can be used to analyze a circuit by writing the current equations at the nodes and solving for the node voltages. For a resistive network, the currents are usually written as the difference between two voltages divided by the impedance (resistance). For a transform circuit, the same principle applies, although the impedance of each element is in general a function of the complex variable s.

Example 9.5: For the circuit shown in Figure 9.5, we want to solve for the voltage $v(t)$ from $t = 0$. Let us assume that there is an initial current $i_L(0^-)$ in the inductor and an initial voltage $v_C(0^-)$ in the capacitor.

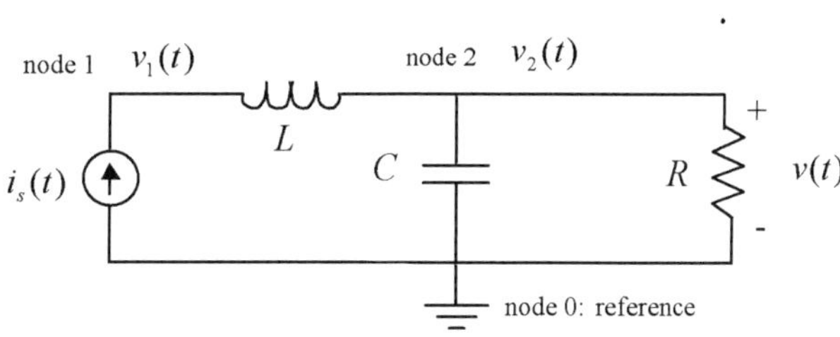

FIGURE 9.5 *RLC* circuit with a current source input.

Using the unilateral Laplace transform, the inductor current can be written as

$$
\begin{aligned}
Ls\mathcal{I}_L(s) - Li_L(0^-) &= \mathcal{V}_L(s) \\
\mathcal{I}_L(s) &= \frac{1}{Ls}\mathcal{V}_L(s) + \frac{1}{s}i_L(0^-)
\end{aligned}
\tag{9.16}
$$

and the corresponding circuit diagram combining the impedance Ls in the Laplace domain and the initial condition seen as a current source for the inductor is shown in Figure 9.6.

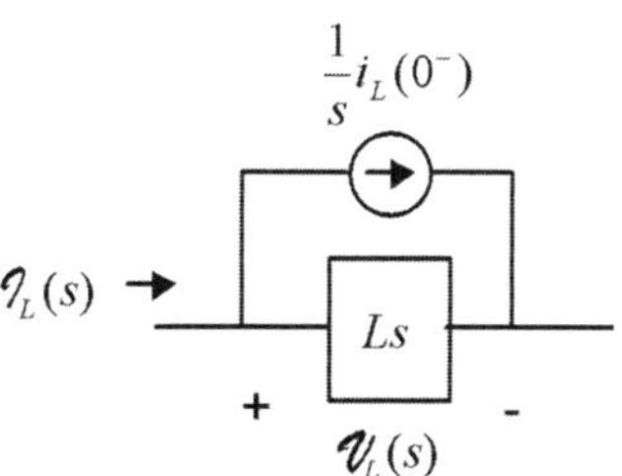

FIGURE 9.6 Equivalent circuit of inductor in the Laplace domain for nodal analysis.

The capacitor's voltage-current relationship in the Laplace domain is written as

$$\mathcal{I}_C(s) = Cs\mathcal{V}_C(s) - Cv_C(0^-) \tag{9.17}$$

and the corresponding circuit diagram combining the impedance $\frac{1}{Cs}$ in the Laplace domain and the initial condition seen as a current source for the capacitor is given in Figure 9.7.

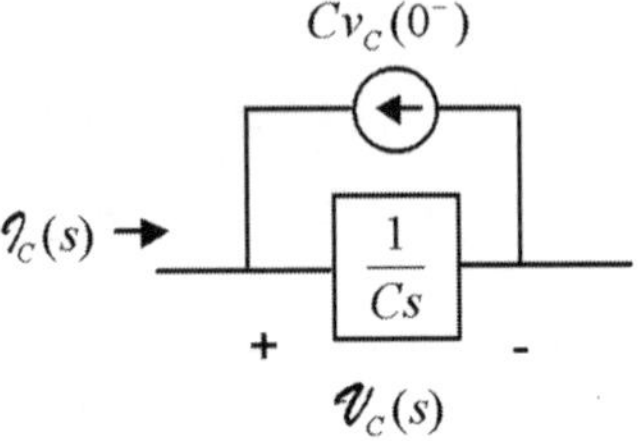

FIGURE 9.7 Equivalent circuit of the capacitor in the Laplace domain for nodal analysis.

A resistor of resistance R is just an impedance R in the Laplace domain. With these impedances and equivalent current sources defined, the transform circuit is depicted in Figure 9.8.

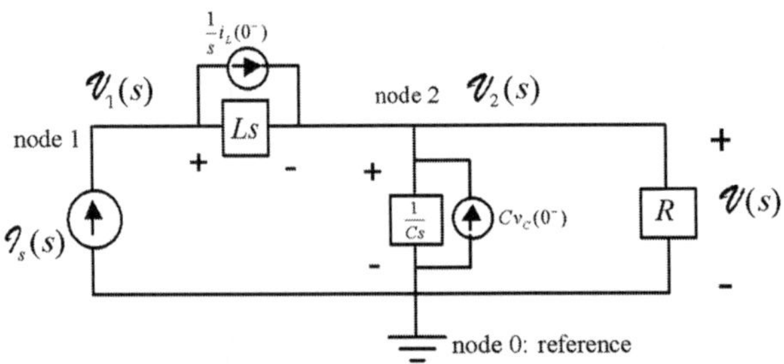

FIGURE 9.8 Transform circuit diagram with current source.

We can solve this circuit by writing the node equations.

Node 1:
$$\mathcal{I}_s(s) + \frac{1}{Ls}[\mathcal{V}_2(s) - \mathcal{V}_1(s)] - \frac{1}{s}i_L(0^-) = 0$$
$$\Rightarrow \quad \mathcal{V}_1(s) = Ls\mathcal{I}_s(s) + \mathcal{V}_2(s) - Li_L(0^-) \tag{9.18}$$

Node 2:

$$\mathcal{I}_s(s) - Cs\mathcal{V}_2(s) + Cv_2(0^-) - \frac{1}{R}\mathcal{V}_2(s) = 0$$

$$\Rightarrow \quad \mathcal{V}_2(s) = \frac{R}{1+RCs}\mathcal{I}_s(s) + \frac{RCv_2(0^-)}{1+RCs} \tag{9.19}$$

Substituting this expression for $\mathcal{V}_2(s)$ in Equation 9.18, we obtain

$$\mathcal{V}_1(s) = Ls\mathcal{I}_s(s) + \frac{R}{1+RCs}\mathcal{I}_s(s) + \frac{RCv_2(0^-)}{1+RCs} - Li_L(0^-) \tag{9.20}$$

Assuming that the source current $i_s(t)$ is a unit step, the voltage $v(t) = v_2(t)$ is obtained by substituting $1/s$ for $\mathcal{I}_s(s)$ in Equation 9.19 first and by taking the inverse Laplace transform:

$$v(t) = R(1 - e^{-\frac{t}{RC}})u(t) + v(0^-)e^{-\frac{t}{RC}}u(t) \tag{9.21}$$

The voltage $\mathcal{V}_1(s)$ is obtained in a similar way by using Equation 9.20.

$$v_1(t) = L[1 - i_L(0^-)]\delta(t) + R(1 - e^{-\frac{t}{RC}})u(t) + v(0^-)e^{-\frac{t}{RC}}u(t) \tag{9.22}$$

Notice that there is an impulse in the node 1 voltage response, which is not surprising since the voltage across the inductor is proportional to the derivative of the unit step current.

Example 9.6: Recall that when voltage sources are present in the circuit, we can create "supernodes" around them, as shown in Figure 9.9.

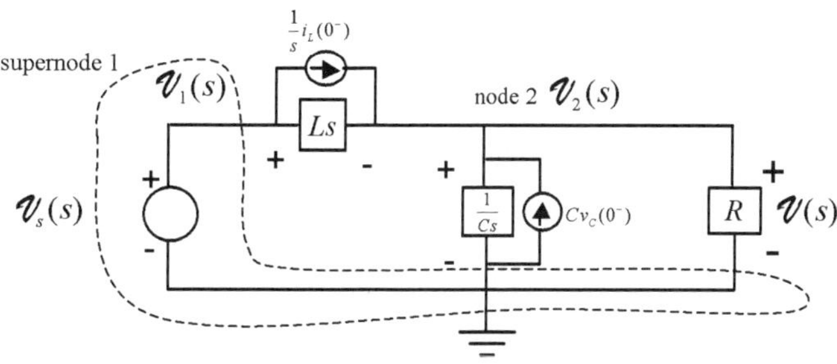

FIGURE 9.9 Transform circuit diagram for a circuit with a supernode.

We have one supernode for which we know that $v_1(t) = v_s(t)$ and one ordinary node; thus, we need only one node equation:

$$\text{Node 2:} \quad \frac{1}{Ls}[\mathcal{V}_s(s) - \mathcal{V}_2(s)] + \frac{1}{s}i_L(0^-) - Cs\mathcal{V}_2(s) + Cv_C(0^-) - \frac{1}{R}\mathcal{V}_2(s) = 0$$

$$\Rightarrow \quad LCs^2\mathcal{V}_2(s) + \frac{L}{R}s\mathcal{V}_2(s) + \mathcal{V}_2(s) = \mathcal{V}_s(s) + Li_L(0^-) + LCsv_C(0^-)$$

$$\mathcal{V}_2(s) = \frac{1}{LCs^2 + \frac{L}{R}s + 1}\mathcal{V}_s(s) + \frac{LCsv_C(0^-) + Li_L(0^-)}{LCs^2 + \frac{L}{R}s + 1} \tag{9.23}$$

Transform Circuit for Mesh Analysis

Mesh analysis can be used to analyze a circuit by applying KVL around the circuit meshes. For a resistive network, the voltages are usually written as the mesh current times the resistances. The same principle applies for a transform circuit, although in this case the impedance of each element is in general a function of the Laplace variable.

Example 9.7: Suppose that we have the circuit in Figure 9.10 and we want to solve for the current $i_c(t) = i_1(t) - i_2(t)$ in the capacitor. Let us assume that there is an initial current $i_L(0^-)$ in the inductor and an initial voltage $v_C(0^-)$ in the capacitor.

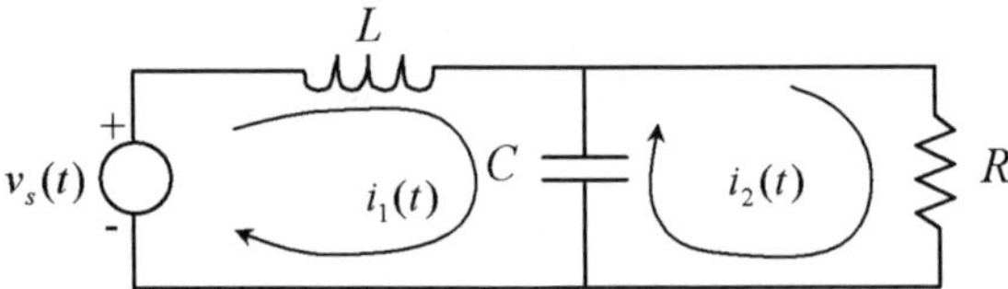

FIGURE 9.10 *RLC* circuit with voltage source input and mesh currents.

Using the unilateral Laplace transform, the inductor voltage can be written as

$$\mathcal{V}_L(s) = Ls\mathcal{I}_L(s) - Li_L(0^-) \tag{9.24}$$

The corresponding circuit diagram combining the impedance Ls in the Laplace domain and the initial condition seen as a voltage source for the inductor is shown in Figure 9.11.

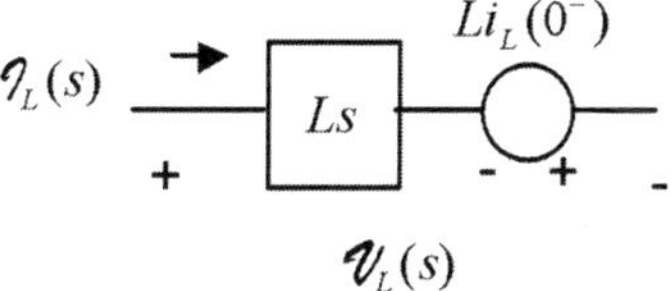

FIGURE 9.11 Equivalent circuit of inductor in the Laplace domain for mesh analysis.

The capacitor voltage-current relationship in the Laplace domain is written as

$$\mathcal{V}_C(s) = \frac{1}{Cs}\mathcal{I}_C(s) + \frac{1}{s}v_C(0^-) \tag{9.25}$$

The corresponding circuit diagram combining the impedance $\frac{1}{Cs}$ in the Laplace domain and the initial condition seen as a voltage source for the capacitor is as shown in Figure 9.12.

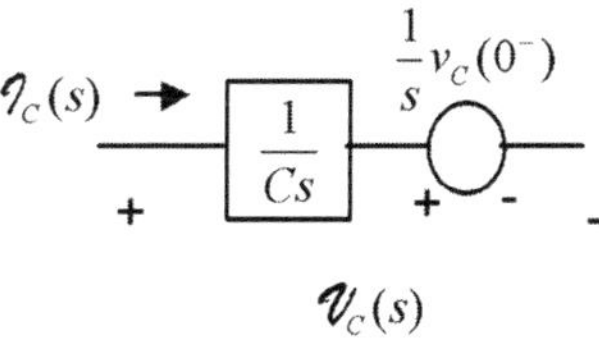

FIGURE 9.12 Equivalent circuit of capacitor in the Laplace domain for mesh analysis.

With these impedances and equivalent current sources defined, the transform circuit can be depicted as in Figure 9.13.

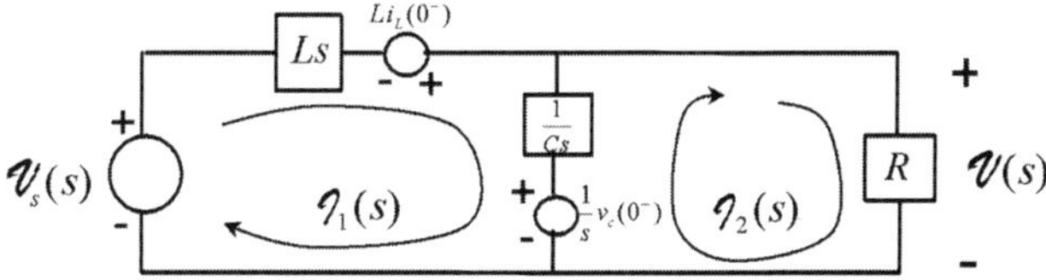

FIGURE 9.13 Transform *RLC* circuit with voltage sources for the input and initial conditions and with mesh currents in the Laplace domain.

Suppose we want to find the capacitor current $i_C(t) = i_1(t) - i_2(t)$. We can solve this circuit by applying KVL to each mesh.

$$\text{Mesh 1: } \mathcal{V}_s(s) - Ls\mathcal{I}_1(s) + Li_L(0^-) - \frac{1}{Cs}[\mathcal{I}_1(s) - \mathcal{I}_2(s)] - \frac{1}{s}v_c(0^-) = 0$$

$$\Rightarrow \mathcal{I}_2(s) = -Cs\mathcal{V}_s(s) + (1 + LCs^2)\mathcal{I}_1(s) + Cv_c(0^-) - LCsi_L(0^-) \quad (9.26)$$

$$\text{Mesh 2: } \frac{1}{Cs}[\mathcal{I}_1(s) - \mathcal{I}_2(s)] + \frac{1}{s}v_c(0^-) - R\mathcal{I}_2(s) = 0$$

$$\Rightarrow \mathcal{I}_1(s) = (1 + RCs)\mathcal{I}_2(s) - Cv_c(0^-) \quad (9.27)$$

Substituting the expression for $\mathcal{I}_2(s)$ in Equation 9.18, we obtain

$$[1 - (1 + RCs)(1 + LCs^2)]\mathcal{I}_1(s) = -(1 + RCs)Cs\mathcal{V}_s(s) + RC^2sv_c(0^-) - (1 + RCs)LCsi_L(0^-)$$

$$\Rightarrow \mathcal{I}_1(s) = \frac{(1 + RCs)}{R(LCs^2 + \frac{L}{R}s + 1)}\mathcal{V}_s(s) + \frac{(1 + RCs)Li_L(0^-)}{R(LCs^2 + \frac{L}{R}s + 1)} - \frac{Cv_c(0^-)}{(LCs^2 + \frac{L}{R}s + 1)} \quad (9.28)$$

Substituting back into Equation 9.7, we obtain

$$\mathcal{I}_2(s) = \frac{1}{R(LCs^2 + \frac{L}{R}s + 1)}\mathcal{V}_s(s) + \frac{Li_L(0^-)}{R(LCs^2 + \frac{L}{R}s + 1)} + \frac{LCv_c(0^-)s}{R(LCs^2 + \frac{L}{R}s + 1)} \quad (9.29)$$

Finally, we can solve for the capacitor current:

$$\mathcal{I}(s) = \mathcal{I}_1(s) - \mathcal{I}_2(s) = \frac{Cs}{(LCs^2 + \frac{L}{R}s + 1)}\mathcal{V}_s(s) + \frac{CLi_L(0^-)s}{(LCs^2 + \frac{L}{R}s + 1)} - \frac{Cv_c(0^-)(1 + \frac{L}{R}s)}{(LCs^2 + \frac{L}{R}s + 1)} \quad (9.30)$$

OPERATIONAL AMPLIFIER CIRCUITS

The operational amplifier (op-amp) is an important building block in analog electronics, notably in the design of active filters. The ideal op-amp is a linear differential amplifier with infinite input impedance, zero output impedance, and a gain A tending to infinity. A schematic of the equivalent circuit of an ideal op-amp is shown in Figure 9.14.

Because of its very high gain, the op-amp is meant to be used in a feedback configuration using additional passive components. Such circuits can implement various types of transfer functions, notably typical first-order leads and lags, and second-order overdamped an underdamped transfer functions.

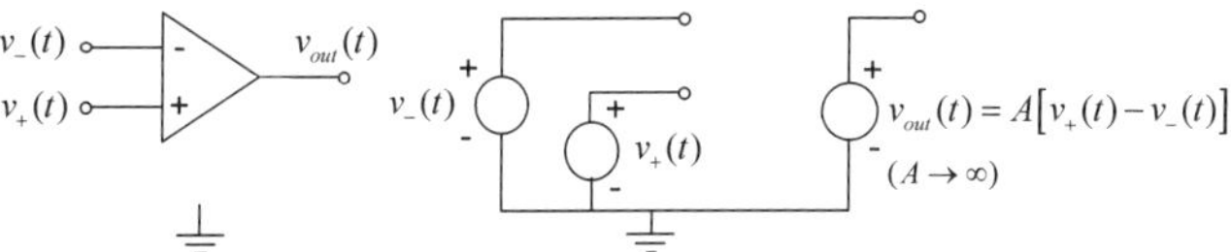

FIGURE 9.14 Equivalent circuit of an ideal op-amp.

Example 9.8: Consider the causal op-amp circuit initially at rest depicted in Figure 9.15. Its LTI circuit model with a voltage-controlled source is also given in the figure. Let us transform the circuit in the Laplace domain and find the transfer function $H_A(s) = V_{out}(s)/V_{in}(s)$. Then, we will let the op-amp gain $A \to +\infty$ to obtain the ideal transfer function $H(s) = \lim_{A \to +\infty} H_A(s)$.

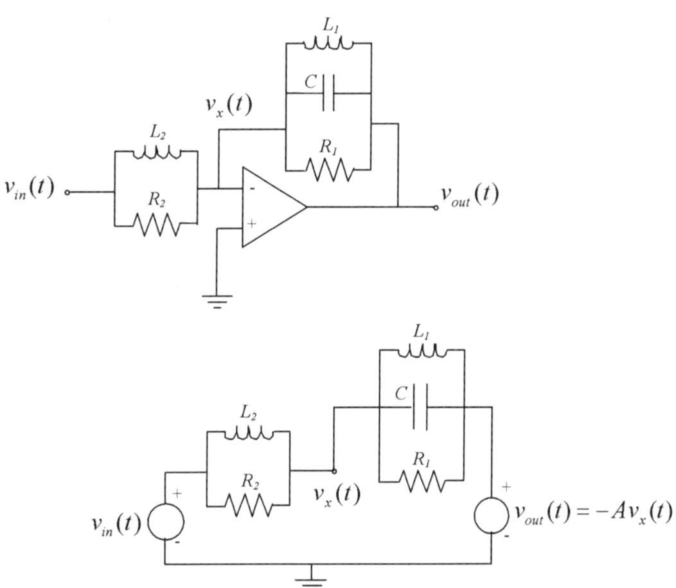

FIGURE 9.15 Op-amp circuit and its equivalent circuit.

The Laplace domain circuit is shown in Figure 9.16.

There are two supernodes for which the nodal voltages are given by the source voltages. The remaining nodal equation is obtained as follows:

$$\frac{V_{in}(s) - V_x(s)}{R_2 \| L_2 s} + \frac{-AV_x(s) - V_x(s)}{R_1 \| \frac{1}{Cs} \| L_1 s} = 0 \qquad (9.31)$$

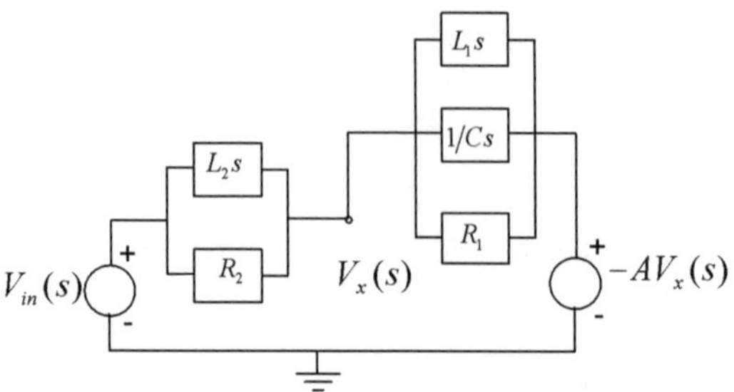

FIGURE 9.16 Laplace transform circuit.

where $R_1 \| \frac{1}{Cs} \| L_1 s = \frac{1}{Cs + \frac{1}{R_1} + \frac{1}{L_1 s}} = \frac{R_1 L_1 s}{R_1 L_1 C s^2 + L_1 s + R_1}$ and $R_2 \| L_2 s = \frac{R_2 L_2 s}{R_2 + L_2 s}$ are the resulting impedances of the parallel connections of the individual impedances. Simplifying the above equation, we get

$$\frac{R_2 + L_2 s}{R_2 L_2 s} V_{in}(s) - \left[\frac{(A+1)(R_1 L_1 C s^2 + L_1 s + R_1)}{R_1 L_1 s} + \frac{R_2 + L_2 s}{R_2 L_2 s} \right] V_x(s) = 0 \quad (9.32)$$

Thus, the transfer function between the input voltage and the node voltage is given by

$$\frac{V_x(s)}{V_{in}(s)} = \frac{\frac{R_2 + L_2 s}{R_2 L_2 s}}{\frac{(A+1)(R_1 L_1 C s^2 + L_1 s + R_1)}{R_1 L_1 s} + \frac{R_2 + L_2 s}{R_2 L_2 s}}$$
$$= \frac{R_1 L_1 s (R_2 + L_2 s)}{R_2 L_2 s (A+1)(R_1 L_1 C s^2 + L_1 s + R_1) + R_1 L_1 s (R_2 + L_2 s)}, \quad (9.33)$$

and the transfer function between the input voltage and the output voltage can be obtained:

$$H_A(s) = \frac{V_{out}(s)}{V_{in}(s)} = \frac{-AV_x(s)}{V_{in}(s)} = \frac{-AR_1 L_1 s (R_2 + L_2 s)}{R_2 L_2 s (A+1)(R_1 L_1 C s^2 + L_1 s + R_1) + R_1 L_1 s (R_2 + L_2 s)} \quad (9.34)$$

The ideal transfer function is obtained as the limit of Equation 9.34 as the op-amp gain tends to infinity:

$$H(s) = \lim_{A \to \infty} H_A(s) = -\frac{R_1 L_1 (R_2 + L_2 s)}{R_2 L_2 (R_1 L_1 C s^2 + L_1 s + R_1)} = -\frac{L_1 (1 + \frac{L_2}{R_2} s)}{L_2 (L_1 C s^2 + \frac{L_1}{R_1} s + 1)} \quad (9.35)$$

This is a second-order system with negative DC gain and one zero $z_1 = -\frac{R_2}{L_2}$. Assume that the desired circuit must have a DC gain of –50, one zero at –1, and two complex conjugate poles with $\omega_n = 10$ rad/s, $\zeta = 0.5$. Let $L_1 = 10$ H. Let us find the values of the remaining circuit components L_2, R_1, R_2, C. These component values are obtained by setting

$$H(s) = -50\frac{s+1}{0.01s^2+0.1s+1} = -\frac{L_1}{L_2}\frac{(\frac{L_2}{R_2}s+1)}{(L_1Cs^2+\frac{L_1}{R_1}s+1)} \tag{9.36}$$

which yields $L_2 = 0.2$ H, $R_1 = 100\ \Omega$, $R_2 = 0.2\ \Omega$, $C = 0.001$ F. With these values, the frequency response of the op-amp circuit is $H(j\omega) = -50\frac{j\omega+1}{0.01(j\omega)^2+0.1(j\omega)+1}$. Figure 9.17 shows the Bode plot of the circuit with the phase expressed in degrees.

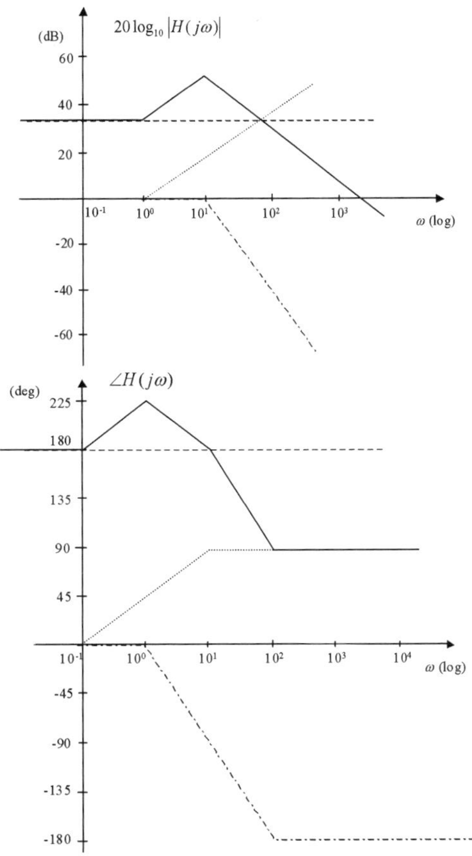

FIGURE 9.17 Bode plot of an op-amp circuit.

SUMMARY

This chapter was a brief overview of the analysis of LTI circuits using the Laplace transform.

- The Laplace transform can be used to solve the differential equation relating an input voltage or current signal to another output signal in the circuit.
- The Laplace transform can also be used to analyze the circuit directly in the Laplace domain. Circuit components are replaced by their impedances, and Kirchhoff's laws are applied to get algebraic equations involving impedances and signals in the Laplace domain.
- The ideal operational amplifier was described, and an active filter op-amp circuit example was solved to illustrate the use of op-amps in realizing transfer functions.

TO PROBE FURTHER

There are many references on circuit analysis. See, for example, Johnson, Johnson, Hilburn, and Scott, 1997. For an in-depth treatment of op-amp circuits, see Schaumann and Van Valkenburg, 2001.

EXERCISES

Exercises with Solutions

Exercise 9.1

The circuit in Figure 9.18 has initial conditions on the capacitor $v_C(0^-)$ and inductor $i_L(0^-)$.

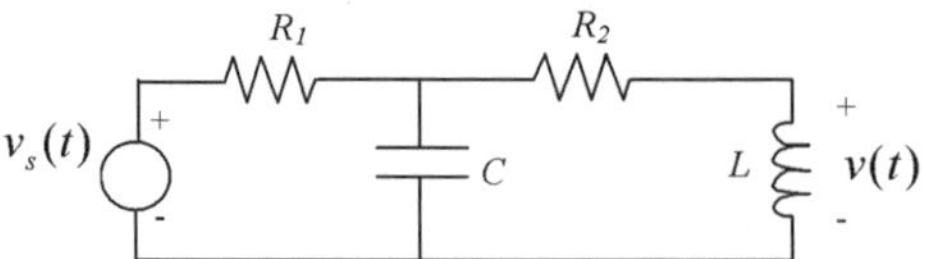

FIGURE 9.18 Circuit of Exercise 9.1.

(a) Transform the circuit using the unilateral Laplace transform.

Answer:
The transform circuit is given in Figure 9.19.

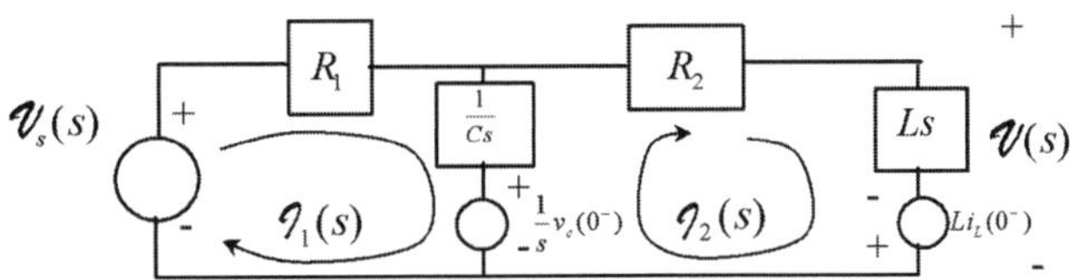

FIGURE 9.19 Transform circuit of Exercise 9.1.

(b) Find the unilateral Laplace transform $\mathcal{V}(s)$ of $v(t)$.

Answer:

Let us use mesh analysis. For mesh 1,

$$\mathcal{V}_s(s) - R_1\mathcal{I}_1(s) - \frac{1}{s}v_C(0^-) - \frac{1}{Cs}[\mathcal{I}_1(s) - \mathcal{I}_2(s)] = 0$$

$$\Rightarrow \quad \mathcal{I}_2(s) = -Cs\mathcal{V}_s(s) + Cv_c(0^-) + (1 + R_1Cs)\mathcal{I}_1(s)$$

For mesh 2,

$$\frac{1}{Cs}[\mathcal{I}_1(s) - \mathcal{I}_2(s)] + \frac{1}{s}v_C(0^-) + Li_L(0^-) - (R_2 + Ls)\mathcal{I}_2(s) = 0$$

$$\Rightarrow \quad \mathcal{I}_1(s) = (1 + R_2Cs + LCs^2)\mathcal{I}_2(s) - Cv_C(0^-) - LCsi_L(0^-)$$

Substituting, we obtain

$\mathcal{I}_2(s) = -Cs\mathcal{V}_s(s) + Cv_c(0^-) + (1 + R_1Cs)\left[(1 + R_2Cs + LCs^2)\mathcal{I}_2(s) - Cv_C(0^-) - LCsi_L(0^-)\right]$.

Solving for $\mathcal{I}_2(s)$, we get

$$\mathcal{I}_2(s) = \frac{\mathcal{V}_s(s)}{LR_1Cs^2 + (R_2R_1C + L)s + R_1 + R_2} + \frac{L(1 + R_1Cs)i_L(0^-) + R_1Cv_c(0^-)}{LR_1Cs^2 + (R_2R_1C + L)s + R_1 + R_2}$$

Finally, the unilateral Laplace transform of the output voltage is given by

$$\mathcal{V}(s) = Ls\mathcal{I}_2(s) - i_L(0^-) = \frac{Ls\mathcal{V}_s(s)}{LR_1Cs^2 + (R_2R_1C + L)s + R_1 + R_2} + \frac{L^2s(1 + R_1Cs)i_L(0^-) + R_1LCsv_c(0^-)}{LR_1Cs^2 + (R_2R_1C + L)s + R_1 + R_2} - i_L(0^-)$$

(c) Give the transfer function $\mathcal{H}(s)$ from the source voltage $\mathcal{V}_s(s)$ to the output voltage $\mathcal{V}(s)$. What type of filter is it (lowpass, highpass, bandpass)? Assuming that the poles of $\mathcal{H}(s)$ are complex, find expressions for its undamped natural frequency ω_n and damping ratio ζ.

Answer:
Notice that the transfer function from the source voltage to the output voltage is *bandpass*. Its gain at DC and infinite frequencies is 0. The transfer function $\mathcal{H}(s)$ from the source voltage $\mathcal{V}_s(s)$ to the output voltage $\mathcal{V}(s)$ is given by

$$\mathcal{H}(s) = \frac{\mathcal{V}(s)}{\mathcal{V}_s(s)} = \frac{Ls}{LR_1Cs^2 + (R_2R_1C + L)s + R_1 + R_2}$$

Its undamped natural frequency is $\omega_n = \sqrt{\frac{R_1+R_2}{LR_1C}}$. The damping ratio is computed from

$$2\zeta\omega_n = \frac{R_2R_1C + L}{LR_1C} \Leftrightarrow \zeta = \frac{\frac{R_2R_1C+L}{LR_1C}}{2\sqrt{\frac{R_1+R_2}{LR_1C}}} = \frac{R_2R_1C+L}{2\sqrt{(R_1+R_2)LR_1C}}$$

(d) Assume that $R_1 = 100\Omega$, $R_2 = 100\,\Omega$, $\omega_n = 10$. Find the values of L and C to get Butterworth poles.

Answer:
The Butterworth poles are for

$$\zeta = \frac{1}{\sqrt{2}} = \frac{R_2R_1C+L}{2\sqrt{(R_1+R_2)LR_1C}} = \frac{10000C+L}{2\sqrt{20000LC}} \Rightarrow 200\sqrt{LC} = 10000C + L$$

Furthermore, $\omega_n = 10 = \sqrt{\frac{2}{LC}} \Rightarrow LC = \frac{1}{50}$, and substituting in the previous equation, we get

$$\begin{aligned}
&200\frac{1}{\sqrt{50}} = 10000C + \frac{1}{50C} \Rightarrow \\
&0 = 500000C^2 - 200\sqrt{50}C + 1 \\
&0 = C^2 - \frac{2\sqrt{50}}{5000}C + \frac{1}{500000} \\
&0 = C^2 - \frac{2}{100\sqrt{50}}C + \frac{1}{500000} \\
&\Rightarrow C = \frac{1}{100\sqrt{50}}\text{ F}
\end{aligned}$$

Finally,

$$L = \frac{1}{50C} = \frac{1}{50\frac{1}{100\sqrt{50}}} = \frac{100}{\sqrt{50}}\ \text{H}$$

Exercises

Exercise 9.2

The circuit in Figure 9.20 has initial conditions on its capacitor $v_C(0^-)$ and inductor $i_L(0^-)$.

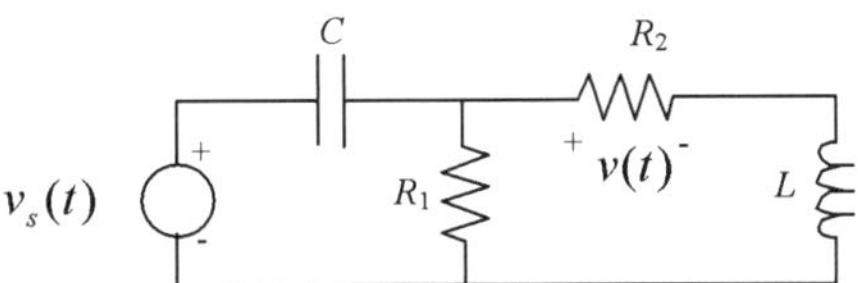

FIGURE 9.20 Circuit in Exercise 9.2.

(a) Transform the circuit using the unilateral Laplace transform.

(b) Find the unilateral Laplace transform $\mathcal{V}(s)$ of v(t).

(c) Give the transfer function $\mathcal{H}(s)$ from the source voltage $\mathcal{V}_s(s)$ to the output voltage $\mathcal{V}(s)$ (it should be second-order). What type of filter is it (lowpass, highpass, bandpass)? Assuming that the poles of $\mathcal{H}(s)$ are complex, find expressions for its undamped natural frequency ω_n and damping ratio ζ.

Exercise 9.3

Consider the causal ideal op-amp circuit in Figure 9.21 (initially at rest), which implements a lowpass filter.

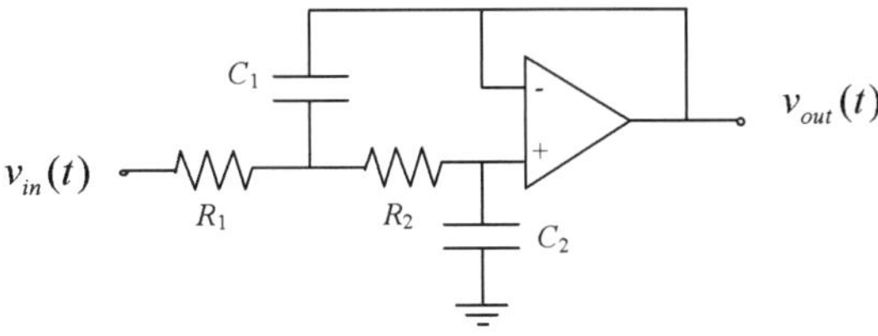

FIGURE 9.21 Op-amp filter circuit of Exercise 9.3.

(a) Sketch the LTI model of the circuit with a voltage-controlled source representing the output of the op-amp, assuming that its input impedance is infinite. Also, assume for this part that the op-amp gain A is finite.

(b) Transform the circuit using the Laplace transform and find the transfer function $H_A(s) = V_{out}(s)/V_{in}(s)$. Then, let the op-amp gain $A \to +\infty$ to obtain the transfer function $H(s) = \lim_{A\to+\infty} H_A(s)$.

(c) Find expressions for the circuit's undamped natural frequency and damping ratio.

Answer:

ON THE CD

Exercise 9.4

Consider the causal op-amp circuit initially at rest depicted in Figure 9.22. Its LTI circuit model with a voltage-controlled source is also given in the figure.

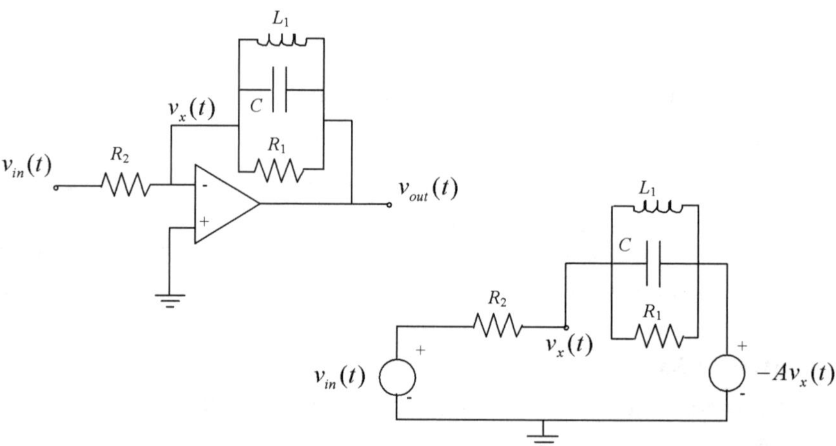

FIGURE 9.22 Op-amp circuit of Exercise 9.4.

(a) Transform the circuit using the Laplace transform and find the transfer function $H_A(s) = V_{out}(s)/V_{in}(s)$. Then, let the op-amp gain $A \to +\infty$ to obtain the ideal transfer function $H(s) = \lim_{A\to+\infty} H_A(s)$.

(b) Assume that the transfer function $H_1(s) = \frac{H(s)}{s}$ has a DC gain of –50 and that $H(s)$ has one zero at 0 and two complex conjugate poles with $\omega_n = 10$ rad/s, $\zeta = 0.5$. Let $L_1 = 10$ H. Find the values of the remaining circuit components R_1, R_2, C.

(c) Give the frequency response of $H(s)$ and sketch its Bode plot.

Exercise 9.5

The circuit in Figure 9.23 has initial conditions on the capacitor $v_C(0^-)$ and inductor $i_L(0^-)$.

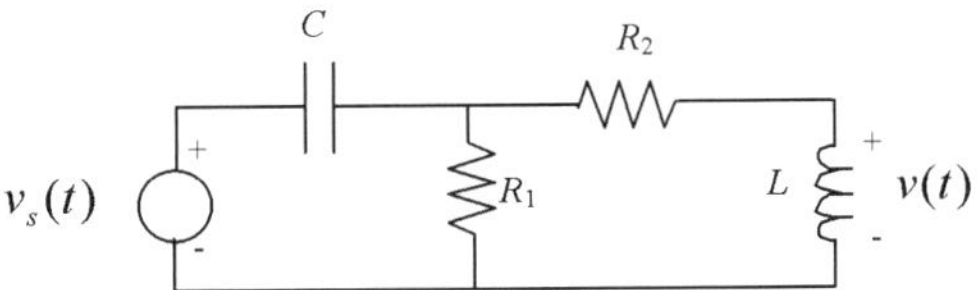

FIGURE 9.23 Circuit of Exercise 9.5.

(a) Transform the circuit using the unilateral Laplace transform.

(b) Find the unilateral Laplace transform of $v(t)$.

(c) Sketch the Bode plot (magnitude and phase) of the frequency response from the input voltage $\mathcal{V}_s(j\omega)$ to the output voltage $\mathcal{V}(j\omega)$. Assume that the initial conditions on the capacitor and the inductor are 0. Use the numerical values $R_1 = 1\,\Omega$, $R_2 = \frac{109}{891}\,\Omega$, $L = \frac{1}{891}$ H, $C = 1$ F.

Answer:

ON THE CD

10 State Models of Continuous-Time LTI Systems

In This Chapter

((Lecture 33: State Models of Continuous-Time LTI Systems))

In Chapter 3 we studied an important class of continuous-time linear time-invariant (LTI) systems defined by linear, causal constant-coefficient differential equations. For a system described by an Nth-order differential equation, it is always possible to find a set of N first-order differential equations and an output equation describing the same input-output relationship. These N first-order differential equations are called the *state equations* of the system. The *states* are the N variables seen as outputs of the state equations.

The concept of state is directly applicable to certain types of engineering systems such as linear circuits and mechanical systems. The state variables in a circuit are the capacitor charges (or equivalently the voltages since $q = Cv$) and the inductor currents. In a mechanical system, the state variables are generally the position and velocity of a body.

Before we move on, an important word on notation: for state-space systems, the *input signal* is conventionally written as $u(t)$ (not to be confused with the unit step) instead of $x(t)$, as the latter is used for the vector of state variables. Hence, in this chapter we will use $q(t)$ to denote the unit step signal.

STATE MODELS OF CONTINUOUS-TIME LTI DIFFERENTIAL SYSTEMS

Consider the general N^{th}-order causal linear constant-coefficient differential equation with $M \le N$:

$$\sum_{k=0}^{N} a_k \frac{d^k y(t)}{dt^k} = \sum_{k=0}^{M} b_k \frac{d^k u(t)}{dt^k}, \tag{10.1}$$

which can be expanded to

$$a_N \frac{d^N y(t)}{dt^N} + \cdots + a_1 \frac{dy(t)}{dt} + a_0 y(t) = b_M \frac{d^M u(t)}{dt^M} + \cdots + b_1 \frac{du(t)}{dt} + b_0 u(t). \tag{10.2}$$

Controllable Canonical Realization

We can derive a state-space model for the system in Equation 10.1 by first finding its *controllable canonical form* (or direct form) realization. The idea is to take the intermediate variable w in the direct form realization introduced in Chapter 7, and its successive $N-1$ derivatives, as state variables. Recall that the Laplace variable s represents the differentiation operator $\frac{d}{dt}$, and its inverse s^{-1} is the integration operator. Let $a_N = 1$ without loss of generality. Taking the Laplace transform on both sides of the differential Equation 10.2, we obtain the transfer function (with the region of convergence [ROC] a right half-plane to the right of the rightmost pole):

$$H(s) = \frac{Y(s)}{U(s)} = \frac{\sum_{k=0}^{M} b_k s^k}{\sum_{k=0}^{N} a_k s^k}$$

$$= \frac{b_M s^M + b_{M-1} s^{M-1} + \cdots + b_0}{s^N + a_{N-1} s^{N-1} + \cdots + a_0}. \tag{10.3}$$

A controllable canonical realization can be obtained by considering the transfer function $H(s)$ as a cascade of two subsystems as shown in Figure 10.1.

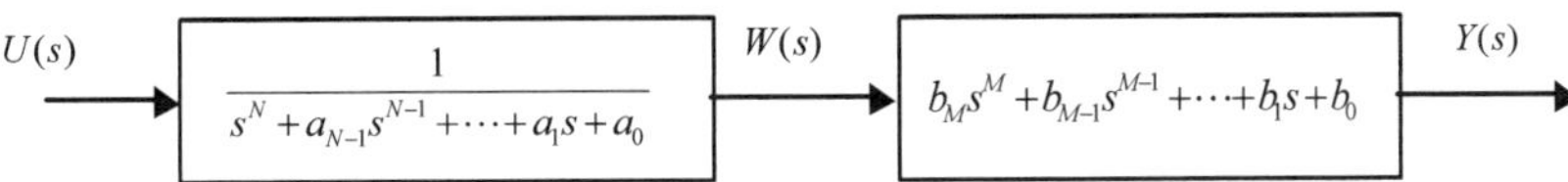

FIGURE 10.1 Transfer function as a cascade of two LTI subsystems.

The input-output system equation of the first subsystem is

$$s^N W(s) = -a_{N-1}s^{N-1}W(s) - \cdots - a_1 sW(s) - a_0 W(s) + U(s), \tag{10.4}$$

which, as seen in Chapter 7, corresponds to feedback loops around a chain of integrators. For the second subsystem we have

$$Y(s) = b_M s^M W(s) + b_{M-1}s^{M-1}W(s) + \cdots + b_1 sW(s) + b_0 W(s). \tag{10.5}$$

The controllable canonical realization is then (assuming $M = N$ without loss of generality) as shown in Figure 10.2.

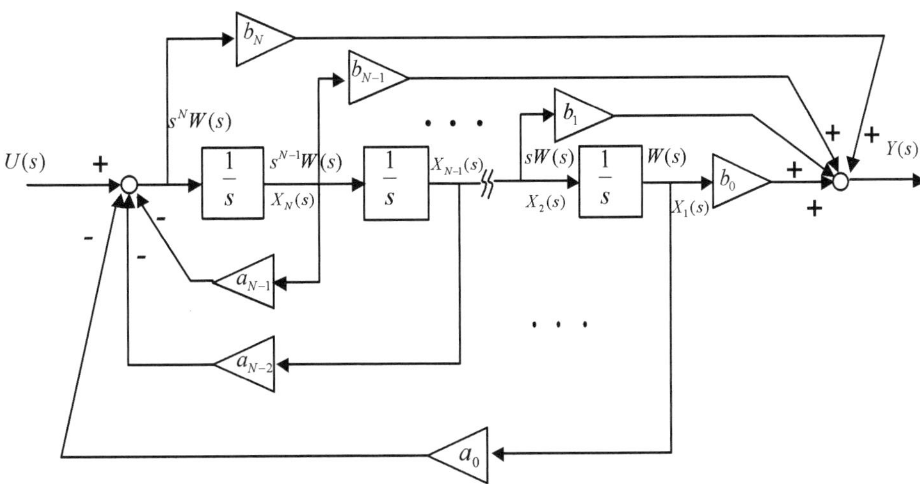

FIGURE 10.2 Controllable canonical realization of transfer function.

From this block diagram, define the state variables $\{x_i\}_{i=1}^{N}$ as follows.

$$
\begin{aligned}
&X_1(s) := W(s) & & \frac{dx_1(t)}{dt} = x_2(t) \\
&X_2(s) := sW(s) & & \frac{dx_2(t)}{dt} = x_3(t) \\
&X_3(s) := s^2W(s) & \Rightarrow & \frac{dx_3(t)}{dt} = x_4(t) \\
&\vdots & & \vdots \\
&X_N(s) := s^{N-1}W(s) & & \frac{dx_N(t)}{dt} = -a_0x_1(t) - a_1x_2(t) - a_2x_3(t) - \cdots - a_{N-1}x_N(t) + u(t)
\end{aligned}
\tag{10.6}
$$

The state equations on the right can be rewritten in vector form:

$$
\begin{bmatrix} \dot{x}_1(t) \\ \dot{x}_2(t) \\ \vdots \\ \dot{x}_{N-1}(t) \\ \dot{x}_N(t) \end{bmatrix}
= \underbrace{\begin{bmatrix} 0 & 1 & \cdots & 0 & 0 \\ 0 & 0 & & 0 & 0 \\ \vdots & & \ddots & & \vdots \\ 0 & 0 & & 0 & 1 \\ -a_0 & -a_1 & \cdots & -a_{N-2} & -a_{N-1} \end{bmatrix}}_{A}
\begin{bmatrix} x_1(t) \\ x_2(t) \\ \vdots \\ x_{N-1}(t) \\ x_N(t) \end{bmatrix}
+ \underbrace{\begin{bmatrix} 0 \\ 0 \\ \vdots \\ 0 \\ 1 \end{bmatrix}}_{B} u(t),
\tag{10.7}
$$

where the constant matrices A and B are defined in Equation 10.7 and the notation $\dot{x}_i(t) := \frac{dx_i(t)}{dt}$ is used for the time derivative. Let the *state vector* (or *state*) be defined as

$$
x(t) := \begin{bmatrix} x_1(t) \\ x_2(t) \\ \vdots \\ x_{N-1}(t) \\ x_N(t) \end{bmatrix}.
\tag{10.8}
$$

The space $\mathbb{R}^N$ in which the state evolves is called the *state space*. Then the *state equation* can be written as

$$
\dot{x}(t) = Ax(t) + Bu(t).
\tag{10.9}
$$

From the block diagram in Figure 10.2, the *output equation* relating the output $y(t)$ to the state vector can be written as follows:

$$\begin{aligned} y(t) &= \underbrace{\begin{bmatrix} b_0 - a_0 b_N & b_1 - a_1 b_N & \cdots & b_{N-1} - a_{N-1} b_N \end{bmatrix}}_{C} x(t) + \underbrace{b_N}_{D} u(t) \\ &= Cx(t) + Du(t) \end{aligned} \tag{10.10}$$

If $H(s)$ is strictly proper, that is, if $M < N$, then the output equation becomes

$$\begin{aligned} y(t) &= \underbrace{\begin{bmatrix} b_0 & b_1 & \cdots & b_{N-1} \end{bmatrix}}_{C} x(t) \\ &= Cx(t) \end{aligned} \tag{10.11}$$

Note that the input has no direct path to the output in this case, as $b_N = 0$ in Figure 10.2 and $D = 0$ in the state model. The *order* of the state-space system defined by Equations 10.9 and 10.10 is N, the dimension of the state vector.

Observable Canonical Realization

We now derive a state-space model for the system of Equation 10.2 by first finding its *observable canonical form* realization. The idea is to write the transfer function $H(s)$ as a rational function of s^{-1}:

$$H(s) = \frac{b_M s^{M-N} + b_{M-1} s^{M-N-1} + \cdots + b_0 s^{-N}}{1 + a_{N-1} s^{-1} + \cdots + a_0 s^{-N}}. \tag{10.12}$$

Assume without loss of generality that $M = N$ (if they are not equal, then just set $b_N = b_{N-1} = \cdots = b_{M+1} = 0$) so that

$$H(s) = \frac{b_N + b_{N-1} s^{-1} + \cdots + b_0 s^{-N}}{1 + a_{N-1} s^{-1} + \cdots + a_0 s^{-N}}. \tag{10.13}$$

Then, the input-output relationship between $U(s)$ and $Y(s)$ can be written as

$$Y(s) = b_N U(s) + [b_{N-1} U(s) - a_{N-1} Y(s)] s^{-1} + [b_{N-2} U(s) - a_{N-2} Y(s)] s^{-2} + \cdots + [b_0 U(s) - a_0 Y(s)] s^{-N}. \tag{10.14}$$

The interpretation is that the output is a linear combination of successive integrals of the output and the input. The block diagram for the observable canonical form consists of a chain of N integrators with summing junctions at the input of each integrator as shown in Figure 10.3.

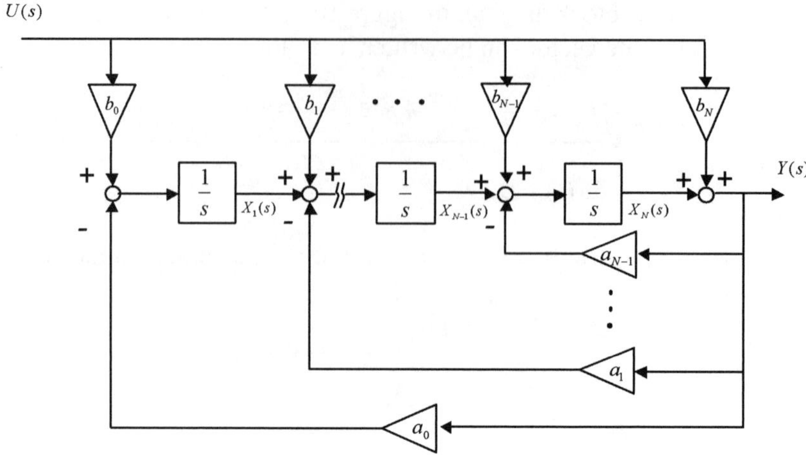

FIGURE 10.3 Observable canonical realization of transfer function.

The state variables are defined as the integrator outputs, which gives us

$$
\begin{aligned}
sX_1(s) &= -a_0 X_N(s) + (b_0 - a_0 b_N)U(s) & & \frac{dx_1(t)}{dt} = -a_0 x_N(t) + (b_0 - a_0 b_N)u(t) \\
sX_2(s) &= X_1(s) - a_1 X_N(s) + (b_1 - a_1 b_N)U(s) & & \frac{dx_2(t)}{dt} = x_1 - a_1 x_N(t) + (b_1 - a_1 b_N)u(t) \\
sX_3(s) &= X_2(s) - a_2 X_N(s) + (b_2 - a_2 b_N)U(s) & \Rightarrow & \frac{dx_3(t)}{dt} = x_2(t) - a_2 x_N(t) + (b_2 - a_2 b_N)u(t) \\
&\vdots & & \vdots \\
sX_N(s) &= X_{N-1}(s) - a_{N-1} X_N(s) + (b_{N-1} - a_{N-1} b_N)U(s) & & \frac{dx_N(t)}{dt} = x_{N-1}(t) - a_{N-1} x_N(t) + (b_{N-1} - a_{N-1} b_N)u(t)
\end{aligned}
\qquad (10.15)
$$

The state equations on the right can be rewritten in vector form:

$$
\begin{bmatrix} \dot{x}_1(t) \\ \dot{x}_2(t) \\ \vdots \\ \dot{x}_{N-1}(t) \\ \dot{x}_N(t) \end{bmatrix} = \underbrace{\begin{bmatrix} 0 & 0 & \cdots & 0 & -a_0 \\ 1 & 0 & & 0 & -a_1 \\ \vdots & & \ddots & & \vdots \\ 0 & 0 & & 0 & -a_{N-2} \\ 0 & 0 & \cdots & 1 & -a_{N-1} \end{bmatrix}}_{A} \begin{bmatrix} x_1(t) \\ x_2(t) \\ \vdots \\ x_{N-1}(t) \\ x_N(t) \end{bmatrix} + \underbrace{\begin{bmatrix} b_0 - a_0 b_N \\ b_1 - a_1 b_N \\ \vdots \\ b_{N-2} - a_{N-2} b_N \\ b_{N-1} - a_{N-1} b_N \end{bmatrix}}_{B} u(t). \qquad (10.16)
$$

The output equation is simply

$$\begin{aligned} y(t) &= \underbrace{\begin{bmatrix} 0 & \cdots & 0 & 1 \end{bmatrix}}_{C} x(t) + \underbrace{b_N}_{D} u(t) \\ &= Cx(t) + Du(t) \end{aligned} \quad (10.17)$$

If $H(s)$ is strictly proper, then, again $b_N = 0$ and hence $D = 0$.

Remarks:

- A general linear time-invariant state-space system has the form $\dot{x}(t) = Ax(t) + Bu(t)$, $y(t) = Cx(t) + Du(t)$ which is often denoted as (A, B, C, D).
- The matrices A, B, C, D are called *state-space matrices*.
- Given a system defined by a proper rational transfer function, a state-space description of it is not unique, as we have shown that there exist at least two: the controllable and observable canonical realizations. It can be shown that there exist infinitely many state-space realizations, as we will find out later.

ON THE CD

MATLAB can be used to get a canonical state-space realization of a transfer function. For example, the following M-file found on the CD-ROM in D:\Chapter10\realization.m generates the controllable canonical realization.

```
%% realization.m State-space realization of a transfer function
% transfer function numerator and denominator
num=[1 100];
den=[1 11 10];
% state-space realization
[A,B,C,D]=tf2ss(num,den)
```

Circuit Example

We will derive controllable and observable canonical state-space representations, and a direct state-space representation for the second-order resistor-inductor-capacitor (RLC) circuit of Figure 10.4. The state variables are the inductor current $i_L(t)$ and the capacitor voltage $v_C(t)$. Suppose that we want to solve for the voltage $v_C(t)$.

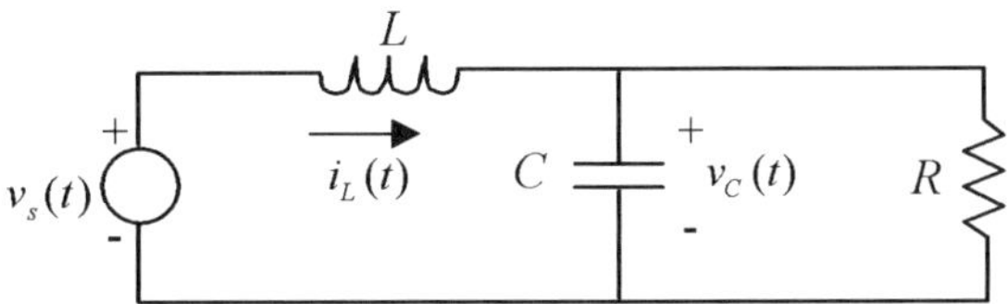

FIGURE 10.4 *RLC* circuit.

Direct State-Space Realization

Left mesh:
$$v_s(t) - L\frac{di_L(t)}{dt} - v_C(t) = 0$$
$$\Rightarrow \frac{di_L(t)}{dt} = -\frac{1}{L}v_C(t) + \frac{1}{L}v_s(t) \tag{10.18}$$

Node:
$$i_L(t) - C\frac{dv_C(t)}{dt} - \frac{1}{R}v_C(t) = 0$$
$$\Rightarrow \frac{dv_C(t)}{dt} = \frac{1}{C}i_L(t) - \frac{1}{RC}v_C(t) \tag{10.19}$$

Letting $x_1(t) := v_C(t),\ x_2(t) := i_L(t),\ u(t) := v_s(t),\ y(t) := v_C(t)$, we can write the system in state-space form:

$$\begin{bmatrix} \dot{x}_1(t) \\ \dot{x}_2(t) \end{bmatrix} = \underbrace{\begin{bmatrix} -\frac{1}{RC} & \frac{1}{C} \\ -\frac{1}{L} & 0 \end{bmatrix}}_{A} \begin{bmatrix} x_1(t) \\ x_2(t) \end{bmatrix} + \underbrace{\begin{bmatrix} 0 \\ \frac{1}{L} \end{bmatrix}}_{B} u(t) \tag{10.20}$$

with the output equation

$$y(t) = \underbrace{\begin{bmatrix} 1 & 0 \end{bmatrix}}_{C} \begin{bmatrix} x_1(t) \\ x_2(t) \end{bmatrix}. \tag{10.21}$$

Controllable Canonical State-Space Realization

Combining Equations 10.18 and 10.19, we get the second-order differential equation

$$\begin{aligned} \frac{d^2 v_C(t)}{dt^2} &= \frac{1}{C}\frac{di_L(t)}{dt} - \frac{1}{RC}\frac{dv_C(t)}{dt} \\ &= -\frac{1}{LC}v_C(t) + \frac{1}{LC}v_s(t) - \frac{1}{RC}\frac{dv_C(t)}{dt}. \end{aligned} \tag{10.22}$$

Upon rearranging, we obtain

$$\frac{d^2 v_C(t)}{dt^2} + \frac{1}{RC}\frac{dv_C(t)}{dt} + \frac{1}{LC}v_C(t) = \frac{1}{LC}v_s(t), \tag{10.23}$$

which in the Laplace domain becomes

$$s^2V_C(s)+\frac{1}{RC}sV_C(s)+\frac{1}{LC}V_C(s)=\frac{1}{LC}V_s(s) \tag{10.24}$$

and has the controllable canonical realization given in Figure 10.5.

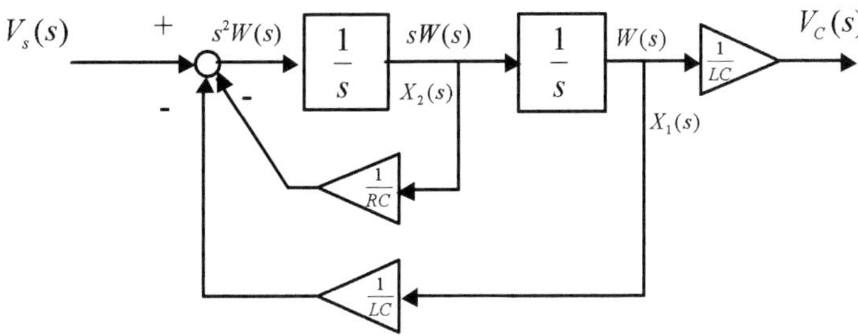

FIGURE 10.5 Controllable canonical realization of a circuit system.

Let $u(t):=v_s(t),\ y(t):=v_C(t)$. The controllable canonical state-space form is then given by

$$\begin{bmatrix}\dot{x}_1(t)\\ \dot{x}_2(t)\end{bmatrix}=\underbrace{\begin{bmatrix}0 & 1\\ -\frac{1}{LC} & -\frac{1}{RC}\end{bmatrix}}_{A}\begin{bmatrix}x_1(t)\\ x_2(t)\end{bmatrix}+\underbrace{\begin{bmatrix}0\\ 1\end{bmatrix}}_{B}u(t), \tag{10.25}$$

and the output equation has the form

$$y(t)=\underbrace{\begin{bmatrix}\frac{1}{LC} & 0\end{bmatrix}}_{C}\begin{bmatrix}x_1(t)\\ x_2(t)\end{bmatrix}. \tag{10.26}$$

Observable Canonical State-Space Realization

Equation 10.24 is divided by s^2 on both sides to obtain

$$V_C(s)+\frac{1}{RCs}V_C(s)+\frac{1}{LCs^2}V_C(s)=\frac{1}{LCs^2}V_s(s), \tag{10.27}$$

which is rewritten as

$$V_C(s) = -\frac{1}{RCs}V_C(s) + \frac{1}{s^2}\left[\frac{1}{LC}V_s(s) - \frac{1}{LC}V_C(s)\right]. \tag{10.28}$$

This equation is represented by the block diagram in Figure 10.6.

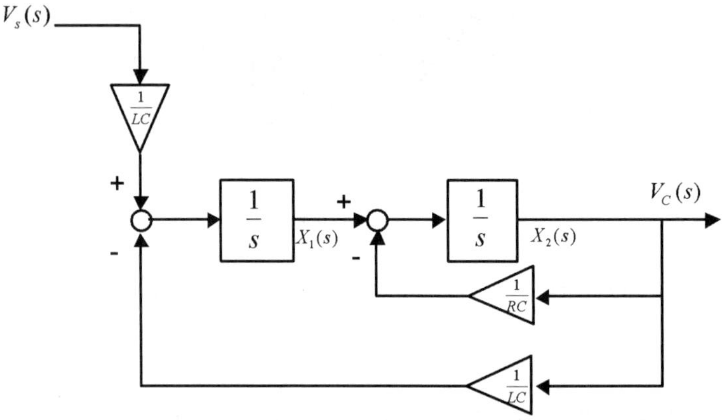

FIGURE 10.6 Observable canonical realization of a circuit system.

Let $u(t) := v_s(t),\ y(t) := v_C(t)$. The observable canonical state-space realization is given by

$$\begin{bmatrix} \dot{x}_1(t) \\ \dot{x}_2(t) \end{bmatrix} = \underbrace{\begin{bmatrix} 0 & -\frac{1}{LC} \\ 1 & -\frac{1}{RC} \end{bmatrix}}_{A} \begin{bmatrix} x_1(t) \\ x_2(t) \end{bmatrix} + \underbrace{\begin{bmatrix} \frac{1}{LC} \\ 0 \end{bmatrix}}_{B} u(t), \tag{10.29}$$

and the output equation is simply

$$y(t) = \underbrace{\begin{bmatrix} 0 & 1 \end{bmatrix}}_{C} \begin{bmatrix} x_1(t) \\ x_2(t) \end{bmatrix}. \tag{10.30}$$

((Lecture 34: Zero-State Response and Zero-Input Response))

ZERO-STATE RESPONSE AND ZERO-INPUT RESPONSE OF A CONTINUOUS-TIME STATE-SPACE SYSTEM

Recall that the response of a system with nonzero initial conditions is composed of a zero-state response due to the input signal only and a zero-input response due to the initial conditions only. For a state-space system, the initial conditions are captured in the *initial state* $x(0)$.

Zero-Input Response

Consider the following general continuous-time, single-input, single-output, N^{th}-order LTI state-space system:

$$\begin{aligned}\dot{x}(t) &= Ax(t) + Bu(t)\\ y(t) &= Cx(t) + Du(t),\end{aligned} \tag{10.31}$$

where $x(t) \in \mathbb{R}^N$, $y(t) \in \mathbb{R}, u(t) \in \mathbb{R}$, and $A \in \mathbb{R}^{N\times N}, B \in \mathbb{R}^{N\times 1}, C \in \mathbb{R}^{1\times N}, D \in \mathbb{R}$. The zero-input response $y_{zi}(t)$ is the response to an initial state $x(0) = x_0$ only. The state equation is then

$$\dot{x}(t) = Ax(t). \tag{10.32}$$

The solution to this homogeneous state equation involves the matrix exponential function, which is defined as a power series of a square matrix $A \in \mathbb{R}^{N\times N}$:

$$e^A := I_N + A + \frac{1}{2}A^2 + \frac{1}{3!}A^3 + \cdots + \frac{1}{k!}A^k + \cdots, \tag{10.33}$$

where I_N is the $N \times N$ identity matrix. It can be shown that this power series converges for any matrix A. Note that this definition generalizes the definition of the scalar exponential function $e^a, a \in \mathbb{R}$. How do we compute e^A? One way is to *diagonalize* the matrix A and take the exponential of the eigenvalues. Specifically, if matrix $T \in \mathbb{C}^{N\times N}$ diagonalizes A, that is,

$$\Lambda := \begin{bmatrix} \lambda_1 & 0 & \cdots & 0 \\ 0 & \lambda_2 & & 0 \\ \vdots & & \ddots & \vdots \\ 0 & 0 & \cdots & \lambda_N \end{bmatrix} = T^{-1}AT \tag{10.34}$$

where $\lambda_i \in \mathbb{C}$ is the ith eigenvalue (all eigenvalues are assumed to be distinct) of the matrix A, then the exponential of A is given by

$$\begin{aligned}
e^{A} = e^{T\Lambda T^{-1}} &= I_N + T\Lambda T^{-1} + \frac{1}{2}T\Lambda^2 T^{-1} + \frac{1}{3!}T\Lambda^3 T^{-1} + \cdots + \frac{1}{k!}T\Lambda^k T^{-1} + \cdots \\
&= T\left[I_N + \Lambda + \frac{1}{2}\Lambda^2 + \frac{1}{3!}\Lambda^3 + \cdots + \frac{1}{k!}\Lambda^k + \cdots \right] T^{-1} \\
&= Te^{\Lambda}T^{-1} \\
&= T\begin{bmatrix} e^{\lambda_1} & 0 & \cdots & 0 \\ 0 & e^{\lambda_2} & & \vdots \\ \vdots & & \ddots & 0 \\ 0 & 0 & \cdots & e^{\lambda_N} \end{bmatrix} T^{-1}
\end{aligned} \tag{10.35}$$

The matrix of eigenvectors of A is diagonalizing, so we can use it as matrix T. The time-dependent matrix exponential e^{At} is simply

$$e^{At} = e^{T\Lambda T^{-1}t} = T\begin{bmatrix} e^{\lambda_1 t} & 0 & \cdots & 0 \\ 0 & e^{\lambda_2 t} & & \vdots \\ \vdots & & \ddots & 0 \\ 0 & 0 & \cdots & e^{\lambda_N t} \end{bmatrix} T^{-1}. \tag{10.36}$$

Now consider the vector-valued function of time

$$x(t) = e^{At}x_0, \tag{10.37}$$

where $x(t) \in \mathbb{R}^N$ and $x(0) = x_0$. The claim is that this function is the state response of the system to the initial state for $t > 0$. To show this, simply substitute Equation 10.37 into the left-hand side of Equation 10.32:

$$\begin{aligned}
\frac{dx(t)}{dt} = \frac{d}{dt}e^{At}x_0 &= \frac{d}{dt}\left[I_n + At + \frac{1}{2}A^2t^2 + \cdots \right] x_0 \\
&= \left[A + A^2 t + \frac{1}{2}A^3 t^2 + \cdots \right] x_0 \\
&= A\left[I_n + At + \frac{1}{2}A^2 t^2 + \cdots \right] x_0 \\
&= Ae^{At}x_0 = Ax(t)
\end{aligned} \tag{10.38}$$

Therefore, the zero-input state response is as given in Equation 10.37 for $t > 0$, and the corresponding zero-input response is

$$y_{zi}(t) = Ce^{At}x_0 q(t), \tag{10.39}$$

where $q(t)$ is the unit step signal.

Example 10.1: Let us revisit the circuit example with its first physically motivated state-space representation:

$$\begin{bmatrix} \dot{x}_1(t) \\ \dot{x}_2(t) \end{bmatrix} = \underbrace{\begin{bmatrix} -\frac{1}{RC} & \frac{1}{C} \\ -\frac{1}{L} & 0 \end{bmatrix}}_{A} \begin{bmatrix} x_1(t) \\ x_2(t) \end{bmatrix} + \underbrace{\begin{bmatrix} 0 \\ \frac{1}{L} \end{bmatrix}}_{B} u(t), \tag{10.40}$$

$$y(t) = \begin{bmatrix} 1 & 0 \end{bmatrix} \begin{bmatrix} x_1(t) \\ x_2(t) \end{bmatrix}. \tag{10.41}$$

Suppose $R = 1\,\Omega$, $L = 1\,\text{H}$, $C = 1\,\text{F}$, the initial capacitor voltage is $x_1(0) = 10$ V, and the initial inductor current is $x_2(0) = 0$ A. With these numerical values, the state equation becomes

$$\begin{bmatrix} \dot{x}_1 \\ \dot{x}_2 \end{bmatrix} = \underbrace{\begin{bmatrix} -1 & 1 \\ -1 & 0 \end{bmatrix}}_{A} \begin{bmatrix} x_1 \\ x_2 \end{bmatrix} + \underbrace{\begin{bmatrix} 0 \\ 1 \end{bmatrix}}_{B} v_s. \tag{10.42}$$

We want to find the zero-input state response of the circuit. We first compute the eigenvalues of A:

$$\begin{aligned} \det(\lambda I_2 - A) &= \det \begin{bmatrix} \lambda + 1 & -1 \\ 1 & \lambda \end{bmatrix} = 0 \\ &\Rightarrow \lambda^2 + \lambda + 1 = 0 \\ \lambda_{1,2} &= -\frac{1}{2} \pm j\frac{\sqrt{3}}{2}. \end{aligned} \tag{10.43}$$

Then, the corresponding eigenvectors v_1, v_2 are computed:

$$
\begin{aligned}
&(\lambda_1 I_2 - A)v_1 = 0\\
&\begin{bmatrix} \frac{1}{2}+j\frac{\sqrt{3}}{2} & -1 \\ 1 & -\frac{1}{2}+j\frac{\sqrt{3}}{2} \end{bmatrix}\begin{bmatrix} v_{11} \\ v_{12} \end{bmatrix}=\begin{bmatrix} 0 \\ 0 \end{bmatrix}\\
&\Rightarrow \begin{bmatrix} v_{11} \\ v_{12} \end{bmatrix}=\begin{bmatrix} \frac{1}{2}-j\frac{\sqrt{3}}{2} \\ 1 \end{bmatrix}\\
&(\lambda_2 I_2 - A)v_2 = 0\\
&\begin{bmatrix} \frac{1}{2}-j\frac{\sqrt{3}}{2} & -1 \\ 1 & -\frac{1}{2}-j\frac{\sqrt{3}}{2} \end{bmatrix}\begin{bmatrix} v_{21} \\ v_{22} \end{bmatrix}=\begin{bmatrix} 0 \\ 0 \end{bmatrix}\\
&\Rightarrow \begin{bmatrix} v_{21} \\ v_{22} \end{bmatrix}=\begin{bmatrix} \frac{1}{2}+j\frac{\sqrt{3}}{2} \\ 1 \end{bmatrix}.
\end{aligned}
\tag{10.44}
$$

Letting

$$
T := \begin{bmatrix} v_1 & v_2 \end{bmatrix} = \begin{bmatrix} \frac{1}{2}-j\frac{\sqrt{3}}{2} & \frac{1}{2}+j\frac{\sqrt{3}}{2} \\ 1 & 1 \end{bmatrix}
\tag{10.45}
$$

and

$$
\Lambda := \begin{bmatrix} -\frac{1}{2}+j\frac{\sqrt{3}}{2} & 0 \\ 0 & -\frac{1}{2}-j\frac{\sqrt{3}}{2} \end{bmatrix},
\tag{10.46}
$$

we check that $T\Lambda T^{-1} = A$:

$$
\begin{aligned}
T\Lambda T^{-1} &= \begin{bmatrix} \frac{1}{2}-j\frac{\sqrt{3}}{2} & \frac{1}{2}+j\frac{\sqrt{3}}{2} \\ 1 & 1 \end{bmatrix} \begin{bmatrix} -\frac{1}{2}+j\frac{\sqrt{3}}{2} & 0 \\ 0 & -\frac{1}{2}-j\frac{\sqrt{3}}{2} \end{bmatrix} \begin{bmatrix} \frac{1}{2}-j\frac{\sqrt{3}}{2} & \frac{1}{2}+j\frac{\sqrt{3}}{2} \\ 1 & 1 \end{bmatrix}^{-1} \\
&= \begin{bmatrix} \frac{1}{2}+j\frac{\sqrt{3}}{2} & \frac{1}{2}-j\frac{\sqrt{3}}{2} \\ -\frac{1}{2}+j\frac{\sqrt{3}}{2} & -\frac{1}{2}-j\frac{\sqrt{3}}{2} \end{bmatrix} \left(\frac{1}{-j\sqrt{3}} \begin{bmatrix} 1 & -\frac{1}{2}-j\frac{\sqrt{3}}{2} \\ -1 & \frac{1}{2}-j\frac{\sqrt{3}}{2} \end{bmatrix} \right) \\
&= \frac{1}{-j\sqrt{3}} \begin{bmatrix} j\sqrt{3} & -j\sqrt{3} \\ j\sqrt{3} & 0 \end{bmatrix} = \begin{bmatrix} -1 & 1 \\ -1 & 0 \end{bmatrix} = A
\end{aligned}
\tag{10.47}
$$

Finally, the zero-input state response is calculated using Equations 10.36 and 10.37:

$$
\begin{aligned}
x(t) &= e^{At}x_0 = Te^{\Lambda t}T^{-1}x_0 \\
&= \begin{bmatrix} \frac{1}{2}-j\frac{\sqrt{3}}{2} & \frac{1}{2}+j\frac{\sqrt{3}}{2} \\ 1 & 1 \end{bmatrix} \begin{bmatrix} e^{(-\frac{1}{2}+j\frac{\sqrt{3}}{2})t} & 0 \\ 0 & e^{(-\frac{1}{2}+j\frac{\sqrt{3}}{2})t} \end{bmatrix} \begin{bmatrix} \frac{1}{2}-j\frac{\sqrt{3}}{2} & \frac{1}{2}+j\frac{\sqrt{3}}{2} \\ 1 & 1 \end{bmatrix}^{-1} \begin{bmatrix} 10 \\ 0 \end{bmatrix} \\
&= \begin{bmatrix} \frac{1}{2}-j\frac{\sqrt{3}}{2} & \frac{1}{2}+j\frac{\sqrt{3}}{2} \\ 1 & 1 \end{bmatrix} \begin{bmatrix} e^{(-\frac{1}{2}+j\frac{\sqrt{3}}{2})t} & 0 \\ 0 & e^{(-\frac{1}{2}+j\frac{\sqrt{3}}{2})t} \end{bmatrix} \begin{bmatrix} 1 & -\frac{1}{2}-j\frac{\sqrt{3}}{2} \\ -1 & \frac{1}{2}-j\frac{\sqrt{3}}{2} \end{bmatrix} \begin{bmatrix} 10 \\ 0 \end{bmatrix} \cdot \frac{1}{-j\sqrt{3}} \\
&= \begin{bmatrix} \frac{1}{2}-j\frac{\sqrt{3}}{2} & \frac{1}{2}+j\frac{\sqrt{3}}{2} \\ 1 & 1 \end{bmatrix} \begin{bmatrix} 10e^{(-\frac{1}{2}+j\frac{\sqrt{3}}{2})t} \\ -10e^{(-\frac{1}{2}-j\frac{\sqrt{3}}{2})t} \end{bmatrix} \cdot \frac{1}{-j\sqrt{3}} \\
&= \frac{1}{-j\sqrt{3}} \begin{bmatrix} 10\left[\left(\frac{1}{2}-j\frac{\sqrt{3}}{2}\right)e^{(-\frac{1}{2}+j\frac{\sqrt{3}}{2})t} - \left(\frac{1}{2}+j\frac{\sqrt{3}}{2}\right)e^{(-\frac{1}{2}-j\frac{\sqrt{3}}{2})t}\right] \\ 10e^{(-\frac{1}{2}+j\frac{\sqrt{3}}{2})t} - 10e^{(-\frac{1}{2}-j\frac{\sqrt{3}}{2})t} \end{bmatrix} \\
&= -\frac{1}{\sqrt{3}} \begin{bmatrix} 20e^{-\frac{1}{2}t}\,\mathrm{Im}\left\{\left(\frac{1}{2}-j\frac{\sqrt{3}}{2}\right)e^{j\frac{\sqrt{3}}{2}t}\right\} \\ 20e^{-\frac{1}{2}t}\,\mathrm{Im}\left\{e^{j\frac{\sqrt{3}}{2}t}\right\} \end{bmatrix}
\end{aligned}
\tag{10.48}
$$

$$= \begin{bmatrix} -\frac{20}{\sqrt{3}} e^{-\frac{1}{2}t} \left(\frac{1}{2} \sin\frac{\sqrt{3}}{2}t - \frac{\sqrt{3}}{2} \cos\frac{\sqrt{3}}{2}t \right) \\ -\frac{20}{\sqrt{3}} e^{-\frac{1}{2}t} \sin\frac{\sqrt{3}}{2}t \end{bmatrix}$$

Zero-State Response

The zero-state response $y_{zs}(t)$ is the response of the system to the input only (initial rest). A recursive solution cannot be obtained in continuous time, so we resort to the impulse response technique. Let $u(t) = \delta(t)$ in Equation 10.31 to find the impulse response.

$$\begin{aligned} \dot{x}(t) &= Ax(t) + B\delta(t) \\ h(t) &= Cx(t) + D\delta(t) \end{aligned} \qquad (10.49)$$

Integrate the state equation in Equation 10.49 from $t = 0^-$ to $t = 0^+$ to "get rid of the impulse" and obtain

$$x(0^+) - \underbrace{x(0^-)}_{=0} = B$$

$$x(0^+) = B. \qquad (10.50)$$

Thus, from $t = 0^+$, we have a zero-input (autonomous) state equation $\dot{x}(t) = Ax(t)$ to solve for $t > 0$ with the initial condition obtained in Equation 10.50. The solution as given by Equation 10.37 is

$$x(t) = e^{At} Bq(t) \qquad (10.51)$$

and hence, the impulse response of the state-space system is given by

$$h(t) = Ce^{At} Bq(t) + D\delta(t). \qquad (10.52)$$

The zero-state response is just the convolution of the input with the impulse response of the system. Assume that the input starts at $t = 0$, that is, $u(t) = 0, t < 0$:

$$\begin{aligned} y_{zs}(t) &= \int_{-\infty}^{+\infty} h(\tau)u(t-\tau)d\tau \\ &= \int_{-\infty}^{+\infty} \left(Ce^{A\tau} Bq(\tau) + D\delta(\tau) \right) u(t-\tau)d\tau \\ &= \int_{0}^{t} Ce^{A\tau} Bu(t-\tau)d\tau + Du(t) \end{aligned} \qquad (10.53)$$

((Lecture 35: Laplace Transform Solution of State-Space Systems))

LAPLACE-TRANSFORM SOLUTION FOR CONTINUOUS-TIME STATE-SPACE SYSTEMS

Consider the state-space system of Equation 10.31 with initial state $x(0^-) = x_0$ depicted in Figure 10.7.

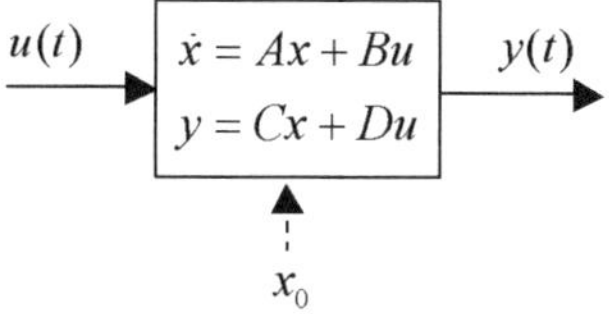

FIGURE 10.7 Block diagram of a state-space system.

Taking the unilateral Laplace transform on both sides of Equation 10.31, we obtain

$$\begin{aligned} s\mathcal{X}(s) - x_0 &= A\mathcal{X}(s) + B\mathcal{U}(s) \\ \mathcal{Y}(s) &= C\mathcal{X}(s) + D\mathcal{U}(s). \end{aligned} \tag{10.54}$$

Solving for the Laplace transform of the state, we get

$$\mathcal{X}(s) = (sI_N - A)^{-1} B\mathcal{U}(s) + (sI_N - A)^{-1} x_0, \tag{10.55}$$

and the Laplace transform of the output is found:

$$\mathcal{Y}(s) = \left[C(sI_N - A)^{-1} B + D \right] \mathcal{U}(s) + C(sI_N - A)^{-1} x_0. \tag{10.56}$$

The first term on the right-hand side is the Laplace transform of the zero-state response of the system to the input $u(t)$, whereas the second term is the Laplace transform of the zero-input response. The time-domain version of Equation 10.56 is thus

$$\begin{aligned} y(t) &= y_{zs}(t) + y_{zi}(t) \\ &= \int_0^t Ce^{A\tau} Bu(t-\tau)d\tau + Du(t) + Ce^{At} x_0 q(t). \end{aligned} \tag{10.57}$$

The transfer function of the system is given by

$$\mathcal{H}(s) = \frac{\mathcal{Y}(s)}{\mathcal{U}(s)} = C(sI_N - A)^{-1}B + D. \tag{10.58}$$

Remark: Earlier, we said that there exist infinitely many state-space realizations of a single transfer function. To convince ourselves of this fact, let us simply consider the (infinitely many) realizations expressed by $(P^{-1}AP, P^{-1}B, CP, D)$, $\forall P \in \mathbb{R}^{N\times N}$, $\det(P) \neq 0$ whose transfer functions are all equal to the one given in Equation 10.58:

$$\begin{aligned} CP(sI_N - P^{-1}AP)^{-1}P^{-1}B + D &= CP(sP^{-1}P - P^{-1}AP)^{-1}P^{-1}B + D \\ &= CP\left[P^{-1}(sI_N - A)P\right]^{-1}P^{-1}B + D \\ &= CPP^{-1}(sI_N - A)^{-1}PP^{-1}B + D \\ &= C(sI_N - A)^{-1}B + D. \end{aligned}$$

Note that in Equation 10.58, we can write the ratio of the two Laplace transforms $\frac{\mathcal{Y}(s)}{\mathcal{U}(s)}$ only because this is a single-input, single-output system. For multi-input, multi-output (MIMO, multivariable) systems, $\mathcal{Y}(s)$ and $\mathcal{U}(s)$ are *vectors* and it would not make sense to have a ratio of two vectors. Nevertheless, the formula for the transfer function matrix of the system is still given by Equation 10.58, and one can write

$$\mathcal{H}(s) = \mathcal{U}(s) \mapsto \mathcal{Y}(s) = C(sI_N - A)^{-1}B + D. \tag{10.59}$$

Recall that the inverse of a square matrix is equal to its *adjoint* (transposed matrix of cofactors) divided by its determinant. Therefore, we have

$$\mathcal{H}(s) = \frac{1}{\det(sI_N - A)} C\,\mathrm{adj}(sI_N - A)B + D. \tag{10.60}$$

The adjoint matrix only contains polynomials; thus, $C\,\mathrm{adj}(sI_N - A)B$ is a polynomial in the Laplace variable s. It follows that the poles of $H(s)$ can only come from the zeros of the polynomial $\det(sI_N - A)$, which are nothing but the eigenvalues of matrix A. This is not to say that the set of poles is equal to the set of eigenvalues of A in all cases (it can be a subset). However, for *minimal* state-space systems as defined below, these two sets are the same.

The ROC of the transfer function will be specified after we give a result relating the eigenvalues of A to the poles of the transfer function for minimal systems.

Bounded-Input, Bounded-Output Stability

Minimal state-space realizations are realizations for which all N eigenvalues of matrix A appear as poles in the transfer function given by Equation 10.58 with their multiplicity. In other words, minimal state-space realizations are those realizations for which the order of the transfer function is the same as the dimension of the state vector.

Fact: *For a minimal state-space realization (A, B, C, D) of a continuous-time system with transfer function H(s), the set of poles of H(s) is equal to the set of eigenvalues of A.*

Since we limit our analysis to causal, minimal state-space realizations, this fact yields the following stability theorem for such continuous-time, LTI state-space systems.

Stability Theorem: *The continuous-time causal, minimal, LTI state-space system (A, B, C, D), where* $A \in \mathbb{R}^{N\times N}, B \in \mathbb{R}^{N\times 1}, C \in \mathbb{R}^{1\times N}, D \in \mathbb{R}$, *is bounded-input, bounded-output (BIBO) stable if and only if all eigenvalues of A have a negative real part.*

Mathematically, (A, B, C, D) *is BIBO stable if and only if* $\mathrm{Re}\{\lambda_i(A)\} < 0$, $\forall i = 1,\ldots,N$.

The ROC of the transfer function in Equation 10.58 is the open right half-plane to the right of $\max\limits_{i=1,\ldots,N} \mathrm{Re}\{\lambda_i(A)\}$.

We found earlier that the impulse response of the state-space system is given by $h(t) = Ce^{At}Bq(t) + D\delta(t)$, where $q(t)$ is the unit step function. Comparing this expression with Equation 10.58, the inverse Laplace transform of $(sI_N - A)^{-1}, \mathrm{Re}\{s\} > \max\limits_{i=1,\ldots,N} \mathrm{Re}\{\lambda_i(A)\}$ is found to be equal to $e^{At}q(t)$; that is,

$$e^{At}q(t) \overset{UL}{\leftrightarrow} (sI_N - A)^{-1}, \mathrm{Re}\{s\} > \max_{i=1,\ldots,N} \mathrm{Re}\{\lambda_i(A)\} \qquad (10.61)$$

Example 10.2: Find the transfer function of the causal minimal state-space system described by

$$\dot{x}(t) = \begin{bmatrix} -2.2 & 0.4 \\ -0.6 & -0.8 \end{bmatrix} x(t) + \begin{bmatrix} 2 \\ -1 \end{bmatrix} u(t)$$
$$y(t) = \begin{bmatrix} -1 & 3 \end{bmatrix} x(t) + 2u(t). \qquad (10.62)$$

First, we compute the eigenvalues of the A matrix by solving $\det(\lambda I - A) = 0$ to obtain $\lambda_1 = -1, \lambda_2 = -2$. Thus, the system is BIBO stable since the poles of the transfer function are negative, being equal to the eigenvalues. We use Equation 10.58 to calculate $H(s)$:

$$H(s)=\begin{bmatrix}-1 & 3\end{bmatrix}\begin{bmatrix}s+2.2 & -0.4\\ 0.6 & s+0.8\end{bmatrix}^{-1}\begin{bmatrix}2\\ -1\end{bmatrix}+2$$
$$=\frac{1}{(s+2.2)(s+0.8)-(-0.4)\cdot 0.6}\begin{bmatrix}-1 & 3\end{bmatrix}\begin{bmatrix}s+0.8 & 0.4\\ -0.6 & s+2.2\end{bmatrix}\begin{bmatrix}2\\ -1\end{bmatrix}+2$$
$$=\frac{1}{s^2+3s+2}\begin{bmatrix}-1 & 3\end{bmatrix}\begin{bmatrix}2s+1.2\\ -s-3.4\end{bmatrix}+2=\frac{-5s-11.4+2(s^2+3s+2)}{s^2+3s+2}$$
$$=\frac{2s^2+s-7.4}{s^2+3s+2}=2\frac{s^2+0.5s-3.7}{s^2+3s+2}=2\frac{(s+2.19)(s-1.69)}{(s+1)(s+2)},\quad \mathrm{Re}\{s\}>-1 \qquad (10.63)$$

The eigenvalues of the A matrix are the same as the poles of the transfer function, as expected since the realization is minimal. Now that the transfer function is known, the output response of the system for a specific input can be found by the usual method of partial fraction expansion of $Y(s) = H(s)U(s)$.

STATE TRAJECTORIES AND THE PHASE PLANE

The time evolution of an N-dimensional state vector $x(t)$ can be depicted using N plots of the state variables $x_i(t)$ versus time. On the other hand, the state trajectory, that is, the locus of points traced by $x(t)$, is a curved line in hyperspace $\mathbb{R}^N$.

For a two-dimensional state vector, we can conveniently plot the state trajectory on a *phase plane* that is a plot of $x_2(t)$ versus $x_1(t)$ (or vice versa). For example, the state trajectory in the phase plane of a second-order system responding to an initial vector as a damped sinusoid will look like a spiral encircling and going toward the origin.

Example 10.3: Consider the causal second-order mass-spring-damper system of Figure 10.8 modeled as a state-space system.

Assume that the mass-spring-damper system is initially at rest, which means that the spring generates a force equal to the force of gravity to support the mass. The balance of forces on the mass and Newton's law gives us an equation for state variable $x_2(t)$:

$$\begin{aligned} m\dot{x}_2(t) &= u(t)-F_k(t)-F_b(t)\\ &= u(t)-kx_1(t)-bx_2(t), \end{aligned} \qquad (10.64)$$

and the second equation simply relates velocity and position:

$$\dot{x}_1(t)=x_2(t). \qquad (10.65)$$

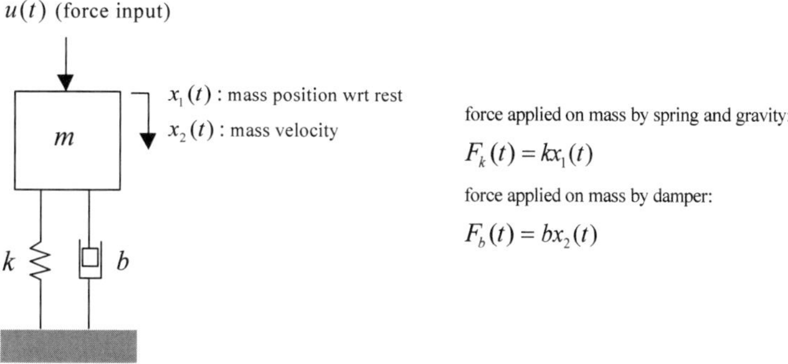

FIGURE 10.8 Mass-spring-damper system.

Let the state vector be $x(t) := \begin{bmatrix} x_1(t) \\ x_2(t) \end{bmatrix}$. The state equation can be written as

$$\dot{x}(t) = \begin{bmatrix} 0 & 1 \\ -k/m & -b/m \end{bmatrix} x(t) + \begin{bmatrix} 0 \\ 1/m \end{bmatrix} u(t). \tag{10.66}$$

Suppose the physical constants have numerical values $m = 10$ kg, $k = 10$ N/m, and $b = 5$ N/$^{\text{m}}\!/_{\text{s}}$. We get

$$\dot{x}(t) = \begin{bmatrix} 0 & 1 \\ -1 & -0.5 \end{bmatrix} x(t) + \begin{bmatrix} 0 \\ 0.1 \end{bmatrix} u(t). \tag{10.67}$$

The zero-input state response to the initial condition of the mass displaced by 5 cm so that $x(0) = \begin{bmatrix} 0.05 \\ 0 \end{bmatrix}$ gives rise to the spiral-shaped state trajectory shown on the phase plane in Figure 10.9.

This phase plane plot was generated by the following MATLAB script, which can be found on the CD-ROM in D:\Chapter10\phaseplane.m.

```
%% Phase plane state trajectory of mass-spring-damper system
% Define state-space system
A=[0 1; -1 -0.5];
B=[0; 0.1];
C=eye(2);
D=zeros(2,1);
x0=[0.05; 0];
% time vector
T=0:.1:100;
% input signal (zero)
U=zeros(length(T),1);
```

```
%simulate
SYS=ss(A,B,C,D);
[YS,TS,XS] = LSIM(SYS,U,T,x0);
plot(100*XS(:,1),100*XS(:,2))
```

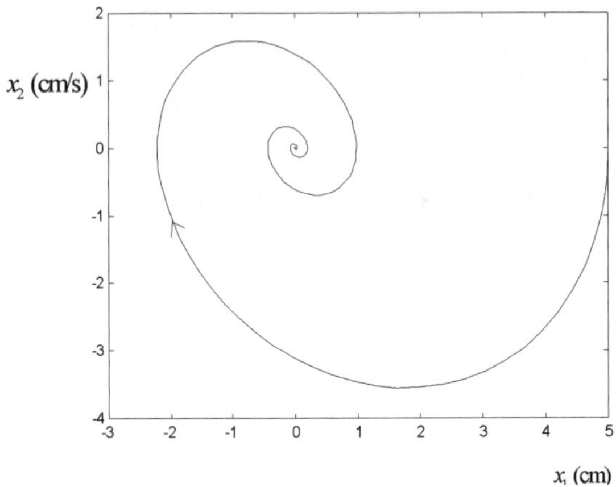

FIGURE 10.9 Phase plane trajectory of a second-order state-space system.

BLOCK DIAGRAM REPRESENTATION OF CONTINUOUS-TIME STATE-SPACE SYSTEMS

The block diagram in Figure 10.10 is often used to describe a continuous-time state-space system. Note that some of the signals represented by arrows are vector-valued and the gains are "matrix gains."

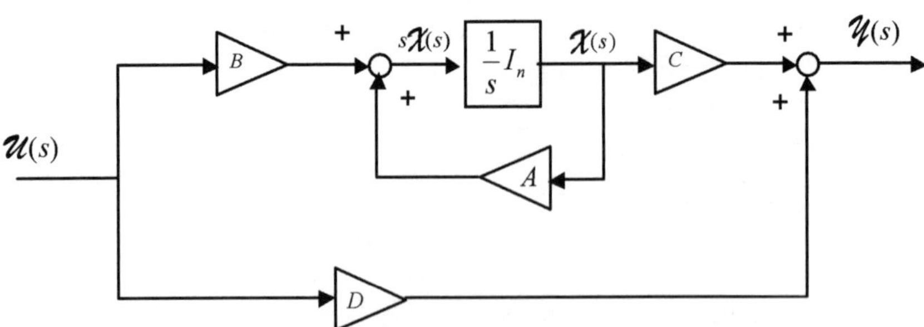

FIGURE 10.10 Block diagram of a state-space system.

One can see that this is a generalization of a scalar first-order system, with N integrators in parallel instead of just one. Remember that matrices do not commute in general, even if they are conformable. Thus, in deriving the equations for the above block diagram, one has to be careful not to write something like $C(sI_N - A)^{-1}B = B(sI_N - A)^{-1}C = CB(sI_N - A)^{-1}$. In other words, the order in which subsystems appear in block diagrams of *multivariable* LTI systems cannot be changed.

SUMMARY

In this chapter, we introduced LTI state-space systems.

- A state model of a physical system can often be obtained from first principles as a collection of first-order differential equations together with an output equation.
- Two state-space realizations of any proper rational transfer function can be easily obtained: the controllable canonical realization and the observable canonical realization. However, there exist infinitely many realizations of any given proper rational transfer function.
- We derived the formulas for the zero-input and zero-state responses, the impulse response, and the transfer function of a general LTI state-space system.
- A causal minimal state-space system was shown to be BIBO stable if and only if all of the eigenvalues of its A matrix lie in the open left half-plane.
- We briefly discussed state trajectories, and the phase plane was illustrated with an example.

TO PROBE FURTHER

State-space modeling of engineering systems is covered in Bélanger, 1995. For an advanced text on state-space systems, see Chen, 1999.

EXERCISES

Exercises with Solutions

Exercise 10.1

Consider the causal LTI state-space system:

$$\dot{x} = Ax + Bu$$
$$y = Cx,$$

where $A = \begin{bmatrix} -1 & 1 \\ -1 & -1 \end{bmatrix}$, $B = \begin{bmatrix} 1 \\ 0 \end{bmatrix}$, $C = \begin{bmatrix} 1 & 1 \end{bmatrix}$.

(a) Is the system stable? Justify your answer.

Answer:
We compute the eigenvalues of the A matrix:

$$\det\begin{bmatrix} \lambda+1 & -1 \\ 1 & \lambda+1 \end{bmatrix} = (\lambda+1)(\lambda+1)+1 = \lambda^2 + 2\lambda + 2$$
$$\Rightarrow \lambda_1 = -1 + j, \lambda_2 = -1 - j,$$

The eigenvalues of the A matrix $\lambda_{1,2} = -1 \pm j$ have a negative real part; therefore the system is stable.

(b) Compute the transfer function $H(s)$ of the system. Specify its ROC.

Answer:

$$\begin{aligned} H(s) &= C(sI_2 - A)^{-1}B \\ &= \begin{bmatrix} 1 & 1 \end{bmatrix}\begin{bmatrix} s+1 & -1 \\ 1 & s+1 \end{bmatrix}^{-1}\begin{bmatrix} 1 \\ 0 \end{bmatrix} \\ &= \frac{1}{s^2+2s+2}\begin{bmatrix} 1 & 1 \end{bmatrix}\begin{bmatrix} s+1 & 1 \\ -1 & s+1 \end{bmatrix}\begin{bmatrix} 1 \\ 0 \end{bmatrix} \\ &= \frac{1}{s^2+2s+2}\begin{bmatrix} 1 & 1 \end{bmatrix}\begin{bmatrix} s+1 \\ -1 \end{bmatrix} = \frac{s}{s^2+2s+2}, \quad \mathrm{Re}\{s\} > -1 \end{aligned}$$

The poles of the transfer function are $-\zeta\omega_n \pm j\omega_n\sqrt{1-\zeta^2} = -\frac{1}{\sqrt{2}}\sqrt{2} \pm j\sqrt{2}\sqrt{\frac{1}{2}}$ $= -1 \pm j1$, equal to the eigenvalues, as expected.

(c) Compute the impulse response $h(t)$ of the system using the matrix exponential.

Answer:

The eigenvectors of the A matrix are computed as follows:

$$(\lambda_1 I - A)v_1 = \begin{bmatrix} -1+j+1 & -1 \\ 1 & -1+j+1 \end{bmatrix}\begin{bmatrix} v_{11} \\ v_{12} \end{bmatrix} = \begin{bmatrix} j & -1 \\ 1 & j \end{bmatrix}\begin{bmatrix} v_{11} \\ v_{12} \end{bmatrix} = \begin{bmatrix} 0 \\ 0 \end{bmatrix}$$

$$\Rightarrow v_{11} = 1, v_{12} = j$$

$$v_2 = v_1^* = \begin{bmatrix} 1 \\ -j \end{bmatrix}$$

Thus, $T = \begin{bmatrix} 1 & 1 \\ j & -j \end{bmatrix}$, $T^{-1} = \frac{1}{-2j}\begin{bmatrix} -j & -1 \\ -j & 1 \end{bmatrix} = \begin{bmatrix} \frac{1}{2} & -j\frac{1}{2} \\ \frac{1}{2} & j\frac{1}{2} \end{bmatrix}$, and

$$h(t) = CT\mathrm{diag}\{e^{(-1+j)t}, e^{(-1-j)t}\}T^{-1}q(t)$$

$$= \begin{bmatrix} 1 & 1 \end{bmatrix}\begin{bmatrix} 1 & 1 \\ j & -j \end{bmatrix}\begin{bmatrix} e^{(-1+j)t} & 0 \\ 0 & e^{(-1-j)t} \end{bmatrix}\begin{bmatrix} \frac{1}{2} & -j\frac{1}{2} \\ \frac{1}{2} & j\frac{1}{2} \end{bmatrix}\begin{bmatrix} 1 \\ 0 \end{bmatrix}q(t)$$

$$= \begin{bmatrix} 1+j & 1-j \end{bmatrix}\begin{bmatrix} e^{(-1+j)t} & 0 \\ 0 & e^{(-1-j)t} \end{bmatrix}\begin{bmatrix} \frac{1}{2} \\ \frac{1}{2} \end{bmatrix}q(t)$$

$$= \left[\left(\frac{1}{2} + j\frac{1}{2}\right)e^{(-1+j)t} + \left(\frac{1}{2} - j\frac{1}{2}\right)e^{(-1-j)t}\right]q(t)$$

$$= e^{-t}\left[\left(\frac{1}{2} + j\frac{1}{2}\right)e^{jt} + \left(\frac{1}{2} - j\frac{1}{2}\right)e^{-jt}\right]q(t)$$

$$= 2e^{-t}\,\mathrm{Re}\left[\left(\frac{1}{2} + j\frac{1}{2}\right)e^{jt}\right]q(t) = e^{-t}\left(\cos t - \sin t\right)q(t),$$

Thus, $h(t) = e^{-t}\left(\cos t - \sin t\right)q(t)$.

Exercise 10.2

Find the controllable and observable canonical state-space realizations for the following LTI system:

$$H(s) = \frac{s^3 + s + 2}{s^3 + 3s}, \quad \mathrm{Re}\{s\} > 0.$$

Answer:

The system's controllable canonical state-space realization is shown in Figure 10.11.

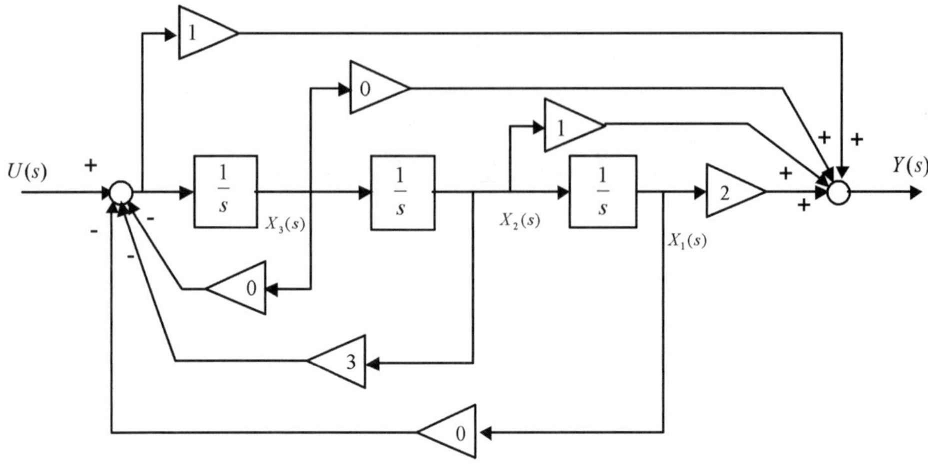

FIGURE 10.11 Controllable canonical realization of the system of Exercise 10.2.

Referring to Figure 10.11, we can write down the state-space equations of the controllable canonical realization of the system:

$$\begin{bmatrix} \dot{x}_1(t) \\ \dot{x}_2(t) \\ \dot{x}_3(t) \end{bmatrix} = \begin{bmatrix} 0 & 1 & 0 \\ 0 & 0 & 1 \\ 0 & -3 & 0 \end{bmatrix} \begin{bmatrix} x_1(t) \\ x_2(t) \\ x_3(t) \end{bmatrix} + \begin{bmatrix} 0 \\ 0 \\ 1 \end{bmatrix} u(t),$$

$$y(t) = \begin{bmatrix} 2 & -2 & 0 \end{bmatrix} \begin{bmatrix} x_1(t) \\ x_2(t) \\ x_3(t) \end{bmatrix} + u(t).$$

The observable canonical realization is the block diagram of Figure 10.12.

From Figure 10.12, the state-space equations of the observable canonical realization of the system can be written as

$$\begin{bmatrix} \dot{x}_1(t) \\ \dot{x}_2(t) \\ \dot{x}_3(t) \end{bmatrix} = \begin{bmatrix} 0 & 0 & 0 \\ 1 & 0 & -3 \\ 0 & 1 & 0 \end{bmatrix} \begin{bmatrix} x_1(t) \\ x_2(t) \\ x_3(t) \end{bmatrix} + \begin{bmatrix} 2 \\ -2 \\ 0 \end{bmatrix} u(t),$$

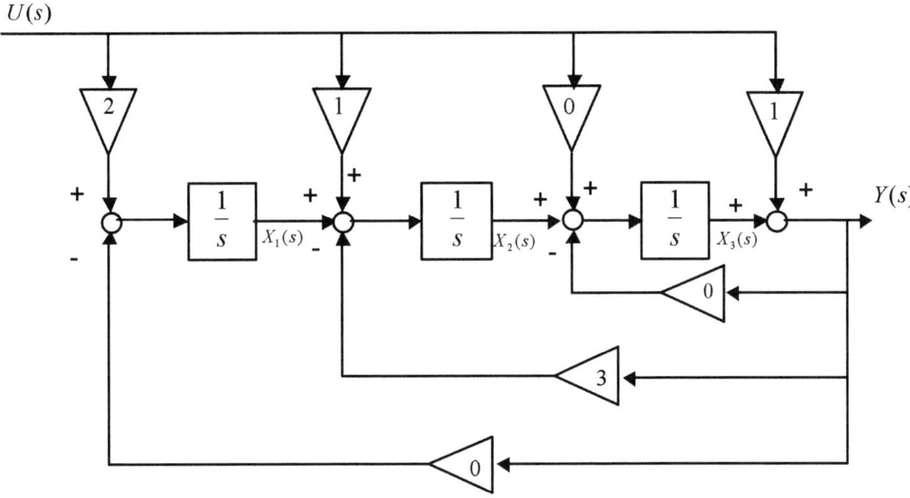

FIGURE 10.12 Observable canonical realization of the system of Exercise 10.2.

$$y(t)=\begin{bmatrix}0 & 0 & 1\end{bmatrix}\begin{bmatrix}x_1(t)\\ x_2(t)\\ x_3(t)\end{bmatrix}+u(t).$$

Exercises

Exercise 10.3

Compute $e^A + I$ for $A=\begin{bmatrix}-2 & 0\\ 3 & 1\end{bmatrix}$.

Answer:

ON THE CD

Exercise 10.4

Consider the causal LTI state-space system

$\dot{x} = Ax + Bu$, where $A=\begin{bmatrix}-1 & 1\\ -1 & -1\end{bmatrix}$, $B=\begin{bmatrix}1\\ 0\end{bmatrix}$, $C=\begin{bmatrix}1 & 1\end{bmatrix}$.

(a) Is the system stable? Justify.

(b) Compute the transfer function $H(s)$ of the system. Specify its ROC.

(c) Compute the impulse response $h(t)$ of the system using the matrix exponential.

Exercise 10.5

Repeat Exercise 10.4 with $A=\begin{bmatrix}0 & 0\\ 1 & 0\end{bmatrix},\quad B=\begin{bmatrix}0 & 0\\ 1 & 0\end{bmatrix},\quad C=\begin{bmatrix}0 & 1\end{bmatrix}$. What type of system is this?

(a) Is the system stable? Justify.

(b) Compute the transfer function $H(s)$ of the system. Specify its ROC.

(c) Compute the impulse response $h(t)$ of the system using the matrix exponential.

Answer:

ON THE CD

Exercise 10.6

Find the controllable and observable canonical state-space realizations for each of the following LTI systems.

(a) $h(t)=e^{-2t}q(t)+te^{2t}q(t)$

(b) $\dfrac{s^3+s^2+2s+1}{s^3+5s^2+2s},\quad \mathrm{Re}\{s\}>0$

Exercise 10.7

Find the controllable and observable canonical state-space realizations for each of the following LTI systems.

(a) $h(t)=e^{-3t}q(t)+e^{-t}q(t)+\delta(t)$

(b) $\dfrac{s^2+5}{s^3+2s^2+2s+1},\quad \mathrm{Re}\{s\}>-0.5$

(c) $\begin{bmatrix}\dot{x}_1\\ \dot{x}_2\end{bmatrix}=\begin{bmatrix}-1 & 0\\ 0 & -2\end{bmatrix}\begin{bmatrix}x_1\\ x_2\end{bmatrix}+\begin{bmatrix}3\\ 1\end{bmatrix}u,\quad y=\begin{bmatrix}2 & 1\end{bmatrix}\begin{bmatrix}x_1\\ x_2\end{bmatrix}+u$, causal

Answer:

ON THE CD

Exercise 10.8

(a) Compute e^{A} for $A=\begin{bmatrix}0 & 1\\ 3 & 2\end{bmatrix}$.

(b) Compute the zero-input state and output responses at time $t_1 = 2$ for the causal LTI state-space system

$$\dot{x} = Ax + Bu,\ y = Cx \text{ where } A = \begin{bmatrix} 0 & 1 \\ 3 & 2 \end{bmatrix},\quad B = \begin{bmatrix} 0 \\ 1 \end{bmatrix},\quad C = \begin{bmatrix} 1 & 0 \end{bmatrix},$$

$$\text{with initial state } x(0) = \begin{bmatrix} 1 \\ -1 \end{bmatrix}.$$

Exercise 10.9

Consider the causal LTI state-space system

$$\dot{x} = Ax + Bu,\ y = Cx \text{ where } A = \begin{bmatrix} -11 & 1 \\ 3 & -9 \end{bmatrix},\quad B = \begin{bmatrix} 2 \\ 3 \end{bmatrix},\quad C = \begin{bmatrix} 1 & 1 \end{bmatrix}.$$

(a) Is the system minimal? Is it stable? Justify.

(b) Compute the transfer function $H(s)$ of the system. Specify its ROC.

(c) Compute the *state transition matrix* defined as $\Phi(t,t_0) := e^{A(t-t_0)}$. This matrix has the property of taking the zero-input state response from the initial state $x(t_0)$ to the state $x(t)$ as follows: $x(t) = \Phi(t,t_0)x(t_0)$.

(d) Compute the impulse response $h(t)$ of the system using the matrix exponential.

Answer:

ON THE CD

Exercise 10.10

Consider the LTI causal state-space system

$$\begin{aligned} \dot{x} &= Ax + Bu \\ y &= Cx + Du, \end{aligned}$$

where $x(t) \in \mathbb{R}^N$, $y(t) \in \mathbb{R}$, $u(t) \in \mathbb{R}$. Show that any state transformation $z = Qx$, where $Q \in \mathbb{R}^{N \times N}$ is invertible, of the above state-space system keeps its transfer function invariant. This means that there are infinitely many state-space representations of any given proper rational transfer function.

11 Application of Transform Techniques to LTI Feedback Control Systems

In This Chapter

- Introduction to LTI Feedback Control Systems
- Closed-Loop Stability and the Root Locus
- The Nyquist Stability Criterion
- Stability Robustness: Gain and Phase Margins
- Summary
- To Probe Further
- Exercises

((Lecture 36: Introduction to LTI Feedback Control Systems))

The use of feedback dates back more than two thousand years to the Greeks and the Arabs, who invented the water clock based on a water level float regulator. Closer to us, and marking the beginning of the industrial revolution in 1769, was the invention by James Watt of the Watt governor, shown in Figure 11.1. The Watt governor was used to regulate automatically the speed of steam engines by feedback. This device measures the angular velocity of the engine shaft with the help of the centrifugal force acting on two spinning masses hinged at the top of the engine shaft. The centrifugal force is counteracted by the gravitational force. When in balance at a constant engine speed, the vertical positions of the masses are given by a function of the shaft angular velocity, and their vertical displacement is linked to a valve controlling the flow of steam to the engine. Thus, the Watt governor is a mechanical implementation of proportional control of the engine shaft velocity.

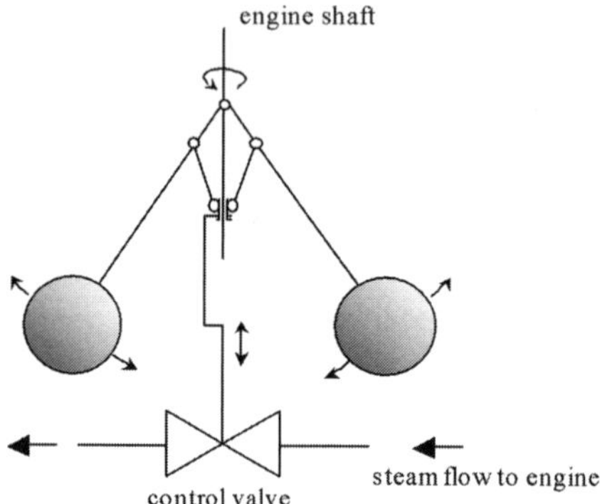

FIGURE 11.1 Schematic of the Watt governor.

It has only been about 70 years since engineers and mathematicians developed the mathematical tools to analyze and design feedback control systems. However, feedback control has proven to be an enabling technology in many industries and it has enjoyed a lot of interest in research and development circles. This chapter only gives a brief introduction to linear time-invariant (LTI) feedback control systems and studies them with the use of the Laplace transform. The most important property of a feedback control system is its stability, and therefore we present various means of ensuring that the closed-loop system will be stable. Tracking systems and regulators are defined and their performance is studied with the introduction of the sensitivity function and the complementary sensitivity function.

INTRODUCTION TO LTI FEEDBACK CONTROL SYSTEMS

A *feedback control system* is a system whose output is controlled using its measurement as a feedback signal. This feedback signal is compared with the *reference signal* to generate an *error signal* that is filtered by a *controller* to produce the system's control input. We will concentrate on single-input, single-output (SISO) continuous-time LTI feedback systems. Thus, the Laplace transform will be our main tool for analysis and design. The block diagram in Figure 11.2 depicts a general feedback control system. Note that all LTI systems represented by transfer functions in this chapter are assumed to be causal, and consequently we omit their regions of convergence (ROCs), which are always understood to be open right half-planes (RHPs).

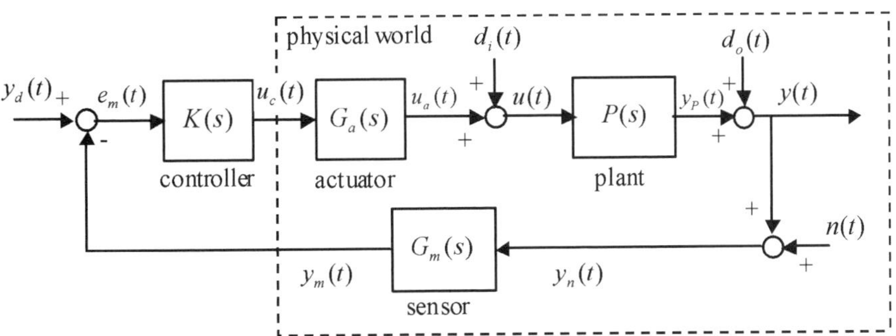

FIGURE 11.2 LTI feedback control system.

The controlled system is called the *plant*, and its LTI model is the transfer function $P(s)$. The disturbed output signal of the plant is $y(t)$ and its noisy measurement is $y_m(t)$, corrupted by the measurement noise $n(t)$. The error between the desired output $y_d(t)$ (or reference) and $y_m(t)$ is the *measured error*, denoted as $e_m(t)$. The actual error between the plant output and the reference is $e(t) := y_d(t) - y(t)$. The *output disturbance* is the signal $d_o(t)$. The feedback measurement sensor dynamics are modeled by $G_m(s)$. The *actuator* (e.g., a valve) modeled by $G_a(s)$ is the device that translates a control signal from the controller $K(s)$ into an action on the plant input. The *input disturbance* signal $d_i(t)$ (e.g., a friction force) disturbs the control signal from the actuator to the plant input.

In many cases, we will assume that the actuator and sensor are perfect (meaning $G_a(s) = G_m(s) = 1$) and that measurement noise can be neglected so that $n(t) = 0$. This will simplify the analysis.

Why do we need feedback anyway? Fundamentally, for three reasons:

- To counteract disturbance signals affecting the output
- To improve system performance in the presence of model uncertainty
- To stabilize an unstable plant

Example 11.1: A classical technique to control the position of an inertial load driven by a permanent-magnet DC motor is to vary the armature current based on a potentiometer measurement of the load angle as shown in Figure 11.3.

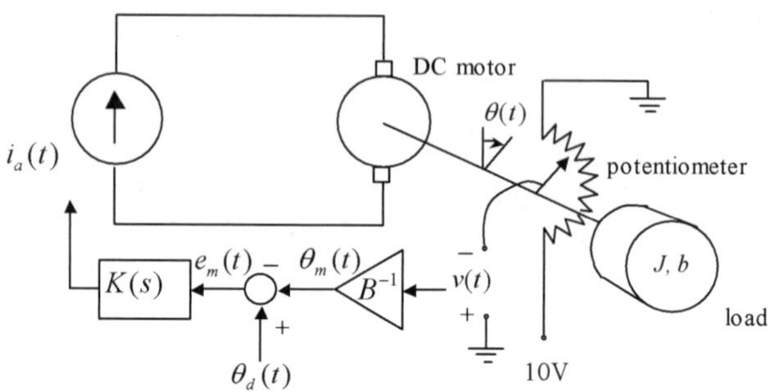

FIGURE 11.3 Schematic of an electromechanical feedback control system.

Let us identify the components of this control system. The plant is the load. The actuator is the DC motor, the sensor is the potentiometer, and the controller $K(s)$ could be an op-amp circuit driving a voltage-to-current power amplifier.

The open-loop dynamics of this system are now described. The torque $\tau(t)$ in newton-meters applied to the load by the motor is proportional to the armature current in amperes: $\tau(t) = Ai_a(t)$, so that

$$G_a(s) = \frac{\hat{\tau}(s)}{\hat{i}_a(s)} = A. \tag{11.1}$$

The plant (or load) is assumed to be an inertia with viscous friction. The equation of motion for the plant is

$$J\frac{d^2\theta(t)}{dt^2} + b\frac{d\theta(t)}{dt} = \tau(t) \tag{11.2}$$

which yields the unstable plant transfer function:

$$P(s) = \frac{\hat{\theta}(s)}{\hat{\tau}(s)} = \frac{1}{s(Js+b)}. \tag{11.3}$$

The potentiometer can be modeled as a pure gain mapping the load angle in the range of $[0,\pi]$ radians to a voltage in the range of $[0\text{V},+10\text{V}]$: $v(t)=B\theta(t)=\frac{10}{\pi}\theta(t)$; thus,

$$G_m(s)=\frac{\hat{\theta}_m(s)}{\hat{\theta}(s)}=\frac{\hat{\theta}_m(s)}{\hat{v}(s)}\cdot\frac{\hat{v}(s)}{\hat{\theta}(s)}=B^{-1}B=1. \qquad (11.4)$$

Assume that the measurement noise is negligible and that there is only an input torque disturbance $\tau_i(t)$ representing unmodeled friction. A block diagram for this example is given in Figure 11.4.

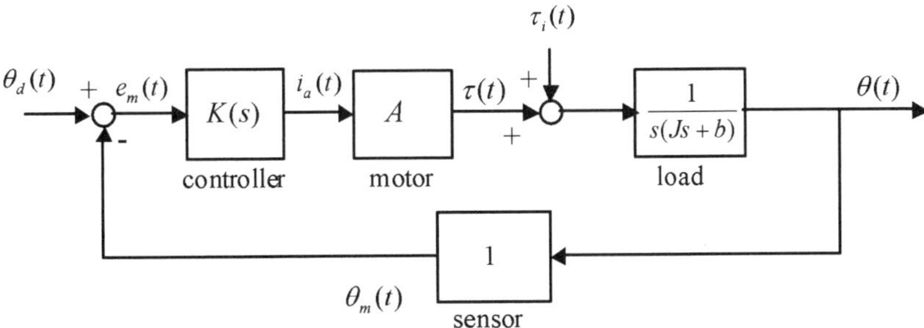

FIGURE 11.4 Block diagram of an electromechanical feedback control system.

Other examples of feedback control systems abound:

- Car cruise control system
- Flight control system (autopilot, fly-by-wire control)
- Satellite attitude control system
- Phase-lock loop (circuit used to tune in to FM radio stations in radio receivers)
- Robot
- Human behavior (this one is hard to model)
- Nuclear reactor

Tracking Systems

Two types of control systems can be distinguished: tracking systems and regulators. As the name implies, a tracking system controls the plant output, so it tracks the reference signal. From the simplified block diagram in Figure 11.5 (no noise or disturbance), good tracking is obtained when the error signal $e(t)\approx 0$ for all desired outputs $y_d(t)$. Then, $y(t)\approx y_d(t)$.

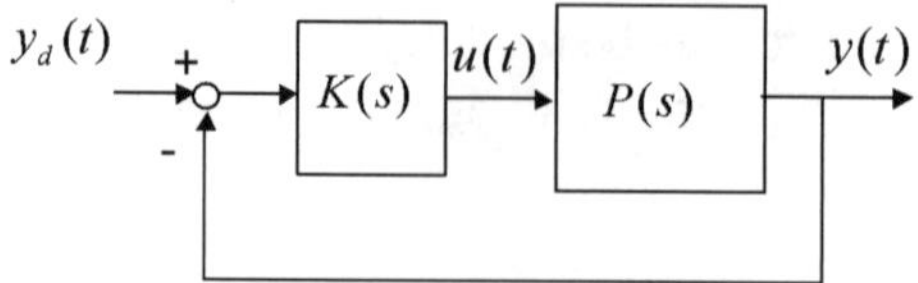

FIGURE 11.5 Unity feedback control system for tracking.

This diagram represents a general *unity feedback system.* Such a system has no dynamics in the feedback path, just a simple unity gain. The mechanical load angle control system in Example 11.1 is a unity feedback tracking system. The closed-loop transfer function from the reference to the output, called the *transmission*, is given by

$$T(s) := \frac{\hat{y}(s)}{\hat{y}_d(s)} = \frac{K(s)P(s)}{1+K(s)P(s)}. \tag{11.5}$$

The tracking objective of $y(t) \approx y_d(t)$ translates into the following requirement on the transmission:

$$T(s) \approx 1. \tag{11.6}$$

We see that this objective will be attained for a "large" *loop gain*, that is, for $|K(s)P(s)| \gg 1$, which, for a given plant, suggests that the magnitude of the controller be made large. However, we will see later that a high-gain controller often leads to instability of the closed-loop transfer function.

Regulators

A *regulator* is a control system whose main objective is to reject the effect of disturbances and maintain the output of the plant to a desired constant value (often taken to be 0 without loss of generality). An example is a liquid tank level regulator. The block diagram shown in Figure 11.6 is for a regulator that must reject the effect of an output disturbance.

The transfer function from the output disturbance to the output, called the *sensitivity*, is obtained from the following loop equation:

$$\hat{y}(s) = -K(s)P(s)\hat{y}(s) + \hat{d}_o(s), \tag{11.7}$$

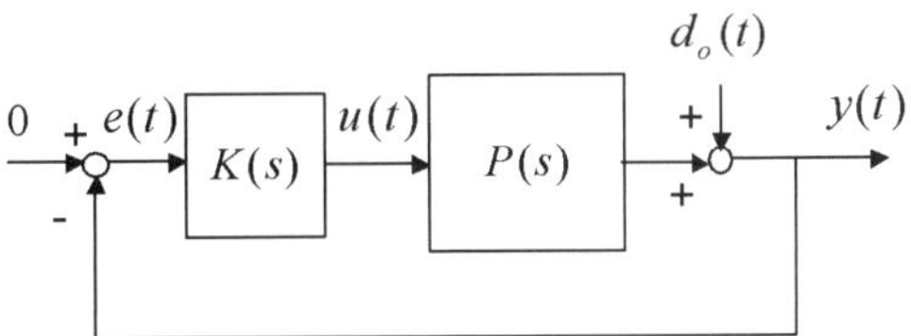

FIGURE 11.6 Unity feedback control system for regulation.

which yields

$$S(s) := \frac{\hat{y}(s)}{\hat{d}_o(s)} = \frac{1}{1+K(s)P(s)}. \tag{11.8}$$

The objective that $y(t) \approx 0$ for expected output disturbance signals translates into the requirement that $S(s) \approx 0$. Again, a high loop gain $|K(s)P(s)| \gg 1$ would appear to be the solution to minimize the sensitivity, but the closed-loop stability constraint often makes this difficult.

((Lecture 37: Sensitivity Function and Transmission))

Sensitivity Function

We introduced the sensitivity function as the transfer function from the output disturbance to the output of the plant,

$$S(s) := \frac{\hat{y}(s)}{\hat{d}_o(s)} = \frac{1}{1+K(s)P(s)}, \tag{11.9}$$

for the standard block diagram in Figure 11.6. The term *sensitivity* can be attributed in part to the fact that the transfer function $S(s)$ represents the level of sensitivity of the output to an output disturbance:

$$\hat{y}(s) = S(s)\hat{d}_0(s). \tag{11.10}$$

If the disturbance signal has a Fourier transform, then (assuming $S(s)$ is stable and hence has a frequency response $S(j\omega)$), the Fourier transform of the output is given by

$$\hat{y}(j\omega) = S(j\omega)\hat{d}_0(j\omega). \tag{11.11}$$

Therefore, the frequency response of the sensitivity $S(j\omega)$ amplifies or attenuates the output disturbance at different frequencies. Note that since the error is simply the negative of the output, we also have

$$\hat{e}(s) = -S(s)\hat{d}_0(s). \tag{11.12}$$

Example 11.2: Suppose $d_0(t) = e^{-t}q(t)$ for the control system depicted in Figure 11.7.

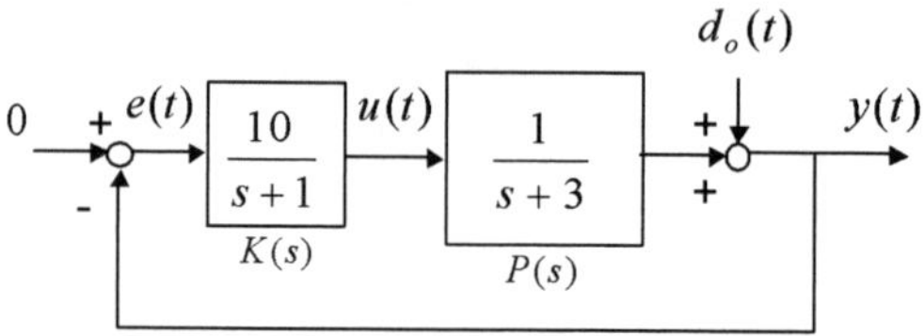

FIGURE 11.7 Regulator with exponential output disturbance.

The Fourier transform of the disturbance signal $d_0(t)$ is given by

$$\hat{d}_0(j\omega) = \frac{1}{1+j\omega}. \tag{11.13}$$

The sensitivity function is calculated as follows:

$$S(s) = \frac{1}{1+\dfrac{10}{(s+1)(s+3)}} = \frac{(s+1)(s+3)}{s^2+4s+13} = \frac{(s+1)(s+3)}{(s+2-j3)(s+2+j3)}. \tag{11.14}$$

This sensitivity function is stable because its complex conjugate poles lie in the open left half-plane (LHP). Its frequency response is given by

$$S(j\omega) = \frac{(j\omega+1)(j\omega+3)}{13-\omega^2+j4\omega}. \tag{11.15}$$

The magnitudes of $S(j\omega), \hat{d}_0(j\omega), \hat{y}(j\omega)$ are plotted using a linear scale in Figure 11.8.

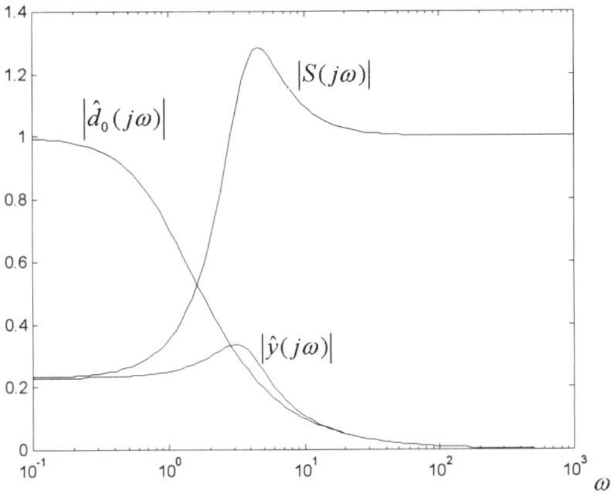

FIGURE 11.8 Magnitude of the output caused by the disturbance in closed loop.

It can be seen that the controller reduces the effect of the output disturbance by roughly a factor of five in the frequency domain, as opposed to the open-loop case. That is, the sensitivity was made small in the bandwidth of the disturbance. In the time domain, the closed-loop plant response

$$y(t) = \mathcal{L}^{-1}\left\{S(s)\hat{d}_0(s)\right\} = e^{-2t}\left(\cos 3t + \frac{1}{3}\sin 3t\right)q(t) \tag{11.16}$$

to the disturbance is smaller in magnitude than the open-loop response $y_{OL}(t) = d_0(t) = e^{-t}q(t)$, as shown in Figure 11.9.

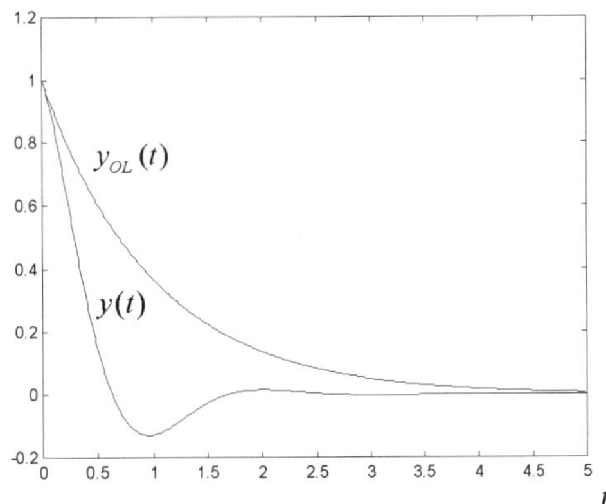

FIGURE 11.9 Open-loop and closed-loop response to disturbance in the time domain.

However, if the disturbance signal had energy around $\omega = 4$ rad/s, it would be *amplified* around this frequency.

The main reason $S(s)$ is called the sensitivity function is because it is equal to the sensitivity of the closed-loop transmission $T(s)$ to an infinitesimally small perturbation of the loop gain defined as $L(s) := K(s)P(s)$. That is, for an infinitesimally small relative change $\frac{dL(s)}{L(s)}$ in the loop gain, the corresponding relative change $\frac{dT(s)}{T(s)}$ in the transmission is given by

$$\frac{\frac{dT(s)}{T(s)}}{\frac{dL(s)}{L(s)}} = \frac{L(s)}{T(s)}\frac{dT(s)}{dL(s)} = [1+L(s)]\frac{d}{dL(s)}\frac{L(s)}{1+L(s)}$$

$$= [1+L(s)]\frac{(1+L(s))-L(s)}{[1+L(s)]^2} = \frac{1}{1+L(s)} = S(s). \tag{11.17}$$

Transmission

The *transmission* is the closed-loop transfer function $T(s)$ introduced earlier. The transmission is also referred to as the *complementary sensitivity function,* as it complements the sensitivity function in the following sense:

$$S(s)+T(s)=1. \tag{11.18}$$

We have seen that $T(s)$ is the closed-loop transfer function,

$$T(s) := \frac{\hat{y}(s)}{\hat{y}_d(s)} = \frac{K(s)P(s)}{1+K(s)P(s)}, \tag{11.19}$$

from the reference signal (desired output) to the plant output in tracking control problems for the standard unity feedback control system shown in Figure 11.10.

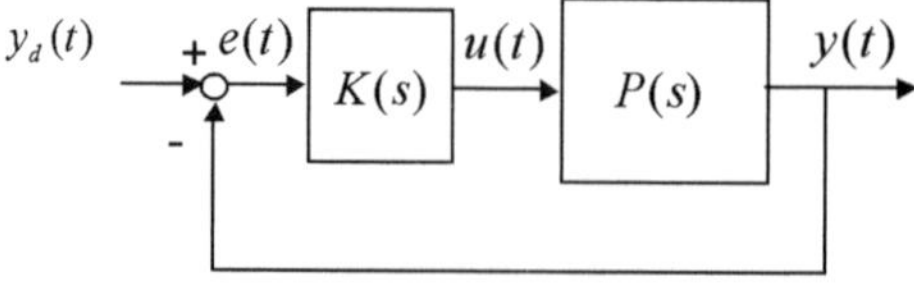

FIGURE 11.10 Feedback control system for input tracking.

Usually, reference signals have the bulk of their energy at low frequencies (e.g., piecewise continuous signals) but not always (e.g., fast robot joint trajectories). The main objective for tracking is to make $T(j\omega)\approx 1$ over the frequency band where the reference has most of its energy.

Example 11.3: Consider the previous regulator example now set up as the tracking system in Figure 11.11.

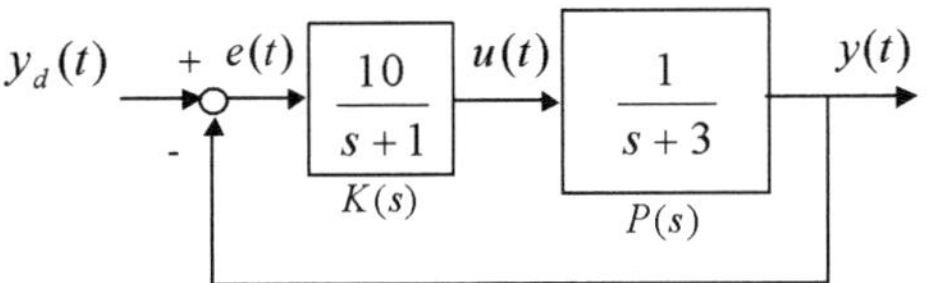

FIGURE 11.11 Feedback control system for input tracking.

The transmission can be calculated using Equation 11.18:

$$T(s)=1-S(s)=1-\frac{s^2+4s+3}{s^2+4s+13}=\frac{10}{s^2+4s+13}. \tag{11.20}$$

Although its DC gain of $T(0)=10/13=0.77$ is not close to 1, the magnitude of its frequency response is reasonably flat and the phase reasonably close to 0 up to $\omega=1$ rad/s, as can be seen in Figure 11.12.

Suppose that the reference signal is a causal rectangular pulse of 10-second duration:

$$y_d(t)=q(t)-q(t-10). \tag{11.21}$$

Its Laplace transform is given by

$$\hat{y}_d(s)=\frac{1-e^{-10s}}{s}, \tag{11.22}$$

so that the Laplace transform of the plant output is

$$\hat{y}(s)=T(s)\hat{y}_d(s)=\frac{10(1-e^{-10s})}{s(s^2+4s+13)}. \tag{11.23}$$

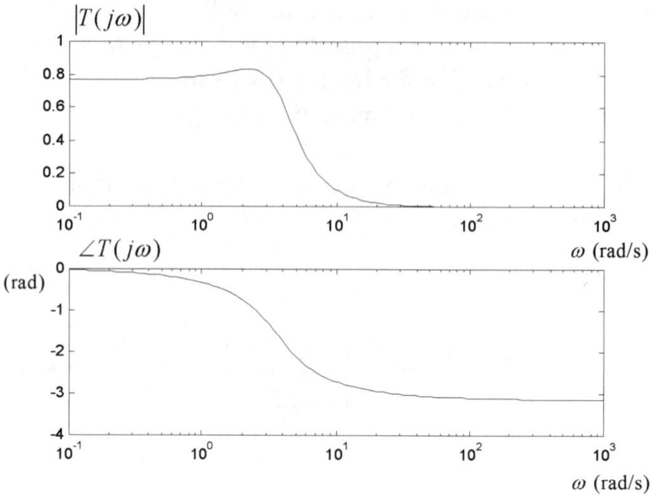

FIGURE 11.12 Frequency response of transmission.

The corresponding time-domain output signal is plotted in Figure 11.13, together with the reference signal.

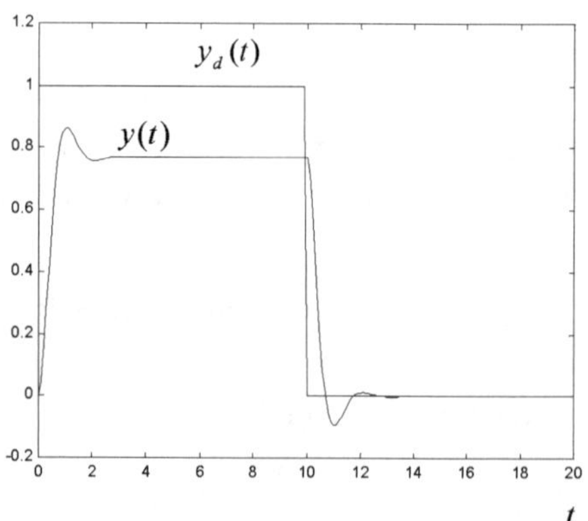

FIGURE 11.13 Closed-loop response of tracking system to a 10-second pulse.

Apart from a settling value lower than 1 due to the DC gain, the response is not too bad. This must mean that in the frequency domain, the Fourier transform of the reference must have most of its energy in the passband of the transmission. It is indeed the case, as seen in the plot of $|\hat{y}_d(j\omega)|$ in Figure 11.14:

$$\hat{y}_d(j\omega) = \frac{10e^{-j5\omega}}{\pi}\operatorname{sinc}(\frac{5\omega}{\pi}). \tag{11.24}$$

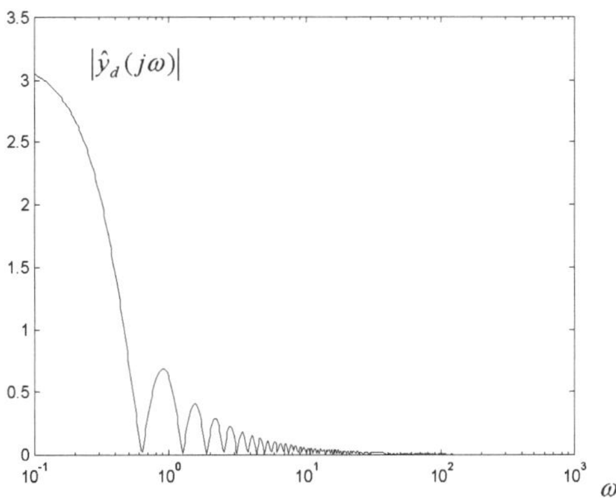

FIGURE 11.14 Magnitude of the input pulse's spectrum.

A Naive Approach to Controller Design

Given a plant model $P(s)$ and a desired stable closed-loop sensitivity or transmission, it is often possible to back solve for the controller $K(s)$ using Equation 11.9 or 11.19.

Example 11.4: A plant is modeled by the transfer function $P(s) = \frac{2}{s+1}$. Let us find the controller that will yield the desired complementary sensitivity function $T(s) = \frac{10}{s+10}$. From Equation 11.19, we have

$$K(s) = \frac{T(s)}{P(s)[1-T(s)]} = \frac{\frac{10}{s+10}}{\frac{2}{s+1}\left[1-\frac{10}{s+10}\right]} = \frac{5(s+1)}{s(s+10)}. \tag{11.25}$$

This looks easy, and it is. However, this approach has many shortcomings, including

- For unstable plant models (i.e., $P(s)$ with at least one pole in the open RHP), the resulting controller $K(s)$ will often have a zero canceling the unstable plant pole in the loop gain, which is unacceptable in practice.
- For a non-minimum phase plant model $P(s)$, that is, with at least one zero in the open RHP, the controller $K(s)$ will often have an unstable pole canceling the RHP plant zero in the loop gain, which may be undesirable in practice.
- This method cannot meet other specifications or requirements on closed-loop time-domain signals, low controller order, etc.
- The controller may not always be proper; that is, its transfer function may sometimes have a numerator of higher order than the denominator. Such a controller is not realizable by a state-space system or by using integrators. One would then need to use differentiators that should be avoided because they tend to amplify the noise.

((Lecture 38: Closed-Loop Stability Analysis))

CLOSED-LOOP STABILITY AND THE ROOT LOCUS

Closing the loop on a stable plant with a stable controller will sometimes result in an unstable closed-loop system; that is, the sensitivity and the transmission will be unstable. Hence, a number of stability tests have been developed over the last century in order to avoid the tedious trial and error approach to obtain closed-loop stability in the design of a controller. The idea is to test for stability, given only the open-loop transfer functions of the plant and the controller.

Closed-Loop Stability

The most fundamental property of a feedback control system is its *stability*. Obviously, an unstable feedback system is useless (unless the goal was to build an oscillator using positive feedback in the first place). In this section, we give four equivalent theorems to check the stability of a unity feedback control system.

We shall use the following definition of bounded-input bounded-output (BIBO) stability (or stability in short) for a unity feedback system. This is a requirement that any bounded-input signal injected at any point in the control system results in bounded-output signals measured at any point in the system.

The unity feedback system in Figure 11.15 is said to be stable if, for all bounded inputs $y_d(t), d_i(t)$, the corresponding outputs $y(t)$, $u_c(t)$ are also bounded.

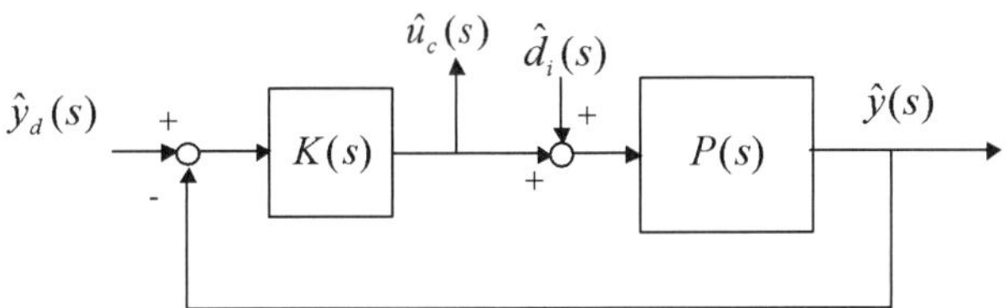

FIGURE 11.15 Setup to test the BIBO stability of a closed-loop system.

The idea behind this definition is that it is not enough to look at a single input-output pair for BIBO stability. Note that some of these inputs and outputs may not appear in the original problem formulation, but they can be defined as fictitious inputs or outputs for stability assessment.

Recall that a transfer function $G(s)$ is BIBO stable if and only if

1. All of its poles are in the open LHP *and*
2. It is *proper*; that is, $\lim_{s\to\infty} G(s) < \infty$ or, equivalently, the order of the numerator is less than or equal to the order of the denominator for $G(s)$ rational.

The second condition is required because otherwise a bounded input $|u(t)| < M$ with arbitrarily fast variations would produce an unbounded output for an improper transfer function. Consider for example a pure differentiator $G(s) = s$ with the input $u(t) = \sin(t^2)$. Its output is $y(t) = 2t\cos(t^2)$, which is unbounded as $t \to +\infty$.

Closed-Loop Stability Theorem I

The closed-loop system in Figure 11.15 is stable if and only if the transfer functions $T(s)$, $P^{-1}(s)T(s)$, and $P(s)S(s)$ are all stable (unstable pole-zero cancellations are allowed in these products).

Proof: It is easy to find the relationship between the inputs and the outputs (do it as an exercise):

$$\begin{bmatrix} \hat{y}(s) \\ \hat{u}_c(s) \end{bmatrix} = \begin{bmatrix} T(s) & P(s)S(s) \\ P^{-1}(s)T(s) & -T(s) \end{bmatrix} \begin{bmatrix} \hat{y}_d(s) \\ \hat{d}_i(s) \end{bmatrix}. \tag{11.26}$$

This matrix of transfer function (called a transfer matrix) is stable if and only if each individual transfer function entry of the matrix is stable. The theorem follows.

Example 11.5: Let us assess the stability of the tracking control system shown in Figure 11.16.

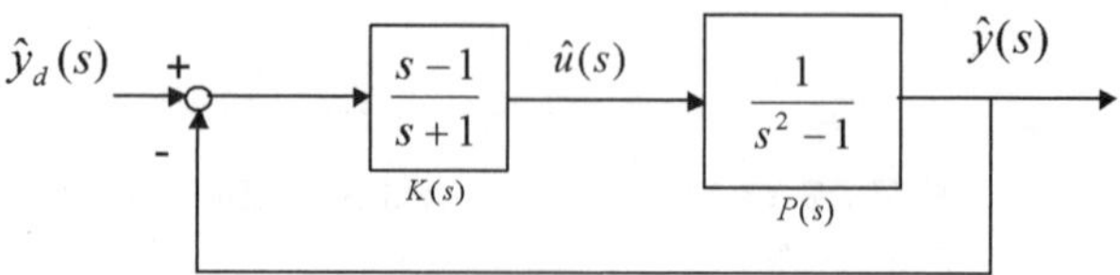

FIGURE 11.16 Closed-loop system whose stability is to be determined.

Note that the open-loop plant $P(s)$ is unstable. We calculate the three transfer functions:

$$\begin{aligned} T(s) &= \frac{K(s)P(s)}{1+K(s)P(s)} = \frac{1}{s^2+2s+2} \; (stable) \\ P^{-1}(s)T(s) &= \frac{K(s)}{1+K(s)P(s)} = \frac{s^2-1}{s^2+2s+2} \; (stable) \\ P(s)S(s) &= \frac{P(s)}{1+K(s)P(s)} = \frac{1}{(s^2-1)(s^2+2s+2)} \; (unstable) \end{aligned} \tag{11.27}$$

and conclude that this closed-loop system is unstable. The problem here is that the controller attempts to cancel out the plant's unstable pole.

We know that stability is directly related to the location of the poles in the s-plane. Since control systems are causal, the ROC of $S(s)$ and $T(s)$ is an open RHP to the right of the rightmost pole. For BIBO stability, the ROC must include the $j\omega$-axis, (including ∞), which means that all the closed-loop poles must be in the open LHP and that $S(s)$ and $T(s)$ must be proper. Note that the poles of $S(s)$ and $T(s)$ are the same, and if either of these two transfer functions is proper, then the other one must also be proper. This is easy to see from the identity:

$$T(s) = 1 - S(s). \tag{11.28}$$

If $S(p_i) = \infty$, then $T(p_i) = \infty$ and vice versa.

Another equivalent closed-loop stability theorem can now be stated (without proof) for a unity feedback control system if we explicitly rule out any pole-zero cancellation occurring in the closed RHP when forming the loop gain $K(s)P(s)$. One only needs to check the stability of either $S(s)$ or $T(s)$.

Closed-Loop Stability Theorem II

The unity feedback control system in Figure 11.15 is stable if and only if

1. *Either S(s) or T(s) is stable, and*
2. *No pole-zero cancellation occurs in the closed RHP when forming the loop gain K(s)P(s).*

Now suppose that the plant and controller transfer functions are written as

$$P(s) = \frac{n_P(s)}{d_P(s)},\ K(s) = \frac{n_K(s)}{d_K(s)}, \tag{11.29}$$

where the plant numerator and denominator $n_P(s), d_P(s)$ are coprime polynomials, that is, they have no common factors, and likewise for the controller numerator and denominator. Define the *characteristic polynomial*

$$p(s) := n_P(s)n_K(s) + d_P(s)d_K(s) \tag{11.30}$$

of the closed-loop system. The *closed-loop poles* of the system are defined to be the zeros of the characteristic polynomial $p(s)$. Our third equivalent stability result follows.

Closed-Loop Stability Theorem III

The unity feedback control system is stable if and only if all of the closed-loop poles of the system lie in the open LHP and the order of p(s) is equal to the order of $d_p(s)d_K(s)$.

Proof (sufficiency only; the proof of necessity is more involved): we use the result of stability Theorem I to write

$$\begin{aligned}
\begin{bmatrix} \hat{y}(s) \\ \hat{u}_c(s) \end{bmatrix} &= \frac{1}{1+P(s)K(s)} \begin{bmatrix} P(s)K(s) & P(s) \\ K(s) & -P(s)K(s) \end{bmatrix} \begin{bmatrix} \hat{y}_d(s) \\ \hat{d}_i(s) \end{bmatrix} \\
&= \frac{d_P(s)d_K(s)}{d_P(s)d_K(s)+n_P(s)n_K(s)} \begin{bmatrix} \dfrac{n_P(s)n_K(s)}{d_P(s)d_K(s)} & \dfrac{n_P(s)}{d_P(s)} \\ \dfrac{n_K(s)}{d_K(s)} & -\dfrac{n_P(s)n_K(s)}{d_P(s)d_K(s)} \end{bmatrix} \begin{bmatrix} \hat{y}_d(s) \\ \hat{d}_i(s) \end{bmatrix} \\
&= \frac{1}{d_P(s)d_K(s)+n_P(s)n_K(s)} \begin{bmatrix} n_P(s)n_K(s) & d_K(s)n_P(s) \\ d_P(s)n_K(s) & -n_P(s)n_K(s) \end{bmatrix} \begin{bmatrix} \hat{y}_d(s) \\ \hat{d}_i(s) \end{bmatrix}
\end{aligned} \tag{11.31}$$

All transfer functions in this matrix are proper and have the characteristic polynomial $p(s)$ as their denominator. Therefore, if all closed-loop poles (i.e., zeros of $p(s)$) are in the open LHP, then the transfer matrix is stable, and by virtue of Theorem I, we conclude that the closed-loop system is stable.

Example 11.6: For Example 11.5, we have

$$n_P(s) = 1,\, d_P(s) = (s+1)(s-1),\, n_K(s) = (s-1),\, d_K(s) = (s+1) \qquad (11.32)$$

and

$$p(s) = (s-1) + (s+1)^2(s-1), \qquad (11.33)$$

which clearly has a zero at $s = 1$. Therefore the control system is unstable.

Finally, we have a fourth equivalent theorem on closed-loop stability, which is really just a restatement of Theorem II (taking $S(s)$).

Closed-Loop Stability Theorem IV

The unity feedback control system is stable if and only if

1. *The transfer function 1 + K(s)P(s) has no closed RHP zeros (including at ∞), and*
2. *No pole-zero cancellation occurs in the closed RHP when forming the loop gain K(s)P(s).*

Routh's Criterion

The stability of a causal LTI system whose transfer function is rational and proper is determined by its poles. An open-loop transfer function is stable if and only if all of its poles lie in the open LHP. A closed-loop system is stable if and only if all of the *closed-loop* poles lie in the open LHP (closed-loop theorem III). In both cases, we need to solve for the N roots of the characteristic equation $a_N s^N + a_{N-1}s^{N-1} + \cdots + a_1 s + a_0 = 0$ to find the poles and determine whether the system is stable or not. There are various ways to do this numerically using a computer, for example, by computing the eigenvalues of the A matrix of a state-space realization of the system. However, in 1877, E. J. Routh devised an extremely simple and clever technique to determine the stability of a system. Routh's criterion is based on an array formed with the coefficients of the denominator of an open-loop transfer function or the closed-loop characteristic polynomial of a feedback system. Assume that $a_N > 0$, and recall that a necessary condition for the system to be stable is that all coefficients of its characteristic polynomial be of the same sign. Thus, if any of the coefficients of the polynomial are negative, the system is unstable. With this necessary condition fulfilled, we want to determine whether the system is stable or not.

The Routh array is formed as follows. The rows are labeled with descending powers of the Laplace variable s. The first two rows of the array are composed of the coefficients of the characteristic polynomial. They can be written down by inspection. The third row of the Routh array is calculated from the first and second rows. The looping arrow on the array attempts to show how the coefficients on a diagonal are multiplied before they are subtracted. Notice that this loop always starts and ends on the first column.

$$
\begin{array}{c|cccc}
s^N & a_N & a_{N-2} & a_{N-4} & \cdots \\
s^{N-1} & a_{N-1} & a_{N-3} & a_{N-5} & \cdots \\
s^{N-2} & \dfrac{a_{N-1}a_{N-2}-a_{N-3}a_N}{a_{N-1}} & \dfrac{a_{N-1}a_{N-4}-a_{N-5}a_N}{a_{N-1}} & \dfrac{a_{N-1}a_{N-6}-a_{N-7}a_N}{a_{N-1}} & \cdots \\
\vdots & \vdots & \vdots & \vdots &
\end{array}
$$

The fourth row is computed in the same manner from the two rows immediately above it, and so on until the last row labeled s^0 is reached. Once this Routh array has been computed, we have the following theorem:

Theorem (Routh): *The system is stable if and only if all the entries in the first column of the Routh array are positive. If there are sign changes in this column, then there are as many unstable poles are there are sign changes.*

Example 11.7: Let us determine whether the following causal system is stable:

$$H(s)=\frac{1}{s^6+5s^5+9s^4+10s^3+11s^2+10s+3}.$$

The Routh array is computed.

$$
\begin{array}{c|cccc}
s^6 & 1 & 9 & 11 & 3 \\
s^5 & 5 & 10 & 10 & \\
s^4 & 7 & 9 & 3 & \\
s^3 & \dfrac{25}{7} & \dfrac{55}{7} & & \\
s^2 & -\dfrac{32}{5} & 3 & & \\
s^1 & \dfrac{305}{32} & & & \\
s^0 & 3 & & &
\end{array}
$$

We conclude that this system is unstable. Furthermore, since there are two sign changes in the first column, that is, from positive to negative to positive, we know that the system has two unstable poles.

Example 11.8: Consider a unity feedback control system with plant $P(s)=\frac{1}{s(s^2+s+1)}$ and a pure gain controller $K(s)=k$. Let us find for what values of k the system is stable. The closed-loop characteristic polynomial is $p(s)=s^3+s^2+s+k$. We compute the Routh array.

$$\begin{array}{c|cc} s^3 & 1 & 1 \\ s^2 & 1 & k \\ s^1 & 1-k & \\ s^0 & k & \end{array}$$

Since it is assumed that controller gain k is positive, the system is stable for $0<k<1$. For $k>1$, there are two sign changes in the first column; therefore the closed-loop system has two unstable poles. The limit case where $k=1$ results in two poles sitting directly on the $j\omega$-axis. This special case of purely imaginary poles is treated in a slightly different way in the Routh array. When the Routh array is computed, this case leads to a row of zeros, for example, the row labeled s^{m-1}. Then we write down the mth-order polynomial whose coefficients are the entries in row s^m, the row above the row of zeros. This polynomial is differentiated and the coefficients of the resulting polynomial are used to replace the zeros in row s^{m-1}.

((Lecture 39: Stability Analysis Using the Root Locus))

The Root Locus

The root locus is the locus in the s-plane described by the closed-loop poles (i.e., the zeros of the characteristic polynomial $p(s)$) as a real parameter k varies from 0 to $+\infty$ in the loop gain. It is a method for studying the effect of a parameter on the locations of the closed-loop poles, in particular to find out for what values of the parameter they become unstable.

The parameter is usually the controller gain, but it could be a parameter of the plant transfer function. The usual setup is shown in Figure 11.17.

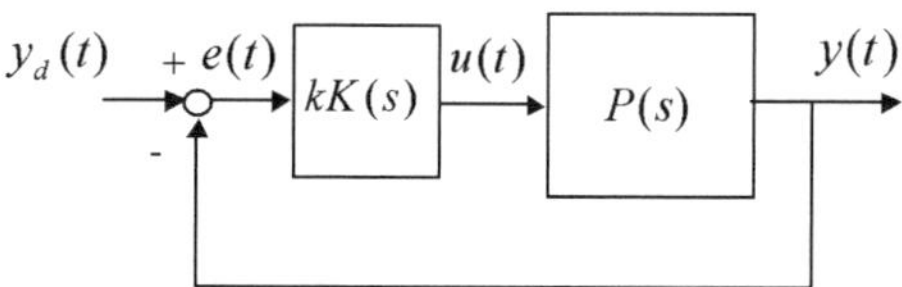

FIGURE 11.17 Closed-loop system with variable gain on the controller for the root locus.

Factor $P(s)$ and $K(s)$ as ratios of coprime polynomials:

$$P(s) = \frac{n_P(s)}{d_P(s)},\ K(s) = \frac{n_K(s)}{d_K(s)}. \tag{11.34}$$

Then, $p(s) = kn_P(s)n_K(s) + d_P(s)d_K(s)$. If $n_P(s)n_K(s)$ and $d_P(s)d_K(s)$ have a common factor, take it out; the zeros of this factor are fixed (i.e., fixed closed-loop poles) with respect to the gain k. Now, assuming there is no common factor, define

$$\begin{aligned} n(s) &:= n_P(s)n_K(s),\ \mu := \text{order}\{n(s)\} \\ d(s) &:= d_P(s)d_K(s),\ \nu := \text{order}\{d(s)\}. \end{aligned} \tag{11.35}$$

Then the loop gain is $L(s) = P(s)K(s) = \frac{n(s)}{d(s)}$. Locate the poles and zeros of $L(s)$ in the s-plane.

We now give a minimal set of rules that help in sketching the root locus.

Rule 1: For $k = 0$, the root locus starts at the poles of $L(s)$.

Proof: The characteristic polynomial is $d(s) + kn(s)\ldots$

Rule 2: As $k \to +\infty$, μ branches of the root locus go to the zeros of $L(s)$, and $\nu - \mu$ branches go to ∞

Proof: There are ν branches of the root locus, that is, roots of $d(s) + kn(s) = 0$. Now, for $k > 0$:

$$\text{zeros of } d(s) + kn(s) \equiv \text{zeros of } \frac{1}{k}d(s) + n(s). \tag{11.36}$$

Let p_0 be a closed-loop pole corresponding to k. Then

$$\frac{1}{k}d(p_0)+n(p_0)=0. \tag{11.37}$$

If $|p_0|$ is bounded as $k\to+\infty$, then

$$\lim_{k\to+\infty}\left[\frac{1}{k}d(p_0)+n(p_0)\right]=\lim_{k\to+\infty}n(p_0)=0. \tag{11.38}$$

That is, the pole p_0 converges to a zero of $L(s)$. Otherwise, $|p_0|$ is unbounded; that is, $p_0\to+\infty$.

Rule 3: The root locus is symmetric with respect to the real axis.

Proof: All complex poles come in conjugate pairs…

Rule 4: A point on the real axis, not a pole or zero of $L(s)$, is on the root locus if and only if it lies to the left of an odd number of real poles and real zeros (counted together) of $L(s)$.

Rule 5: For the branches of the root locus going to infinity, their asymptotes are described by

$$\text{Center of asymptotes}=\frac{\sum\text{poles of }L(s)-\sum\text{zeros of }L(s)}{\nu-\mu}.$$

$$\text{Angles of asymptotes}=\frac{2k+1}{\nu-\mu}\pi\text{ rad},\quad k=0,1,\ldots,\nu-\mu-1.$$

Example 11.9: Sketch the root locus of the tracking system shown in Figure 11.17, where

$$P(s)=\frac{s(0.2s+1)}{2s^3+10s^2+20},\quad K(s)=1.$$

We find $p(s)=2s^3+10s^2+20+ks(0.2s+1)$. The loop gain is $L(s)=P(s)=\frac{s(0.2s+1)}{2s^3+10s^2+20}$. Its poles are at $p_{1,2}=0.1747\pm j1.356$ and $p_3=-5.349$. The root locus starts at these poles for k = 0, and two branches tend to the zeros $z_1=0$, $z_2=-5$ of $L(s)$ as $k\to+\infty$. There is only one asymptote on the real line going to $-\infty$. A sketch of the root locus based on the preceding rules is shown in Figure 11.18.

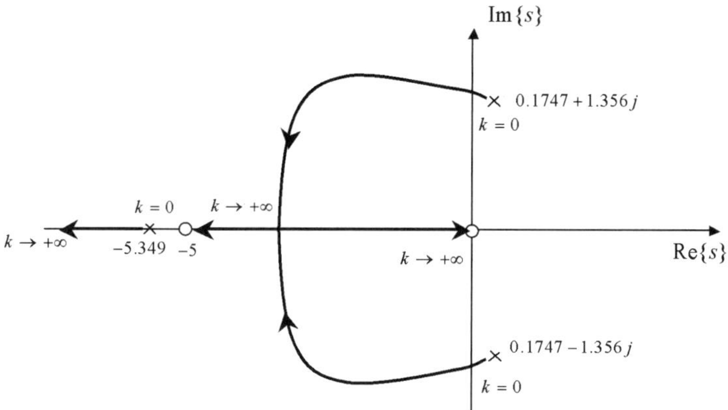

FIGURE 11.18 Root locus of a closed-loop system with variable gain on the controller.

The root locus is a technique for conducting interactive control analysis and design. Factors limiting its usefulness include the following:

- The closed-loop poles do not completely characterize a system's behavior.
- The root locus can be used for one varying parameter only.

Thus, the root locus is a tool that can be useful for simple problems. It is best computed and plotted using a CAD software such as MATLAB.

Example 11.10: Root locus using MATLAB

Suppose we want to plot the root locus of a unity feedback control system with plant $P(s)=\frac{1}{s^2+2s+4}$ and controller $K(s)=k\frac{2s+1}{s-1}$ for a controller gain k varying between 0 and 1000. The following MATLAB program does the job, producing the root locus in Figure 11.19. This M-file can be found on the companion CD-ROM in D:\Chapter11\rootlocus.m

```
%% rootlocus.m Root locus of a feedback control system
% vector of gains
K=0:1:1000;
% loop gain
numK=[2 1];
denK=[1 -1];
numP=[1];
denP=[1 2 4];
numL=conv(numK,numP);
```

```
denL=conv(denK,denP);
polesL=roots(denL);
zerosL=roots(numL);
L=tf(numL,denL);
% root locus
rlocus(L,K);
```

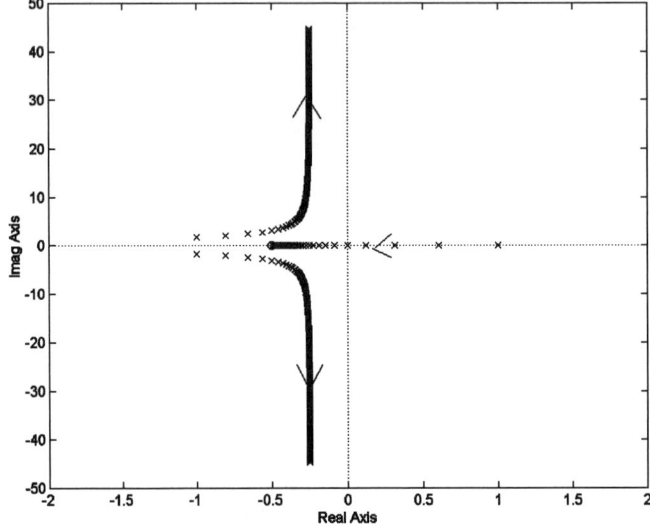

FIGURE 11.19 Root locus of a closed-loop system using MATLAB.

((Lecture 40: The Nyquist Stability Criterion))

THE NYQUIST STABILITY CRITERION

The Nyquist criterion uses a plot of the frequency response of the loop gain, called the Nyquist plot, to determine the stability of a closed-loop system. It can also be used to find measures of stability robustness called the gain margin and the phase margin. These margins represent the additional gain or negative phase on the loop gain that would take the feedback system to the verge of instability.

The Principle of the Argument and the Encirclement Property

The *Principle of the Argument* states that *the net change in phase (argument) of a transfer function G(s) (as the complex variable s describes a closed contour C* *clockwise in the complex plane) is equal to the number of poles of G(s) enclosed in C minus the number of zeros of G(s) enclosed in C, times 2π.*

This is a particular case of conformal mappings in the complex plane, where a closed contour is mapped to the locus of $G(s)$ in the complex plane. One result that is of interest to us from conformal mapping theory is that a closed contour in the s-plane is mapped by $G(s)$ to another closed contour in the complex plane.

Another equivalent form of the principle of the argument is the *encirclement property*, which states that *as a closed contour C in the s-plane is traversed once in the clockwise direction, the corresponding plot of G(s) (for values of s along C) encircles the origin in the clockwise direction a net number of times equal to the number of zeros of G(s) minus the number of poles of G(s) contained within the contour C.*

In applying this property, a counterclockwise encirclement of the origin is interpreted as one negative clockwise encirclement.

The Nyquist Criterion

The Nyquist criterion is an application of the encirclement property to the Nyquist plot of the loop gain to determine the stability of a closed-loop system. It provides a check for stability but says nothing about where the closed-loop poles are. The root locus can provide that information, but it requires analytical descriptions of the controller and the plant, that is, transfer functions. On the other hand, the Nyquist criterion can be applied to a plant or loop gain whose frequency response has been measured experimentally, but whose transfer function is unavailable.

Recall our closed-loop stability theorem IV: the unity feedback control system is stable if and only if the transfer function $1 + K(s)P(s)$ has no closed RHP zeros, and no pole-zero cancellation occurs in the closed right half-plane when forming the loop gain $K(s)P(s)$. Assume the latter condition holds and suppose the controller can be factorized as a pure gain times a transfer function: $kK(s)$. Then for stability we must ensure that $1 + kK(s)P(s)$ has no closed RHP zeros. Further assume that $1 + kK(s)P(s)$ is proper.

Nyquist Contour

To use the encirclement property, we must choose a closed contour that includes the closed RHP. This contour is called the *Nyquist contour* and is shown in Figure 11.20. It produces the Nyquist plot of a transfer function. The Nyquist contour includes the entire imaginary axis (including $\pm j\infty$) and a semicircle of radius $R \to \infty$ to the right of the $j\omega$-axis. Because we assumed that $1 + kK(s)P(s)$ is proper, the Nyquist plot will remain at the constant value $\lim_{s\to\infty} 1 + kK(s)P(s) =: b$ as the Laplace variable describes the infinite semicircle.

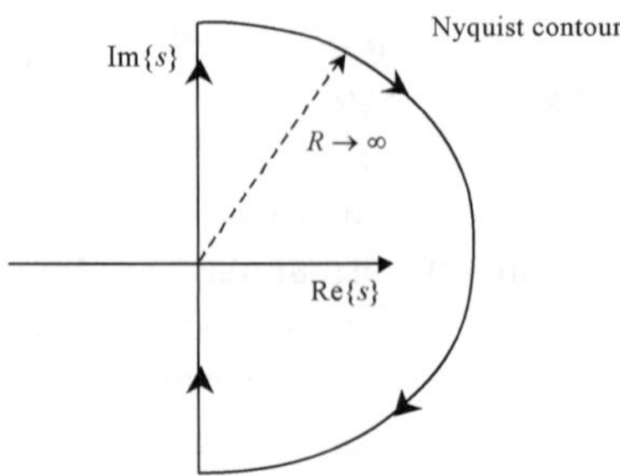

FIGURE 11.20 Definition of the Nyquist contour.

If there are any poles or zeros on the $j\omega$-axis, they can be included in the Nyquist contour by indenting it to the left of (but infinitesimally close to) them.

Nyquist Plot of L(s)

The Nyquist plot of a transfer function $L(s)$ is the locus of $L(s)$ as the complex variable s describes the Nyquist contour. Because of the special shape of the Nyquist contour, the Nyquist plot is basically the locus of the frequency response $L(j\omega)$ in the complex plane as ω goes from $-\infty$ to $+\infty$. In other words, for every fixed ω, the complex number $L(j\omega)$ is represented by a point in the complex plane. The locus of all these points forms the Nyquist plot of $L(j\omega)$.

Example 11.11: The Nyquist plot of the first-order loop gain $L(s)=\frac{1}{0.1s+1}$ is shown in Figure 11.21. It starts at 0 (magnitude of 0, phase of $\pi/2$) at $\omega=-\infty$; then the phase of $L(j\omega)$ starts to decrease, while its magnitude increases, as ω increases towards 0. At DC, $L(j0)=1$ (the phase is 0). The magnitude begins to decrease again as ω increases from 0 to $+\infty$, while the phase becomes negative. It eventually tends to $-\pi/2$ as $\omega \to +\infty$.

We now have all the elements in place to derive the Nyquist criterion. The transfer function $1 + kK(s)P(s)$ must not have any zero within the Nyquist contour for stability. The encirclement property states that

$$\begin{array}{c}\#\text{clockwise encirclements of the origin}\\ \text{by the Nyquist plot of }(1+kL(s))\end{array} = \underbrace{\begin{array}{c}-\#\text{closed RHP poles of }(1+kL(s))\\ +\#\text{closed RHP zeros of }(1+kL(s))\end{array}}_{0}$$

where # means "number of." An equivalent stability condition is that the loop gain $L(s)$ must not be equal to $-\frac{1}{k}$ within the Nyquist contour. Also, since $L(s)=$

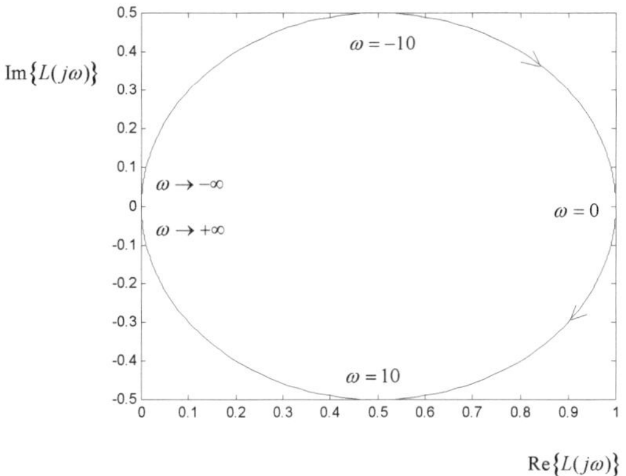

FIGURE 11.21 Nyquist plot of a first-order system.

$\frac{1}{k}(1+kL(s))-\frac{1}{k}$, the number of encirclements of the point $-\frac{1}{k}$ by the Nyquist plot of $L(s)$ is exactly the same as the number of encirclements of the origin by the Nyquist plot of $1 + kL(s)$. Furthermore, the closed RHP poles of $L(s)$ are the same as those of $1 + kL(s)$. Therefore, we have the equivalent stability condition, called the *Nyquist criterion.*

The Nyquist Criterion: *Assuming that no pole-zero cancellation occurs in the closed right half-plane when forming the loop gain $K(s)P(s)$, the unity feedback closed-loop system is stable if and only if:*

$$\#\text{counterclockwise encirclements of } -\frac{1}{k} \text{ by the Nyquist plot of } L(s) = \#\text{closed RHP poles of } L(s).$$

Remarks:

- The Nyquist plot is simply a representation of the frequency response of a system as a locus in the complex plane, parameterized by the frequency. As previously mentioned, the Nyquist criterion could be checked for a loop gain whose frequency response is known, but not its transfer function.
- The frequency-response magnitude and phase plots of $L(j\omega)$ can be used to draw its Nyquist plot: for each frequency, read off the magnitude and phase of $L(j\omega)$ and mark the corresponding point in the complex plane.
- For LTI systems with a real impulse response (real coefficients for rational transfer functions), the Nyquist plot is symmetric with respect to the real axis.

Example 11.12: We want to check whether the feedback control system in Figure 11.22 is stable, where $K(s)=\frac{1}{s+1}$, $P(s)=\frac{1}{0.5s+1}$ and $k=2$.

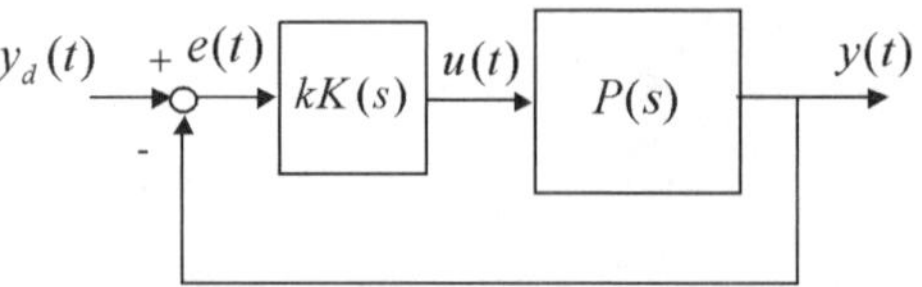

FIGURE 11.22 Closed-loop system whose stability is assessed using the Nyquist criterion.

The frequency response of the loop gain is $L(j\omega)=K(j\omega)P(j\omega)=\frac{1}{(0.5j\omega+1)(j\omega+1)}$. Note that this loop gain is stable, as both poles are in the open LHP. Moreover, there is no pole-zero cancellation. Therefore, the closed-loop system will be stable if and only if the net number of counterclockwise encirclements of the critical point $-\frac{1}{2}$ by the Nyquist plot of $L(j\omega)$ is 0. We see in Figure 11.23 that for $\omega \to \pm\infty$, that is, on the infinite semicircle of the Nyquist contour, the Nyquist plot of $L(j\omega)$ stays at the origin. We also have $L(j0) = 1$.

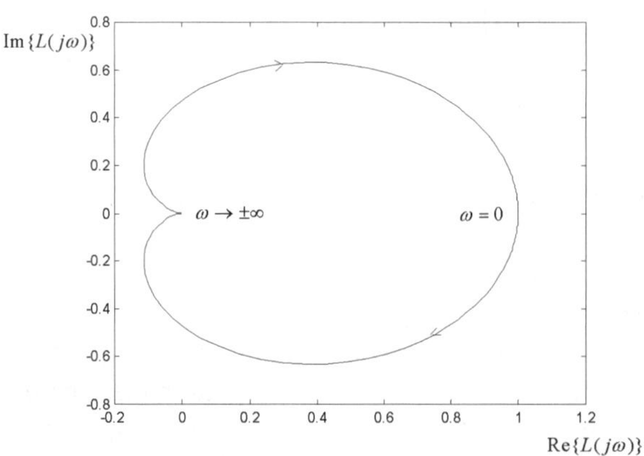

FIGURE 11.23 Nyquist plot of a second-order system.

We can see that the point $-\frac{1}{2}$ is to the left of the Nyquist plot, and hence the control system is stable. We can actually find the range of k's for which the control system would be stable. From the Nyquist plot, we can see that all points $-\frac{1}{k}$

to the left of the origin lie outside of the loop formed by the Nyquist plot, as well as all points to the right of 1. This implies that the system is stable for $k \geq 0$ and for $-1 < k < 0$. Therefore the complete range of gains to get stability is $k > -1$.

((Lecture 41: Gain and Phase Margins))

STABILITY ROBUSTNESS: GAIN AND PHASE MARGINS

Bode Plot of Loop Gain

The Nyquist criterion gives us the ability to check the stability of a unity feedback system by looking at the Nyquist plot of its loop gain only. This is useful for at least two reasons.

- We can design a controller $K(s)$ based on a plant transfer function $P(s)$ or just its frequency response $P(j\omega)$ and ensure that the closed-loop system will be stable by looking at the frequency response of the loop gain $L(j\omega) = K(j\omega)P(j\omega)$. We do not have to compute the characteristic polynomial (which cannot be done anyway if only $P(j\omega)$ is available).
- Closed-loop *stability robustness* can be assessed by looking at the Nyquist plot. Stability robustness refers to how much variation in the loop gain's frequency response $L(j\omega)$ (mostly coming from uncertainty in the plant's frequency response) can be tolerated without inducing instability of the control system. Think of stability robustness as how far away the Nyquist plot is from the critical point $-\frac{1}{k}$. Here we are assuming that the Nyquist criterion was satisfied to start with, meaning that the nominal closed-loop system is stable. In this case, the closed loop will become unstable when $L(j\omega)$ varies to the point of touching the critical point $-\frac{1}{k}$.

Note that we will set $k = 1$ in the remainder of this section, such that the critical point is now -1, that is, the controller is thought to be the fixed transfer function $K(s)$. An example is shown in Figure 11.24, where the nominal Nyquist plot of $L(j\omega)$ (no closed RHP poles in $L(s)$) of a closed-loop stable system is perturbed to $L_p(j\omega)$, which touches the critical point -1. The closed-loop system with loop gain $L_p(j\omega)$ is unstable.

By conjugate symmetry, the magnitude and phase plots (the Bode plot) of the loop gain's frequency response $L(j\omega)$ convey the same information as the Nyquist plot. Therefore, it is possible to use the Nyquist criterion to check closed-loop stability by looking at the Bode plot of $L(j\omega)$, although this often proves to be difficult. It is relatively easy only for low-order, "well-behaved" loop gains, which

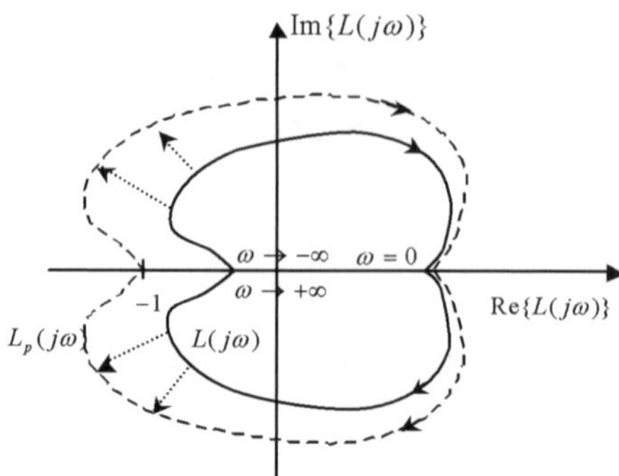

FIGURE 11.24 Perturbed Nyquist plot of loop gain touching the critical point.

fortunately make up many of the SISO control systems that we have to analyze or design in practice.

For a stable loop gain, the Nyquist plot should neither encircle, nor touch the critical point −1 for closed-loop stability. Let us further restrict our attention to stable and "well-behaved" loop gains (including many low-order, minimum-phase, proper rational transfer functions $L(s)$ with positive DC gains.) For the Bode plot of a well-behaved loop gain, the above requirement translates into the following: the magnitude of the loop gain in decibels should be less than 0 dB at frequencies where the phase is −π or less, that is, $\angle L(j\omega) \le -180°$.

Example 11.13: Consider the second-order plant model and pure gain controller $P(s) = \frac{1}{(0.1s+1)(0.01s+1)}$, $K(s) = 100$ of a unity feedback control system. The Bode plot of $L(s)$ and its Nyquist plot are shown in Figure 11.25.

The loop gain is stable, and hence the Nyquist criterion is satisfied since the Nyquist plot of $L(j\omega)$ does not encircle the critical point −1. On the Bode plot, we see that for any finite frequency, the critical point −1 (i.e., 0 dB and phase of −180°) is not reached. It would be if, for example, the phase of $L(j\omega)$ was −180° at the frequency where the magnitude is 0 dB (around 300 rad/s). This additional negative phase is similar to (but not the same as) a clockwise rotation of the lower part of the Nyquist plot (and a corresponding counterclockwise rotation of its upper part to keep the symmetry) until it touches the critical point.

Gain and Phase Margins

In this section, we assume that the Nyquist criterion is satisfied for $L(j\omega)$ so that the closed-loop system is stable. Let us define the *crossover frequency* ω_{co} as the frequency where the magnitude of the loop gain is 0 dB (or 1). The crossover

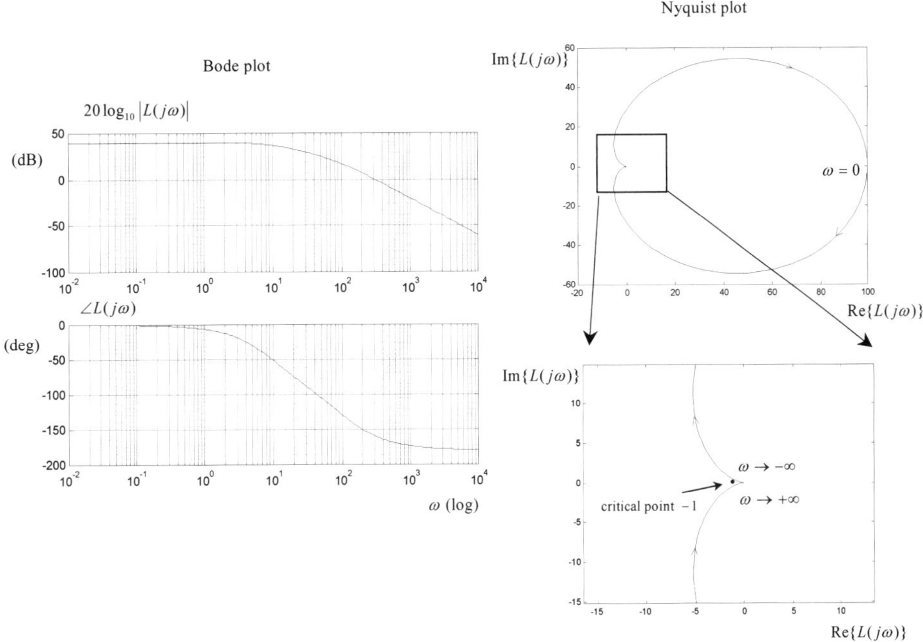

FIGURE 11.25 Bode plot and Nyquist plot of a second-order loop gain.

frequency is easy to find on the Bode plot. In the previous example, the crossover frequency is $\omega_{co} = 300$ rad/s . We saw in that example that the closed-loop system was stable, but additional negative phase at the crossover frequency could destabilize it. The absolute value of this additional negative phase (at ω_{co}) taking the control system to the verge of instability is called the *phase margin* ϕ_m of the feedback control system.

The phase margin is easy to read off a Bode plot of the loop gain. For the above example, the phase margin is approximately $\phi_m = 20^0$ since the phase at the crossover frequency is $\angle L(j\omega_{co}) \cong -160^\circ$. This means that additional negative phase coming, for example, from a time delay of τ seconds in the loop gain with frequency response $e^{-j\omega\tau}$ could destabilize the control system. We can compute the minimum time delay that would destabilize the system as follows:

$$\begin{aligned} \omega_{co}\tau &= \frac{\pi}{180}\phi_m \\ \Rightarrow \tau &= \frac{\pi}{180\omega_{co}}\phi_m = \frac{20\pi}{180 \cdot 300} = 0.0012 \text{ s}, \end{aligned} \tag{11.39}$$

which means that a time delay of 1.2 ms or more in the loop gain (e.g., if the plant is $P(s) = \frac{e^{-s\tau}}{(0.1s+1)(0.01s+1)}$ with $\tau > 1.2$ ms) would destabilize the feedback system. The phase margin can also be found on the Nyquist plot as the angle between the point where the locus crosses the unit circle and the real line.

Similarly, the *gain margin* k_m is defined as the minimum additional positive gain such that the closed-loop system is taken to the verge of instability. The gain margin is also easy to read off the Bode plot. It is the negative of the magnitude of the loop gain in decibels at the frequency where the phase is –180° (call it $\omega_{-\pi}$). On the Nyquist plot, the gain margin is the negative of the inverse of the real value where the locus of $L(j\omega)$ crosses the real line in the left half-plane.

For our previous example, the gain margin is actually infinite because $\omega_{-\pi} = +\infty$ and $-20\log_{10}|L(j\infty)| = +\infty$. This means that no matter how large the controller gain is, the feedback system will always be stable.

Example 11.14: Consider the second-order plant model $P(s) = \frac{1}{(0.1s+1)(0.01s+1)}$ and the controller $K(s) = \frac{10}{s+1}$ of a unity feedback control system. The Bode plot of $L(s)$ and its Nyquist plot are shown in Figure 11.26.

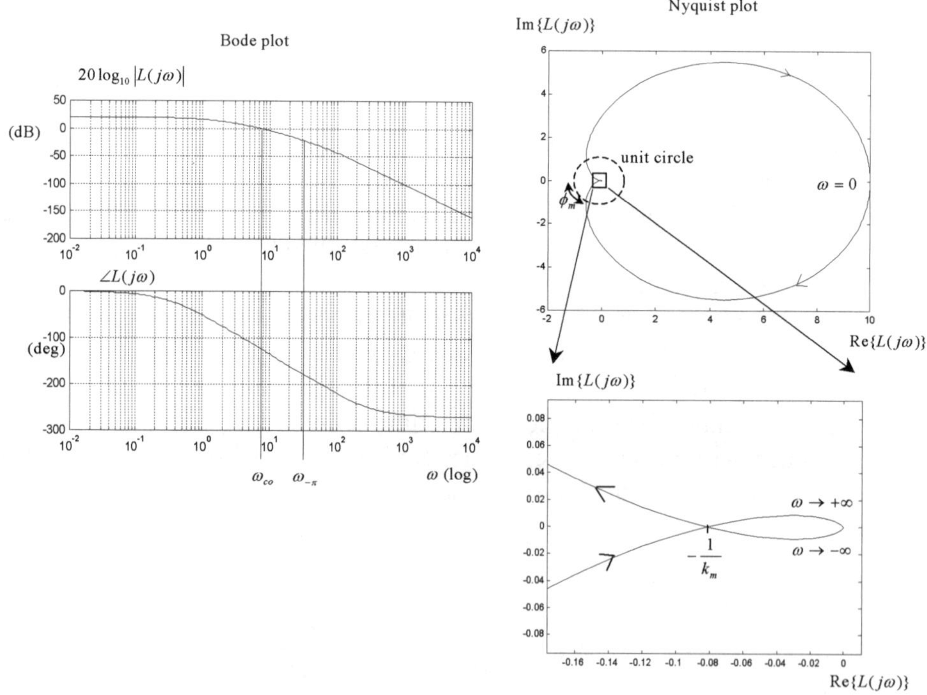

FIGURE 11.26 Bode plot and Nyquist plot of a third-order loop gain.

For this example, the crossover frequency is approximately $\omega_{co} = 7.8$ rad/s, and the frequency where the phase is $-180°$ is approximately $\omega_{-\pi} = 33.7$ rad/s. The phase margin is given by

$$\angle L(j\omega_{co}) \cong -125^\circ \Rightarrow \phi_m = 55^\circ. \tag{11.40}$$

The phase margin is also indicated on the Nyquist plot as the angle between the point where the locus crosses the unit circle and the real line.

The gain margin is given by

$$k_m = -20\log_{10}\left|L(j\omega_{-\pi})\right| = 22 \text{ dB}. \tag{11.41}$$

SUMMARY

In this chapter, we analyzed LTI feedback control systems.

- Feedback control has the ability to reject system output disturbances, reduce the effect of uncertainty, and stabilize unstable systems.
- We distinguished between two types of feedback control systems: regulators and tracking systems.
- Closed-loop stability is a necessary requirement for any feedback system. We gave four equivalent stability theorems for unity-feedback control systems. We also introduced Routh's criterion, the root locus, and the Nyquist criterion as different means of assessing closed-loop stability.
- Two simple measures of closed-loop stability robustness were defined: the gain margin and the phase margin.

TO PROBE FURTHER

Feedback control systems are studied in detail in control engineering texts (Bélanger, 1995; Kuo and Golnaraghi, 2002). For a more theoretical treatment of control systems, see Doyle, Francis and Tannenbaum, 1992.

EXERCISES

Exercises with Solutions

Exercise 11.1

Consider the causal LTI unity feedback regulator in Figure 11.27, where $P(s) = \frac{(s-1)}{(s+1)(s^2+5\sqrt{2}s+25)}$, $K(s) = \frac{s^2+3\sqrt{2}s+9}{(s+2)(s+3)}$ and $k \in [0,+\infty)$.

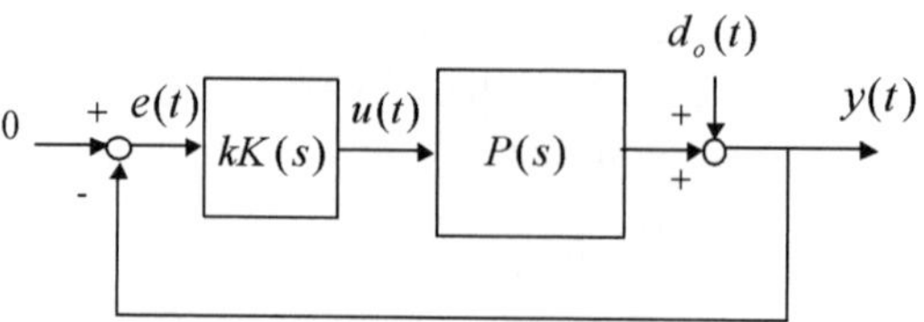

FIGURE 11.27 Regulator of root locus Exercise 11.1.

(a) Use properties of the root locus to sketch it. Check your sketch using MATLAB (*rlocus* command).

Answer:

The loop gain is $L(s) = kP(s)K(s) = \frac{k(s-1)(s^2+3\sqrt{2}s+9)}{(s+1)(s+2)(s+3)(s^2+5\sqrt{2}s+25)}$.

- The root locus starts at the (open-loop) poles of $L(s)$: $-1, -2, -3, -\frac{5}{\sqrt{2}} \pm \frac{5}{\sqrt{2}}j$ for $k=0$. It ends at the zeros of $L(s)$: $1, -\frac{3}{\sqrt{2}} \pm j\frac{3}{\sqrt{2}}$ ∞, ∞ for $k=+\infty$.
- On the real line, the root locus will have one branch between the pole at -1 and the zero at -2, and also one branch between the poles at -3 and -2 (Rule 4).
- Let $\nu = \deg\{d\} = 5$ and $\mu = \deg\{n\} = 3$. For the two branches of the root locus going to infinity, the asymptotes are described by

$$\text{Center of asymptotes: } = \frac{\sum \text{poles of } L(s) - \sum \text{zeros of } L(s)}{\nu - \mu}$$

$$= \frac{(-1-2-3-5\sqrt{2})-(1-3\sqrt{2})}{2} = \frac{-7-2\sqrt{2}}{2} = -4.9$$

$$\text{Angles of asymptotes: } = \frac{2k+1}{\nu-\mu}\pi, \quad k = 0,1$$

$$= \begin{cases} \pi/2, k=0 \\ 3\pi/2, k=1 \end{cases}$$

Root locus: See Figure 11.28.

(b) Compute the value of the controller gain k for which the control system becomes unstable.

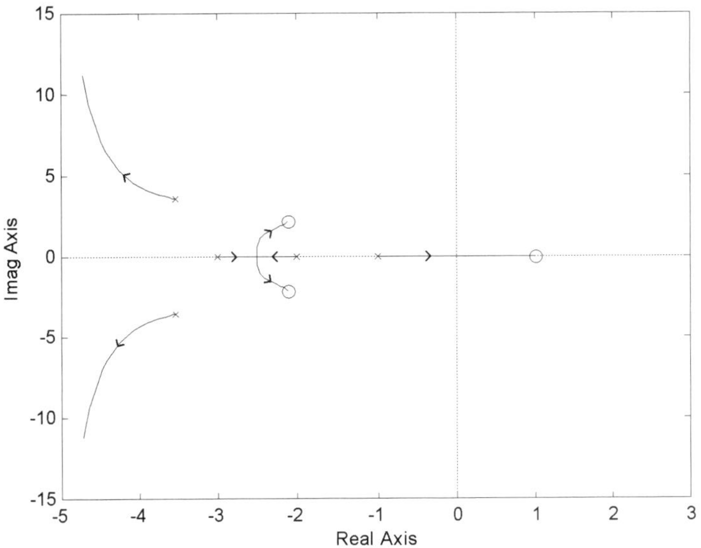

FIGURE 11.28 Root locus for Exercise 11.1.

Answer:
The characteristic polynomial is obtained:

$$\begin{aligned} p(s) &= n(s) + d(s) \\ &= k(s-1)(s^2 + 3\sqrt{2}s + 9) + (s+1)(s+2)(s+3)(s^2 + 5\sqrt{2}s + 25) \\ &= s^5 + a_4 s^4 + a_3 s^3 + a_2 s^2 + a_1 s + (-9k + 150). \end{aligned}$$

From the root locus, we see that the onset of instability occurs when a real pole crosses the imaginary axis at 0. At that point, we have

$$\begin{aligned} p(s)\big|_{s=0} &= -9k + 150 = 0 \\ \Rightarrow k &= \frac{50}{3} = 16.67. \end{aligned}$$

Exercise 11.2

We want to analyze the stability of the tracking control system shown in Figure 11.29, where $P(s) = \frac{4s+1}{(s-1)(0.1s+1)}$ and $K(s) = \frac{10(0.5s+1)}{0.1s+1}$.

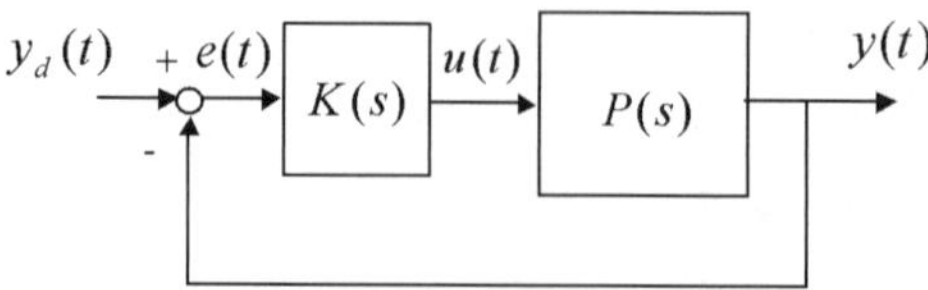

FIGURE 11.29 Tracking system of Exercise 11.2.

(a) Assess the stability of this closed-loop system using any two of the four stability theorems.

Using Theorem I: We have to show that $T(s)$, $P^{-1}(s)T(s)$ and $P(s)S(s)$ are all stable.

$$T(s)=\frac{P(s)K(s)}{1+P(s)K(s)}=\frac{\dfrac{10(4s+1)(0.5s+1)}{(s-1)(0.1s+1)^2}}{1+\dfrac{10(4s+1)(0.5s+1)}{(s-1)(0.1s+1)^2}}=\frac{20s^2+45s+10}{0.01s^3+20.19s^2+45.8s+9}$$

is stable (all three poles in LHP, strictly proper). The poles are –2017, –2.1, and –0.2.

$$P^{-1}(s)T(s)=\frac{\dfrac{10(0.5s+1)}{0.1s+1}}{1+\dfrac{10(4s+1)(0.5s+1)}{(s-1)(0.1s+1)^2}}=\frac{(0.1s^2+0.9s-1)(5s+10)}{0.01s^3+20.19s^2+45.8s+9}$$

is also stable (same poles as above, proper).

$$P(s)S(s)=\frac{P(s)}{1+P(s)K(s)}=\frac{\dfrac{4s+1}{(s-1)(0.1s+1)}}{1+\dfrac{10(4s+1)(0.5s+1)}{(s-1)(0.1s+1)^2}}=\frac{0.4s^2+4.1s+1}{0.01s^3+20.19s^2+45.8s+9}$$

is stable (same poles as above, strictly proper). Therefore the feedback system is stable.

Using Theorem II: We have to show that either $T(s)$ or $S(s)$ is stable and that no pole-zero cancellation occurs in the closed RHP in forming the loop gain. The latter condition holds, and

$$T(s) = \frac{P(s)K(s)}{1+P(s)K(s)} = \frac{\dfrac{10(4s+1)(0.5s+1)}{(s-1)(0.1s+1)^2}}{1+\dfrac{10(4s+1)(0.5s+1)}{(s-1)(0.1s+1)^2}} = \frac{20s^2+45s+10}{0.01s^3+20.19s^2+45.8s+9}$$

is stable (all three poles in LHP, strictly proper). The poles are –2017, –2.1, and –0.2. Therefore the feedback system is stable.

Using Theorem III: We have to show that the closed-loop poles, that is, the zeros of the characteristic polynomial $p(s)$, are all in the open LHP. The plant and the controller are already expressed as ratios of coprime polynomials.

$$p(s) = n_K n_P + d_K d_P = 0.01s^3 + 20.19s^2 + 45.8s + 9$$

All three closed-loop poles –2017, –2.1, and –0.2 lie in the open LHP, and therefore the feedback system is stable.

Using Theorem IV: We have to show that 1 + $K(s)P(s)$ has no zero in the closed RHP and that no pole-zero cancellation occurs in the closed RHP in forming the loop gain. The latter condition obviously holds, and

$$1+K(s)P(s) = \frac{1}{S(s)} = 1+\frac{10(4s+1)(0.5s+1)}{(s-1)(0.1s+1)^2} = \frac{0.01s^3+20.19s^2+45.8s+9}{0.01s^3+0.19s^2+0.8s-1}.$$

All three zeros of this transfer function –2017, –2.1, and –0.2 lie in the open LHP, and therefore the feedback system is stable.

(b) Use MATLAB to sketch the Nyquist plot of the loop gain $L(s) = K(s)P(s)$. Give the critical point and discuss the stability of the closed-loop system using the Nyquist criterion.

Answer:
The Nyquist plot given in Figure 11.30 was produced using the Nyquist command in MATLAB.

The loop gain has one RHP pole, and according to the Nyquist criterion, the Nyquist plot should encircle the critical point –1 once counterclockwise. This is indeed what we can observe here, and hence the closed-loop system is stable.

Exercise 11.3

We want to analyze the stability of the tracking control system in Figure 11.31, where $P(s) = \frac{s+1}{10s+1}$ and $K(s) = \frac{10}{s}$.

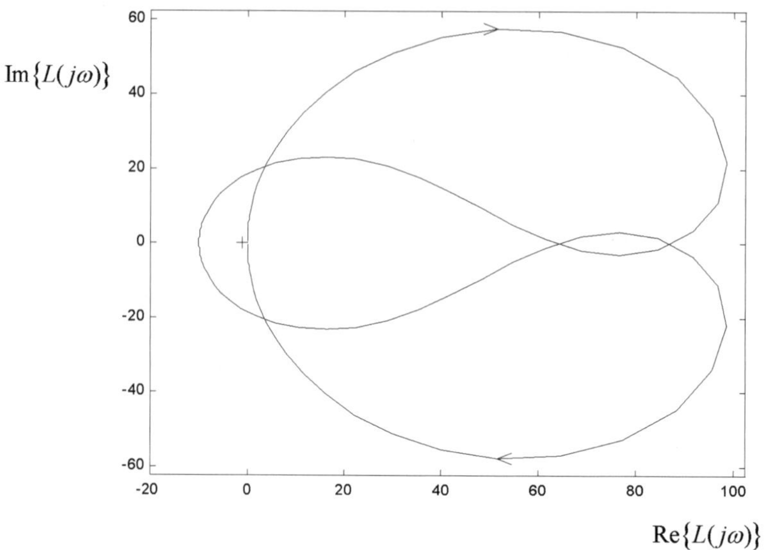

FIGURE 11.30 Nyquist plot of Exercise 11.2(b).

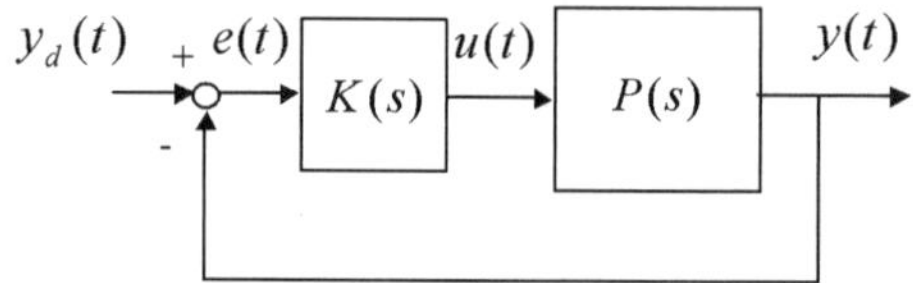

FIGURE 11.31 Tracking control system of Exercise 11.3.

Sketch the Bode plot in decibels (magnitude) and degrees (phase) of the loop gain (you can use MATLAB to check if your sketch is right). Find the frequencies ω_{co} and $\omega_{-\pi}$. Assess the stability robustness by finding the gain margin k_m and phase margin ϕ_m of the system. Compute the minimum time delay in the plant that would cause instability.

Answer:

The loop gain is $L(s) = \frac{10(s+1)}{s(10s+1)}$ and its Bode plot is shown in Figure 11.32.

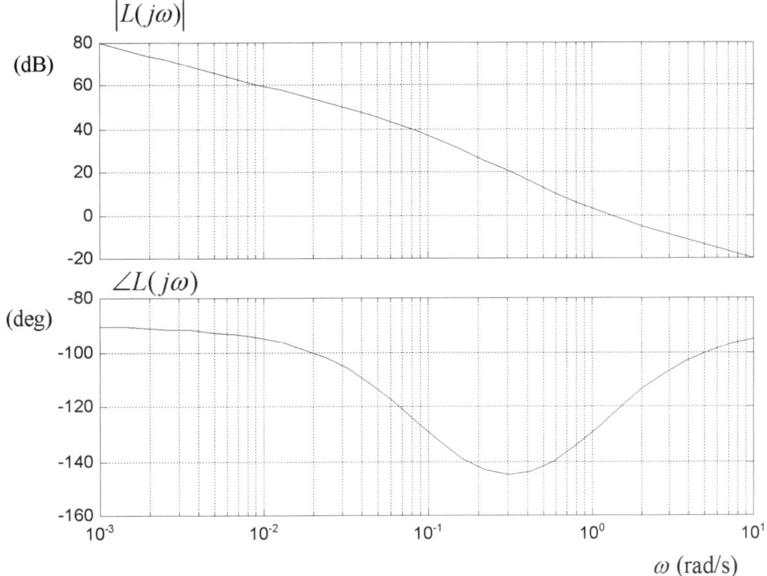

FIGURE 11.32 Bode plot of loop gain in Exercise 11.3.

Frequency $\omega_{-\pi}$ is undefined, as the phase never reaches –180°. Thus, the gain margin k_m is infinite, and the phase margin is $\phi_m \cong 58^\circ$ at $\omega_{co} \cong 1.3$ rad/s. The minimum time delay τ in the plant that would cause instability is obtained as follows:

$$\omega_{co}\tau = \frac{\pi}{180}\phi_m$$
$$\Rightarrow \tau = \frac{\pi}{180\omega_{co}}\phi_m = \frac{58\pi}{180 \cdot 1.3} = 0.78\,\text{s}.$$

Exercises

Exercise 11.4

Consider the LTI feedback control system shown in Figure 11.33.

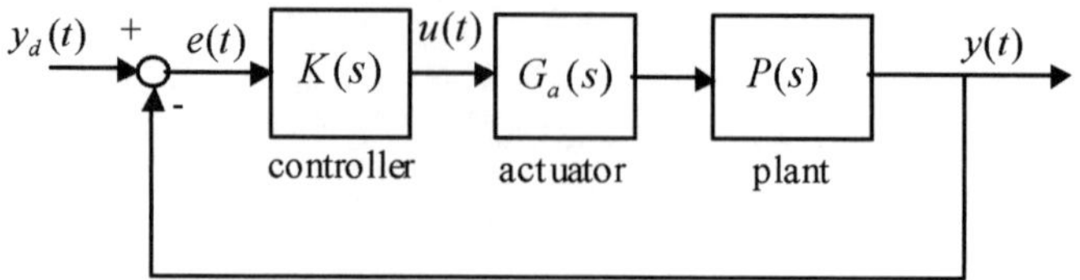

FIGURE 11.33 Feedback control system of Exercise 11.4.

The transfer functions of the different causal components of the control system are $G_a(s)=\frac{1}{s+1}$, $K(s)=\frac{4s+8}{s+10}$, and $P(s)=\frac{s-1}{10s+1}$.

(a) Compute the loop gain $L(s)$ and the closed-loop characteristic polynomial $p(s)$. Is the closed-loop system stable?

(b) Find the sensitivity $S(s)$ and complementary sensitivity $T(s)$ functions.

(c) Find the steady-state error signal of the closed-loop response $y(t)$ to the input $y_d(t)=\sin(t)$.

(d) Assume that the real parameter k is an additional gain on the controller; that is, the controller is $kK(s)$. Sketch the root locus for the real parameter varying in $k\in[0,+\infty)$.

Exercise 11.5

We want to analyze the stability of the tracking control system shown in Figure 11.34, where $P(s)=\frac{-0.1s+1}{(0.01s+1)(0.1s+1)}$ and $K(s)=\frac{10(0.5s+1)}{s}$. Assess the stability of this closed-loop system using any two of the four stability theorems.

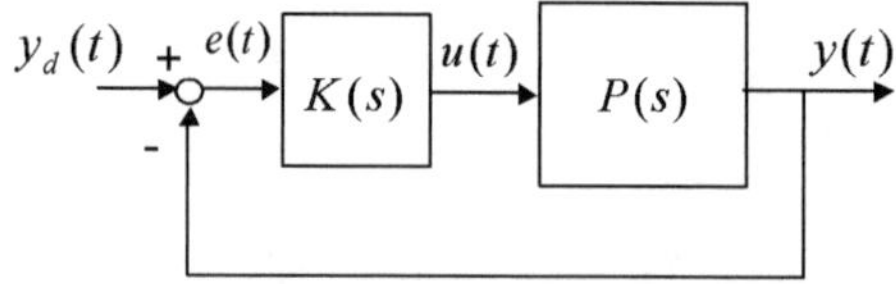

FIGURE 11.34 Feedback control system of Exercise 11.5.

Answer:

Exercise 11.6

Consider the LTI unity feedback regulator in Figure 11.35.

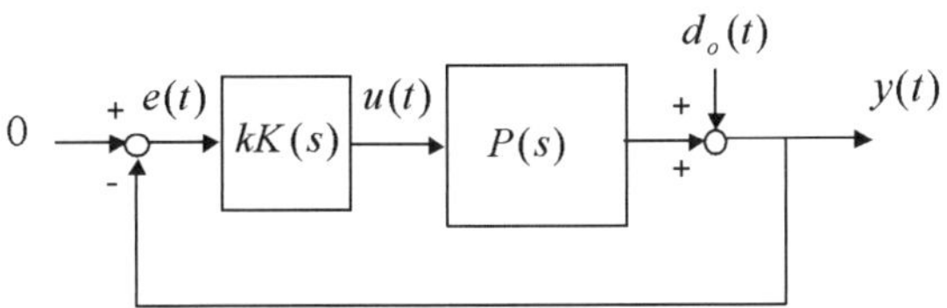

FIGURE 11.35 Feedback regulator of Exercise 11.6.

The transfer functions in this regulator are $P(s)=\frac{(s^2-4s+4)}{(s-1)(s^2+\sqrt{2}s+1)}$, $K(s)=\frac{1}{s+2}$, and $k\in[0,+\infty)$. Use properties of the root locus to sketch it. Check your sketch using MATLAB (*rlocus* command).

Exercise 11.7

Consider the LTI feedback control system shown in Figure 11.36, where $G_a(s)=\frac{10}{(s+3)}$, $K(s)=\frac{100(2s+1)}{(s+1)}$, and the plant model P is $P(s)=\frac{s+2}{s}$.

(a) Compute the loop gain $L(s)$ and the closed-loop characteristic polynomial $p(s)$. Is the closed-loop system stable?

(b) Find the sensitivity function $S(s)$ and the complementary sensitivity function $T(s)$.

(c) Find the steady-state error of the closed-loop step response $y(t)$, that is, for the step reference $y_d(t)=q(t)$.

(d) Assume that the real parameter k is an additional gain on the controller, that is, the controller is $kK(s)$. Sketch the root locus for the real parameter varying in $k\in[0,+\infty)$.

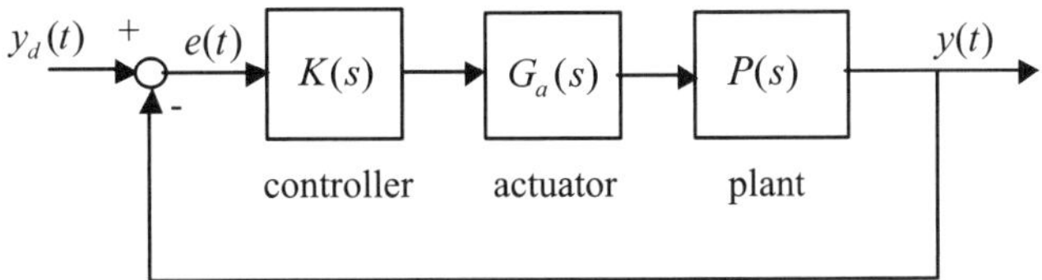

FIGURE 11.36 Feedback control system of Exercise 11.7.

Answer:

Exercise 11.8

Sketch the Nyquist plots of the following loop gains. Assess closed-loop stability (use the critical point –1.)

(a) $L(s)=\frac{1}{(s+1)^2}$

(b) $L(s)=\frac{1}{(s+1)(s-1)}$

Exercise 11.9

We want to analyze the stability of the tracking control system in Figure 11.37, where $P(s)=\frac{-0.1s+1}{(s+1)(10s+1)}$ and $K(s)=\frac{(s+1)}{s}$.

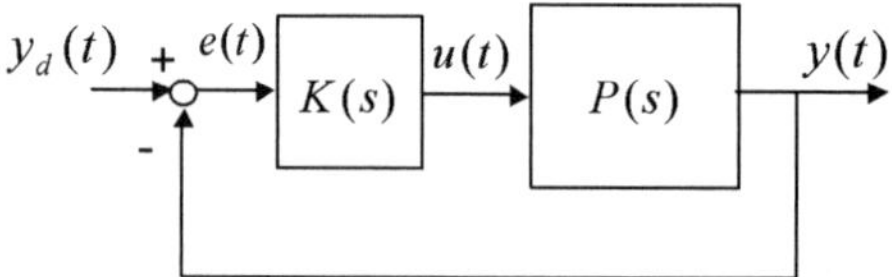

FIGURE 11.37 Feedback control system of Exercise 11.9.

Hand sketch the Bode plot in decibels (magnitude) and degrees (phase) of the loop gain. You can use MATLAB to check if your sketch is right. Find the crossover frequency ω_{co} and the frequency where the phase is –180°: $\omega_{-\pi}$. Assess the stability robustness by finding the gain margin k_m and phase margin ϕ_m of the system. Compute the minimum time delay in the plant that would cause instability.

Answer:

Exercise 11.10

Sketch the Nyquist plot of the loop gain $L(s)=\frac{s+2}{(s+1)(10s+1)}$. Identify the frequencies where the locus of $L(j\omega)$ crosses the unit circle and the real axis (if it does.)

Exercise 11.11

Consider the spacecraft shown in Figure 11.38, which has to maneuver in order to dock on a space station.

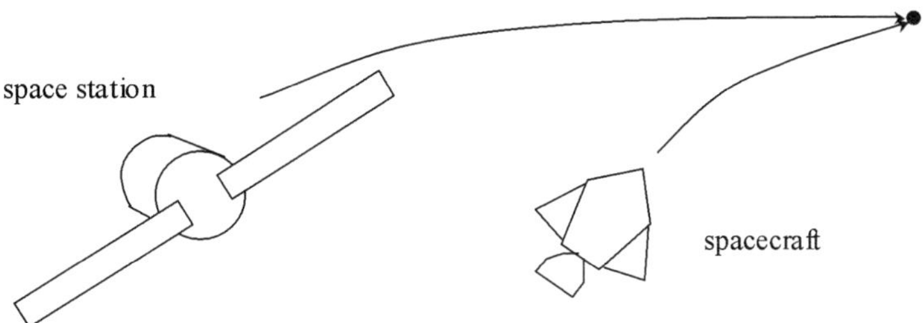

FIGURE 11.38 Spacecraft docking on a space station in Exercise 11.11.

For simplicity, we consider the one-dimensional case where the state of each vehicle consists of its position and velocity along a single axis z. Assume that the space station moves autonomously according to the state equation

$$\dot{x}_s(t) = A_s x_s(t),$$

where $x_s = \begin{bmatrix} z_s \\ \dot{z}_s \end{bmatrix}$, $A_s = \begin{bmatrix} 0 & 1 \\ 0 & 0 \end{bmatrix}$, and the spacecraft's equation of motion is

$$\dot{x}_c(t) = A_c x_c(t) + B_c u_c(t)$$

where $x_c = \begin{bmatrix} z_c \\ \dot{z}_c \end{bmatrix}$, $u_c(t)$ is the thrust, $A_c = \begin{bmatrix} 0 & 1 \\ 0 & 0 \end{bmatrix}$, and $B_c = \begin{bmatrix} 0 \\ 0.1 \end{bmatrix}$.

(a) Write down the state-space system of the state error $e := x_c - x_s$, which describes the evolution of the difference in position and velocity between the spacecraft and the space station. The output is the difference in position.

(b) A controller is implemented in a unity feedback control system shown in Figure 11.39 to drive the position difference to zero for automatic docking. The controller is given by

$$K(s) = \frac{100(s+1)}{0.01s+1}, \quad \text{Re}\{s\} > -100$$

Find $G(s)$ and assess the stability of this feedback control system (hint: one of the closed-loop poles is at -10).

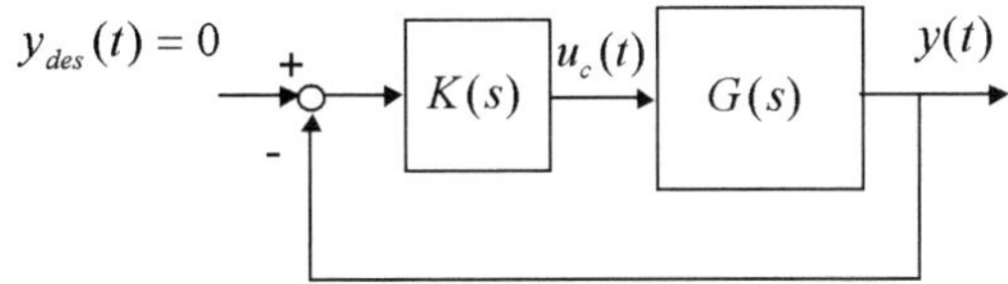

FIGURE 11.39 Feedback control system of Exercise 11.11.

(c) Find the loop gain, sketch its Bode plot, and compute the phase margin of the closed-loop system. Assuming for the moment that the controller would be implemented on Earth, what would be the longest communication delay that would not destabilize the automatic docking system?

(d) Compute the sensitivity function of the system and give the steady-state error to a unit step disturbance on the output.

Answer:

12 Discrete-Time Fourier Series and Fourier Transform

In This Chapter

((Lecture 42: Definition of the Discrete-Time Fourier Series))

In this chapter, we go back to the study of discrete-time signals, this time focusing on the frequency domain. We will see that periodic discrete-time signals can be expanded in a finite Fourier sum of complex harmonics. However, aperiodic discrete-time signals require a continuum of complex exponentials to represent them. Thus, the Fourier transform of a discrete-time signal is a continuous function of frequency.

RESPONSE OF DISCRETE-TIME LTI SYSTEMS TO COMPLEX EXPONENTIALS

Recall that complex exponentials of the type Cz^n are eigenfunctions of discrete-time linear time-invariant (DLTI) systems; that is, they remain basically invariant under the action of delays. For example, they are used to find homogeneous responses of difference systems. The response of a DLTI system to a complex exponential input is the same complex exponential with only a change in (complex) amplitude: $z^n * h[n] = H(z)z^n$. The complex amplitude factor is in general a function of the complex number z. To show that the complex exponential z^n is an eigenfunction of a DLTI system, we write,

$$\begin{aligned} y[n] &= \sum_{k=-\infty}^{+\infty} h[k]x[n-k] = \sum_{k=-\infty}^{+\infty} h[k]z^{n-k} \\ &= z^n \sum_{k=-\infty}^{+\infty} h[k]z^{-k}. \end{aligned} \tag{12.1}$$

The system's response has the form $y[n] = H(z)z^n$, where $H(z) = \sum_{k=-\infty}^{+\infty} h[k]z^{-k}$, assuming that the sum converges. The function $H(z)$ is called the z-transform of the impulse response of the system. For Fourier analysis, we will restrict our attention to complex exponentials that have z lying on the unit circle, that is, of the form $e^{j\omega n}$.

FOURIER SERIES REPRESENTATION OF DISCRETE-TIME PERIODIC SIGNALS

The complex exponential $e^{j\omega_1 n}$ of frequency $\omega_1 = \frac{2\pi}{N}$ is periodic with fundamental period N and fundamental frequency $\omega_0 := \frac{2\pi}{N} = \omega_1$. The set of all discrete-time complex exponentials that are periodic with (not necessarily fundamental) period N is given by

$$\phi_k[n] = e^{jk\omega_0 n} = e^{jk\frac{2\pi}{N}n}, \quad k = \ldots, -2, -1, 0, 1, 2, \ldots. \tag{12.2}$$

This set of harmonically related complex exponentials is actually redundant, as there are only N distinct exponentials in it. For example, $e^{j\frac{2\pi}{N}n} = e^{j(N+1)\frac{2\pi}{N}n}$, so $\phi_1[n] = \phi_{N+1}[n]$, and in general, for any integer r,

$$\phi_k[n] = \phi_{k+rN}[n]. \tag{12.3}$$

Remarks:

- The set of harmonically related complex exponentials $\phi_k[n]=e^{jk\frac{2\pi}{N}n}$ are distinct only over an interval $\langle N\rangle$ of N consecutive values of k (starting at any k). This set is denoted as $\{\phi_k[n]\}_{k=\langle N\rangle}$.
- The set $\{\phi_k[n]\}_{k=\langle N\rangle}$ is orthogonal. To prove this, first consider the case $k=r$:

$$\begin{aligned}\sum_{n=p}^{p+N-1}\phi_k[n]\phi_k[n]^* &= \sum_{n=p}^{p+N-1} e^{jk\frac{2\pi}{N}n}e^{-jk\frac{2\pi}{N}n}\\ &= \sum_{n=p}^{p+N-1} e^{j(k-k)\frac{2\pi}{N}n} = N.\end{aligned} \tag{12.4}$$

Then for $k\neq r$,

$$\begin{aligned}\sum_{n=p}^{p+N-1}\phi_k[n]\phi_r[n]^* &= \sum_{n=p}^{p+N-1} e^{jk\frac{2\pi}{N}n}e^{-jr\frac{2\pi}{N}n},\quad r,k\in\langle N\rangle, r\neq k\\ &= \sum_{n=p}^{p+N-1} e^{j(k-r)\frac{2\pi}{N}n},\quad \text{let } m=n-p,\\ &= \sum_{m=0}^{N-1} e^{j(k-r)\frac{2\pi}{N}(m+p)}\\ &= e^{j(k-r)p\frac{2\pi}{N}}\sum_{m=0}^{N-1} e^{j(k-r)\frac{2\pi}{N}m}\\ &= e^{j(k-r)p\frac{2\pi}{N}}\left(\frac{1-e^{j(k-r)\frac{2\pi}{N}N}}{1-e^{j(k-r)\frac{2\pi}{N}}}\right) = e^{j(k-r)p\frac{2\pi}{N}}\left(\frac{1-1}{1-e^{j(k-r)\frac{2\pi}{N}}}\right) = 0.\end{aligned} \tag{12.5}$$

The fundamental period of distinct harmonically related complex exponentials is not necessarily N for all. For example, the case $N=6$ is considered in Table 12.1.

TABLE 12.1 Frequencies of Discrete-Time Complex Harmonics for N = 6

$\phi_k[n]$	$e^{j0\frac{2\pi}{6}n}=1$	$e^{j\frac{2\pi}{6}n}$	$e^{j2\frac{2\pi}{6}n}$	$e^{j3\frac{2\pi}{6}n}$	$e^{j4\frac{2\pi}{6}n}$	$e^{j5\frac{2\pi}{6}n}$
Frequency ω_1	0	$\frac{\pi}{3}$	$\frac{2\pi}{3}$	π	$\frac{4\pi}{3}$	$\frac{5\pi}{3}$
Fundamental frequency ω_0	2π (or 0)	$\frac{\pi}{3}$	$\frac{2\pi}{3}$	π	$\frac{2\pi}{3}$	$\frac{\pi}{3}$
Fundamental period	1	6	3	2	3	6

Fourier Series Representation

We consider a periodic discrete-time signal of period N that has the form of a linear combination of the exponentials in $\{\phi_k[n]\}_{k=\langle N\rangle}$:

$$\tilde{x}[n]=\sum_{k=\langle N\rangle} a_k\phi_k[n]=\sum_{k=\langle N\rangle} a_k e^{jk\omega_0 n}=\sum_{k=\langle N\rangle} a_k e^{jk\frac{2\pi}{N}n}. \tag{12.6}$$

Noticing that the set $\{\phi_k[n]\}_{k=\langle N\rangle}$ of N harmonically related complex exponentials is orthogonal, we can compute the coefficients a_k by multiplying Equation 12.6 by $\phi_k[n]^*=e^{-jk\frac{2\pi}{N}n}$ and summing over the interval of time $\langle N\rangle$:

$$\sum_{n=\langle N\rangle}\tilde{x}[n]\phi_k[n]^*=\sum_{n=\langle N\rangle}\tilde{x}[n]e^{-jk\frac{2\pi}{N}n}=\sum_{n=\langle N\rangle}\sum_{p=\langle N\rangle} a_p e^{jp\frac{2\pi}{N}n}e^{-jk\frac{2\pi}{N}n}=Na_k. \tag{12.7}$$

Hence,

$$a_k=\frac{1}{N}\sum_{n=\langle N\rangle}\tilde{x}[n]e^{-jk\frac{2\pi}{N}n}. \tag{12.8}$$

The remaining question is, Can *any* discrete-time periodic signal $x[n]$ of period N be written as a linear combination of complex exponentials as in Equation 12.6? To show that this is true, we need to show that the relationship between $x[n]$ and a_k is invertible. In other words, given any $x[n]$ of period N, the corresponding set of N coefficients computed using Equation 12.8 should be unique, and vice-versa. Expanding and repeating Equation 12.8, and choosing $k=0,1,2,\ldots,N-1$ as the interval $\langle N\rangle$, we obtain

$$\begin{aligned}
a_0&=\frac{1}{N}(x[0]+x[1]+x[2]+\cdots+x[N-1])\\
a_1&=\frac{1}{N}\left(x[0]+x[1]e^{-j\frac{2\pi}{N}}+x[2]e^{-j\frac{2\pi}{N}2}+\cdots+x[N-1]e^{-j\frac{2\pi}{N}(N-1)}\right)\\
&\vdots\\
a_{N-1}&=\frac{1}{N}\left(x[0]+x[1]e^{-j(N-1)\frac{2\pi}{N}}+x[2]e^{-j(N-1)\frac{2\pi}{N}2}+\cdots+x[N-1]e^{-j(N-1)\frac{2\pi}{N}(N-1)}\right),
\end{aligned} \tag{12.9}$$

which can be written in matrix-vector form as follows:

$$\begin{bmatrix} a_0 \\ a_1 \\ \vdots \\ a_{N-1} \end{bmatrix} = \frac{1}{N} \begin{bmatrix} 1 & 1 & 1 & \cdots & 1 \\ 1 & e^{-j\frac{2\pi}{N}} & e^{-j\frac{2\pi}{N}2} & \cdots & e^{-j\frac{2\pi}{N}(N-1)} \\ \vdots & \vdots & \vdots & \vdots & \vdots \\ 1 & e^{-j(N-1)\frac{2\pi}{N}} & e^{-j(N-1)\frac{2\pi}{N}2} & \cdots & e^{-j(N-1)\frac{2\pi}{N}(N-1)} \end{bmatrix} \begin{bmatrix} x[0] \\ x[1] \\ x[2] \\ \vdots \\ x[N-1] \end{bmatrix}. \qquad (12.10)$$

The matrix in this equation can be shown to be invertible; hence, a unique set of coefficients $\{a_k\}_{k=\langle N\rangle}$ corresponds to each $x[n]$ of period N, and vice versa.

The coefficients $\{a_k\}_{k=\langle N\rangle}$ are called the *discrete-time Fourier series (DTFS) coefficients* of $x[n]$. The *DTFS pair* is given by

$$x[n] = \sum_{k=\langle N\rangle} a_k e^{jk\omega_0 n} = \sum_{k=\langle N\rangle} a_k e^{jk\frac{2\pi}{N}n} \qquad (12.11)$$

$$a_k = \frac{1}{N}\sum_{n=\langle N\rangle} x[n]e^{-jk\omega_0 n} = \frac{1}{N}\sum_{n=\langle N\rangle} x[n]e^{-jk\frac{2\pi}{N}n}, \qquad (12.12)$$

where Equation 12.11 is the *synthesis equation* (or the *Fourier series of* $x[n]$), and Equation 12.12 is the *analysis equation*.

Remarks:

- The coefficients $\{a_k\}_{k=\langle N\rangle}$ can be seen as a periodic sequence with $k \in \mathbb{Z}$, as they repeat with period N.
- All summations are *finite,* which means that the sums *always converge*. Thus, the DTFS could be more accurately described as the discrete-time Fourier *sum*.

Example 12.1: Consider the following discrete-time periodic signal $x[n]$ of period $N = 4$ shown in Figure 12.1.

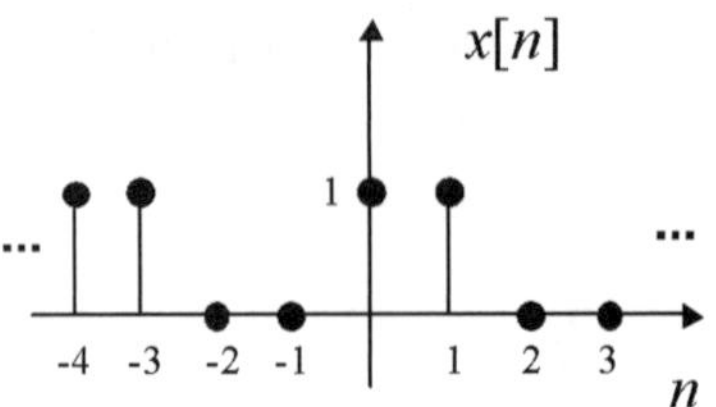

FIGURE 12.1 Discrete-time square wave signal.

We can compute its four distinct Fourier series coefficients using Equation 12.12.

$$
\begin{aligned}
a_0 &= \frac{1}{4}\sum_{n=0}^{3} x[n] = \frac{1}{2} \\
a_1 &= \frac{1}{4}\sum_{n=0}^{3} x[n]e^{-j\frac{2\pi}{4}n} = \frac{1}{4}\left(1+e^{-j\frac{\pi}{2}}\right) = \frac{1}{4}(1-j) = \frac{1}{2\sqrt{2}}e^{-j\frac{\pi}{4}} \\
a_2 &= \frac{1}{4}\sum_{n=0}^{3} x[n]e^{-j2\frac{2\pi}{4}n} = \frac{1}{4}\left(1+e^{-j\pi}\right) = \frac{1}{4}(1-1) = 0 \\
a_3 &= \frac{1}{4}\sum_{n=0}^{3} x[n]e^{-j3\frac{2\pi}{4}n} = \frac{1}{4}\left(1+e^{-j\frac{3\pi}{2}}\right) = \frac{1}{4}(1+j) = \frac{1}{2\sqrt{2}}e^{+j\frac{\pi}{4}}
\end{aligned} \tag{12.13}
$$

Let us see if we can recover $x[1]$ using the synthesis equation:

$$
x[1] = \sum_{k=0}^{3} a_k e^{jk\frac{2\pi}{4}} = \frac{1}{2} + \frac{1}{2\sqrt{2}}e^{-j\frac{\pi}{4}}e^{j\frac{\pi}{2}} + 0 + \frac{1}{2\sqrt{2}}e^{j\frac{\pi}{4}}e^{-j\frac{\pi}{2}} = \frac{1}{2} + \frac{1}{\sqrt{2}}\mathrm{Re}\{e^{j\frac{\pi}{4}}\} = 1 \tag{12.14}
$$

((Lecture 43: Properties of the Discrete-Time Fourier Series))

PROPERTIES OF THE DISCRETE-TIME FOURIER SERIES

We will use the notation $x[n] \overset{FS}{\leftrightarrow} a_k$ to represent a DTFS pair. The properties of the DTFS are similar to those of continuous-time Fourier series. All signals in the following subsections are assumed to be periodic with fundamental period N, unless otherwise specified. The DTFS coefficients are often called the *spectral coefficients*. The properties of the DTFS are summarized in Table D.9 in Appendix D.

Linearity

The operation of calculating the DTFS of a periodic signal is linear.

For $x[n]\overset{FS}{\leftrightarrow}a_k$, $y[n]\overset{FS}{\leftrightarrow}b_k$, if we form the linear combination $z[n]=\alpha x[n]+\beta y[n]$, $\alpha,\beta\in\mathbb{C}$, we have

$$z[n]\overset{FS}{\leftrightarrow}\alpha a_k+\beta b_k. \tag{12.15}$$

Time Shifting

Time shifting leads to a multiplication by a complex exponential. For $x[n]\overset{FS}{\leftrightarrow}a_k$,

$$x[n-n_0]\overset{FS}{\leftrightarrow}e^{-jk\frac{2\pi}{N}n_0}a_k, \tag{12.16}$$

where n_0 is an integer.

Remarks:

- The magnitudes of the Fourier series coefficients are not changed; only their phases are.
- A time shift by an integer number of periods, that is, of $n_0=pN, p\in\mathbb{Z}$ does not change the DTFS coefficients, as expected.

Time Reversal

Time reversal leads to a "frequency reversal" of the corresponding sequence of Fourier series coefficients:

$$x[-n]\overset{FS}{\leftrightarrow}a_{-k}. \tag{12.17}$$

Interesting consequences are that

- For $x[n]$ even, the sequence of coefficients is also even ($a_{-k}=a_k$).
- For $x[n]$ odd, the sequence of coefficients is also odd ($a_{-k}=-a_k$).

Time Scaling

Let us first examine the periodicity of $x_{\downarrow m}[n]:=x[mn]$ and $x_{\uparrow m}[n]$ (defined in Equation 12.18), where m is a positive integer. The first signal $x_{\downarrow m}[n]$ is called a *decimated,* or *downsampled,* version of $x[n]$; that is, only every m^{th} sample of $x[n]$ is retained. It is periodic if $\exists M$, such that $x[mn]=x[m(n+M)]=x[mn+mM]$.

This condition is verified if $\exists p, M \in \mathbb{Z}$, such that $mM = pN$, which is always satisfied by picking $p = m,\ M = N$. Therefore, the signal $x_{\downarrow m}[n]$ is periodic of period N. However, its fundamental period can be smaller than N. For example, if N is a multiple of m, we can select $p = 1,\ M = \frac{N}{m}$, and the fundamental period of $x_{\downarrow m}[n]$ is $M = \frac{N}{m}$. In order to find the DTFS coefficients of $x_{\downarrow m}[n]$, we would need to use results in sampling theory for discrete-time signals. This will be covered in Chapter 15.

Consider the signal defined as

$$x_{\uparrow m}[n] := \begin{cases} x[n/m], & \text{if } n \text{ is a multiple of } m \\ 0, & \text{otherwise} \end{cases}, \tag{12.18}$$

where m is a positive integer. This is called an *upsampled* version of the original signal $x[n]$. Thus, the *upsampling operation* inserts $m - 1$ zeros between consecutive samples of the original signal. The upsampled signal is periodic as shown below, but its fundamental period is mN and its fundamental frequency is $\frac{2\pi}{mN}$.

$$x_{\uparrow m}[n+mN] := \begin{cases} x[(n+mN)/m] = x[n/m+N] = x[n/m], & \text{if } n \text{ is a multiple of } m \\ 0, \text{ if } n \text{ is not a multiple of } m \end{cases} \tag{12.19}$$

Example 12.2: Upsampling of a periodic square wave signal is shown in Figure 12.2.

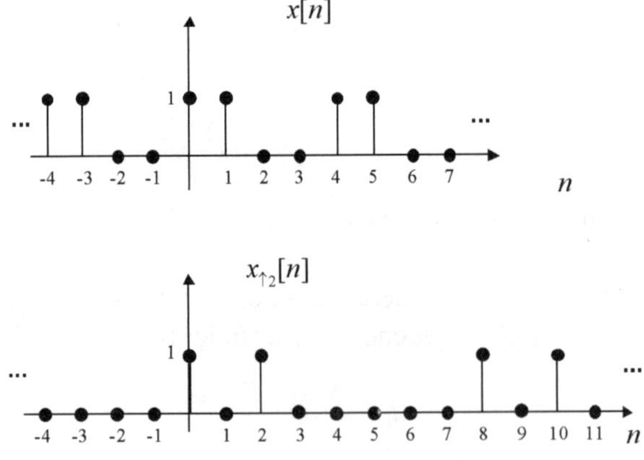

FIGURE 12.2 Upsampling a discrete-time square wave signal.

The Fourier series coefficients of the upsampled signal $x_{\uparrow m}[n]$ are given by

$$x_{\uparrow m}[n] \overset{FS}{\leftrightarrow} \frac{1}{m} a_k, \tag{12.20}$$

where $\left\{\frac{1}{m} a_k\right\}$ is viewed as a periodic sequence of period mN.

Proof:

$$\begin{aligned} b_k &= \frac{1}{mN} \sum_{n=\langle mN \rangle} x_{\uparrow m}[n] e^{-jk\frac{2\pi}{mN}n} = \frac{1}{mN} \sum_{n=0,m,..,m(N-1)} x[n/m] e^{-jk\frac{2\pi}{mN}n} \\ &= \frac{1}{mN} \sum_{p=\langle N \rangle} x[p] e^{-jk\frac{2\pi}{N}p} = \frac{1}{m} a_k \end{aligned} \tag{12.21}$$

Periodic Convolution of Two Signals

Suppose that $x[n]$ and $y[n]$ are both periodic with period N. For $x[n] \overset{FS}{\leftrightarrow} a_k$, $y[n] \overset{FS}{\leftrightarrow} b_k$, we have

$$\sum_{m=\langle N \rangle} x[m] y[n-m] \overset{FS}{\leftrightarrow} N a_k b_k. \tag{12.22}$$

Remarks:

- The periodic convolution is itself periodic of period N (show it as an exercise).
- What is the use of a periodic convolution? It is useful in periodic signal filtering. The DTFS coefficients of the input signal are the a_k's, and the b_k's are chosen by the filter designer to attenuate or amplify certain frequencies. The resulting discrete-time output signal is given by the periodic convolution above. But it is mostly useful for convolving signals of finite support: with sufficient zero-padding, we can pretend that each one of the zero-padded signals represents a period of a periodic signal and use Equation 12.22 to compute the convolution in the frequency domain. The zero padding has the effect of turning the periodic convolution into an ordinary convolution. We can then obtain the corresponding time-domain signal by solving Equation 12.10. This idea leads to the discrete Fourier transform (DFT) and the fast Fourier transform (FFT) algorithm, which are widely used techniques although beyond the scope of this book.

Multiplication of Two Signals

The time domain multiplication of the two signals defined earlier yields

$$x[n]y[n] \overset{FS}{\leftrightarrow} \sum_{l=\langle N \rangle} a_l b_{k-l}, \tag{12.23}$$

that is, a periodic convolution of the two sequences of spectral coefficients. This property is used in discrete-time modulation of a periodic signal.

First Difference

The first difference of a periodic signal (often used as an approximation to the continuous-time derivative) has the following spectral coefficients:

$$x[n] - x[n-1] \overset{FS}{\leftrightarrow} (1 - e^{-jk\frac{2\pi}{N}})a_k. \tag{12.24}$$

Running Sum

The running sum of a signal is the inverse of the first difference "system." Note that the running sum of a periodic signal is periodic if and only if $a_0 = 0$; that is, the DC component of the signal is 0. In this case,

$$\sum_{m=-\infty}^{n} x[m] \overset{FS}{\leftrightarrow} \frac{1}{(1 - e^{-jk\frac{2\pi}{N}})} a_k. \tag{12.25}$$

Conjugation and Conjugate Symmetry

The complex conjugate of a periodic signal yields complex conjugation and frequency reversal of the spectral coefficients:

$$x^*[n] \overset{FS}{\leftrightarrow} a^*_{-k} \tag{12.26}$$

Interesting consequences are that

- For $x[n]$ real, the sequence of coefficients is *conjugate symmetric* ($a_{-k} = a_k^*$). This implies $|a_{-k}| = |a_k|$, $\angle(a_{-k}) = -\angle(a_k)$, $a_0 \in \mathbb{R}$, $\text{Re}\{a_{-k}\} = \text{Re}\{a_k\}$, $\text{Im}\{a_{-k}\} = -\text{Im}\{a_k\}$.
- For $x[n]$ real and even, the sequence of coefficients is also real and even ($a_{-k} = a_k \in \mathbb{R}$).

- For $x[n]$ real and odd, the sequence of coefficients is purely imaginary and odd ($a_{-k} = -a_k \in j\mathbb{R}$).
- For an even-odd decomposition of the signal $x[n] = x_e[n] + x_o[n]$, we have $x_e[n] \overset{FS}{\leftrightarrow} \mathrm{Re}\{a_k\}$, $x_o[n] \overset{FS}{\leftrightarrow} j\,\mathrm{Im}\{a_k\}$.

((Lecture 44: Definition of the Discrete-Time Fourier Transform))

DISCRETE-TIME FOURIER TRANSFORM

We now turn our attention to Fourier transforms of aperiodic discrete-time signals. The development of the Fourier transform is based on the Fourier series of a periodic discrete-time signal whose period tends to infinity. Consider the following periodic signal $\tilde{x}[n]$ of period $N = 7$, shown in Figure 12.3.

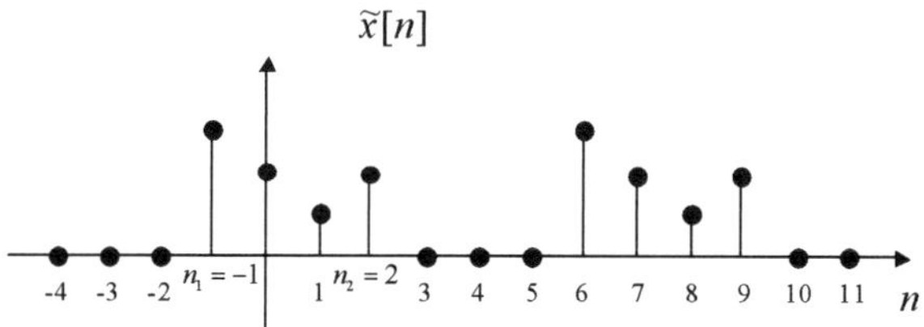

FIGURE 12.3 Discrete-time periodic signal.

Define $x[n]$ to be equal to $\tilde{x}[n]$ over one period, and zero elsewhere, as shown in Figure 12.4.

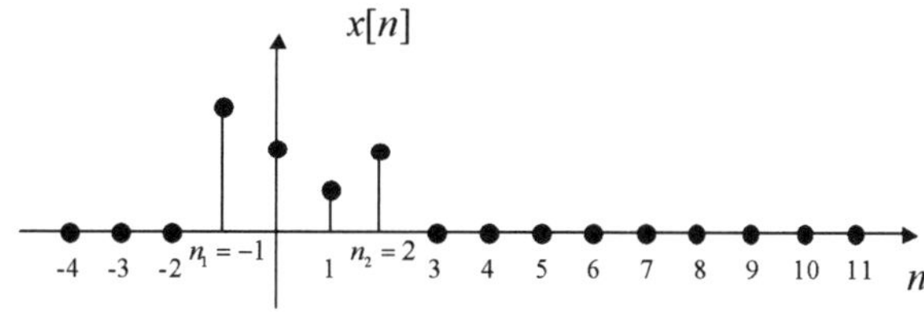

FIGURE 12.4 A periodic discrete-time signal corresponding to one period of the periodic signal.

Let us examine the DTFS pair of $\tilde{x}[n]$ given by

$$\tilde{x}[n] = \sum_{k=\langle N\rangle} a_k e^{jk\frac{2\pi}{N}n}, \tag{12.27}$$

$$a_k = \frac{1}{N}\sum_{n=\langle N\rangle} \tilde{x}[n] e^{-jk\frac{2\pi}{N}n}. \tag{12.28}$$

Referring to Figure 12.4, if we pick the summation interval such that $-n_1 \le n \le n_2 \subseteq \langle N\rangle$, we can substitute $x[n]$ for $\tilde{x}[n]$ in Equation 12.6:

$$a_k = \frac{1}{N}\sum_{n=\langle N\rangle} x[n] e^{-jk\frac{2\pi}{N}n} = \frac{1}{N}\sum_{n=-\infty}^{+\infty} x[n] e^{-jk\frac{2\pi}{N}n}. \tag{12.29}$$

Define the function

$$X(e^{j\omega}) := \sum_{n=-\infty}^{+\infty} x[n] e^{-j\omega n}. \tag{12.30}$$

We see that the DTFS coefficients a_k are scaled *samples* of this continuous function of frequency ω. That is,

$$a_k = \frac{1}{N} X(e^{j\frac{2\pi}{N}k}) = \frac{1}{N} X(e^{j\omega_0 k}). \tag{12.31}$$

Using this expression for a_k in Equation 12.27, we obtain

$$\tilde{x}[n] = \sum_{k=\langle N\rangle} \frac{1}{N} X(e^{jk\omega_0}) e^{jk\omega_0 n} = \frac{1}{2\pi}\sum_{k=\langle N\rangle} X(e^{jk\omega_0}) e^{jk\omega_0 n}\omega_0. \tag{12.32}$$

At the limit, as $N \to +\infty$ in Equation 12.32, we get

- $\omega_0 \to d\omega$.
- $k\omega_0 \to \omega$.
- The summation over $N \to \infty$ small frequency intervals of width $\omega_0 = \frac{2\pi}{N} \to d\omega$ tends to an integral over a frequency interval of width 2π.
- $\tilde{x}[n] \to x[n]$.

Then Equation 12.32 becomes

$$x[n] = \frac{1}{2\pi}\int_{2\pi} X(e^{j\omega}) e^{j\omega n} d\omega, \tag{12.33}$$

which, together with Equation 12.11, rewritten here for convenience,

$$X(e^{j\omega}) = \sum_{n=-\infty}^{+\infty} x[n]e^{-j\omega n}, \tag{12.34}$$

form the *discrete-time Fourier transform (DTFT) pair*. Equation 12.33 is the *synthesis equation*, meaning that we can synthesize the discrete-time signal from the knowledge of its frequency spectrum. The function $X(e^{j\omega})$ in the *analysis equation* (Equation 12.34) is the *Fourier transform* of $x[n]$. It is periodic of period 2π as we now show:

$$X(e^{j(\omega+2\pi)}) = \sum_{n=-\infty}^{+\infty} x[n]e^{-j(\omega+2\pi)n} = \sum_{n=-\infty}^{+\infty} x[n]e^{-j\omega n}e^{-j2\pi n} = \sum_{n=-\infty}^{+\infty} x[n]e^{-j\omega n} = X(e^{j\omega}). \tag{12.35}$$

Example 12.3: Consider the exponential signal $x[n] = a^n u[n],\ a \in \mathbb{R},\ |a| < 1$, as shown in Figure 12.5 for $0 < a < 1$.

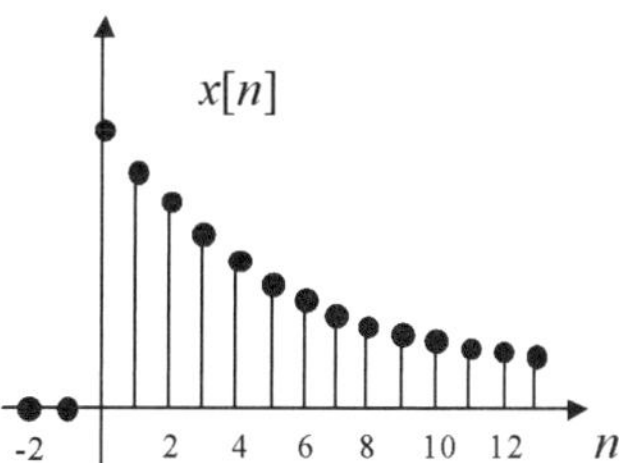

FIGURE 12.5 Discrete-time exponential signal.

Its Fourier transform is

$$X(e^{j\omega}) = \sum_{n=0}^{+\infty} a^n e^{-j\omega n} = \sum_{n=0}^{+\infty} (ae^{-j\omega})^n = \frac{1}{1-ae^{-j\omega}}. \tag{12.36}$$

Note that this infinite sum converges because $\left|ae^{-j\omega}\right| = |a| < 1$. The magnitude of $X(e^{j\omega})$ for $0 < a < 1$ is plotted in Figure 12.6.

Example 12.4: Consider the even rectangular pulse signal of width $2n_0 + 1$ as shown in Figure 12.7 for the case $n_0 = 2$.

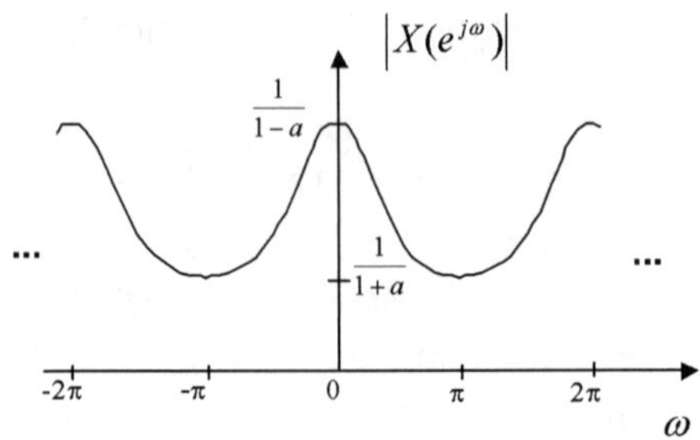

FIGURE 12.6 Magnitude of Fourier transform of discrete-time exponential signal.

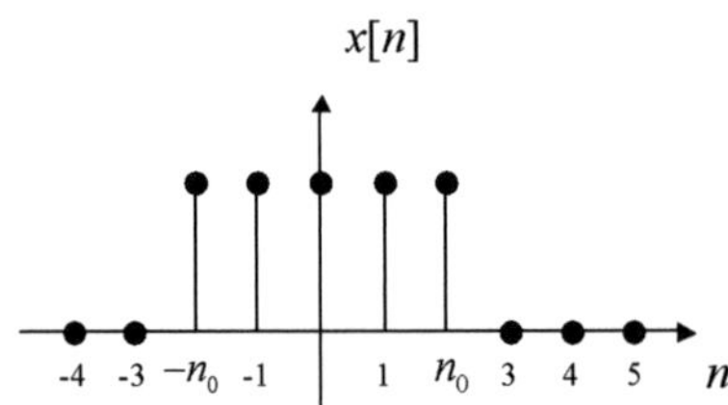

FIGURE 12.7 Rectangular pulse signal.

Its Fourier transform is given by

$$\begin{aligned}
X(e^{j\omega}) &= \sum_{n=-\infty}^{+\infty} x[n]e^{-j\omega n} = \sum_{n=-n_0}^{n_0} e^{-j\omega n} \\
&= e^{j\omega n_0} \sum_{m=0}^{2n_0} e^{-j\omega m} \\
&= e^{j\omega n_0} \frac{1-e^{-j\omega(2n_0+1)}}{1-e^{-j\omega}} \\
&= \frac{e^{j\omega n_0} - e^{-j\omega(n_0+1)}}{1-e^{-j\omega}} \\
&= \frac{e^{-j\omega/2}}{e^{-j\omega/2}} \frac{e^{j\omega(n_0+1/2)} - e^{-j\omega(n_0+1/2)}}{e^{j\omega/2} - e^{-j\omega/2}} \\
&= \frac{\sin\omega(n_0+1/2)}{\sin(\omega/2)}.
\end{aligned} \tag{12.37}$$

This function is the discrete-time counterpart of the sinc function that was the Fourier transform of the continuous-time rectangular pulse. However, the function in Equation 12.37 is periodic of period 2π, whereas the sinc function is aperiodic. The Fourier transform of a pulse with $n_0 = 2$ is shown in Figure 12.8.

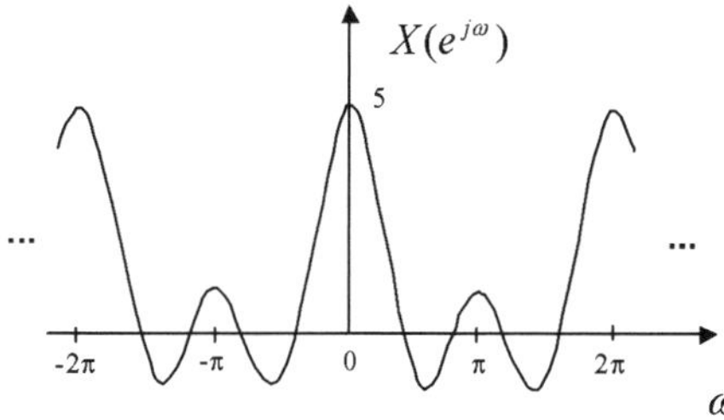

FIGURE 12.8 Fourier transform of discrete-time rectangular pulse signal.

Convergence of the Discrete-Time Fourier Transform

We now give sufficient conditions for convergence of the infinite summation of the DTFT. The DTFT of Equation 12.34 will converge either if the signal is *absolutely summable*, that is,

$$\sum_{n=-\infty}^{+\infty} \left| x[n] \right| < \infty, \qquad (12.38)$$

or if the sequence has finite energy, that is,

$$\sum_{n=-\infty}^{+\infty} \left| x[n] \right|^2 < \infty. \qquad (12.39)$$

In contrast, the finite integral in the synthesis Equation 12.33 always converges.

((Lecture 45: Properties of the Discrete-Time Fourier Transform))

PROPERTIES OF THE DISCRETE-TIME FOURIER TRANSFORM

We use the notation $x[n] \overset{F}{\leftrightarrow} X(e^{j\omega})$ to represent a DTFT pair. The following properties of the DTFT are similar to those of the DTFS. These properties are summarized in Table D.8 in Appendix D.

Linearity

The operation of calculating the DTFT of a signal is linear. For $x[n] \overset{F}{\leftrightarrow} X(e^{j\omega})$, $y[n] \overset{F}{\leftrightarrow} Y(e^{j\omega})$, if we form the linear combination $z[n] = ax[n] + by[n]$, $a,b \in \mathbb{C}$, then we have:

$$z[n] \overset{F}{\leftrightarrow} aX(e^{j\omega}) + bY(e^{j\omega}). \tag{12.40}$$

Time Shifting

Time shifting the signal by $n_0 \in \mathbb{Z}$ leads to a multiplication of the Fourier transform by a complex exponential:

$$x[n - n_0] \overset{F}{\leftrightarrow} e^{-j\omega n_0} X(e^{j\omega}). \tag{12.41}$$

Remark: Only the phase of the DTFT is changed.

Frequency Shifting

A frequency shift by $\omega_0 \in \mathbb{R}$ leads to a multiplication of $x[n]$ by a complex exponential:

$$e^{j\omega_0 n} x[n] \overset{F}{\leftrightarrow} X(e^{j(\omega - \omega_0)}). \tag{12.42}$$

Time Reversal

Time reversal leads to a frequency reversal of the corresponding DTFT:

$$x[-n] \overset{F}{\leftrightarrow} X(e^{-j\omega}). \tag{12.43}$$

Proof:

$$\sum_{n=-\infty}^{+\infty} x[-n] e^{-j\omega n} = \sum_{m=-\infty}^{\infty} x[m] e^{j\omega m} = X(e^{-j\omega}) \tag{12.44}$$

Consequences: For $x[n]$ even, $X(e^{j\omega})$ is also even; for $x[n]$ odd, $X(e^{j\omega})$ is also odd.

Time Scaling

Upsampling (Time Expansion)

Recall that the *upsampled* version of signal $x[n]$, denoted as $x_{\uparrow m}[n]$, has $m - 1$ zeros inserted between consecutive samples of the original signal. Thus, upsampling can be seen as a time expansion of the signal. The Fourier transform of the upsampled signal is given by

$$x_{\uparrow m}[n] \overset{F}{\leftrightarrow} X(e^{jm\omega}). \tag{12.45}$$

Note that the resulting spectrum is compressed around the frequency $\omega = 0$, but since $X(e^{j\omega})$ is periodic of period 2π, its compressed version can still have a significant magnitude around $\omega = \pi$, which is the highest possible frequency in any discrete-time signal. This energy at high frequencies corresponds to the fast transitions between the original signal values and the zeros that were inserted in the upsampling operation. Figure 12.9 shows the Fourier transform of a rectangular pulse signal $x[n]$ before and after upsampling by a factor of 2, giving $x_{\uparrow 2}[n]$. Although not shown in the figure, the phase undergoes the same compression effect. Notice how the magnitude of the upsampled signal is larger than the original at high frequencies (around $\omega = \pi$). Because of this effect, the upsampling operator is often followed by a discrete-time lowpass filter (more on this in Chapter 15).

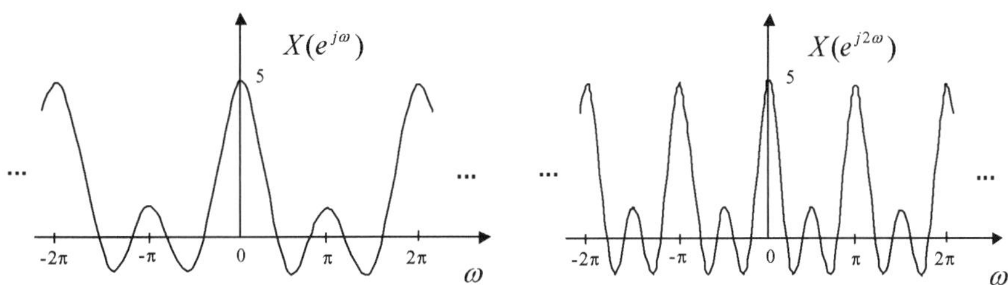

FIGURE 12.9 Effect of upsampling on the Fourier transform of a discrete-time rectangular pulse signal.

Downsampling (Decimation)

Recall that the signal $x_{\downarrow m} := x[mn]$ is a *decimated* or *downsampled* version of $x[n]$; that is, only every m^{th} sample of $x[n]$ is retained. Since aliasing may occur, we will postpone this analysis until Chapter 15, where sampling is studied.

Differentiation in Frequency

Differentiation of the DTFT with respect to frequency gives a multiplication of the signal by n:

$$nx[n] \overset{F}{\leftrightarrow} j\frac{dX(e^{j\omega})}{d\omega}. \tag{12.46}$$

Convolution of Two Signals

For $x[n] \overset{F}{\leftrightarrow} X(e^{j\omega}),\ y[n] \overset{F}{\leftrightarrow} Y(e^{j\omega})$, we have

$$\sum_{m=-\infty}^{\infty} x[m]y[n-m] \overset{F}{\leftrightarrow} X(e^{j\omega})Y(e^{j\omega}). \tag{12.47}$$

Proof: Under the appropriate assumption of convergence, to be able to interchange the order of summations, we have

$$\begin{aligned}\sum_{n=-\infty}^{+\infty}\sum_{m=-\infty}^{\infty} x[m]y[n-m]e^{-j\omega n} &= \sum_{m=-\infty}^{+\infty} x[m]\sum_{n=-\infty}^{\infty} y[n-m]e^{-j\omega n}\\ &= \sum_{m=-\infty}^{+\infty} x[m]\sum_{p=-\infty}^{\infty} y[p]e^{-j\omega(p+m)}\\ &= \sum_{m=-\infty}^{+\infty} x[m]e^{-j\omega m}\sum_{p=-\infty}^{\infty} y[p]e^{-j\omega p}\\ &= X(e^{j\omega})Y(e^{j\omega}).\end{aligned} \tag{12.48}$$

Remarks:

- The basic use of this property is to compute the output signal of a system for a particular input signal, given its impulse response or DTFT.
- The convolution property is also useful in discrete-time filter design and feedback controller design.

Example 12.5: Given a system with $h[n]=(-0.8)^n u[n]$ and an input $x[n]=(0.5)^n u[n]$, the DTFT of the output is given by

$$Y(e^{j\omega}) = H(e^{j\omega})X(e^{j\omega}) = \frac{1}{1+0.8e^{-j\omega}}\frac{1}{1-0.5e^{-j\omega}}. \tag{12.49}$$

We perform a partial fraction expansion of $Y(e^{j\omega})$ to be able to use Table D.7 in Appendix D to obtain $y[n]$. Note that the first-order terms in the partial fraction expansion should have the form $\frac{A}{1-ae^{-j\omega}}$, not $\frac{A}{e^{j\omega}-a}$, which usually leads to a wrong solution. Let $z=e^{j\omega}$ for convenience.

$$\frac{1}{(1+0.8z^{-1})(1-0.5z^{-1})}=\frac{A}{1+0.8z^{-1}}+\frac{B}{1-0.5z^{-1}} \tag{12.50}$$

$$\left.\frac{1}{(1-0.5z^{-1})}\right|_{z=-0.8}=A+\left.\frac{B(1+0.8z^{-1})}{1-0.5z^{-1}}\right|_{z=-0.8} \Rightarrow A=\frac{1}{(1-\frac{0.5}{-0.8})}=\frac{8}{13} \tag{12.51}$$

$$\left.\frac{1}{(1+0.8z^{-1})}\right|_{z=0.5}=B+\left.\frac{A(1-0.5z^{-1})}{1+0.8z^{-1}}\right|_{z=0.5} \Rightarrow B=\frac{1}{(1+\frac{0.8}{0.5})}=\frac{5}{13} \tag{12.52}$$

Finally, we use Table D.7 to get

$$y[n]=\frac{8}{13}(-0.8)^n u[n]+\frac{5}{13}(0.5)^n u[n]. \tag{12.53}$$

Multiplication of Two Signals

With the two signals as defined above,

$$x[n]y[n]\overset{F}{\leftrightarrow}\frac{1}{2\pi}\int_{2\pi} X(e^{j\upsilon})Y(e^{j(\omega-\upsilon)})d\upsilon. \tag{12.54}$$

Remarks:

- Note that the resulting DTFT is a periodic convolution of the two DTFTs.
- This property is used in discrete-time modulation and sampling.

First Difference

The first difference of a signal has the following spectrum:

$$x[n]-x[n-1]\overset{F}{\leftrightarrow}(1-e^{-j\omega})X(e^{j\omega}). \tag{12.55}$$

Running Sum (Accumulation)

The running sum of a signal is the inverse of the first difference:

$$\sum_{m=-\infty}^{n} x[m] \overset{F}{\leftrightarrow} \frac{1}{(1-e^{-j\omega})} X(e^{j\omega}) + \pi X(e^{j0}) \sum_{k=-\infty}^{+\infty} \delta(\omega - k2\pi). \tag{12.56}$$

The frequency-domain impulses at DC account for the possibility that signal $x[n]$ has a nonzero DC component $X(e^{j0}) \neq 0$.

Conjugation and Conjugate Symmetry

Taking the conjugate of a signal has the effect of conjugation and frequency reversal of the DTFT:

$$x^*[n] \overset{F}{\leftrightarrow} X^*(e^{-j\omega}). \tag{12.57}$$

Interesting consequences are that

- For $x[n]$ real, the DTFT is *conjugate symmetric:* $X(e^{j\omega}) = X^*(e^{-j\omega})$. This implies $|X(e^{-j\omega})| = |X(e^{j\omega})|$ (even magnitude), $\angle X(e^{-j\omega}) = -\angle X(e^{j\omega})$ (odd phase), $X(e^{j0}) \in \mathbb{R}$, $\mathrm{Re}\{X(e^{-j\omega})\} = \mathrm{Re}\{X(e^{j\omega})\}$ (even), $\mathrm{Im}\{X(e^{-j\omega})\} = -\mathrm{Im}\{X(e^{j\omega})\}$ (odd)
- For $x[n]$ real and even, the DTFT is also real and even: $X(e^{j\omega}) = X(e^{-j\omega}) \in \mathbb{R}$.
- For $x[n]$ real and odd, the DTFT is purely imaginary and odd: $X(e^{j\omega}) = -X(e^{-j\omega}) \in j\mathbb{R}$.
- For an even-odd decomposition of the signal $x[n] = x_e[n] + x_o[n]$, $x_e[n] \overset{F}{\leftrightarrow} \mathrm{Re}\{X(e^{j\omega})\}$, $x_o[n] \overset{F}{\leftrightarrow} j\,\mathrm{Im}\{X(e^{j\omega})\}$.

Parseval Equality and Energy Density Spectrum

The Parseval equality establishes a correspondence between the energy of the signal and the energy in its spectrum:

$$\sum_{n=-\infty}^{+\infty} |x[n]|^2 = \frac{1}{2\pi} \int_{2\pi} |X(e^{j\omega})|^2 \, d\omega. \tag{12.58}$$

The squared magnitude of the DTFT $|X(e^{j\omega})|^2$ is referred to as the *energy-density spectrum* of the signal $x[n]$.

((Lecture 46: DTFT of Periodic and Step Signals, Duality))

DTFT OF PERIODIC SIGNALS AND STEP SIGNALS

Fourier transforms of discrete-time periodic signals can be defined by using impulses in the frequency domain.

DTFT of Complex Exponentials

Consider the complex exponential signal $x[n]=e^{j\omega_0 n}$. Its Fourier transform is given by

$$X(e^{j\omega})=\sum_{n=-\infty}^{+\infty}x[n]e^{-j\omega n}=\sum_{n=-\infty}^{+\infty}e^{j\omega_0 n}e^{-j\omega n}=\sum_{n=-\infty}^{+\infty}e^{-j(\omega-\omega_0)n}. \qquad (12.59)$$

This last sum does not converge to a regular function, but rather to a distribution, that is, an impulse train. For example, consider the finite sum

$$X_N(e^{j\omega})=\sum_{n=-N}^{+N}e^{-j(\omega-\omega_0)n}=e^{j(\omega-\omega_0)N}\sum_{m=0}^{2N}e^{-j(\omega-\omega_0)m}=\frac{\sin[(N+1/2)(\omega-\omega_0)]}{\sin[(\omega-\omega_0)/2]}. \qquad (12.60)$$

It is basically the DTFT of a rectangular pulse, but shifted in frequency, as shown in Figure 12.10. Notice that the amplitude of the main lobes grows with N, while their width decreases with N. Their area tends to 2π.

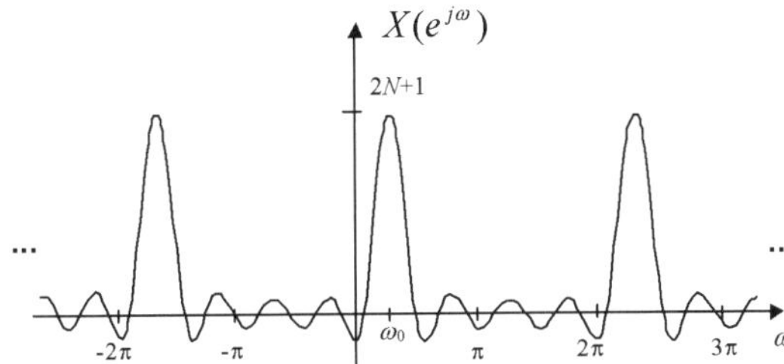

FIGURE 12.10 Truncated Fourier transform sum of a complex exponential signal.

Thus, as $N\to\infty$, we get an impulse located at ω_0 for the DTFT of the complex exponential $e^{j\omega_0 n}$, and this impulse is repeated every 2π radians, since any DTFT is periodic of period 2π.

$$X_N(e^{j\omega})\underset{N\to\infty}{\to}X(e^{j\omega})=\sum_{l=-\infty}^{+\infty}2\pi\delta(\omega-\omega_0-2\pi l). \qquad (12.61)$$

Check: Inverse Fourier transform. Note that there is only one impulse per interval of width 2π.

$$x[n] = \frac{1}{2\pi}\int_{2\pi}\sum_{l=-\infty}^{+\infty} 2\pi\delta(\omega-\omega_0-2\pi l)e^{j\omega n}d\omega = e^{j\omega_0 n} \tag{12.62}$$

DTFT of the Step Signal

Since the constant signal $x[n] = 1$ can be written as $x[n] = e^{j0n}$, it follows that its DTFT in the interval $[-\pi,\pi]$ is an impulse located at $\omega = 0$. Thus,

$$x[n] = 1 \overset{F}{\leftrightarrow} \sum_{l=-\infty}^{+\infty} 2\pi\delta(\omega - 2\pi l). \tag{12.63}$$

In order to find the Fourier transform of the unit step $u[n]$, for which the analysis Equation 12.34 does not converge, we write this signal as the limit of two exponential signals pieced together at the origin plus the constant $1/2$, as shown in Figure 12.11:

$$u[n] = \frac{1}{2} + \lim_{\alpha\to 1}\left(-\frac{1}{2}\alpha^{-(n+1)}u[-(n+1)] + \frac{1}{2}\alpha^n u[n]\right). \tag{12.64}$$

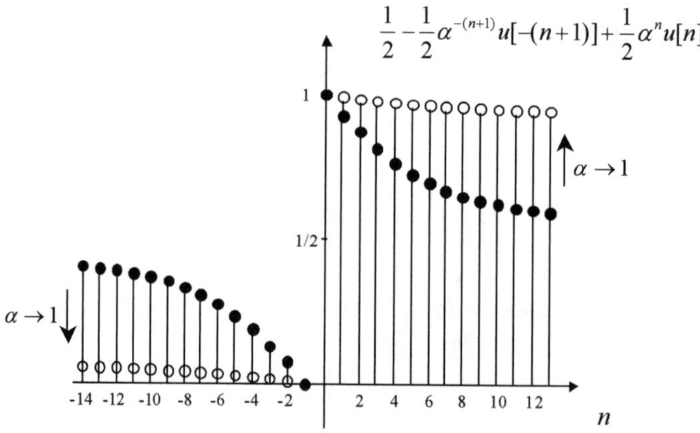

FIGURE 12.11 Piecewise exponential signal tending to the unit step.

We already know that the DTFT of $\frac{1}{2}\alpha^n u[n]$ is $\frac{1}{2}\frac{1}{1-\alpha e^{-j\omega}}$, and by the time reversal and time shifting properties, we have $-\frac{1}{2}\alpha^{-(n+1)}u[-(n+1)] \overset{F}{\leftrightarrow} -\frac{1}{2}\frac{e^{j\omega}}{1-\alpha e^{j\omega}}$.

Taking the Fourier transform of the right-hand side of Equation 12.64 before taking the limit, we obtain

$$\begin{aligned}
U(e^{j\omega}) &= \sum_{l=-\infty}^{+\infty} \pi\delta(\omega - 2\pi l) + \lim_{\alpha\to 1}\left(-\frac{1}{2}\frac{e^{j\omega}}{1-\alpha e^{j\omega}} + \frac{1}{2}\frac{1}{1-\alpha e^{-j\omega}} \right) \\
&= \sum_{l=-\infty}^{+\infty} \pi\delta(\omega - 2\pi l) + \frac{1}{2}\lim_{\alpha\to 1}\left(\frac{-e^{j\omega}(1-\alpha e^{-j\omega}) + (1-\alpha e^{j\omega})}{(1-\alpha e^{j\omega})(1-\alpha e^{-j\omega})} \right) \\
&= \sum_{l=-\infty}^{+\infty} \pi\delta(\omega - 2\pi l) + \frac{1}{2}\lim_{\alpha\to 1}\left(\frac{(\alpha+1)-(\alpha+1)e^{j\omega}}{(1-\alpha e^{j\omega})(1-\alpha e^{-j\omega})} \right) \\
&= \sum_{l=-\infty}^{+\infty} \pi\delta(\omega - 2\pi l) + \frac{1}{2}\left(\frac{2(1-e^{j\omega})}{(1-e^{j\omega})(1-e^{-j\omega})} \right) \\
&= \sum_{l=-\infty}^{+\infty} \pi\delta(\omega - 2\pi l) + \frac{1}{1-e^{-j\omega}}.
\end{aligned} \tag{12.65}$$

Hence, the Fourier transform of the unit step is given by $u[n] \overset{F}{\leftrightarrow} \frac{1}{1-e^{-j\omega}} + \sum_{k=-\infty}^{+\infty} \pi\delta(\omega - 2\pi k)$.

From the Fourier Series to the Fourier Transform

Recall that a periodic signal of fundamental period N can be represented as a Fourier series as follows:

$$x[n] = \sum_{k=\langle N\rangle} a_k e^{jk\omega_0 n} = \sum_{k=\langle N\rangle} a_k e^{jk\frac{2\pi}{N}n}. \tag{12.66}$$

Using the DTFT formula and the above result, we obtain

$$\begin{aligned}
X(e^{j\omega}) &= \sum_{n=-\infty}^{\infty} \sum_{k=\langle N\rangle} a_k e^{jk\frac{2\pi}{N}n} e^{-j\omega n} \\
&= \sum_{k=\langle N\rangle} a_k \sum_{n=-\infty}^{\infty} e^{-j(\omega - k\frac{2\pi}{N})n} \\
&= \sum_{k=\langle N\rangle} 2\pi a_k \sum_{l=-\infty}^{\infty} \delta(\omega - k\frac{2\pi}{N} - 2\pi l) \\
&= \sum_{k=-\infty}^{\infty} 2\pi a_k \delta(\omega - k\frac{2\pi}{N}).
\end{aligned} \tag{12.67}$$

Thus, we can write the DTFT of a periodic signal by inspection from the knowledge of its Fourier series coefficients (recall that they are periodic).

Example 12.6: Let us find the DTFT of $x[n]=1+\sin(\frac{2\pi}{3}n)-\cos(\frac{2\pi}{7}n)$. We first have to determine whether this signal is periodic. The sine term repeats every three time steps, whereas the cosine term repeats every seven time steps. Thus, the signal is periodic of fundamental period $N=21$. Write

$$x[n]=1+\frac{1}{2j}\left(e^{j\frac{2\pi 7}{21}n}-e^{-j\frac{2\pi 7}{21}n}\right)-\frac{1}{2}\left(e^{j\frac{2\pi 3}{21}n}+e^{-j\frac{2\pi 3}{21}n}\right). \tag{12.68}$$

The nonzero DTFS coefficients of the signal are $a_0=1, a_{-7}=j\frac{1}{2}, a_7=-j\frac{1}{2}$, $a_{-3}=a_3=\frac{1}{2}$; hence we have

$$\begin{aligned}
X(e^{j\omega}) &= \sum_{k=-10}^{10} 2\pi a_k \sum_{l=-\infty}^{\infty}\delta(\omega-k\frac{2\pi}{21}-2\pi l)\\
&=1+\pi\sum_{l=-\infty}^{\infty}\delta(\omega+\frac{6\pi}{21}-2\pi l)+\pi\sum_{l=-\infty}^{\infty}\delta(\omega-\frac{6\pi}{21}-2\pi l)\\
&\quad+j\pi\sum_{l=-\infty}^{\infty}\delta(\omega+\frac{14\pi}{21}-2\pi l)-j\pi\sum_{l=-\infty}^{\infty}\delta(\omega-\frac{14\pi}{21}-2\pi l)\\
&=1+\sum_{l=-\infty}^{\infty}\left[\pi\delta(\omega+\frac{6\pi}{21}-2\pi l)+\pi\delta(\omega-\frac{6\pi}{21}-2\pi l)+j\pi\delta(\omega+\frac{14\pi}{21}-2\pi l)-j\pi\delta(\omega-\frac{14\pi}{21}-2\pi l)\right]
\end{aligned} \tag{12.69}$$

DTFT of a Periodic Discrete-Time Impulse Train

Let us now find the DTFT of the discrete-time impulse train $x[n]=\sum_{k=-\infty}^{\infty}\delta[n-kN]$. This signal is periodic of period N. Its DTFS coefficients are given by

$$a_k=\frac{1}{N}\sum_{n=0}^{N-1}x[n]e^{-jk\frac{2\pi}{N}n}=\frac{1}{N}\sum_{n=0}^{N-1}\delta[n]e^{-jk\frac{2\pi}{N}n}=\frac{1}{N}, \tag{12.70}$$

and hence, the DTFT of the impulse train is simply a train of impulses in the frequency domain, equally spaced by $\frac{2\pi}{N}$ radians.

$$\begin{aligned}
X(e^{j\omega}) &= \sum_{k=0}^{N-1}\frac{2\pi}{N}\sum_{l=-\infty}^{\infty}\delta(\omega-k\frac{2\pi}{N}-2\pi l)\\
&=\frac{2\pi}{N}\sum_{k=-\infty}^{\infty}\delta(\omega-k\frac{2\pi}{N})
\end{aligned} \tag{12.71}$$

This transform is shown in Figure 12.12.

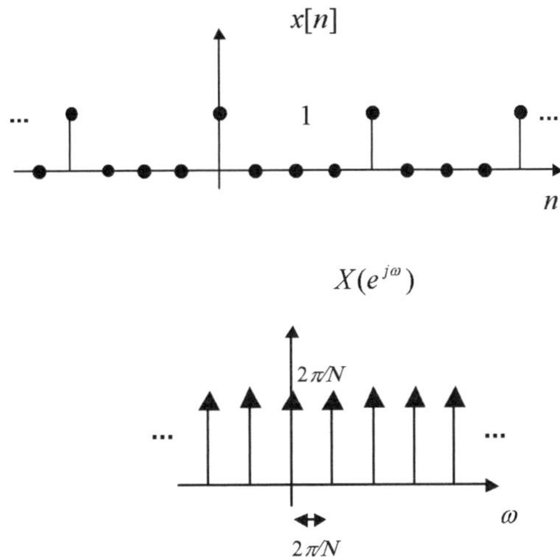

FIGURE 12.12 Impulse train and its Fourier transform.

DUALITY

There is an obvious duality between the analysis and synthesis equations of the discrete-time Fourier series. The Fourier series coefficients can be seen as a periodic signal, and the time-domain signal as the coefficients. Specifically, the spectral coefficients of the sequence a_k are $\frac{1}{N}\, x[-n]$. That is, we have

$$\underset{time}{x[n]} \overset{FS}{\leftrightarrow} \underset{freq}{a_k}, \tag{12.72}$$

$$\underset{time}{a_n} \overset{FS}{\leftrightarrow} \underset{freq}{\frac{1}{N} x[-k]}. \tag{12.73}$$

This duality can be useful in solving problems for which we are given, for example, a time-domain signal that has the form of a known spectral coefficient sequence whose corresponding periodic signal is also given. Properties of the DTFS also display this duality. For example, consider a time-shift and coefficient index shift (frequency shift):

$$x[n-n_0] \overset{FS}{\leftrightarrow} a_k e^{-j\frac{k2\pi}{N}n_0} \tag{12.74}$$

$$e^{jm\frac{2\pi}{N}n}x[n] \overset{FS}{\longleftrightarrow} a_{k-m}. \tag{12.75}$$

There is no such duality for the DTFT since it is continuous, whereas the signal is discrete.

SUMMARY

This chapter introduced Fourier analysis for discrete-time signals.

- Periodic discrete-time signals of fundamental period N have a Fourier series representation, where the series is a finite sum of N complex harmonics.
- Many aperiodic discrete-time signals have a Fourier transform representation, for instance the class of finite-energy signals. The discrete-time Fourier transform is typically a continuous function of frequency, and it is always periodic of period 2π radians.
- The inverse discrete-time Fourier transform is given by an integral over one period of 2π radians. If the DTFT is a rational function of $e^{j\omega}$, then a partial fraction expansion approach can be used to get the time-domain signal.
- The DTFT of a periodic discrete-time signal can be defined with the help of frequency-domain impulses.

TO PROBE FURTHER

For more details on Fourier analysis of discrete-time signals, see Oppenheim, Schafer and Buck, 1999.

EXERCISES

Exercises with Solutions

Exercises 12.1

Compute the Fourier series coefficients $\{a_k\}$ of the signal $x[n]$ shown in Figure 12.13. Sketch the magnitude and phase of the coefficients. Write $x[n]$ as a Fourier series.

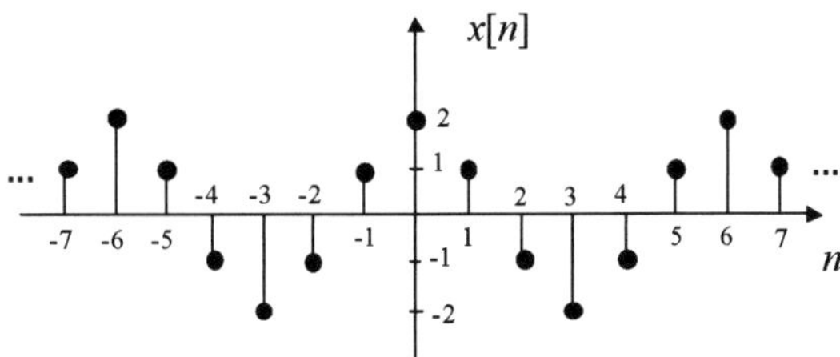

FIGURE 12.13 Periodic signal of Exercise 12.1.

Answer:

The fundamental period of this signal is $N = 6$ and its fundamental frequency is $\omega_0 = \frac{2\pi}{6}$. The DC component is $a_0 = 0$. The other coefficients are obtained using the analysis equation of the DTFS:

$$\begin{aligned}
a_k &= \frac{1}{6}\sum_{n=0}^{5} x[n]e^{-jk\frac{2\pi}{6}n} \\
&= \frac{1}{6}\left(2 + e^{-jk\frac{2\pi}{6}} - e^{-jk\frac{4\pi}{6}} - 2e^{-jk\frac{6\pi}{6}} - e^{-jk\frac{8\pi}{6}} + e^{-jk\frac{10\pi}{6}}\right) \\
&= \frac{1}{6}\left(2(1-(-1)^k) + e^{-jk\frac{\pi}{3}} - e^{-jk\frac{2\pi}{3}} - e^{-jk\frac{4\pi}{3}} + e^{-jk\frac{5\pi}{3}}\right) \\
&= \frac{1}{6}\left(2(1-(-1)^k) + (1-(-1)^k)e^{-jk\frac{\pi}{3}} - (1-(-1)^k)e^{-jk\frac{2\pi}{3}}\right) \\
&= \frac{(1-(-1)^k)}{6}\left(2 + e^{-jk\frac{\pi}{3}} - e^{-jk\frac{2\pi}{3}}\right).
\end{aligned}$$

Numerically,

$$a_0 = 0, a_1 = 1, a_2 = 0, a_3 = 0, a_4 = 0, a_5 = 1.$$

All coefficients are real, as the signal is real and even. The magnitude and phase of the spectrum are shown in Figure 12.14.

We can write the Fourier series of $x[n]$ as

$$x[n] = \sum_{k=0}^{5} a_k e^{jk\omega_0 n} = e^{j\frac{2\pi}{6}n} + e^{j\frac{2\pi}{6}5n}.$$

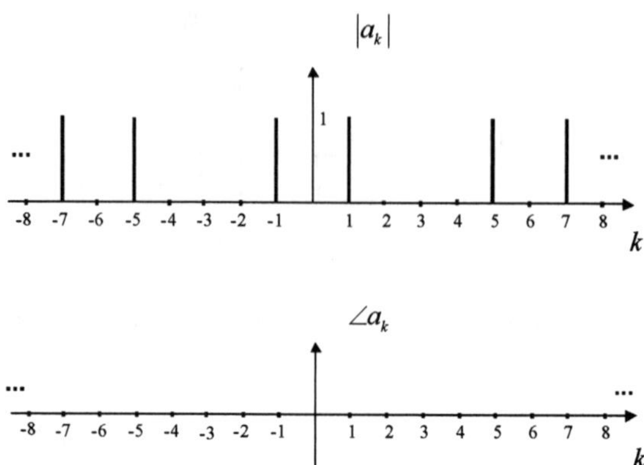

FIGURE 12.14 Magnitude and phase of DTFS of Exercise 12.1.

Exercise 12.2

(a) Compute the Fourier transform $X(e^{j\omega})$ of the signal $x[n]$ shown in Figure 12.15 and plot its magnitude and phase over the interval $\omega \in [-\pi, \pi]$.

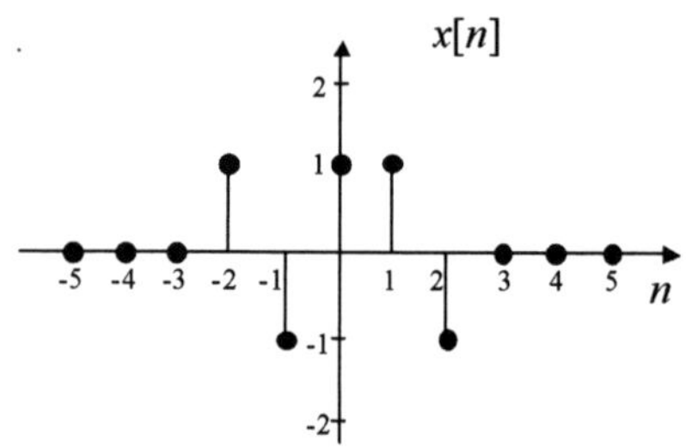

FIGURE 12.15 Signal of Exercise 12.2.

Answer:

$$
\begin{aligned}
X(e^{j\omega}) &= \sum_{n=-\infty}^{\infty} x[n]e^{-j\omega n} \\
&= e^{j\omega 2} - e^{j\omega} + 1 + e^{-j\omega} - e^{-j\omega 2} \\
&= 1 - 2j\sin\omega + 2j\sin 2\omega = 1 - 2j(\sin\omega - \sin 2\omega)
\end{aligned}
$$

The magnitude given below is shown in Figure 12.16 for $\omega \in [-\pi, \pi]$.

$$
\begin{aligned}
\left|X(e^{j\omega})\right| &= \sqrt{1 + 4\left[\sin\omega - \sin 2\omega\right]^2} \\
&= \sqrt{1 + 4\sin^2\omega - 8\sin(2\omega)\sin\omega + 4\sin^2(2\omega)}
\end{aligned}
$$

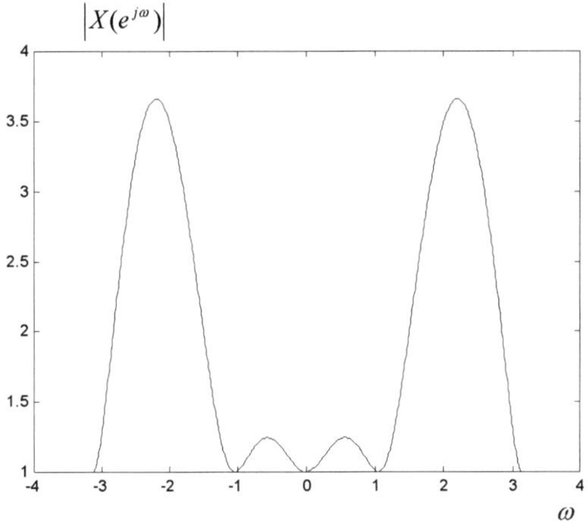

FIGURE 12.16 Magnitude of DTFT of Exercise 12.2.

The phase is given by

$$\angle X(e^{j\omega}) = \arctan\frac{2\sin(2\omega) - 2\sin\omega}{1}$$

and is plotted in Figure 12.17 for $\omega \in [-\pi, \pi]$.

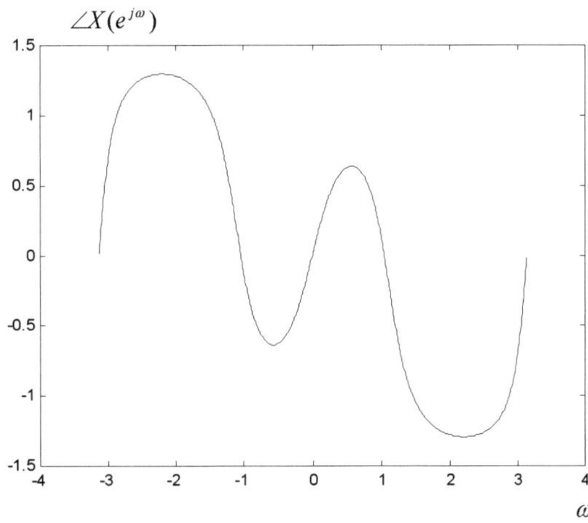

FIGURE 12.17 Phase of DTFT of Exercise 12.2.

Exercise 12.3

Compute the Fourier transforms $X(e^{j\omega})$ of the following discrete-time signals.

(a) $x[n]=[\alpha^n \sin(\omega_0 n)+\beta^n]u[n], \quad |\alpha|<1, |\beta|<1.$

Answer:

$$x[n]=\left[\frac{1}{2j}\alpha^n\left(e^{j\omega_0 n}-e^{-j\omega_0 n}\right)+\beta^n\right]u[n]$$
$$=\frac{1}{2j}(\alpha e^{j\omega_0})^n u[n]-\frac{1}{2j}(\alpha e^{-j\omega_0})^n u[n]+(\beta)^n u[n]$$

Using Table D.7, we obtain the DTFT:

$$X(e^{j\omega})=\frac{1}{2j}\left[\frac{1}{1-\alpha e^{-j(\omega-\omega_0)}}-\frac{1}{1-\alpha e^{-j(\omega+\omega_0)}}\right]+\frac{1}{1-\beta e^{-j\omega}}$$
$$=\frac{(-0.5j)(1-\alpha e^{-j(\omega+\omega_0)})+(0.5j)(1-\alpha e^{-j(\omega-\omega_0)})}{1-2\alpha\cos\omega_0 e^{-j\omega}+\alpha^2 e^{-j2\omega}}+\frac{1}{1-\beta e^{-j\omega}}$$
$$=\frac{-(0.5j)\alpha e^{-j(\omega+\omega_0)}+(0.5j)\alpha e^{-j(\omega-\omega_0)})}{1-2\alpha\cos\omega_0 e^{-j\omega}+\alpha^2 e^{-j2\omega}}+\frac{1}{1-\beta e^{-j\omega}}$$
$$=\frac{-\alpha\sin\omega_0 e^{-j\omega}}{1-2\alpha\cos\omega_0 e^{-j\omega}+\alpha^2 e^{-j2\omega}}+\frac{1}{1-\beta e^{-j\omega}}$$
$$=\frac{-\alpha\sin\omega_0 e^{-j\omega}(1-\beta e^{-j\omega})+1-2\alpha\cos\omega_0 e^{-j\omega}+\alpha^2 e^{-j2\omega}}{(1-2\alpha\cos\omega_0 e^{-j\omega}+\alpha^2 e^{-j2\omega})(1-\beta e^{-j\omega})}$$
$$=\frac{1-\alpha(\sin\omega_0+2\cos\omega_0)e^{-j\omega}+\alpha(\alpha+\beta\sin\omega_0)e^{-j2\omega}}{(1-2\alpha\cos\omega_0 e^{-j\omega}+\alpha^2 e^{-j2\omega})(1-\beta e^{-j\omega})}.$$

(b) $x[n]=(u[n+2]-u[n-3])*(u[n+2]-u[n-3])$, where * is the convolution operator.

Answer:

First consider the DTFT of the pulse signal $y[n]:=u[n+2]-u[n-3]$, which is

$$Y(e^{j\omega})=\frac{\sin(5/2\omega)}{\sin(\omega/2)}.$$

Now, $x[n] = y[n] * y[n]$, and hence,

$$X(e^{j\omega}) = Y(e^{j\omega})Y(e^{j\omega}) = \left[\frac{\sin(5/2\omega)}{\sin(\omega/2)}\right]^2$$

Exercises

Exercise 12.4

Given an LTI system with $h[n] = u[n]$ and an input $x[n] = (0.8)^n u[n]$, compute the DTFT of the output $Y(e^{j\omega})$ and its inverse DTFT $y[n]$.

Exercise 12.5

Consider the signal $x[n] = \cos(\frac{\pi}{5}n + 2)(j)^n$.

(a) Is this signal periodic? If the signal is periodic, what is its fundamental period?

(b) Compute the discrete-time Fourier series coefficients of $x[n]$.

Answer:

ON THE CD

Exercise 12.6

Compute the Fourier transforms $X(e^{j\omega})$ of the following signals:

(a) $x[n] = \alpha^n[\sin(\omega_0 n) + 2\cos(\omega_0 n)]u[n]$,

(b) $x[n] = (u[n+2] - u[n-3]) * \sum_{k=-\infty}^{+\infty} e^{j\pi k}\delta[n - 15k]$, where * is the convolution operator

Exercise 12.7

Compute the Fourier transform $H(e^{j\omega})$ of the impulse response $h[n]$ shown in Figure 12.18 and find its magnitude over the interval $\omega \in [-\pi, \pi]$.

Answer:

ON THE CD

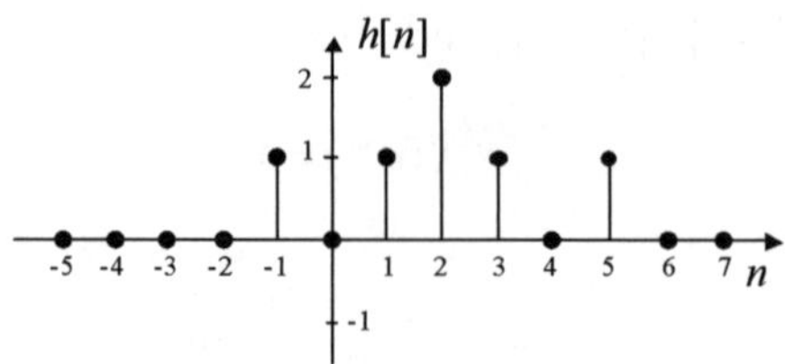

FIGURE 12.18 Signal in Exercise 12.7.

Exercise 12.8

Compute the Fourier transform $X(e^{j\omega})$ of the signal $x[n]$ shown in Figure 12.19 and sketch its magnitude and phase over the interval $\omega \in [-\pi, \pi]$.

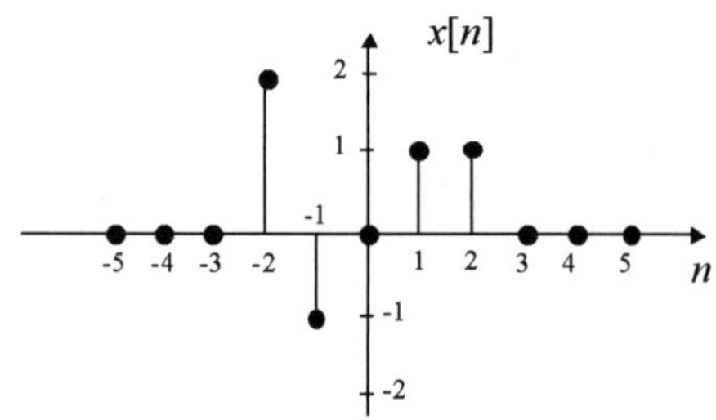

FIGURE 12.19 Signal in Exercise 12.8.

Exercise 12.9

Compute the Fourier series coefficients $\{a_k\}$ of the signal $x[n]$ shown in Figure 12.20. Sketch the magnitude and phase of the coefficients. Write $x[n]$ as a Fourier series.

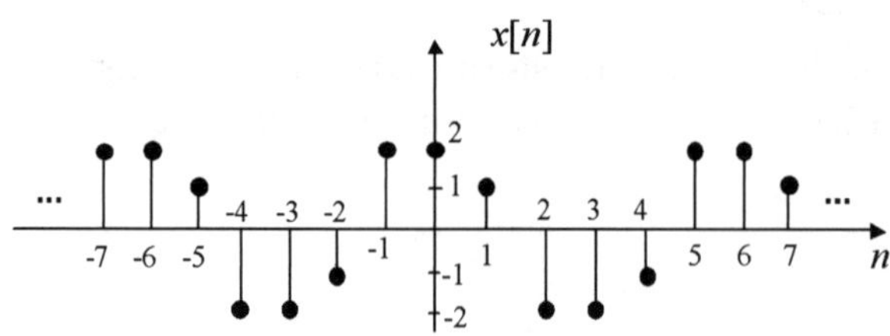

FIGURE 12.20 Periodic signal in Exercise 12.9.

Answer:

Exercise 12.10

Consider a DLTI system with impulse response $h[n]=(-0.4)^n u[n]-(0.5)^{n-2}u[n-2]$. Compute the output signal $y[n]$ for the input $x[n]=(0.2)^n u[n]$. Use the DTFT.

Exercise 12.11

Compute the Fourier transform $X(e^{j\omega})$ of the signal $x[n]=ne^{j\frac{\pi}{8}n}\alpha^{n-3}u[n-3]$, $|\alpha|<1$.

Answer:

13 The *z*-Transform

In This Chapter

((Lecture 47: Definition and Convergence of the z-Transform))

Recall that the Laplace transform was introduced as being a more general tool to represent continuous-time signals than the Fourier transform. For example, the latter could not be used for signals tending to infinity. In discrete time, the z-transform defined as a Laurent series plays the role of the Laplace transform in that it can be used to analyze signals going to infinity—as long as an appropriate region of convergence (ROC) is determined for the Laurent series. In this chapter, we will define the z-transform and study its properties. We will see that the z-transform of the impulse response of a discrete-time linear time-invariant (DLTI) system, called the transfer function, together with its region of convergence, completely define the system. In particular, the transfer function evaluated on the unit circle in the complex plane is nothing but the frequency response of the system.

DEVELOPMENT OF THE TWO-SIDED *Z*-TRANSFORM

The response of a DLTI system to a complex exponential input z^n is the same complex exponential, with only a change in (complex) amplitude: $z^n * h[n] = H(z)z^n$, as shown below. The complex amplitude factor is in general a function of the complex variable z.

$$\begin{aligned} y[n] &= \sum_{k=-\infty}^{+\infty} h[k]x[n-k] = \sum_{k=-\infty}^{+\infty} h[k]z^{n-k} \\ &= z^n \sum_{k=-\infty}^{+\infty} h[k]z^{-k} \\ &= H(z)z^n \end{aligned} \tag{13.1}$$

The system's response has the form $y[n] = H(z)z^n$, where $H(z) = \sum_{n=-\infty}^{+\infty} h[n]z^{-n}$, assuming that this infinite sum converges. The function $H(z)$ is called the *z-transform* of the impulse response of the system. The z-transform is also defined for a general discrete-time signal $x[n]$:

$$X(z) := \sum_{n=-\infty}^{+\infty} x[n]z^{-n}, \tag{13.2}$$

which in expanded form is seen to be a Laurent series:

$$X(z) = \ldots + x[-3]z^3 + x[-2]z^2 + x[-1]z^1 + x[0] + x[1]z^{-1} + x[2]z^{-2} + x[3]z^{-3} + \ldots. \tag{13.3}$$

Note that the discrete-time Fourier transform (DTFT) is a special case of the z-transform:

$$X(e^{j\omega}) = X(z)\Big|_{z=e^{j\omega}} = \sum_{n=-\infty}^{+\infty} x[n]e^{-j\omega n}. \tag{13.4}$$

In the z-plane, the DTFT is simply $X(z)$ evaluated on the unit circle, as depicted in Figure 13.1.

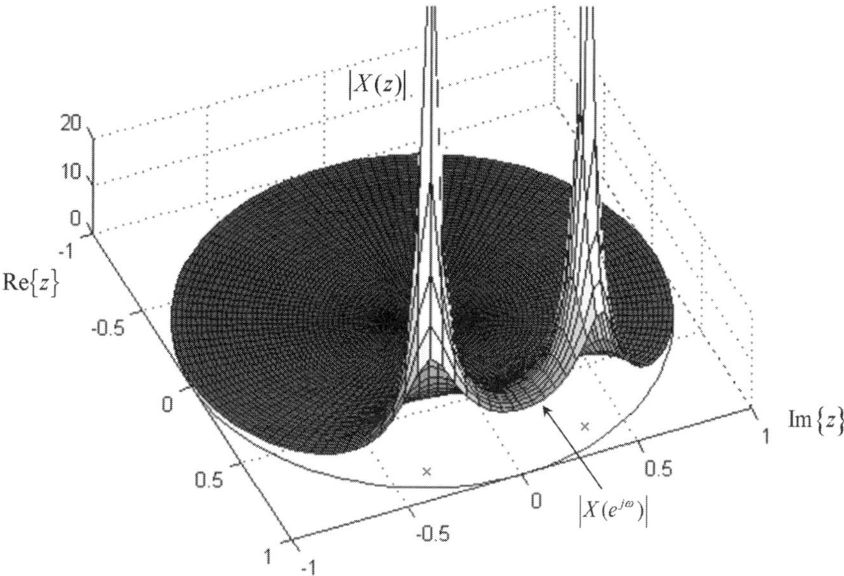

FIGURE 13.1 Relationship between the magnitudes of a z-transform and its corresponding Fourier transform.

Figure 13.1 was done with the MATLAB script zTFmagsurface.m, which is located on the companion CD-ROM in D:\Chapter13.

Analogously, the continuous-time Fourier transform is the Laplace transform evaluated on the $j\omega$-axis. Thus, the $j\omega$-axis of the s-plane in continuous time corresponds to the unit circle of the z-plane in discrete time.

Writing $z = re^{j\omega}$, we can analyze the convergence of the infinite summation in Equation 13.2:

$$X(re^{j\omega}) = \sum_{k=-\infty}^{+\infty} (x[k]r^{-k})e^{-j\omega k}. \tag{13.5}$$

We see that the convergence of the z-transform is equivalent to the convergence of the DTFT of the signal $x[n]r^{-n}$ for any given circle in the z-plane of radius r. That is,

$$X(re^{j\omega}) = \mathcal{F}\left\{x[n]r^{-n}\right\}. \tag{13.6}$$

Thus, the convergence of the z-transform will be described in terms of disk-shaped or annular regions of the z-plane centered at $z=0$. Note that the exponential weight r^{-n}, $r \ge 0$ multiplying the signal is either a constant-magnitude or decaying exponential ($r \ge 1$), or a growing exponential ($0 < r < 1$).

Example 13.1: The z-transform of the basic exponential signal $x[n] = a^n u[n]$, $a \in \mathbb{C}$ is computed as follows:

$$X(z) = \sum_{n=0}^{+\infty} a^n z^{-n} = \sum_{n=0}^{+\infty} (az^{-1})^n. \tag{13.7}$$

The ROC of this z-transform is the region in the complex plane where values of z guarantee that $|az^{-1}| < 1$, or equivalently $|z| > |a|$. Then

$$X(z) = \sum_{n=0}^{+\infty} (az^{-1})^n = \frac{1}{1-az^{-1}} = \frac{z}{z-a}, \quad |z| > |a|. \tag{13.8}$$

A special case is the unit step signal $u[n]$ ($a=1$), whose z-transform is

$$U(z) = \frac{1}{1-z^{-1}} = \frac{z}{z-1}, \quad |z| > 1. \tag{13.9}$$

Example 13.2: Consider the signal

$$x[n] = \left(\frac{1}{3}\right)^n u[n] + 2\left(\frac{1}{2}\right)^n u[-n-1]. \tag{13.10}$$

Its z-transform is computed as follows.

$$\begin{aligned} X(z) &= \sum_{n=-\infty}^{+\infty} \left[\left(\frac{1}{3}\right)^n u[n] + 2\left(\frac{1}{2}\right)^n u[-n-1] \right] z^{-n} \\ &= \sum_{n=0}^{+\infty} \left(\frac{1}{3}\right)^n z^{-n} + 2\sum_{n=-\infty}^{-1} \left(\frac{1}{2}\right)^n z^{-n} \\ &= \sum_{n=0}^{+\infty} \left(\frac{1}{3}\right)^n z^{-n} + 4z\sum_{n=0}^{+\infty} 2^n z^n \end{aligned}$$

$$= \underbrace{\frac{1}{1-\frac{1}{3}z^{-1}}}_{|z|>\frac{1}{3}} + \underbrace{\frac{4z}{1-2z}}_{|z|<\frac{1}{2}}$$

$$= \underbrace{\frac{z}{z-\frac{1}{3}}}_{|z|>\frac{1}{3}} + \underbrace{\frac{4z}{1-2z}}_{|z|<\frac{1}{2}}$$

$$= \frac{2z(z-\frac{1}{6})}{(z-\frac{1}{3})(1-2z)}, \quad \frac{1}{3} < |z| < \frac{1}{2} \tag{13.11}$$

The ROC of $X(z)$ can be displayed on a pole-zero plot as shown in Figure 13.2.

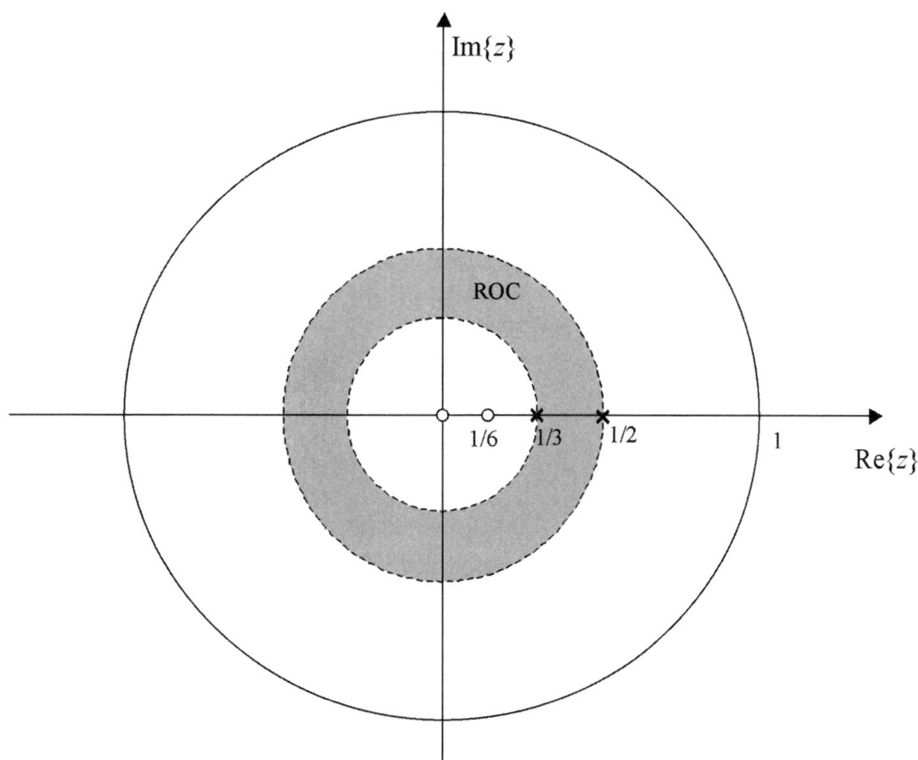

FIGURE 13.2 Pole-zero plot of a z-transform.

Note that a z-transform $X(z)$ is rational whenever the signal $x[n]$ is a linear combination of real or complex exponentials.

ROC OF THE Z-TRANSFORM

Similar to the ROC of the Laplace transform, the ROC of the z-transform has several properties that can help us find it. The ROC is the region of the z-plane ($z = re^{j\omega}$) where the signal $x[n]r^{-n}$ has a DTFT. That is, the ROC consists of values of z where the signal $x[n]r^{-n}$ is absolutely summable; that is, $\sum_{k=-\infty}^{+\infty} |x[k]| r^{-k} < \infty$. Convergence is dependent only on r, not on ω. Hence, if $X(z)$ exists at $z_0 = r_0 e^{j\omega_0}$, then it also converges on the circle $z = r_0 e^{j\omega}, 0 \le \omega \le 2\pi$. This guarantees that the ROC will be composed of concentric rings. It can be shown that it is a single ring. This ring can extend inward to zero, in which case it becomes a disk, or extend outward to infinity. However, it is often bounded by poles, and the boundary of the ring is open. We list some of the properties of ROCs of z-transforms.

- The ROC of $X(z)$ does not contain any poles.
- If $x[n]$ is of finite duration, then the ROC is the entire z-plane, except possibly $z = 0$ and $z = \infty$.

In this case, the finite sum of the z-transform converges for (almost) all z. The only two exceptions are $z = 0$ because of the negative powers of z and $z = \infty$ because of the positive powers of z in $X(z) = \sum_{n=n_1}^{n_2} x[n]z^{-n}$.

- If $x[n]$ is right-sided, then the ROC of $X(z)$ contains the exterior of a disk that either extends to $z = \infty$ in the case $x[n] = 0, n < 0$, or does not include $z = \infty$. If in addition, $X(z)$ is rational, then the ROC is the open exterior of a disk bounded by the farthest pole from the origin.
- If $x[n]$ is left-sided, then the ROC of $X(z)$ contains the interior of a disk that either includes $z = 0$ in the case $x[n] = 0, n > 0$ or does not include $z = 0$. If in addition, $X(z)$ is rational, then the ROC is the open disk bounded by the closest pole to the origin.
- If $x[n]$ is two-sided, then the ROC of $X(z)$ contains a ring with open boundaries in the z-plane. If in addition, $X(z)$ is rational, then the ROC is an open ring bounded by poles of $X(z)$.

Remarks:

- For a given pole-zero pattern, or equivalently, a rational $X(z)$, there are a limited number of ROCs that are consistent with the properties just described.
- The DTFT of a signal exists if the ROC of its z-transform includes the unit circle.

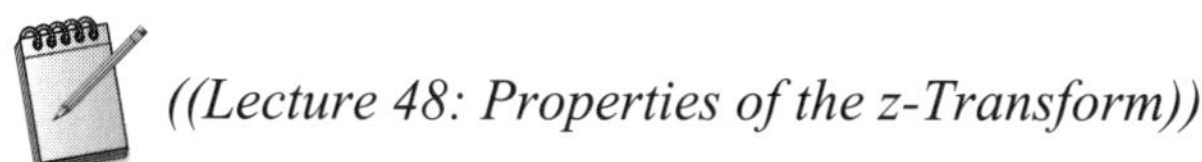

PROPERTIES OF THE TWO-SIDED Z-TRANSFORM

The notation $x[n] \overset{Z}{\leftrightarrow} X(z)$ is used to represent a z-transform pair. In this section, we discuss the main properties of the z-transform. These properties are summarized in Table D.11 in Appendix D.

Linearity

The operation of calculating the z-transform of a signal is linear.

For $x[n] \overset{Z}{\leftrightarrow} X(z), z \in \mathrm{ROC}_X$, $y[n] \overset{Z}{\leftrightarrow} Y(z), z \in \mathrm{ROC}_Y$; if we form the linear combination $z[n] = ax[n] + by[n]$, $a, b \in \mathbb{C}$, then we have

$$z[n] \overset{Z}{\leftrightarrow} aX(z) + bY(z), \ \mathrm{ROC} \supseteq \mathrm{ROC}_X \cap \mathrm{ROC}_Y. \tag{13.12}$$

Time Shifting

Time shifting leads to a multiplication by a complex exponential:

$$x[n-n_0] \overset{Z}{\leftrightarrow} z^{-n_0} X(z), \ \mathrm{ROC} = \mathrm{ROC}_X, \text{except possible addition/removal of 0 or } \infty. \tag{13.13}$$

Scaling in the z-Domain

$$z_0^{\,n} x[n] \overset{Z}{\leftrightarrow} X\left(\frac{z}{z_0}\right), \ \mathrm{ROC} = |z_0| \mathrm{ROC}_X, \tag{13.14}$$

where the ROC is the scaled version of ROC_X. Also, if $X(z)$ has a pole or zero at $z = a$, then $X(z/z_0)$ has a pole or zero at $z = z_0 a$. An important special case is when $z_0 = e^{j\omega_0}$. In this case $|z_0| \mathrm{ROC}_X = \mathrm{ROC}_X$, and

$$e^{j\omega_0 n} x[n] \overset{Z}{\leftrightarrow} X\left(e^{-j\omega_0} z\right). \tag{13.15}$$

This corresponds to a counterclockwise rotation by an angle of ω_0 radians of the pole-zero pattern of $X(z)$. On the unit circle (i.e., the DTFT), this rotation corresponds to a frequency shift.

Time Reversal

Reversing the time in signal $x[n]$ leads to

$$x[-n]\overset{Z}{\leftrightarrow} X(z^{-1}),\ \text{ROC}=\text{ROC}_X^{\ -1}; \tag{13.16}$$

that is, if $z\in \text{ROC}_X$, then $z^{-1}\in \text{ROC}$.

Upsampling

The upsampled signal

$$x_{\uparrow m}[n] := \begin{cases} x[n/m], & \text{if } n \text{ is a multiple of } m \\ 0, & \text{otherwise} \end{cases} \tag{13.17}$$

has a z-transform given by:

$$x_{\uparrow m}[n]\overset{Z}{\leftrightarrow} X(z^m),\ \text{ROC}=\text{ROC}_X^{1/m}. \tag{13.18}$$

That is, if $z_0\in \text{ROC}_X$, then $z_0^{1/m}=r_0^{1/m}e^{j(\frac{\omega_0}{m}+\frac{2\pi k}{m})}\in \text{ROC},\ k=0,\ldots,m-1$. Also, if $X(z)$ has a pole (or a zero) at $z_0=r_0e^{j\omega_0}$, then the z-transform of $x_{\uparrow m}[n]$ has m poles (or m zeros) at $z_0^{1/m}=r_0^{1/m}e^{j(\frac{\omega_0}{m}+\frac{2\pi k}{m})}$, $k=0,\ldots,m-1$. The upsampling property can be interpreted through the power series representation of the z-transform in Equation 13.18:

$$X(z^m)=\sum_{n=-\infty}^{+\infty} x[n]z^{-mn} = \sum_{n=\ldots,-2m,-m,0,m,2m,\ldots} x[n]z^{-n} = \sum_{n=-\infty}^{+\infty} x_{\uparrow m}[n]z^{-n}. \tag{13.19}$$

Differentiation in the *z*-Domain

Differentiation of the z-transform with respect to z yields

$$nx[n]\overset{Z}{\leftrightarrow} -z\frac{dX(z)}{dz},\ \text{ROC}=\text{ROC}_X. \tag{13.20}$$

Convolution of Two Signals

The convolution of $x[n]$ and $y[n]$ has a resulting z-transform given by

$$x[n]*y[n]=\sum_{m=-\infty}^{\infty} x[m]y[n-m]\overset{Z}{\leftrightarrow} X(z)Y(z),\ \text{ROC}\supseteq \text{ROC}_X\cap \text{ROC}_Y \tag{13.21}$$

Remark: The ROC can be larger than $\mathrm{ROC_X} \cap \mathrm{ROC_Y}$ if pole-zero cancellations occur when forming the product $X(z)Y(z)$.

First Difference

The first difference of a signal has the following z-transform:

$$x[n]-x[n-1]\overset{Z}{\leftrightarrow}(1-z^{-1})X(z),\ \mathrm{ROC}\supseteq\mathrm{ROC_X}\cap\left\{z\in\mathbb{C}:|z|>0\right\}. \quad (13.22)$$

Running Sum

The running sum, or accumulation, of a signal is the inverse of the first difference.

$$\sum_{m=-\infty}^{n} x[m]\overset{Z}{\leftrightarrow}\frac{1}{(1-z^{-1})}X(z),\ \mathrm{ROC}\supseteq\mathrm{ROC_X}\cap\{z\in\mathbb{C}:|z|>1\} \quad (13.23)$$

Conjugation

$$x^{*}[n]\overset{Z}{\leftrightarrow}X^{*}(z^{*}),\ \mathrm{ROC}=\mathrm{ROC_X}. \quad (13.24)$$

Remark: For $x[n]$ real, we have: $X(z)=X^{*}(z^{*})$. Thus, if $X(z)$ has a pole (or a zero) at $z=a$, it must also have a pole (or a zero) at $z=a^{*}$. That is, all complex poles and zeros come in conjugate pairs in the z-transform of a real signal.

Initial-Value Theorem

If $x[n]$ is a signal that starts at $n=0$, that is, $x[n]=0, n<0$, we have

$$x[0]=\lim_{z\to\infty}X(z). \quad (13.25)$$

This property follows from the power series representation of $X(z)$:

$$\lim_{z\to\infty}X(z)=\lim_{z\to\infty}\left(x[0]+x[1]z^{-1}+x[2]z^{-2}+\ldots\right)=x[0]. \quad (13.26)$$

Remark: For a transform $X(z)$ expressed as a ratio of polynomials in z, the order of its numerator cannot be greater than the order of its denominator for this property to apply, because then $x[n]$ would have at least one nonzero value at negative times.

Final-Value Theorem

If $x[n]$ is a signal that starts at $n = 0$, that is, $x[n] = 0, n < 0$, we have

$$\lim_{n\to\infty} x[n] = \lim_{z\to 1}\left(1 - z^{-1}\right)X(z). \tag{13.27}$$

This formula gives us the residue at the pole $z = 1$ (which corresponds to DC). If this residue is nonzero, then $X(z)$ has a nonzero final value.

((Lecture 49: The Inverse z-Transform))

THE INVERSE *Z*-TRANSFORM

The inverse z-transform is obtained by contour integration in the z-plane. This section presents a derivation of this result and discusses the use of the partial fraction expansion technique to invert a z-transform.

Contour Integral

Consider the z-transform $X(z)$ and let $z = re^{j\omega}$ be in its ROC. Then, we can write

$$X(re^{j\omega}) = \mathcal{F}\left\{x[n]r^{-n}\right\}, \tag{13.28}$$

where $\mathcal{F}\{\cdot\}$ denotes the operation of taking the Fourier transform. The inverse DTFT is then

$$x[n]r^{-n} = \mathcal{F}^{-1}\left\{X(re^{j\omega})\right\}, \tag{13.29}$$

and hence,

$$\begin{aligned} x[n] &= r^n \mathcal{F}^{-1}\left\{X(re^{j\omega})\right\} \\ &= \frac{r^n}{2\pi}\int_{2\pi} X(re^{j\omega})e^{j\omega n}\,d\omega \\ &= \frac{1}{2\pi}\int_{2\pi} X(re^{j\omega})(re^{j\omega})^n\,d\omega. \end{aligned} \tag{13.30}$$

From $z = re^{j\omega}$, we get

$$dz = \frac{dz}{d\omega} d\omega = \frac{d}{d\omega}\left(re^{j\omega}\right) d\omega = rje^{j\omega} d\omega$$

$$\Rightarrow d\omega = \frac{e^{-j\omega}}{jr} dz = \frac{z^{-1} dz}{j} \tag{13.31}$$

so that

$$\begin{aligned} x[n] &= \frac{1}{2\pi} \int_{2\pi} X(re^{j\omega})(re^{j\omega})^n d\omega \\ &= \frac{1}{2\pi j} \oint_{C} X(z) z^n z^{-1} dz \\ &= \frac{1}{2\pi j} \oint_{C} X(z) z^{n-1} dz, \end{aligned} \tag{13.32}$$

where the integral is evaluated counterclockwise around the closed circular contour $C := \left\{ z \in \mathbb{C} : |z| = r \right\}$ lying in the ROC (or any other circle centered at the origin in the ROC) in the z-plane. Thus, the inverse z-transform formula is

$$x[n] = \frac{1}{2\pi j} \oint_{C} X(z) z^{n-1} dz. \tag{13.33}$$

From the theory of complex functions, we find that this integral is equal to the sum of the residues at the poles of $X(z)z^{n-1}$ contained in the closed contour (this is the residue theorem). That is,

$$x[n] = \sum \text{Residues}\left\{ X(z) z^{n-1} \right\}. \tag{13.34}$$

Example 13.3: Suppose that we want to compute the inverse z-transform of $X(z) = \frac{z}{z-a}, |z| > |a|$. First, we form the product $X(z)z^{n-1} = \frac{z^n}{z-a}$. Then, we take the circle $|z| = |a| + \varepsilon, \varepsilon > 0$ as the closed contour in the ROC. The function has only one pole at $z = a$, and hence it has a single residue given by

$$\text{Res}_{z=a}\left\{ X(z) z^{n-1} \right\} = (z-a) X(z) z^{n-1}\Big|_{z=a} = a^n. \tag{13.35}$$

Now, because the ROC of $X(z)$ is the exterior of a disk (including infinity) of radius equal to the magnitude of the outermost pole, the corresponding signal must be right-sided and causal. Therefore the inverse z-transform of $X(z)$ is

$$x[n] = a^n u[n]. \tag{13.36}$$

Partial Fraction Expansion

An easier way to get the inverse z-transform is to expand $X(z)$ in partial fractions and use Table D.10 (Appendix D) of basic z-transform pairs. This technique is illustrated by two examples.

Example 13.4: Find the signal with z-transform

$$X(z)=\frac{z+z^{-1}}{(1+\tfrac{1}{2}z^{-1})(z-\tfrac{1}{3})},\quad \frac{1}{3}<|z|<\frac{1}{2}. \tag{13.37}$$

We first write $X(z)$ as a rational function of z in order to find the poles and zeros:

$$X(z)=\frac{z^2+1}{(z+\tfrac{1}{2})(z-\tfrac{1}{3})},\quad \frac{1}{3}<|z|<\frac{1}{2}. \tag{13.38}$$

It is clear that the poles are $p_1=-\frac{1}{2}$, $p_2=\frac{1}{3}$ and the zeros are $z_1=j, z_2=-j$. The pole-zero plot with the ROC is shown in Figure 13.3.

Noting that the transform in Equation 13.38 is a *biproper* rational function, that is, the numerator and denominator are of the same order, we write the partial fraction expansion of $X(z)$ as

$$X(z)=\frac{1+z^{-2}}{(1+\tfrac{1}{2}z^{-1})(1-\tfrac{1}{3}z^{-1})}=A+\underbrace{\frac{B}{1+\tfrac{1}{2}z^{-1}}}_{|z|<\frac{1}{2}}+\underbrace{\frac{C}{1-\tfrac{1}{3}z^{-1}}}_{|z|>\frac{1}{3}}, \tag{13.39}$$

where the ROCs of the individual terms are selected for consistency with the ROC $\frac{1}{3}<|z|<\frac{1}{2}$. Coefficients A, B, and C are computed as follows.

$$A=X(z)\big|_{z=0}=-6 \tag{13.40}$$

$$B=(1+\tfrac{1}{2}z^{-1})X(z)\big|_{z=-\frac{1}{2}}=\left.\frac{1+z^{-2}}{(1-\tfrac{1}{3}z^{-1})}\right|_{z=-\frac{1}{2}}=\frac{5}{(\frac{5}{3})}=3 \tag{13.41}$$

$$C=(1-\tfrac{1}{3}z^{-1})X(z)\big|_{z=\frac{1}{3}}=\left.\frac{1+z^{-2}}{(1+\tfrac{1}{2}z^{-1})}\right|_{z=\frac{1}{3}}=\frac{10}{(\frac{5}{2})}=4 \tag{13.42}$$

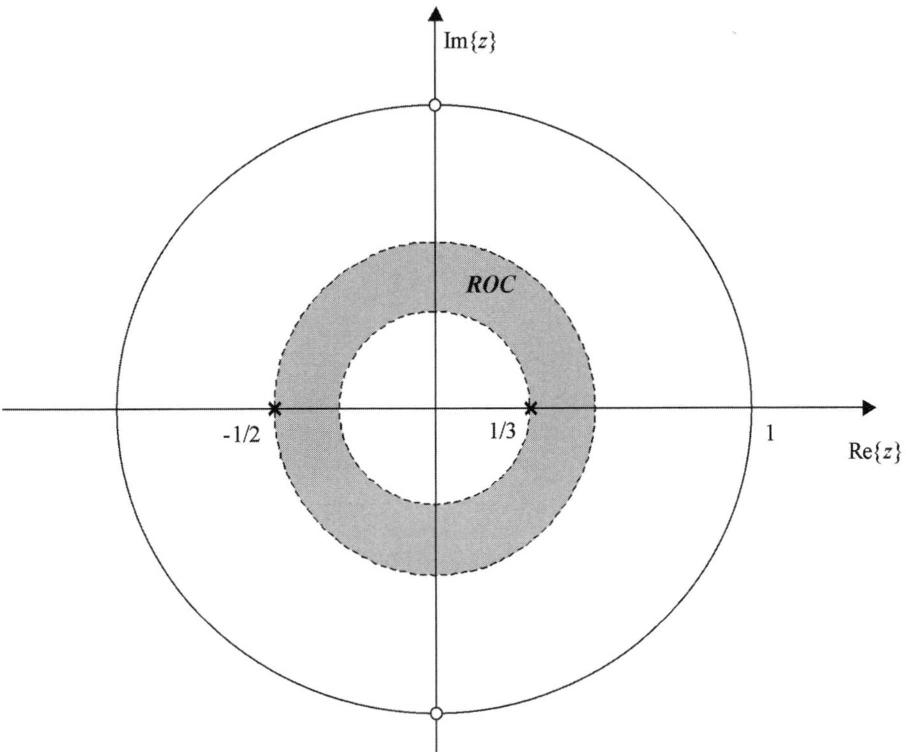

FIGURE 13.3 Pole-zero plot of a *z*-transform.

Thus,

$$X(z) = -6 + \underbrace{\frac{3}{1+\frac{1}{2}z^{-1}}}_{|z|<\frac{1}{2}} + \underbrace{\frac{4}{1-\frac{1}{3}z^{-1}}}_{|z|>\frac{1}{3}} \quad \overset{Z}{\leftrightarrow} \quad x[n] = -6\delta[n] - 3\left(-\frac{1}{2}\right)^n u[-n-1] + 4\left(\frac{1}{3}\right)^n u[n]. \quad (13.43)$$

Had the ROC of $X(z)$ been specified as $|z| > \frac{1}{2}$, then the inverse *z*-transform would have been

$$x[n] = -6\delta[n] + 3\left(-\frac{1}{2}\right)^n u[n] + 4\left(\frac{1}{3}\right)^n u[n]. \quad (13.44)$$

In the next example, the *z*-transform has a double pole.

Example 13.5: Find the signal with z-transform:

$$X(z)=\frac{z^{-1}+z^{-2}}{(1+\frac{1}{2}z^{-1})^2(1-\frac{1}{3}z^{-1})},\ |z|>\frac{1}{2}. \qquad (13.45)$$

We write $X(z)$ as a rational function of z in order to find the poles and zeros:

$$X(z)=\frac{z(z+1)}{(z+\frac{1}{2})^2(z-\frac{1}{3})},\ |z|>\frac{1}{2}. \qquad (13.46)$$

The poles are $p_1=-\frac{1}{2}$ (multiplicity $m = 2$), $p_2=\frac{1}{3}$ and the zeros are $z_1=0, z_2=-1$. The partial fraction expansion of $X(z)$ can be expressed as follows, where partial fractions of order 1 to $m = 2$ are included for the multiple pole:

$$X(z)=\frac{z^{-1}+z^{-2}}{(1+\frac{1}{2}z^{-1})^2(1-\frac{1}{3}z^{-1})}=\underbrace{\frac{A}{1+\frac{1}{2}z^{-1}}}_{|z|>\frac{1}{2}}+\underbrace{\frac{B}{(1+\frac{1}{2}z^{-1})^2}}_{|z|>\frac{1}{2}}+\underbrace{\frac{C}{1-\frac{1}{3}z^{-1}}}_{|z|>\frac{1}{3}}, \qquad (13.47)$$

where the ROCs of the individual terms are selected for consistency with the ROC $|z|>\frac{1}{2}$. Coefficients A, B, and C are computed as follows.

$$C=(1-\tfrac{1}{3}z^{-1})X(z)\Big|_{z=\frac{1}{3}}=\frac{z^{-1}+z^{-2}}{(1+\frac{1}{2}z^{-1})^2}\bigg|_{z=\frac{1}{3}}=\frac{3+9}{(\frac{5}{2})^2}=\frac{48}{25} \qquad (13.48)$$

$$B=(1+\tfrac{1}{2}z^{-1})^2X(z)\Big|_{z=-\frac{1}{2}}=\frac{z^{-1}+z^{-2}}{(1-\frac{1}{3}z^{-1})}\bigg|_{z=-\frac{1}{2}}=\frac{-2+4}{(\frac{5}{3})}=\frac{6}{5} \qquad (13.49)$$

$$\begin{aligned}A&=X(z)\Big|_{z\to\infty}-\frac{B}{(1+\frac{1}{2}z^{-1})^2}\bigg|_{z\to\infty}-\frac{C}{(1-\frac{1}{3}z^{-1})}\bigg|_{z\to\infty}\\&=0-B-C=-\frac{30}{25}-\frac{48}{25}=-\frac{78}{25}\end{aligned} \qquad (13.50)$$

Finally, the signal is obtained using Table D.10:

$$X(z)=-\underbrace{\frac{78}{25}\frac{1}{1+\frac{1}{2}z^{-1}}}_{|z|>\frac{1}{2}}+\underbrace{\frac{6}{5}\frac{1}{(1+\frac{1}{2}z^{-1})^2}}_{|z|>\frac{1}{2}}+\underbrace{\frac{48}{25}\frac{1}{1-\frac{1}{3}z^{-1}}}_{|z|>\frac{1}{3}}$$

$$\overset{Z}{\leftrightarrow}\ x[n]=-\frac{78}{25}\left(-\frac{1}{2}\right)^n u[n]+\frac{6}{5}(n+1)\left(-\frac{1}{2}\right)^n u[n]+\frac{48}{25}\left(\frac{1}{3}\right)^n u[n]. \qquad (13.51)$$

Power Series Expansion

The definition of the z-transform is a power series whose coefficients equal the signal values. Thus, given $X(z)$, we can expand it in a power series and directly identify the signal values to obtain the inverse z-transform.

Example 13.6: Usually the power series of a z-transform is infinite, and we can use long division to obtain the signal values. For example, consider $X(z)=\frac{1}{1-0.5z^{-1}}$, $|z|>0.5$. Long division yields

$$\begin{array}{r l} & 1+0.5z^{-1}+(0.5)^2z^{-2}+\ldots \\ 1-0.5z^{-1} \big) & 1 \\ & \underline{1-0.5z^{-1}} \\ & \quad 0.5z^{-1} \\ & \quad \underline{0.5z^{-1}-(0.5)^2z^{-2}} \\ & \qquad (0.5)^2z^{-2} \\ & \qquad \ddots \end{array} \tag{13.52}$$

Note that the resulting power series converges because the ROC implies $|0.5z^{-1}|<1$. Here, we can see a pattern, that is,

$$x[n]=1\delta[n]+0.5\delta[n-1]+(0.5)^2\delta[n-2]+\ldots+(0.5)^k\delta[n-k]+\ldots, \tag{13.53}$$

so that

$$x[n]=(0.5)^n u[n]. \tag{13.54}$$

Now suppose that the ROC is specified as the disk $|z|<0.5$ for the same z-transform. Then, $|(0.5)^{-1}z|<1$, and we can expand $X(z)=\frac{1}{1-0.5z^{-1}}=\frac{(0.5)^{-1}z}{-1+(0.5)^{-1}z}$ as a power series with positive powers of z by long division:

$$\begin{array}{r l} & -2z-2^2z^2-2^3z^3\ldots \\ -1+2z \big) & 2z \\ & \underline{2z-2^2z^2} \\ & \quad 2^2z^2 \\ & \quad \underline{2^2z^2-2^3z^3} \\ & \qquad 2^3z^3 \\ & \qquad \ddots \end{array} \tag{13.55}$$

Again, we can see a pattern:

$$x[n] = -2\delta[n+1] - 2^2\delta[n+2] - \ldots - 2^k\delta[n+k] - \ldots, \tag{13.56}$$

so that

$$x[n] = -2^{-n}u[-n-1] = -(0.5)^n u[-n-1]. \tag{13.57}$$

((Lecture 50: Transfer Function Characterization of DLTI Systems))

ANALYSIS AND CHARACTERIZATION OF DLTI SYSTEMS USING THE *Z*-TRANSFORM

Transfer Function Characterization of DLTI systems

Suppose we have the DLTI system in Figure 13.4.

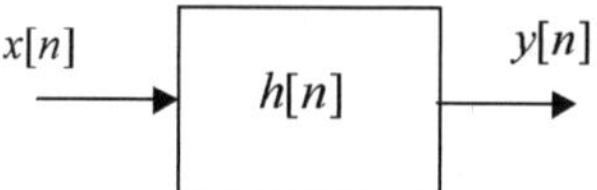

FIGURE 13.4 DLTI system.

The convolution property of the *z*-transform allows us to write

$$Y(z) = H(z)X(z),\ \ \mathrm{ROC} \supseteq \mathrm{ROC}_X \cap \mathrm{ROC}_H \tag{13.58}$$

so that we can find the response by computing the inverse *z*-transform of $Y(z)$:

$$y[n] = \mathcal{Z}^{-1}\{Y(z)\}. \tag{13.59}$$

The *z*-transform $H(z)$ of the impulse response $h[n]$ is called the *transfer function* of the DLTI system. The transfer function together with its ROC uniquely define the DLTI system. Properties of DLTI systems are associated with some characteristics of their transfer functions (poles, zeros, ROC.)

Causality

Recall that $h[n] = 0$ for $n < 0$ for a causal system, and thus the impulse response is right-sided. We have seen that the ROC of a right-sided signal is the exterior of a disk. If $z = \infty$ is also included in the ROC, then the signal is also causal because the power series expansion of $H(z)$ does not contain any positive powers of z. Therefore, *A DLTI system is causal if and only if the ROC of its transfer function $H(z)$ is the exterior of a circle including infinity.*

If the transfer function $H(z)$ is rational, then we can interpret this result as follows. *A DLTI system with a rational transfer function $H(z)$ is causal if and only if:*

1. *The ROC is the exterior of a circle of radius equal to the magnitude of the outermost pole, and*
2. *With $H(z)$ expressed as a ratio of polynomials in z, the order of the numerator is less than or equal to the order of the denominator.*

Stability

We have seen that the bounded-input bounded-output (BIBO) stability of a DLTI system is equivalent to its impulse response being absolutely summable, in which case its Fourier transform converges. This also implies that the ROC contains the unit circle. We have just shown necessity (the "only if" part) of the following result on stability: *A DLTI system is stable if and only if the ROC of its transfer function contains the unit circle.*

For a DLTI system with a *rational* and *causal* transfer function, the above stability condition translates into the following: *A causal DLTI system with rational transfer function $H(z)$ is stable if and only if all of its poles lie inside the unit circle.*

Remarks:

- A DLTI system can be stable without being causal.
- A DLTI system can be causal without being stable.

Example 13.7 Consider the transfer function of a third-order system with two complex poles at $p_1 = 0.9e^{j\frac{\pi}{4}}$, $p_2 = 0.9e^{-j\frac{\pi}{4}}$ and one real pole at $p_3 = -1.5$:

$$\begin{aligned} H(z) &= \frac{1}{(1-0.9e^{j\frac{\pi}{4}}z^{-1})(1-0.9e^{-j\frac{\pi}{4}}z^{-1})(1+1.5z^{-1})} \\ &= \frac{1}{(1-0.9\sqrt{2}z^{-1}+0.81z^{-2})(1+1.5z^{-1})}. \end{aligned} \tag{13.60}$$

This system can have three ROCs:

ROC 1: $\{z : |z| < 0.9\}$, corresponding to an anticausal and unstable system
ROC 2: $\{z : 0.9 < |z| < 1.5\}$, corresponding to a noncausal but stable system
ROC 3: $\{z : |z| > 1.5\}$, corresponding to a causal and unstable system

These ROCs are shown on the pole-zero plots in Figure 13.5.

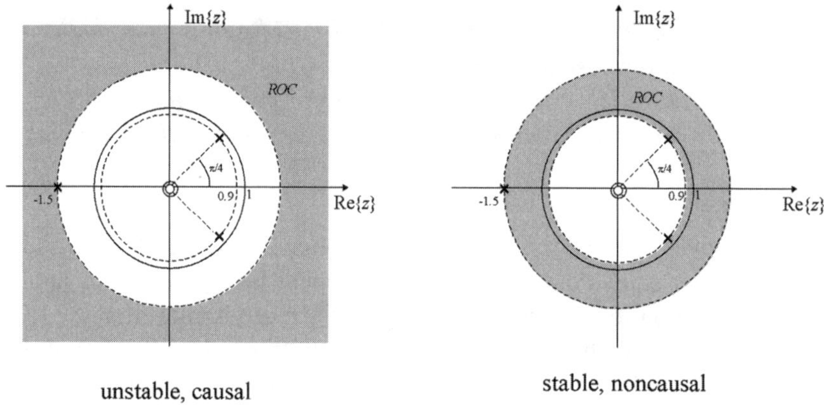

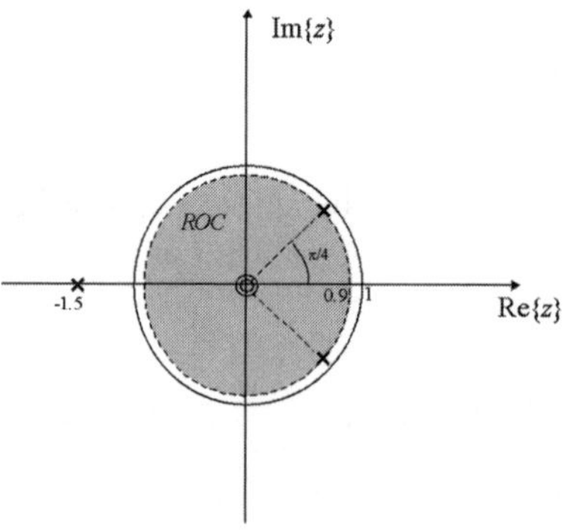

FIGURE 13.5 Possible ROCs of transfer function.

Transfer Function Algebra and Block Diagram Representations

Just like Laplace-domain transfer functions of continuous-time LTI systems can be interconnected to form more complex systems, we can interconnect transfer functions in the z-domain to form new DLTI systems. Transfer functions form an *algebra,* which means that the usual operations of addition, subtraction, division, and multiplication of transfer functions always result in new transfer functions.

Cascade Interconnection

A cascade interconnection of two DLTI systems, as shown in Figure 13.6, results in the product of their transfer functions:

$$Y(z) = H_2(z)H_1(z)X(z), \tag{13.61}$$

$$H(z) = H_2(z)H_1(z), \quad \mathrm{ROC} \supseteq \mathrm{ROC}_1 \cap \mathrm{ROC}_2. \tag{13.62}$$

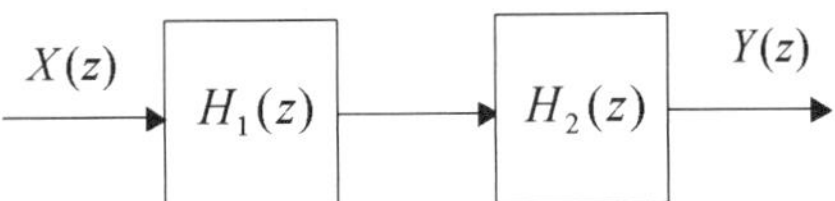

FIGURE 13.6 Cascade interconnection of transfer functions.

Parallel Interconnection

A parallel interconnection of two DLTI systems, as shown in Figure 13.7, results in the sum of their transfer functions:

$$Y(z) = [H_2(z) + H_1(z)]X(z), \tag{13.63}$$

$$H(z) = H_2(z) + H_1(z), \quad \mathrm{ROC} \supseteq \mathrm{ROC}_1 \cap \mathrm{ROC}_2. \tag{13.64}$$

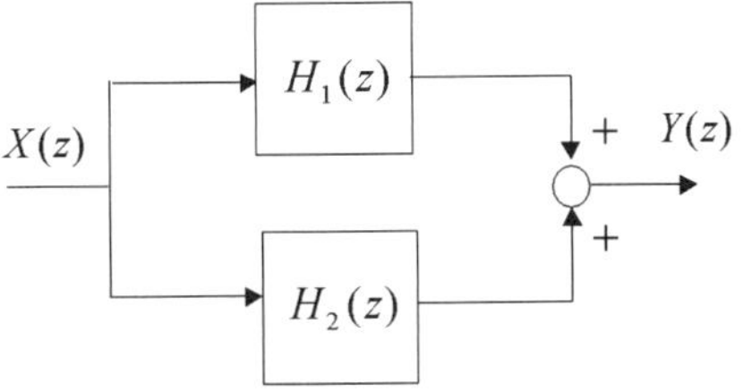

FIGURE 13.7 Parallel interconnection of transfer functions.

Feedback Interconnection

A feedback interconnection of two DLTI systems is depicted in the block diagram in Figure 13.8. Feedback systems are causal, but their poles are usually different from the poles of $H_1(z)$ and $H_2(z)$, so they have to be computed on a case-by-case basis. The ROC of the closed-loop transfer function $H(z)$ can be determined afterwards as the exterior of a disk of radius equal to the magnitude of the farthest pole from the origin.

$$\begin{aligned} E(z) &= X(z) - H_2(z)Y(z) \\ Y(z) &= H_1(z)E(z) \end{aligned} \tag{13.65}$$

$$\begin{aligned} E(z) &= X(z) - H_2(z)H_1(z)E(z) \\ E(z) &= \frac{1}{1+H_1(z)H_2(z)}X(z) \\ Y(z) &= \underbrace{\frac{H_1(z)}{1+H_1(z)H_2(z)}}_{H(z)}X(z) \end{aligned} \tag{13.66}$$

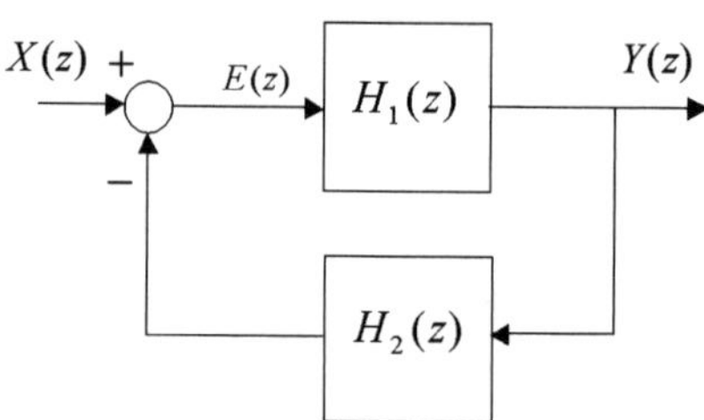

FIGURE 13.8 Feedback interconnection of transfer functions.

((Lecture 51: LTI Difference Systems and Rational Transfer Functions))

Transfer Function Characterization of LTI Difference Systems

For systems characterized by linear constant-coefficient difference equations, the z-transform provides an easy way to obtain the transfer function, the Fourier transform, and the time-domain system response to a specific input.

Consider the Nth-order difference equation:

$$\sum_{k=0}^{N} a_k y[n-k] = \sum_{k=0}^{M} b_k x[n-k], \tag{13.67}$$

which can be expanded into

$$a_0 y[n] + a_1 y[n-1] + \cdots + a_N y[n-N] = b_0 x[n] + b_1 x[n-1] + \cdots + b_M x[n-M]. \tag{13.68}$$

Using the time-shifting property of the z-transform, we directly obtain the z-transform on both sides of this equation:

$$\sum_{k=0}^{N} a_k z^{-k} Y(z) = \sum_{k=0}^{M} b_k z^{-k} X(z) \tag{13.69}$$

or

$$(a_0 + a_1 z^{-1} + \cdots + a_N z^{-N}) Y(z) = (b_0 + b_1 z^{-1} + \cdots + b_M z^{-M}) X(z). \tag{13.70}$$

The transfer function is then given by the z-transform of the output divided by the z-transform of the input:

$$H(z) = \frac{Y(z)}{X(z)} = \frac{b_0 + b_1 z^{-1} + \cdots + b_M z^{-M}}{a_0 + a_1 z^{-1} + \cdots + a_N z^{-N}}. \tag{13.71}$$

Hence, the transfer function of an LTI difference system is always rational. If the difference equation is causal, which is the case in real-time signal processing, then the region of convergence of the transfer function will be the open exterior of a disk of radius equal to the magnitude of the farthest pole from the origin. The region of convergence of a transfer function obtained by taking the ratio of transforms of specific input and output signals must be consistent with the ROCs of $Y(z)$ and $X(z)$. Specifically, it must satisfy $\mathrm{ROC}_Y \supseteq \mathrm{ROC}_X \cap \mathrm{ROC}_H$. If the rational transfer function is given without an ROC, then knowledge of system properties such as causality or stability can help us find it.

Example 13.8: Consider a DLTI system defined by the difference equation

$$y[n] + \frac{1}{3} y[n-1] = 2x[n-1]. \tag{13.72}$$

Taking the z-transform, we get

$$Y(z) + \frac{1}{3} z^{-1} Y(z) = 2z^{-1} X(z), \tag{13.73}$$

which yields the transfer function:

$$H(z) = \frac{2z^{-1}}{1+\frac{1}{3}z^{-1}}. \tag{13.74}$$

This provides the algebraic expression for $H(z)$, but not the ROC. There are two impulse responses that are consistent with the difference equation.

A right-sided impulse response corresponds to the ROC $|z| > \frac{1}{3}$. Using the time-shifting property, we get

$$h[n] = 2\left(-\frac{1}{3}\right)^{n-1} u[n-1]. \tag{13.75}$$

In this case the system is causal and stable.

A left-sided impulse response corresponds to the ROC $|z| < \frac{1}{3}$. Using the time-shifting property again, we get

$$h[n] = -2\left(-\frac{1}{3}\right)^{n-1} u[-n]. \tag{13.76}$$

This case leads to an unstable, anticausal system. It is hard to imagine the effect of an anticausal system on an input signal, especially if we think of the difference equation as being implemented as a filter in a real-time signal processing system (more on this in Chapter 15). When the constraint of real time is not an issue, such as in off-line image processing or time-series analysis, then one can define the time $n = 0$ at will, time reverse a signal stored in a vector in a computer without any consequence, use anticausal systems, etc.

Block Diagram Realization of a Rational Transfer Function

It is possible to obtain a realization of the transfer function of a DLTI difference system as a combination of three basic elements: the gain, the summing junction, and the unit delay. These elements are shown in Figure 13.9.

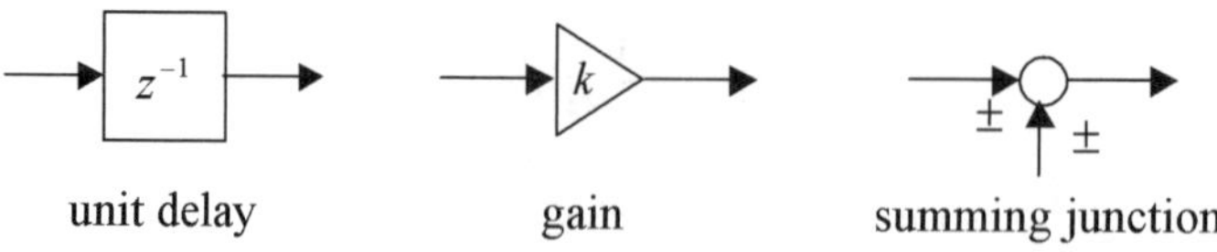

FIGURE 13.9 Three basic elements used to realize any transfer function.

Simple First-Order Transfer Function

Consider the transfer function $H(z)=\frac{1}{1-az^{-1}}$, which corresponds to the first-order difference equation

$$y[n]=ay[n-1]+x[n]. \tag{13.77}$$

It can be realized by a feedback interconnection of the three basic elements as shown in Figure 13.10.

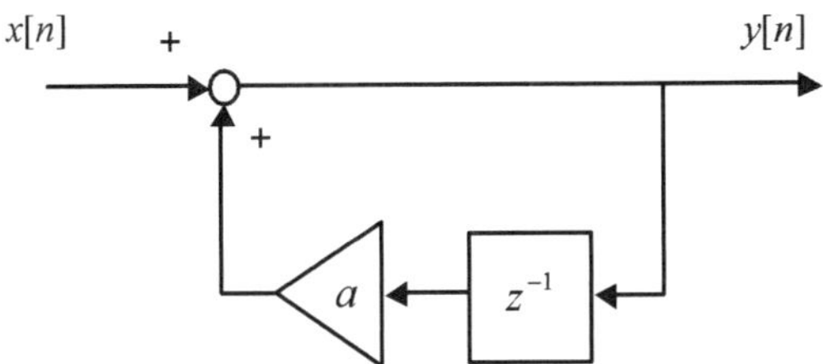

FIGURE 13.10 Realization of a first-order transfer function.

With this block diagram, we can realize any transfer function of any order in parallel form after it is written as a partial fraction expansion.

Simple Second-Order Transfer Function

Consider the transfer function $H(z)=\frac{1}{1+a_1z^{-1}+a_2z^{-2}}$. It can be realized with a feedback interconnection of the three basic elements in a number of ways. One way is to expand the transfer function as a sum of two first-order transfer functions (partial fraction expansion). The resulting form is called the *parallel form*, which is a parallel interconnection of the two first-order transfer functions. Another way is to break up the transfer function as a cascade (multiplication) of two first-order transfer functions. Yet another way to realize the second-order transfer function is the so-called *direct form* or *controllable canonical form*. To derive this form, consider the system equation

$$Y(z)=-a_1z^{-1}Y(z)-a_2z^{-2}Y(z)+X(z). \tag{13.78}$$

This equation can be realized as in Figure 13.11 with two unit delays.

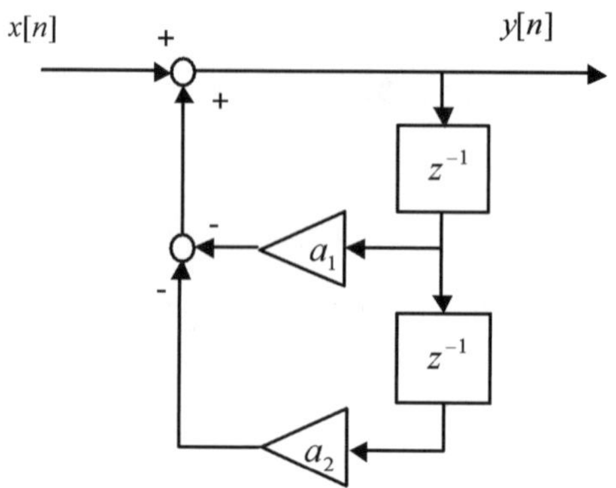

FIGURE 13.11 Realization of a second-order transfer function.

Direct Form (Controllable Canonical Form)

A direct form can be obtained by breaking up the general transfer function in Equation 13.79 into two subsystems as shown in Figure 13.12.

$$H(z)=\frac{Y(z)}{X(z)}=\frac{b_0+b_1z^{-1}+\cdots+b_Mz^{-M}}{a_0+a_1z^{-1}+\cdots+a_Nz^{-N}} \tag{13.79}$$

Assume without loss of generality that $a_0 = 1$ (if not, just divide all b_i's by a_0.)

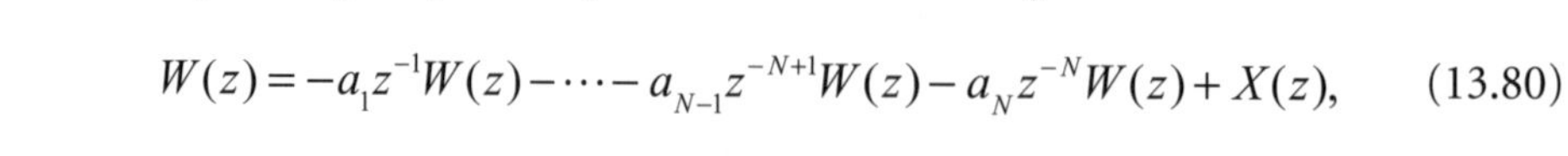

$X(z)$ → $\boxed{\dfrac{1}{1+a_1z^{-1}+\cdots+a_{N-1}z^{-N+1}+a_Nz^{-N}}}$ → $W(z)$ → $\boxed{b_0+b_1z^{-1}+\cdots+b_{M-1}z^{-M+1}+b_Mz^{-M}}$ → $Y(z)$

FIGURE 13.12 Transfer function as a cascade of two DLTI subsystems.

The input-output system equation of the first subsystem is

$$W(z)=-a_1z^{-1}W(z)-\cdots-a_{N-1}z^{-N+1}W(z)-a_Nz^{-N}W(z)+X(z), \tag{13.80}$$

and for the second subsystem, we have

$$Y(z)=b_0W(z)+b_1z^{-1}W(z)+\cdots+b_{M-1}z^{-M+1}W(z)+b_Mz^{-M}W(z). \tag{13.81}$$

The direct form realization is then as shown in Figure 13.13 for a second-order system.

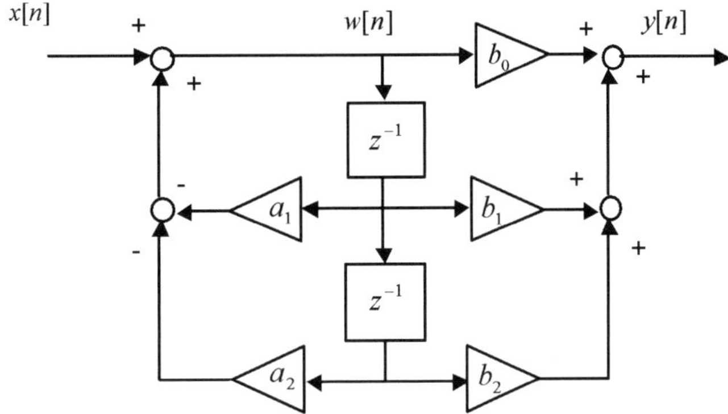

FIGURE 13.13 Direct form realization of a second-order system.

((Lecture 52:The Unilateral z-Transform))

THE UNILATERAL *Z*-TRANSFORM

Recall from Chapter 7 that the unilateral Laplace transform was used for the causal part of continuous-time signals and systems. We now study the analogous unilateral z-transform defined for the causal part of discrete-time signals and systems.

The unilateral z-transform of a sequence $x[n]$ is defined as

$$\mathcal{X}(z) := \sum_{n=0}^{+\infty} x[n]z^{-n}, \tag{13.82}$$

and the signal/transform pair is denoted as $x[n] \overset{UZ}{\longleftrightarrow} \mathcal{X}(z) = \mathcal{UZ}\{x[n]\}$.

The series in Equation 13.82 only has negative powers of z since the summation runs over nonnegative times. One implication is that

$$\mathcal{UZ}\{x[n]\} = \mathcal{UZ}\{x[n]u[n]\}. \tag{13.83}$$

Another implication is that *the ROC of a unilateral z-transform is always the exterior of a circle.*

Example 13.9: Consider the step signal starting at time $n = -2$:

$$x[n] = u[n+2]. \tag{13.84}$$

The bilateral z-transform of $x[n]$ is obtained by using the time-shifting property:

$$X(z) = \frac{z^2}{1-z^{-1}} = \frac{z^3}{z-1}, \quad |z| > 1,\ z \neq \infty. \tag{13.85}$$

The unilateral z-transform of $x[n]$ is computed as

$$\begin{aligned}\mathcal{X}(z) &= \sum_{n=0}^{+\infty} z^{-n} \\ &= \frac{1}{1-z^{-1}} = \frac{z}{z-1}, \quad |z| > 1.\end{aligned} \tag{13.86}$$

Thus, in this case, the two z-transforms are different.

Inverse Unilateral *z*-Transform

The inverse unilateral z-transform can be obtained by performing a partial fraction expansion, selecting all the ROCs of the individual first-order fractions to be exteriors of disks. The power series expansion technique using long division can be used as well. The series must be in negative powers of z.

Properties of the Unilateral *z*-Transform Differing from Those of the Bilateral *z*-Transform

The properties of the bilateral z-transform apply to the unilateral z-transform, except the ones listed below. Consider the unilateral z-transform pair $x[n] \overset{UZ}{\leftrightarrow} \mathcal{X}(z)$ in the following.

Time Delay

$$x[n-1] \overset{UZ}{\leftrightarrow} z^{-1}\mathcal{X}(z) + x[-1], \quad \text{ROC} = \text{ROC}_X, \text{except possible addition of } 0 \tag{13.87}$$

The value $x[-1]$ originally at time $n = -1$ "reappears" at $n = 0$, within the summation interval of the unilateral z-transform, after the shift by one time step to the right. The result is the power series

$$z^{-1}\mathcal{X}(z) + x[-1] = x[-1] + x[0]z^{-1} + x[1]z^{-2} + x[2]z^{-3} + \cdots \tag{13.88}$$

Time Advance

$$x[n+1] \overset{UZ}{\leftrightarrow} z\mathcal{X}(z) - zx[0], \quad \text{ROC} = \text{ROC}_X, \text{except possible removal of } 0 \tag{13.89}$$

After a time advance, the first value of the signal $x[0]$ is shifted to the left, outside of the interval of the unilateral z-transform. The resulting power series is

$$z\mathcal{X}(z) - zx[0] = x[1] + x[2]z^{-1} + x[3]z^{-2} + \cdots. \tag{13.90}$$

Convolution

For signals that are nonzero only for $n \geq 0$, $x_1[n] \overset{UZ}{\leftrightarrow} \mathcal{X}_1(z)$, and $x_2[n] \overset{UZ}{\leftrightarrow} \mathcal{X}_2(z)$, we have the familiar result

$$x_1[n] * x_2[n] \overset{UZ}{\leftrightarrow} \mathcal{X}_1(z)\mathcal{X}_2(z), \qquad \text{ROC} \supseteq \text{ROC}_1 \cap \text{ROC}_2. \tag{13.91}$$

Note that the resulting signal will also be causal since

$$\begin{aligned} y[n] &= x_1[n] * x_2[n] \\ &= \sum_{m=-\infty}^{+\infty} x_1[m]x_2[n-m] \\ &= \sum_{m=-\infty}^{+\infty} x_1[m]u[m]x_2[n-m]u[n-m] \\ &= \sum_{m=0}^{n} x_1[m]x_2[n-m] \end{aligned} \tag{13.92}$$

and the last sum is equal to 0 for $n < 0$.

Solution of Difference Equations with Initial Conditions

The main use of the unilateral z-transform is for solving difference equations with nonzero initial conditions. The time delay property can be used recursively to show that

$$x[n-m] \overset{UZ}{\leftrightarrow} z^{-m}\mathcal{X}(z) + z^{-m+1}x[-1] + \cdots + z^{-1}x[-m+1] + x[-m]. \tag{13.93}$$

Thus, we can deal with the initial conditions of a difference system by using the unilateral z-transform.

Example 13.10: Consider the causal difference equation

$$y[n] - 0.8y[n-1] = 2x[n], \tag{13.94}$$

where the input signal is $x[n] = (0.5)^n u[n]$ and the initial condition is $y[-1] = y_{-1}$.

Taking the unilateral z-transform on both sides of Equation 13.94, we obtain

$$\begin{aligned}\mathcal{Y}(z)-0.8z^{-1}\mathcal{Y}(z)-0.8y[-1]&=2\mathcal{X}(z)\\(1-0.8z^{-1})\mathcal{Y}(z)-0.8y_{-1}&=\frac{2}{1-0.5z^{-1}},\end{aligned}\tag{13.95}$$

which yields

$$\mathcal{Y}(z)=\frac{0.8y_{-1}}{(1-0.8z^{-1})}+\frac{2}{(1-0.8z^{-1})(1-0.5z^{-1})},\quad |z|>0.8.\tag{13.96}$$

The first term on the right-hand side is nonzero if and only if the initial condition is nonzero. It is called the *zero-input response* of the system for the obvious reason that if the input is 0, then the output depends only on the initial condition.

The second term on the right-hand side of Equation 13.96 is the response of the system when the initial condition is zero ($y_{-1}=0$). It is called the *zero-state response* (we will study the notion of the *discrete-time state* in Chapter 17). Here, we need to expand the zero-state response in partial fractions:

$$\frac{2}{(1-0.8z^{-1})(1-0.5z^{-1})}=\frac{1.23}{1-0.8z^{-1}}+\frac{0.77}{1-0.5z^{-1}}.\tag{13.97}$$

Finally, the unilateral z-transform of the system is given by

$$\mathcal{Y}(z)=\underbrace{\frac{0.8y_{-1}+1.23}{1-0.8z^{-1}}}_{|z|>0.8}+\underbrace{\frac{0.77}{1-0.5z^{-1}}}_{|z|>0.5},\tag{13.98}$$

and its corresponding time-domain signal is

$$y[n]=(0.8y_{-1}+1.23)(0.8)^{n}u[n]+0.77(0.5)^{n}u[n].\tag{13.99}$$

SUMMARY

In this chapter, we introduced the z-transform for discrete-time signals.

- The bilateral z-transform was defined as a Laurent series whose coefficients are the signal values. It is a generalization of the discrete-time Fourier transform that applies to a larger class of signals. Every z-transform has an associated region of convergence, and together they uniquely define a time-domain signal.

- The DTFT of a signal is simply equal to its z-transform evaluated on the unit circle, provided the latter is contained in the ROC.
- The inverse z-transform is given by a contour integral, but in most cases it is easier to expand the transform in partial fractions and use Table D.10 of basic z-transform pairs to obtain the signal. A power series expansion approach can also be used to obtain the signal in simple cases.
- Discrete-time LTI systems were studied using the z-transform. It was shown that the z-transform of the impulse response, that is, the transfer function and its ROC, completely characterize a system.
- Difference systems were shown to have rational transfer functions. These can be realized through an interconnection of three basic elements: the gain, the summing junction, and the unit delay.
- The unilateral z-transform considers only the portion of discrete-time signals at nonnegative times. Its time-delay property makes it useful in the solution of causal difference equations with initial conditions.

TO PROBE FURTHER

For a detailed coverage of the z-transform, see Oppenheim, Schafer and Buck, 1999 and Proakis and Manolakis, 1995.

EXERCISES

Exercises with Solutions

Exercise 13.1

Sketch the pole-zero plot and compute the impulse response $h[n]$ of the system with transfer function

$$H(z)=\frac{z(1-0.8z^{-1})}{(z^2-0.8z+0.64)(1+2z^{-1})}$$

and with ROC: $0.8<|z|<2$. Specify whether or not the system is causal and stable.

Answer:

$$H(z)=\frac{z(z-0.8)}{(z^2-0.8z+0.64)(z+2)}=\frac{z^{-1}(1-0.8z^{-1})}{(1-0.8e^{j\frac{\pi}{3}}z^{-1})(1-0.8e^{-j\frac{\pi}{3}}z^{-1})(1+2z^{-1})},\quad 0.8<|z|<2$$

$$=\underbrace{\frac{A}{(1-0.8e^{j\frac{\pi}{3}}z^{-1})}}_{|z|>0.8}+\underbrace{\frac{A^*}{(1-0.8e^{-j\frac{\pi}{3}}z^{-1})}}_{|z|>0.8}+\underbrace{\frac{C}{(1+2z^{-1})}}_{|z|<2}$$

The coefficients are given by

$$A=\left.\frac{z^{-1}(1-0.8z^{-1})}{(1-0.8e^{-j\frac{\pi}{3}}z^{-1})(1+2z^{-1})}\right|_{z=0.8e^{j\frac{\pi}{3}}}=\frac{1.25e^{-j\frac{\pi}{3}}(1-e^{-j\frac{\pi}{3}})}{(1-e^{-j\frac{2\pi}{3}})(1+2.5e^{-j\frac{\pi}{3}})}=\frac{1.25e^{-j\frac{\pi}{3}}(1-e^{-j\frac{\pi}{3}})}{(3.5-e^{-j\frac{2\pi}{3}}+2.5e^{-j\frac{\pi}{3}})}=$$

$$=\frac{1.25\left(\frac{1}{2}-j\frac{\sqrt{3}}{2}-(-\frac{1}{2}-j\frac{\sqrt{3}}{2})\right)}{(5.25-1.5j\frac{\sqrt{3}}{2})}=\frac{\frac{5}{4}}{\frac{1}{4}(21-j3\sqrt{3})}=\frac{5(21+j3\sqrt{3})}{468}=0.224+0.0555j$$

$$C=\left.\frac{z^{-1}(1-0.8z^{-1})}{(1-0.8e^{j\frac{\pi}{3}}z^{-1})(1-0.8e^{-j\frac{\pi}{3}}z^{-1})}\right|_{z=-2}=\frac{-0.7}{(1+0.4+0.16)}=-0.449$$

Thus,

$$H(z)=\underbrace{\frac{0.224+0.0555j}{(1-0.8e^{j\frac{\pi}{3}}z^{-1})}}_{|z|>0.8}+\underbrace{\frac{0.224-0.0555j}{(1-0.8e^{-j\frac{\pi}{3}}z^{-1})}}_{|z|>0.8}-\underbrace{\frac{0.449}{(1+2z^{-1})}}_{|z|<2}$$

The inverse z-transform is obtained using Table D.10:

$$h[n]=(0.22+j0.056)\left(0.8e^{j\frac{\pi}{3}}\right)^n u[n]+(0.22-j0.056)\left(0.8e^{-j\frac{\pi}{3}}\right)^n u[n]-0.45(-2)^n u[-n-1]$$

$$=2\,\mathrm{Re}\left\{e^{j\frac{\pi}{3}n}(0.22+j0.056)\right\}(0.8)^n u[n]-0.45(-2)^n u[-n-1].$$

$$=2(0.8)^n\left(0.22\cos\frac{\pi}{3}n-0.056\sin\frac{\pi}{3}n\right)u[n]-0.45(-2)^n u[-n-1]$$

The pole-zero plot is shown in Figure 13.14.

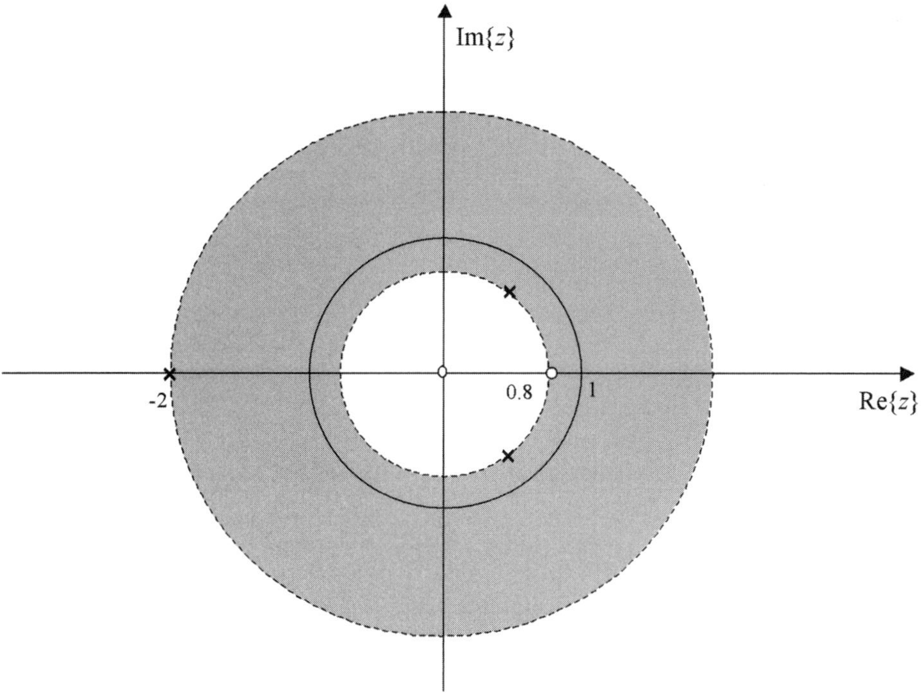

FIGURE 13.14 Pole-zero plot of transfer function in Exercise 13.1.

The system is not causal since the ROC is a ring, but it is stable, as it includes the unit circle.

Exercise 13.2

Compute the inverse z-transform of $X(z)=\frac{z}{(1-0.5z^{-1})}$, $|z|<0.5$ using the power series expansion method.

Answer:

$$X(z)=\frac{z}{(1-0.5z^{-1})}=\frac{2z^2}{2z-1},$$

Long division yields

$$\begin{array}{r} -2z^2-4z^3-(2)^3z^4-\ldots \\ -1+2z\overline{)\ 2z^2\qquad\qquad\qquad} \\ 2z^2-4z^3 \\ \hline 4z^3 \\ 4z^3-8z^4 \\ \hline 8z^4 \end{array}.$$

Note that the resulting power series converges because the ROC implies $|2z|<1$. The signal is

$$\begin{aligned} x[n] &= -2\delta[n+2]-4\delta[n+3]-8\delta[n+4]\ldots \\ &= -(\frac{1}{2})^{n+1}u[-n-2]. \end{aligned}$$

Exercise 13.3

Consider the stable LTI system defined by its transfer function

$$H(z)=\frac{z^2+z-2}{z^2+z+0.5}.$$

(a) Sketch the pole-zero plot for this transfer function and give its ROC. Is the system causal?

Answer:

The poles are $p_1=-0.5+j0.5, p_2=-0.5-j0.5$. The zeros are $z_1=-2, z_2=1$. The system is stable, so its ROC must include the unit circle. Because $H(\infty)$ is finite, we can conclude that the system is causal. The pole-zero plot is shown in Figure 13.15.

(b) Find the corresponding difference system relating the output $y[n]$ to the input $x[n]$.

Answer:

We first write the transfer function as a function of z^{-1} of the form

$$H(z)=\frac{1+z^{-1}-2z^{-2}}{1+z^{-1}+0.5z^{-2}}.$$

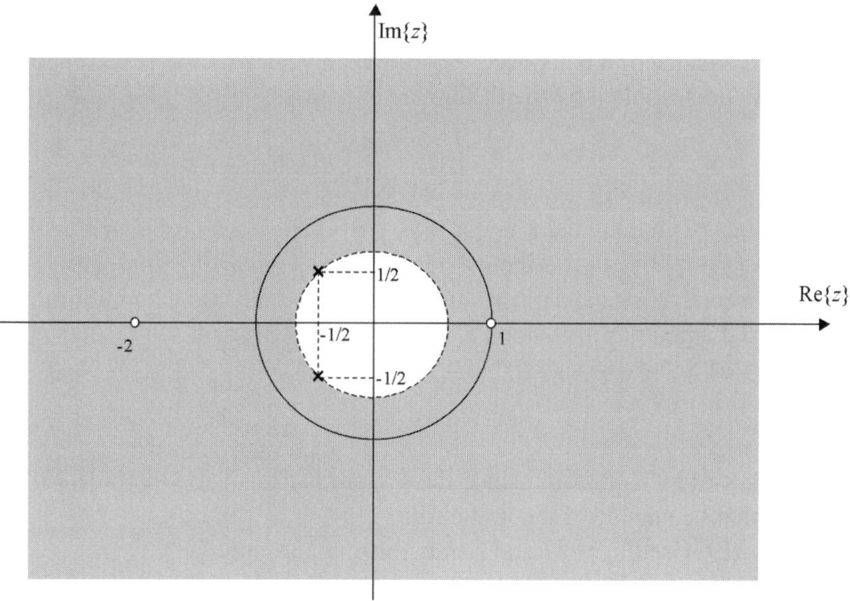

FIGURE 13.15 Pole-zero plot of transfer function in Exercise 13.3(a).

The corresponding difference system is

$$y[n]+y[n-1]+0.5y[n-2]=x[n]+x[n-1]-2x[n-2].$$

(c) Sketch the direct form realization of this system.

Answer:
The direct form realization of the system is given in Figure 13.16.

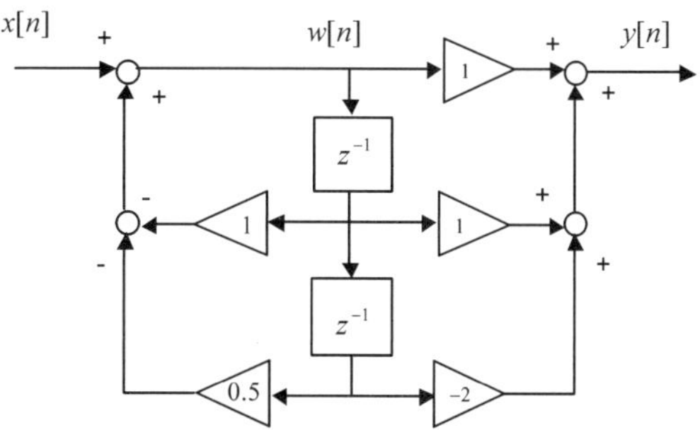

FIGURE 13.16 Direct form realization of transfer function in Exercise 13.3.

Exercise 13.4 (*a bit of actuarial mathematics using the unilateral z-transform...*)

The balance of a bank account after each year with interest compounded annually may be described by the difference equation

$$y[n]=(1+r)y[n-1]+x[n],$$

where r is the annual interest rate, $y[n]$ is the account balance at the beginning of the $(n+1)^{st}$ year, the input "signal" $x[n]=M(u[n]-u[n-L])$ is composed of L consecutive annual deposits of M dollars, and the initial condition $y[-1]=y_{-1}$ is the initial amount in the account before the first deposit.

(a) Is this system stable?

Answer:
The system is unstable since the system is causal and the pole $1+r$ is larger than 1, that is, outside of the unit circle.

(b) Use the unilateral z-transform to compute $\mathcal{Y}(z)$.

Answer:
Taking the unilateral z-transform on both sides, we obtain

$$\mathcal{Y}(z)-(1+r)\left(z^{-1}\mathcal{Y}(z)+y[-1]\right)=\mathcal{X}(z)$$

$$\mathcal{Y}(z)=\frac{(1+r)y[-1]}{1-(1+r)z^{-1}}+\frac{\mathcal{X}(z)}{1-(1+r)z^{-1}}$$

$$\mathcal{Y}(z)=\frac{(1+r)y[-1]}{1-(1+r)z^{-1}}+\frac{M(1-z^{-L})}{\left[1-(1+r)z^{-1}\right](1-z^{-1})}$$

$$=\frac{(1+r)y[-1](1-z^{-1})+M(1-z^{-L})}{\left[1-(1+r)z^{-1}\right](1-z^{-1})}$$

more useful form:

$$=\frac{(1+r)y[-1]+M\sum_{k=0}^{L-1}z^{-k}}{\left[1-(1+r)z^{-1}\right]}.$$

(c) Find the annual deposit M as a function of the final balance in the account after L years, $y[L-1]$, and the interest rate r. Compute the annual deposit M if you want to accrue \$100,000 after 20 years at 5% annual interest rate with an initial balance of $y_{-1}=\$1000$.

Answer:
The account balance at the beginning of the $(n+1)^{st}$ year is

$$\begin{aligned} y[n] &= \mathcal{Z}^{-1}\left\{\mathcal{Y}(z)\right\} \\ &= \mathcal{Z}^{-1}\left\{\frac{(1+r)y[-1]+M\sum_{k=0}^{L-1}z^{-k}}{\left[1-(1+r)z^{-1}\right]}\right\} \\ &= \left[(1+r)y[-1]\right](1+r)^n u[n]+M\sum_{k=0}^{L-1}(1+r)^{n-k}u[n-k]. \end{aligned}$$

When the last payment is made at $n=L-1$, we get

$$\begin{aligned} y[L-1] &= \left[(1+r)y[-1]\right](1+r)^{L-1}+M\sum_{k=0}^{L-1}(1+r)^{L-1-k} \\ &= (1+r)^L y[-1]+M\sum_{m=0}^{L-1}(1+r)^m, \end{aligned}$$

which yields

$$M=\frac{y[L-1]-(1+r)^L y[-1]}{\sum_{m=0}^{L-1}(1+r)^m}=\frac{y[L-1]-(1+r)^L y[-1]}{\dfrac{1-(1+r)^L}{1-(1+r)}}=\frac{r\left[y[L-1]-(1+r)^L y[-1]\right]}{(1+r)^L-1}$$

$$\begin{aligned} M &= \frac{r\left[y[L-1]-(1+r)^L y[-1]\right]}{(1+r)^L-1} \\ &= \frac{0.05\left[\$100000-(1.05)^{20}\cdot\$1000\right]}{(1.05)^{20}-1} \\ &= \$2944. \end{aligned}$$

Exercises

Exercise 13.5

Compute the z-transform of each of the following signals and sketch its pole-zero plot, indicating the ROC.

(a) $x[n]=\alpha^n\cos(\omega_0 n+\theta)u[n],\ |\alpha|>1$. Use the values $\alpha=1.5,\ \omega_0=\frac{3\pi}{4}$, $\theta=-\frac{\pi}{4}$ for the pole-zero plot.

(b) $x[n]=u[n+4]-u[n]$

(c) $x[n]=(-2)^n u[-n+3]$

Answer:

ON THE CD

Exercise 13.6

Compute the inverse z-transform of $X(z)=\frac{z^2}{z+0.2},\ 0.2<|z|<\infty$ using the power series expansion method.

Exercise 13.7

Consider the following so-called auto-regressive moving-average causal filter S initially at rest:

$$S:\ y[n]-0.9y[n-1]+0.81y[n-2]=x[n]-x[n-2]$$

(a) Compute the z-transform of the impulse response of the filter $H(z)$ (the transfer function) and give its ROC. Sketch the pole-zero plot.

(b) Compute the impulse response $h[n]$ of the filter.

(c) Compute the frequency response of the filter. Plot its magnitude. What type of filter is it (lowpass, highpass, or bandpass)?

(d) Compute and sketch the step response $s[n]$ of the filter.

Answer:

ON THE CD

Exercise 13.8

Consider a DLTI system with transfer function $H(z)=\frac{z^{-3}-1.2z^{-4}}{(z-0.8)(z+0.8)}$.

(a) Sketch the pole-zero plot of the system.

(b) Find the ROC that makes this system stable.

(c) Is the system causal with the ROC that you found in (b)? Justify your answer.

(d) Suppose that $H(e^{j\omega})$ is bounded for all frequencies. Find the response of the system $y[n]$ to the input $x[n]=u[n]$.

Exercise 13.9

Compute the inverse z-transform $x[n]$ of $X(z)=\frac{1}{z(z+0.4)}$, $|z|>0.4$ using the method of long division and sketch it.

Answer:

ON THE CD

Exercise 13.10

Sketch the pole-zero plot and compute the impulse response $h[n]$ of the stable system with transfer function

$$H(z)=\frac{2000z^3+1450z^2+135z}{(100z^2-81)(5z+4)}.$$

Specify its ROC. Specify whether or not the system is causal.

Exercise 13.11

Consider the DLTI system with transfer function $H(z)=\frac{z-1}{z^{-1}(z+0.4)}$.

(a) Sketch the pole-zero plot of the system.

(b) Find the ROC that makes this system stable.

(c) Is the system causal with the ROC that you found in (b)? Justify your answer.

(d) Suppose that $H(e^{j\omega})$ is bounded for all frequencies. Calculate the response of the system $y[n]$ to the input $x[n]=u[n]$.

Answer:

ON THE CD

14 Time and Frequency Analysis of Discrete-Time Signals and Systems

In This Chapter

((Lecture 53: Relationship Between the DTFT and the z-Transform))

We have seen that the discrete-time Fourier transform (DTFT) of a system's impulse response (the *frequency response* of the system) exists whenever the system is bounded-input bounded-output stable or, equivalently, whenever the region of convergence (ROC) of the system's transfer function includes the unit circle. Then, the frequency response of the system is simply its transfer function $H(z)$ evaluated on the unit circle $|z|=1$, that is, $z=e^{j\omega}$. In this chapter, we discuss the geometric relationship between the poles and zeros of the z-transform of a signal and its corresponding Fourier transform. It is possible to estimate qualitatively the frequency response of a system just by looking at the pole-zero plot of its transfer function. For example, referring back to Figure 13.1, complex poles close to the unit circle will tend to raise the magnitude of the frequency response at nearby frequencies.

We will look in some detail at the connections between the frequency responses of first-order and second-order systems and their time-domain impulse and step responses. Finally, the analysis and design of discrete-time infinite impulse response filters and finite impulse response filters will be discussed. In particular, the window design technique of finite impulse response filters will be introduced.

GEOMETRIC EVALUATION OF THE DTFT FROM THE POLE-ZERO PLOT

If we write the rational transfer function $H(z)$ of a causal stable system in the pole-zero form,

$$H(z) = A\frac{(z-z_1)\cdots(z-z_M)}{(z-p_1)\cdots(z-p_N)}, \tag{14.1}$$

then its magnitude is given by

$$|H(z)| = |A|\frac{|z-z_1|\cdots|z-z_M|}{|z-p_1|\cdots|z-p_N|}. \tag{14.2}$$

Evaluating this magnitude on the unit circle, we obtain

$$|H(e^{j\omega})| = |A|\frac{|e^{j\omega}-z_1|\cdots|e^{j\omega}-z_M|}{|e^{j\omega}-p_1|\cdots|e^{j\omega}-p_N|}. \tag{14.3}$$

Since the system is assumed to be stable, all poles lie inside the unit circle, but the zeros do not have that restriction. The magnitude of the frequency response, as a function of frequency ω varying over the range $[-\pi,\pi]$, can be analyzed qualitatively as the point $e^{j\omega}$ moves along the unit circle. The contribution of each pole and zero to the magnitude can be analyzed by viewing $|e^{j\omega}-p_k|, |e^{j\omega}-z_k|$ as the length of the vector from the pole to the point $e^{j\omega}$ and from the zero to the point $e^{j\omega}$, respectively. In particular,

- A pole $p_k = r_k e^{j\theta_k}$ close to the unit circle will tend to increase the magnitude at frequencies $\omega \approx \theta_k$ because the distance between $e^{j\omega}$ and $p_k = r_k e^{j\theta_k}$ in the z-plane is small.

- A zero $z_k = r_k e^{j\theta_k}$ close to the unit circle will tend to decrease the magnitude at frequencies $\omega \approx \theta_k$.

The phase of $H(e^{j\omega})$ is given by

$$\begin{aligned}\angle H(e^{j\omega}) = \angle A + \angle(e^{j\omega} - z_1) + \angle(e^{j\omega} - z_2) + \cdots + \angle(e^{j\omega} - z_M) \\ - \angle(e^{j\omega} - p_1) - \angle(e^{j\omega} - p_2) - \cdots - \angle(e^{j\omega} - p_M).\end{aligned} \tag{14.4}$$

Thus, the total phase is the sum of the individual angles of the pole and zero factors $e^{j\omega} - p_k, e^{j\omega} - z_k$ seen as vectors in the z-plane and the phase of the gain A.

First-Order Systems

Consider the first-order causal system with $|a| < 1$:

$$H(z) = \frac{1}{1 - az^{-1}} = \frac{z}{z - a}, \quad |z| > |a|. \tag{14.5}$$

This system is stable, and hence it has a Fourier transform given by

$$H(e^{j\omega}) = \frac{1}{1 - ae^{-j\omega}} = \frac{e^{j\omega}}{e^{j\omega} - a}. \tag{14.6}$$

The geometric interpretation described above can be depicted on the pole-zero plot shown in Figure 14.1, where a is real, $0 < a < 1$.

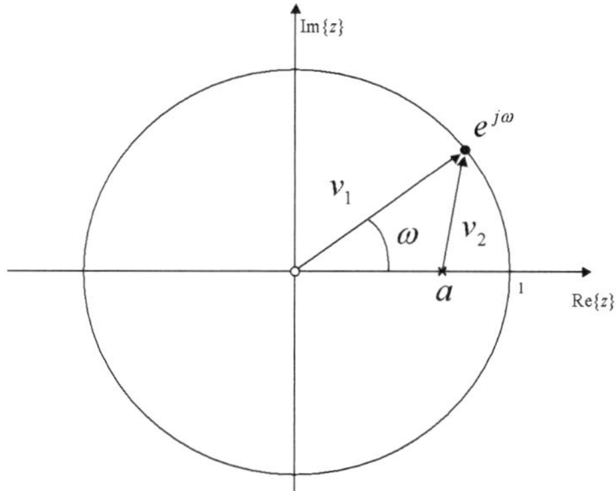

FIGURE 14.1 Pole-zero plot showing the vectors associated with the pole-zero form of a first-order transfer function with one real positive pole.

When the tip of the vector v_1 is at 1 ($\omega = 0$), the magnitude of v_2 is minimum, and hence the magnitude of $H(e^{j\omega})$ is maximized as $\left|H(e^{j\omega})\right| = \frac{|v_1|}{|v_2|} = \frac{1}{|v_2|}$. When ω goes from 0 to π, or from 0 to $-\pi$, the length of v_2 increases monotonically, which means that the magnitude will decrease monotonically. Hence, this is a lowpass filter. Thus, for $0 < a < 1$, the magnitude plot will look like the one shown in Figure 14.2.

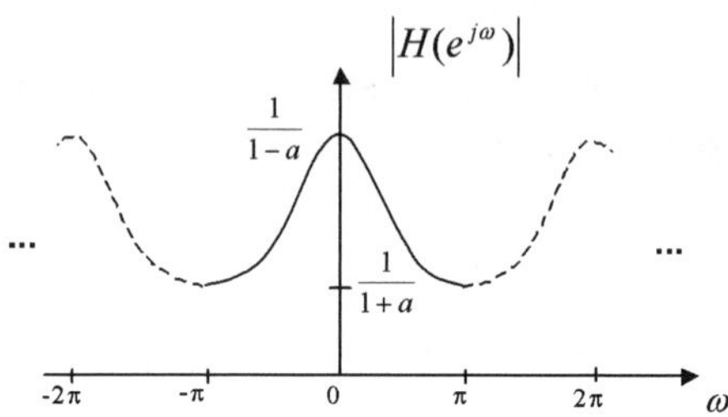

FIGURE 14.2 Magnitude sketch of the frequency response of a first-order transfer function with a positive pole.

The phase $\angle H(e^{j\omega})$ is given by the angle of v_1 minus the angle of v_2:

$$\begin{aligned}\angle H(e^{j\omega}) &= \angle v_1 - \angle v_2 \\ &= \omega - \arctan\left(\frac{\sin\omega - \mathrm{Im}\{a\}}{\cos\omega - \mathrm{Re}\{a\}}\right) \\ &= \omega - \arctan\left(\frac{\sin\omega}{\cos\omega - a}\right), \quad \text{for } a \in \mathbb{R}. \end{aligned} \tag{14.7}$$

Thus, the phase plot looks like the one sketched in Figure 14.3.

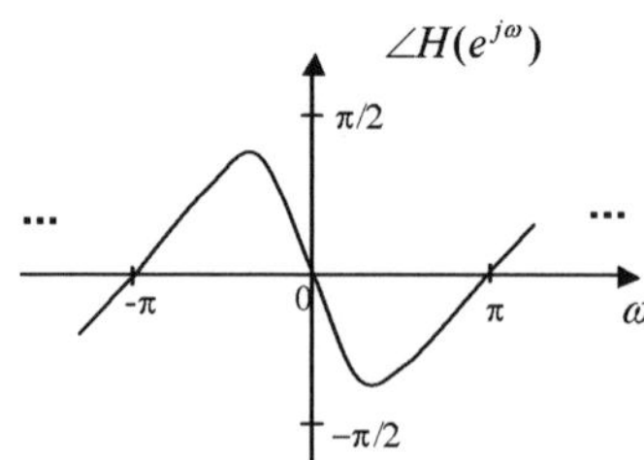

FIGURE 14.3 Phase sketch of the frequency response of a first-order transfer function with a positive real pole.

For the case $-1 < a < 0$, the vectors are shown on the pole-zero plot of Figure 14.4.

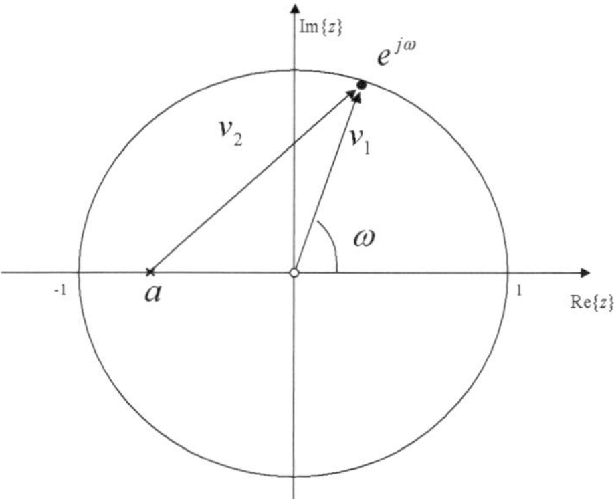

FIGURE 14.4 Pole-zero plot showing the vectors associated with the pole-zero form of a first-order transfer function with one real negative pole.

When the tip of the vector v_1 is at 1 ($\omega = 0$), the magnitude of v_2 is at its maximum, and hence the magnitude of $H(e^{j\omega})$ is minimized as $\left|H(e^{j\omega})\right| = \frac{|v_1|}{|v_2|} = \frac{1}{|v_2|}$. When ω goes from 0 to π, or from 0 to $-\pi$, the length of v_2 decreases monotonically, which means that the magnitude will increase monotonically. At the highest frequencies $\omega = \pm\pi$, the magnitude of v_2 is at its minimum, so the magnitude of $H(e^{j\omega})$ is at its maximum. Hence, this is a highpass filter, and its magnitude plot will look like the one in Figure 14.5 for $-1 < a < 0$.

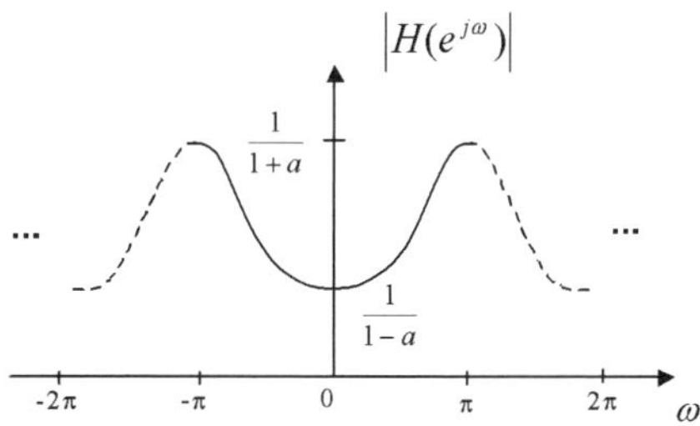

FIGURE 14.5 Magnitude sketch of the frequency response of a first-order transfer function with a negative pole.

The phase $\angle H(e^{j\omega})$ is again given by the angle of v_1 minus the angle of v_2 as expressed in Equation 14.7. It should look like the phase sketched in Figure 14.6.

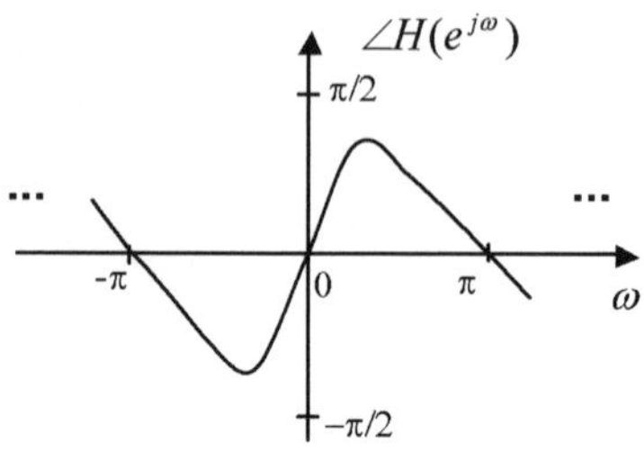

FIGURE 14.6 Phase sketch of the frequency response of a first-order transfer function with a negative real pole.

Second-Order Systems

Consider the stable second-order causal system with poles at $p_{1,2} = re^{\pm j\theta},\ 0 < r < 1$:

$$H(z) = \frac{1}{1 - 2r\cos\theta z^{-1} + r^2 z^{-2}} = \frac{z^2}{z^2 - 2r\cos\theta z + r^2}, \quad |z| > r. \tag{14.8}$$

The impulse response of this system is obtained from Table D.10 and by using the linearity and time-advance properties of the z-transform:

$$h[n] = \frac{1}{\sin\theta} r^n \sin((n+1)\theta) u[n]. \tag{14.9}$$

Its Fourier transform is given by

$$\begin{aligned} H(e^{j\omega}) &= \frac{e^{j2\omega}}{e^{j2\omega} - 2r\cos\theta e^{j\omega} + r^2} \\ &= \frac{e^{j2\omega}}{(e^{j\omega} - re^{j\theta})(e^{j\omega} - re^{-j\theta})}. \end{aligned} \tag{14.10}$$

The magnitude of $H(e^{j\omega})$ can be analyzed qualitatively by looking at the pole-zero plot in Figure 14.7 showing the vectors as defined above.

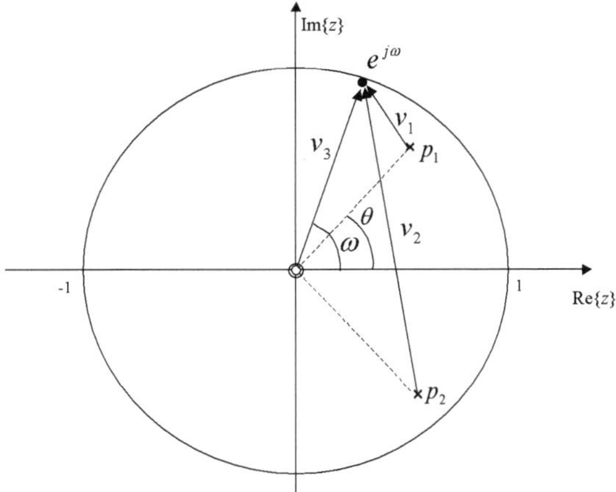

FIGURE 14.7 Pole-zero plot showing the vectors associated with the pole-zero form of a second-order transfer function with complex poles.

The magnitude is given by $\left|H(e^{j\omega})\right| = \frac{|v_3|^2}{|v_1||v_2|} = \frac{1}{|v_1||v_2|} = \frac{1}{|v_1||v_2|}$, which gets large as the frequency approaches $\pm\theta$ (see Figure 14.8).

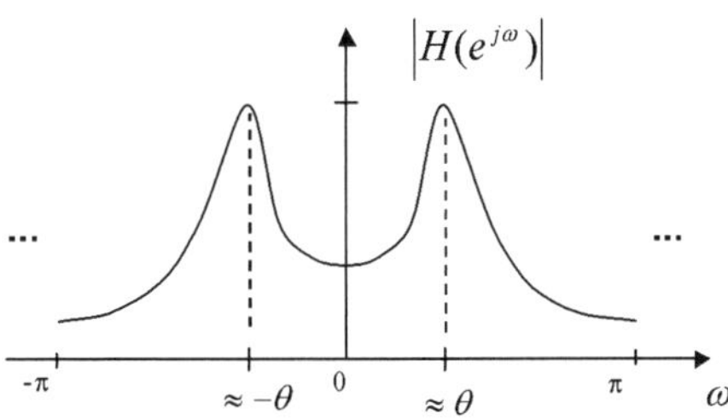

FIGURE 14.8 Magnitude sketch of the frequency response of a second-order transfer function with complex poles.

It is clear that the peaks on the magnitude sketch of Figure 14.8 will get larger as the poles get closer to the unit circle ($r \to 1$), the limit being poles sitting directly on the unit circle and peaks going to infinity. Thus, r has an effect similar to the damping ratio ζ of continuous-time second-order systems.

The phase of $H(e^{j\omega})$ is given by twice the angle of v_3 minus the sum of the angles of v_1 and v_2:

$$\begin{aligned}\angle H(e^{j\omega}) &= 2\angle v_3 - \angle v_1 - \angle v_2 \\ &= 2\omega - \arctan\left(\frac{\sin\omega - \mathrm{Im}\{p_1\}}{\cos\omega - \mathrm{Re}\{p_1\}}\right) - \arctan\left(\frac{\sin\omega - \mathrm{Im}\{p_2\}}{\cos\omega - \mathrm{Re}\{p_2\}}\right). \quad (14.11)\end{aligned}$$

The phase might look like the one sketched in Figure 14.9, although it varies greatly with pole locations. Typically, the closer the poles are to the unit circle, the sharper the phase drop near $\omega = \theta$, since the angle of the vector v_1 changes more rapidly with ω in that frequency band.

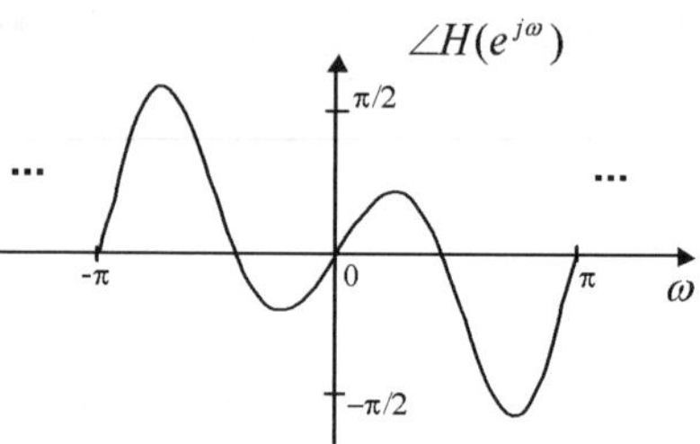

FIGURE 14.9 Phase sketch of the frequency response of a second-order transfer function with complex poles.

((Lecture 54: Frequency Analysis of First-Order and Second-Order Systems))

FREQUENCY ANALYSIS OF FIRST-ORDER AND SECOND-ORDER SYSTEMS

In this section, we look in a bit more detail at the frequency responses of first-order and second-order discrete-time linear time-invariant (DLTI) systems.

First-Order Systems

Let us consider again a first-order causal, stable system with $|a| < 1$:

$$H(z) = \frac{1}{1 - az^{-1}} = \frac{z}{z - a}, \quad |z| > |a|. \quad (14.12)$$

Its Fourier transform is given by

$$H(e^{j\omega}) = \frac{1}{1 - ae^{-j\omega}} = \frac{e^{j\omega}}{e^{j\omega} - a}. \quad (14.13)$$

Its impulse response is

$$h[n] = a^n u[n], \tag{14.14}$$

and its unit step response is computed as the running sum of its impulse response:

$$s[n] = \sum_{k=-\infty}^{n} a^k u[k] = \sum_{k=0}^{n} a^k = \frac{1-a^{n+1}}{1-a} u[n]. \tag{14.15}$$

The magnitude of the parameter a plays a role similar to that of the time constant τ of a continuous-time first-order system. Specifically, $|a|$ determines the rate at which the system responds. For small $|a|$, the impulse response decays sharply and the step response settles quickly. For $|a|$ close to 1, the transients are much slower. Figure 14.10 shows the step responses of two first-order systems, one with $a = 0.5$ and the other with $a = 0.8$.

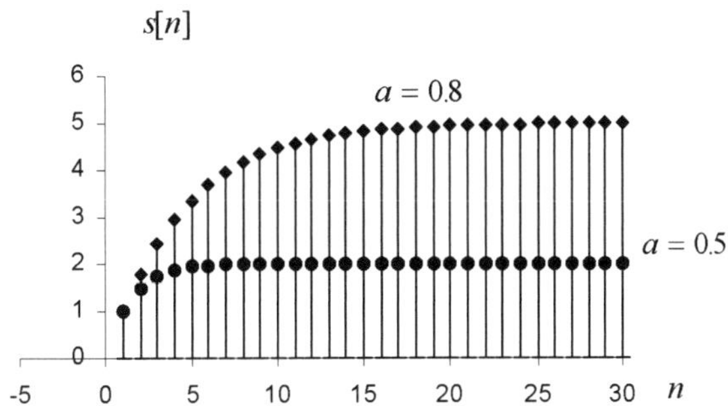

FIGURE 14.10 Step responses of two first-order DLTI systems with a real positive pole.

From a frequency point of view, the lowpass frequency response of the system corresponding to small $|a|$ has a wider bandwidth than for $|a|$ close to 1. This is easier to see when the frequency response $H(e^{j\omega})$ is normalized to have a unity DC gain:

$$\begin{aligned} \left|H(e^{j\omega})\right| &= \left|(1-a)\frac{1}{1-ae^{-j\omega}}\right| \\ &= \frac{1-a}{(1-a\cos\omega)^2 + (a\sin\omega)^2} \\ &= \frac{1-a}{(1+a^2-2a\cos\omega)^{1/2}} \end{aligned} \tag{14.16}$$

The magnitude in Equation 14.16 is plotted in Figure 14.11 for the cases $a = 0.5$ and $a = 0.8$.

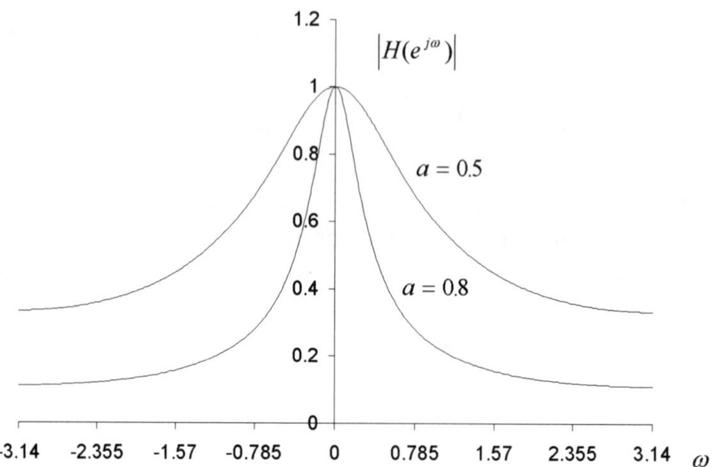

FIGURE 14.11 Magnitude of the frequency responses of first-order transfer functions with positive poles.

The phase changes more abruptly around DC for $|a|$ close to 1, as shown in Figure 14.12.

$$\angle H(e^{j\omega}) = \omega - \arctan\left(\frac{\sin\omega}{\cos\omega - a}\right), \quad \text{for } a \in \mathbb{R}. \tag{14.17}$$

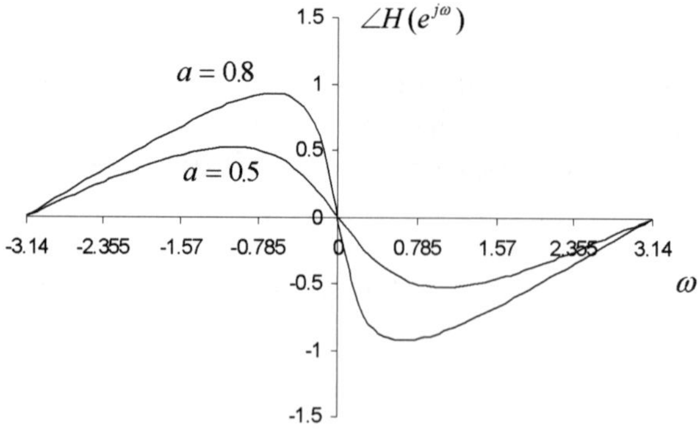

FIGURE 14.12 Phase of the frequency responses of first-order transfer functions with positive poles.

Second-Order Systems

We now turn to a second-order causal, stable system with poles at $p_{1,2} = re^{\pm j\theta}$, $0 < r < 1$:

$$H(z) = \frac{1}{1 - 2r\cos\theta z^{-1} + r^2 z^{-2}} = \frac{z^2}{z^2 - 2r\cos\theta z + r^2}, \quad |z| > r. \tag{14.18}$$

Its frequency response is given by

$$H(e^{j\omega}) = \frac{e^{j2\omega}}{e^{j2\omega} - 2r\cos\theta e^{j\omega} + r^2}, \tag{14.19}$$

whose magnitude is

$$\begin{aligned}
\left|H(e^{j\omega})\right| &= \left|\frac{1}{e^{j2\omega} - 2r\cos\theta e^{j\omega} + r^2}\right| \\
&= \frac{1}{\left|e^{j\omega} - re^{-j\theta}\right|\left|e^{j\omega} - re^{j\theta}\right|} \\
&= \frac{1}{\left|e^{j(\omega+\theta)} - r\right|\left|e^{j(\omega-\theta)} - r\right|} \\
&= \frac{1}{\left[1 + r^2 - 2r\cos(\omega+\theta)\right]^{\frac{1}{2}}\left[1 + r^2 - 2r\cos(\omega-\theta)\right]^{\frac{1}{2}}}.
\end{aligned} \tag{14.20}$$

We see that the magnitude will peak around $\omega = \pm\theta$. The DC gain is obtained by substituting $\omega = 0$ in this expression, and we get

$$\left|H(e^{j0})\right| = \frac{1}{\left[1 + r^2 - 2r\cos\theta\right]}. \tag{14.21}$$

For comparison, let us normalize the system so that its DC gain is unity for any pole parameters r, θ:

$$H(z) = \frac{1 + r^2 - 2r\cos\theta}{1 - 2r\cos\theta z^{-1} + r^2 z^{-2}}, \quad |z| > r. \tag{14.22}$$

Then,

$$\left|H(e^{j\omega})\right| = \frac{1+r^2-2r\cos\theta}{\left[1+r^2-2r\cos(\omega+\theta)\right]^{\frac{1}{2}}\left[1+r^2-2r\cos(\omega-\theta)\right]^{\frac{1}{2}}}. \qquad (14.23)$$

Figure 14.13 shows the frequency response magnitude of the second-order system for $\theta = \frac{\pi}{4}$ and two values of pole magnitude, namely $r = 0.6$ and $r = 0.8$.

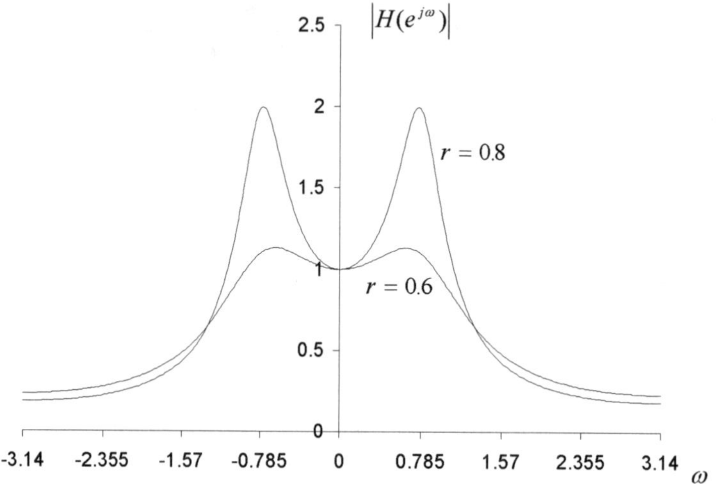

FIGURE 14.13 Frequency response magnitude of second-order transfer functions with two pole magnitudes.

The phase of the frequency response for $\theta = \frac{\pi}{4}$ in Equation 14.24 is shown in Figure 14.14 for $r = 0.6$ and $r = 0.8$.

$$\angle H(e^{j\omega}) = 2\omega - \arctan\left(\frac{\sin\omega - r\sin\theta}{\cos\omega - r\cos\theta}\right) - \arctan\left(\frac{\sin\omega + r\sin\theta}{\cos\omega - r\cos\theta}\right). \qquad (14.24)$$

The impulse response of this system for $\theta = \frac{\pi}{4}$ is

$$h[n] = \sqrt{2}r^n \sin\left[(n+1)\frac{\pi}{4}\right]u[n]. \qquad (14.25)$$

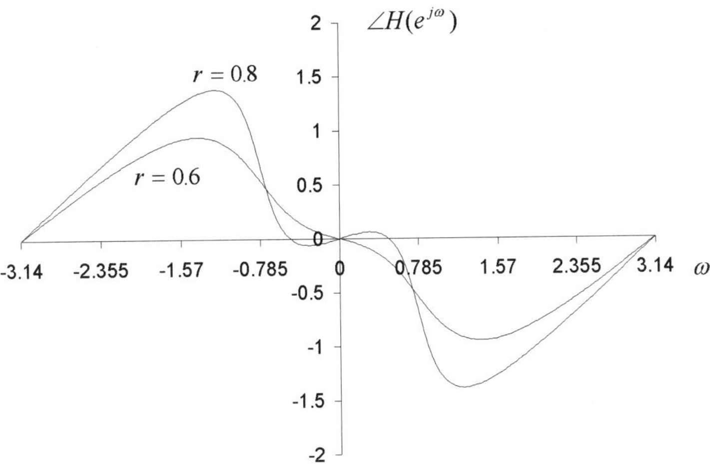

FIGURE 14.14 Frequency response phase of second-order transfer functions with two pole magnitudes.

This impulse response is shown in Figure 14.15, again for the cases $r = 0.6$ and $r = 0.8$.

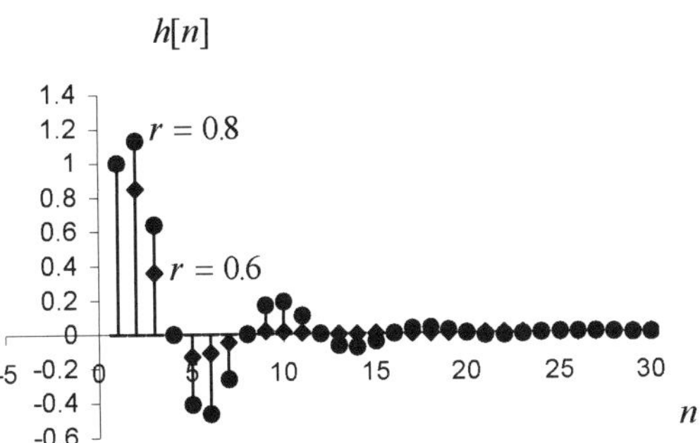

FIGURE 14.15 Impulse responses of second-order transfer functions with two pole magnitudes.

We can see that the impulse response for $r = 0.8$ displays larger oscillations, which corresponds to the higher peaks in the frequency response.

((Lecture 55: Ideal Discrete-Time Filters))

IDEAL DISCRETE-TIME FILTERS

Ideal frequency-selective filters are filters that let frequency components over a given frequency band (the *passband*) pass through undistorted, while components at other frequencies (the *stopband*) are completely cut off.

The usual scenario where filtering is needed is when a *noise* $w[n]$ is added to a signal $x[n]$, but the noise has most of its energy at frequencies outside of the bandwidth of the signal. We want to recover the original signal from its noisy measurement. Note that the "noise" can be composed of other modulated signals as in the frequency division multiplexing technique.

Ideal Lowpass Filter

An ideal lowpass filter with the proper bandwidth can recover a signal $x[n]$ from its noisy measurement $\tilde{x}[n]$ as illustrated in the filtering block diagram of Figure 14.16.

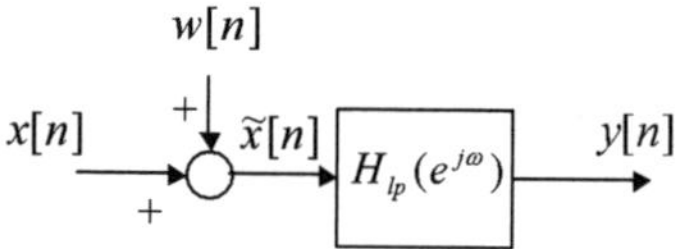

FIGURE 14.16 Typical discrete-time filtering problem.

In this idealized problem, the noise spectrum is assumed to have all of its energy at frequencies higher than the bandwidth W of the signal, as shown in Figure 14.17. Thus, an ideal lowpass filter would perfectly recover the signal, that is, $y[n] = x[n]$.

The frequency response of the ideal lowpass filter with cutoff frequency ω_c depicted in Figure 14.18 is simply given by

$$H_{lp}(e^{j\omega}) = \begin{cases} 1, & |\omega - k2\pi| \le \omega_c,\ k = \ldots,-1,0,1,\ldots \\ 0, & \text{otherwise} \end{cases} \tag{14.26}$$

Its impulse response (from Table D.7 in Appendix D) is noncausal, real, and even:

$$h_{lp}[n] = \frac{\sin \omega_c n}{\pi n} = \frac{\omega_c}{\pi} \operatorname{sinc}\left(\frac{\omega_c n}{\pi}\right), \tag{14.27}$$

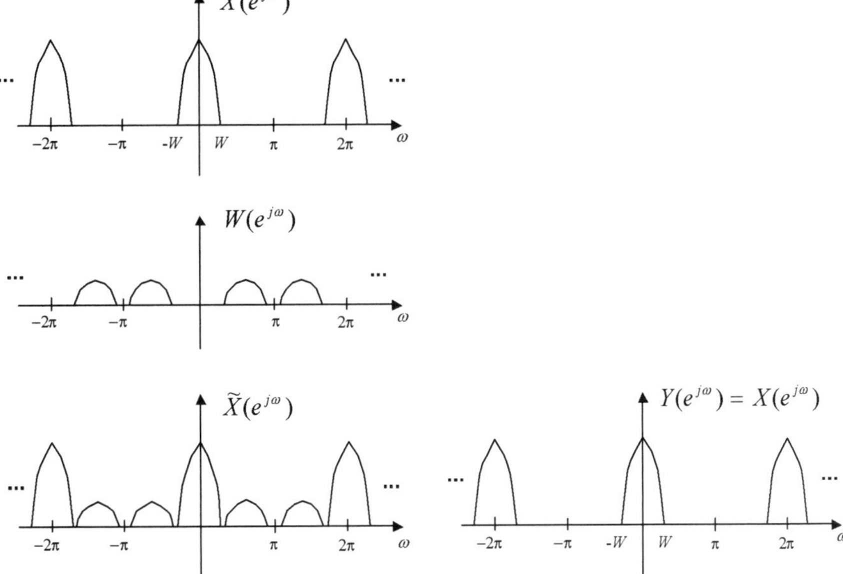

FIGURE 14.17 Fourier transforms of signals in filtering problem.

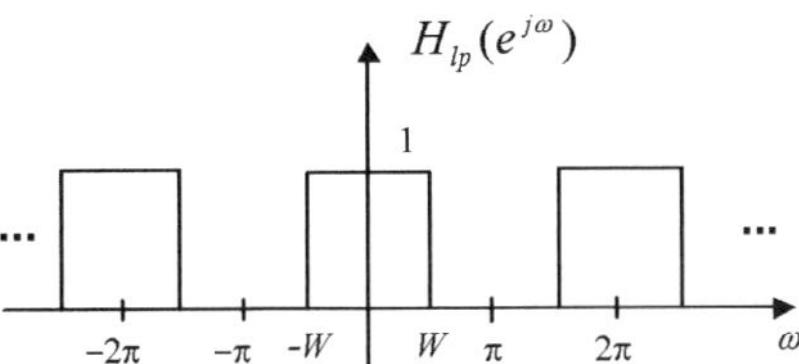

FIGURE 14.18 Frequency response of an ideal discrete-time lowpass filter.

which unfortunately makes a real-time implementation of this filter impossible.

First-Order Approximation

We have seen that the frequency response magnitude of a normalized causal, stable, first-order filter is given by

$$|H(e^{j\omega})| = \left|(1-a)\frac{1}{1-ae^{-j\omega}}\right| = \frac{1-a}{(1+a^2-2a\cos\omega)^{1/2}}. \tag{14.28}$$

Suppose the cutoff frequency ω_c (bandwidth) of the filter is defined as the frequency where the magnitude is –3 dB. Then, we can find an expression for the real pole $0 < a < 1$ in terms of the cutoff frequency ω_c.

$$\begin{aligned}
-3\text{ dB} &= 20\log_{10}\left(\frac{1-a}{(1+a^2-2a\cos\omega_c)^{1/2}}\right)\\
10^{-\frac{3}{20}} &= \frac{1-a}{(1+a^2-2a\cos\omega_c)^{1/2}}\\
10^{-\frac{3}{10}}(1+a^2-2a\cos\omega_c) &= (1-a)^2\\
-10^{-\frac{3}{10}}(1+a^2-2a\cos\omega_c) &= -1+2a-a^2\\
(1-10^{-\frac{3}{10}})a^2+(2\cdot 10^{-\frac{3}{10}}\cos\omega_c-2)a+1-10^{-\frac{3}{10}} &= 0\\
0.4988a^2-(2-1.0024\cos\omega_c)a+0.4988 &= 0
\end{aligned} \tag{14.29}$$

This quadratic equation can be solved for the pole

$$\begin{aligned}
a &= \frac{(2-1.0024\cos\omega_c)}{0.9976} \pm \frac{1}{2}\sqrt{\frac{(2-1.0024\cos\omega_c)^2}{0.2488}-4}\\
&= \frac{(2-1.0024\cos\omega_c)}{0.9976} \pm \frac{1}{0.9976}\sqrt{(2-1.0024\cos\omega_c)^2-0.9952}
\end{aligned} \tag{14.30}$$

Note that the plus sign leads to a pole larger than one; hence we select

$$a = \frac{(2-1.0024\cos\omega_c)}{0.9976} - \frac{1}{0.9976}\sqrt{(2-1.0024\cos\omega_c)^2-0.9952}. \tag{14.31}$$

The poles corresponding to different cutoff frequencies as given by Equation 14.31 are listed in Table 14.1.

TABLE 14.1 Pole of First-Order Lowpass Filter vs. Cutoff Frequency

ω_c	$\frac{\pi}{16}$	$\frac{\pi}{8}$	$\frac{3\pi}{16}$	$\frac{\pi}{4}$	$\frac{5\pi}{16}$	$\frac{3\pi}{8}$
a	0.821841	0.677952	0.563235	0.472582	0.401309	0.3454

Example 14.1: For the cutoff frequencies $\frac{\pi}{16}$ and $\frac{\pi}{4}$, the poles are $a = 0.821841$ and $a = 0.472582$, respectively. The magnitudes of the first-order filters with these poles are plotted over the ideal brickwall magnitudes in Figure 14.19. We can see from this figure that a first-order filter is a very crude approximation to an ideal lowpass filter.

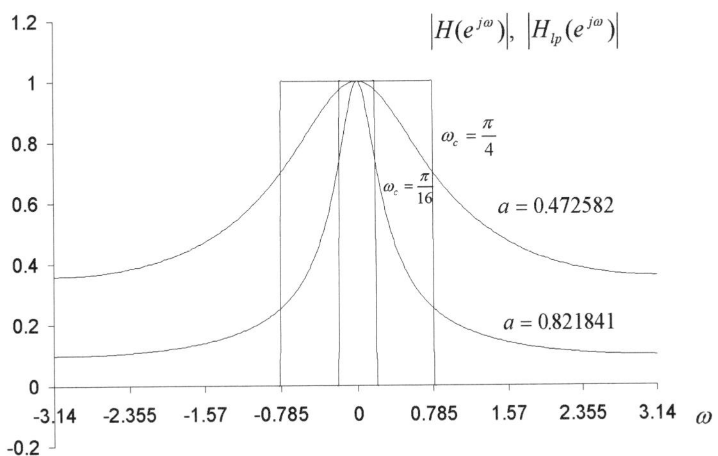

FIGURE 14.19 Frequency response magnitudes of first-order discrete-time lowpass filters.

Second-Order Approximation

The frequency response magnitude of a normalized causal, stable, second-order filter with complex poles and two zeros at $z = 0$ was computed as

$$\left|H(e^{j\omega})\right| = \frac{1 + r^2 - 2r\cos\theta}{\left[1 + r^2 - 2r\cos(\omega + \theta)\right]^{\frac{1}{2}}\left[1 + r^2 - 2r\cos(\omega - \theta)\right]^{\frac{1}{2}}}. \qquad (14.32)$$

Here, we have two parameters to shape the frequency response, namely r and θ. Without getting into specific optimal design techniques, we could see by trial and error using a software package such as MATLAB that it is possible to get a better approximation to an ideal lowpass filter using a second-order filter. For example, the magnitude of a second-order lowpass filter with $\omega_c = \frac{\pi}{4}$ rad is plotted over that of a first-order filter with the same cutoff in Figure 14.20. An easy improvement to the second-order lowpass filter would be to move one of its two zeros to $z = -1$, forcing the magnitude down to zero at $\omega_c = \pm\pi$.

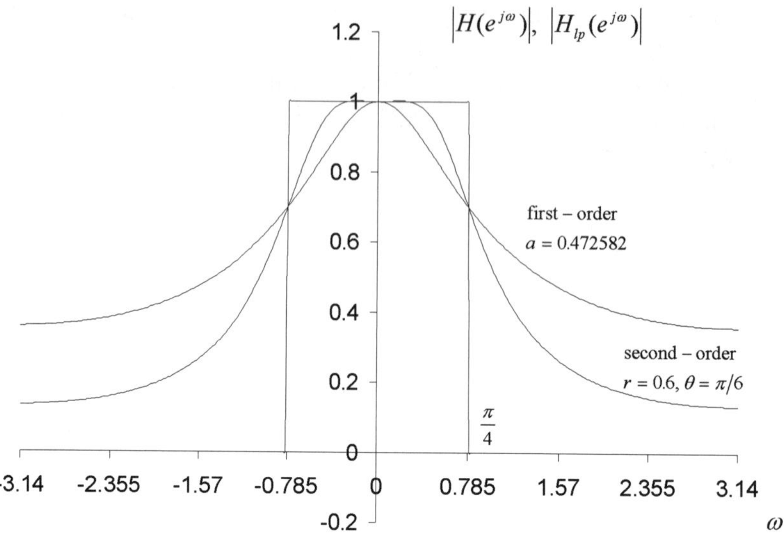

FIGURE 14.20 Frequency response magnitudes of second-order and first-order discrete-time lowpass filters.

Ideal Highpass Filter

An ideal highpass filter with cutoff frequency ω_c is given by

$$H_{hp}(e^{j\omega}) = \begin{cases} 1, & |\omega-(2k+1)\pi| < \pi - \omega_c, k \in \mathbb{Z} \\ 0, & \text{otherwise} \end{cases}. \qquad (14.33)$$

This highpass frequency response is shown in Figure 14.21.

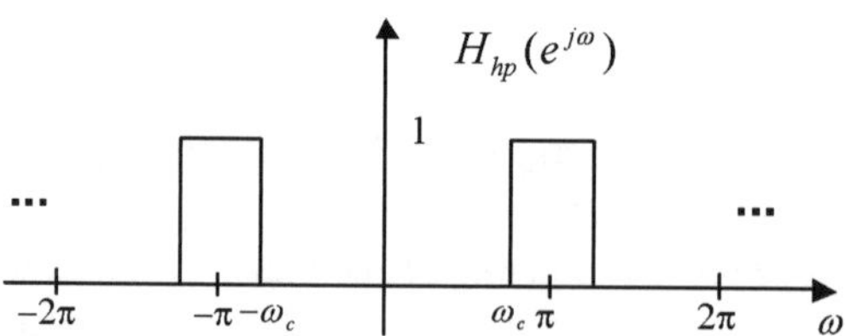

FIGURE 14.21 Frequency response of an ideal discrete-time highpass filter.

The ideal highpass frequency response can be seen as the ideal lowpass spectrum with cutoff frequency $\pi - \omega_c$ and frequency-shifted by π radians. From the frequency shifting property of the DTFT, we find that the impulse response of the ideal highpass filter is:

$$\begin{aligned} h_{hp}[n] &= e^{j\pi n} h_{lp}[n] \\ &= (-1)^n \frac{\sin(\pi - \omega_c)n}{\pi n} \\ &= (-1)^n \frac{\sin \omega_c n}{\pi n}. \end{aligned} \tag{14.34}$$

Unfortunately, this highpass filter is also impossible to implement in real time, as it is noncausal and the impulse response extends to infinity both toward the negative times and the positive times.

First-Order Approximation

The ideal highpass frequency response can be approximated by a normalized causal, stable, first-order filter with a negative pole $-1 < a < 0$. The normalization is done at the highest frequency $\omega = \pi$; that is, $z = -1$ so that $H(-1) = 1$.

$$H(z) = (1 + a)\frac{1}{1 - az^{-1}} \tag{14.35}$$

$$\left|H(e^{j\omega})\right| = \frac{1 + a}{(1 + a^2 - 2a\cos\omega)^{1/2}} \tag{14.36}$$

Note that the relationship between the cutoff frequency ω_c and the pole a is given by Equation14.31, but using the "new" pole $|a|$ and the "new" cutoff frequency $\pi - \omega_c$. After $|a|$ is obtained from the equation, the pole of the highpass filter is just $a = -|a|$.

Example 14.2: The poles corresponding to the cutoff frequencies $\frac{3\pi}{4}$ and $\frac{15\pi}{16}$ of a first-order highpass filter are $a = -0.472582$ and $a = -0.821841$, respectively. The corresponding filter magnitudes are plotted in Figure 14.22 over the ideal brickwall highpass frequency responses.

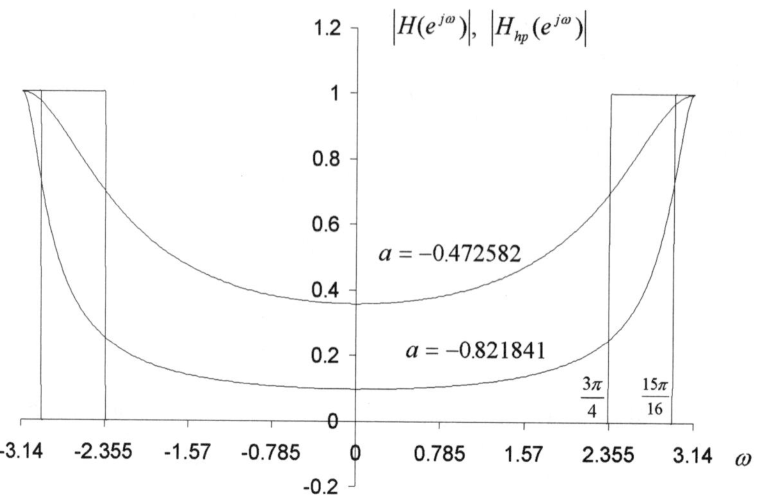

FIGURE 14.22 Frequency response magnitudes of first-order discrete-time highpass filters.

Second-Order Approximation

The frequency response of a normalized (at $z=-1$) causal, stable, second-order filter with two zeros at 0 is given by

$$|H(e^{j\omega})| = \frac{1+r^2+2r\cos\theta}{\left[1+r^2-2r\cos(\omega+\theta)\right]^{\frac{1}{2}}\left[1+r^2-2r\cos(\omega-\theta)\right]^{\frac{1}{2}}}. \tag{14.37}$$

Here, we restrict the poles to be in the left half of the unit disk; that is, $\frac{\pi}{2}<\theta<\pi$.

Example 14.3: Let us compare a second-order highpass filter, designed by trial and error to get $\omega_c = \frac{3\pi}{4}$, with a first-order filter with the same cutoff frequency, as shown in Figure 14.23. The complex poles' magnitude and angles obtained were $r=0.6, \theta=\pm 5\pi/6$. Clearly, the second-order filter offers a better approximation to the ideal highpass filter than the first-order filter.

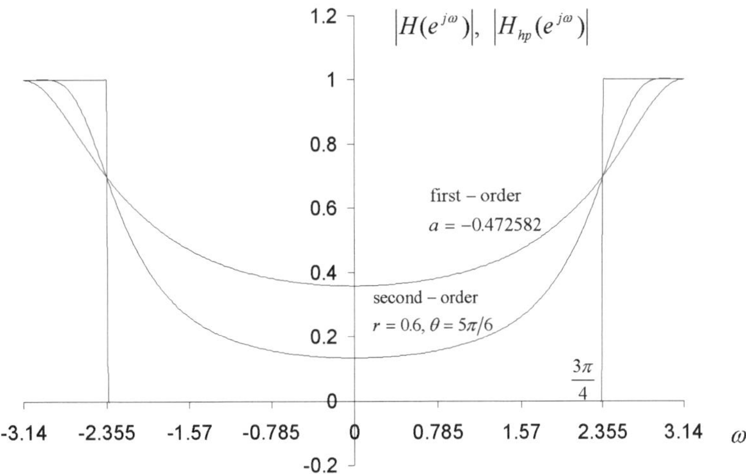

FIGURE 14.23 Frequency response magnitudes of first-order discrete-time highpass filters.

Ideal Bandpass Filter

As shown in Figure 14.24, an ideal bandpass filter with a passband between ω_{c1}, ω_{c2} has a frequency response given by

$$H_{bp}(e^{j\omega}) = \begin{cases} 1, & \left|\omega - (2k\pi + \frac{\omega_{c2}+\omega_{c1}}{2})\right| \le \frac{\omega_{c2}-\omega_{c1}}{2}, \ k = \ldots,-1,0,1,\ldots \\ 1, & \left|\omega - (2k\pi - \frac{\omega_{c2}+\omega_{c1}}{2})\right| \le \frac{\omega_{c2}-\omega_{c1}}{2}, \ k = \ldots,-1,0,1,\ldots. \\ 0, & \text{otherwise} \end{cases} \tag{14.38}$$

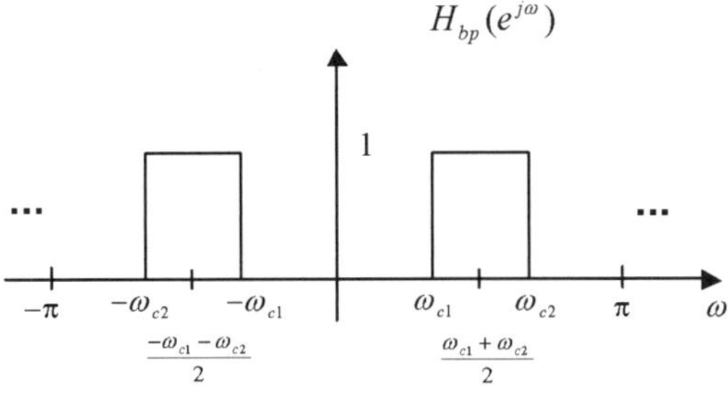

FIGURE 14.24 Frequency response of an ideal discrete-time bandpass filter.

Second-Order Approximation

The second-order frequency response is normalized at the frequencies $\pm\omega_p$ where the peaks occur. These frequencies are found to be:

$$\omega_p = \pm\arccos\left\{\frac{1+r^2}{2r}\cos\theta\right\}. \tag{14.39}$$

Thus, the normalized magnitude of the second-order frequency response is

$$\left|H(e^{j\omega})\right| = \frac{\left[1+r^2-2r\cos(\omega_p+\theta)\right]^{\frac{1}{2}}\left[1+r^2-2r\cos(\omega_p-\theta)\right]^{\frac{1}{2}}}{\left[1+r^2-2r\cos(\omega+\theta)\right]^{\frac{1}{2}}\left[1+r^2-2r\cos(\omega-\theta)\right]^{\frac{1}{2}}}. \tag{14.40}$$

We can use this expression to carry out a design by trial and error. Suppose we are given the frequencies ω_{c1}, ω_{c2} of the ideal bandpass filter that we have to approximate with a second-order filter. We first set $\omega_p = \frac{\omega_{c1}+\omega_{c2}}{2}$, and we compute the pole angle θ by using the inverse of the relationship in Equation 14.39:

$$\cos\theta = \frac{2r}{1+r^2}\cos\omega_p$$

$$\Rightarrow$$

$$\theta = \arccos\left\{\frac{2r}{1+r^2}\cos\omega_p\right\}. \tag{14.41}$$

Then, we can try out different values of $0<r<1$ to obtain the proper passband.

Example 14.4: Let us design a second-order bandpass filter approximating the ideal bandpass frequency response with $\omega_{c1} = \frac{\pi}{4}$, $\omega_{c1} = \frac{\pi}{2}$. We compute $\omega_p = \frac{\omega_{c1}+\omega_{c2}}{2} = \frac{3\pi}{8} = 1.1781$. Table 14.2 shows the pole angle for different values of r.

TABLE 14.2 Magnitude and Angle of Complex Pole for the Design of a Second-Order Bandpass Filter.

r	0.6	0.7	0.8	0.9
θ	1.226366	1.202992	1.18818	1.180386

The magnitude plot in Figure 14.25 shows that a (more or less) reasonable approximation is obtained with $r = 0.7, \theta = 1.203$.

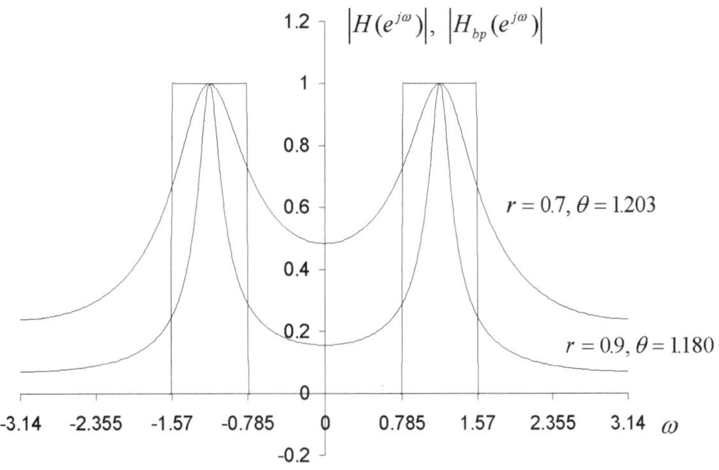

FIGURE 14.25 Frequency response magnitudes of second-order bandpass filters.

((Lecture 56:IIR and FIR Filters))

INFINITE IMPULSE RESPONSE AND FINITE IMPULSE RESPONSE FILTERS

There exist two broad classes of discrete-time filters: infinite impulse response (IIR) filters and finite impulse response (FIR) filters. This section introduces both classes of filters and gives some basic analysis and design strategies for each.

IIR Filters

IIR filters have impulse responses extending to $n \to \infty$. This includes the class of DLTI *recursive* filters, that is, filters represented by difference equations including delayed versions of the output $y[n]$. Consider the general N^{th}-order difference equation of a stable, causal system with $a_0 \neq 0$:

$$a_0 y[n] + a_1 y[n-1] + \cdots + a_N y[n-N] = b_0 x[n] + b_1 x[n-1] + \cdots + b_M x[n-M]. \quad (14.42)$$

This equation represents an IIR filter if at least one of the coefficients $\{a_i\}_{i=1}^{N}$ is nonzero. In terms of transfer functions, IIR filters have transfer functions with at least one pole p_m different from 0:

$$H(z) = \frac{(b_0 + b_1 z^{-1} + \cdots + b_M z^{-M})}{(a_0 + a_1 z^{-1} + \cdots + a_N z^{-N})} = A\frac{\prod_{k=1}^{M}(1 - z_k z^{-1})}{\prod_{k=1}^{N}(1 - p_k z^{-1})} = Az^{N-M}\frac{\prod_{k=1}^{M}(z - z_k)}{\prod_{k=1}^{N}(z - p_k)}. \tag{14.43}$$

The usual first-order and second-order filters are examples of IIR filters, for example,

$$H(z) = \frac{1 + \frac{1}{3}z^{-1}}{1 - \frac{1}{2}z^{-1}}, \quad |z| > \frac{1}{2}, \tag{14.44}$$

whose associated recursive difference equation is

$$y[n] = \frac{1}{2}y[n-1] + x[n] + \frac{1}{3}x[n-1]. \tag{14.45}$$

We have already studied simple design methods for these types of filters (with their zeros restricted to be at 0) to approximate ideal filters in the previous section. There exist several approaches to design accurate high-order IIR filters. One of them is to design the filter in continuous time (in the Laplace domain), using, for example, the Butterworth, Chebyshev, or elliptic pole patterns and then transforming the Laplace-domain transfer function into the z-domain using the bilinear transformation. Other computer-aided techniques use iterative optimization methods on the discrete-time filter coefficients to minimize the error between the desired frequency response and the filter's actual frequency response.

Benefits of IIR filters include the following:

- Low-order filters can offer relatively sharp transition bands.
- They have low memory requirements when implemented as a recursive equation.

One disadvantage of IIR filters is that a frequency response with an approximately linear phase is difficult to obtain. A linear phase, corresponding to a time delay, is important in communication systems in order to avoid signal distortion caused by signal harmonics being subjected to different delays.

FIR Filters

FIR filters have, as the name implies, impulse responses of finite duration. For instance, causal FIR filters are non-recursive DLTI filters in the sense that their corresponding difference equations in the regular form have only $a_0 y[n]$ on the left-hand side:

$$a_0 y[n] = b_0 x[n] + b_1 x[n-1] + \cdots + b_M x[n-M]. \tag{14.46}$$

Even though this difference equation is 0th-order according to our original definition, as an FIR filter the system is said to be M^{th}-order. Moving-average filters are of the FIR type. The impulse response of a causal FIR filter (with $a_0 = 1$ without loss of generality) is simply

$$h[n] = b_0 \delta[n] + b_1 \delta[n-1] + \cdots + b_M \delta[n-M]. \tag{14.47}$$

That is,

$$h[n] = \begin{cases} b_n, & n = 0, \ldots, M \\ 0, & \text{otherwise} \end{cases}. \tag{14.48}$$

The transfer function of a causal FIR filter is given by

$$\begin{aligned} H(z) &= b_0 + b_1 z^{-1} + \cdots + b_M z^{-M} \\ &= \frac{b_0 z^M + b_1 z^{M-1} + \cdots + b_M}{z^M} \\ &= A \frac{\prod_{k=1}^{M} (z - z_k)}{z^M} \end{aligned} \tag{14.49}$$

Note that all the poles are at $z = 0$. Thus, only the zeros' locations in the z-plane will determine the filter's frequency response. A realization of a second-order causal FIR filter with unit delays is shown in Figure 14.26.

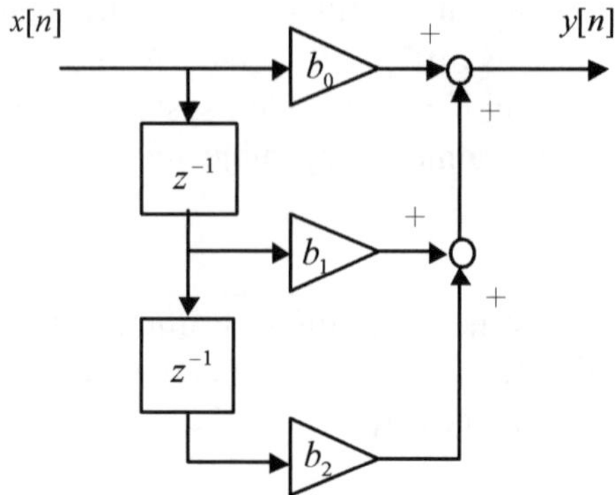

FIGURE 14.26 Realization of a second-order causal FIR filter.

Moving-Average Filters

A special type of FIR filter is the causal *moving-average filter,* whose coefficients are all equal to a constant (chosen so that the DC gain is 1); that is, the impulse response is a rectangular pulse:

$$h[n]=\begin{cases}\dfrac{1}{M+1}, & n=0,\ldots,M\\ 0, & \text{otherwise}\end{cases}. \tag{14.50}$$

This impulse response is shown in Figure 14.27 for $M=4$.

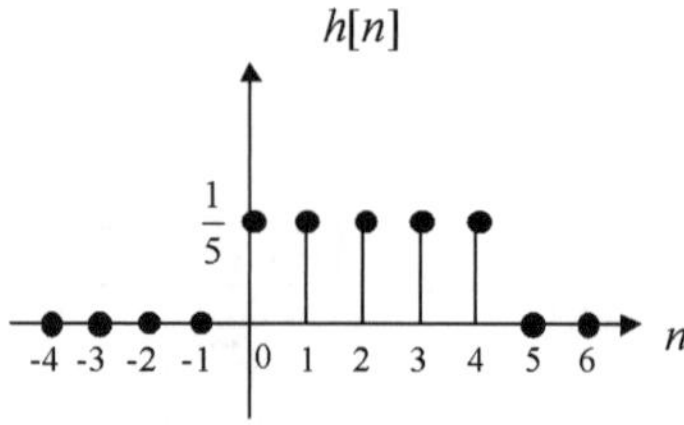

FIGURE 14.27 Impulse response of fourth-order moving average filter.

The moving average filter is often used to smooth economic data in order to find the underlying trend of a variable. Its transfer function is

$$
\begin{aligned}
H(z) &= \frac{1}{M+1}\left(1+z^{-1}+\cdots+z^{-M}\right) \\
&= \frac{1}{M+1}\frac{z^{M}+z^{M-1}+\cdots+1}{z^{M}}.
\end{aligned}
\tag{14.51}
$$

The frequency response of the causal moving average filter is computed as follows.

$$
\begin{aligned}
H(e^{j\omega}) &= \frac{1}{M+1}\left(1+e^{-j\omega}+\cdots+e^{-j\omega M}\right) \\
&= \frac{1}{M+1}e^{-j\omega\frac{M}{2}}\left(e^{j\omega\frac{M}{2}}+e^{j\omega(\frac{M}{2}-1)}+\cdots+e^{-j\omega(\frac{M}{2}-1)}+e^{-j\omega\frac{M}{2}}\right) \\
&= \begin{cases} \dfrac{1}{M+1}e^{-j\omega\frac{M}{2}}\left(1+2\displaystyle\sum_{k=0}^{M/2-1}\cos\left[\omega(\frac{M}{2}-k)\right]\right), & M \text{ even} \\ \dfrac{2}{M+1}e^{-j\omega\frac{M}{2}}\displaystyle\sum_{k=0}^{(M-1)/2}\cos\left[\omega(\frac{M}{2}-k)\right], & M \text{ odd} \end{cases}
\end{aligned}
\tag{14.52}
$$

Alternatively, we can use the finite geometric sum formula in Table B.2 (Appendix B) to obtain a single equivalent expression for $H(e^{j\omega})$:

$$
\begin{aligned}
H(e^{j\omega}) &= \frac{1}{M+1}\sum_{0}^{M}e^{-j\omega k} \\
&= \frac{1}{M+1}\frac{1-e^{-j\omega(M+1)}}{1-e^{-j\omega}} \\
&= \frac{e^{-j\omega\frac{M+1}{2}}}{(M+1)e^{-j\frac{\omega}{2}}}\frac{e^{j\omega\frac{M+1}{2}}-e^{-j\omega\frac{M+1}{2}}}{e^{j\frac{\omega}{2}}-e^{-j\frac{\omega}{2}}} \\
&= \frac{e^{-j\omega\frac{M}{2}}}{M+1}\frac{\sin\left(\omega\dfrac{M+1}{2}\right)}{\sin\left(\dfrac{\omega}{2}\right)}.
\end{aligned}
\tag{14.53}
$$

The magnitude of this frequency response displays M zeros, the first one being at $\omega = \frac{2\pi}{M+1}$, as shown in Figure 14.28. Thus, the bandwidth of this lowpass filter depends only on its length and cannot be specified otherwise.

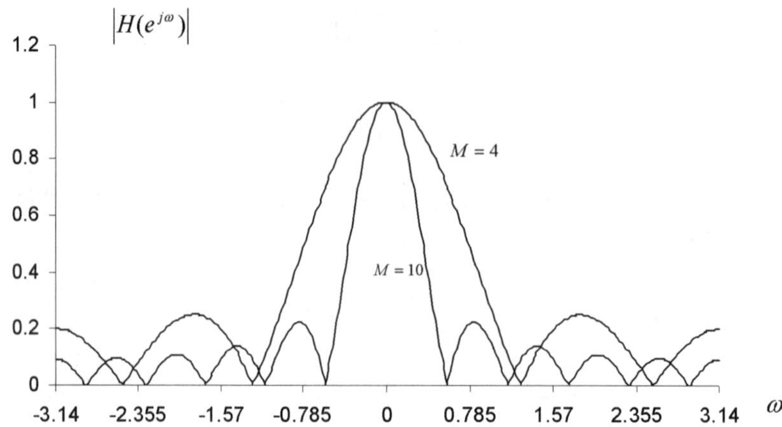

FIGURE 14.28 Frequency response magnitudes of moving average FIR filters.

Also, since there are M zeros in $H(e^{j\omega})$, these zeros must be zeros of $H(z)$ on the unit circle. Thus, the pole-zero plot of a moving average filter is as shown in Figure 14.29 (case $M = 4$.)

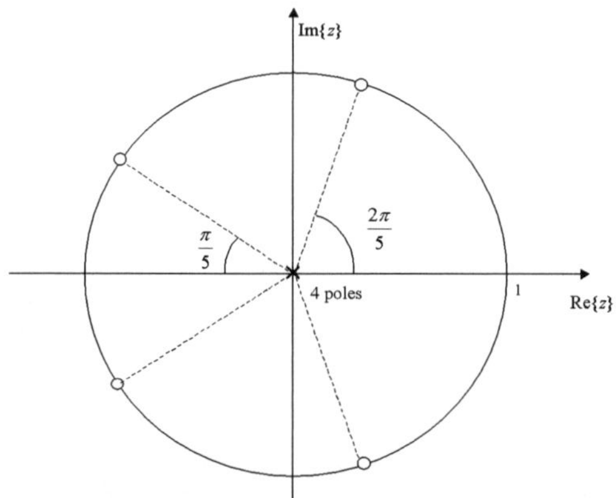

FIGURE 14.29 Pole-zero plot of moving average FIR filter of order 4.

The zeros are equally spaced on the unit circle as though there were $M + 1$ zeros, with the one at $z = 1$ removed.

((Lecture 57:FIR Filter Design by Windowing))

FIR Filter Design by Impulse Response Truncation

FIR filters can be designed via a straight truncation of a desired infinite impulse response. This method is very effective and popular because it is straightforward, and one can get extremely sharp transitions *and* linear phases, but at the cost of long filter lengths.

Consider for example the noncausal, real, even, infinite impulse response of the ideal lowpass filter:

$$h_{lp}[n] = \frac{\omega_c}{\pi}\operatorname{sinc}\left(\frac{\omega_c n}{\pi}\right) = \frac{\sin(\omega_c n)}{\pi n}. \tag{14.54}$$

This impulse response is plotted in Figure 14.30 for the cutoff frequency $\omega_c = \frac{\pi}{4}$.

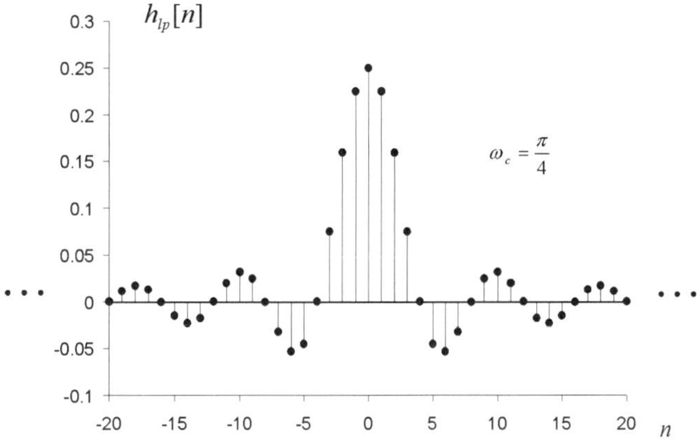

FIGURE 14.30 Impulse response of ideal lowpass IIR filter.

A first attempt would be to truncate this response and keep only the first M + 1 values of the causal part. However, this does not produce very good results. For a given filter length M + 1 and assuming that M is even, it is much better to time-delay the impulse response by $M/2$ first and then truncate it to retain only the values for $n = 0, \ldots, M$.

Example 14.5: Suppose we select M = 40, and we want to have a cutoff frequency of $\omega_c = \frac{\pi}{4}$. Then, we delay the impulse response shown above by 20 time steps and truncate it to obtain the finite impulse response $h[n] = h_{lp}[n-20](u[n] - u[n-41])$ shown in Figure 14.31.

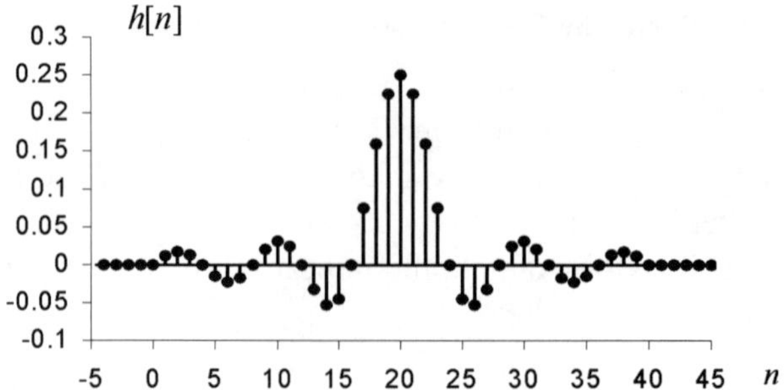

FIGURE 14.31 Impulse response of a causal FIR filter obtained by truncation and time shifting of an ideal lowpass IIR filter.

The frequency response of this causal FIR filter can be obtained numerically from the following expression:

$$\begin{aligned} H(e^{j\omega}) &= h[0] + h[1]e^{-j\omega} + \cdots + h[40]e^{-j\omega 40} \\ &= e^{-j\omega 20}\left(0.25 + 2\sum_{k=0}^{19} h[k]\cos[\omega(20-k)]\right). \end{aligned} \tag{14.55}$$

Its magnitude is plotted in Figure 14.32 and is compared to the ideal lowpass filter with cutoff frequency $\omega_c = \frac{\pi}{4}$.

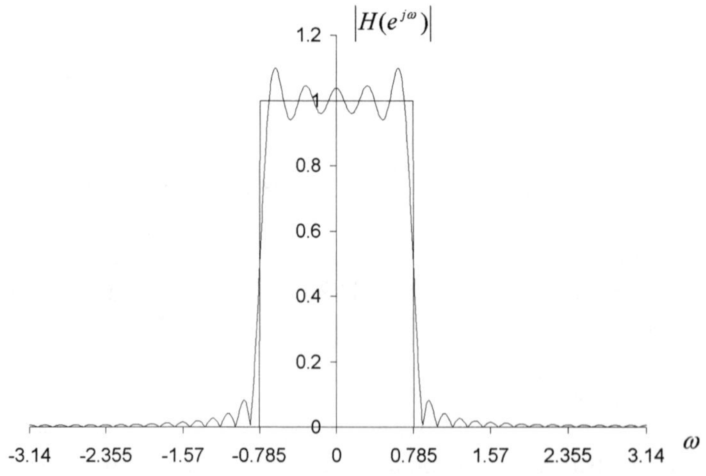

FIGURE 14.32 Frequency response magnitudes of causal FIR and ideal lowpass filters for $M = 40$ and $\omega_c = \frac{\pi}{4}$.

The phase is piecewise linear and linear in the passband where $\angle H(e^{j\omega}) = -20\omega$.

Remarks:

- Longer finite impulse responses yield increasingly better filters.
- The causal FIR filter equation $y[n] = h[0]x[n] + h[1]x[n-1] + \cdots + h[M]x[n-M]$ is nothing but the discrete-time convolution sum.

FIR Filter Design Using Windows

A straight truncation of a desired infinite impulse response can be seen as the multiplication in the time domain of a rectangular window $w[n]$ with the infinite impulse response of the filter. Then, the resulting finite impulse response centered at $n = 0$ is time-delayed to make it causal. The resulting effect in the frequency domain is the periodic convolution of the Fourier transforms of the infinite impulse response $H_{lp}(e^{j\omega})$ and of the rectangular window $W(e^{j\omega})$.

Example 14.6: Suppose we select $M = 20$. The even rectangular window

$$w[n] = u[n+10] - u[n-11] \tag{14.56}$$

is applied to the impulse response $h_{lp}[n]$ of the ideal lowpass filter with cutoff frequency $\omega_c = \frac{\pi}{2}$ in order to truncate it. The impulse response of the FIR filter before the time shift is given by

$$h_0[n] = w[n]h_{lp}[n]. \tag{14.57}$$

Its corresponding frequency response is the convolution of the spectra of the rectangular window and the ideal lowpass filter:

$$H_0(e^{j\omega}) = \frac{1}{2\pi}\int_{-\pi}^{\pi} W(e^{j\upsilon})H_{lp}(e^{j(\omega-\upsilon)})d\upsilon. \tag{14.58}$$

This convolution operation in the frequency domain is illustrated in Figure 14.33.

The subsequent time shift $h[n] = h_0[n-10]$ only adds a linear negative phase component to $H_0(e^{j\omega})$, but it does not change its magnitude. The magnitude of $H(e^{j\omega})$ is shown in Figure 14.34.

The truncation method can be improved upon by using windows of different shapes that have "better" spectra. Note that the best window would be the infinite rectangular window, since its DTFT is an impulse at $\omega = 0$. Then the convolution of $W(e^{j\omega}) = \delta(\omega)$ with the rectangular spectrum of the lowpass filter would leave it

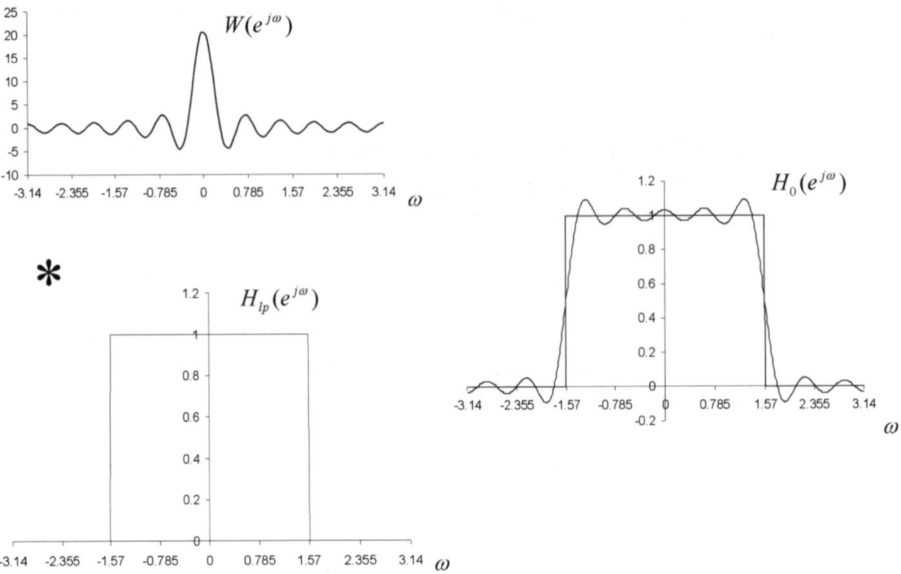

FIGURE 14.33 Convolution of the frequency response of an ideal lowpass filter with the DTFT of a rectangular window.

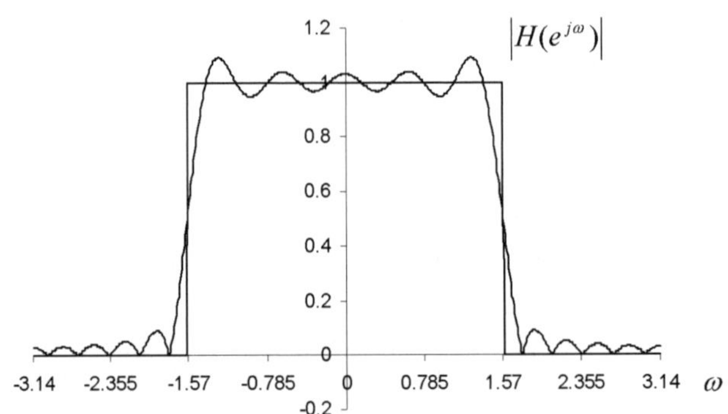

FIGURE 14.34 Frequency response magnitudes of causal FIR and ideal lowpass filters for $M = 20$ and $\omega_c = \frac{\pi}{2}$.

unchanged. This limit case helps us understand that the Fourier transform of a good window should have as narrow a main lobe as possible and very small side lobes. Essentially, the narrower the main lobe is, the sharper the transition will be around the cutoff frequency. Large side lobes in $W(e^{j\omega})$ lead to larger ripples in the passband and stopband of the filter.

In general, there is a tradeoff in selecting an appropriate window: *For a fixed order M, windows with a narrow main lobe have larger side lobes, and windows with smaller side lobes have wider main lobes.*

This tradeoff led researchers to propose different windows such as the Hanning, Hamming, Bartlett, Blackman window, etc. Note that as the window length $M+1$ gets longer, the main lobe gets narrower, leading to a sharper transition, but the maximum magnitude of the side lobes does not decrease. The even *Hamming window* with M even, shown in Figure 14.35, is defined as follows:

$$w[n]=\left[0.54+0.46\cos\left(\frac{2\pi n}{M}\right)\right]\left(u[n+M/2]-u[n-M/2-1]\right). \quad (14.59)$$

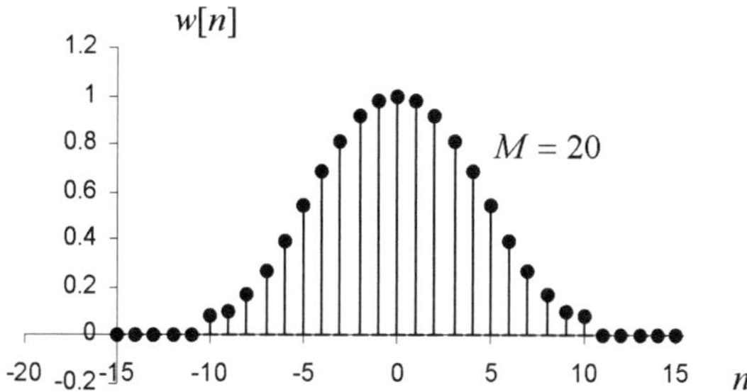

FIGURE 14.35 Hamming window for $M = 20$.

The Fourier transform of the Hamming window has smaller side lobes but a slightly wider main lobe than the rectangular window, as can be seen in Figure 14.36.

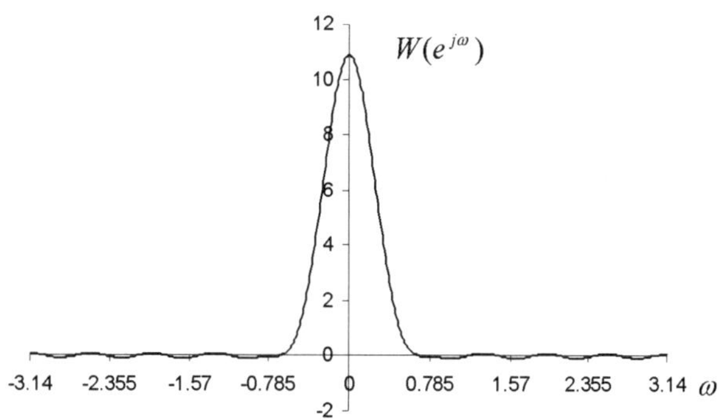

FIGURE 14.36 DTFT of a Hamming window for $M = 20$.

For the same lowpass FIR filter design as above, namely $M = 20$ and $\omega_c = \frac{\pi}{2}$, but this time using the Hamming window instead of the rectangular window, we obtain the finite impulse response of Figure 14.37.

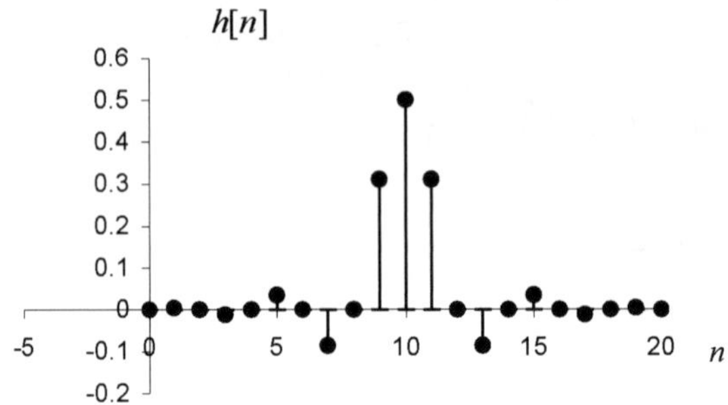

FIGURE 14.37 Impulse response of a causal FIR filter obtained by windowing and time shifting of an ideal lowpass IIR filter, using a Hamming window with $M = 20$.

The magnitude of the filter's frequency response is shown in Figure 14.38. We can see that the passband and stopband are essentially flat, but the transition band is wider than the previous design done by truncation.

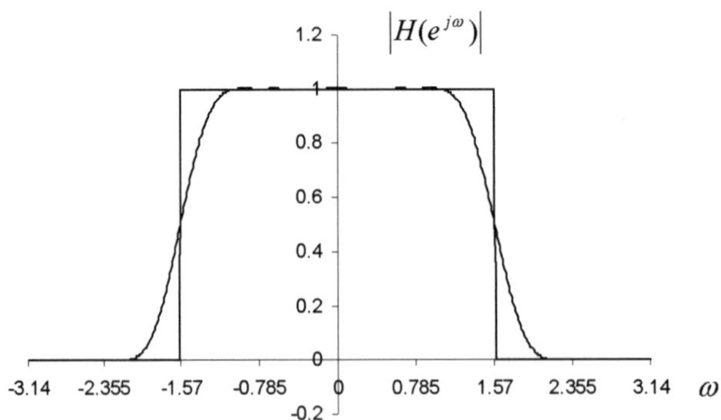

FIGURE 14.38 Magnitudes of causal FIR and ideal lowpass filters for $M = 20$ and $\omega_c = \frac{\pi}{2}$, designed using a Hamming window.

Linear Phase Condition

A causal FIR filter of order M has a linear phase if and only if its impulse response satisfies the following condition:

$$h[n] = h[M-n]. \tag{14.60}$$

This simply means that the filter is symmetric around its middle point. For a filter $h_0[n]$ centered at $n = 0$ (before it is time-shifted to make it causal), the linear phase condition becomes the zero-phase condition, and it holds if $h_0[n]$ is even.

It turns out that only FIR, not IIR, filters can have a linear phase. The frequency response of a linear phase FIR filter is given by

$$\begin{aligned} H(e^{j\omega}) &= h[0] + h[1]e^{-j\omega} + \cdots + h[M]e^{-j\omega M} \\ &= \begin{cases} e^{-j\omega\frac{M}{2}}\left(h[M/2] + 2\sum_{k=0}^{M/2-1} h[k]\cos\left[\omega(M/2-k)\right]\right), & M \text{ even} \\ e^{-j\omega\frac{M}{2}}\left(2\sum_{k=0}^{(M-1)/2} h[k]\cos\left[\omega(M/2-k)\right]\right), & M \text{ odd} \end{cases} \end{aligned} \tag{14.61}$$

SUMMARY

In this chapter, we analyzed the behavior of DLTI systems in both the time and frequency domains.

- The frequency response can be characterized in a qualitative fashion just by looking at the pole-zero plot. The frequency, impulse, and step responses of first-order and second-order systems were analyzed.
- Ideal frequency-selective discrete-time filters were discussed, and first and second-order approximations were given.
- Discrete-time IIR and FIR filters were introduced, and the windowing technique for FIR filter design was presented.

TO PROBE FURTHER

For comprehensive treatments of discrete-time systems and filter design, see Oppenheim, Schafer and Buck, 1999; Proakis and Manolakis, 1995; and Winder, 2002.

EXERCISES

Exercises with Solutions

Exercise 14.1

(a) Design a discrete-time second-order IIR bandpass filter approximating the ideal bandpass filter with frequencies $\omega_{c1} = \frac{\pi}{4}, \omega_{c2} = \frac{3\pi}{4}$ and normalize it to have a passband-frequency gain of 1.

Answer:

We compute $\omega_p = \frac{\omega_{c1}+\omega_{c2}}{2} = \frac{\pi}{2}$. The pole angle is independent of r, as

$$\theta = \arccos\left\{\frac{2r}{1+r^2}\cos\omega_p\right\} = \arccos\{0\} = \frac{\pi}{2}.$$

The transfer function is

$$\begin{aligned}
H(z) &= \frac{\left[1+r^2-2r\cos(\omega_p+\theta)\right]^{\frac{1}{2}}\left[1+r^2-2r\cos(\omega_p-\theta)\right]^{\frac{1}{2}}}{1-2r\cos\theta z^{-1}+r^2z^{-2}}, \quad |z|>r \\
&= \frac{\left[1+r^2-2r\cos(\pi)\right]^{\frac{1}{2}}\left[1+r^2-2r\cos(0)\right]^{\frac{1}{2}}}{1-2r\cos\frac{\pi}{2}z^{-1}+r^2z^{-2}}, \quad |z|>r \\
&= \frac{\left[1+r^2+2r\right]^{\frac{1}{2}}\left[1+r^2-2r\right]^{\frac{1}{2}}}{1+r^2z^{-2}} = \frac{\left[(1+r^2)^2-4r^2\right]}{1+r^2z^{-2}} = \frac{(1-r^2)^2}{1+r^2z^{-2}}, \quad |z|>r.
\end{aligned}$$

The magnitude plot in Figure 14.39 shows that a "reasonable" design is obtained with $r = 0.52$.

(b) Plot the magnitude of its frequency response and the magnitude of the ideal bandpass filter on the same graph.

Answer:

The frequency response magnitudes of the bandpass filters are plotted in Figure 14.39.

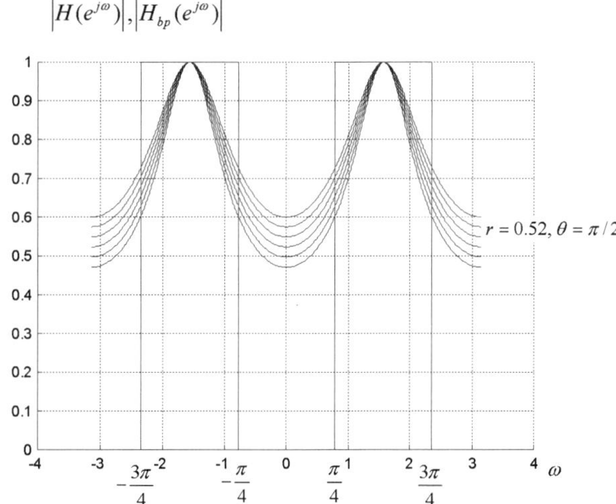

FIGURE 14.39 Magnitudes of second-order IIR and ideal bandpass filters (Exercise 14.1).

Exercise 14.2

(a) First, design a lowpass FIR filter of length $M + 1 = 17$ with cutoff frequency $\omega_c = \frac{\pi}{4}$ using a Hamming window. Plot its magnitude over the magnitude of the ideal filter.

Answer:

Windowed ideal lowpass filter:

$$h_0[n] = w[n]h_{lp}[n] = w[n]\frac{\sin\omega_c n}{\pi n},$$

where the Hamming window is

$$w[n] = \left[0.54 + 0.46\cos\left(\frac{2\pi n}{16}\right)\right]\left(u[n+8] - u[n-9]\right)$$

After the shift:

$$h[n] = w[n-8]\frac{\sin[\omega_c(n-8)]}{\pi(n-8)} = w[n-8]\frac{\omega_c}{\pi}\operatorname{sinc}\left[\frac{\omega_c}{\pi}(n-8)\right]$$

Frequency response:

$$
\begin{aligned}
H(e^{j\omega}) &= h[0]+h[1]e^{-j\omega}+\cdots+h[16]e^{-j\omega 16} \\
&= e^{-j\omega 8}\left(h[8]+2\sum_{k=0}^{7}h[k]\cos\left(\omega(8-k)\right)\right) \\
&= e^{-j\omega 8}\left(\frac{1}{4}+2\sum_{k=0}^{7}\frac{\sin\left(\frac{\pi}{4}(k-8)\right)}{\pi(k-8)}\left[0.54+0.46\cos\left(\frac{2\pi(k-8)}{16}\right)\right]\cos\left(\omega(8-k)\right)\right).
\end{aligned}
$$

The magnitude of this frequency response, which is just the absolute value of the big bracket in the last line of the above equation, is plotted in Figure 14.40.

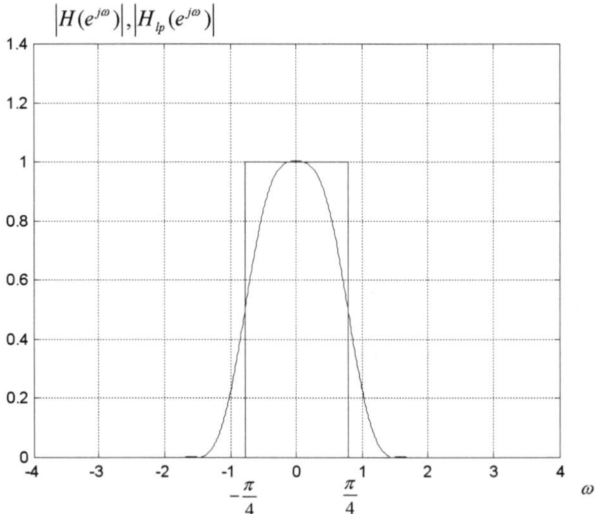

FIGURE 14.40 Magnitudes of 16th-order Hamming-windowed FIR and ideal lowpass filters (Exercise 14.2).

The following MATLAB M-file used to design the FIR filter can be found on the companion CD-ROM in D:\Chapter14\FIRdesign.m.

```
%% Freq resp of FIR filter
% number of points in FIR filter is M+1
M=16;
% cutoff frequency of lowpass
wc=pi/4;
% freq vector
w=[-pi:0.01:pi]';
% FR computation using cosine formula
Hjw=(wc/pi)*ones(length(w),1);
for k=0:M/2-1
Hjw=Hjw+2*sin((k-M/2)*wc)/((k-M/2)*pi)*(0.54+0.46*cos(2*pi*(k-
M/2)/M))*cos(w*(M/2-k));
end
% Ideal lowpass
Hlp=zeros(length(w),1);
for k=1:length(w)
if (abs(w(k)) < wc)
Hlp(k)=1;
end
end
%plot frequency response
plot(w,abs(Hjw),w,Hlp);
```

(b) Use the filter in (a) to form a real bandpass FIR filter with cutoff frequencies $\frac{\pi}{4}, \frac{3\pi}{4}$. Give its impulse response and plot its magnitude over the magnitude of the ideal bandpass filter and that of the IIR filter in Exercise 14.1.

Answer:
Using frequency shifting,

$$\begin{aligned}
H_1(e^{j\omega}) &= H(e^{j(\omega+\frac{\pi}{2})}) + H(e^{j(\omega-\frac{\pi}{2})}) \\
&= \left\{ h[0] + h[1]e^{-j(\omega+\frac{\pi}{2})} + \cdots + h[16]e^{-j(\omega+\frac{\pi}{2})16} \right\} + \left\{ h[0] + h[1]e^{-j(\omega-\frac{\pi}{2})} + \cdots + h[16]e^{-j(\omega-\frac{\pi}{2})16} \right\} \\
&= 2h[0] + \sum_{k=1}^{16} (e^{-j\frac{\pi}{2}k} + e^{j\frac{\pi}{2}k}) h[k] e^{-jk\omega} \\
&= 2h[0] + \sum_{k=1}^{16} 2\cos(\frac{\pi}{2}k) h[k] e^{-jk\omega}.
\end{aligned}$$

The impulse response is given by $h_1[k]=2\cos(\frac{\pi}{2}k)h[k]$; thus,

$$H_1(e^{j\omega})=e^{-j\omega 8}\left(h_1[8]+2\sum_{k=0}^{7}h_1[k]\cos\big(\omega(8-k)\big)\right)$$

$$=e^{-j\omega 8}\left(\frac{1}{2}+2\sum_{k=0}^{7}2\cos(\frac{\pi}{2}k)\frac{\sin\left(\frac{\pi}{4}(k-8)\right)}{\pi(k-8)}\left[0.54+0.46\cos\left(\frac{2\pi(k-8)}{16}\right)\right]\cos\big(\omega(8-k)\big)\right).$$

The frequency response magnitudes of this FIR bandpass filter and of the second-order IIR filters of Exercise 14.1 are shown in Figure 14.41.

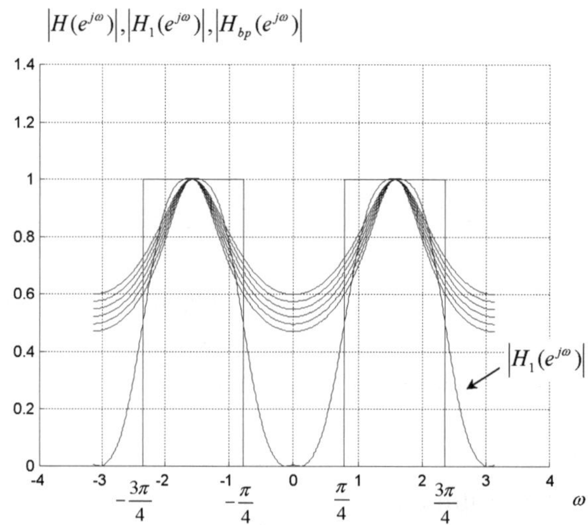

FIGURE 14.41 Magnitudes of bandpass filters (Exercise 14.2).

(c) Give an expression for the phase in the passband of the FIR bandpass filter.

Answer:
The phase in the passband is -8ω.

Exercises

Exercise 14.3

Consider the following moving-average filter S initially at rest:

$$S: \qquad y[n] = \frac{1}{4}x[n+1] + \frac{1}{4}x[n] + \frac{1}{4}x[n-1] + \frac{1}{4}x[n-2].$$

(a) Find the impulse response $h[n]$ of the filter. Is it causal?

(b) Find the transfer function of the filter $H(z)$ and give its region of convergence. Sketch the pole-zero plot.

(c) Find the frequency response of the filter. Sketch its magnitude.

(d) Compute the –3 dB cutoff frequency ω_c.

Answer:

ON THE CD

Exercise 14.4

Suppose we want to design a causal, stable, first-order highpass filter of the type

$$H(z) = \frac{B}{1 - az^{-1}}, |z| > |a|$$

with –3 dB cutoff frequency $\omega_c = \frac{2\pi}{3}$ and a real.

(a) Express the real constant B in terms of the pole a to obtain unity gain at the highest frequency $\omega = \pi$.

(b) Design the filter; that is, find the numerical values of the pole a and the constant B.

(c) Sketch the magnitude of the filter's frequency response.

Exercise 14.5

(a) Design a discrete-time second-order IIR lowpass filter approximating the ideal lowpass filter with –3 dB cutoff frequency $\omega_c = \frac{\pi}{6}$ and normalize it to have a DC gain of 1. You can proceed by trial and error. Plot the magnitude of its frequency response (use MATLAB) and the magnitude of the ideal lowpass filter on the same figure.

(b) Add a zero at $\omega = \pi$ to your design to improve the response at high frequency. Plot the resulting frequency response magnitude as well as the response in (a) and discuss the results.

Answer:

ON THE CD

Exercise 14.6

(a) First, design a lowpass FIR filter of order $M = 256$ with cutoff frequency $\omega_c = \frac{\pi}{6}$ radians using a Hamming window. Plot its magnitude over the magnitudes of the ideal filter and the filters in Exercise 14.5.

(b) Give an expression for the phase in the passband of the FIR bandpass filter.

(c) Simulate the filter for the input $x[n] = \cos(\frac{\pi}{8}n)u[n] + \cos(\frac{\pi}{4}n)u[n]$ until the output reaches steady-state and plot the results. Also plot the input on a separate graph.

Exercise 14.7

(a) Design a first-order discrete-time lowpass filter with a –3 dB cutoff frequency $\omega_c = \frac{\pi}{12}$ and a DC gain of 1.

(b) Plot the magnitude of its frequency response.

(c) Write the filter as a difference equation and plot the first 20 values of the filtered signal $y[n]$ for the input signal $x[n] = u[n] - u[n-10]$ with the filter being initially at rest.

Answer:

ON THE CD

Exercise 14.8

(a) Design a DT second-order IIR bandpass filter approximating the ideal bandpass filter with frequencies $\omega_{c1} = \frac{3\pi}{8}, \omega_{c2} = \frac{\pi}{2}$ and normalize it to have a passband-frequency gain of 5.

(b) Plot the magnitude of its frequency response and the magnitude of the ideal bandpass filter on the same figure.

Exercise 14.9

(a) Design a first-order DT lowpass filter with a –3 dB cutoff frequency $\omega_c = \frac{\pi}{12}$ and a DC gain of 1.

(b) Plot the magnitude of its frequency response.

(c) Write the filter as a difference equation, and plot the first 15 values of the filtered signal $y[n]$ for the input signal $x[n] = u[n-2]$.

Answer:

Exercise 14.10

(a) Design a 20th-order (i.e., $M = 20$) DT causal FIR highpass filter approximating the ideal highpass filter with $\omega_c = \frac{2\pi}{3}$ and normalized to have a high-frequency gain of 1. Use the straight truncation (rectangular window) technique.

(b) Repeat (a) using the Hamming window.

(c) Plot the magnitudes of the frequency responses of the two FIR filters, the magnitude of the IIR filter obtained in Exercise 14.4, and the magnitude of the ideal highpass filter on the same figure.

(d) Plot the first 20 values of the two filtered signals $y[n]$, i.e., the output of each filter, for the step input signal $x[n] = u[n]$.

15 Sampling Systems

In This Chapter

- Sampling of Continuous-Time Signals
- Signal Reconstruction
- Discrete-Time Processing of Continuous-Time Signals
- Sampling of Discrete-Time Signals
- Summary
- To Probe Further
- Exercises

((Lecture 58: Sampling))

This chapter introduces the important bridge between continuous-time and discrete-time signals provided by the *sampling* process. Sampling records discrete values of a continuous-time signal at periodic instants of time, either for real-time processing or for storage and subsequent off-line processing. Sampling opens up a world of possibilities for the processing of continuous-time signals through the use of discrete-time systems such as infinite impulse response (IIR) and finite impulse response (FIR) filters.

SAMPLING OF CONTINUOUS-TIME SIGNALS

Recall that the Fourier transform of the continuous-time signal $x(t)$ is given by

$$X(j\omega) = \int_{-\infty}^{+\infty} x(t)e^{-j\omega t}\,dt. \tag{15.1}$$

Under certain conditions, a continuous-time signal can be completely represented by (and recovered from) its samples taken at periodic instants of time. The sampling operation can be seen as the multiplication of a continuous-time signal with a periodic impulse train of period T_s, as depicted in Figure 15.1. The spectrum of the sampled signal is the convolution of the Fourier transform of the signal with the spectrum of the impulse train, which is itself a frequency-domain impulse train of period equal to the sampling frequency $\omega_s = 2\pi/T_s$. This frequency-domain analysis of sampling is illustrated in Figure 15.2.

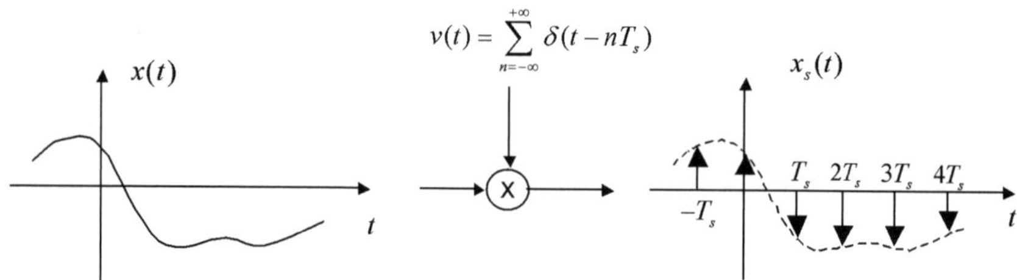

FIGURE 15.1 Impulse train sampling of a continuous-time signal.

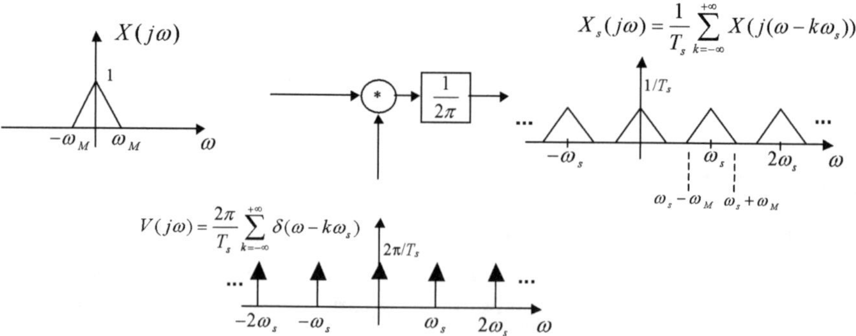

FIGURE 15.2 Frequency domain representation of impulse train sampling of a continuous-time signal.

The resulting sampled signal in the time domain is a sequence of impulses given by

$$x_s(t) = \sum_{n=-\infty}^{+\infty} x(nT_s)\delta(t - nT_s), \tag{15.2}$$

where the impulse at time $t = nT_s$ has an area equal to the signal value at that time. In the frequency domain, the spectrum of the sampled signal is a superposition of frequency-shifted replicas of the original signal spectrum, scaled by $1/T_s$.

$$\begin{aligned} X_s(j\omega) &= \frac{1}{T_s}\int_{-\infty}^{+\infty} X(j\upsilon)\sum_{k=-\infty}^{+\infty} \delta(\omega - \upsilon - k\omega_s)d\upsilon \\ &= \frac{1}{T_s}\int_{-\infty}^{+\infty}\sum_{k=-\infty}^{+\infty} X(j(\omega - k\omega_s))\delta(\omega - \upsilon - k\omega_s)d\upsilon \\ &= \frac{1}{T_s}\sum_{k=-\infty}^{+\infty} X(j(\omega - k\omega_s)) \end{aligned} \tag{15.3}$$

The Sampling Theorem

The extremely useful *sampling theorem*, also known as the *Nyquist theorem*, or the *Shannon theorem*, gives a sufficient condition to recover a continuous-time signal from its samples $x(nT_s),\ n \in \mathbb{Z}$.

Sampling theorem: Let x(t) be a band-limited signal with $X(j\omega) = 0$ for $|\omega| > \omega_M$. *Then x(t) is uniquely determined by its samples* $x(nT_s),\ -\infty < n < +\infty$ *if*

$$\omega_s > 2\omega_M, \tag{15.4}$$

where $\omega_s = \frac{2\pi}{T_s}$ *is the sampling frequency.*

Figure 15.2 suggests that given the signal samples, we can recover the signal $x(t)$ by filtering $x_s(t)$ using an ideal lowpass filter with DC gain T_s and with a cut-off frequency between ω_M and $\omega_s - \omega_M$, usually chosen as $\frac{\omega_s}{2}$, which is called the *Nyquist frequency*. It is indeed the case, and the setup to recover the signal is shown in Figure 15.3.

The sampling theorem expresses a fact that is easy to observe from the example plot of $X_s(j\omega)$ in Figure 15.2: the original spectrum centered at $\omega = 0$ can be recovered undistorted provided it does not overlap with its neighboring replicas.

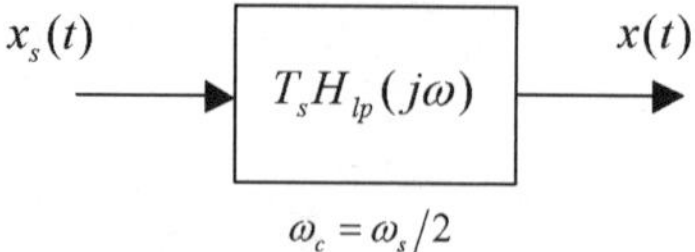

FIGURE 15.3 Ideal lowpass filter used to recover the continuous-time signal from the impulse train sampled signal.

Sampling Using a Sample-and-Hold Operator

The *sample-and-hold* (SH) operator retains the value of the signal sample up until the following sampling instant. It basically produces a "staircase" signal, that is, a piecewise constant signal from the samples. A schematic of an ideal circuit implementing a sample-and-hold is shown in Figure 15.4. The switch, which is assumed to close only for an infinitesimal period of time at the sampling instants to charge the capacitor to its new voltage, is typically implemented using a field effect transistor.

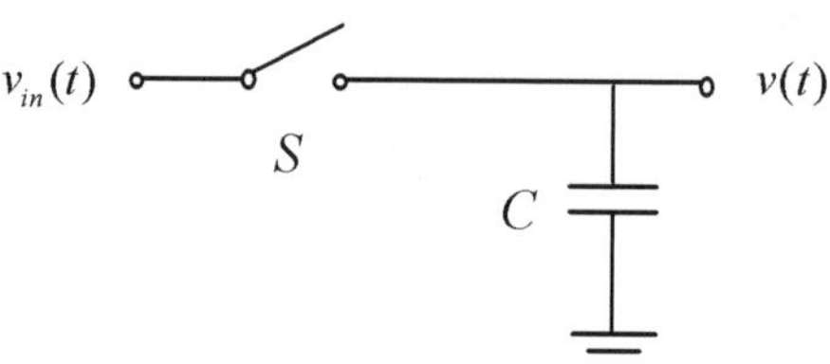

FIGURE 15.4 Simplified sample-and-hold circuit.

The theoretical representation of a sample-and-hold shown in Figure 15.5 consists of a sampling operation (multiplication by an impulse train), followed by filtering with a linear time-invariant (LTI) system of impulse response $h_0(t)$, which is a unit pulse of duration equal to the sampling period T_s. Note that the sample-and-hold operator is sometimes called zero-order-hold (ZOH), although here we call zero-order-hold only the LTI system block with impulse response $h_0(t)$ in Figure 15.5.

Example 15.1: The continuous-time signal $x(t)$ shown in Figure 15.6 is sampled using a sample-and-hold operator, resulting in the continuous-time piecewise constant signal $x_0(t)$.

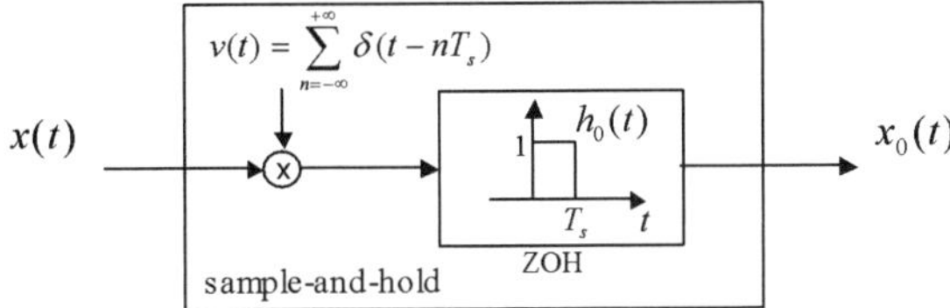

FIGURE 15.5 Sample-and-hold operator.

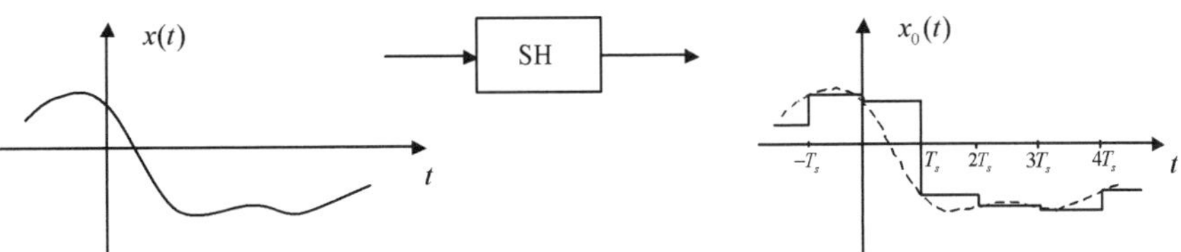

FIGURE 15.6 Effect of sample-and-hold operator on an input signal.

Note that the sampled signal $x_0(t)$ carries the same information as the samples themselves, so according to the sampling theorem, we should be able to recover the entire signal $x(t)$. It is indeed the case. From the block diagram of the sample-and-hold, what we would need to do is find the inverse of the ZOH system with impulse response $h_0(t)$ and then use a perfect lowpass filter. The frequency response $H_0(j\omega)$ is given by the usual sinc function for an even rectangular pulse signal, multiplied by $e^{-j\omega\frac{T_s}{2}}$ because of the time delay of $T_s/2$ seconds to make the pulse causal:

$$H_0(j\omega)=T_s e^{-j\omega\frac{T_s}{2}}\operatorname{sinc}\left(\frac{T_s}{2\pi}\omega\right)=2e^{-j\omega\frac{T_s}{2}}\frac{\sin(\omega\frac{T_s}{2})}{\omega}. \tag{15.5}$$

The inverse of $H_0(j\omega)$ is given by

$$H_1(j\omega)=H_0^{-1}(j\omega)=\frac{1}{2}e^{j\omega\frac{T_s}{2}}\frac{\omega}{\sin(\omega\frac{T_s}{2})}. \tag{15.6}$$

The *reconstruction filter* is the cascade of the inverse filter and the lowpass filter,

$$H_r(j\omega):=T_s H_{lp}(j\omega)H_1(j\omega), \tag{15.7}$$

whose magnitude and phase are sketched in Figure 15.8.

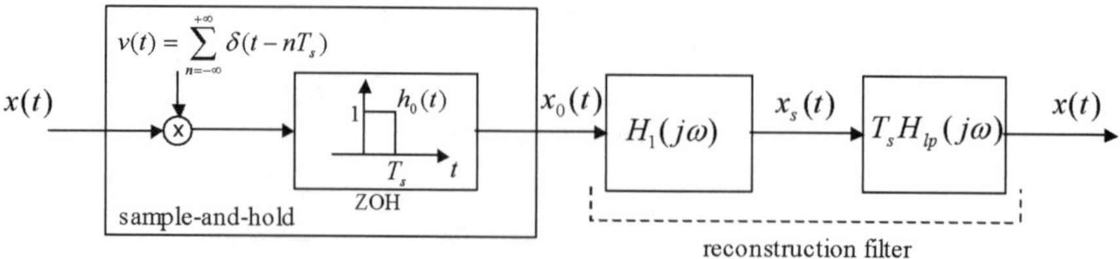

FIGURE 15.7 Signal reconstruction from the output of the sample-and-hold.

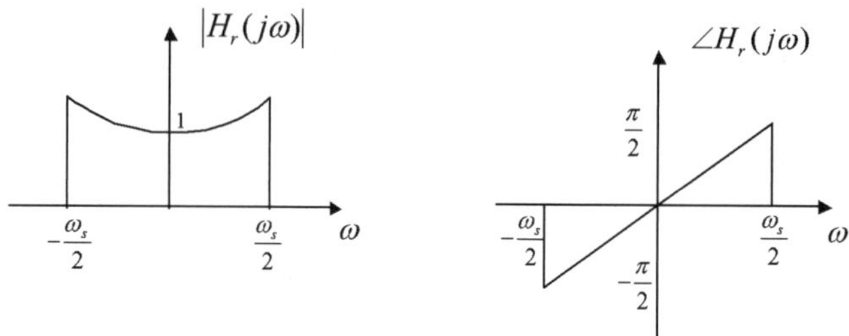

FIGURE 15.8 Frequency response of the reconstruction filter.

Unfortunately, this frequency response cannot be realized exactly in practice, one of the difficulties being that its phase reflects a time advance of $T_s/2$ seconds, but it can be approximated with a causal filter. In fact, in many practical situations, it is often sufficient to use a simple (nonideal) lowpass filter with a relatively flat magnitude in the passband to recover a good approximation of the signal. For example, many audio systems have a ZOH at the output of each channel and rely on the natural lowpass frequency responses of the loudspeakers and the human ear to smooth the signal.

((Lecture 59: Signal Reconstruction and Aliasing))

SIGNAL RECONSTRUCTION

Assume that a band-limited signal is sampled at the frequency $\omega_s = \frac{2\pi}{T_s}$ that satisfies the condition of the sampling theorem. What we have as a result is basically a discrete-time signal $x(nT_s)$ from which we would like to recover the original continuous-time signal.

Perfect Signal Interpolation Using Sinc Functions

As seen above, the ideal scenario to reconstruct the signal would be to construct a train of impulses $x_s(t)$ from the samples and then to filter this signal with an ideal lowpass filter. In the time domain, this is equivalent to interpolating the samples using time-shifted sinc functions with zeros at nT_s for $\omega_c = \omega_s/2$ as shown in Figure 15.9. Each impulse in $x_s(t)$ triggers the impulse response of the lowpass filter (the sinc signal), and the resulting signal $x(t)$ at the output of the filter is the sum of all of these time-shifted sinc signals with amplitudes equal to the samples $x(nT_s)$.

$$x(t) = \sum_{k=-\infty}^{+\infty} x(nT_s)\text{sinc}(\frac{t - nT_s}{T_s}) \tag{15.8}$$

This is clearly unfeasible, at least in real time. However, there are a number of ways to reconstruct the signal by using different types of interpolators and reconstruction filters.

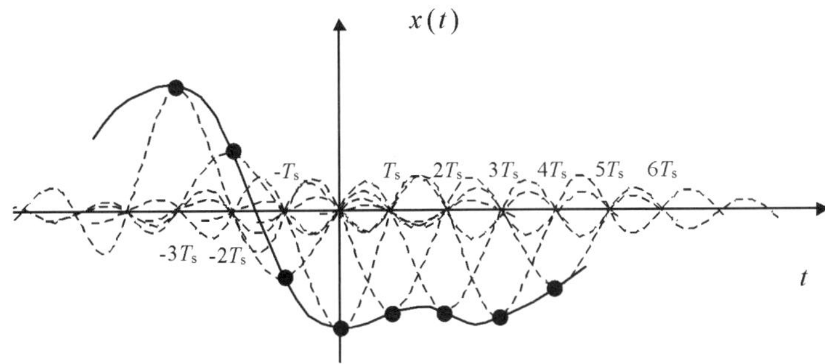

FIGURE 15.9 Perfect signal interpolation using an ideal lowpass filter.

Zero-Order Hold

The ZOH, now viewed as an interpolator in Figure 15.10, offers a coarse way to reconstruct the signal. It interpolates the signal samples with a constant line segment over a sampling period for each sample. Another way to look at it is to observe that the frequency response $H_0(j\omega)$ is a (poor) approximation to the ideal lowpass filter's, as shown in Figure 15.11, where the spectrum of the signal $x(t)$ is a triangle.

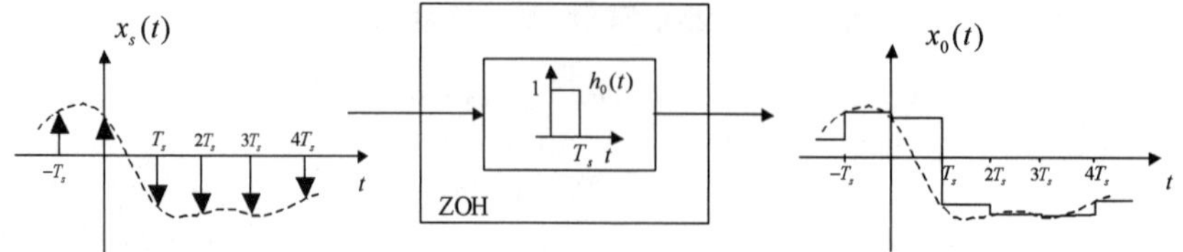

FIGURE 15.10 Signal interpolation using a ZOH.

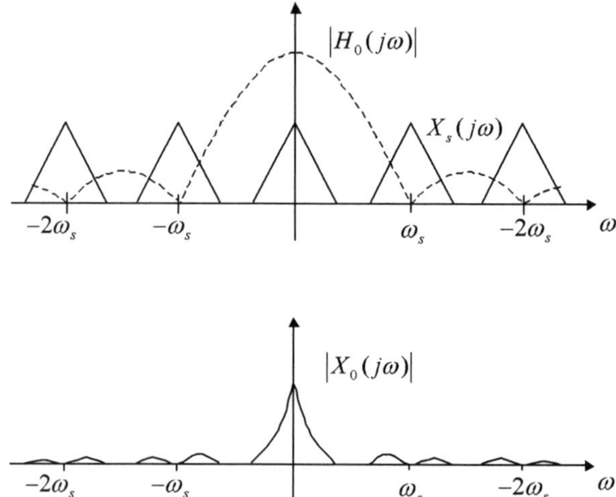

FIGURE 15.11 Spectrum of a signal interpolated using a ZOH.

First-Order Hold (Linear Interpolation)

The first-order hold (FOH) has a triangular impulse response instead of a rectangular pulse. The resulting interpolation is linear between each sample. It is closer to the signal than what a ZOH could achieve but it is noncausal. However, the FOH can be made causal by delaying its impulse response by T_s seconds, although this also causes a delay T_s between the original signal and its interpolated version. In the frequency domain, the Fourier transform of $h_1(t)$ is also a better approximation to the ideal lowpass filter than $H_0(j\omega)$ is, essentially because the magnitude $|H_1(j\omega)|$ is the square of the sinc function; that is, $|H_1(j\omega)| = |H_0(j\omega)|^2$, as shown in Figure 15.12.

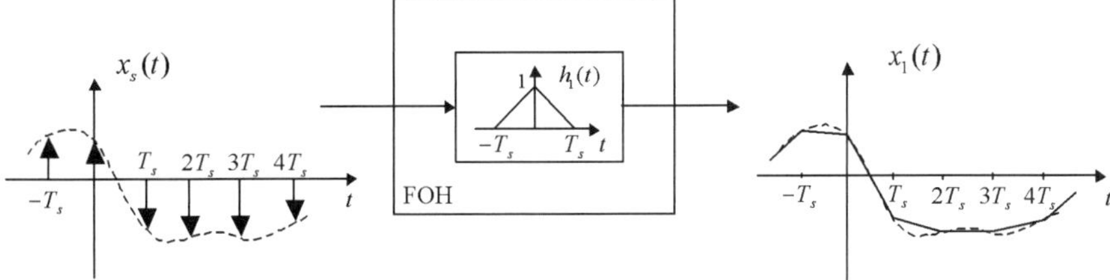

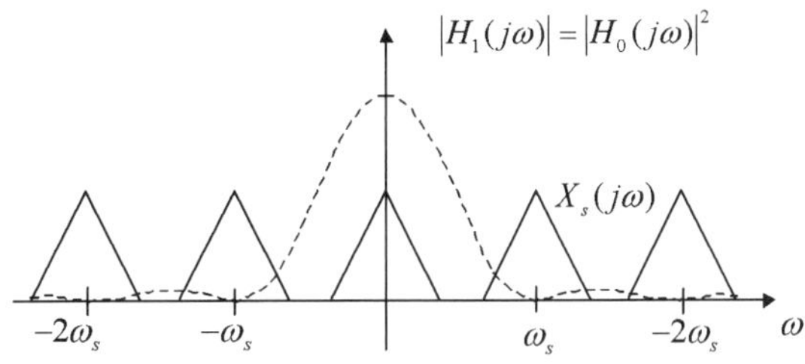

FIGURE 15.12 Signal interpolated using an FOH.

Aliasing

When a sampling frequency is too low to avoid overlapping between the spectra, we say that there is *aliasing*. Aliasing occurs when sampling is performed at too low a frequency that violates the sampling theorem, that is, when $\omega_s < 2\omega_m$. Looking at Figure 15.13, we see that the high frequencies in the replicas of the original spectrum shifted to the left and to the right by ω_s get mixed with lower frequencies in the original spectrum centered at 0. With aliasing creating distortion in the spectrum, the original signal cannot be recovered by lowpass filtering.

The effect of aliasing can sometimes be observed on television, particularly in video footage of cars whose wheels appear to be slowing down when the car is in fact accelerating. The video frames have a frequency of 30 frames per second (30 Hz), which is the standard video sampling rate. Aliasing can occur when the identical wheel spokes repeat their geometrical pattern (e.g., with one spoke vertical) for example, 20 times per second. This could produce the impression that the wheel pattern is repeating 10 times a second (30–20 Hz), making the wheels appear to be spinning slower than the speed of the car would suggest.

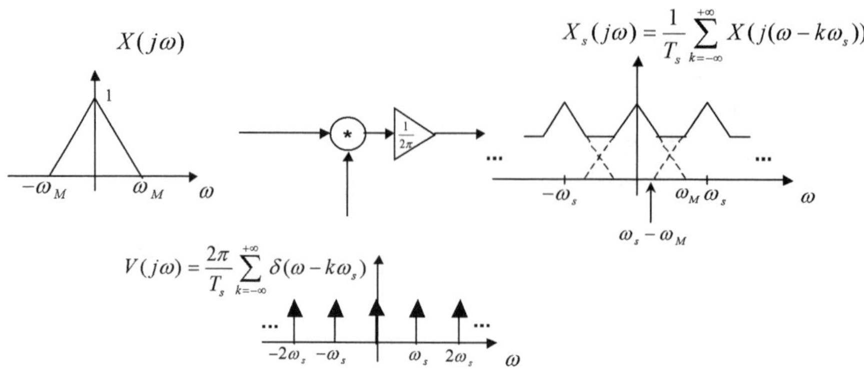

FIGURE 15.13 Aliasing due to a low sampling frequency.

Another classical way to illustrate aliasing is the sampling of a sinusoidal signal at less than twice its fundamental frequency, as given in the following example.

Example 15.2: Assume signal $x(t) = \cos(\omega_0 t)$ is sampled at the rate of $\omega_s = 1.5\omega_0$, violating the sampling theorem. Figure 15.14 shows the resulting effect of aliasing in the frequency domain, which brings two impulses at the frequencies $\pm\omega_1 = \pm(\omega_s - \omega_0) = \pm 0.5\omega_0$. If the sampled signal were lowpass filtered with a prescribed cutoff frequency of $\omega_c = 0.5\omega_s$ and a gain of T_s, then only those two impulses would remain at the output of the filter, corresponding to the signal $x_1(t) = \cos(\omega_1 t) = \cos(0.5\omega_0 t)$. Figure 15.15 shows that this sinusoidal signal of a fundamental frequency half that of the original sinusoidal signal also interpolates the samples.

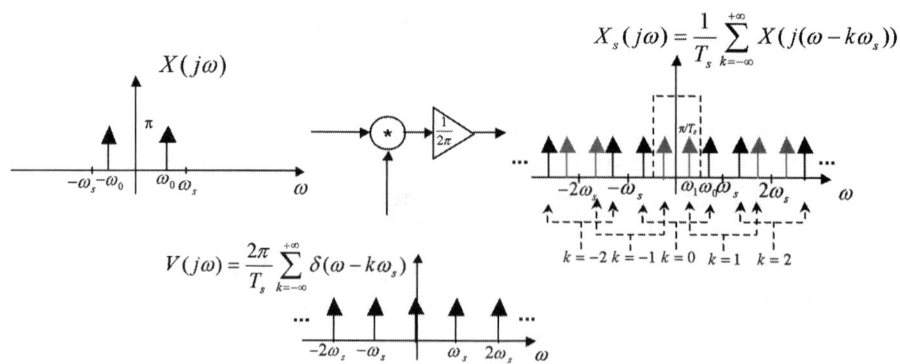

FIGURE 15.14 Aliasing of a sinusoidal signal.

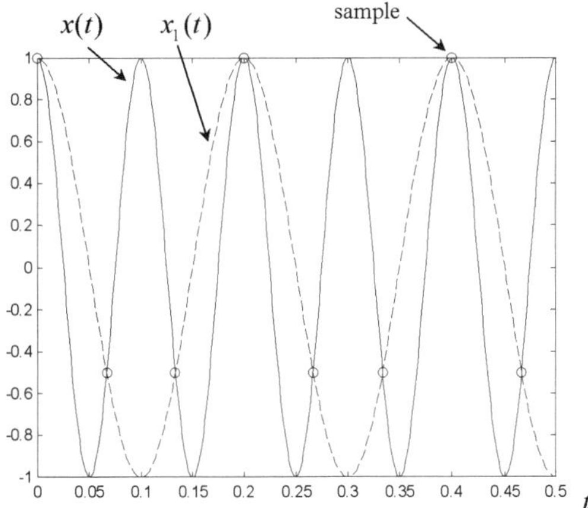

FIGURE 15.15 Aliasing effect: two sinusoidal signals of different frequencies interpolate the samples.

Remarks:

- Most continuous-time signals in practical situations have a spectrum that is not band-limited, but instead tapers off to zero as the frequency goes to infinity. Sampling such signals will produce aliasing and therefore distort the base spectrum of the sampled signal, centered around $\omega = 0$, with a resulting loss of information. In order to avoid this situation, a continuous-time *antialiasing filter* must be used to band-limit the signal *before* sampling. An antialiasing filter is a lowpass filter whose cutoff frequency is set lower than half the sampling frequency. Though it will introduce some distortion at high frequencies in the original spectrum, it is often a better solution than introducing aliasing distortion at lower frequencies by not using an antialiasing filter. Comparing for example the spectrum of the sampled signal in Figure 15.16 with the aliased spectrum in Figure 15.13, we can see that the use of an antialiasing filter has significantly reduced the distortion.
- It is also possible to increase the sampling rate such that the spectrum of the signal has negligible energy past the Nyquist frequency ($\omega_s/2$). Care must be exercised though, since any noise energy present at frequencies higher than $\omega_s/2$ will be aliased to low frequencies as well, generating distortion. Thus, this is typically not a good solution.
- In practice, a generally safe rule of thumb is to choose the sampling frequency to be five to ten times higher than the bandwidth of the signal. However, this choice may prove too conservative for some applications.

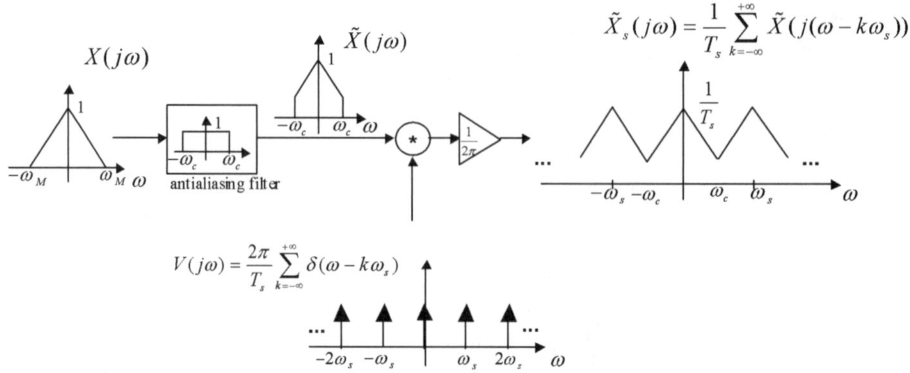

FIGURE 15.16 Aliasing avoided using an antialiasing filter.

((Lecture 60: Discrete-Time Processing of Continuous-Time Signals))

DISCRETE-TIME PROCESSING OF CONTINUOUS-TIME SIGNALS

Discrete-time processing of continuous-time signals has been made possible by the advent of the digital computer. With today's fast, inexpensive microprocessors and dedicated digital signal processor chips, it is advantageous to implement sophisticated filters and controllers for continuous-time signals as discrete-time systems.

We have reviewed all the mathematical machinery needed to analyze and design these *sampled-data systems*. The fundamental result provided by the sampling theorem allows us to make the connection between continuous time and discrete time. Consider the block diagram of a sampled-data system in Figure 15.17. The blocks labeled CT/DT and DT/CT are conversion operators described in the next section.

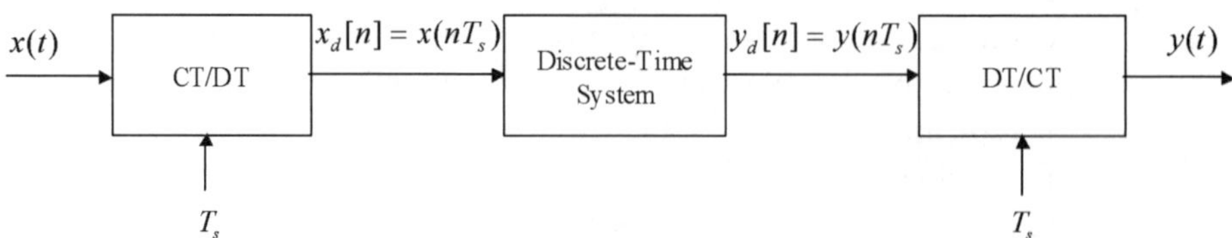

FIGURE 15.17 Sampled-data system for discrete-time processing of continuous-time signals.

CT/DT Operator

As indicated in Figure 15.17, the continuous-time to discrete-time operator CT/DT is simply defined by

$$\text{CT/DT:} \quad x_d[n] = x(nT_s), \ n \in \mathbb{Z}. \qquad (15.9)$$

It is also useful to think of the CT/DT operator as impulse train sampling followed by a conversion of the impulse areas to values of a discrete-time signal represented by the operator $\mathcal{V}$ in Figure 15.18. To be fancy, operator $\mathcal{V}$, which maps the set of impulse-sampled signals $\mathcal{X}_s$ into the set of discrete-time signals $\mathcal{X}_d$, can be defined as follows:

$$\mathcal{V}: \mathcal{X}_s \to \mathcal{X}_d, \quad x_d[n] = \int_{nT_s - \frac{T_s}{2}}^{nT_s + \frac{T_s}{2}} x_s(t)dt, \quad n \in \mathbb{Z}. \qquad (15.10)$$

Note that the information is the same in both representations $x_s(t)$ and $x_d[n]$ of the sampled signal, as suggested by Figure 15.19.

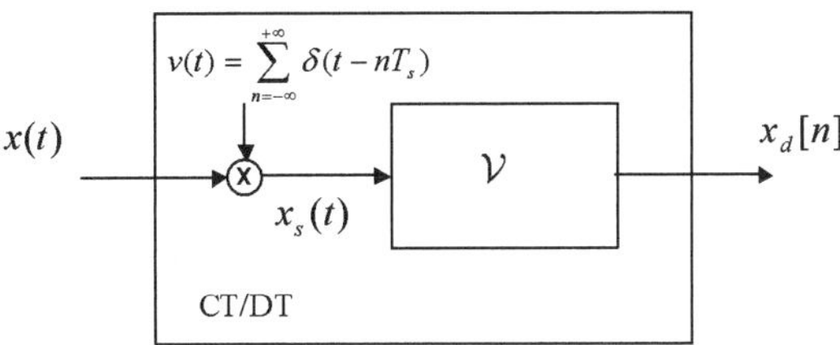

FIGURE 15.18 CT/DT conversion operator.

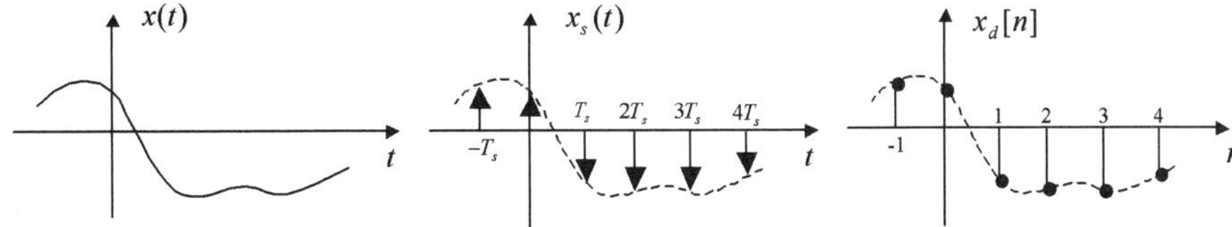

FIGURE 15.19 Impulse train sampled signal and its discrete-time counterpart in the CT/DT operation.

The sampling period of T_s seconds is normalized to 1 in the discrete-time signal $x_d[n]$. For the remainder of this section, let the continuous-time frequency variable be denoted as ω, and the discrete-time frequency variable as Ω. Recall that the spectrum $X_s(j\omega)$ of the sampled signal $x_s(t)$ is an infinite sum of replicas of $X(j\omega)$ shifted at integer multiples of the sampling frequency $\omega_s = \frac{2\pi}{T_s}$. Hence, $X_s(j\omega)$ is periodic of period ω_s. The discrete-time Fourier transform (DTFT) $X_d(e^{j\Omega})$ of $x_d[n]$ is also periodic, but of period 2π. The relationship between the two spectra is then simply

$$X_d(e^{j\Omega}) = X_s(j\underbrace{\Omega/T_s}_{\omega}) \tag{15.11}$$

as we now show.

$$\begin{aligned}
X_s(j\omega) &= \int_{-\infty}^{+\infty} \sum_{n=-\infty}^{+\infty} x(nT_s)\delta(t-nT_s)e^{-j\omega t}\,dt \\
&= \sum_{n=-\infty}^{+\infty} x(nT_s)e^{-j\omega nT_s} \\
&= \sum_{n=-\infty}^{+\infty} x_d[n]e^{-j\omega nT_s} \\
&= \sum_{n=-\infty}^{+\infty} x_d[n]e^{-j\Omega n} \quad \text{for } \omega = \frac{\Omega}{T_s}. \\
&= X_d(e^{j\omega T_s})
\end{aligned} \tag{15.12}$$

Thus, we have $X_s(j\omega) = X_d(e^{j\omega T_s})$, or equivalently Equation 15.11. This important result means that the shape of the spectrum of the discrete-time signal $x_d[n]$ is the same as the shape of the spectrum of the sampled signal $x_s(t)$. The only difference is that the former is *compressed* in frequency in such a way that the frequency range $[-\omega_s/2, \omega_s/2]$ is mapped to the discrete-time frequency range $[-\pi, \pi]$. Figure 15.20 shows an example of a continuous-time signal with a triangular spectrum that is sampled and converted to a discrete-time signal with the CT/DT operator.

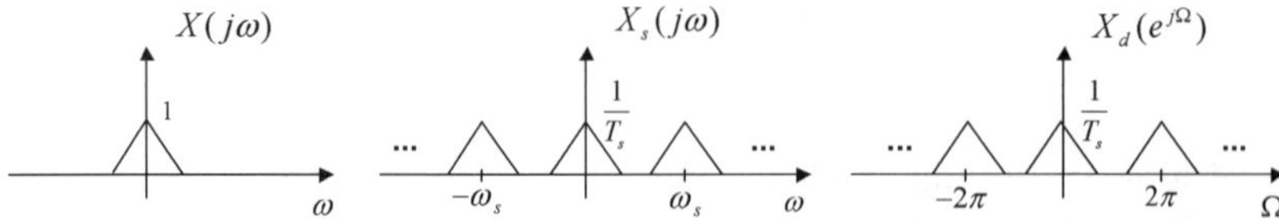

FIGURE 15.20 Frequency-domain view of sampled signal and its discrete-time counterpart in the CT/DT operation.

The last step in characterizing the CT/DT operator is to relate $X_d(e^{j\Omega})$ to $X(j\omega)$. Recall that

$$X_s(j\omega) = \frac{1}{T_s}\sum_{k=-\infty}^{+\infty} X(j(\omega - k\omega_s)). \qquad (15.13)$$

Thus, from Equation 15.11 we obtain

$$\begin{aligned} X_d(e^{j\Omega}) &= X_s(j\Omega/T_s) \\ &= \frac{1}{T_s}\sum_{k=-\infty}^{+\infty} X\left(j\frac{(\Omega - k2\pi)}{T_s}\right). \end{aligned} \qquad (15.14)$$

Remarks:

- An *analog-to-digital (A/D) converter* is the practical device used to implement the ideal CT/DT operation. However, an A/D converter quantizes the signal values with a finite number of bits, for example, a 12-bit A/D.
- If the sampling rate satisfies the sampling theorem, that is, $\omega_s > 2\omega_M$, where ω_M is the bandwidth of the continuous-time signal, then there will not be any aliasing in $X_d(e^{j\Omega})$.

DT/CT Operator

The discrete-time to continuous-time DT/CT conversion operator in Figure 15.17 consists first of forming a train of impulses occurring every T_s seconds, with the impulse at time nT_s having an area $y_d[n]$. This operation is simply the inverse of operator $\mathcal{V}$ defined in Equation 15.10, denoted as $\mathcal{V}^{-1}$. Then, an ideal lowpass filter with its cutoff frequency set at the Nyquist frequency $\omega_c = \omega_s/2$ and with a gain of T_s is applied to the impulse train, as shown in Figure 15.21.

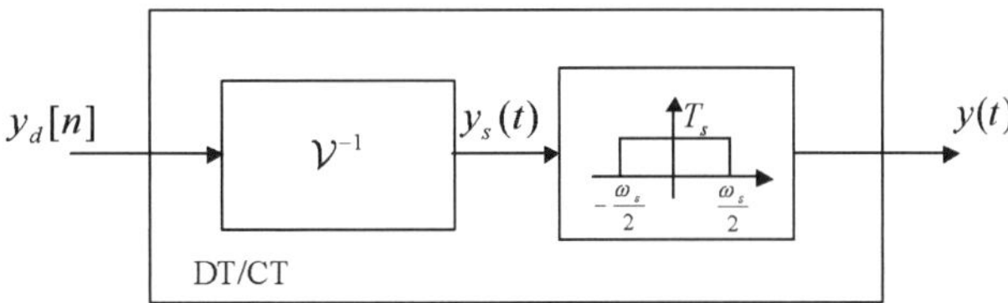

FIGURE 15.21 DT/CT conversion operator.

Remarks:

- A *digital-to-analog (D/A) converter* is the practical device used to implement the ideal DT/CT operation. Typical D/A converters use a ZOH in place of the ideal lowpass filter.
- If the discrete-time signal comes from a sampled continuous-time signal for which the sampling theorem was satisfied, then it should be clear that DT/CT will recover the continuous-time signal perfectly.

((Lecture 61: Equivalence to Continuous-Time Filtering; Sampling of Discrete-Time Signals))

Equivalence to a Continuous-Time LTI System

Can the system depicted in Figure 15.22 be equivalent to a purely continuous-time LTI system as represented by its frequency response $H(j\omega)$? The answer is *yes, but only for input signals of bandwidth* $\omega_M < \frac{\omega_s}{2}$. In this case, the frequency response up to the Nyquist frequency of the equivalent continuous-time LTI system is given by

$$H(j\omega) = H_d(e^{j\omega T_s}). \tag{15.15}$$

Thus, an input signal of bandwidth $\omega_M < \frac{\omega_s}{2}$ in the block diagram of Figure 15.22 would have its spectrum compressed from the frequency interval $[-\omega_s/2, \omega_s/2]$ to the discrete-time frequency interval $[-\pi, \pi]$ via the mapping $\Omega = \omega T_s$ before being filtered by $H_d(e^{j\Omega})$.

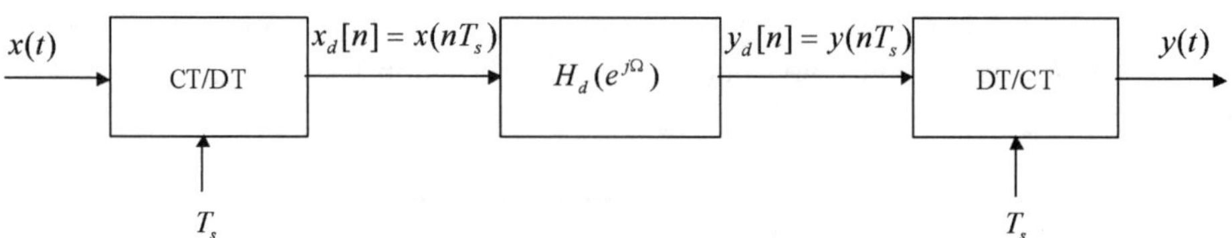

FIGURE 15.22 Sampled-data system.

An important question remains: suppose we want to design a sampled-data system that would match the behavior of, for instance, a high-order Butterworth filter that was previously designed as a continuous-time system with transfer function $H_B(s)$. Further assume that the input signals are known to have a bandwidth lower than the Nyquist frequency. How can we design such a system? What is required is a discrete-time version of the Butterworth filter represented by a transfer function in the z-domain $H_{Bd}(z)$, which can be obtained through *discretization* of the system $H_B(s)$. Discretization of a continuous-time system is discussed in Chapter 17. In an algorithm implementing the middle block of the sampled-data system of Figure 15.22, the discretized system $H_{Bd}(z)$ would be programmed either as a recursive difference equation, a convolution, or sometimes as a recursive state-space system.

SAMPLING OF DISCRETE-TIME SIGNALS

With the growing popularity of digital signal processing and digital communications, more and more operations on signals normally carried out in continuous time are implemented in discrete time. For example, modulation and sampling can be done entirely in discrete time. In this section, we look at the process of sampling discrete-time signals and the related operations of decimation and upsampling.

Impulse Train Sampling

Let $v[n]$ be a discrete-time impulse train of period N_s; that is, $v[n]=\sum_{k=-\infty}^{+\infty}\delta[n-kN_s]$. Then, impulse train sampling of $x[n]$ is defined as

$$x_s[n]:=x[n]v[n]=\sum_{k=-\infty}^{+\infty}x[kN_s]\delta[n-kN_s]. \tag{15.16}$$

In the frequency domain, this corresponds to the periodic convolution of the DTFTs:

$$X_s(e^{j\omega})=\frac{1}{2\pi}\int_{2\pi}V(e^{j\theta})X(e^{j(\omega-\theta)})d\theta, \tag{15.17}$$

where

$$V(e^{j\omega})=\frac{2\pi}{N_s}\sum_{k=-\infty}^{+\infty}\delta(\omega-k\omega_s), \tag{15.18}$$

and $\omega_s:=\frac{2\pi}{N_s}$, $0<\omega_s\le 2\pi$, is the discrete-time sampling frequency. Thus, the spectrum of the sampled signal is given by

$$X_s(e^{j\omega}) = \frac{1}{N_s}\sum_{k=0}^{N_s-1} X(e^{j(\omega - k\omega_s)}). \tag{15.19}$$

Note that $X_s(e^{j\omega})$ is a finite sum over $k = 0,\ldots,N_s - 1$, as the convolution in Equation 15.17 is computed over an interval of width 2π, for example, over $[-\pi,\pi]$, and there are only N_s impulses in $V(e^{j\omega})$ in this interval.

Example 15.3: A signal $x[n]$ with DTFT shown at the top of Figure 15.23 is band-limited to $\pi/4$. The signal is sampled at twice the bandwidth of the signal, that is, with a sampling frequency $\omega_s = \frac{\pi}{2}$ corresponding to the sampling period $N_s = 4$ and yielding $x_s[n] = x[n]v[n]$. The DTFT $V(e^{j\omega})$ of the impulse train $v[n]$, which is convolved with the signal spectrum, is composed of impulses located at integer multiples of $\omega_s = \frac{\pi}{2}$.

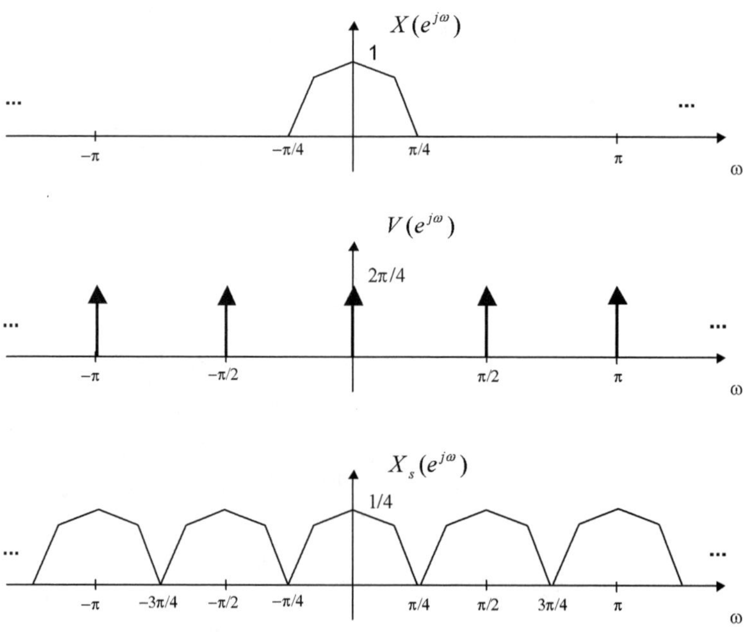

FIGURE 15.23 Discrete-time sampling in the frequency domain.

((Lecture 62: Decimation, Upsampling and Interpolation))

Decimation

Recall that impulse train sampling of $x[n]$, defined as $x_s[n]=x[n]v[n]=\sum_{k=-\infty}^{+\infty} x[kN_s]\delta[n-kN_s]$, yields the spectrum $X_s(e^{j\omega})=\frac{1}{N_s}\sum_{k=0}^{N_s-1} X(e^{j(\omega-k\omega_s)})$. The purpose of decimation is to compress a discrete-time signal, but the sampled signal $x_s[n]$ still has $N_s - 1$ zeros in between the values of $x[nN_s]$, carrying no information. Decimation gets rid of these zeros after sampling, thereby compressing the number of values in $x[n]$ and $x_s[n]$ by a factor N_s.

The signal $x_{\downarrow N_s}[n] := x[N_s n]$ is called a *decimated,* or *downsampled,* version of $x[n]$, that is, only every N_s^{th} sample of $x[n]$ is retained. Also note that $x_{\downarrow N_s}[n]=x_s[N_s n]$.

In a real-time communication system, this means that the decimated signal can be transmitted at a rate N_s times slower than the rate of the original signal. It also means that for a given channel with a fixed bit rate, more decimated signals can be transmitted through the channel at the same time using time-division multiplexing (more on this in Chapter 16).

Frequency Spectra of Decimated Signals

Let the integer $N > 1$ be the sampling period. The DTFT of a downsampled signal is given by

$$\begin{aligned} X_{\downarrow N}(e^{j\omega}) &= \sum_{n=-\infty}^{+\infty} x_{\downarrow N}[n]e^{-j\omega n} \\ &= \sum_{n=-\infty}^{+\infty} x[nN]e^{-j\omega n} \\ &= \sum_{m=-\infty}^{+\infty} x_s[m]e^{-j\omega\frac{m}{N}} = X_s(e^{j\frac{\omega}{N}}). \end{aligned} \tag{15.20}$$

Thus, $X_{\downarrow N}(e^{j\omega})=X_s(e^{j\frac{\omega}{N}})$; that is, the spectrum of the decimated signal $x_{\downarrow N}[n]$ is the *frequency-expanded* version of the spectrum of the sampled signal $x_s[n]$.

Example 15.4: Consider the signal $x[n]$, whose Fourier transform shown in the top plot in Figure 15.24 has a bandwidth of $\pi/4$. The signal $x_{\downarrow 4}[n]$, decimated by a factor of 4, has the DTFT shown at the bottom of the figure, while the signal $x_s[n]$, sampled at frequency $\omega_s = \frac{\pi}{2}$ corresponding to the sampling period $N = 4$, has the DTFT in the middle. It can be seen that the spectrum $X_{\downarrow 4}(e^{j\omega})$ is a stretched version of $X_s(e^{j\omega})$, expanded by a factor of $N = 4$.

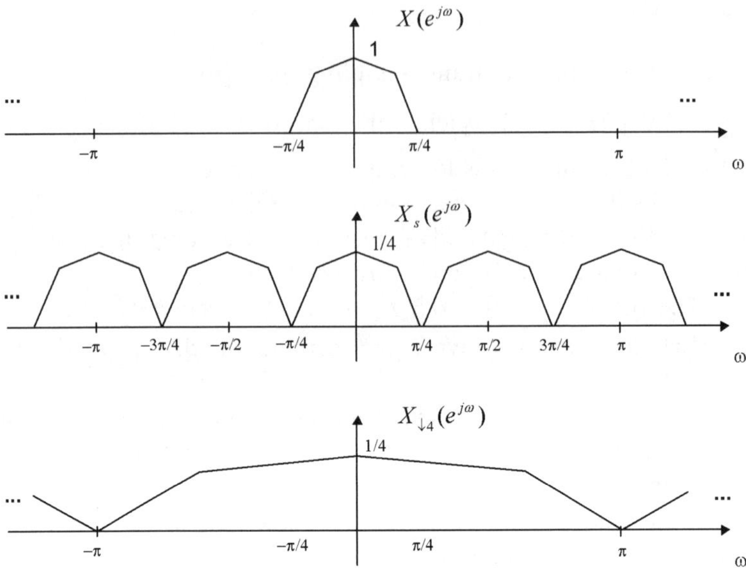

FIGURE 15.24 Effect of downsampling in the frequency domain.

Aliasing

What happens if the sampling period N is a large number? Can $X_{\downarrow N}(e^{j\omega}) = X_s(e^{j\frac{\omega}{N}})$ expand so much that it is no longer a periodic spectrum of period 2π? No. In this case, aliasing occurs in $X_s(e^{j\omega})$, but the center of the first (distorted) copy of the spectrum to the right of the main one (centered at $\omega = 0$) is at frequency $\frac{2\pi}{N}$ in $X_s(e^{j\omega})$. This means that the aliased $X_s(e^{j\omega})$ is periodic of period 2π. Its subsequent expansion through decimation by a factor of N brings back $X_{\downarrow N}(e^{j\omega}) = X_s(e^{j\frac{\omega}{N}})$ to a period of 2π, with the first copy of the spectrum to the right of the main one now being centered at $\omega = 2\pi$.

Aliasing occurs when $\omega_s = \frac{2\pi}{N} < 2\omega_M$, where ω_M is the bandwidth of the signal, in both operations of sampling and decimation. This is the discrete-time version of the sampling theorem.

Reconstruction of Decimated Signals: Upsampling and Interpolation

Recall that the upsampling operation is defined as:

$$x_{\uparrow N}[n] := \begin{cases} x[n/N], & \text{if } n \text{ is a multiple of } N \\ 0, & \text{otherwise} \end{cases}. \tag{15.21}$$

The upsampling operation inserts $N-1$ zeros between consecutive samples of the original signal. The Fourier transform of the upsampled signal $x_{\uparrow N}[n]$ is given by

$$x_{\uparrow N}[n] \overset{F}{\leftrightarrow} X(e^{jN\omega}); \tag{15.22}$$

that is, its spectrum is a frequency-compressed version of $X(e^{j\omega})$.

Assume that a signal $x[n]$ was downsampled to $x_{\downarrow N}[n]$ without aliasing. The signal $x[n]$ can be recovered from its downsampled version by first upsampling the decimated signal, shown as the block labeled $\uparrow N$ in Figure 15.25, followed by lowpass filtering with an ideal lowpass filter of cutoff frequency $\omega_c = \frac{\omega_s}{2} = \frac{\pi}{N}$ and gain N.

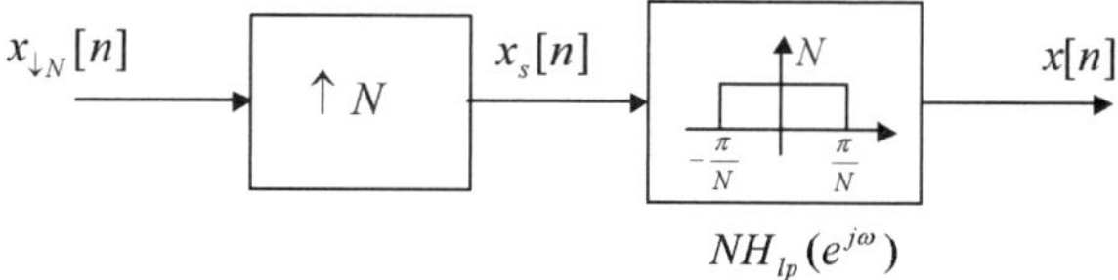

FIGURE 15.25 Upsampling followed by lowpass filtering for signal reconstruction after decimation.

Example 15.5: The decimated signal $x_{\downarrow 4}[n]$ of the previous example is upsampled by a factor of 4, yielding the signal $x_s[n]$, with three zeros inserted in-between each sample. The ideal lowpass filter interpolates the samples and turns the inserted zeros into the original values of the signal, as shown in Figure 15.26. Figure 15.27 illustrates the operations used to reconstruct the decimated signal in the frequency domain.

Notice in Figure 15.27 how the upsampled signal has copies of the main part of the spectrum at high frequencies (around $\pm\pi$). These high-frequency components (coming from the fast variations in the upsampled signal that flips between sample values and the inserted zeros) must be removed by the lowpass filter $4H_{lp}(e^{j\omega})$ to recover $x[n]$.

Maximum Decimation

Maximum signal compression through decimation (without aliasing) can be achieved by expanding the bandwidth ω_M of the original signal spectrum up to π. However, it is usually not possible to do this exactly, as decimation results in spectral expansion by an *integer* factor N.

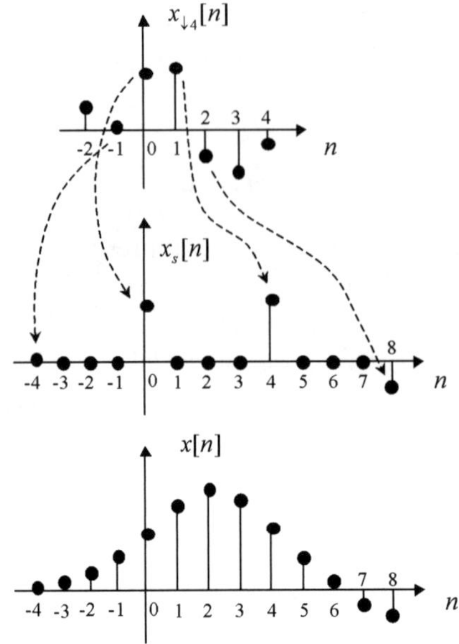

FIGURE 15.26 Time-domain view of upsampling followed by lowpass filtering for signal reconstruction after decimation.

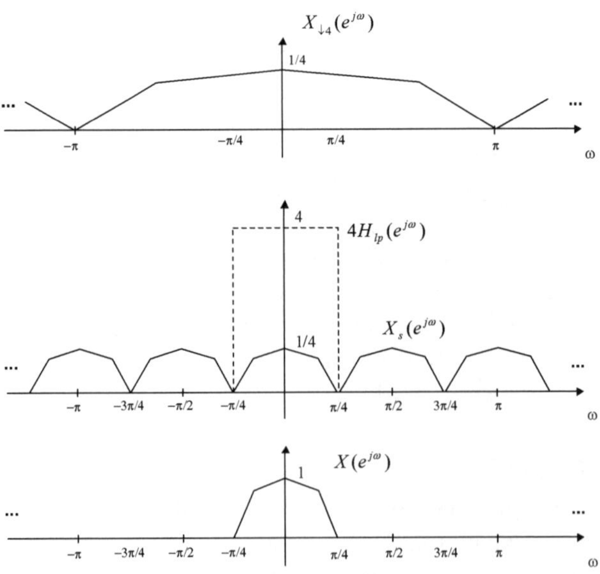

FIGURE 15.27 Frequency-domain view of upsampling followed by lowpass filtering for signal reconstruction after decimation.

One way to expand the spectrum up to, or close to, π is to upsample the signal first (followed by lowpass filtering) and then to decimate it. This two-stage procedure can produce a rational spectral expansion factor, which can bring the edge of the spectrum arbitrarily close to π.

Example 15.6: Suppose that the discrete-time signal to be downsampled to reach maximal decimation has a bandwidth of $\omega_M = \frac{2\pi}{5}$. Then, we require a rational spectral expansion factor of $\frac{5}{2}$ to bring the edge of the DTFT of the signal to π. This is clearly impossible to achieve with decimation alone, which at best could expand the spectrum by a factor of 2 without aliasing with $N = 2$. The trick here is to upsample by a factor of 2 (insert a 0 between each value of $x[n]$) first, thereby compressing the spectrum to a bandwidth of $\frac{\pi}{5}$, and then to apply an ideal lowpass filter to remove the unwanted replicas centered at frequencies ±π in $X_{\uparrow 2}(e^{j\omega})$, which could cause aliasing to occur. Finally, the upsampled filtered signal with DTFT $X_{\uparrow 2lp}(e^{j\omega})$ is decimated by a factor of 5 to obtain a bandwith of π. These operations are shown in Figure 15.28.

Remark: Because aliasing of the spectrum of the upsampled signal can easily occur in the decimation operation, upsampling should be followed by lowpass filtering with unity gain and cutoff frequency $\omega_c = \frac{\pi}{N}$, where N is the upsampling factor.

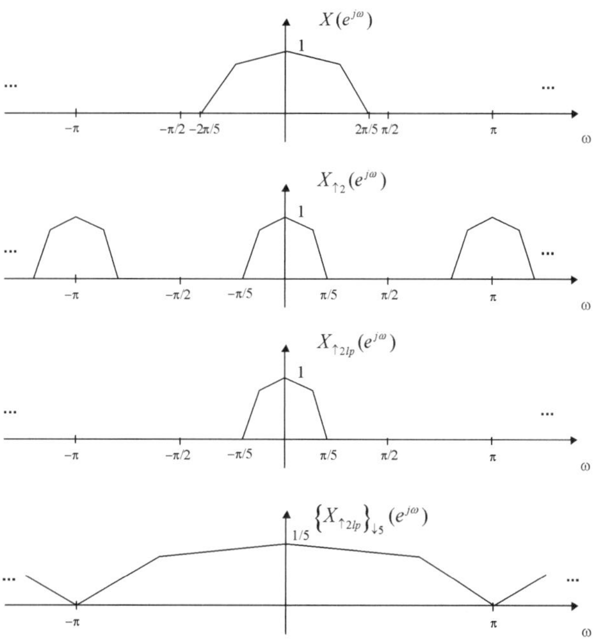

FIGURE 15.28 Maximal decimation via upsampling followed by decimation.

SUMMARY

Sampling was introduced in this chapter as an important bridge between continuous-time and discrete-time signals, with the focus of processing continuous-time signals using discrete-time systems.

- The sampling theorem establishes a sufficient condition on the sampling rate for a continuous-time signal to be reconstructed from its sampled version. Sampling is easier to understand in the frequency domain.
- Perfect signal reconstruction from the samples can be done with a perfect lowpass filter. Imperfect, but simpler, signal reconstruction can be performed using a zero-order hold or a first-order hold.
- Discrete-time processing of a continuous-time signal is theoretically equivalent to filtering with a corresponding continuous-time system within a frequency band extending to half of the sampling frequency, provided the proper setup is in place.
- Sampling of discrete-time signals leads to the important operations of decimation and upsampling. These operations can be used for discrete-time signal compression in communication systems.

TO PROBE FURTHER

On sampling systems, see Oppenheim, Schafer and Buck, 1999 and Proakis and Manolakis, 1995. Decimation and upsampling are covered in Oppenheim, Willsky, and Nawab, 1997 and in Haykin and Van Veen, 2002.

EXERCISES

Exercises with Solutions

Exercise 15.1

The system shown in Figure 15.29 filters the continuous-time noisy signal $x_n(t) = x(t) + n(t)$ composed of the sum of a signal $x(t)$ and a noise $n(t)$.

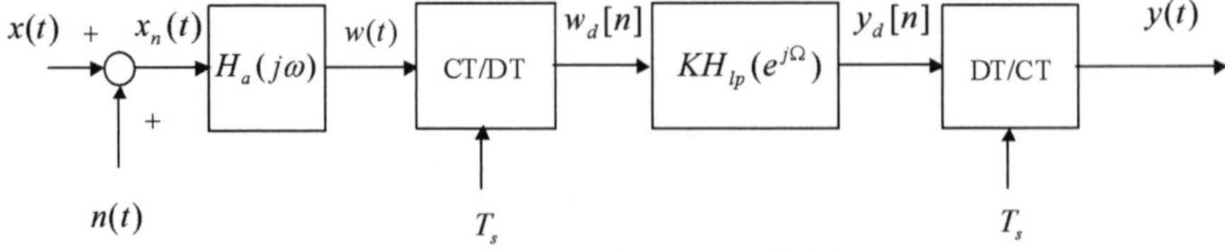

FIGURE 15.29 Sampled-data system with antialiasing filter of Exercise 15.1.

The signal and noise have their respective spectrum, $X(j\omega)$, $N(j\omega)$ shown in Figure 15.30. The frequency response of the antialiasing lowpass filter is also shown in the figure.

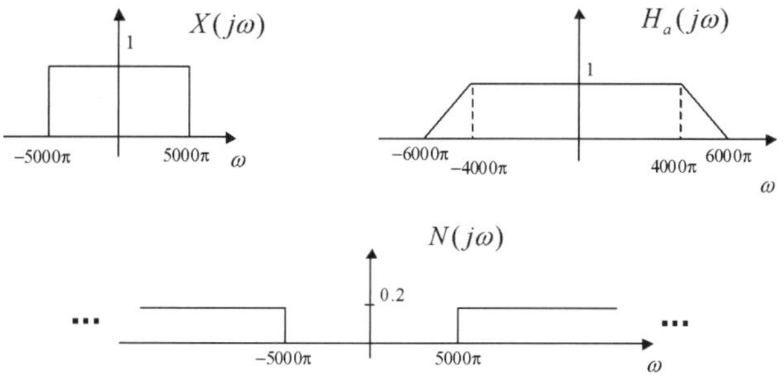

FIGURE 15.30 Antialiasing filter and signal and noise spectra in Exercise 15.1.

(a) Let the sampling frequency be $\omega_s = 11000\pi$ rad/s. Sketch the spectrum $W(j\omega)$ of the signal $w(t)$. Also sketch the spectrum $W_d(e^{j\Omega})$. Indicate the important frequencies and magnitudes on your sketch. Discuss the results.

Answer:

The Nyquist frequency is $\frac{\omega_s}{2} = 5500\pi$. The spectra $W(j\omega)$ and $W_d(e^{j\Omega})$ are shown in Figure 15.31.

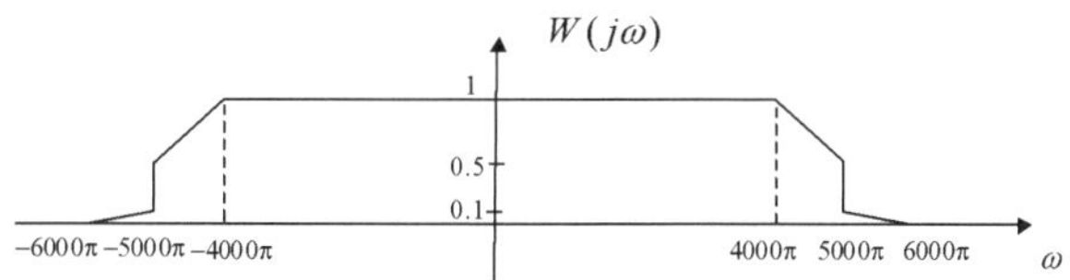

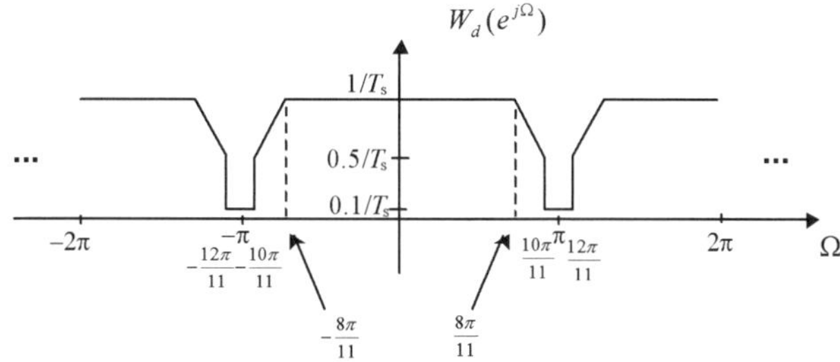

FIGURE 15.31 Fourier transform of output of antialiasing filter and DTFT of signal after CT/DT (Exercise 15.1).

(b) Design an ideal discrete-time lowpass filter $KH_{lp}(e^{j\Omega})$ (give its cutoff frequency Ω_c and gain K) so that the signal $x(t)$ (possibly distorted by linear filtering) can be approximately recovered at the output. Sketch the spectrum $Y_d(e^{j\Omega})$ with this filter.

Answer:

From Figure 15.31, the ideal lowpass would have a cutoff frequency $\Omega_c = \frac{10\pi}{11}$ in order to remove the remaining noise, and unity gain since the DT/CT operator already contains a gain of T_s. The frequency response of the lowpass filter $H_{lp}(e^{j\Omega})$ is shown in Figure 15.32, and the DTFT of the output of the filter $Y_d(e^{j\Omega})$ is in Figure 15.33.

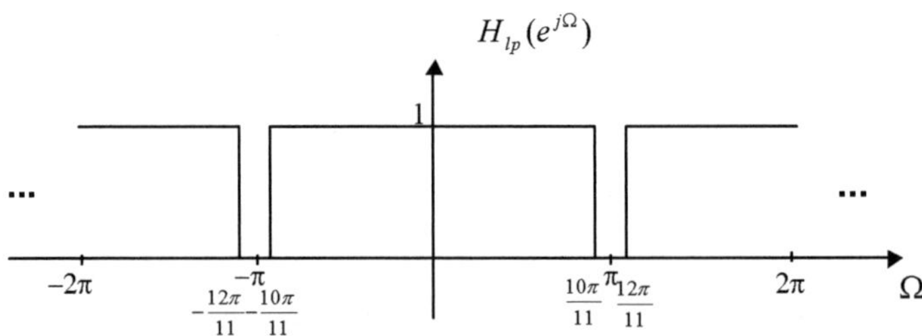

FIGURE 15.32 Frequency response of ideal lowpass filter (Exercise 15.1).

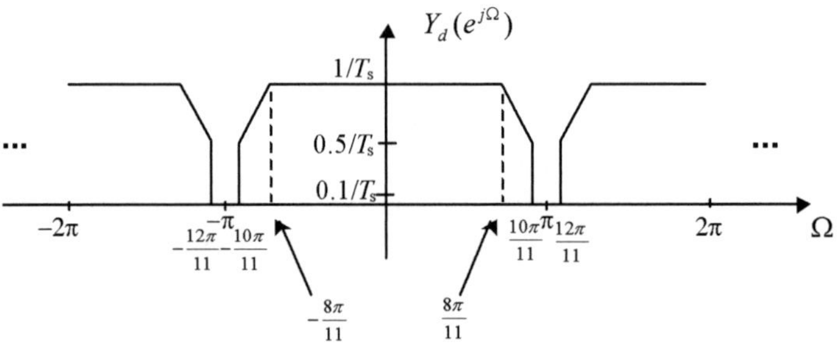

FIGURE 15.33 DTFT of output of ideal lowpass filter (Exercise 15.1).

(c) Sketch the spectrum $Y(j\omega)$ and compute the ratio of linear distortion in the output $y(t)$ with respect to the input signal; that is, compute $100 \times \frac{E_{error}}{E_x}$ in percent, where E_{error} : energy of $x(t) - y(t)$, E_x : energy of $x(t)$.

Answer:

The Fourier transforms of the output $Y(j\omega)$ and the error signal $X(j\omega) - Y(j\omega)$ are sketched in Figure 15.34.

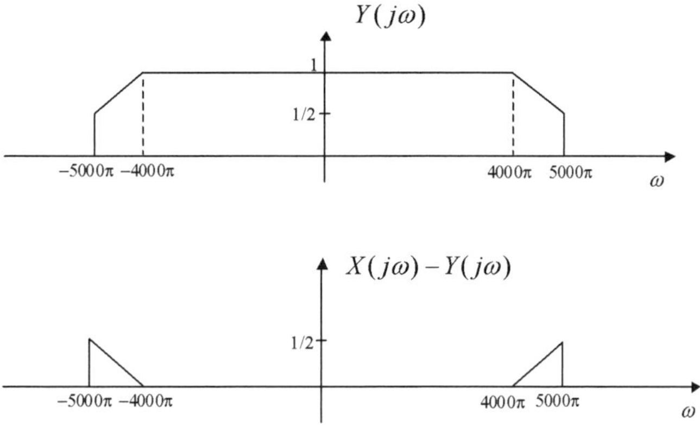

FIGURE 15.34 Fourier transforms of continuous-time output signal and error signal (Exercise 15.1).

The energy of the signal and the energy of the error signal are computed using the Parseval equality as follows.

$$E_x = \frac{1}{2\pi}\int_{-5000\pi}^{5000\pi} |X(j\omega)|^2\, d\omega = \frac{1}{2\pi}\int_{-5000\pi}^{5000\pi} d\omega = 5000$$

$$E_{error} = 2\frac{1}{2\pi}\int_{4000\pi}^{5000\pi} |X(j\omega) - Y(j\omega)|^2\, d\omega = \frac{1}{\pi}\int_{4000\pi}^{5000\pi}\left|\frac{1}{2000\pi}(\omega - 4000\pi)\right|^2 d\omega$$

$$= \frac{1}{2000^2\pi^3}\int_{4000\pi}^{5000\pi}(\omega - 4000\pi)^2\, d\omega = \frac{1}{(3)(2000^2)\pi^3}\left[(\omega - 4000\pi)^3\right]_{4000\pi}^{5000\pi}$$

$$= \frac{1}{(3)(2000^2)\pi^3}\left[(5000\pi - 4000\pi)^3 - 0\right] = \frac{1000^3\pi^3}{(3)(2000^2)\pi^3} = \frac{1000}{12} = 83.3$$

Ratio of linear distortion:

$$\frac{E_{error}}{E_x} = \frac{1000/12}{5000}\times 100\% = 1.67\%$$

Exercise 15.2

Consider the discrete-time system shown in Figure 15.35, where $\downarrow N$ represents decimation by N. The operator $\{\uparrow N\}_{lp}$ denotes upsampling by N followed by an ideal unity-gain lowpass filter with cutoff frequency $\frac{\pi}{N}$. This system transmits a signal $x[n]$ that comes in at a rate of 100 kilosamples/second over a channel with limited bit-rate capacity. At each time n, the 16-bit quantizer rounds offs the real value $x_2[n]$ to a 16-bit value $y[n]$.

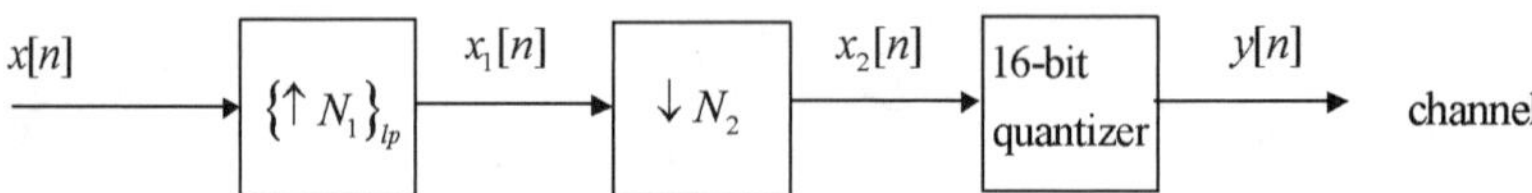

FIGURE 15.35 Block diagram of discrete-time system (Exercise 15.2).

(a) Given that the input signal $x[n]$ is bandlimited to 0.13π radians, find the integers N_1, N_2 that will minimize the sample rate for transmission over the channel. Give the bit rate that you obtain.

Answer:
Bandwidth of signal $x[n]$: $\omega_m = \frac{13\pi}{100} = \frac{13(2\pi)}{200}$. We want the DTFT of $x_2[n]$ to cover as much of the frequency interval $[-\pi, \pi]$ as possible using upsampling and decimation. We can upsample first by a factor of $N_1 = 13$, which compresses the bandwidth to $\frac{\pi}{100}$, and then we can decimate by a factor of $N_2 = 100$ to expand the spectrum up to π. The resulting sample rate is reduced by a factor of $\frac{N_2}{N_1} = \frac{100}{13}$ to 13 kilosamples/s. With a 16-bit quantizer, the bit rate needed to transmit the signal $y[n]$ is 16 bits/sample $\times$ 13,000 samples/s = 208,000 bits/s.

(b) With the values obtained in (a), assume a triangular spectrum for $x[n]$ of unit amplitude at DC and sketch the spectra $X(e^{j\omega})$, $X_1(e^{j\omega})$, $X_2(e^{j\omega})$, indicating the important frequencies and magnitudes.

Answer:
The spectra $X(e^{j\omega})$, $X_1(e^{j\omega})$, $X_2(e^{j\omega})$ are sketched in Figure 15.36.

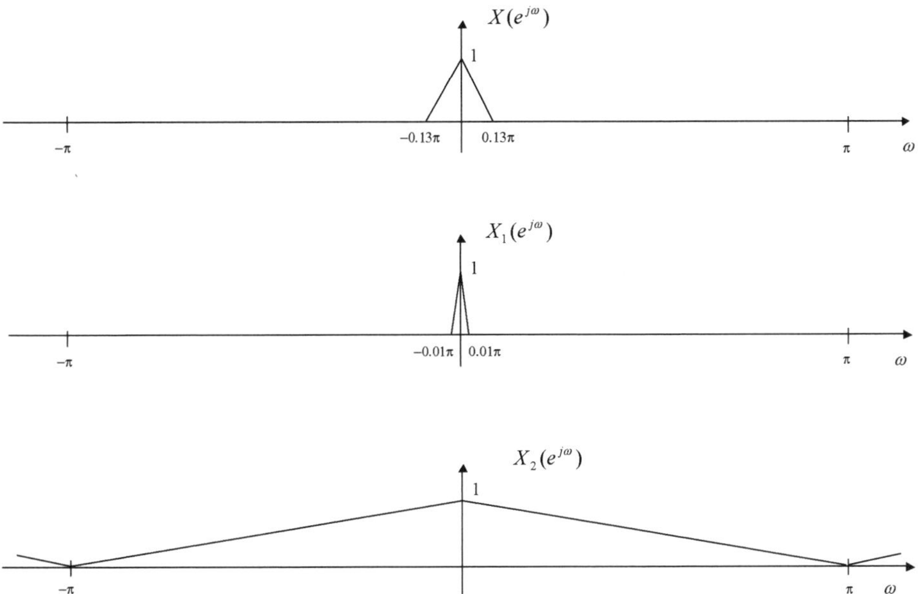

FIGURE 15.36 DTFTs of upsampled filtered and decimated signals (Exercise 15.2).

Exercises

Exercise 15.3

The signals below are sampled with sampling period T_s. Determine the bounds on T_s that guarantee there will be no aliasing.

(a) $x(t) = \cos(10\pi t)\dfrac{\sin(\pi t)}{2t}$

(b) $x(t) = e^{-4t}u(t) * \dfrac{\sin(Wt)}{\pi t}$

Answer:

Exercise 15.4

A continuous-time voltage signal lies in the frequency band $|\omega| < 5\pi$ rad/s. This signal is contaminated by a large sinusoidal signal of frequency 120π rad/s. The contaminated signal is sampled at a sampling rate of $\omega_s = 13\pi$ rad/s.

(a) After sampling, at what frequency does the interfering sinusoidal signal appear?

(b) Now suppose the contaminated signal is passed through an antialiasing filter consisting of an RC circuit with frequency response $H(j\omega) = \frac{1}{RCj\omega + 1}$. Find the value of the time constant RC required for the sinusoid to be attenuated by a factor of 1000 (60 dB) prior to sampling.

Exercise 15.5

Consider the sampling system in Figure 15.37 with an ideal unit-gain, lowpass antialiasing filter $H_{lp}(j\omega)$, with cutoff frequency ω_c, and where the sampling frequency is $\omega_s = \frac{2\pi}{T_s}$.

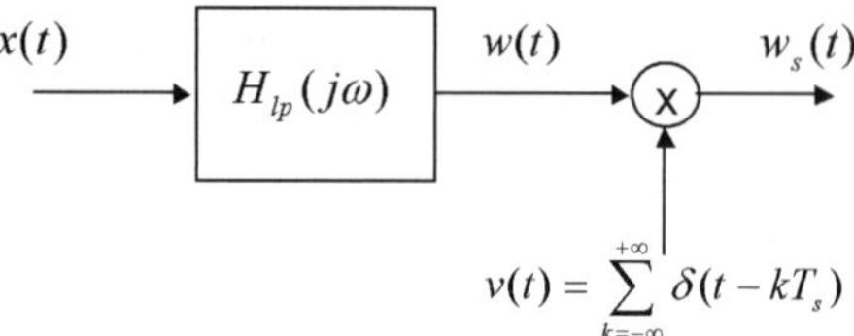

FIGURE 15.37 Sampling system in Exercise 15.5.

The input signal is $x(t) = e^{-t}u(t)$, and the sampling period is set at $T_s = \frac{\pi}{\sqrt{3}}$.

(a) Give a mathematical expression for $X(j\omega)$, the Fourier transform of the input signal, and sketch it (magnitude and phase.) Design the antialiasing filter (i.e., find its cutoff frequency) so that its bandwidth is maximized while avoiding aliasing of its output $w(t)$ in the sampling operation. With this value of ω_c, sketch the magnitudes of the Fourier transforms $W(j\omega)$ and $W_s(j\omega)$.

(b) Compute the ratio of total energies $r = 100\frac{E_{\infty w}}{E_{\infty x}}$ in percent, where $E_{\infty w}$ is the total energy in signal $w(t)$ and $E_{\infty x}$ is the total energy in signal $x(t)$. This ratio gives us an idea of how similar $w(t)$ is to $x(t)$ before sampling. How similar is it? (Hint: $\int \frac{du}{a^2+u^2} = \frac{1}{a}\arctan\left(\frac{u}{a}\right) + C$)

Answer:

Exercise 15.6

Consider the sampling system in Figure 15.38, where the sampling frequency is $\omega_s = \frac{2\pi}{T_s}$.

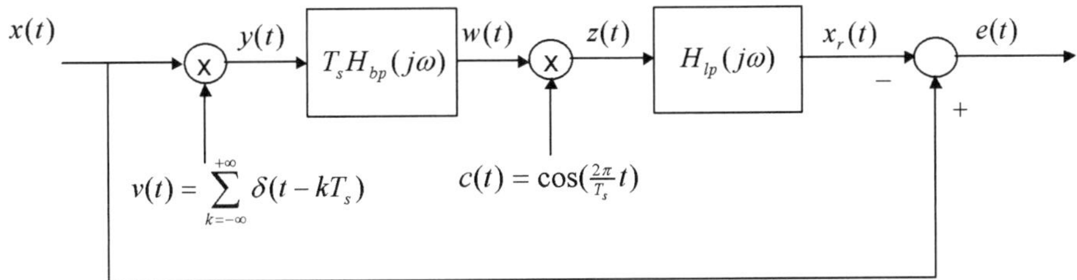

FIGURE 15.38 Sampling system in Exercise 15.6.

The input signal is $x(t) = \frac{W^2}{2\pi}\,\mathrm{sinc}^2\left(\frac{W}{2\pi}t\right)$ and the spectra of the ideal bandpass filter and the ideal lowpass filter are shown in Figure 15.39.

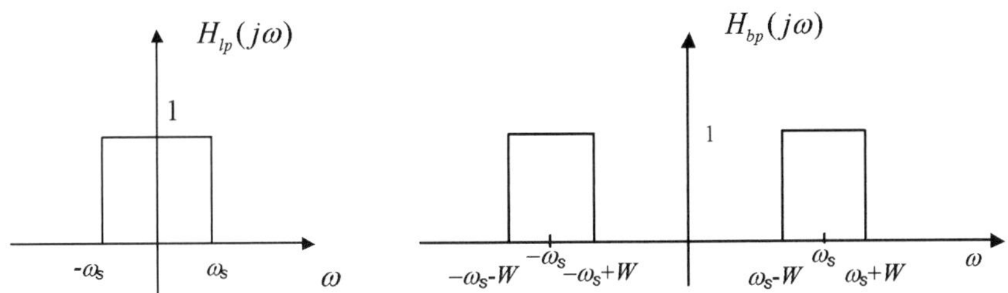

FIGURE 15.39 Frequency responses of ideal lowpass and bandpass filters in Exercise 15.6.

(a) Compute and sketch $X(j\omega)$, the Fourier transform of the input signal. For what range of sampling frequencies $\omega_s = \frac{2\pi}{T_s}$ is the sampling theorem satisfied for the first sampler?

(b) Assume that the sampling theorem is satisfied with the slowest sampling frequency ω_s in the range found in (a). Sketch the spectra $Y(j\omega)$, $W(j\omega)$, and $Z(j\omega)$ for this case.

(c) Sketch the Fourier transforms $X_r(j\omega)$ and $E(j\omega)$. Compute the total energy in the error signal $e(t) := x(t) - x_r(t)$.

Exercise 15.7

Consider the sampling system in Figure 15.40, where the input signal is $x(t) = \frac{W}{\pi}\operatorname{sinc}\left(\frac{W}{\pi}t\right)$ and the spectra of the ideal bandpass filter and the ideal lowpass filter are shown in Figure 15.41.

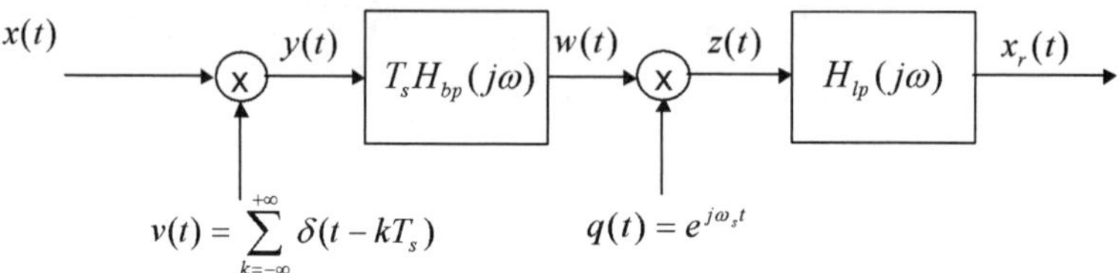

FIGURE 15.40 Sampling system in Exercise 15.7.

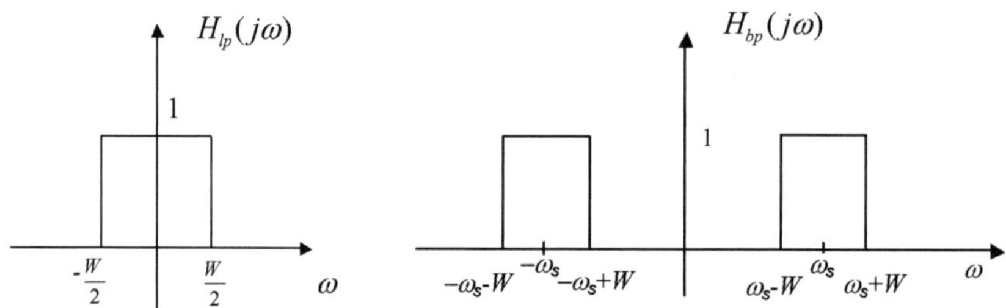

FIGURE 15.41 Frequency responses of the ideal lowpass and bandpass filters in Exercise 15.7.

(a) Find and sketch $X(j\omega)$, the Fourier transform of the input signal $x(t) = \frac{W}{\pi}\operatorname{sinc}\left(\frac{W}{\pi}t\right)$. For what range of sampling frequencies $\omega_s = \frac{2\pi}{T_s}$ is the sampling theorem satisfied?

(b) Assume that the sampling theorem is satisfied with $\omega_s = 3W$ for the remaining questions. Sketch the Fourier transforms $Y(j\omega)$ and $W(j\omega)$.

(c) Sketch the Fourier transforms $Z(j\omega)$ and $X_r(j\omega)$.

(d) Using the Parseval equality, find the total energy of the error signal $e(t)$, defined as the difference between the input signal $x(t)$ and the "reconstructed" output signal $x_r(t)$.

Answer:

Exercise 15.8

The system depicted in Figure 15.42 is used to implement a continuous-time bandpass filter. The discrete-time filter $H_d(e^{j\Omega})$ has frequency response on $[-\pi, \pi]$ given as

$$H_d(e^{j\Omega}) = \begin{cases} 1, & \Omega_a \le |\Omega| \le \Omega_b \\ 0, & \text{otherwise} \end{cases}$$

Find the sampling period T_s, and frequencies Ω_a, Ω_b, and W_1 so that the equivalent continuous-time frequency response $G(j\omega)$ satisfies $G(j\omega) = 1$ for $100\pi < |\omega| < 200\pi$, and $G(j\omega) = 0$ elsewhere. In solving this problem, choose W_1 as small as possible and choose T_s as large as possible.

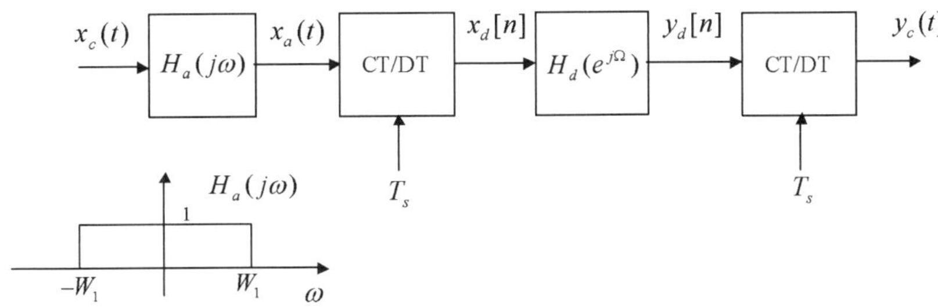

FIGURE 15.42 System implementing a continuous-time bandpass filter in Exercise 15.8.

Exercise 15.9

The signal $x[n]$ with DTFT depicted in Figure 15.43 is decimated to obtain $x_{\downarrow 4}[n] = x[4n]$. Sketch $X_{\downarrow 4}(e^{j\omega})$.

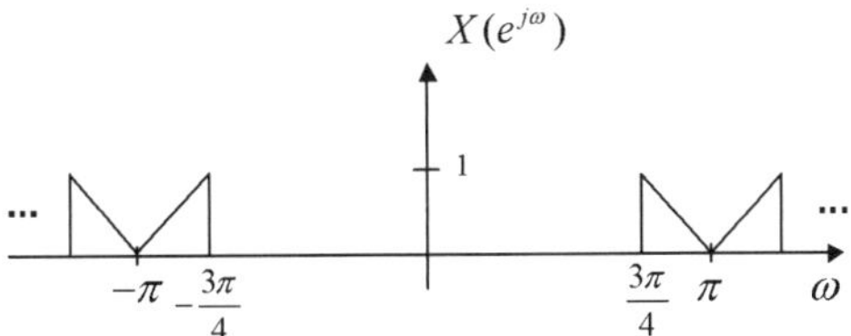

FIGURE 15.43 DTFT of signal in Exercise 15.9.

Answer:

Exercise 15.10

Suppose that you need to transmit a discrete-time signal whose DTFT is shown in Figure 15.44 with a sample rate of 1 MHz. The specification is that the signal should be transmitted at the lowest possible rate, but in real time; that is, the signal at the receiver must be exactly the same with a sample rate of 1 MHz. Design a system (draw a block diagram) that meets these specs. Both before transmission and after reception, you can use upsampling-filtering denoted as $\{\uparrow N\}_{lp}$, decimation denoted as $\downarrow N$, ideal filtering, modulation, demodulation, and summing junctions. (You might want to read the section on amplitude modulation and synchronous demodulation in Chapter 16 first.)

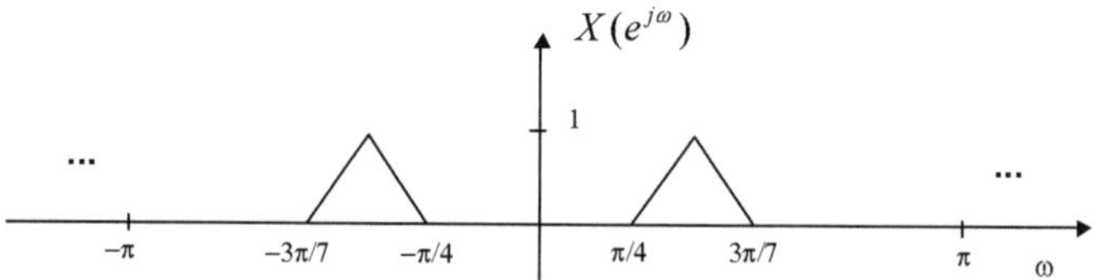

FIGURE 15.44 Spectrum of discrete-time signal to be transmitted in Exercise 15.10.

Exercise 15.11

Consider the decimated multirate system shown in Figure 15.45 used for voice data compression. This system transmits a signal $x[n]$ over two low-bit-rate channels. The sampled voice signal is bandlimited to $\omega_M = \frac{2\pi}{5}$.

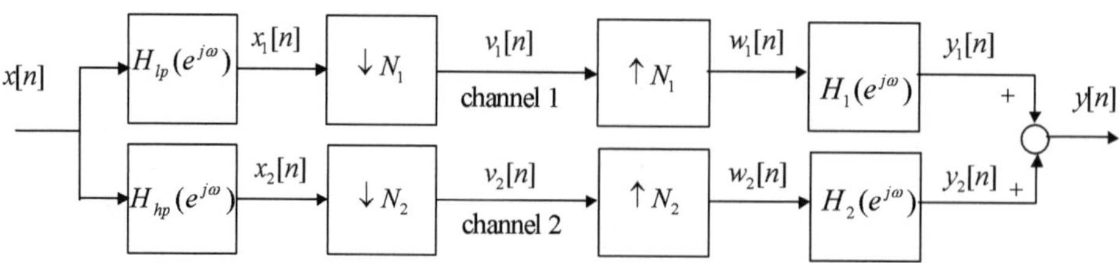

FIGURE 15.45 Decimated multirate system in Exercise 15.11.

Numerical values:

- Input lowpass filter's cutoff frequency $\omega_{clp} = \frac{\pi}{3}$
- Input highpass filter's cutoff frequency $\omega_{chp} = \frac{\pi}{3}$
- Signal's spectrum over [–π, π]: $X(e^{j\omega}) = \begin{cases} 1 - \frac{5}{2\pi}|\omega|, & |\omega| \leq \frac{2\pi}{5} \\ 0, & \frac{2\pi}{5} < |\omega| < \pi \end{cases}$

(a) Sketch the spectra $X(e^{j\omega})$, $X_1(e^{j\omega})$, and $X_2(e^{j\omega})$, indicating the important frequencies and magnitudes.

(b) Find the maximum decimation factors N_1 and N_2, avoiding aliasing, and sketch the corresponding spectra $V_1(e^{j\omega})$, $V_2(e^{j\omega})$, $W_1(e^{j\omega})$, and $W_2(e^{j\omega})$, indicating the important frequencies and magnitudes. Specify what the ideal output filters $H_1(e^{j\omega})$ and $H_2(e^{j\omega})$ should be for perfect signal reconstruction. Sketch their frequency responses, indicating the important frequencies and magnitudes.

(c) Compute the ratio of total energies at the output between the high-frequency subband $y_2[n]$ and the output signal $x[n]$; that is, compute $r := 100\frac{E_{\infty y_2}}{E_{\infty y}}\%$, where the energy is given by $E_{\infty y} := \sum_{n=-\infty}^{+\infty} |y[n]|^2$.

(d) Now suppose each of the two signal subbands $v_1[n]$ and $v_2[n]$ are quantized with a different number of bits to achieve good data compression, without losing intelligibility of the voice message. According to your result in (c), it would seem to make sense to use fewer bits to quantize the high-frequency subband. Suppose that the filter bank operates at an input/output sample rate of 10 kHz, and you decide to use 12 bits to quantize $v_1[n]$ and 4 bits to quantize $v_2[n]$. Compute the bit rates of channel 1 and channel 2 and the overall bit rate of the system.

Answer:

ON THE CD

16 Introduction to Communication Systems

In This Chapter

- Complex Exponential and Sinusoidal Amplitude Modulation
- Demodulation of Sinusoidal AM
- Single-Sideband Amplitude Modulation
- Modulation of a Pulse-Train Carrier
- Pulse-Amplitude Modulation
- Time-Division Multiplexing
- Frequency-Division Multiplexing
- Angle Modulation
- Summary
- To Probe Further
- Exercises

((Lecture 63: Amplitude Modulation and Synchronous Demodulation))

The field of telecommunications engineering has radically changed our lives by allowing us to communicate with other people from virtually any location on earth and even from space. Who could have imagined two hundred years ago that this could ever be possible? The study of communication systems is largely based on signals and systems theory. In particular, the time-domain multiplication property of Fourier transforms is used in amplitude modulation. This chapter is a brief introduction to the basic theory of modulation for signal transmission.

COMPLEX EXPONENTIAL AND SINUSOIDAL AMPLITUDE MODULATION

Recall the time-domain multiplication property for Fourier transforms: the multiplication of two signals results in the convolution of their spectra:

$$x(t)y(t)\overset{FT}{\leftrightarrow}\frac{1}{2\pi}X(j\omega)*Y(j\omega). \tag{16.1}$$

Amplitude modulation (AM) is based on this property. For example, consider the modulation system described by

$$y(t)=x(t)c(t), \tag{16.2}$$

where the *modulated signal* $y(t)$ is the product of the *carrier signal* $c(t)$ and the *modulating signal* $x(t)$, also called the *message*. The carrier signal can be a complex exponential or a sinusoid, or even a pulse train.

An important objective in modulation is to produce a signal whose frequency range is suitable for transmission over the communication channel to be used. In telephone systems, long-distance transmission is often accomplished over microwave (300 MHz to 300 GHz) or satellite links (300 MHz to 40 GHz), but most of the energy of a voice signal is in the range of 50 Hz to 5 kHz. Hence, voice signals have to be shifted to much higher frequencies for efficient transmission. This can be achieved by amplitude modulation.

Amplitude Modulation with a Complex Exponential Carrier

In amplitude modulation with a complex exponential carrier, the latter can be written as

$$c(t)=e^{j(\omega_c t+\theta_c)}, \tag{16.3}$$

where the frequency ω_c is called the *carrier frequency*. Let $\theta_c = 0$ for convenience. We have seen that the Fourier transform of a complex exponential is an impulse of area 2π, so that

$$C(j\omega)=2\pi\delta(\omega-\omega_c). \tag{16.4}$$

The frequency-domain convolution of $C(j\omega)$ and $X(j\omega)$ yields

$$
\begin{aligned}
Y(j\omega) &= \frac{1}{2\pi} X(j\omega) * C(j\omega) \\
&= \int_{-\infty}^{+\infty} X(j\upsilon)\delta(\omega - \upsilon - \omega_c)d\upsilon \\
&= \int_{-\infty}^{+\infty} X(j\upsilon)\delta(-(\upsilon - (\omega - \omega_c))d\upsilon \\
&= \int_{-\infty}^{+\infty} X(j\upsilon)\delta(\upsilon - (\omega - \omega_c))d\upsilon \\
&= X(j(\omega - \omega_c)).
\end{aligned} \tag{16.5}
$$

Thus, the spectrum of the modulated signal $y(t)$ is that of the modulating signal $x(t)$ frequency-shifted to the carrier frequency, as shown in Figure 16.1.

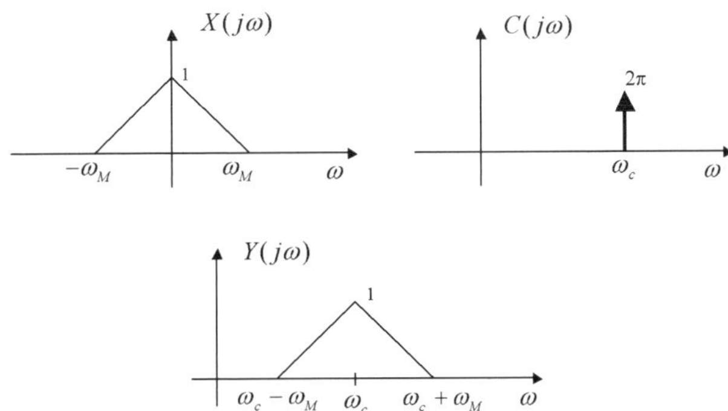

FIGURE 16.1 Amplitude modulation with a complex exponential carrier.

An obvious *demodulation* strategy would be to multiply the modulated signal by $e^{-j\omega_c t}$

$$
y(t)e^{-j\omega_c t} = x(t)e^{j\omega_c t}e^{-j\omega_c t} = x(t). \tag{16.6}
$$

In the frequency domain, this operation simply brings the spectrum back around $\omega = 0$.

Amplitude Modulation with a Sinusoidal Carrier

In sinusoidal amplitude modulation, the carrier signal is given by

$$
c(t) = \cos(\omega_c t + \theta_c). \tag{16.7}
$$

Sinusoidal AM can be represented by the diagram in Figure 16.2, where the modulated signal $y(t)$ is fed into an antenna for transmission.

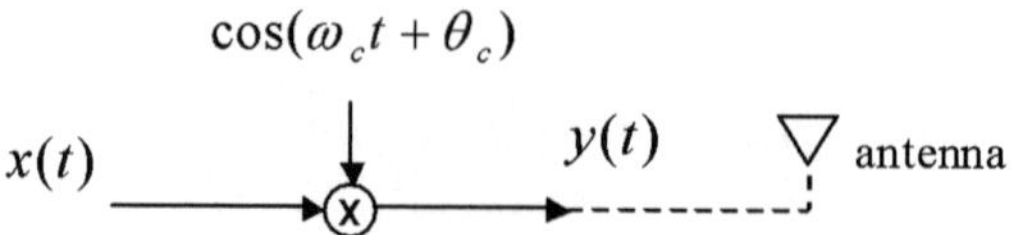

FIGURE 16.2 Diagram of sinusoidal AM.

Again, let $\theta_c = 0$ for convenience. The spectrum of the carrier signal is

$$C(j\omega) = \pi\delta(\omega + \omega_c) + \pi\delta(\omega - \omega_c), \tag{16.8}$$

and the spectrum of the modulated signal is obtained through a convolution:

$$\begin{aligned} Y(j\omega) &= \frac{1}{2\pi} X(j\omega) * C(j\omega) \\ &= \frac{1}{2} X(j(\omega + \omega_c)) + \frac{1}{2} X(j(\omega - \omega_c)). \end{aligned} \tag{16.9}$$

We see in Figure 16.3 that there are two replicas of $X(j\omega)$, one at ω_c and the other at $-\omega_c$.

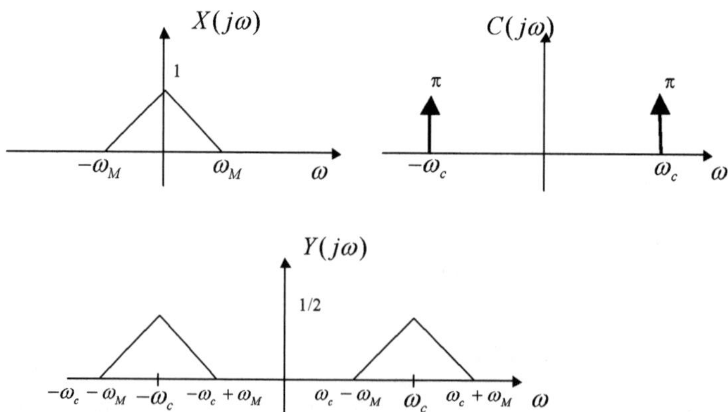

FIGURE 16.3 Sinusoidal AM in the frequency domain.

Note that the two copies of the original spectrum can overlap if the carrier frequency is not high enough, that is, if $\omega_c < \omega_M$, which is not the case for AM with a complex exponential carrier. The modulating signal may be unrecoverable if this happens.

DEMODULATION OF SINUSOIDAL AM

In a communication system, the information-bearing (modulating) signal $x(t)$ is recovered at the receiver end through demodulation. There are two commonly used methods for sinusoidal AM demodulation: *synchronous demodulation,* in which the transmitter and receiver are synchronized and in phase, and *asynchronous demodulation,* which does not require accurate knowledge of the carrier signal.

Synchronous Demodulation

Assuming that $\omega_c > \omega_M$, synchronous demodulation is straightforward. Consider the modulated signal to be demodulated:

$$y(t) = x(t)\cos(\omega_c t). \tag{16.10}$$

If we multiply this signal again by the carrier $\cos(\omega_c t)$ at the receiver, that is,

$$w(t) = y(t)\cos(\omega_c t), \tag{16.11}$$

then the two replicas of $Y(j\omega)$ will be such that the left part of one adds up to the right part of the other, thereby reforming the original spectrum of $x(t)$ around $\omega = 0$. Then $x(t)$ can be recovered by an ideal lowpass filter with a gain of 2 and cutoff frequency ω_{co}, satisfying $\omega_M < \omega_{co} < 2\omega_c - \omega_M$. This principle of synchronous demodulation is illustrated by Figure 16.4.

Also, using the trigonometric identity,

$$\cos^2(\omega_c t) = \frac{1}{2} + \frac{1}{2}\cos(2\omega_c t), \tag{16.12}$$

we can express the signal $\omega(t)$ as follows:

$$\begin{aligned} w(t) &= x(t)\cos^2(\omega_c t) \\ &= \frac{1}{2}x(t) + \frac{1}{2}x(t)\cos(2\omega_c t), \end{aligned} \tag{16.13}$$

where it is clear that the message is recovered in the first term, and the second term is akin to an amplitude modulation at twice the carrier frequency, which is subsequently removed by lowpass filtering.

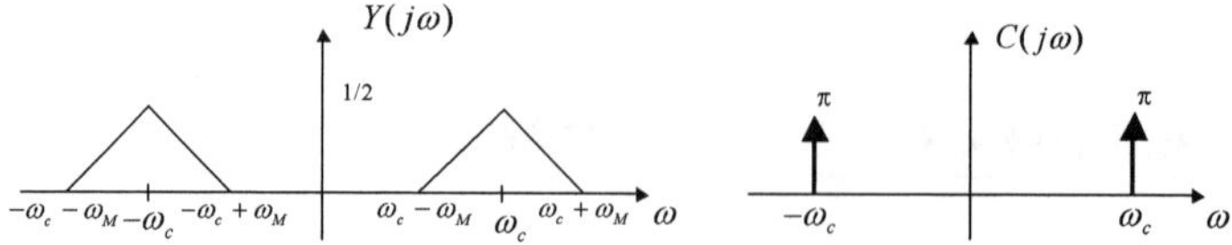

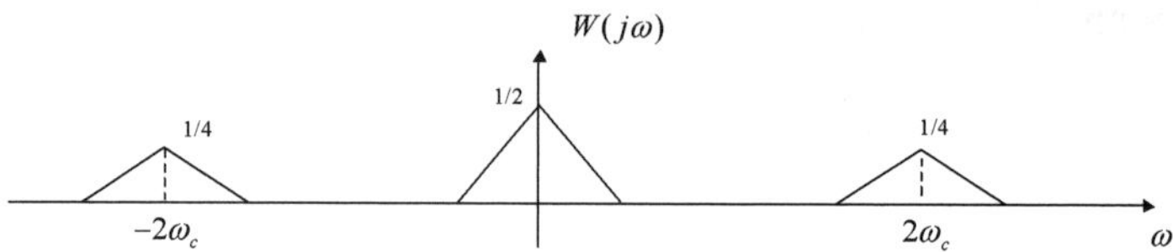

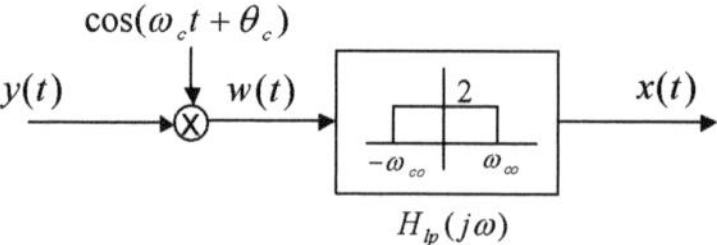

FIGURE 16.4 Synchronous demodulation of sinusoidal AM.

Now, suppose that the receiver and the transmitter use exactly the same carrier frequency, but with a phase difference, that is,

$$c_{transm}(t) = \cos(\omega_c t + \theta_c), \tag{16.14}$$

and

$$c_{rec}(t) = \cos(\omega_c t + \phi_c). \tag{16.15}$$

Then, using the trigonometric identity

$$\cos(\omega_c t + \theta_c)\cos(\omega_c t + \phi_c) = \frac{1}{2}\cos(\theta_c - \phi_c) + \frac{1}{2}\cos(2\omega_c t + \theta_c + \phi_c), \tag{16.16}$$

we have

$$w(t) = \frac{1}{2}x(t)\cos(\theta_c - \phi_c) + \frac{1}{2}x(t)\cos(2\omega_c t + \theta_c + \phi_c). \tag{16.17}$$

This means that the amplitude of the signal recovered at the output of the lowpass filter is smaller than the original amplitude by a factor of $\cos(\theta_c - \phi_c)$. In particular, when the demodulating carrier is out of phase by $\pi/2$, the output of the demodulator is zero.

Equation 16.17 also helps explain the *beating* phenomenon heard on some older radio receivers in which the volume of a demodulated voice or music signal seems to periodically go up and down. Suppose that the phase of the receiver's carrier is actually the linear function of time $\phi_c = \delta t$, where δ is a very small real number in proportion to the carrier frequency. In this case, the carrier frequency used by the receiver is slightly off with respect to the carrier frequency used to modulate the signal as

$$c_{rec}(t) = \cos(\omega_c t + \phi_c(t)) = \cos((\omega_c + \delta)t). \tag{16.18}$$

Then, Equation 16.17 becomes

$$w(t) = \frac{1}{2}x(t)\cos(\delta t + \theta_c) + \frac{1}{2}x(t)\cos(2\omega_c t + \theta_c + \phi_c), \tag{16.19}$$

where the amplitude of the first term containing the message is affected by a sinusoidal gain $\cos(\delta t + \theta_c)$, which produces the beating effect.

((Lecture 64: Asynchronous Demodulation))

Asynchronous Demodulation

In contrast to synchronous demodulation of AM signals, asynchronous demodulation does not require that the receiver have very accurate knowledge of the carrier's phase and frequency. Asynchronous demodulation is used in simple AM radio receivers: it is a cheap, but lower quality, alternative to synchronous demodulation.

Asynchronous demodulation involves a nonlinear operation and is therefore easier to understand in the time domain. Suppose that we add a positive constant to the signal to be transmitted before modulation:

$$y(t) = \left[A + x(t)\right]\cos(\omega_c t), \tag{16.20}$$

where A is large enough to make $A + x(t) > 0, \forall t$. This amounts to transmitting the carrier signal as well as the modulated signal. Let K be the maximum amplitude of $x(t)$, that is, $|x(t)| < K$, and assume $A \geq K$. The modulation index m is the ratio

$$m := K/A. \tag{16.21}$$

The modulating signal $x(t)$ turns out to be the envelope of the modulated signal $y(t)$, as the example in Figure 16.5 shows with $A = 1$ and $m = 0.3$.

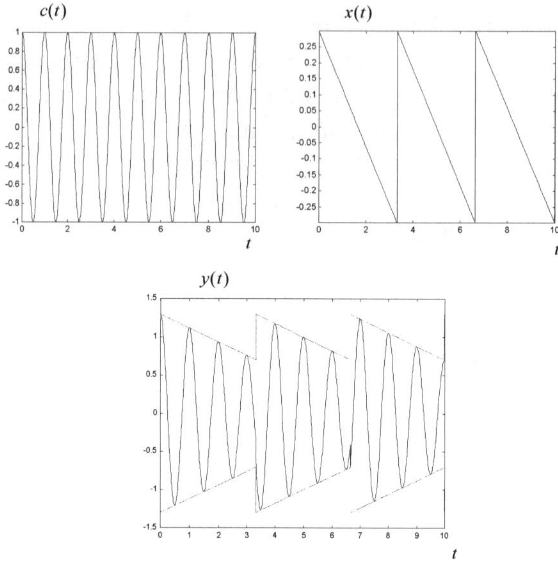

FIGURE 16.5 AM signal with a 0.3 modulation index.

Thus, the asynchronous demodulator should be an *envelope detector*. An envelope detector such as the one in Figure 16.6 can be implemented with a simple *RC* circuit and a diode.

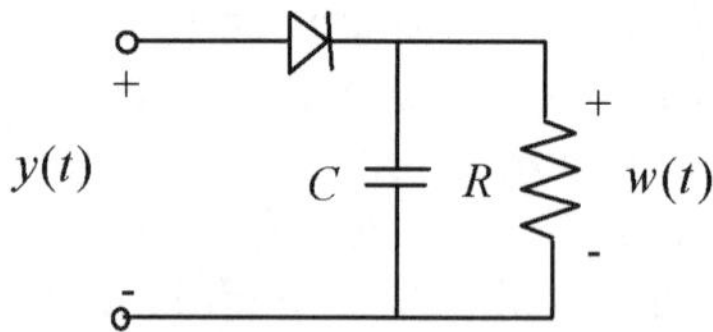

FIGURE 16.6 Envelope detector

The diode half-wave rectifies the signal. When the voltage $y(t)$ gets higher than the capacitor voltage, the latter follows $y(t)$. When $y(t)$ drops below the voltage of the capacitor, the diode switches off and the capacitor discharges through the resistor with time constant $\tau = RC$. The resulting signal $w(t)$ is shown in Figure 16.7.

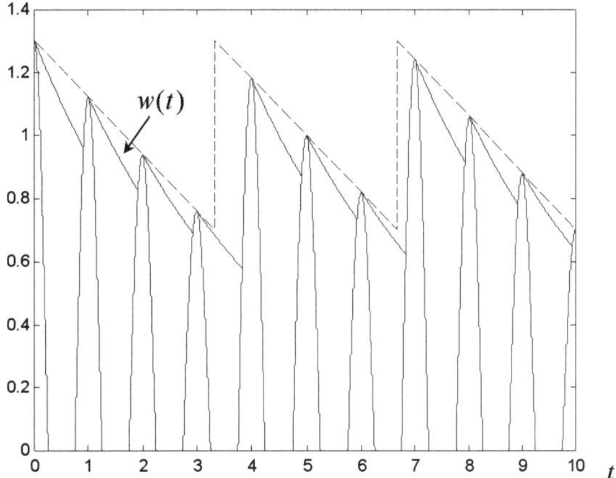

FIGURE 16.7 Detector output in asynchronous demodulation of an AM signal.

The envelope detector circuit is normally followed by a lowpass filter to get rid of the components at frequencies around the carrier frequency. This would smooth out the jagged graph of signal $w(t)$ in Figure 16.7.

Example 16.1: Let us design an envelope detector to demodulate the AM signal:

$$y(t) = [1 + 0.5\cos(200\pi t)]\cos(2\pi 10^6 t). \tag{16.22}$$

The output voltage of the detector, going from one peak at voltage v_1 to the next when it intersects the modulated carrier at voltage v_2 after approximately one period $T = 1\ \mu$s of the carrier, is given by:

$$v_2 \cong v_1 e^{-T/RC}. \tag{16.23}$$

Since the time constant $\tau = RC$ of the detector should be large with respect to $T = 1\ \mu$s we can use a first-order approximation of the exponential such that

$$v_2 \cong v_1(1 - T/RC). \tag{16.24}$$

This is a line of negative slope $-\frac{v_1}{RC}$ between the initial voltage v_1 and the final voltage v_2 so that

$$\frac{v_2 - v_1}{T} \cong -\frac{v_1}{RC}. \tag{16.25}$$

This negative slope must be steeper than the maximum negative slope of the envelope of $y(t)$, denoted as $\mathrm{env}\{y(t)\}$, which is obtained as follows.

$$\frac{d\,\mathrm{env}\{y(t)\}}{dt} = -100\pi \sin(200\pi t)$$
$$\Rightarrow \min_t \frac{d\,\mathrm{env}\{y(t)\}}{dt} = -100\pi \tag{16.26}$$

Taking the worst-case voltage $v_1 = 0.5$, in the sense that $-\frac{v_1}{RC}$ must still be below -100π with this voltage, we must have

$$-\frac{0.5}{RC} < -100\pi$$
$$\Leftrightarrow$$
$$RC < \frac{0.5}{100\pi} = 0.0016 \text{ s.} \tag{16.27}$$

Thus, we could take $R = 1\,\mathrm{k}\Omega,\ C = 1\,\mu\mathrm{F}$ to get $RC = 0.001$ s.

Remarks:

- The envelope detector circuit works best when the modulation index m is small. This is because large variations in the envelope (negative derivative) for m close to 1 are "difficult to follow" by the detector since the capacitor discharge rate is fixed. The tradeoff in the choice of the time constant of the detector is that a small time constant is desirable for such fast variations of negative slope, but on the other hand, a large time constant is desirable to minimize the amount of high-frequency ripple on $w(t)$.
- A small modulation index m means that a large part of the power transmitted is "wasted" on the carrier, which makes the system inefficient.
- AM radio broadcasting uses sinusoidal AM, and the previous generation of receivers typically used asynchronous envelope detectors.

((Lecture 65: Single Sideband Amplitude Modulation))

SINGLE-SIDEBAND AMPLITUDE MODULATION

There is redundancy of information in sinusoidal AM. Two copies of the spectrum of the original real signal of bandwidth ω_M are shifted to ω_c and $-\omega_c$, each one now occupying a frequency band of width $2\omega_M$. Because bandwidth is a valuable commodity, we would like to use the redundancy in the positive and negative frequencies to our advantage.

The idea behind *single-sideband AM* (SSB-AM) is to keep only one half of the original spectrum around ω_c and to keep the other half around $-\omega_c$, as shown in Figure 16.8. The net result is that instead of having a positive-frequency bandwidth of $2\omega_M$, the modulated signal uses a bandwidth of ω_M only.

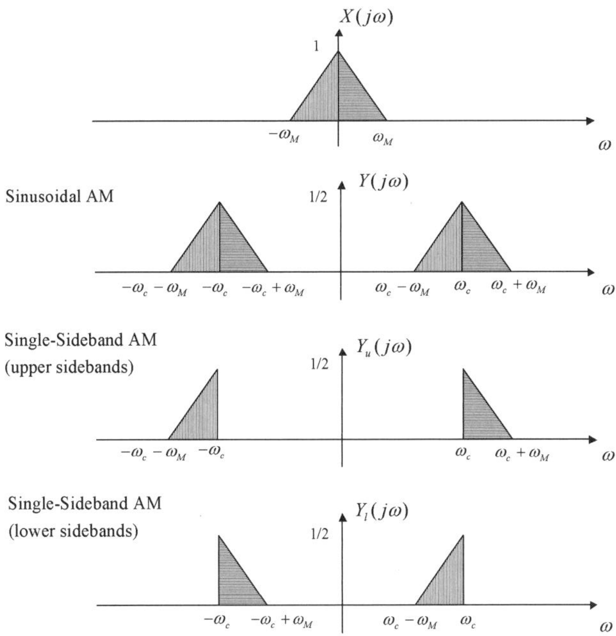

FIGURE 16.8 Upper and lower single-sideband AM compared to sinusoidal AM.

We can see from this figure that demodulation will consist of bringing the two halves of the original spectrum together around $\omega = 0$.

Generating the Sidebands

One obvious method to generate the upper sidebands is to use an ideal highpass filter with cutoff frequency ω_c at the output of a sinusoidal AM modulator, as shown in Figure 16.9.

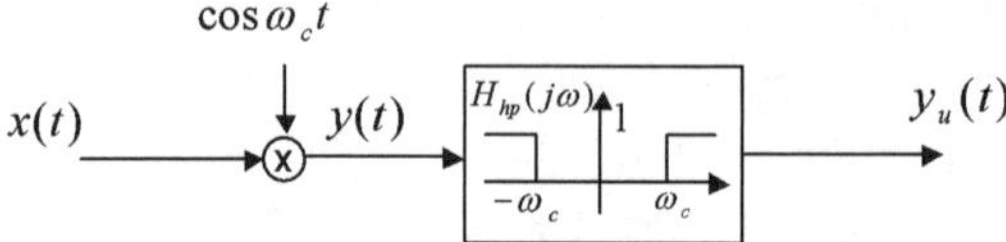

FIGURE 16.9 Upper SSB-AM using a highpass filter.

Similarly, the lower sidebands can be generated using an ideal lowpass filter (an ideal bandpass filter would also work) with cutoff frequency ω_c following a sinusoidal AM modulator (see Figure 16.10).

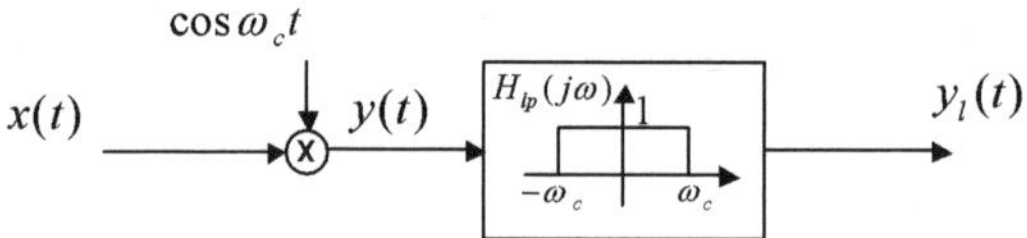

FIGURE 16.10 Lower SSB-AM using a lowpass filter.

In practice, these techniques would require quasi-ideal filters with high cutoff frequencies, which can be difficult to design. Yet another technique to generate upper or lower sidebands is to use the system in Figure 16.11 with two modulation operations and a $\pi/2$ phase-shift filter (this one keeps the lower sidebands).

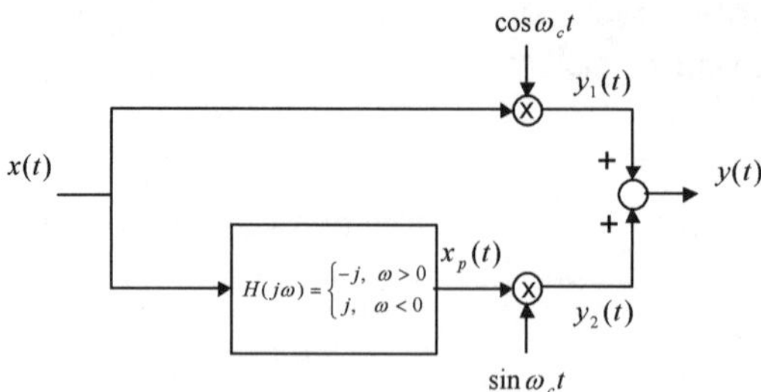

FIGURE 16.11 Lower SSB-AM using a phase-shift filter.

The upper path of the block diagram in Figure 16.11 produces the usual double-sideband spectrum $Y_1(j\omega)$, while the lower path produces a negative copy of the upper sidebands in $Y_2(j\omega)$, but keeping the lower sidebands intact. Thus, the sum of $Y_1(j\omega)$ and $Y_2(j\omega)$ cancels off the upper sidebands and keeps only the lower sidebands. Note that the perfect phase-shifter, also called a *Hilbert transformer,* is impossible to obtain in practice, but good approximations can be designed.

To understand how the lower path works, let the spectrum of the modulating signal be decomposed as

$$X(j\omega) = X_{-}(j\omega) + X_{+}(j\omega), \tag{16.28}$$

where $X_{-}(j\omega)$ is the component at negative frequencies, and $X_{+}(j\omega)$ is the component at positive frequencies. Then, after filtering $x(t)$ with the phase-shifter $H(j\omega)$, we obtain

$$X_p(j\omega) = jX_{-}(j\omega) - jX_{+}(j\omega). \tag{16.29}$$

The spectrum of the sinusoidal carrier is

$$C(j\omega) = j\pi\delta(\omega + \omega_c) - j\pi\delta(\omega - \omega_c), \tag{16.30}$$

and that of the modulated signal $y_2(t)$ is

$$\begin{aligned} Y_2(j\omega) &= \frac{1}{2\pi} X_p(j\omega) * C(j\omega) \\ &= j\frac{1}{2} X_p(j(\omega + \omega_c)) - j\frac{1}{2} X_p(j(\omega - \omega_c)) \\ &= \frac{1}{2}\left[-X_{-}(j(\omega + \omega_c)) + X_{+}(j(\omega + \omega_c)) + X_{-}(j(\omega - \omega_c)) - X_{+}(j(\omega - \omega_c))\right]. \end{aligned} \tag{16.31}$$

Now,

$$\begin{aligned} Y_1(j\omega) &= \frac{1}{2} X(j(\omega + \omega_c)) + \frac{1}{2} X(j(\omega - \omega_c)) \\ &= \frac{1}{2}\left[X_{-}(j(\omega + \omega_c)) + X_{+}(j(\omega + \omega_c)) + X_{-}(j(\omega - \omega_c)) + X_{+}(j(\omega - \omega_c))\right]. \end{aligned} \tag{16.32}$$

Hence,

$$Y(j\omega) = Y_1(j\omega) + Y_2(j\omega) = X_{+}(j(\omega + \omega_c)) + X_{-}(j(\omega - \omega_c)) \tag{16.33}$$

is composed of the lower sidebands only.

Demodulation

Synchronous demodulation is required for SSB-AM/SC (single-sideband amplitude modulation, suppressed carrier). In SSB-AM/WC (single-sideband amplitude modulation with carrier), synchronous demodulation could be implemented with a highly selective bandpass filter to recover the carrier. Here it is assumed that the spectrum of the original signal has no energy around DC. A block diagram of the demodulator and the signal spectra are shown in Figure 16.12.

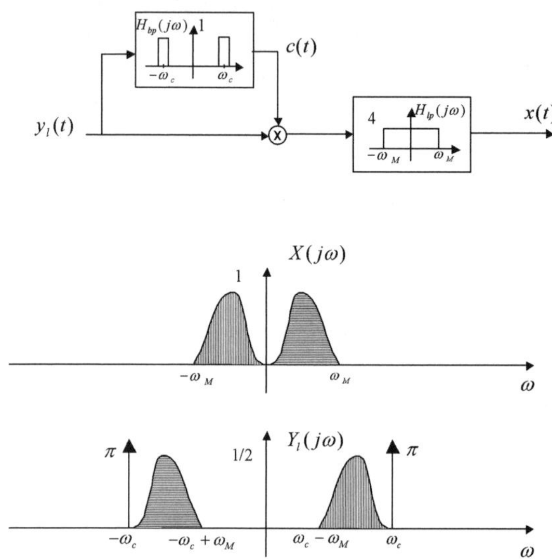

FIGURE 16.12 Demodulation of lower single-sideband AM signal using a bandpass filter.

Remarks:

- High resolution digital TV broadcasting (HDTV) uses a form of SSB-AM for signal transmission.
- Regular sinusoidal AM is often called *double-sideband AM* (DSB-AM).
- A phase-lock loop is sometimes used in the receiver to reproduce the carrier accurately and use it in a synchronous demodulator. The phase-lock loop is discussed in the section on angle modulation.

((Lecture 66: Pulse-Train and Pulse Amplitude Modulation))

MODULATION OF A PULSE-TRAIN CARRIER

The carrier signal can be a train of finite rectangular pulses in the modulation system shown in Figure 16.13 and characterized by the equation $y(t)=x(t)c(t)$. Define the rectangular pulse

$$p(t):=\begin{cases}1, & |t|<\dfrac{\Delta}{2} \\ 0, & \text{otherwise}\end{cases}, \tag{16.34}$$

and the pulse train

$$c(t):=\sum_{n=-\infty}^{+\infty} p(t-nT). \tag{16.35}$$

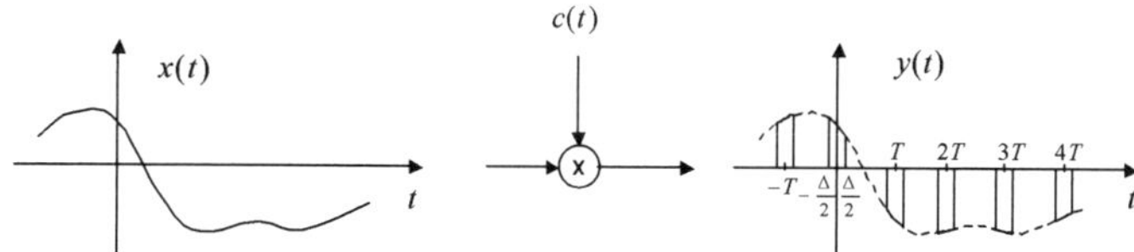

FIGURE 16.13 Pulse-train modulation.

Let $\omega_c = \frac{2\pi}{T}$ In the frequency domain, this modulation is quite similar to impulse train sampling, as we can see from Figure 16.14. The only difference is that the Fourier transform of $c(t)$ in impulse train sampling is an impulse train of constant area, whereas here the areas of the impulses follow the "sinc envelope" of the Fourier transform $P(j\omega)$ of the pulse $p(t)$. That is, the impulse areas are the Fourier series coefficients a_k of $c(t)$.

The spectrum of the modulated signal is given by

$$Y(j\omega)=\sum_{k=-\infty}^{+\infty} a_k X(j(\omega-k\omega_c)), \tag{16.36}$$

where

$$a_k=\frac{\sin(k\omega_c\Delta/2)}{\pi k}. \tag{16.37}$$

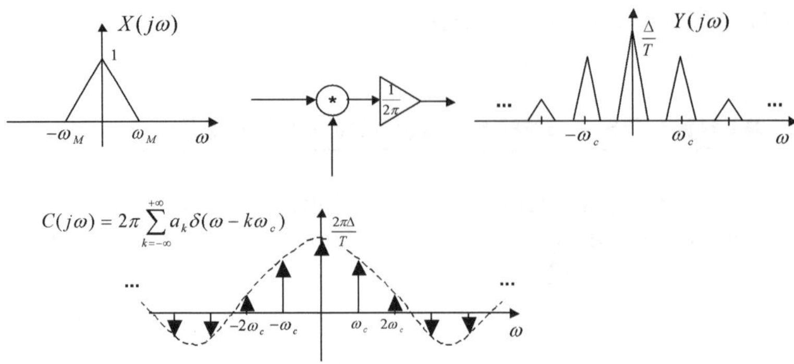

FIGURE 16.14 Pulse-train modulation in the frequency domain.

The replicated spectra do not overlap in $Y(j\omega)$ if the sampling theorem is satisfied, that is, if $\omega_c > 2\omega_M$. The original modulating signal $x(t)$ can then be recovered by lowpass filtering. Note that bandpass filtering around $\omega_c = \frac{2\pi}{T}$ would produce a DSB-AM spectrum.

What is pulse-train modulation used for? It is used in *time-division multiplexing,* which will be studied later.

PULSE-AMPLITUDE MODULATION

We have seen that pulse-train modulation basically corresponds to time-slicing of the signal $x(t)$. Based on the sampling theorem, it should be sufficient to use only *one* sampled value of the signal $x(nT)$ rather than its whole continuous range of values over the pulse duration. This type of modulation is called *pulse-amplitude modulation* (PAM). The analysis is different from pulse-;train modulation: rather than obtaining scaled, undistorted copies of the original spectrum in the modulated signal $y(t)$, PAM creates some distortion in the spectral replicas in $Y(j\omega)$. This distortion comes from the zero-order-hold (ZOH)–like operation as shown in Figure 16.15.

The frequency response $H_0(j\omega)$ of $h_0(t)$ is given by

$$H_0(j\omega) = \Delta e^{-j\omega\frac{\Delta}{2}} \operatorname{sinc}\left(\tfrac{\Delta}{2\pi}\omega\right) = 2e^{-j\omega\frac{\Delta}{2}} \frac{\sin(\omega\frac{\Delta}{2})}{\omega}, \tag{16.38}$$

and the spectrum $Y(j\omega)$ shown in Figure 16.16 is given by

$$Y(j\omega) = \frac{1}{T}\sum_{k=-\infty}^{+\infty} X(j(\omega - k\omega_c))H_0(j\omega). \tag{16.39}$$

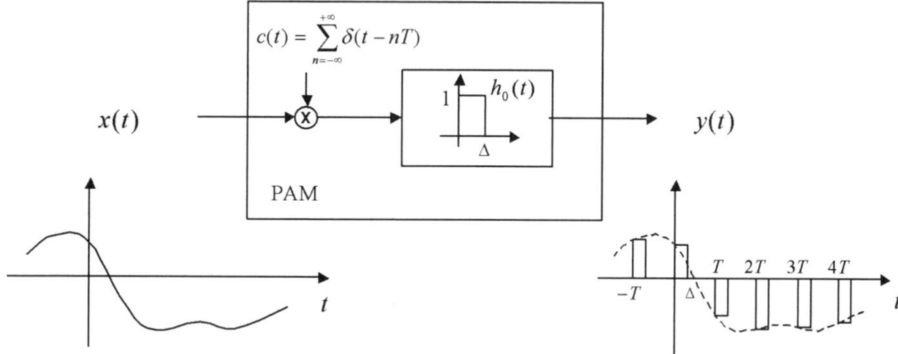

FIGURE 16.15 Pulse-amplitude modulation.

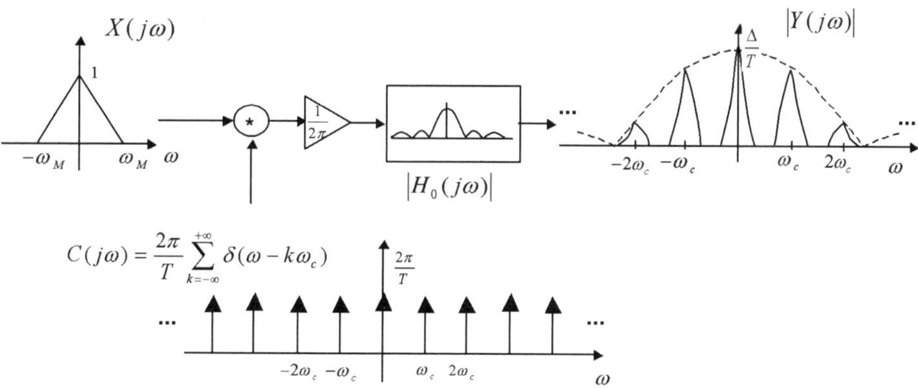

FIGURE 16.16 Pulse-amplitude modulation in the frequency domain.

The distortion caused by the sinc frequency response $H_0(j\omega)$ can be substantially decreased by using narrow pulses, that is, choosing Δ small (although this may lead to a low signal-to-noise power ratio), and by using an inverse filter $H_1(j\omega) \cong H_0^{-1}(j\omega)$ before lowpass filtering at the receiving end.

On the other hand, pulse-amplitude modulation is often demodulated by a CT/DT sampling operator at the receiver to create a discrete-time signal, which automatically resolves the distortion problem.

Intersymbol Interference in PAM Systems

PAM systems are time-domain based. The transmission of a PAM signal over a real communication channel is not easy. For example, let us consider a finite-bandwidth communication channel with a frequency response similar to a first-order system. The amplitude modulated pulses will get distorted and delayed through the channel, to the point where each pulse gets "smeared" in time and interferes with its neighbors. This is called *intersymbol interference.*

Example 16.2: A PAM signal representing signal samples $x(nT) = 1$ with $T = 1$, $\Delta = 0.3$ is transmitted through a first-order channel with frequency response $H_{ch}(j\omega) = \frac{1}{0.2j\omega + 1}$. The pulses at the output of the channel are plotted in Figure 16.17, where we can see that each received pulse has an effect on the next ones.

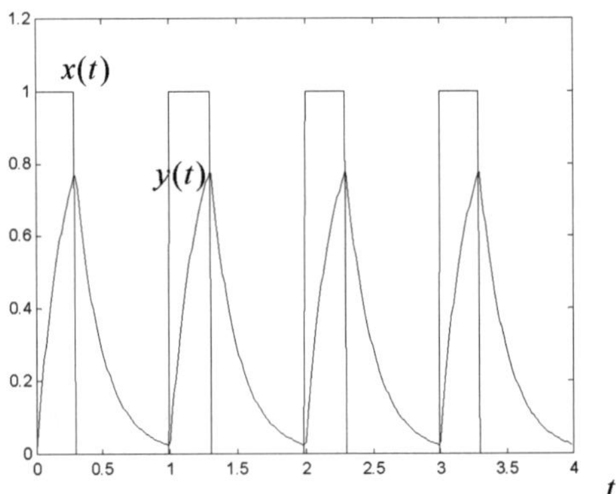

FIGURE 16.17 Transmission of a PAM signal through a first-order channel.

If the intersymbol interference is only due to the limited bandwidth of the channel, for example,

$$H_{ch}(j\omega) = \begin{cases} 1, & |\omega| < W \\ 0, & |\omega| \geq W \end{cases}, \tag{16.40}$$

then one way to get rid of it is to use a bandlimited pulse, for example, a sinc pulse:

$$p(t) = T\frac{\sin(\pi t/T)}{\pi t}, \tag{16.41}$$

so that the pulse is transmitted undistorted since

$$P(j\omega) = \begin{cases} 1, & |\omega| < \dfrac{\pi}{T} \\ 0, & |\omega| > \dfrac{\pi}{T} \end{cases}, \tag{16.42}$$

and we assume that $\frac{\pi}{T} < W$. One potential problem with this strategy is that the sinc pulse is of infinite duration. However, $p(t)$ has zero crossings at each sampling instant so that only the contribution of the current pulse is sampled at the receiver. Obviously, the CT/DT operation at the receiver must be very well synchronized to sample $y(t)$ at the right time.

This may not be obvious, but with the ideal sinc pulse $p(t)$, the PAM signal is *equal* to $x(t)$ (refer back to Figure 15.9). One might as well transmit the signal $x(t)$ directly. The main benefit of using sinc pulses is for time-division multiplexing (TDM), where many signals are pulse-amplitude modulated and multiplexed for transmission over a single channel. Then it is crucial to separate the pulses at the sampling instants; otherwise a phenomenon called *crosstalk* can occur. An example of crosstalk is when one is having a conversation on the phone and suddenly hears in the background someone else's voice on a different call.

((Lecture 67: Frequency-Division and Time-Division Multiplexing; Angle Modulation))

TIME-DIVISION MULTIPLEXING

TDM is used to transmit more than one pulse-amplitude modulated signal over a single channel. TDM can be represented as a rotating switch connecting each signal to the channel for a brief period of time, as shown in Figure 16.18.

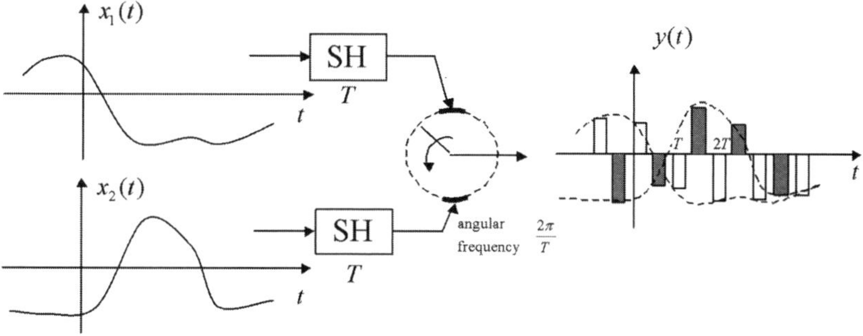

FIGURE 16.18 Time-division multiplexing of two signals.

As mentioned before, it is crucial to avoid intersample interference in such a system when $y(t)$ is transmitted over a communication channel. Intersample interference occurs in bandlimited channels (even with flat frequency responses). The use of sinc pulses, or other types of bandlimited pulses with zero crossings at the sampling instants, can greatly reduce intersample interference.

Demodulation

The ideal demodulator for TDM in Figure 16.19 is composed of impulse train samplers synchronized with each PAM subsignal of $y(t)$ (an operation called demultiplexing), followed by ideal lowpass filters to reconstruct the continuous-time signals.

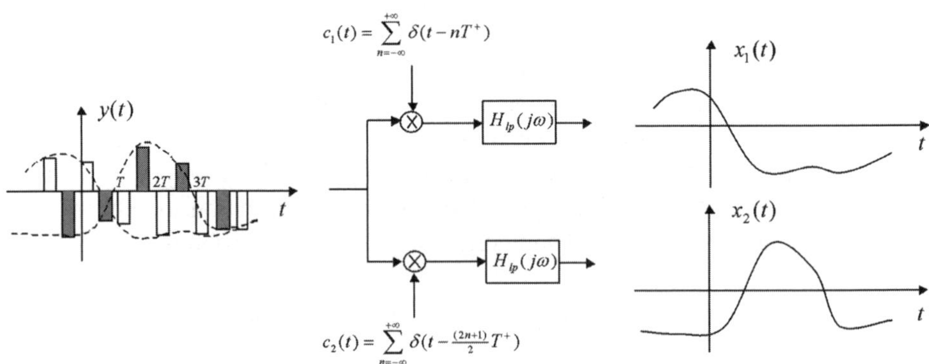

FIGURE 16.19 Demodulation of a TDM signal.

The structure of the demodulator depends on what format the demultiplexed signals should take at the receiver. For example, since TDM is often used for digital communication systems, it might be desirable to generate discrete-time signals following the demultiplexing operation. In this case a CT/DT operation would replace the impulse train samplers and the filters in Figure 16.19. A practical implementation might use a synchronized analog-to-digital (A/D) converter sampling $y(t)$ at the rate of $\omega_s = 4\pi/T$. Demultiplexing is then performed digitally in the processor.

Non-Ideal Channels

At least three types of distortion can occur when a TDM signal is transmitted over a realistic (non-ideal) communication channel:

- Distortion caused by a finite bandwidth channel: the ideal rectangular pulse has a spectrum extending to infinite frequencies, and the high-frequency part of the spectrum cut off by the channel results in a distorted pulse causing intersymbol interference. A solution to this problem is to use bandlimited pulses as previously mentioned.
- Distortion caused by a channel with non-flat magnitude or nonlinear phase: this can distort the pulse so that its amplitude is changed and can also cause intersymbol interference. Channel equalization at the receiver using an equalizer can improve this situation.
- Distortion caused by additive noise: this situation can be improved by filtering if the power spectral density of the noise is outside of the bandwith of the TDM signal (using bandlimited pulses). If the noise cannot be filtered out, then pulse-code modulation (PCM) can be used if it is acceptable to quantize the amplitude of the original PAM signals to be transmitted. Suppose that the signal amplitudes are quantized using 8 bits (256 values); then each of the 8 bits can be transmitted successively. In this case, the transmitted voltage pulses would represent either a 0 (e.g., 0 V) or a 1 (e.g., 10 V), and it should be easy to decide at the receiver whether it was a 0 or a 1 being transmitted, even in the presence of significant additive noise.

FREQUENCY-DIVISION MULTIPLEXING

Frequency-division multiplexing (FDM) is used to transmit more than one amplitude modulated (or frequency modulated) signal over a single channel. Note that FDM and TDM are dual modes of communication: TDM multiplexes and demultiplexes signals in the time domain using PAM and sampling at the receiver, whereas FDM does the same thing in the frequency domain with AM (or FM), bandpass filters, and demodulation.

An FDM system for DSB-AM/SC signals is shown in Figure 16.20.

The individual input signals are allocated distinct segments of the frequency band. To recover the individual channels in the demultiplexing process requires two steps (see Figure 16.21):

1. Bandpass filtering to extract the modulated signal of interest in the band

$$\left[\omega_{ci}-\omega_M,\omega_{ci}+\omega_M\right]$$

2. Synchronous or asynchronous demodulation to recover the original signal

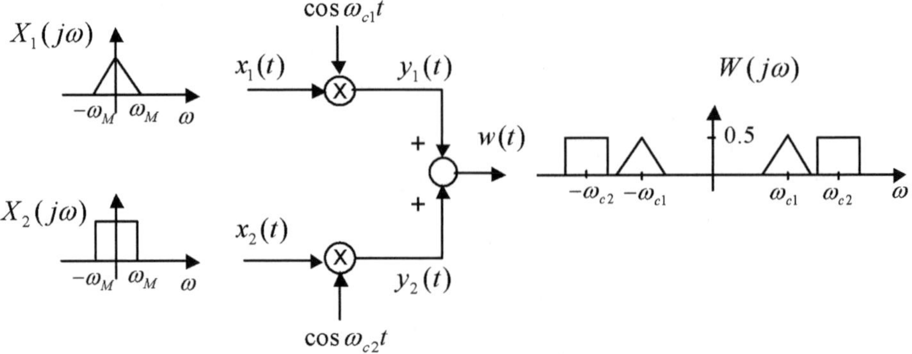

FIGURE 16.20 Frequency-division multiplexing of two signals.

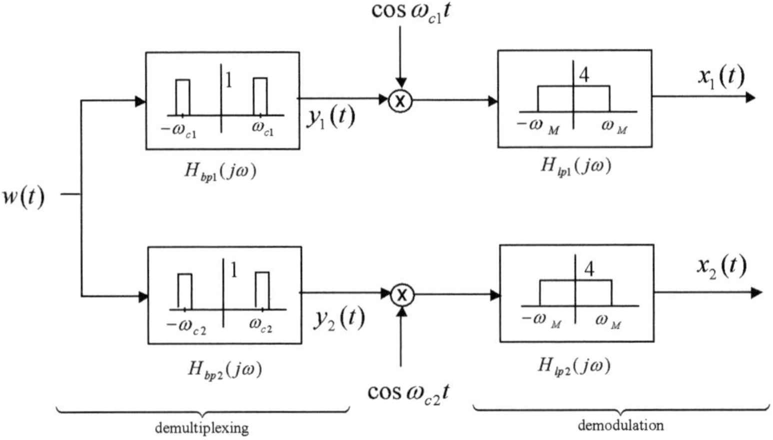

FIGURE 16.21 Demultiplexing and demodulation of an FDM signal.

In a simple AM radio receiver such as the one in Figure 16.22, there is only one bandpass filter at a fixed intermediate frequency ω_{IF}. Two copies of the spectrum of the received FDM signal $w(t)$ are shifted to $\omega_{ci} + \omega_{IF}$ and to $-\omega_{ci} - \omega_{IF}$ so that the spectrum of the desired radio station is aligned with the bandpass filter. This process is called the *superheterodyne receiver*. It avoids the use of a complex, expensive tunable bandpass filter. An envelope detector (or a synchronous demodulator) does the rest.

Note that the envelope detector also does not have to be tunable. Rather, it is designed to be optimal for the intermediate frequency. Also note that in practice there would normally be a coarse tunable filter applied on $w(t)$ before the superheterodyning operation to remove the possibility of spectral overlaps.

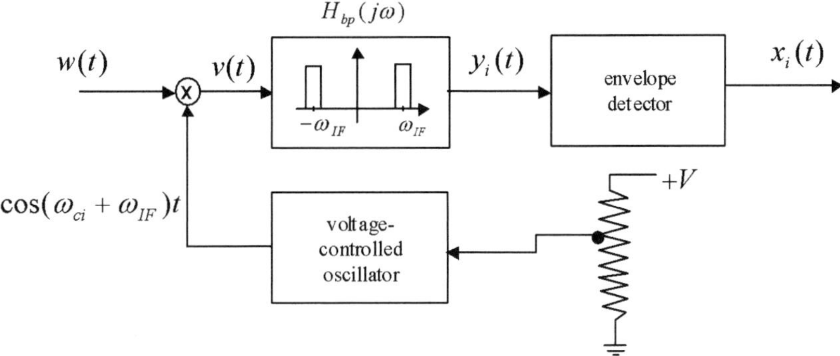

FIGURE 16.22 Superheterodyne AM receiver.

For the above example with two signals (radio stations) and the tuner set to receive station 1, the spectra would be as shown in Figure 16.23.

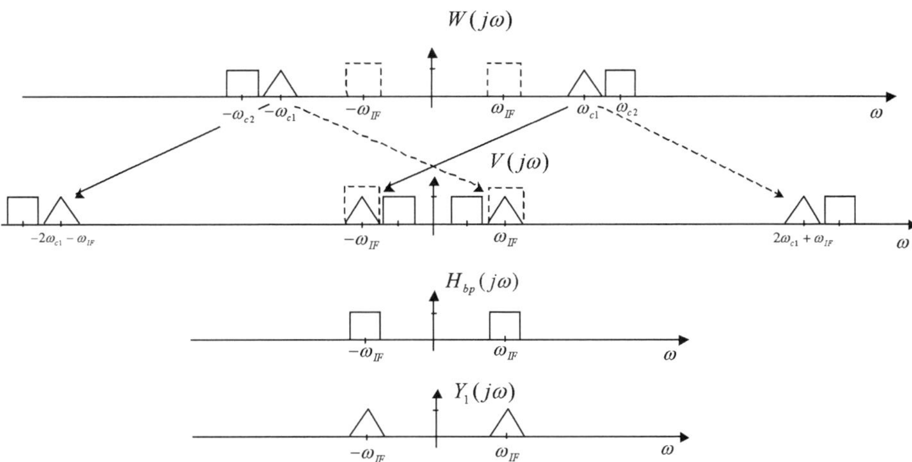

FIGURE 16.23 Tuning the superheterodyne AM receiver to receive signal 1.

ANGLE MODULATION

Instead of modulating the amplitude of the carrier, it is often preferable to modulate its frequency or phase. This section is a brief overview of *angle modulation,* encompassing these two techniques. Define the *instantaneous frequency* $\omega_i(t)$ as the derivative of the angle of the carrier $c(t) = \cos(\phi(t))$.

$$\omega_i(t) := \frac{d}{dt}\phi(t) \tag{16.43}$$

The integral form is

$$\phi(t) = \int_{-\infty}^{t} \omega_i(\tau)d\tau. \tag{16.44}$$

In amplitude modulation, we have $\phi(t) = \omega_c t$ and $\omega_i(t) = \omega_c$. Note that angle modulation is difficult to analyze in the frequency domain, so this is outside of the scope of this book.

Frequency Modulation

In frequency modulation, the instantaneous modulation frequency is set to

$$\omega_i(t) = \omega_c + k_f x(t), \tag{16.45}$$

so that

$$\phi(t) = \omega_c t + k_f \int_{-\infty}^{t} x(\tau)d\tau, \tag{16.46}$$

and the frequency modulated signal is given by

$$y(t) = A\cos\left(\omega_c t + k_f \int_{-\infty}^{t} x(\tau)d\tau\right). \tag{16.47}$$

Note that its amplitude is constant.

Phase Modulation

In phase modulation, the angle is set to

$$\phi(t) = \omega_c t + k_f x(\tau), \tag{16.48}$$

and the phase modulated signal is given by

$$y(t) = A\cos\left(\omega_c t + k_f x(t)\right). \tag{16.49}$$

Demodulation of FM Signals: The Discriminator and the Phase-Lock Loop

Demodulation of angle-modulated signals can be carried out using a *discriminator*, which is composed of a differentiator followed by an envelope detector, as shown in Figure 16.24.

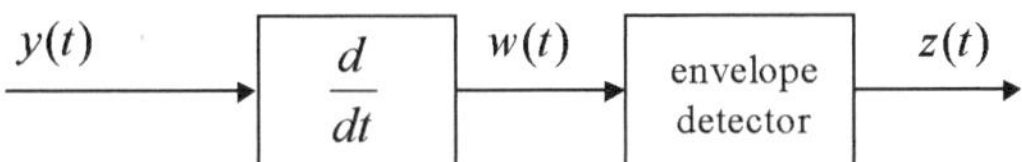

FIGURE 16.24 Discriminator for demodulation of FM signals.

At the output of the differentiator, signal $w(t) = -A[\omega_c + k_f x(t)]\sin\left(\omega_c t + k_f \int_{-\infty}^{t} x(\tau)d\tau\right)$ is essentially an AM signal because the frequency of the FM "sine" wave (acting as a carrier) is much higher than the bandwidth of the modulating signal. Therefore, an envelope detector will generate $z(t) \cong A[\omega_c + k_f x(t)]$, a scaled version of the modulating signal.

Demodulation of angle-modulated signals can also be carried out more efficiently using a system called a *phase-lock loop* (PLL). This is a feedback control system that tracks the frequency of the modulated signal by reducing the phase error between the modulated signal and a sinusoid generated by a local oscillator. A block diagram of a typical phase-lock loop is shown in Figure 16.25.

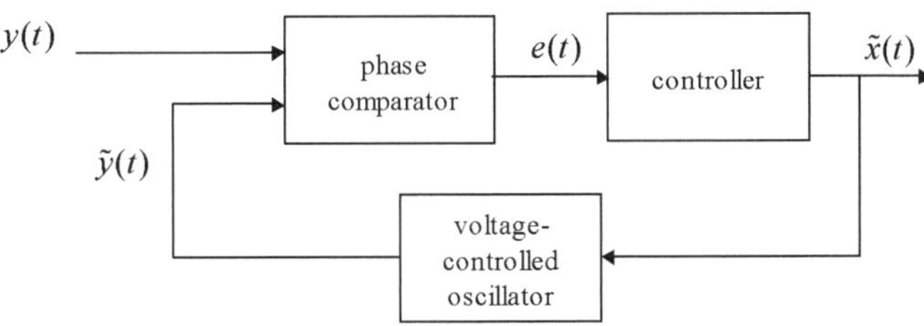

FIGURE 16.25 Phase-lock loop.

The voltage controlled oscillator (VCO) outputs a sine wave $\tilde{y}(t)$ with a frequency proportional to its input voltage. If this frequency is below the frequency of the FM signal, the phase difference between $y(t)$ and $\tilde{y}(t)$ will increase linearly, causing the output of the controller to increase the VCO frequency until it "locks" on the FM signal's frequency.

Let us analyze a basic implementation of the phase-lock loop. An important assumption is that the frequencies, and furthermore the angles, of the modulated signal and the sinusoid at the output of the VCO are very close. The phase comparator can be implemented by multiplying the signals $y(t)$ and $\tilde{y}(t)$.

$$\begin{aligned} y(t)\tilde{y}(t) &= A\cos\left(\omega_c t + k_f \int_{-\infty}^{t} x(\tau)d\tau\right)\sin\left(\omega_c t + \theta(t)\right) \\ &= \frac{A}{2}\sin\left(\theta(t) - k_f \int_{-\infty}^{t} x(\tau)d\tau\right) + \frac{A}{2}\sin\left(2\omega_c t + \theta(t) + k_f \int_{-\infty}^{t} x(\tau)d\tau\right) \end{aligned} \quad (16.50)$$

To first order, the first term is proportional to the phase difference. The second term is at twice the carrier frequency and can easily be removed by a lowpass filter (with a gain of –1 to get negative feedback.) The resulting phase error signal is then:

$$\begin{aligned} e(t) &= -\frac{A}{2}\sin\left(\theta(t) - k_f \int_{-\infty}^{t} x(\tau)d\tau\right) \\ &\cong \frac{A}{2}\left(k_f \int_{-\infty}^{t} x(\tau)d\tau - \theta(t)\right) \quad \text{(to first order).} \end{aligned} \quad (16.51)$$

A block diagram of the phase comparator is shown in Figure 16.26.

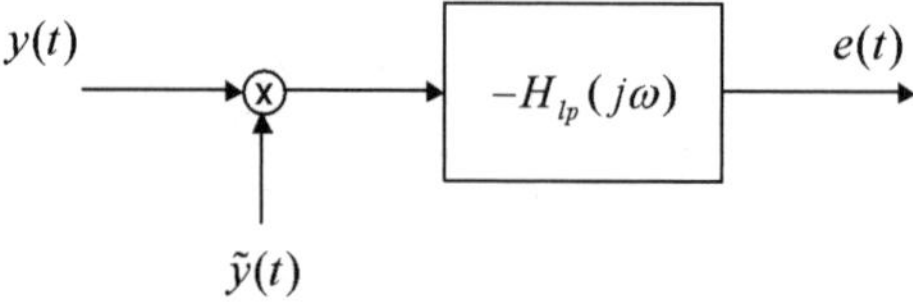

FIGURE 16.26 Phase comparator.

The PLL is in *phase lock* when the error is equal to zero, that is, when $\theta(t) = r(t) := k_f \int_{-\infty}^{t} x(\tau)d\tau$. In this case, the instantaneous frequency of the output of the VCO $\tilde{y}(t)$ is given by

$$\omega_{VCO} := \frac{d}{dt}\left[\omega_c t + \theta(t)\right] = \omega_c + k_f x(t). \quad (16.52)$$

Generally, a VCO produces an instantaneous frequency that is proportional to its input voltage, which we denoted as $\tilde{x}(t)$. Here, we assume that for a zero input voltage, the VCO oscillates at frequency ω_c.

$$\omega_{VCO} = \omega_c + \frac{d\theta(t)}{dt} = \omega_c + k_{VCO}\tilde{x}(t) \tag{16.53}$$

Therefore, the phase of the VCO is the integral of its input voltage:

$$\theta(t) = k_{VCO}\int_{-\infty}^{t} \tilde{x}(\tau)d\tau. \tag{16.54}$$

The PLL can now be analyzed as a linear time-invariant (LTI) feedback control system with the block diagram in Figure 16.27, where the controller block is an LTI controller with transfer function $K(s)$, and its output $\tilde{x}(t)$ is the signal that should be proportional to the message signal $x(t)$.

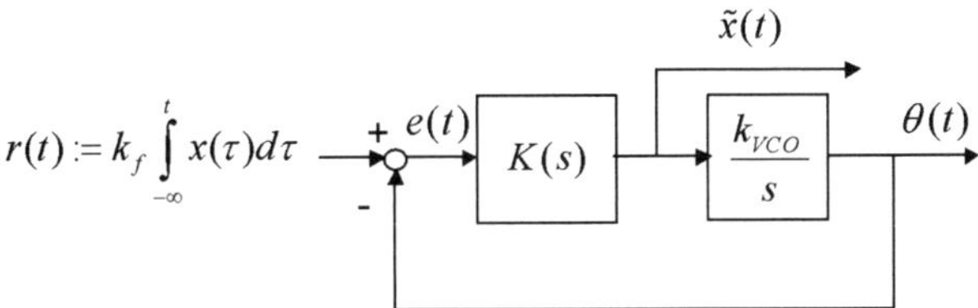

FIGURE 16.27 LTI feedback control model of PLL.

Recall from Chapter 11 that the closed-loop transmission of this feedback tracking system can be computed as follows:

$$T(s) := \frac{\hat{\theta}(s)}{\hat{r}(s)} = \frac{K(s)\frac{k_{VCO}}{s}}{1 + K(s)\frac{k_{VCO}}{s}}. \tag{16.55}$$

Assuming that $K(s) = k$ is a pure gain controller, we obtain what is called a PLL of order 1, whose transmission is

$$T(s) = \frac{kk_{VCO}}{s + kk_{VCO}} = \frac{1}{\frac{1}{kk_{VCO}}s + 1}. \tag{16.56}$$

The DC gain of this closed-loop transfer function is 1, which represents near-perfect tracking of the phase of the FM signal when it changes slowly. The magnitude of the Bode plot of $T(s)$ stays close to 1 (0 dB) up until the break frequency $\omega_0 = kk_{VCO}$. This frequency must be made higher than the bandwidth of the reference signal, which is essentially the bandwidth of the message signal (modulo the $1/j\omega$ effect of integration), by selecting the controller gain k appropriately. Also recall that the linear approximation of the sine function of the phase error holds for small angles only. This is another important consideration to keep in mind in the design of $K(s)$, as the PLL could "unlock" if the error becomes too large.

Finally, the message-bearing signal of interest in the PLL is the output of the controller, which is given by

$$\hat{\tilde{x}}(s) = \frac{k}{1 + k\frac{k_{VCO}}{s}} = \frac{ks}{s + kk_{VCO}}\hat{r}(s) = \frac{1}{k_{VCO}}\frac{s}{\frac{1}{kk_{VCO}}s + 1}\hat{r}(s). \tag{16.57}$$

Thus, signal $\tilde{x}(t)$ is a filtered version of $\frac{d}{dt}r(t) = \frac{k_f}{k_{VCO}}x(t)$, where the derivative comes from the numerator s, but the effect of the first-order lowpass filter $\frac{1}{\frac{1}{kk_{VCO}}s+1}$ can be neglected if the controller gain k is chosen high enough, which pushes the cutoff frequency outside of the bandwidth of the message signal. Therefore, with a large controller gain, the first-order PLL effectively demodulates the FM signal by giving the voltage signal:

$$\tilde{x}(t) \cong \frac{k_f}{k_{VCO}}x(t). \tag{16.58}$$

SUMMARY

This chapter was a brief introduction to the theory of communication systems.

- Amplitude modulation of a message signal is obtained by multiplying the signal with a sinusoidal carrier. This shifts the spectrum of the message and recenters it around the carrier frequency. The AM signal can be demodulated by a synchronous demodulator whose frequency must be made equal to the carrier frequency, or by a simpler asynchronous demodulator essentially consisting of an envelope detector.

- Many AM signals can be transmitted over the same channel using frequency division multiplexing.
- We discussed pulse-train modulation and pulse-amplitude modulation for transmitting sampled signals. Time-division multiplexing can be used to transmit many PAM signals at the same time, but intersymbol interference can become a problem if the pulses are not sufficiently bandlimited.
- Angle modulation was discussed with an emphasis on frequency modulation. The basic discriminator and phase-lock loop were analyzed as two possible demodulators of FM signals.

TO PROBE FURTHER

For a more complete introduction to communication systems, see Roden, 1995 and Haykin, 2000.

EXERCISES

Exercises with Solutions

Exercise 16.1

Consider the DSB-AM/WC signal:

$$y(t) = [1 + 0.2x(t)]\cos(2\pi 10^5 t),$$

where the periodic modulating signal is $x(t) = \left|\sin(1000\pi t)\right|$.

(a) Sketch the modulating signal $x(t)$ and the spectrum of the modulated signal $Y(j\omega)$.

Answer:
The modulating signal $x(t)$ sketched in Figure 16.28 is a full-wave rectified sine wave.

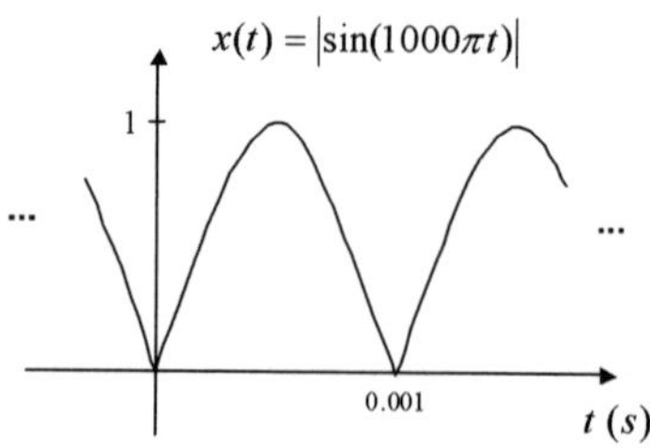

FIGURE 16.28 Modulating signal of Exercise 16.1.

Let $T_1 = 0.001$ be the fundamental period of the signal $x(t)$, let $\omega_1 = 2\pi/T_1$ be its fundamental frequency, and $\omega_0 = 1000\pi = 0.5\omega_1$ be the fundamental frequency of $\sin(1000\pi t)$. The spectrum of the modulated signal is obtained by first computing the Fourier series coefficients of the message signal:

$$
\begin{aligned}
a_k &= \frac{1}{T_1}\int_0^{T_1} v(t)e^{-jk\omega_1 t}\,dt \\
&= \frac{1}{T_1}\int_0^{T_1} \sin(\omega_0 t)e^{-jk\omega_1 t}\,dt \\
&= \frac{1}{2jT_1}\int_0^{T_1} \left(e^{j\omega_0 t} - e^{-j\omega_0 t}\right)e^{-jk\omega_1 t}\,dt \\
&= \frac{1}{2jT_1}\int_0^{\frac{\pi}{\omega_0}} \left(e^{j\omega_0(1-2k)t} - e^{-j\omega_0(1+2k)t}\right)dt \\
&= \frac{\omega_0}{2\pi j}\left[\frac{-2}{j\omega_0(1-2k)} - \frac{2}{j\omega_0(1+2k)}\right] \\
&= \frac{2}{\pi(1-4k^2)}.
\end{aligned}
$$

Thus, the spectrum $X(j\omega)$ is given by

$$
\begin{aligned}
X(j\omega) &= 2\pi\sum_{k=-\infty}^{+\infty} a_k\delta(\omega - k\omega_1) \\
&= \sum_{k=-\infty}^{+\infty} \frac{4}{(1-4k^2)}\delta(\omega - k2000\pi)
\end{aligned}
$$

and the spectrum of the modulated signal is found to be

$$Y(j\omega)=\sum_{k=-\infty}^{+\infty}\frac{2}{(1-4k^2)}\delta(\omega-200000\pi-k2000\pi)+\sum_{k=-\infty}^{+\infty}\frac{2}{(1-4k^2)}\delta(\omega+200000\pi-k2000\pi)$$

This spectrum is sketched in Figure 16.29.

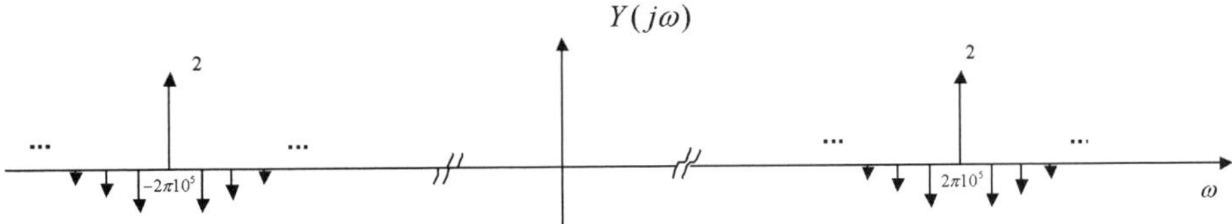

FIGURE 16.29 Spectrum of modulated signal of Exercise 16.1.

(b) Design an envelope detector to demodulate the AM signal. That is, draw a circuit diagram of the envelope detector and compute the values of the circuit components. Justify all of your approximations and assumptions. Provide rough sketches of the carrier signal, the modulated signal, and the signal at the output of the detector. What is the modulation index m of the AM signal?

Answer:
An envelope detector can be implemented with the simple *RC* circuit with a diode shown in Figure 16.30.

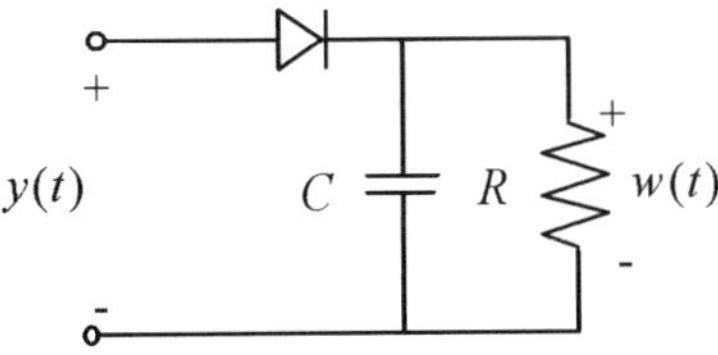

FIGURE 16.30 Envelope detector in Exercise 16.1.

The output voltage of the detector, when it goes from one peak at voltage v_1 to the next when it intersects the modulated carrier at voltage v_2 after approximately one period $T = 10\ \mu$s of the carrier, is given by $v_2 \cong v_1 e^{-T/RC}$. Since the time constant $\tau = RC$ of the detector should be large with respect to $T = 10\ \mu$s, we can use a first-order approximation of the exponential such that $v_2 \cong v_1(1 - T/RC)$. This is a line of negative slope $-\frac{v_1}{RC}$ between the initial voltage v_1 and the final voltage v_2 so that

$$\frac{v_2 - v_1}{T} \cong -v_1/RC.$$

This slope must be "more negative" than the maximum negative slope of the envelope of v_1; thus we have to solve the following minimization problem:

$$\min_t \frac{d(0.2\sin(1000\pi t))}{dt} = -200\pi.$$

Taking the worst-case $v_1 = 1$, we must have

$$-\frac{1}{RC} < -200\pi$$

$$\Leftrightarrow$$

$$RC < \frac{1}{200\pi} = 0.00159.$$

We could take $R = 1$ kΩ, $C = 1\ \mu$F to get $RC = 0.001$s.

Let K be the maximum amplitude of $0.2x(t)$, that is, $|0.2x(t)| < 0.2 = K$, and let $A = 1$. The modulation index m is computed as $m = K/A = 0.2$.

Exercise 16.2

The system shown in Figure 16.31 demodulates the noisy modulated continuous-time signal $y_n(t) = y(t) + n(t)$ composed of the sum of

- Signal $y(t)$ which is a lower SSB-AM/SC of $x(t)$ (assume a magnitude of half that of $X(j\omega)$)
- A noise signal $n(t)$

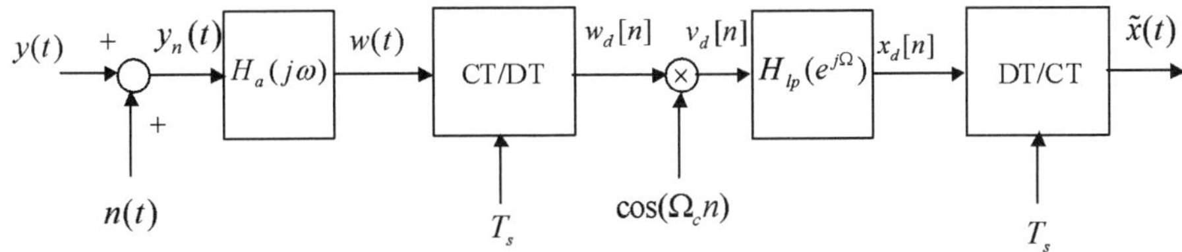

FIGURE 16.31 Discrete-time SSB-AM demodulator in Exercise 16.2.

The carrier signal is $\cos(\omega_c t)$, where $\omega_c = 100000\pi$ rad/s. The antialiasing filter $H_a(j\omega)$ is a perfect unity-gain lowpass filter with cutoff frequency ω_a.

The modulating signal $x(t)$ has a triangular spectrum $X(j\omega)$ as shown in Figure 16.32. The spectrum $N(j\omega)$ of the noise signal is also shown in Figure 16.32.

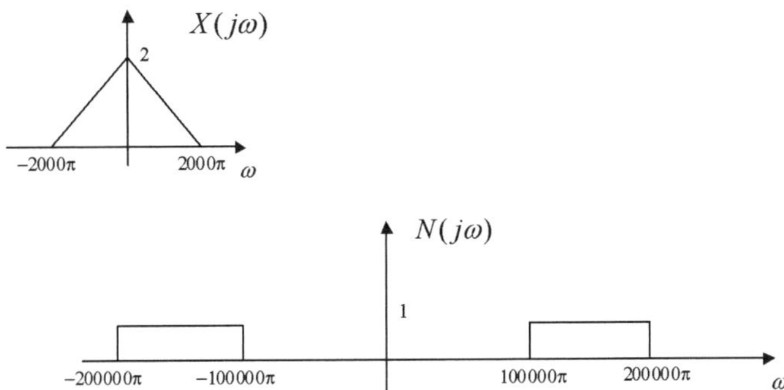

FIGURE 16.32 Fourier transforms of signal and noise in Exercise 16.2.

(a) Find the minimum antialiasing filter's cutoff frequency ω_a that will avoid any unrepairable distortion of the modulated signals due to the additive noise $n(t)$. Sketch the spectra $Y_n(j\omega)$ and $W(j\omega)$ of signals $y_n(t)$ and $w(t)$ for the frequency ω_a that you found. Indicate the important frequencies and magnitudes on your sketch.

Answer:

Minimum cutoff frequency of antialiasing filter: $\omega_a = 100{,}000\pi$ rad/s The spectra $Y_n(j\omega)$ and $W(j\omega)$ are sketched in Figure 16.33.

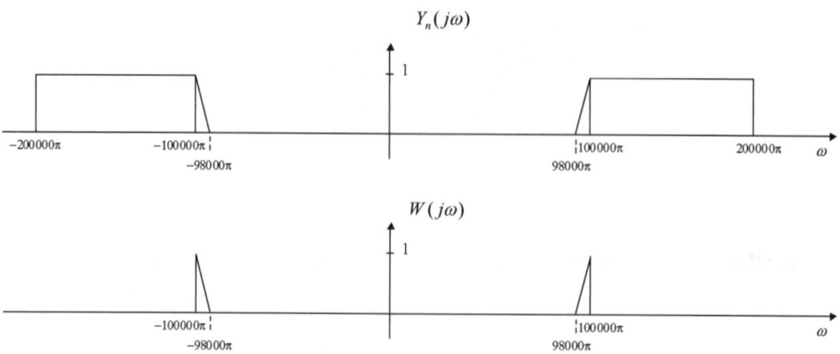

FIGURE 16.33 Fourier transforms of signal and noise in Exercise 16.2.

(b) Find the minimum sampling frequency $\omega_s = \frac{2\pi}{T_s}$ and its corresponding sampling period T_s that would allow perfect reconstruction of the modulated signal. Give the corresponding cutoff frequency Ω_1 of the perfect unity-gain lowpass filter and the demodulation frequency Ω_c. (What does the discrete-time synchronous demodulation amount to here?) Using these frequencies, sketch the spectra $W_d(e^{j\Omega}), V_d(e^{j\Omega}), X_d(e^{j\Omega})$.

Answer:

Sampling frequency: $\omega_s = 2\omega_a = 200000\pi$ rad/s, $T_s = \dfrac{2\pi}{\omega_s} = \dfrac{1}{100000} = 10^{-5}$ s

Demodulation frequency: $\Omega_c = \pi$. The synchronous demodulation amounts to multiplying the signal by $(-1)^n$.

Cutoff frequencies: $\Omega_1 = 2000\pi T_s = 0.02\pi$. The DTFTs $W_d(e^{j\Omega}), V_d(e^{j\Omega})$, $X_d(e^{j\Omega})$ are shown in Figure 16.34.

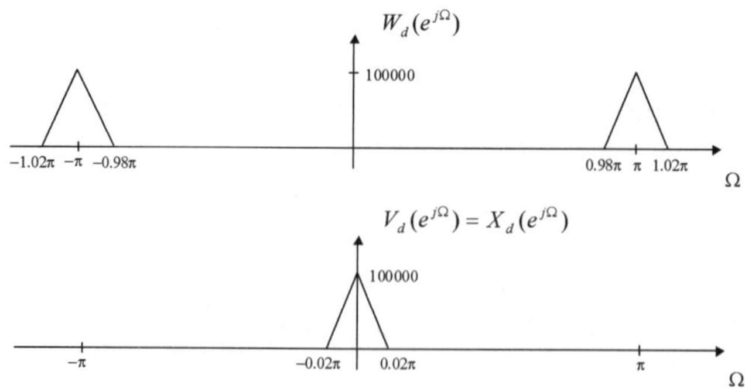

FIGURE 16.34 Fourier transforms of signal and noise in Exercise 16.2.

Exercise 16.3

You have to design an upper SSB amplitude modulator in discrete-time as an implementation of the continuous-time modulator shown in Figure 16.35.

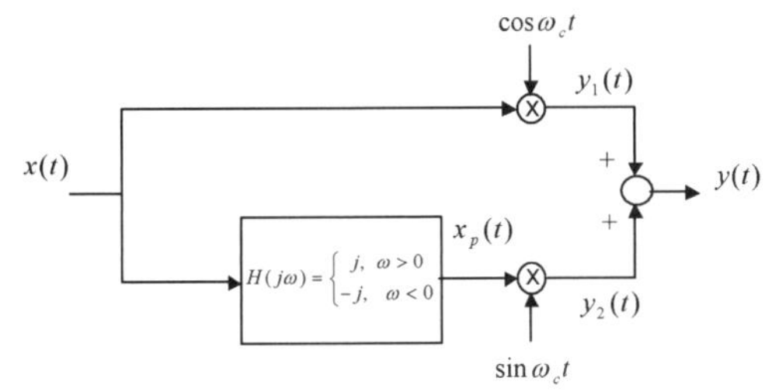

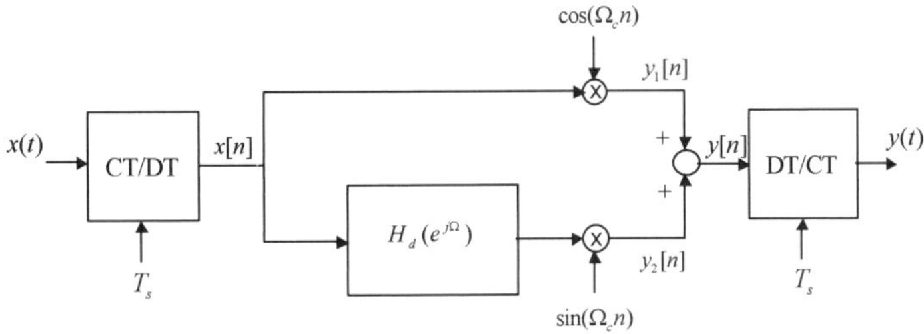

FIGURE 16.35 Continuous-time and discrete-time upper SSB-AM modulators of Exercise 16.3.

The modulating signal has the Fourier transform shown in Figure 16.36, and the carrier frequency is $\omega_c = 2{,}000{,}000\pi$ rad/s (1 MHz).

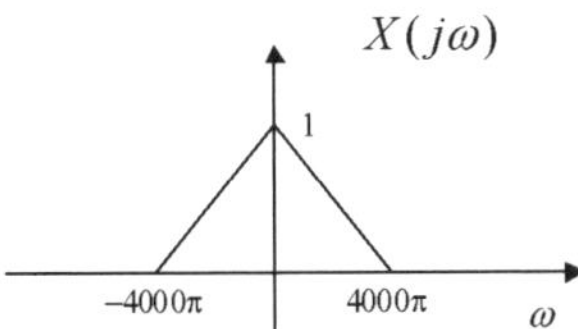

FIGURE 16.36 Spectrum of the message signal in Exercise 16.3.

Design the modulation system (with ideal components) for the slowest possible sampling rate. Find an expression for the ideal discrete-time phase shift filter $H_d(e^{j\Omega})$ and compute its impulse response $h_d[n]$. Explain how you could implement an approximation to this ideal filter and describe modifications to the overall system so that it would work in practice.

Answer:
First, the ideal phase-shift filter should have the following frequency response:

$$H_d(e^{j\Omega}) = \begin{cases} j, & 0 < \Omega < \pi \\ -j, & -\pi < \Omega < 0 \end{cases}.$$

The inverse Fourier transform yields

$$h_d[n] = \frac{1}{2\pi} \int_{-\pi}^{\pi} H_d(e^{j\Omega}) e^{j\Omega n} d\Omega = \frac{1}{\pi n}[1 - (-1)^n].$$

To compute the slowest sampling frequency, we start from the desired upper SSB-AM signal at the output, whose bandwidth is $\omega_M = 2{,}004{,}000\pi$, which should correspond to the highest discrete-time frequency $\Omega = \pi$. Thus, we can compute the sampling period from the relationship $\frac{\Omega}{T} = \omega \Rightarrow \frac{\pi}{\omega_M} = T$, which yields $T = 4.99 \times 10^{-7} s$.

This system could be implemented in practice using an FIR approximation to the ideal phase-shift filter. Starting from $h_d[n]$, a windowed impulse response of length $M + 1$ time-delayed by $M/2$ to make it causal would work. However, the resulting delay of $M/2$ samples introduced in the lower path of the modulator should be balanced out by the introduction of an equivalent delay block $z^{-M/2}$ in the upper path.

Exercises

Exercise 16.4

The superheterodyne receiver in Figure 16.22 consists of taking the product of the AM radio signal with a carrier whose frequency is tuned by a variable-frequency oscillator. Then, the resulting signal is filtered by a fixed bandpass filter centered at the intermediate frequency (IF) ω_{IF}. The goal is to have a fixed high-quality filter, which is cheaper than a high-quality tunable filter. The output of the IF bandpass filter is then demodulated with an oscillator at constant frequency to tune in to your favorite radio station. Suppose that the input signal is an AM wave of bandwidth 10 kHz and carrier frequency ω_c that may lie anywhere in the range 0.535 MHz to 1.605 MHz (typical of AM radio broadcasting). Find the range of tuning that must be provided in the local oscillator ω_{VCO} in order to achieve this requirement.

Exercise 16.5

In the operation of the superheterodyne receiver in Figure 16.22, it should be clear from Figure 16.23 that even though the receiver is tuned in to station 1, the "ghost" spectrum of a radio station at a carrier frequency higher than ω_{c1} could appear in the passband of the IF bandpass filter if an additional filter is not implemented. Determine that ghost carrier frequency.

Answer:

Exercise 16.6

Design an envelope detector to demodulate the AM signal

$$y(t) = [1 + 0.4x(t)]\cos(2\pi 10^3 t),$$

where $x(t)$ is the periodic modulating signal shown in Figure 16.37. That is, draw a circuit diagram of the envelope detector and compute the values of the circuit components. Justify all of your approximations and assumptions. Provide rough sketches of the carrier signal, the modulated signal, and the signal at the output of the detector. What is the modulation index m of the AM signal?

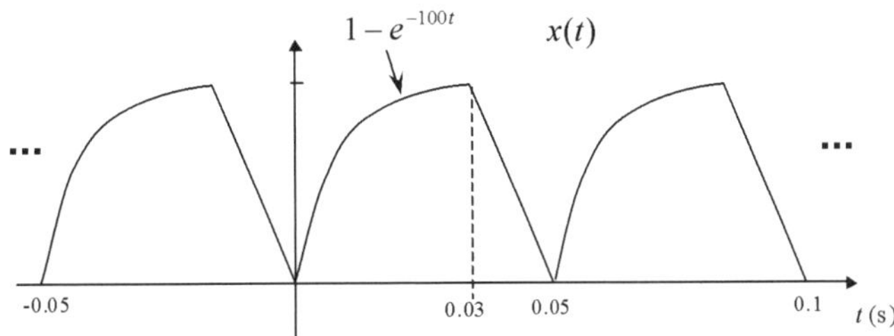

FIGURE 16.37 Modulating signal in Exercise 16.6.

Exercise 16.7

The sampled-data system shown in Figure 16.38 provides amplitude modulation of the continuous-time signal $x(t)$. The impulse train signal is $p[n] = \sum_{k=-\infty}^{+\infty} \delta[n-kN]$.

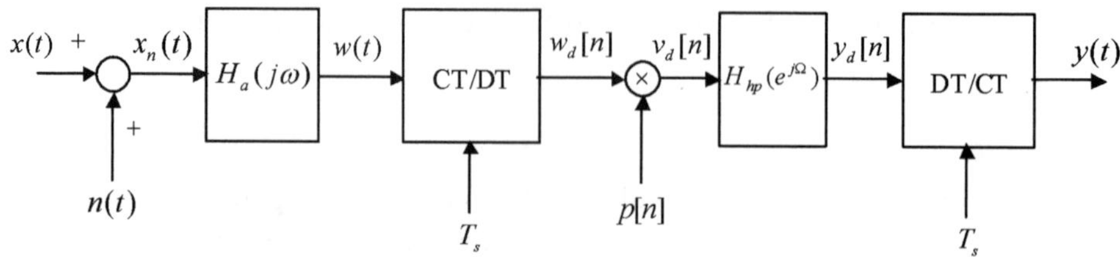

FIGURE 16.38 Modulation system in Exercise 16.7.

The antialiasing filter $H_a(j\omega)$ is an ideal unity-gain lowpass filter with cutoff frequency ω_a, and the perfect discrete-time highpass filter $H_{hp}(e^{j\Omega})$ has gain N (which is also the period of $p[n]$) and cutoff frequency $\Omega_1 = 0.6\pi$.

The modulating (or message) signal $x(t)$ has spectrum $X(j\omega)$ as shown in Figure 16.39. The spectrum of the noise signal $N(j\omega)$ is also shown in the figure.

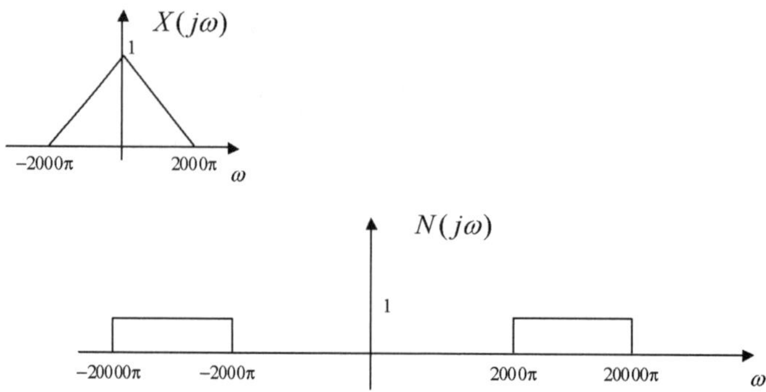

FIGURE 16.39 Fourier transforms of signal and noise in Exercise 16.5.

(a) Find the minimum antialiasing filter's cutoff frequency ω_a that will avoid any unrepairable distortion of the signal $x(t)$ due to the additive noise $n(t)$. Sketch the spectra $X_n(j\omega)$ and $W(j\omega)$ of signals $x_n(t)$ and $w(t)$ for the frequency ω_a that you found. Indicate the important frequencies and magnitudes on your sketches.

(b) Find the minimum sampling frequency $\omega_s = \dfrac{2\pi}{T_s}$ and its corresponding sampling period T_s that would allow amplitude modulation of the signal $x(t)$ at a carrier frequency of $\omega_c = 8000\pi$ rad/s. Find the corresponding discrete-time sampling period N of $p[n]$ for the system to work. Using these frequencies, sketch the spectra $W_d(e^{j\Omega})$, $V_d(e^{j\Omega})$, $Y_d(e^{j\Omega})$ and $Y(j\omega)$.

Answer:

Exercise 16.8

The system shown in Figure 16.40 is a lower single-sideband, suppressed-carrier AM modulator implemented in discrete time. The message signal $x(t)$ is corrupted by an additive noise $n(t)$: $x_n(t) = x(t) + n(t)$ before sampling. We want the modulator to operate at a carrier frequency $\omega_c = 2\pi \times 10^6$ rad/s (1 MHz).

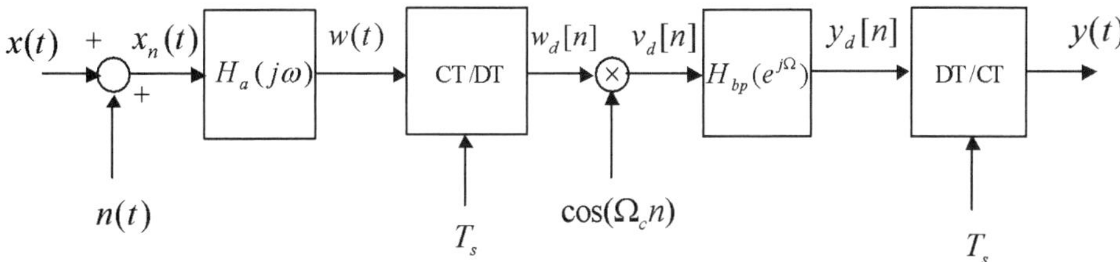

FIGURE 16.40 Discrete-time SSB modulator of Exercise 16.8.

The antialiasing filter $H_a(j\omega)$ is a perfect unity-gain lowpass filter with cutoff frequency ω_a. The antialiased signal $w(t)$ is first converted to a discrete-time signal $w_d[n]$ via the CT/DT operator. Signal $w_d[n]$ is modulated with frequency Ω_c and bandpass filtered by $H_{bp}(e^{j\Omega})$ to create the lower sidebands. Finally, the DT/CT operator produces the continuous-time lower SSB/SC AM signal $y(t)$.

The Fourier transforms of the modulating signal $x(t)$ and the noise $X(j\omega)$ and $N(j\omega)$ are shown in Figure 16.41.

(a) The antialiasing filter's cutoff frequency is given as $\omega_a = 3000\pi$. Sketch the spectra $X_n(j\omega)$ and $W(j\omega)$ of signals $x_n(t)$ and $w(t)$. Indicate the important frequencies and magnitudes on your sketch.

(b) Find the minimum sampling frequency ω_s and corresponding sampling period T_s that will produce the required modulated signal. Find the discrete-time modulation frequency Ω_c that will result in a continuous-time carrier frequency $\omega_c = 2\pi \times 10^6$ rad/s. Give the cutoff frequencies $\Omega_1 < \Omega_2$ of the bandpass filter to obtain a lower SSB-AM/SC signal. Using these frequencies, sketch the spectra $W_d(e^{j\Omega})$, $V_d(e^{j\Omega})$, $Y_d(e^{j\Omega})$ and $Y(j\omega)$.

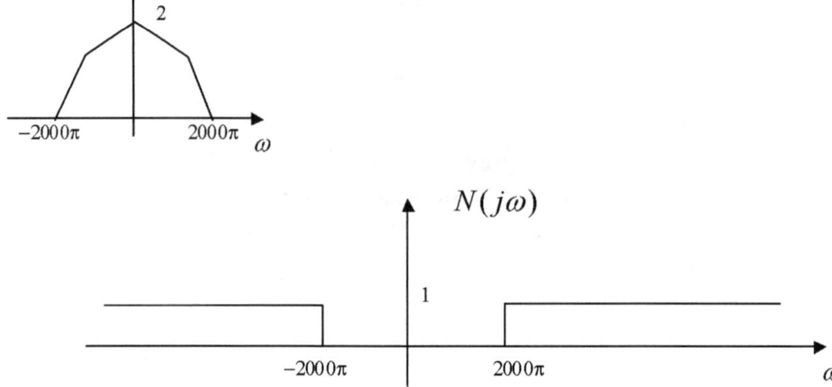

FIGURE 16.41 Fourier transforms of signal and noise in Exercise 16.8.

Exercise 16.9

A DSB/SC AM signal $y(t)$ is generated with a carrier signal $c_{transm}(t) = \cos(\omega_c t)$. Suppose that the oscillator of the synchronous AM demodulator at the receiver in Figure 16.42 is slightly off:

$$c_{rec}(t) = \cos((\omega_c + \Delta)t).$$

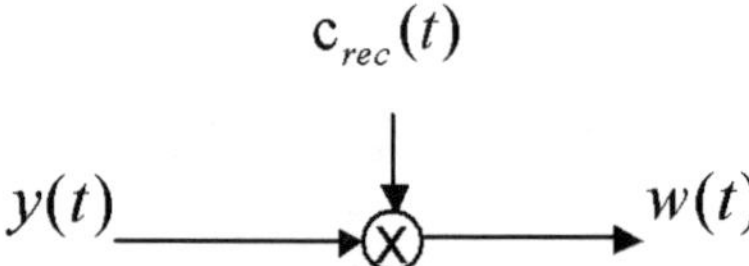

FIGURE 16.42 Synchronous demodulator at the receiver in Exercise 16.9.

(a) Denoting the modulating signal as $x(t)$, write the expression for $w(t)$, and for $z(t)$ after perfect unity-magnitude lowpass filtering with cutoff at ω_c.

(b) Let $\omega_c = 2\pi 10^6$, $\Delta = 2\pi 10^3$ rad/s. Plot $z(t)$ for the modulating signal $x(t) = \sin(20000\pi t)$.

Answer:

17 System Discretization and Discrete-Time LTI State-Space Models

In This Chapter

((Lecture 68: State Models of LTI Difference Systems))

In this last chapter, causal discrete-time state-space models of linear time-invariant (LTI) systems are introduced mainly as a means of providing methods to discretize continuous-time LTI systems. The topic of system discretization is an important one for at least two reasons. First, engineers often need to simulate the behavior of continuous-time systems, and analytical solutions can be very difficult to obtain for systems of order three or more. Second, many filter design and controller design techniques have been developed in continuous time. Discretizing the resulting system often yields a sampled-data implementation that performs just as well as the intended continuous-time design.

Of course, discrete-time LTI (DLTI) state-space models are of interest in their own right, particularly in advanced multivariable discrete-time filter design and controller design techniques, which are beyond the scope of this textbook. An important word on notation before we move on: for discrete-time state-space systems, the *input signal* is conventionally written as $u[n]$ (not to be confused with the unit step) instead of $x[n]$, as the latter is used for the vector of state variables. Hence, in this chapter we will use $q[n]$ to denote the unit step signal.

CONTROLLABLE CANONICAL FORM

In general, an Nth-order linear constant-coefficient causal difference equation with $M \leq N$ has the form

$$\sum^{N} a_k y[n-k] = \sum^{M} b_k x[n-k], \tag{17.1}$$

which can be expanded into

$$a_0 y[n] + a_1 y[n-1] + \cdots + a_N y[n-N] = b_0 x[n] + b_1 x[n-1] + \cdots + b_M x[n-M]. \tag{17.2}$$

Just like the continuous-time case, we can derive a state-space model for this system by first finding its *controllable canonical form* (direct form) realization. We take the intermediate variable $w[n]$ and its successive $N-1$ delayed versions as state variables. Let $a_0 = 1$ without loss of generality. Taking the z-transform on both sides of the difference Equation 17.1, we obtain the transfer function (with region of convergence [ROC] the exterior of a disk of radius equal to the magnitude of the outermost pole):

$$\begin{aligned} H(z) = \frac{Y(z)}{U(z)} &= \frac{\sum_{k=0}^{M} b_k z^{-k}}{\sum_{k=0}^{N} a_k z^{-k}} \\ &= \frac{b_0 + b_1 z^{-1} \cdots + b_{M-1} z^{-M+1} + b_M z^{-M}}{1 + a_1 z^{-1} + \cdots + a_{N-1} z^{-N+1} + a_N z^{-N}}. \end{aligned} \tag{17.3}$$

A direct form can be obtained by considering the transfer function $H(z)$ as a cascade of two subsystems as shown in Figure 17.1.

The input-output system equation of the first subsystem is

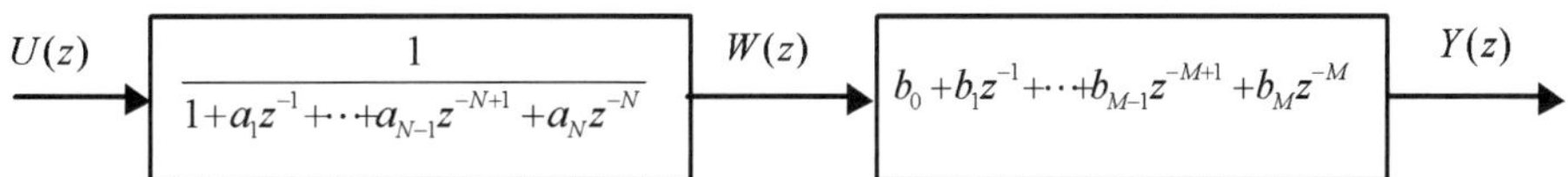

FIGURE 17.1 Discrete-time transfer function as cascade of two LTI systems.

$$W(z) = -a_1 z^{-1} W(z) - \cdots - a_{N-1} z^{-N+1} W(z) - a_N z^{-N} W(z) + U(z). \qquad (17.4)$$

For the second subsystem we have

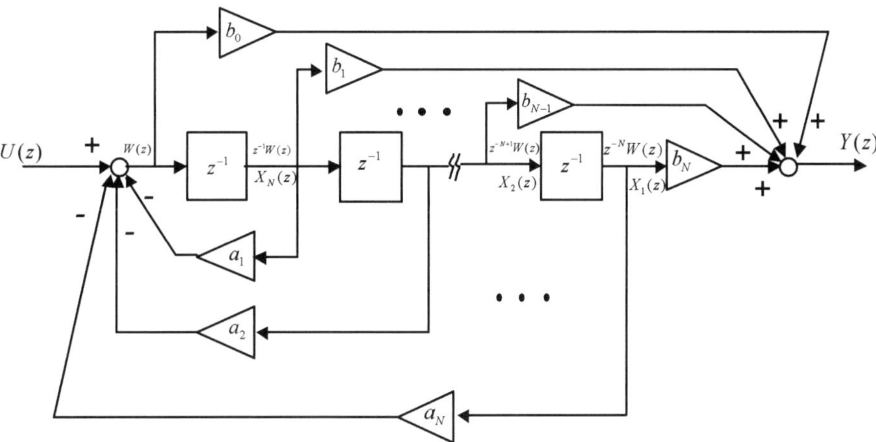

FIGURE 17.2 Direct form realization of a discrete-time transfer function.

$$Y(z) = b_0 W(z) + b_1 z^{-1} W(z) + \cdots + b_{M-1} z^{-M+1} W(z) + b_M z^{-M} W(z). \qquad (17.5)$$

The direct form realization is shown in Figure 17.2, where it is assumed that $M = N$ without loss of generality.

From this block diagram, define the state variables $\left\{x_i\right\}_{i=1}^{N}$ as follows.

$$
\begin{aligned}
&X_1(z) := z^{-N}W(z) && x_1[n+1] = x_2[n] \\
&X_2(z) := z^{-N+1}W(z) && x_2[n+1] = x_3[n] \\
&\vdots && \vdots \\
&X_{N-1}(z) := z^{-2}W(z) && x_{n-1}[n+1] = x_N[n] \\
&X_N(z) := z^{-1}W(z) && x_N[n+1] = -a_1x_N[n] - a_2x_{N-1}[n] - \cdots - a_Nx_1[n] + u[n]
\end{aligned}
\tag{17.6}
$$

The state equations on the right can be rewritten in vector form:

$$
\begin{bmatrix} x_1[n+1] \\ x_2[n+1] \\ \vdots \\ x_{N-1}[n+1] \\ x_N[n+1] \end{bmatrix} = \underbrace{\begin{bmatrix} 0 & 1 & \cdots & 0 & 0 \\ 0 & 0 & & 0 & 0 \\ \vdots & & \ddots & & \vdots \\ 0 & 0 & & 0 & 1 \\ -a_N & -a_{N-1} & \cdots & -a_2 & -a_1 \end{bmatrix}}_{A} \begin{bmatrix} x_1[n] \\ x_2[n] \\ \vdots \\ x_{N-1}[n] \\ x_N[n] \end{bmatrix} + \underbrace{\begin{bmatrix} 0 \\ 0 \\ \vdots \\ 0 \\ 1 \end{bmatrix}}_{B} u[n]. \tag{17.7}
$$

Let the *state vector* (or *state*) be defined as

$$
x[n] := \begin{bmatrix} x_1[n] \\ x_2[n] \\ \vdots \\ x_{N-1}[n] \\ x_N[n] \end{bmatrix}. \tag{17.8}
$$

Then the *state equation* (Equation 17.7) can be written as

$$
x[n+1] = Ax[n] + Bu[n] \tag{17.9}
$$

From the block diagram in Figure 17.2, the *output equation* relating the output $y[n]$ to the state vector can be written as follows.

$$
\begin{aligned}
y[n] &= \underbrace{\begin{bmatrix} b_N - a_Nb_0 & b_{N-1} - a_{N-1}b_0 & \cdots & b_1 - a_1b_0 \end{bmatrix}}_{C} x[n] + \underbrace{b_0}_{D} u[n] \\
&= Cx[n] + Du[n]
\end{aligned}
\tag{17.10}
$$

If $H(z)$ is strictly proper as a rational function of z, that is, the order of the numerator is less than the order of the denominator, then the output equation becomes

$$y[n] = Cx[n] \tag{17.11}$$

Note that the input has no direct path to the output in this case, as $D = b_0 = 0$.

OBSERVABLE CANONICAL FORM

We now derive an observable canonical state-space realization for the system of Equation 17.1. Assume without loss of generality that $M = N$. First, let us rewrite the transfer function $H(z)$ of Equation 17.3 for convenience:

$$H(z) = \frac{b_0 + b_1 z^{-1} \cdots + b_{N-1} z^{-N+1} + b_N z^{-N}}{1 + a_1 z^{-1} + \cdots + a_{N-1} z^{-N+1} + a_N z^{-N}}. \tag{17.12}$$

Then, the input-output relationship between $U(z)$ and $Y(z)$ can be written as

$$Y(z) = b_0 U(z) + (b_1 U(z) - a_1 Y(z))z^{-1} + (b_2 U(z) - a_2 Y(z))z^{-2} + \cdots + (b_N U(z) - a_N Y(z))z^{-N} \tag{17.13}$$

The block diagram of Figure 17.3 for the observable canonical form consists of a chain of N unit delays with a summing junction at the input of each.

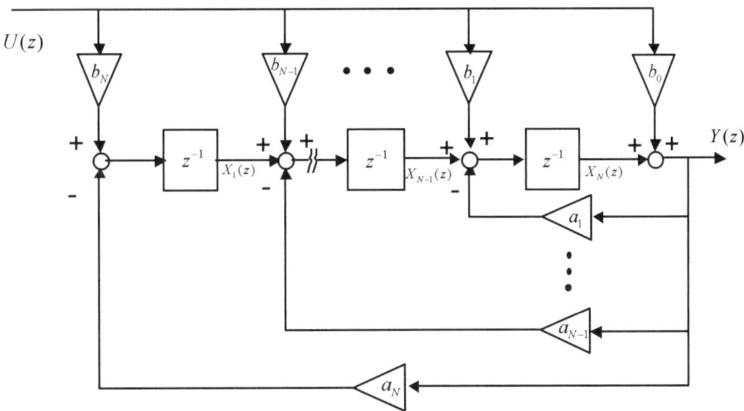

FIGURE 17.3 Observable canonical form realization of a discrete-time transfer function.

The state variables are defined as the outputs of the unit delays, which gives us:

$$\begin{aligned}
&zX_1(z)=-a_N X_N(z)+(b_N-a_N b_0)U(z) && x_1[n+1]=-a_N x_N[n]+(b_N-a_N b_0)u[n]\\
&zX_2(z)=X_1(z)-a_{N-1}X_N(z)+(b_{N-1}-a_{N-1}b_0)U(z) && x_2[n+1]=x_1[n]-a_{N-1}x_N[n]+(b_{N-1}-a_{N-1}b_0)u[n]\\
&zX_3(z)=X_2(z)-a_{N-2}X_N(z)+(b_{N-2}-a_{N-2}b_0)U(z) \;\Rightarrow && x_3[n+1]=x_2[n]-a_{N-2}x_N[n]+(b_{N-2}-a_{N-2}b_0)u[n].\\
&\vdots && \vdots\\
&zX_N(z)=X_{N-1}(z)-a_1 X_N(z)+(b_1-a_1 b_0)U(z) && x_N[n+1]=x_{N-1}[n]-a_1 x_N[n]+(b_1-a_1 b_0)u[n]
\end{aligned} \quad (17.14)$$

The state equations on the right can be rewritten in vector form:

$$\begin{bmatrix} x_1[n+1] \\ x_2[n+1] \\ \vdots \\ x_{N-1}[n+1] \\ x_N[n+1] \end{bmatrix} = \underbrace{\begin{bmatrix} 0 & 0 & \cdots & 0 & -a_N \\ 1 & 0 & & 0 & -a_{N-1} \\ \vdots & & \ddots & & \vdots \\ 0 & 0 & & 0 & -a_2 \\ 0 & 0 & \cdots & 1 & -a_1 \end{bmatrix}}_{A} \begin{bmatrix} x_1[n] \\ x_2[n] \\ \vdots \\ x_{N-1}[n] \\ x_N[n] \end{bmatrix} + \underbrace{\begin{bmatrix} b_N - a_N b_0 \\ b_{N-1} - a_{N-1} b_0 \\ \vdots \\ b_2 - a_2 b_0 \\ b_1 - a_1 b_0 \end{bmatrix}}_{B} u[n]. \quad (17.15)$$

Again this state equation can be written as in Equation 17.9. From the block diagram in Figure 17.3, the *output equation* relating the output $y[n]$ to the state vector can be written as follows.

$$\begin{aligned} y[n] &= \underbrace{\begin{bmatrix} 0 & 0 & \cdots & 0 & 1 \end{bmatrix}}_{C} x[n] + \underbrace{b_0}_{D} u[n] \\ &= Cx[n] + Du[n] \end{aligned} \quad (17.16)$$

((Lecture 69: Zero-State and Zero-Input Responses of Discrete-Time State Models))

ZERO-STATE AND ZERO-INPUT RESPONSES OF A DISCRETE-TIME STATE-SPACE SYSTEM

Recall that the response of a causal LTI difference system with nonzero initial conditions is composed of a zero-state response due to the input signal only and a zero-input response due to the initial conditions only. For a discrete-time state-space system, the initial conditions are captured in the *initial state* $x[0]$.

Zero-Input Response

The zero-input response of a state-space system is the response to a nonzero initial state only. Consider the following general state-space system:

$$\begin{aligned} x[n+1] &= Ax[n] + Bu[n], \\ y[n] &= Cx[n] + Du[n] \end{aligned} \tag{17.17}$$

where (the values, not the signals) $x[n] \in \mathbb{R}^N$, $y[n] \in \mathbb{R}$, $u[n] \in \mathbb{R}$ and $A \in \mathbb{R}^{N\times N}, B \in \mathbb{R}^{N\times 1}, C \in \mathbb{R}^{1\times N}, D \in \mathbb{R}$, with initial state $x[0] \neq 0$ and input $u[n] = 0$. Let the unit step signal be denoted as $q[n]$. A solution can be readily obtained recursively:

$$\begin{aligned} x[1] &= Ax[0] \\ y_{zi}[0] &= Cx[0] \\ x[2] &= A^2x[0] \\ y_{zi}[0] &= CAx[0] \\ x[3] &= A^3x[0] \\ y_{zi}[2] &= CA^2x[0] \\ &\vdots \\ x[n+1] &= A^{n+1}x[0] \\ y_{zi}[n] &= CA^n x[0]. \end{aligned} \tag{17.18}$$

Hence, the zero-input response is $y_{zi}[n] = CA^n x[0]q[n]$, and the corresponding state response is $x[n] = A^n x[0]q[n]$.

Zero-State Response

The zero-state response $y_{zs}[n]$ is the response of the system to the input only (zero initial conditions). A recursive solution yields

$$\begin{aligned}
x[0] &= 0 \\
y_{zs}[-1] &= 0 \\
x[1] &= Bu[0] \\
y_{zs}[0] &= Du[0] \\
x[2] &= ABu[0] + Bu[1] \\
y_{zs}[1] &= CBu[0] + Du[1] \\
x[3] &= A^2 Bu[0] + ABu[1] + Bu[2] \\
y_{zs}[2] &= CABu[0] + CBu[1] + Du[2] \\
&\vdots \\
x[n+1] &= A^n Bu[0] + A^{n-1} Bu[1] + \cdots + ABu[n-1] + Bu[n] \\
y_{zs}[n] &= CA^{n-1} Bu[0] + CA^{n-2} Bu[1] + \cdots + CBu[n-1] + Du[n].
\end{aligned} \tag{17.19}$$

These last two equations look like convolutions, and indeed they are. The impulse response of the state-space system of Equation 17.17 is obtained by setting $u[n] = \delta[n]$ with a zero initial state.

$$\begin{aligned}
x[n+1] &= Ax[n] + B\delta[n] \\
y[n] &= Cx[n] + D\delta[n]
\end{aligned} \tag{17.20}$$

The recursive solution for the impulse response yields

$$\begin{aligned}
x[1] &= B \\
h[0] &= D \\
x[2] &= AB \\
h[1] &= CB \\
x[3] &= A^2 B \\
h[2] &= CAB \\
&\vdots \\
x[n+1] &= A^n B \\
h[n] &= CA^{n-1} B.
\end{aligned} \tag{17.21}$$

Thus, the impulse response of the system is given by

$$h[n] = CA^{n-1}Bq[n-1] + D\delta[n]. \tag{17.22}$$

State-space systems are not different from other LTI systems, in that the zero-state response of an LTI state-space system is the convolution of the impulse response with the input. Assume that the input is zero at negative times, then

$$\begin{aligned} y_{zs}[n] &= h[n]*u[n] = CA^{n-1}Bq[n-1]*u[n] + D\delta[n]*u[n] \\ &= \sum_{k=-\infty}^{+\infty} CA^{k-1}Bq[k-1]u[n-k] + Du[n] \\ &= \sum_{k=1}^{n} CA^{k-1}Bu[n-k] + Du[n]. \end{aligned} \tag{17.23}$$

This last expression for the zero-state response is the same as the last equality in Equation 17.19. Finally, the overall response of a causal DLTI state-space system is the combination of the zero-state and the zero-input response:

$$\begin{aligned} y[n] &= y_{zi}[n] + y_{zs}[n] \\ &= CA^{n}x[0]q[n] + \left(\sum_{k=1}^{n} CA^{k-1}Bu[n-k] \right) q[n-1] + Du[n]. \end{aligned} \tag{17.24}$$

Z-TRANSFORM SOLUTION OF DISCRETE-TIME STATE-SPACE SYSTEMS

Consider the general LTI discrete-time state-space system:

$$\begin{aligned} x[n+1] &= Ax[n] + Bu[n] \\ y[n] &= Cx[n] + Du[n], \end{aligned} \tag{17.25}$$

where $x[n] \in \mathbb{R}^N$, $y[n] \in \mathbb{R}$, $u[n] \in \mathbb{R}$ and $A \in \mathbb{R}^{N\times N}$, $B \in \mathbb{R}^{N\times 1}$, $C \in \mathbb{R}^{1\times N}$, $D \in \mathbb{R}$, with initial state $x[0] = x_0$. Taking the unilateral *z*-transform on both sides of Equation 17.25, we obtain

$$\begin{aligned} z\mathcal{X}(z) - zx_0 &= A\mathcal{X}(z) + B\mathcal{U}(z) \\ \mathcal{Y}(z) &= C\mathcal{X}(z) + D\mathcal{U}(z). \end{aligned} \tag{17.26}$$

Solving for the z-transform of the state in Equation 17.26, we get

$$\mathcal{X}(z) = (zI_n - A)^{-1} B\mathcal{U}(z) + z(zI_n - A)^{-1} x_0, \tag{17.27}$$

and the z-transform of the output is

$$\mathcal{Y}(z) = \left[C(zI_n - A)^{-1} B + D \right] \mathcal{U}(z) + zC(zI_n - A)^{-1} x_0. \tag{17.28}$$

The first term on the right-hand side of Equation 17.28 is the z-transform of the zero-state response of the system to the input $u[n]$, whereas the second term is the z-transform of the zero-input response. Thus, the transfer function of the system is given by:

$$\mathcal{H}(z) = \frac{\mathcal{Y}(z)}{\mathcal{U}(z)} = C(zI_n - A)^{-1} B + D. \tag{17.29}$$

Note that we have not specified an ROC yet. First, we need a result relating the eigenvalues of matrix A to the poles of the transfer function.

Bounded-Input Bounded-Output Stability

Minimal state-space realizations are realizations for which all N eigenvalues of A appear as poles in the transfer function given by Equation 17.29 with their multiplicity. In other words, minimal state-space realizations are those realizations for which the order of the transfer function as obtained from Equation 17.29 is the same as the dimension N of the state.

Fact: For a minimal state-space realization (A, B, C, D) of a system with transfer function $H(z)$ the set of poles of $H(z)$ is equal to the set of eigenvalues of A.

Since we limit our analysis to minimal state-space realizations, this fact yields the following stability theorem for DLTI state-space systems.

Stability theorem: *The minimal causal DLTI state-space system* (A, B, C, D), *where* $A \in \mathbb{R}^{N\times N}, B \in \mathbb{R}^{N\times 1}, \ C \in \mathbb{R}^{1\times N}, D \in \mathbb{R}$ *is bounded-input, bounded-output (BIBO) stable if and only if all eigenvalues of A have a magnitude less than one.* Mathematically: (A, B, C, D) *is BIBO stable if and only if* $|\lambda_i(A)| < 1, \forall i = 1, \ldots, N.$

Furthermore, since the eigenvalues of A are equal to the poles of $H(z)$ the ROC of the transfer function in Equation 17.29 is the exterior of a disk of radius

$\rho := \max_{i=1,\ldots,N} |\lambda_i(A)|$. This radius is called the *spectral radius* of the matrix A, denoted as $\rho(A)$.

We found earlier that the impulse response of the system in Equation 17.25 is given by $h[n] = CA^{n-1}Bq[n-1] + D\delta[n]$. Hence, by identification with Equation 17.29, the inverse z-transform of $(zI_N - A)^{-1}, |z| > \rho(A)$ must be $A^{n-1}q[n-1]$, which is indeed the case. (Show it as an exercise using a power series expansion of the matrix function $(zI_N - A)^{-1}, |z| > \rho(A)$.) That is, we have

$$A^{n-1}q[n-1] \overset{UZ}{\leftrightarrow} (zI_N - A)^{-1}, |z| > \rho(A). \tag{17.30}$$

Example 17.1: Let us find the transfer function of the causal system described by

$$\begin{aligned} x[n+1] &= \begin{bmatrix} 0.8286 & -0.2143 \\ -0.1429 & 0.4714 \end{bmatrix} x[n] + \begin{bmatrix} 2 \\ -1 \end{bmatrix} u[n] \\ y[n] &= \begin{bmatrix} -1 & 3 \end{bmatrix} x[n] + 2u[n]. \end{aligned} \tag{17.31}$$

First, we compute the eigenvalues of the A matrix to obtain $\lambda_1 = 0.4, \lambda_2 = 0.9$. Therefore, the spectral radius of the matrix is $\rho(A) = 0.9$ and the ROC should contain $|z| > 0.9$ (or be equal to it if the realization is found to be minimal). We use Equation 17.29 to calculate $H(z)$.

$$\begin{aligned} H(z) &= \begin{bmatrix} -1 & 3 \end{bmatrix} \begin{bmatrix} z-0.8286 & 0.2143 \\ 0.1429 & z-0.4714 \end{bmatrix}^{-1} \begin{bmatrix} 2 \\ -1 \end{bmatrix} + 2, \quad |z| > 0.9 \\ &= \frac{1}{(z-0.8286)(z-0.4714) - 0.1429 \cdot 0.2143} \begin{bmatrix} -1 & 3 \end{bmatrix} \begin{bmatrix} z-0.4714 & -0.2143 \\ -0.1429 & z-0.8286 \end{bmatrix} \begin{bmatrix} 2 \\ -1 \end{bmatrix} + 2 \\ &= \frac{1}{z^2 - 1.3z + 0.36} \begin{bmatrix} -1 & 3 \end{bmatrix} \begin{bmatrix} 2z - 0.7285 \\ -z + 0.5428 \end{bmatrix} + 2 = \frac{-5z + 2.3569 + 2(z^2 - 1.3z + 0.36)}{z^2 - 1.3z + 0.36} \\ &= \frac{2z^2 - 7.6z + 3.0769}{z^2 - 1.3z + 0.36} = 2\frac{z^2 - 3.8z + 1.5385}{z^2 - 1.3z + 0.36} = 2\frac{(z-0.461)(z-3.339)}{(z-0.4)(z-0.9)}, \quad |z| > 0.9 \end{aligned} \tag{17.32}$$

The eigenvalues of the A matrix are the same as the poles of the transfer function, and hence the realization is minimal.

((Lecture 70: Discretization of Continuous-Time LTI Systems))

DISCRETIZATION OF CONTINUOUS-TIME SYSTEMS

Continuous-time differential systems can be discretized to obtain difference equations. This is usually done for simulation purposes, that is, to obtain a numerical solution of the differential system's response. In particular, discretization of a continuous-time state-space system (A, B, C, D) yields the discrete-time state-space system (A_d, B_d, C_d, D_d).

Discretization Using the Step-Invariant Transformation (c2d operator)

One way to discretize a continuous-time system is to use the *step-invariant transformation*. It consists of a zero-order-hold (ZOH)–like operator at the input of the state-space system, which we call DT/ZOH, and a CT/DT operator at its output. A block diagram of the step-invariant transformation, also known as the *c2d operator*, is given in Figure 17.4.

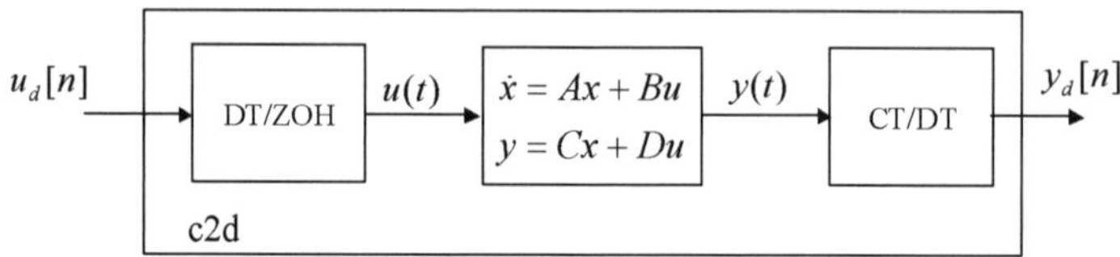

FIGURE 17.4 c2d discretization operator.

The overall mapping of (A, B, C, D) to the discrete-time state-space system (A_d, B_d, C_d, D_d) through the step-invariant transformation is called the c2d operator in reference to the *c2d* command in the MATLAB Control Systems Toolbox, and we can write

$$(A_d, B_d, C_d, D_d) = c2d\{(A, B, C, D)\}. \tag{17.33}$$

The DT/ZOH operator shown in Figure 17.5 is defined as a mapping from a discrete-time signal to an impulse train (operator $\mathcal{V}^{-1}$ consisting of forming a train of impulses occurring every T_s seconds, with the impulse at time nT_s having an area $u_d[n]$), followed by a ZOH function that holds each value for a period T_s.

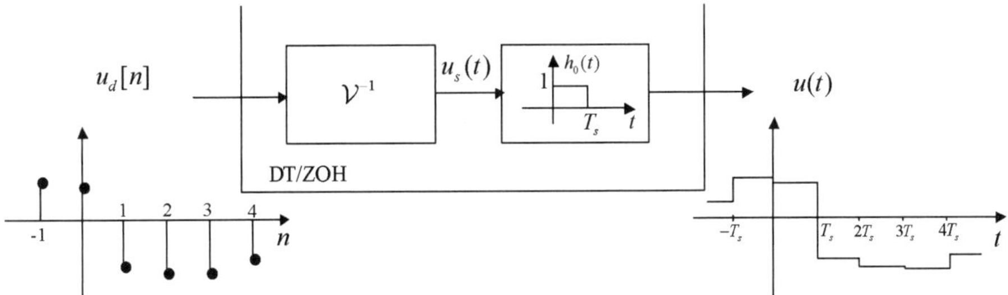

FIGURE 17.5 DT/ZOH operator.

The CT/DT operator defined in Chapter 15 is shown in Figure 17.6.

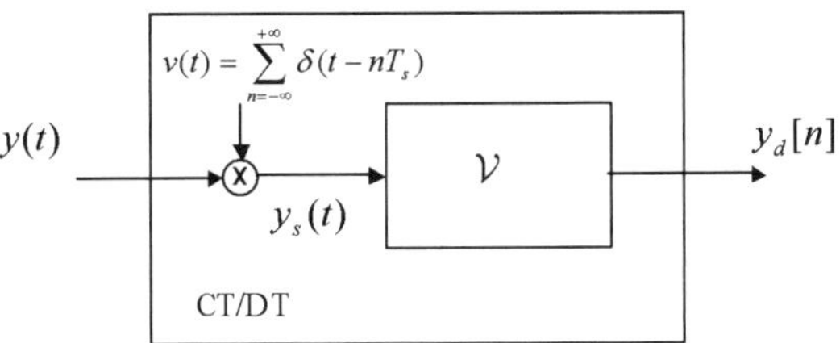

FIGURE 17.6 CT/DT conversion operator.

It is easy to see why c2d is a step-invariant transformation in Figure 17.4: the continuous-time step response $y(t)$ to a step $u(t) = q(t)$ is the same whether the step is applied in continuous time, $u(t) = q(t)$, or in discrete time, $u_d[n] = q[n]$. Therefore, the discrete-time step response will be the sampled continuous-time step response: $y_d[n] = y(nT_s)$.

Let us have a second look at the matrix exponential e^{At}. It is called the *state transition matrix* when it is time shifted to t_0, since for the continuous-time system (A, B, C, D) it takes the state $x(t_0)$ to the state $x(t)$ for $t > t_0$ when the input is zero:

$$x(t) = e^{A(t-t_0)}x(t_0). \tag{17.34}$$

The state response of the state-space system (A, B, C, D) to be discretized is given by the combination of the zero-input state response and the zero-state state response.

$$
\begin{aligned}
x(t) &= e^{A(t-t_0)}x(t_0) + \int_{t_0}^{t} e^{A\tau} Bu(t-\tau)d\tau \\
&= e^{A(t-t_0)}x(t_0) + \int_{t_0}^{t} e^{A(t-\tau)} Bu(\tau)d\tau
\end{aligned}
\tag{17.35}
$$

Notice that the input signal $u(t)$ is a "staircase" function, as it is held constant between sampling instants. Thus, if we take $t_0 = kT_s$ and $t = (k+1)T_s$ in Equation 17.35, we can write

$$
\begin{aligned}
x((n+1)T_s) &= e^{AT_s}x(nT_s) + \int_{nT_s}^{(n+1)T_s} e^{A((n+1)T_s-\tau)} d\tau\, Bu(nT_s) \\
&= e^{AT_s}x(nT_s) + e^{A(n+1)T_s} \int_{nT_s}^{(n+1)T_s} e^{-A\tau} d\tau\, Bu(nT_s) \\
&= e^{AT_s}x(nT_s) - e^{A(n+1)T_s} A^{-1} \left[e^{-A\tau} \right]_{nT_s}^{(n+1)T_s} Bu(nT_s) \\
&= e^{AT_s}x(nT_s) - A^{-1} e^{A(n+1)T_s} \left[e^{-A(n+1)T_s} - e^{-AnT_s} \right] Bu(nT_s) \\
&= e^{AT_s}x(nT_s) - A^{-1} \left[I_N - e^{AT_s} \right] Bu(nT_s) \\
&= \underbrace{e^{AT_s}}_{A_d} x(nT_s) + \underbrace{A^{-1}\left[e^{AT_s} - I_N \right] B}_{B_d} u(nT_s).
\end{aligned}
\tag{17.36}
$$

where we use the fact that A^{-1} (assuming it exists) commutes with $e^{A(n+1)T_s}$. If we define the discrete-time state $x_d[n] := x(nT_s)$, the last equality in Equation 17.36 can be rewritten as a discrete-time state equation as follows, while the output equation does not change:

$$
\begin{aligned}
x_d[n+1] &= A_d x_d[n] + B_d u_d[n] \\
y_d[n] &= C_d x_d[n] + D_d u_d[n],
\end{aligned}
\tag{17.37}
$$

where

$$\begin{aligned} A_d &:= e^{AT_s} \\ B_d &:= A^{-1}\left[e^{AT_s} - I_N\right]B \\ C_d &:= C \\ D_d &:= D. \end{aligned} \tag{17.38}$$

Discretization Using the Bilinear Transformation

The bilinear transformation (also called Tustin's method) is a mapping from the Laplace domain to the z-domain via

$$s = \frac{2}{T_s}\frac{1-z^{-1}}{1+z^{-1}}. \tag{17.39}$$

Example 17.2: Let us discretize the causal first-order lag $H(s) = \frac{s+1}{5s+1}$ using a sampling period of $T_s = 0.1\,s$ using the bilinear transformation. We have

$$\begin{aligned} H_d(z) &= \left.\frac{1+s}{1+5s}\right|_{s=20\frac{1-z^{-1}}{1+z^{-1}}} = \frac{1+20\frac{1-z^{-1}}{1+z^{-1}}}{1+100\frac{1-z^{-1}}{1+z^{-1}}} = \frac{1+z^{-1}+20-20z^{-1}}{1+z^{-1}+100-100z^{-1}} \\ &= \frac{21-19z^{-1}}{101-99z^{-1}} = \frac{0.2079(1-0.9048z^{-1})}{(1-0.9802z^{-1})}, \quad |z| > 0.9802 \end{aligned} \tag{17.40}$$

The DC gain of this discretized system is given by $H_d(e^{j0}) = H_d(1) = \frac{21-19}{101-99} = 1 = H(j0)$, and hence both systems have the same low-frequency gain. In fact, the bilinear transformation provides a very good approximation to the frequency response of the continuous-time transfer function, at least up to frequencies close to the Nyquist rate $\omega_s/2$, as seen in the Bode plots of- Figure 17.7.

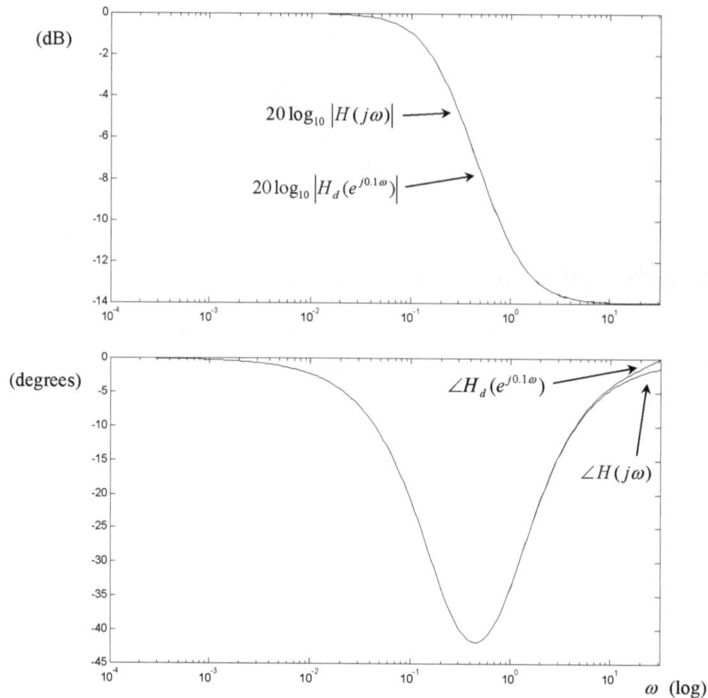

FIGURE 17.7 Bode plots of first-order lag and its bilinear discretization up to the Nyquist frequency.

Remark: Once a system has been discretized, it must be simulated off-line or run in real-time *at the same sampling frequency* as was used in the discretization process. Otherwise, the poles and zeros migrate and the correspondence with the original continuous-time system is lost. It is a common mistake to only change the sampling rate of a sampled-data system while neglecting to replace the discretized filter with a new one obtained by discretizing again with the new sampling period.

The formula in Equation 17.39 comes from the trapezoidal approximation to an integral which is s^{-1} in the Laplace domain.

Suppose we want to approximate the continuous-time integrator system of Figure 17.8. Consider the plot of a signal $v(t)$ to be integrated between $t_0 = (n-1)T_s$, $t_1 = nTs$, as shown in Figure 17.9.

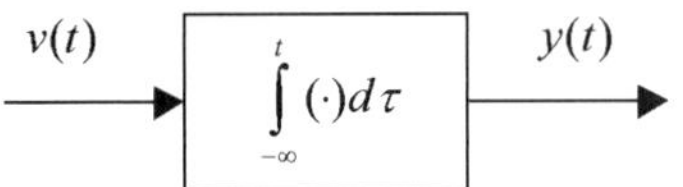

FIGURE 17.8 Integrator system.

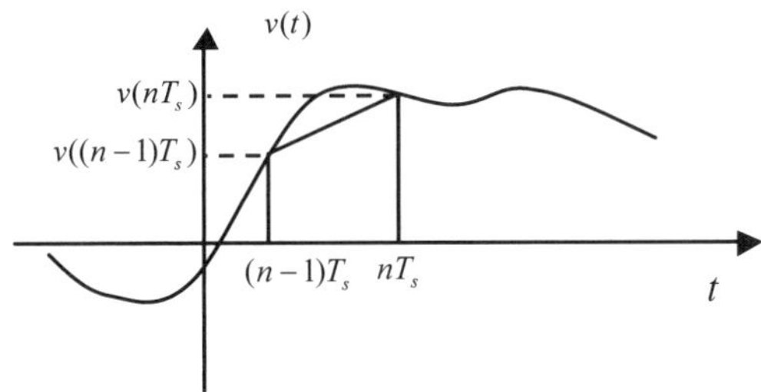

FIGURE 17.9 Trapezoidal approximation to an integral.

The trapezoidal approximation of the integral system s^{-1} is given by

$$y(nT_s) - y((n-1)T_s) = \int_{(n-1)T_s}^{nT_s} v(t)dt \cong \frac{T_s}{2}\left[v(nT_s) + v((n-1)T_s)\right], \qquad (17.41)$$

which in discrete time can be written as (taking the approximation as an equality)

$$y_d[n] - y_d[n-1] = \frac{T_s}{2}\left[v_d[n] + v_d[n-1]\right]. \qquad (17.42)$$

In the z-domain, the transfer function of this system is given by $\frac{T_s}{2}\left(\frac{1+z^{-1}}{1-z^{-1}}\right)$. Thus, we have $\frac{1}{s} = \frac{T}{2}\left(\frac{1+z^{-1}}{1-z^{-1}}\right)$, and Equation 17.39 follows.

Now, applying this bilinear transformation to the state equation of our continuous-time state-space system in the Laplace domain

$$\begin{aligned} sX(s) &= AX(s) + BU(s) \\ Y(s) &= CX(s) + DU(s), \end{aligned} \qquad (17.43)$$

we obtain

$$\frac{2}{T_s}\frac{1-z^{-1}}{1+z^{-1}}X(z)=AX(z)+BU(z)$$

$$\Rightarrow$$

$$(1-z^{-1})X(z)=\frac{T_s}{2}(1+z^{-1})AX(z)+\frac{T_s}{2}(1+z^{-1})BU(z). \tag{17.44}$$

Note that the following derivation of the formulas in Equation 17.51 is not essential. Multiplying Equation 17.44 on both sides by z, we get

$$(z-1)X(z)=\frac{T_s}{2}(z+1)AX(z)+\frac{T_s}{2}(z+1)BU(z)$$

$$\left(I_N-\frac{T_s}{2}A\right)zX(z)=\left(\frac{T_s}{2}A+I_N\right)X(z)+\frac{T_s}{2}BU(z)+\frac{T_s}{2}zBU(z)$$

$$zX(z)=\left(I_N-\frac{T_s}{2}A\right)^{-1}\left(\frac{T_s}{2}A+I_N\right)X(z)+\frac{T_s}{2}\left(I_N-\frac{T_s}{2}A\right)^{-1}BU(z)+\frac{T_s}{2}z\left(I_N-\frac{T_s}{2}A\right)^{-1}BU(z) \tag{17.45}$$

In the time domain,

$$x[n+1]=\left(I_N-\frac{T_s}{2}A\right)^{-1}\left(\frac{T_s}{2}A+I_N\right)x[n]+\frac{T_s}{2}\left(I_N-\frac{T_s}{2}A\right)^{-1}Bu[n]+\frac{T_s}{2}\left(I_N-\frac{T_s}{2}A\right)^{-1}Bu[n+1]. \tag{17.46}$$

We have to get rid of the last term on the right-hand side in order to obtain the usual form of a state-space system. That term is a direct path to the state, and hence to the output $y[n+1]$. In order to do this, let us define the new state

$$\tilde{x}[n]:=x[n]-\frac{T_s}{2}\left(I_N-\frac{T_s}{2}A\right)^{-1}Bu[n]. \tag{17.47}$$

Then, the state equation becomes

$$\begin{aligned}\tilde{x}[n+1] &= \left(I_N - \frac{T_s}{2}A\right)^{-1}\left(\frac{T_s}{2}A + I_N\right)\tilde{x}[n] + \frac{T_s}{2}\left[\left(I_N - \frac{T_s}{2}A\right)^{-1}\left(\frac{T_s}{2}A + I_N\right) + I_N\right]\left(I_N - \frac{T_s}{2}A\right)^{-1} Bu[n] \\ &= \left(I_N - \frac{T_s}{2}A\right)^{-1}\left(\frac{T_s}{2}A + I_N\right)\tilde{x}[n] + \frac{T_s}{2}\left(I_N - \frac{T_s}{2}A\right)^{-1}\left[\left(\frac{T_s}{2}A + I_N\right) + \left(I_N - \frac{T_s}{2}A\right)\right]\left(I_N - \frac{T_s}{2}A\right)^{-1} Bu[n] \\ &= \underbrace{\left(I_N - \frac{T_s}{2}A\right)^{-1}\left(\frac{T_s}{2}A + I_N\right)}_{A_d}\tilde{x}[n] + \underbrace{T_s\left(I_N - \frac{T_s}{2}A\right)^{-2}}_{B_d} Bu[n] \end{aligned} \quad (17.48)$$

and the output equation is computed as follows:

$$\begin{aligned} y[n] &= C\tilde{x}[n] + \frac{T_s}{2}C\left(I_N - \frac{T_s}{2}A\right)^{-1} Bu[n] + Du[n] \\ &= \underbrace{C}_{C_d}\tilde{x}[n] + \underbrace{\left[D + \frac{T_s}{2}C\left(I_N - \frac{T_s}{2}A\right)^{-1} B\right]}_{D_d} u[n]. \end{aligned} \quad (17.49)$$

Hence, the state-space system discretized using the bilinear transformation is given by

$$\begin{aligned} \tilde{x}[n+1] &= A_d\tilde{x}[n] + B_d u[n] \\ y[n] &= C_d\tilde{x}[n] + D_d u[n], \end{aligned} \quad (17.50)$$

where

$$\begin{aligned} A_d &:= \left(I_N - \frac{T_s}{2}A\right)^{-1}\left(I_N + \frac{T_s}{2}A\right) \\ B_d &:= T_s\left(I_N - \frac{T_s}{2}A\right)^{-2} B \\ C_d &:= C \\ D_d &:= D + \frac{T_s}{2}C\left(I_N - \frac{T_s}{2}A\right)^{-1} B. \end{aligned} \quad (17.51)$$

Remark: The MATLAB *c2d* command with the "tustin" option implements the bilinear transformation

$$A_d = \left(I_N - \frac{T_s}{2} A \right)^{-1} \left(I_N + \frac{T_s}{2} A \right)$$

$$B_d = \left(I_N - \frac{T_s}{2} A \right)^{-1} B$$

$$C_d = CT_s \left(I_N - \frac{T_s}{2} A \right)^{-1}$$

$$D_d = D + \frac{T_s}{2} C \left(I_N - \frac{T_s}{2} A \right)^{-1} B \qquad (17.52)$$

with different B_d and C_d matrices from those given in Equation 17.51 but yielding the same transfer function as the state-space realization. Either realization can be used.

SUMMARY

This chapter introduced discrete-time state-space LTI systems and the discretization of continuous-time systems.

- Difference LTI systems represented by proper rational transfer functions can be realized as state-space systems. We gave procedures to compute the controllable and the observable canonical realizations, but just like the continuous-time case, there exist infinitely many realizations of any given proper rational transfer function.
- We derived the formulas for the zero-input and zero-state responses, the impulse response, and the transfer function of a general discrete-time state-space system.
- A minimal state-space system was shown to be BIBO stable if and only if all of the eigenvalues of its A matrix lie in the open unit disk centered at the origin.
- Two system discretization techniques were derived: the step-invariant transformation, called c2d, and the bilinear transformation.

TO PROBE FURTHER

Discrete-time state-space systems and discretization are discussed in Chen, 1999.

EXERCISES

Exercises with Solutions

Exercise 17.1

We want to implement a causal continuous-time LTI Butterworth filter of the second order as a discrete-time system. The transfer function of the Butterworth filter is given by $H(s)=\dfrac{1}{\frac{1}{\omega_n^2}s^2+\frac{2\zeta}{\omega_n}s+1}$, where $\omega_n=2000\pi$ and $\zeta=\dfrac{1}{\sqrt{2}}$.

(a) Find a state-space realization of the Butterworth filter and discretize it with a sampling frequency 10 times higher than the cutoff frequency of the filter. Use the bilinear transformation.

Answer:

$$H(s)=\frac{1}{\frac{1}{\omega_n^2}s^2+\frac{2\zeta}{\omega_n}s+1}=\frac{\omega_n^2}{s^2+2\zeta\omega_n s+\omega_n^2}$$
$$=\frac{4\pi^2\times10^6}{s^2+2000\pi\sqrt{2}s+4\pi^2\times10^6}$$

The controllable canonical state-space realization is given by

$$\begin{bmatrix}\dot{x}_1\\ \dot{x}_2\end{bmatrix}=\underbrace{\begin{bmatrix}0 & 1\\ -4\pi^2\times10^6 & -2000\pi\sqrt{2}\end{bmatrix}}_{A}\begin{bmatrix}x_1\\ x_2\end{bmatrix}+\underbrace{\begin{bmatrix}0\\ 1\end{bmatrix}}_{B}u,\quad y=\underbrace{\begin{bmatrix}4\pi^2\times10^6 & 0\end{bmatrix}}_{C}\begin{bmatrix}x_1\\ x_2\end{bmatrix},$$

and $D=0$.

The cutoff frequency of the filter is $\omega_n=2000\pi$ rad/s, so we set the sampling frequency at $\omega_s=20000\pi$ rad/s, so that $T_s=10^{-4}$ s.

$$A_{bilin} := \left(I_2 - \frac{T_s}{2}A\right)^{-1}\left(I_2 + \frac{T_s}{2}A\right)$$

$$= \left(I_2 - 5\times 10^{-5}\begin{bmatrix} 0 & 1 \\ -4\pi^2\times 10^6 & -2000\pi\sqrt{2}\end{bmatrix}\right)^{-1}\left(I_2 + 5\times 10^{-5}\begin{bmatrix} 0 & 1 \\ -4\pi^2\times 10^6 & -2000\pi\sqrt{2}\end{bmatrix}\right)$$

$$= \begin{bmatrix} 0.8721 & 0.00006481 \\ -2559 & 0.2962 \end{bmatrix}$$

$$B_{bilin} := T_s\left(I_2 - \frac{T_s}{2}A\right)^{-2} B = \begin{bmatrix} 0.00000000513 \\ 0.0000379 \end{bmatrix}$$

$$C_{bilin} := C = \begin{bmatrix} 3.948\times 10^7 & 0 \end{bmatrix}$$

$$D_{bilin} := D + \frac{T_s}{2}C\left(I_2 - \frac{T_s}{2}A\right)^{-1} B = 0.06396$$

(b) Plot the frequency responses of both the continuous-time and the discrete-time filters on the same graph up to the Nyquist frequency (half of the sampling frequency) in radians/second. Discuss the results and how you would implement this filter.

Answer: The transfer function is computed as

$$G_{bilin}(z) = C_{bilin}(zI_n - A_{bilin})^{-1}B_{bilin} + D_{bilin}$$
$$= \frac{0.06396 + 0.1279z^{-1} + 0.06396z^{-2}}{1 - 1.1683z^{-1} + 0.4241z^{-2}}, \quad |z| > 0.65.$$

ON THE CD

The Bode plots of $H(j\omega)$ and $H_{bilin}(e^{j0.0001\omega})$ up to the Nyquist frequency 10,000π rad/s are computed using the following MATLAB program, which is located in D:\Chapter17\discretized.m on the companion CD-ROM.

```
%% Exercise 17.1 discretization of Butterworth filter
% transfer function and CT state-space model
num=[1];
den=[1/(2000*pi)^2 sqrt(2)/(2000*pi) 1];
[A,B,C,D]=tf2ss(num,den);
T=[0 1; 1 0]; % permutation matrix to get same form as in Chapter 10
A=inv(T)*A*T;
B=inv(T)*B;
C=C*T;
```

```
H=ss(A,B,C,D);
% bilinear transf
Ts=0.0001
Ab=inv(eye(2)-0.5*Ts*A)*(eye(2)+0.5*Ts*A);
Bb=Ts*inv(eye(2)-0.5*Ts*A)*inv(eye(2)-0.5*Ts*A)*B;
Cb=C;
Db=D+0.5*Ts*C*inv(eye(2)-0.5*Ts*A)*B;
Hb=ss(Ab,Bb,Cb,Db,Ts);
% Frequency response of CT Butterworth and its discretized version
w=logspace(1,log10(10000*pi),200);
w=w(1,1:199);
[MAG,PHASE] = bode(H,w);
[MAGbilin,PHASEbilin] = bode(Hb,w);
figure(1)
semilogx(w,20*log10(MAGbilin(:,:)),w,20*log10(MAG(:,:)))
figure(2)
semilogx(w,PHASEbilin(:,:),w,PHASE(:,:))
```

The resulting Bode plots are shown in Figure 17.10.

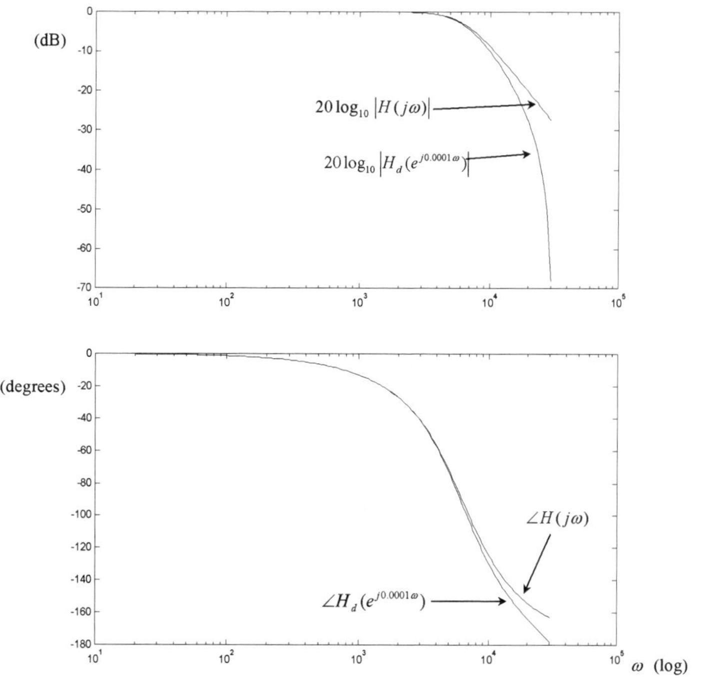

FIGURE 17.10 Bode plots of second-order Butterworth filter and its bilinear discretization up to the Nyquist frequency.

The filter can be implemented as a second-order recursive difference equation: $y[n]=1.1683y[n-1]-0.4241y[n-2]+0.06396x[n]+0.1279x[n-1]+0.06396x[n-2]$.

(c) Compute and plot on the same graph the first 30 points of the step response of the Butterworth filter and its discretized version.

Answer: The following MATLAB script (last part of discretized.m, run after the script given in (b)) computes the continuous-time step response using the *lsim* command (which internally uses a c2d discretization) with a sampling period 10 times shorter than T_s.

```
% Step responses
figure(3)
t=[0:0.00001:.00299]; % time vector to plot step resp of CT system
[y,ts,x]=lsim(H,ones(1,300),t);
plot(ts,y)
hold on
[yb,tsb,xb]=lsim(Hb,ones(1,30));
plot(tsb,yb,'o')
hold off
```

The resulting plot is shown in Figure 17.11.

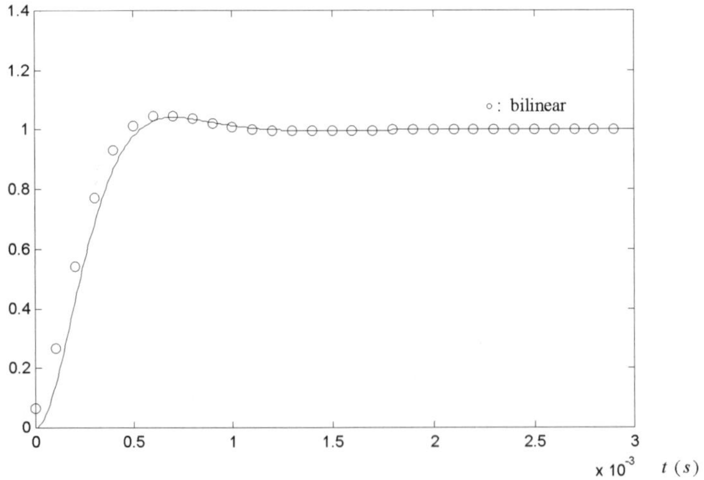

FIGURE 17.11 Step responses of second-order Butterworth filter and its bilinear discretization.

Exercise 17.2

Consider the causal DLTI system given by its transfer function

$$H(z) = \frac{z^2 - z}{z^2 + 0.1z - 0.72}, \quad |z| > 0.9.$$

(a) Find the controllable canonical state-space realization (A,B,C,D) of the system (draw the block diagram and give the realization.) Assess its stability based on the eigenvalues of A.

Answer: The direct form realization is shown in Figure 17.12.

$$H(z) = \frac{1 - z^{-1}}{1 + 0.1z^{-1} - 0.72z^{-2}}, \quad |z| > 0.9$$

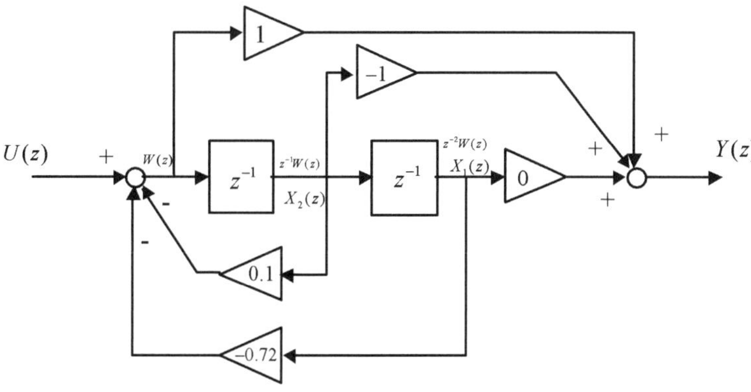

FIGURE 17.12 Direct form realization in Exercise 17.2.

Controllable canonical state-space realization:

$$x[n+1] = \underbrace{\begin{bmatrix} 0 & 1 \\ 0.72 & -0.1 \end{bmatrix}}_{A} x[n] + \underbrace{\begin{bmatrix} 0 \\ 1 \end{bmatrix}}_{B} u[n]$$

$$y[n] = \underbrace{\begin{bmatrix} 0.72 & -1.1 \end{bmatrix}}_{C} x[n] + \underbrace{1}_{D} u[n]$$

Eigenvalues of A: $0.8, -0.9$ are inside the unit circle, and therefore the system is stable.

(b) Compute the impulse response of the system $h[n]$ by diagonalizing the A matrix.

Answer: The impulse response of the system $h[n]$ is given by

$$\begin{aligned}
h[n] &= CA^{n-1}Bq[n-1] + D\delta[n] \\
&= \begin{bmatrix} 0.72 & -1.1 \end{bmatrix} \begin{bmatrix} 0 & 1 \\ 0.72 & -0.1 \end{bmatrix}^{n-1} \begin{bmatrix} 0 \\ 1 \end{bmatrix} q[n-1] + \delta[n] \\
&= \begin{bmatrix} 0.72 & -1.1 \end{bmatrix} \left(\begin{bmatrix} 0.7809 & -0.7433 \\ 0.6247 & 0.6690 \end{bmatrix} \begin{bmatrix} 0.8 & 0 \\ 0 & -0.9 \end{bmatrix} \begin{bmatrix} 0.7809 & -0.7433 \\ 0.6247 & 0.6690 \end{bmatrix}^{-1} \right)^{n-1} \begin{bmatrix} 0 \\ 1 \end{bmatrix} q[n-1] + \delta[n] \\
&= \begin{bmatrix} 0.72 & -1.1 \end{bmatrix} \left(\begin{bmatrix} 0.7809 & -0.7433 \\ 0.6247 & 0.6690 \end{bmatrix} \begin{bmatrix} 0.8^{n-1} & 0 \\ 0 & (-0.9)^{n-1} \end{bmatrix} \begin{bmatrix} 0.7809 & -0.7433 \\ 0.6247 & 0.6690 \end{bmatrix}^{-1} \right) \begin{bmatrix} 0 \\ 1 \end{bmatrix} q[n-1] + \delta[n] \\
&= [-0.0941(0.8)^{n-1} - 1.0059(-0.9)^{n-1}]q[n-1] + \delta[n].
\end{aligned}$$

Exercises

Exercise 17.3

The causal continuous-time LTI system with transfer function $G(s) = \frac{1}{0.1s+1}$ is discretized with a sampling period of $T_s = 0.01$ s for simulation purposes. Use the c2d transformation first to get $G_{c2d}(z)$, then the bilinear transformation to get $G_{bilin}(z)$.

Answer:

ON THE CD

Exercise 17.4

The causal continuous-time LTI system with transfer function $G(s) = \frac{s}{(s+1)(s+2)}$ is discretized with a sampling period of $T_s = 0.1$ s for simulation purposes. The c2d transformation will be used first, and then it will be compared to the bilinear transformation.

(a) Find a continuous-time state-space realization of the system.

(b) Compute the discrete-time state-space system $(A_{c2d}, B_{c2d}, C_{c2d}, D_{c2d})$ for $G(s)$ and its associated transfer function $G_{c2d}(z)$, specifying its ROC.

(c) Compute the discrete-time state-space system representing the bilinear transformation of $G(s)$, $(A_{bilin}, B_{bilin}, C_{bilin}, D_{bilin})$ and its associated transfer function $G_{bilin}(z)$, specifying its ROC.

(d) Use MATLAB to plot the frequency responses $G(j\omega), G_{bilin}(e^{j\omega T_s}), G_{c2d}(e^{j\omega T_s})$ up to frequency $\frac{\omega_s}{2}$ on the same graph, where ω is the continuous-time frequency. Use a decibel scale for the magnitude and a log frequency scale for both magnitude and phase plots. Discuss any difference you observe.

Exercise 17.5

Consider the causal DLTI system specified by its transfer function:

$$H(z) = \frac{z^2 - z}{z^2 - z + 0.5}, \quad |z| > \frac{1}{\sqrt{2}}.$$

(a) Find the controllable canonical state-space realization (A, B, C, D) of the system. Assess its stability based on the eigenvalues of A.

(b) Compute the zero-input response of the system $y_{zi}[n]$ for the initial state $x[0] = \begin{bmatrix} 1 \\ 0 \end{bmatrix}$ by diagonalizing the A matrix.

Answer:

ON THE CD

Exercise 17.6

Consider the causal DLTI system with transfer function $H(z) = \frac{z+0.5}{z^2 - 0.64}, \quad |z| > 0.8.$

(a) Find the observable canonical state-space realization (A, B, C, D) of the system. Assess its stability based on the eigenvalues of A.

(b) Compute the zero-input response of the system $y_{zi}[n]$ for the initial state

$$x[0] = \begin{bmatrix} 1 \\ 1 \end{bmatrix}$$

Exercise 17.7

Find the controllable canonical state-space realization of the causal LTI system defined by the difference equation $y[n]-0.4y[n-1]=2x[n]-0.4x[n-1]$ and compute its transfer function from the state-space model, specifying its ROC.

Answer:

ON THE CD

Exercise 17.8

The causal continuous-time LTI system with transfer function $G(s)=\frac{s+2}{s+1}$ is discretized with sampling period $T_s=0.1$ s for simulation purposes. The c2d transformation is used first, and then it is compared to the bilinear transformation.

(a) Find a state-space realization of $G(s)=\frac{s+2}{s+1}$, $\mathrm{Re}\{s\}>-1$.

(b) Compute the discrete-time state-space system for $G(s)$ using c2d and its associated transfer function $G_{c2d}(z)$, specifying its ROC.

(c) Find the bilinear transformation $G_{bilin}(z)$ of $G(s)$, specifying its ROC. Compute the difference between the two frequency responses obtained with c2d and the bilinear transformation; that is, compute $E(e^{j\omega}):=G_{bilin}(e^{j\omega})-G_{c2d}(e^{j\omega})$. Evaluate this difference at DC and at the highest discrete-time frequency.

Appendix

A Using MATLAB

MATLAB® is a useful and widespread software package developed by The MathWorks Inc. for numerical computation in engineering and science. MATLAB is easy to use and can be learned quickly. It comes with very good manuals. The purpose of this appendix is simply to provide a brief overview on how to use MATLAB and present some of its capabilities.

In order to perform computations, one can use the command line, or write a program as a script, called an M-file, in MATLAB's own language. This language is well suited to handling large vectors and matrices as single objects. Consider the following script:

```
% Simple matrix-vector computations...
% Define 3x3 matrix A
A=[1 2 3; 4 0 -2; 1 2 -3]
% Define 3x1 vector x
x=[-1; 0; 1]
% Compute eigenvalues and eigenvectors of A
[T,L]=eig(A)
% L is the diagonal matrix of eigenvalues,
T is the matrix of eigenvectors
% Diagonalize matrix A with T
D=inv(T)*A*T
% Compute the product A.x
y=A*x
```

Also, mathematical functions can be used on an entire vector or matrix in one shot. This greatly simplifies the code. For example, the following script plots ten cycles of a sine wave in only three lines.

```
% time vector
t=0:.01:1;y=sin(20*pi*t);
plot(t,y)
```

The help command tells the user how to use any other command. For instance,

```
» help eig
    EIG    Eigenvalues and eigenvectors.
E = EIG(X) is a vector containing the eigenvalues of a square
matrix X.

[V,D] = EIG(X) produces a diagonal matrix D of eigenvalues and a
full matrix V whose columns are the corresponding eigenvectors so
that X*V = V*D.
```

Finally, many people have developed MATLAB *toolboxes* over the years, which are collections of functions targeted at specific areas of engineering. For example, in this book we use commands from the Control System Toolbox, such as *lsim* to simulate the response of LTI systems.

```
%simulate state-space LTI system
SYS=ss(A,B,C,D);
[YS,TS,XS] = LSIM(SYS,U,T,x0);
plot(XS(:,1),XS(:,2))
```

Appendix

B Mathematical Notation and Useful Formulas

TABLE B.1 Mathematical Notation

Notation	Meaning	Remark
$\mathbb{R}$	Real numbers	
$\mathbb{Z}$	Integers	
$\mathbb{C}$	Complex numbers	
j	$j := \sqrt{-1}$	Imaginary number
$\forall$	For every, for all	
$\exists$	There exists	
$\in$	Element of	
$:=$	Defined as being equal to	
$N!$	$N! := N \cdot (N-1) \cdots 3 \cdot 2 \cdot 1$	Factorial, $0! = 1$
$\delta(t)$, $\delta[n]$	CT, DT unit impulse	
$u(t)$, $u[n]$	CT, DT unit step signal	Except for state-space systems for which $u(t)$, $u[n]$ are the inputs, notably in Chapters 10 and 17
$q(t)$, $q[n]$	CT, DT unit step signal	In Chapters 10, 11 and 17
$h(t)$, $h[n]$	CT, DT impulse response	
$s(t)$, $s[n]$	CT, DT step response	
$\dot{x}$	(dx/dt)	
ω_n	Undamped natural frequency	Second-order systems
ζ	Damping ratio	Second-order systems
ω	Continuous-time frequency	Units of rad/s
ω, Ω	Discrete-time frequency	Units of rad
$\lambda_i(A)$	i^{th} eigenvalue of square matrix *A*	
$\rho(A)$	Spectral radius of $N \times N$ matrix *A*	$\rho(A) := \max_{i=1,\ldots,N} \lvert \lambda_i(A) \rvert$
$\arctan\left(\frac{\beta}{\alpha}\right)$	Four-quadrant arctan $\alpha . \beta \in \mathbb{R}$ are displayed with their own sign	

TABLE B.2 Useful Formulas

Formula	Remark
$\cos(\theta)=\frac{1}{2}e^{j\theta}+\frac{1}{2}e^{-j\theta}=\mathrm{Re}\{e^{j\theta}\}$	
$\sin(\theta)=\frac{1}{2j}e^{j\theta}-\frac{1}{2j}e^{-j\theta}=\mathrm{Im}\{e^{j\theta}\}$	
$e^{j\theta}=\cos(\theta)+j\sin(\theta)$	
$\cos(\theta)\cos(\phi)=\frac{1}{2}\cos(\theta-\phi)+\frac{1}{2}\cos(\theta+\phi)$	
$\sin(\theta)\cos(\phi)=\frac{1}{2}\sin(\theta-\phi)+\frac{1}{2}\sin(\theta+\phi)$	
$\sin(\theta)\sin(\phi)=\frac{1}{2}\cos(\theta-\phi)-\frac{1}{2}\cos(\theta+\phi)$	
$\sum_{k=0}^{N}a^k=\frac{1-a^{N+1}}{1-a},\ \forall a\in\mathbb{C}$	Geometric sum
$\sum_{k=0}^{+\infty}a^k=\frac{1}{1-a},\ a\in\mathbb{C},\ \lvert a\rvert<1$	Geometric series
$z=\alpha+j\beta=re^{j\theta}\in\mathbb{C},\ z^*=\alpha-j\beta=re^{-j\theta}$ $r=\lvert z\rvert=\sqrt{\alpha^2+\beta^2},\ \theta=\angle z=\arctan\left(\frac{\beta}{\alpha}\right)$ $\alpha=r\cos\theta,\ \beta=r\sin\theta$	Various representations of complex number z and its conjugate

Appendix C About the CD-ROM

CD-ROM FOLDERS

Applets: The Learnware applets

Chapter folders: Solutions to selected problems, MATLAB scripts, and all of the figures from the book, organized by chapter

Sample exams: Sample midterm and final examinations

The companion CD-ROM to the textbook contains files for

- Solutions to odd-numbered problems in each chapter plus sample exams in PDF format

  The detailed solutions to odd-numbered problems at the end of Chapter $k \in \{1,2,...,17\}$, are given in the file D:\Chapter*k*\Chapter*k*problems.pdf, where D: is assumed to be the CD-ROM drive. The sample midterm tests and final exams are located in D:\Sample Exams\Covering Chapters 1 to 9, and D:\Sample Exams\Covering Chapters 10 to 17. All of the figures from each chapter can be found as TIFF files in D:\Chapter*k*\Figures.
- Learnware applets (discrete-time convolution, Fourier series, Bode plot)

  The discrete-time convolution Java applet allows the user to enter the values of an input signal and an impulse response and to visualize the convolution either as a sum of scaled and time-shifted impulse responses or as the sum of the values of a signal that is the product of the input signal and the time-reversed and shifted impulses response. The convolution applet can be run by pointing a Java-enabled browser to

  D:\Applets\Convolution\SignalGraph\Convolution.html.

  The Fourier series Java applet uses an intuitive graphical user interface. One period of a periodic signal can be drawn using a mouse or a touchpad, and the applet computes the Fourier series coefficients and displays a truncated sum as an approximation to the signal at hand. The convolution applet can be run by pointing a Java-enabled browser to

D:\Applets\FourierSeries\FourierApplet.html.

The Bode applet is a Windows executable (.exe) file and can be found at D:\Applets\BodePlot\Bode.exe. Just double-click on it and you will be able to build a transfer function by dragging poles and zeros onto a pole-zero plot. Add a value for the DC gain of the overall transfer function and you will get the Bode plot showing the actual frequency response of the system together with its broken line approximation discussed in the text.

- MATLAB M-files of selected examples in the text.

  These MATLAB script files, called M-files (with a .m extension) contain sequences of MATLAB commands that perform a desired computation for an example. The selected M-files are located in the Chapter*k* folders.

SYSTEM REQUIREMENTS

Minimum: Pentium II PC running Microsoft Windows 98. Microsoft Internet Explorer 5 or Netscape 7 browser with Java Plug-in 1.4 (*www.sun.com*). Acrobat Reader 5 (*www.adobe.com*). MATLAB 5.3 with Control System Toolbox (*www.mathworks.com*).

Recommended: Pentium 4 PC running Microsoft Windows XP or Windows 2000. Microsoft Internet Explorer 6 or Netscape 7 browser with Java Plug-in 1.4 (*www.sun.com*). Acrobat Reader 5 (*www.adobe.com*). MATLAB 6.5 with Control System toolbox (*www.mathworks.com*).

Appendix D Tables of Transforms

TABLE D.1 Fourier Transform Pairs

Time domain $x(t)$		**Frequency domain** $X(j\omega)$
$\delta(t)$		1
$u(t)$		$\frac{1}{j\omega}+\pi\delta(\omega)$
$e^{at}u(t)$	$a\in\mathbb{C}, \mathrm{Re}\{a\}<0$	$\frac{1}{j\omega-a}$
$-e^{at}u(-t)$	$a\in\mathbb{C}, \mathrm{Re}\{a\}>0$	$\frac{1}{j\omega-a}$
$te^{at}u(t)$	$a\in\mathbb{C}, \mathrm{Re}\{a\}<0$	$\frac{1}{(j\omega-a)^2}$
$e^{-\alpha t}\sin(\omega_0 t)u(t)$	$\alpha,\omega_0\in\mathbb{R},\ \alpha>0$	$\frac{\omega_0}{(j\omega+\alpha)^2+\omega_0^2}$
$e^{-\alpha t}\cos(\omega_0 t)u(t)$	$\alpha,\omega_0\in\mathbb{R},\ \alpha>0$	$\frac{j\omega+\alpha}{(j\omega+\alpha)^2+\omega_0^2}$
1		$\delta(\omega)$
$e^{j\omega_0 t}$	$\omega_0\in\mathbb{R}$	$\delta(\omega-\omega_0)$
$\sum_{-\infty}^{+\infty}\delta(t-kT)$	$T\in\mathbb{R},\ T>0$	$\frac{2\pi}{T}\sum_{k=-\infty}^{+\infty}\delta(\omega-k\frac{2\pi}{T})$
$\begin{cases}1, & \lvert t\rvert<t_0\\ 0, & \lvert t\rvert>t_0\end{cases}$	$t_0\in\mathbb{R},\ t_0>0$	$2t_0\mathrm{sinc}(\frac{t_0}{\pi}\omega)$
$\frac{\omega_c}{\pi}\mathrm{sinc}\left(\frac{\omega_c}{\pi}t\right)=\frac{\sin(\omega_c t)}{\pi t}$	$\omega_c\in\mathbb{R},\ \omega_c>0$	$\begin{cases}1, & \lvert\omega\rvert<\omega_c\\ 0, & \lvert\omega\rvert>\omega_c\end{cases}$
$\sum_{k=-\infty}^{+\infty}a_k e^{jk\omega_0 t}$ (Fourier series)	$a_k\in\mathbb{C}$, $\omega_0\in\mathbb{R},\ \omega_0>0$	$\sum_{k=-\infty}^{+\infty}2\pi a_k\delta(\omega-k\omega_0)$

TABLE D.2 Properties of the Fourier Transform

Time domain		Frequency domain
$x(t)=\frac{1}{2\pi}\int_{-\infty}^{+\infty}X(j\omega)e^{j\omega t}d\omega$		$X(j\omega)=\int_{-\infty}^{+\infty}x(t)e^{-j\omega t}dt$
$ax(t)+by(t)$	$a,b\in\mathbb{C}$	$aX(j\omega)+bY(j\omega)$
$x(t-t_0)$	$t_0\in\mathbb{R}$	$e^{-j\omega t_0}X(j\omega)$
$x(\alpha t)$	$\alpha\in\mathbb{R}$	$\frac{1}{\lvert\alpha\rvert}X\left(j\frac{\omega}{\alpha}\right)$
$\frac{d}{dt}x(t)$		$j\omega X(j\omega)$
$\int_{-\infty}^{t}x(\tau)d\tau$	$\left\lvert\int_{-\infty}^{\infty}x(\tau)d\tau\right\rvert<+\infty$	$\frac{1}{j\omega}X(j\omega)+\pi X(0)\delta(\omega)$
$x(t)*y(t)$		$X(j\omega)Y(j\omega)$
$x(t)y(t)$		$\frac{1}{2\pi}X(j\omega)*Y(j\omega)$
$x^*(t)$		$X^*(-j\omega)$
$x(t)\in\mathbb{R}$		$\lvert X(j\omega)\rvert=\lvert X(-j\omega)\rvert,\ \angle X(j\omega)=-\angle X(-j\omega)$
$x(t)=x(-t)\in\mathbb{R}$		$X(j\omega)=X(-j\omega)\in\mathbb{R}$
$x(t)=-x(-t)\in\mathbb{R}$		$X(j\omega)=-X(-j\omega)\in j\mathbb{R}$ i.e., purely imaginary
Parseval Equality: $\int_{-\infty}^{+\infty}\lvert x(t)\rvert^2dt=\frac{1}{2\pi}\int_{-\infty}^{+\infty}\lvert X(j\omega)\rvert^2d\omega$		

TABLE D.3 Properties of the Fourier Series

Time domain $x(t), y(t)$ periodic of fundamental period T		Frequency domain $x(t)\overset{FS}{\leftrightarrow}a_k,\ y(t)\overset{FS}{\leftrightarrow}b_k$
$x(t)=\sum_{k=-\infty}^{+\infty}a_k e^{jk\omega_0 t}$	$\omega_0\in\mathbb{R},\ \omega_0=\frac{2\pi}{T}>0$	$a_k=\frac{1}{T}\int_T x(t)e^{-jk\omega_0 t}dt$
$x(t)=a_0+2\sum_{k=1}^{+\infty}\lvert a_k\rvert\cos(k\omega_0 t+\angle a_k)$	$x(t)\in\mathbb{R}$	a_k
$x(t)=a_0+$ $2\sum_{k=1}^{+\infty}\left[\mathrm{Re}\{a_k\}\cos(k\omega_0 t)-\mathrm{Im}\{a_k\}\sin(k\omega_0 t)\right]$	$x(t)\in\mathbb{R}$	a_k
$\alpha x(t)+\beta y(t)$	$\alpha,\beta\in\mathbb{C}$	$\alpha a_k+\beta b_k$
$x(t-t_0)$	$t_0\in\mathbb{R}$	$e^{-jk\omega_0 t_0}a_k$
$x(\alpha t)$	$\alpha\in\mathbb{R},\alpha>0$	a_k (fund. freq. is now $\alpha\omega_0$)
$x(-t)$		a_{-k}
$\frac{d}{dt}x(t)$		$jk\omega_0 a_k$
$\int_{-\infty}^{t}x(\tau)d\tau$	$a_0=\int_{-\infty}^{+\infty}x(\tau)d\tau=0$	$\frac{1}{jk\omega_0}a_k$
$x(t)*h(t)$	$\int_{-\infty}^{\infty}\lvert h(t)\rvert dt<+\infty$ (system must be stable)	$a_k H(jk\omega_0)$
$x(t)y(t)$		$\sum_{m=-\infty}^{+\infty}a_m b_{k-m}$
$x^*(t)$		a^*_{-k}
$x(t)\in\mathbb{R}$		$\lvert a_k\rvert=\lvert a_{-k}\rvert,\ \angle a_k=-\angle a_{-k}$
$x(t)=x(-t)\in\mathbb{R}$		$a_k=a_{-k}\in\mathbb{R}$
$x(t)=-x(-t)\in\mathbb{R}$		$a_k=-a_{-k}\in j\mathbb{R}$
Parseval Equality: $\frac{1}{T}\int_T \lvert x(t)\rvert^2 dt=\sum_{k=-\infty}^{+\infty}\lvert a_k\rvert^2$		

TABLE D.4 Laplace Transform Pairs

Time domain $x(t)$		**Laplace domain** $X(s)$	ROC
$x(t)=\frac{1}{j2\pi}\int_{\alpha-j\infty}^{\alpha+j\infty}X(s)e^{st}ds$	$\{s\in\mathbb{C}:\mathrm{Re}\{s\}=\alpha\}$ $\in ROC$	$X(s)=\int_{-\infty}^{+\infty}x(t)e^{-st}dt$	$s\in\mathrm{ROC}$
$\delta(t)$		1	$\forall s$
$u(t)$		$\frac{1}{s}$	$\mathrm{Re}\{s\}>0$
$tu(t)$		$\frac{1}{s^2}$	$\mathrm{Re}\{s\}>0$
$t^k u(t)$	$k=1,2,3,\ldots$	$\frac{1}{k!}\frac{1}{s^k}$	$\mathrm{Re}\{s\}>0$
$e^{at}u(t)$	$a\in\mathbb{C}$	$\frac{1}{s-a}$	$\mathrm{Re}\{s\}>\mathrm{Re}\{a\}$
$-e^{at}u(-t)$	$a\in\mathbb{C}$	$\frac{1}{s-a}$	$\mathrm{Re}\{s\}<\mathrm{Re}\{a\}$
$e^{-\alpha t}\sin(\omega_0 t)u(t)$	$\alpha,\omega_0\in\mathbb{R}$	$\frac{\omega_0}{(s+\alpha)^2+\omega_0^2}$	$\mathrm{Re}\{s\}>-\alpha$
$e^{-\alpha t}\cos(\omega_0 t)u(t)$	$\alpha,\omega_0\in\mathbb{R}$	$\frac{s+\alpha}{(s+\alpha)^2+\omega_0^2}$	$\mathrm{Re}\{s\}>-\alpha$
$\sin(\omega_0 t)u(t)$	$\omega_0\in\mathbb{R}$	$\frac{\omega_0}{s^2+\omega_0^2}$	$\mathrm{Re}\{s\}>0$
$\cos(\omega_0 t)u(t)$	$\omega_0\in\mathbb{R}$	$\frac{s}{s^2+\omega_0^2}$	$\mathrm{Re}\{s\}>0$
$\begin{cases}1, & \lvert t\rvert<t_0\\ 0, & \lvert t\rvert>t_0\end{cases}$	$t_0\in\mathbb{R},\ t_0>0$	$\frac{e^{t_0 s}-e^{-t_0 s}}{s}$	$x(t)$

TABLE D.5: Properties of the Laplace Transform

Time domain		Laplace domain	ROC
$e^{-sto}\mathcal{X}(s)$		$X(s),\ Y(s)$	$\mathrm{ROC_X}, \mathrm{ROC_Y}$
$ax(t)+by(t)$	$a,b \in \mathbb{C}$	$aX(s)+bY(s)$	$\mathrm{ROC} \supseteq \mathrm{ROC_X} \cap \mathrm{ROC_Y}$
$x(t-t_0)$	$t_0 \in \mathbb{R}$	$e^{-st_0}X(s)$	$\mathrm{ROC_X}$
$x(\alpha t)$	$\alpha \in \mathbb{R}$	$\frac{1}{\lvert\alpha\rvert}X\left(\frac{s}{\alpha}\right)$	$\frac{1}{\alpha}\mathrm{ROC_X}$
$\frac{d}{dt}x(t)$		$sX(s)$	$\mathrm{ROC} \supseteq \mathrm{ROC_X}$
$\int_{-\infty}^{t} x(\tau)d\tau$		$\frac{1}{s}X(s)$	$\mathrm{ROC} \supseteq \mathrm{ROC_X} \cap \{s:\mathrm{Re}\{s\}>0\}$
$e^{s_0 t}x(t)$	$s_0 \in \mathbb{C}$	$X(s-s_0)$	$\mathrm{ROC_X} + \mathrm{Re}\{s_0\}$
$x(t)*y(t)$		$X(s)Y(s)$	$\mathrm{ROC} \supseteq \mathrm{ROC_X} \cap \mathrm{ROC_Y}$
$x^*(t)$		$X^*(s^*)$	$\mathrm{ROC_X}$
$x(0^+)$	$x(t)=0, t<0$	$x(0^+) = \lim_{s\to+\infty} sX(s)$	Initial value theorem
$\lim_{t\to+\infty} x(t)$	$x(t)=0,\ t<0,$ $\left\lvert\lim_{t\to+\infty} x(t)\right\rvert < \infty$	$\lim_{t\to+\infty} x(t) = \lim_{s\to 0} sX(s)$	Final value theorem
$-tx(t)$		$\frac{dX(s)}{ds}$	$\mathrm{ROC_X}$

TABLE D.6 Properties of the Unilateral Laplace Transform

Time domain $x(t)$		**Laplace domain** $X(s)$	ROC
$x(t),\ y(t),$ $x(t)=y(t)=0, t<0$		$\mathcal{X}(s),\ \mathcal{Y}(s)$	ROC_X, ROC_Y
$ax(t)+by(t)$	$a,b\in\mathbb{C}$	$a\mathcal{X}(s)+b\mathcal{Y}(s)$	$ROC \supseteq ROC_X \cap ROC_Y$
$x(t-t_0)$	$t_0\in\mathbb{R}, t_0>0$	$e^{-sto}\mathcal{X}(s)$	ROC_X
$x(\alpha t)$	$\alpha\in\mathbb{R}, \alpha>0$	$\frac{1}{\alpha}\mathcal{X}\left(\frac{s}{\alpha}\right)$	$\frac{1}{\alpha}ROC_X$
$\frac{d}{dt}x(t)$		$s\mathcal{X}(s)-x(0^-)$	$ROC \supseteq ROC_X$
$\int_0^t x(\tau)d\tau$		$\frac{1}{s}\mathcal{X}(s)$	$ROC \supseteq ROC_X \cap \{s:\mathrm{Re}\{s\}>0\}$
$e^{s_0t}x(t)$	$s_0\in\mathbb{C}$	$\mathcal{X}(s-s_0)$	$ROC_X+\mathrm{Re}\{s_0\}$
$x(t)*y(t)$		$\mathcal{X}(s)\mathcal{Y}(s)$	$ROC \supseteq ROC_X \cap ROC_Y$
$x^*(t)$		$\mathcal{X}^*(s^*)$	ROC_X
$x(0^+)$		$x(0^+)=\lim_{s\to+\infty} s\mathcal{X}(s)$	Initial value theorem
$\lim_{t\to+\infty} x(t)$	$\left\|\lim_{t\to+\infty} x(t)\right\|<\infty$	$\lim_{t\to+\infty} x(t)=\lim_{s\to 0} s\mathcal{X}(s)$	Final value theorem
$-tx(t)$		$\frac{d\mathcal{X}(s)}{ds}$	ROC_X

TABLE D.7 Discrete-Time Fourier Transform Pairs

Time domain $x[n]$		**Frequency domain** $X(e^{j\omega})$ always periodic of period 2π
$x[n]=\frac{1}{2\pi}\int_{2\pi} X(e^{j\omega})e^{j\omega n}d\omega$		$X(e^{j\omega})=\sum_{n=-\infty}^{+\infty} x[n]e^{-j\omega n}$
$\delta[n]$		1
$\delta[n-n_0]$	$n_0\in\mathbb{Z}$	$e^{-j\omega n_0}$
$u[n]$		$\frac{1}{1-e^{-j\omega}}+\sum_{k=-\infty}^{+\infty}\pi\delta(\omega-2\pi k)$
1		$\sum_{k=-\infty}^{+\infty}2\pi\delta(\omega-2\pi k)$
$u[n+n_0]-u[n-n_0-1]$	$n_0\in\mathbb{Z}, n_0>0$	$\frac{\sin\omega(n_0+1/2)}{\sin(\omega/2)}$
$a^n u[n]$	$a\in\mathbb{C},\ \lvert a\rvert<1$	$\frac{1}{1-ae^{-j\omega}}$
$(n+1)a^n u[n]$	$a\in\mathbb{C},\ \lvert a\rvert<1$	$\frac{1}{(1-ae^{-j\omega})^2}$
$a^n u[-n-1]$	$a\in\mathbb{C},\ \lvert a\rvert>1$	$\frac{1}{1-ae^{-j\omega}}$
$r^n\cos(\omega_0 n)u[n]$	$r,\omega_0\in\mathbb{R}, r>0$	$\frac{1-r\cos(\omega_0)e^{-j\omega}}{1-2r\cos(\omega_0)e^{-j\omega}+r^2e^{-j2\omega}}$
$r^n\sin(\omega_0 n)u[n]$	$r,\omega_0\in\mathbb{R}, r>0$	$\frac{r\sin(\omega_0)e^{-j\omega}}{1-2r\cos(\omega_0)e^{-j\omega}+r^2e^{-j2\omega}}$
$\cos(\omega_0 n)$	$\omega_0\in\mathbb{R}$	$\pi\sum_{k=-\infty}^{+\infty}\delta(\omega-\omega_0-2\pi k)+\delta(\omega+\omega_0-2\pi k)$
$\sin(\omega_0 n)$	$\omega_0\in\mathbb{R}$	$j\pi\sum_{k=-\infty}^{+\infty}-\delta(\omega-\omega_0-2\pi k)+\delta(\omega+\omega_0-2\pi k)$
$\frac{\sin\omega_c n}{\pi n}=\frac{\omega_c}{\pi}\operatorname{sinc}\left(\frac{\omega_c n}{\pi}\right)$	$\omega_c\in\mathbb{R},$ $0<\omega_c<\pi$	$\begin{cases}1, & \lvert\omega-k2\pi\rvert\le\omega_c,\ k\in\mathbb{Z}\\ 0, & \text{otherwise}\end{cases}$

→

$x[n]=\sum_{k=\langle N\rangle} a_k e^{jk\frac{2\pi}{N}n}$ (DTFS)	$a_k \in \mathbb{C}$	$\sum_{k=-\infty}^{\infty} 2\pi a_k \delta(\omega - k\frac{2\pi}{N})$
$\sum_{k=-\infty}^{\infty} \delta[n-kN]$	$N \in \mathbb{Z}, N>0$	$\frac{2\pi}{N}\sum_{k=-\infty}^{\infty} \delta(\omega - k\frac{2\pi}{N})$

TABLE D.8: Properties of the Discrete-Time Fourier Transform

Time domain		Frequency domain
$x[n]=\frac{1}{2\pi}\int_{2\pi} X(e^{j\omega})e^{j\omega n}d\omega$		$X(e^{j\omega})=\sum_{n=-\infty}^{+\infty} x[n]e^{-j\omega n}$
$ax[n]+by[n]$	$a,b\in\mathbb{C}$	$aX(e^{j\omega})+bY(e^{j\omega})$
$x[n-n_0]$	$n_0\in\mathbb{Z}$	$e^{-j\omega n_0}X(e^{j\omega})$
$x[-n]$		$X(e^{-j\omega})$
$e^{j\omega_0 n}x[n]$	$\omega_0\in\mathbb{R}$	$X(e^{j(\omega-\omega_0)})$
$nx[n]$		$j\frac{dX(e^{j\omega})}{d\omega}$
$\sum_{m=-\infty}^{n} x[m]$		$\frac{1}{(1-e^{-j\omega})}X(e^{j\omega})$
$x[n]-x[n-1]$		$(1-e^{-j\omega})X(e^{j\omega})$
$x_{\uparrow m}[n]$	$m\in\mathbb{Z}$, $m>0$	$X(e^{jm\omega})$
$x[n]*y[n]$		$X(e^{j\omega})Y(e^{j\omega})$
$x[n]y[n]$		$\frac{1}{2\pi}\int_{2\pi} X(e^{j\upsilon})Y(e^{j(\omega-\upsilon)})d\upsilon$
$x^*[n]$		$X^*(e^{-j\omega})$
$x[n]\in\mathbb{R}$		$\lvert X(e^{j\omega})\rvert=\lvert X(e^{-j\omega})\rvert$, $\angle X(e^{j\omega})=-\angle X(e^{-j\omega})$
$x[n]=x[-n]\in\mathbb{R}$		$X(e^{j\omega})=X(e^{-j\omega})\in\mathbb{R}$
$x[n]=-x[-n]\in\mathbb{R}$		$X(e^{j\omega})=-X(e^{-j\omega})\in j\mathbb{R}$, i.e., purely imaginary
Parseval Equality: $\sum_{-\infty}^{+\infty}\lvert x[n]\rvert^2=\frac{1}{2\pi}\int_{2\pi}\lvert X(e^{j\omega})\rvert^2 d\omega$		

TABLE D.9: Properties of the Discrete-Time Fourier Series

Time domain $x[n], y[n]$ periodic, fund. period N, fund. freq. $\omega_0 = \frac{2\pi}{N}$		**Frequency domain** $x[n] \overset{FS}{\leftrightarrow} a_k,\ y[n] \overset{FS}{\leftrightarrow} b_k$
$x[n] = \sum_{k=\langle N\rangle} a_k e^{jk\omega_0 n} = \sum_{k=\langle N\rangle} a_k e^{jk\frac{2\pi}{N}n}$	$a_k \in \mathbb{C}$	$a_k,\ k \in \langle N\rangle$
$\alpha x[n] + \beta y[n]$	$\alpha, \beta \in \mathbb{C}$	$\alpha a_k + \beta b_k$
$x[n - n_0]$	$n_0 \in \mathbb{Z}$	$e^{-jk\omega_0 n_0} a_k$
$x[-n]$		a_{-k}
$e^{jm\omega_0 n} x[n]$	$m \in \mathbb{Z}$	a_{k-m}
$\sum_{m=-\infty}^{n} x[m]$	$a_0 = 0$	$\frac{1}{(1 - e^{-jk\omega_0})} a_k$
$x[n] - x[n-1]$		$(1 - e^{-jk\omega_0}) a_k$
$x_{\uparrow m}[n]$	$m \in \mathbb{Z}$, $m > 0$	$\frac{1}{m} a_k,\ k \in \langle mN\rangle$
$\sum_{m=\langle N\rangle} x[m] y[n-m]$		$N a_k b_k$
$x[n] y[n]$		$\sum_{l=\langle N\rangle} a_l b_{k-l}$
$x^*[n]$		a^*_{-k}
$x[n] \in \mathbb{R}$		$\lvert a_k \rvert = \lvert a_{-k} \rvert, \angle a_k = -\angle a_{-k}$
$x[n] = x[-n] \in \mathbb{R}$		$a_k = a_{-k} \in \mathbb{R}$
$x[n] = -x[-n] \in \mathbb{R}$		$a_k = -a_{-k} \in j\mathbb{R}$ i.e., purely imaginary
Parseval Equality:	$\frac{1}{N}\sum_{n\in\langle N\rangle} \lvert x[n]\rvert^2 = \sum_{k\in\langle N\rangle} \lvert a_k\rvert^2$	

TABLE D.10 *z*-Transform Pairs

Time domain $x[n]$		**z domain** $X(z)$	ROC
$x[n]=\frac{1}{j2\pi}\oint_{C} X(z)z^{n-1}dz$	$C:=\{z\in \mathrm{ROC}: \lvert z\rvert = r\}$	$X(z)=\sum_{n=-\infty}^{+\infty} x[n]z^{-n}$	$z\in \mathrm{ROC}$
$\delta[n]$		1	$\forall z$
$\delta[n-n_0]$	$n_0\in\mathbb{Z}$	z^{-n_0}	$\forall z/\{0\},\ n_0>0$ $\forall z/\{\infty\},\ n_0<0$
$u[n]$		$\frac{1}{1-z^{-1}}$	$\lvert z\rvert>1$
$u[n+n_0]-u[n-n_0-1]$	$n_0\in\mathbb{Z}$	$\frac{z^{n_0}-z^{-n_0-1}}{1-z^{-1}}$	$\forall z/\{0,\infty\}$
$a^n u[n]$	$a\in\mathbb{C},\ \lvert a\rvert<1$	$\frac{1}{1-az^{-1}}$	$\lvert z\rvert>\lvert a\rvert$
$-a^n u[-n-1]$	$a\in\mathbb{C},\ \lvert a\rvert>1$	$\frac{1}{1-az^{-1}}$	$\lvert z\rvert<\lvert a\rvert$
$(n+1)a^n u[n]$	$a\in\mathbb{C},\ \lvert a\rvert<1$	$\frac{1}{(1-az^{-1})^2}$	$\lvert z\rvert>\lvert a\rvert$
$r^n\cos(\omega_0 n)u[n]$	$r,\omega_0\in\mathbb{R},\ r>0$	$\frac{1-r\cos(\omega_0)z^{-1}}{1-2r\cos(\omega_0)z^{-1}+r^2z^{-2}}$	$\lvert z\rvert>r$
$r^n\sin(\omega_0 n)u[n]$	$r,\omega_0\in\mathbb{R},\ r>0$	$\frac{r\sin(\omega_0)z^{-1}}{1-2r\cos(\omega_0)z^{-1}+r^2z^{-2}}$	$\lvert z\rvert>r$

TABLE D.11: Properties of the *z*-Transform Pairs

Time domain		***z* domain**	ROC
$x[n], y[n]$		$X(z),\ Y(z)$	$\mathrm{ROC_X}, \mathrm{ROC_Y}$
$ax[n]+by[n]$	$a,b\in\mathbb{C}$	$aX(z)+bY(z)$	$\mathrm{ROC}\supseteq\mathrm{ROC_X}\cap\mathrm{ROC_Y}$
$x[n-n_0]$	$n_0\in\mathbb{Z}$	$z^{-n_0}X(z)$	$\mathrm{ROC_X}$, except possible addition/removal of 0 or ∞
$x[-n]$		$X(z^{-1})$	$\{z^{-1}:z\in\mathrm{ROC_X}\}$
$z_0^{\,n}x[n]$	$z_0\in\mathbb{C}$	$X\left(\dfrac{z}{z_0}\right)$	$\lvert z_0\rvert\mathrm{ROC_X}$
$nx[n]$		$-z\dfrac{dX(z)}{dz}$	$\mathrm{ROC_X}$
$\sum_{m=-\infty}^{n}x[m]$		$\dfrac{1}{(1-z^{-1})}X(z)$	$\mathrm{ROC}\supseteq\mathrm{ROC_X}\cap\{\lvert z\rvert>1\}$
$x[n]-x[n-1]$		$(1-z^{-1})X(z)$	$\mathrm{ROC}\supseteq\mathrm{ROC_X}\cap\{\lvert z\rvert>0\}$
$x_{\uparrow m}[n]$	$m\in\mathbb{Z}$, $m>0$	$X(z^m)$	$\{z^{1/m}:z\in\mathrm{ROC_X}\}$
$x[n]*y[n]$		$X(z)Y(z)$	$\mathrm{ROC}\supseteq\mathrm{ROC_X}\cap\mathrm{ROC_Y}$
$x^*[n]$		$X^*(z^*)$	$\mathrm{ROC_X}$

TABLE D.12: Properties of the Unilateral *z*-Transform

Time domain		***z* domain**	ROC
$x[n], y[n]$		$\mathcal{X}(z),\ \mathcal{Y}(z)$	$\mathrm{ROC_X}, \mathrm{ROC_Y}$
$ax[n]+by[n]$	$a,b \in \mathbb{C}$	$a\mathcal{X}(z)+b\mathcal{Y}(z)$	$\mathrm{ROC} \supseteq \mathrm{ROC_X} \cap \mathrm{ROC_Y}$
$x[n-1]$		$z^{-1}\mathcal{X}(z)+x[-1]$	$\mathrm{ROC_X}$, except possible removal of 0
$x[n+1]$		$z\mathcal{X}(z)-zx[0]$	$\mathrm{ROC_X}$, except possible addition of 0
$x[n-n_0]$	$n_0 \in \mathbb{Z}$	$z^{-n_0}\mathcal{X}(z)+z^{-n_0+1}x[-1]+\ldots +x[-n_0]$	$\mathrm{ROC_X}$, except possible removal of 0
$z_0{}^n x[n]$	$z_0 \in \mathbb{C}$	$\mathcal{X}\left(\dfrac{z}{z_0}\right)$	$\lvert z_0\rvert \mathrm{ROC_X}$
$nx[n]$		$-z\dfrac{d\mathcal{X}(z)}{dz}$	$\mathrm{ROC_X}$
$\sum_{m=-0}^{n} x[m]$		$\dfrac{1}{(1-z^{-1})}\mathcal{X}(z)$	$\mathrm{ROC} \supseteq \mathrm{ROC_X} \cap \{\lvert z\rvert > 1\}$
$x[n]-x[n-1]$		$(1-z^{-1})\mathcal{X}(z)$	$\mathrm{ROC} \supseteq \mathrm{ROC_X} \cap \{\lvert z\rvert > 0\}$
$x_{\uparrow m}[n]$	$m \in \mathbb{Z}$, $m > 0$	$\mathcal{X}(z^m)$	$\{z^{1/m} : z \in \mathrm{ROC_X}\}$
$x[n] * y[n]$ $x[n]=y[n]=0, n<0$		$\mathcal{X}(z)\mathcal{Y}(z)$	$\mathrm{ROC} \supseteq \mathrm{ROC_X} \cap \mathrm{ROC_Y}$
$x^*[n]$		$\mathcal{X}^*(z^*)$	$\mathrm{ROC_X}$

Index

Q

R

S